CREEDS
OF THE
CHURCHES

A Reader in Christian Doctrine
from the Bible to the Present

THIRD EDITION

Edited by
JOHN H. LEITH

Pemberton Professor of Theology
Union Theological Seminary in Virginia

JOHN KNOX PRESS
ATLANTA

TO ANN

ANCHOR BOOKS EDITION, 1963

REVISED EDITION, 1973

Third Edition, 1982

Library of Congress Cataloging in Publication Data
Main entry under title:

Creeds of the churches.

1. Creeds—Collected works. 2. Theology,
Doctrinal—Collected works. I. Leith, John H.
BT990.C655   1982   238   82-48029
ISBN   0-8042-0526-4   (pkb.)

PRINTED IN THE UNITED STATES OF AMERICA
JOHN KNOX PRESS
ATLANTA, GEORGIA 30365

ACKNOWLEDGMENT is made to the following publishers and authors for permission to reprint selections from copyrighted material:

THE CHRISTIAN CENTURY FOUNDATION Excerpt from "Jesus Christ as Divine Human Savior" by Albert C. Outler in May 3, 1961 issue. Copyright 1961 Christian Century Foundation. Reprinted by permission.

HODDER & STOUGHTON LIMITED Excerpt from *The Apostolic Preaching and Its Developments* by C. H. Dodd. Reprinted by permission of the publishers.

STUDENT CHRISTIAN MOVEMENT PRESS LIMITED Excerpt from *The Third World Conference on Faith and Order,* edited by Oliver S. Tomkins. Reprinted by permission.

WESTMINSTER PRESS Excerpt from *Christology of the Later Fathers,* Volume III, Library of Christian Classics. Published 1954, The Westminster Press. Reprinted by permission of Westminster Press and Student Christian Movement Press Limited.

JOHN KNOX PRESS Excerpt from ANSELM: *Fides Quaerens Intellectum* by Karl Barth. Reprinted by permission of John Knox Press and Student Christian Movement Press Limited.

MENNONITE PUBLISHING HOUSE Excerpt from *The Doctrines of the Mennonites* by John C. Wenger. Reprinted by permission of the publishers.

THE MACMILLAN COMPANY "The Grace of Our Lord Jesus Christ" and "Affirmation of Union" from *The Second Conference on Faith and Order, Held at Edinburgh, August 3–18, 1937,* edited by Leonard Hodgson. Reprinted by permission.

B. HERDER AND COMPANY "The Creed of the Council of Trent" from *The Church Teaches,* Documents of the Church in English Translation. Reprinted by permission of the publisher.

HARPER & BROTHERS Excerpt from *The Creeds of Christendom* Vol. 3 by Philip Schaff; *Man's Disorder and God's Design* (The Message of the First Assembly of the World Council of Churches). All reprinted by permission of the publisher.

NATIONAL COUNCIL OF THE CHURCHES OF CHRIST IN THE U. S. A. The Scripture quotations in this publication are from the *Revised Standard Version of the Bible,* copyrighted 1946 and 1952 by the Division of Christian Education, National Council of Churches, and used by permission; "The Relation of the Churches to the World in the Light of Christian Faith" from the 1943 Study of the Federal Council of Churches. Reprinted by permission.

MUHLENBERG PRESS "Augsburg Confession" and "The Small Catechism" from *Book of Concord,* edited by Theodore G. Tappert. Reprinted by permission.

THE AMERICAN BAPTIST PUBLICATION SOCIETY "The New Hampshire Declaration of Faith" from *Baptist Confessions of Faith* by William L. Lumpkin. Published by The Judson Press (1959). Reprinted by permission.

NATIONAL CATHOLIC WELFARE CONFERENCE Translations of *Munificentissimus Deus* and *Humani Generis.* Reprinted by permission.

SAINT ANTHONY'S GUILD Excerpt from *Ineffabilis Deus,* translated by Rev. Dominic J. Unger. Copyright 1946 by St. Anthony's Guild, Paterson, N. J.

THE SOCIETY FOR PROMOTING CHRISTIAN KNOWLEDGE Excerpts from Sellers: *The Council of Chalcedon* and Ernest Evans: *Tertullian's Treatise Against Praxeas.* Reprinted by permission.

OXFORD UNIVERSITY PRESS Excerpt from *Christian Tradition and the Unity We Seek* by Albert C. Outler. Reprinted by permission of the publisher.

T. & T. CLARK Excerpt from Irenaeus: *Ante-Nicene Christian Library,* Edinburgh; excerpt from *The Nicene and Post-Nicene Fathers.* Reprinted by permission.

ESTATE OF WILLISTON WALKER Excerpt from *The Creeds and Platforms of Congregationalism* by Williston Walker. Reprinted by permission of The First New Haven National Bank.

ASSOCIATION PRESS Excerpt from *New Delhi Speaks about Christian Witness, Service, Unity,* edited by W. A. Visser 't Hooft. Reprinted by permission.

DOUBLEDAY & COMPANY, INC. *The German Phoenix* by Franklin Hamlin Littell. Copyright © 1960 by Franklin Hamlin Littell. Reprinted by permission.

PREFACE

The purpose of this work is to provide in one volume the major theological affirmations of the Christian churches. The selection has been limited to documents which have some measure of official status in the Church's history. In some cases the selection has been arbitrary, but an effort has been made to include creeds which are as representative as possible of the Christian community and which illustrate the developing intellectual consensus of the Church.

The limitation of the selection to "official" documents is due to the demands of space and to the increasing availability of good anthologies of theological literature in sets and in single volumes. A single volume containing the "official" theological documents is not so readily available. In some instances I have chosen to omit a well-known creed which is easily accessible to make room for a less well-known but significant document which is not conveniently available.

The introductions are not intended to be exhaustive or complete. Their purpose is to identify and to indicate something of the significance of each document in the history of the Church's theological enterprise. References to literature which does provide adequate introductory material have been included. References to German and French works have been included where no adequate or corresponding works are available in English.

Documents have been printed in their entirety insofar as space has permitted. Generally speaking, it is better to have a document in its entirety; and for this reason some breadth of selection has been sacrificed.

No one can acknowledge the full debt which he owes to family, teachers, and friends. Mention can be made only of

Preface

those who have given specific help in the preparation of this volume. I am indebted to Professor Franklin H. Littell of Chicago Theological Seminary for his suggestion that this volume be undertaken and for his encouragement and advice. I am also indebted to President James A. Jones of Union Theological Seminary in Virginia for the encouragement and assistance which he has provided; to the staff of the Union Theological Seminary library; and to Reverend Ross Mackenzie of Westminster Presbyterian Church, Richmond, Virginia, and Professor James Mays of Union Theological Seminary in Virginia for their help in the translation of documents. I owe an especially important debt to Professor Albert C. Outler of Southern Methodist University, who was my teacher and who has given invaluable advice in the preparation of this volume. Mrs. Dorothy P. Trible and my wife, Ann W. Leith, have rendered yeoman service in typing the manuscript. The assistance of Mr. Carl Morse and the Doubleday editors has been indispensable. This is a much better volume than it would have been because of the help which I have received, but all those who have helped must be completely absolved from any faults which remain.

REVISED EDITION

The publication of a new edition of CREEDS OF THE CHURCHES by John Knox Press provides an opportunity to include portions of a document of Vatican Council II, Dogmatic Constitution on the Church, and two contemporary statements of faith of the churches. It also provides an opportunity to thank again friends and associates whose reviews and comments have contributed to this volume.

JOHN H. LEITH
UNION THEOLOGICAL SEMINARY
IN VIRGINIA
MARCH 1973

PREFACE TO THIRD EDITION

This revision brings up-to-date declarations on the mission and unity of the church. It makes possible the addition of some older documents which are needed by many users of the book: the Athanasian Creed, the London Confession of 1644, and the Dogmatic Constitution on Divine Revelation, 1965. I am grateful for the advice of friends and reviewers, and especially my teacher in history of doctrine, Albert C. Outler, William L. Lumpkin, an authority on Baptist statements of faith, and T. Watson Street, historian of the church and missions.

JOHN H. LEITH
UNION THEOLOGICAL SEMINARY
IN VIRGINIA

CONTENTS

Contents ix

x   *Contents*

THE CREEDS AND THEIR ROLE
IN THE CHURCH

Christianity has always been a "creedal" religion in that it has always been theological. It was rooted in the theological tradition of ancient Israel, which was unified by its historical credos and declaratory affirmations of faith. No pretheological era has been discovered in the New Testament or in the history of the Christian community. From the beginning Christianity has been theological, involving men in theological reflection and calling them to declarations of faith. A nontheological Christianity has simply never endured, although such has been attempted, for instance, by individual seers (*Spiritualisten*) in the sixteenth century and also by collaborators with totalitarian ideologies (e.g., the *positives Christentum* of the German Christians) in the twentieth century.

The need for theology and for creeds arises from two basic facts. One is the nature of man as an intelligent being. "Just because he is *intelligens* the Christian, of all men, has to learn to discern with agonizing clarity what is conceivable by him about God himself."[1] What cannot be thought through critically and expressed with reasonable clarity cannot demand the allegiance of man's whole being. Understanding is necessary for man's full commitment. Hence faith must be spoken and made intelligible. This is not to say that faith must be enclosed within the limits of reason, but it does mean that faith must require neither the closing of the mind nor the sacrifice of the integrity of the mind.

Christian faith also holds that God is the Truth and that

[1] *Anselm: Fides Quaerens Intellectum* by Karl Barth (London: SCM Press, Ltd., 1960), pp. 20–21.

he is the source of all truth. To be sure, God is love as
well as truth, will as well as mind. While God may be
truth, truth is not God. Yet if God is to be known and
served, he must be known and served with the mind as well
as with the heart and will. A commitment that does not
serve God with the mind is always dangerous and irresponsible. Indeed the articulation of faith in intelligible
words not only clarifies faith but becomes itself the means
of deeper commitment of heart and mind. Theology and
creeds are the service of God through the life of the mind
and are indispensable to any other service which may be
rendered to God.

I.

While creeds are an attempt to give articulate, intelligible
expression to Christian faith, they, at least the great ones,
are not intellectualistic. They are fashioned in history, not
in the relative isolation of a scholar's study. Christianity
is first of all a historical religion, not simply in the sense
that it has a history but in its conviction that God has de-
cisively acted and made himself known in history. The great
creedal affirmations of the Old and New Testaments are
recitals of and reflections upon the historic events in which
God is believed to have disclosed himself.

The great creeds, however, are not only rooted in history
as their source and basis, but they are also framed in history
and bear the marks of history. Generally speaking, creeds
have not been written in the quiet periods of history but
in those moments of historical intensity when the Church
has been engaged by foes from without, or when its mission or life has been endangered from within. This is not
to suggest that creeds are merely the products of external
forces pressing upon the Church from without or of conflicts within. The Church would have had creeds even if
there had been no threatening heresy such as Gnosticism
in the second century or National Socialism in the twentieth, even if there had been no internal disagreements as
to the content of the faith at Nicaea in the fourth century
or in the Reformation in the sixteenth. The Christian faith
of its own volition comes to some sort of articulate expres-

sion, and the affirmation of faith is part of the Christian's praise and thanksgiving to his God. Yet it is true that history is the *milieu* in which the creed-making process takes place, and it adds its intensity to that process and leaves its marks upon it.

Creeds have to be expressed in the language of a particular time and place. The concepts and terms which they use are datable in a particular history. The *Sitz im Leben* determines even the style and form of the creed. In certain situations the only confession needed is the simple Christological affirmation "Jesus is Lord" or "Jesus is the Christ." Other situations demand the binitarian affirmation concerning God and Christ, and in still other situations only a trinitarian confession will do. At Nicaea and at Chalcedon it was necessary to deal with particular doctrines, but in the Reformation the situation demanded comprehensive confessions. In recent times a notable instance of the historicity of creeds is seen in the Barmen Declaration, which reasserted the historic Christian faith against the renascent paganism of National Socialism.

Once creeds have come into being, they begin to shape history also. The Nicene faith, for example, influenced the piety, worship, and cultural involvement of subsequent generations of Christians. The theological reflections that are embodied in creeds become part of the theological memory of the Church and are the source and context for future theological decisions. None of the great creeds of the Church were produced independently of what the Church thought and said in previous generations.

Creeds are likewise judged by history as well as produced in history. The Creed of Nicaea is a notable example of a creed that had to wait the confirmation of history. It was debated by the Church for fifty years before it became the consensus of the Church. Creeds cannot be imposed by simple fiat upon the Church. They are examined, corrected, rejected, and confirmed by history. In the long run, they have to be confirmed not by some assembly so much as by the common-sense wisdom of the Christian community. To use a Quaker term, they must become the "sense of the meeting" to have abiding authority.

The great creeds are not only marked by historicity but also by catholicity. They are never intentionally sectarian. They intend to state the faith of the Christian Church. In the Ancient Church the creed-making process was itself notably catholic. The Definition of Chalcedon was the product of the theology of Antioch, of Alexandria, and of Rome and the West. The result was different from and better than that which these schools of theology could have produced alone. Never since the fifth century has the theological enterprise been so catholic, but surely one of the most hopeful signs in contemporary theology is the recovery of catholicity.

Many creeds that have been catholic in intention have not been catholic in fact. Indeed some creeds have been written with the purpose of excluding persons who considered themselves Christian. Yet even this restriction of the Christian community is done in the name of a true catholicity. Perhaps creeds are most catholic when they claim to be so only in intention and purpose. The absolute claim to have achieved catholicity has never yet been fully confirmed and becomes in itself destructive of catholicity. The creeds with the greatest claim to catholicity, such as the Nicene, are limited to basic affirmation; and their catholicity has been achieved, and in some measure produced by them, in a long history.

Closely related to the catholicity of the creedal process is its communal character. Some creeds, such as the Apostles' Creed, are wholly anonymous. They simply grew out of the life of the Church. Even the great creeds of Nicaea and Chalcedon were not so much produced as they were amended or collected from the creedal store of the Church. The creeds that are largely the work of one man, such as the Second Helvetic Confession or the Augsburg Confession, are unintelligible apart from the community of faith in which the author participated. Theology is the servant of the community. The *lex orandi* in no small measure determines the *lex credendi*. The great doctrines of the Church were affirmed in worship and experience before they were written on paper or authorized by councils. "A doctrinal system, a developed liturgy, a settled polity, all these are achievements possible only *within* a community that has its life and power from another originating source than these."[2]

The creeds of the Church, in addition to being the products of the community of faith more than of individual effort, can only be used within the Christian community. A confession, to be sure, is always an individual act; but it is an act that takes place in community. In many of the creeds the communal nature of the confession is explicitly affirmed in the affirmation of the holy catholic Church and the communion of saints. The corporate confession of the creed realizes the communion of saints and bolsters the faith of the individual by the faith of the Church.

II.

The church liturgy has been one of the primary occasions that called for the development of creeds; for worship is incomplete without an affirmation of faith in hymn, prayer, and sermon. The confession of faith is an essential moment in the life of a Christian. In confession the believer speaks out before men and with men the silent thought and affirmation of his heart and mind. He makes outward what is inward.[3] In confession the believer takes his stand, commits his life, declares what he believes to be true, affirms his ultimate loyalty, and defies every false claim upon his life. The confession of faith is the seal of faith and the courage of faith.

The confession of faith is never merely a matter of the mind, as important as the mind may be. For the confession commits more than the mind. It commits all of life. It must be affirmed with the whole person. Hence creeds can never be learned simply from books, though this learning is surely important. They must be learned in the midst of the community of worshiping and believing people who share in a common life of which the creed is a common affirmation. The confession of faith is a living sacrifice when the be-

[2] *The Christian Tradition and the Unity We Seek* by Albert Outler (New York: Oxford University Press, 1957), p. 66.
[3] *Creed and the Creeds* by John Huntley Skrine (London: Longmans, Green & Co., 1911), pp. 34 ff.

liever offers by the help of words his whole personality to his Creator.[4]

The liturgical life of the Church called for creeds of various types. A creedal statement was needed as a guide for preaching. Such a statement, in contrast to a creed used in baptism, could be flexible both as to form and content and of greater length. Flexibility and lack of precise language were in fact desirable as they allowed for creative theological work. The Rules of Faith in the Ancient Church served this purpose admirably as they kept theologians in bounds on the one hand and on the other hand did not stifle creativity, as is well demonstrated by Origen. For a similar reason Bullinger and others were hesitant to commit themselves to any one confession at the time of the Reformation. The Rules of Faith could serve the needs of instruction and preaching without being cast in settled form. Declarations of faith by the worshiping congregation, in distinction from such Rules of Faith, had to be precise, fixed, and economical in the use of words. The evidence indicates that such declaratory creeds were late (third and fourth centuries) in developing.

Creedal statements were from the beginning associated with baptism. The importance of this rite for the development of creeds is very considerable. Hans Lietzmann went so far as to say that the root of all creeds is the formula of belief pronounced by the baptizand or pronounced in his hearing and assented to by him before baptism. This statement does not do justice to the great variety of situations that called for creedal affirmation in the life of the Church, but it does indicate the importance of baptism for the development of creeds.

One of the oldest confessions of the Church is reflected in the baptism of the Ethiopian eunuch. Here the eunuch himself asks, "What is to prevent my being baptized?" (Acts 8:36–38). Philip replied, "If you believe with all your heart, you may," and he answered, "I believe that Jesus Christ is the Son of God." The fact that this part of the text may be an interpolation does not affect its signifi-

[4] *Ibid.*, p. 197.

cance as an indication of the importance of baptism in creedal development.

The creedal form that was apparently most commonly used in the baptismal rites of the second and third centuries was interrogatory. The affirmation of faith took place through the baptizand's response to the officiant's questions. One of the best examples of the interrogatory creed is found in the *Apostolic Tradition* of Hippolytus, which is printed on page 23.

The creed had been introduced into the Holy Communion by the latter part of the fifth century. By this time creedal patterns were already established. The sacrament of the Holy Communion did probably have a part in such additions to the creed as the *filioque*.

Another important source of creedal development was the teaching ministry of the Church. This was focused in the preparation of candidates for baptism. Creedal statements served as the basis for the famous catechetical lectures that were given in this preparation. The candidate was taught the faith that had been maintained in the Church since the days of the Apostles. Catechetical instruction was not a free-lance operation but was the responsible traditioning, the authoritative delivery, of the faith. The Rules of Faith that we find in Justin Martyr, Irenaeus, Tertullian, Clement, and Origen served as the basis for the teaching ministry of the Church; and they all intended to transmit the faith of the Apostles.

A practice developed in catechetical instruction that called for a more precise and fixed creed. This was the act of the *traditio symboli* and the *redditio symboli*. At an important moment in the training of the catechumen the faith was authoritatively delivered (traditioned) to him in the form of a creed. The catechumen then learned the creed and rendered it back as his own. Recent scholars are convinced that in the traditioning and rendering of the creed we find the most significant source of the declaratory creed.

The teaching ministry also served as the source of another important creedal form, the catechism. Augustine recognized the importance of the question-and-answer method of theological education, and the Church increasingly made use of it. The Protestant Reformers with their emphasis on the priesthood of all believers were especially given to catechetical instruction. The Reformation gave birth to a whole bevy of catechisms, which for the most part were based upon the traditional instruction in the Creed, the Decalogue, and the Lord's Prayer, with sections on the sacraments and in some instances on preaching. The catechetical method had the advantage not only of providing clear and precise statements of Christian theology, but also of raising the important questions and in particular the questions for which Christian faith is the answer. In less stereotyped forms, as Augustine pointed out, it enabled the teacher to understand the theological development and insight of the pupil.

Still another need that was served by the creeds was the Church's concern for hermeneutics. Originally, the Church had to declare how it would understand the Old Testament and what the substance of the Apostolic tradition was. After the Apostolic witness was put into writing, the Church had to have some measure by which to determine which books were canonical, that is, genuinely apostolic. After the canon of the New Testament was fixed, it was still necessary to provide some principle of interpretation to distinguish the centrally important from the peripheral and to put together in some coherent way the diversity of the New Testament testimony. As Oscar Cullmann has put it, every interpreter has to distinguish between the central principle and what is derived from it. Hence every theology presupposes a rule of faith.[5]

The creed is simply the Church's understanding of the meaning of Scripture. The creed says, Here is how the Church reads and receives Scripture.[6] The whole history of theology is the history of the interpretation of Scripture, even though the theologians do not always cite Biblical

[5] *The Earliest Christian Confessions* by Oscar Cullmann, tr. by J. K. S. Reid (London: Lutterworth Press, 1949), p. 11.
[6] *Explication de la Confession de Foi de la Rochelle* by Roger Mehl (Paris: Collection "Les Bergers et les Mages"), pp. 10 ff.

references. In general, the victories in the great theological debates have gone to those who have been the most convincing interpreters of Scripture. The creeds are the record of the Church's interpretation of the Bible in the past and the authoritative guide to hermeneutics in the present.

The rise of heresy was still another situation that created the need for creeds. Heresy is so important a factor in the origin of creeds that it tempts the commentator to exaggerate its role. As was said long ago, creeds are signposts to heresies. The task of the creed was to defend the Church against heresy. The creed has the negative role of shutting the heretic out and setting the boundaries within which authentic Christian theology and life can take place. These functions of the creed account in some instances for the choice of words and also for the items of theological affirmation. Yet it is a mistake to attribute creeds simply to heresy, for there would be creeds even if there were no heretics. In fact, theology can become the subject of debate apart from heresy. It may well be that the creeds, without the heretics, would not be as good as they are; for the heretics made their contributions. They required the Church to think through theological issues when it did not want to do so. They made the Church exercise care in theological language so that the language of theology would say what the Christian community wanted to say. Creeds are not due simply to the heretics, but they would be much poorer creeds without the heretics.

Creeds are also a standard, a battle cry, a testimony and witness to the world. In the Ancient Church persecution afforded an occasion for a Christian confession. In the twentieth century the paganism of National Socialism challenged confession from Christians. Communism likewise calls for a declaration of belief. These radical situations illustrate a need that is always present, the need for commitment. Christian faith is not only the gift of God's grace; it is also a command, a task. It is a battle against the "world, the flesh, and the devil." The creed is a marching song, a battle cry. In this fact resides some of the truth in the assertion that creeds are to be sung.

III.

The word creed suggests authority, but the exact nature and extent of creedal authority is a difficult question. There is no one answer that satisfies all Christians. On one extreme the creed is almost identified with the Word of God. On the other extreme creeds are minimized and dogmatic Christianity is regarded as a mistake, or at best an unfortunate necessity.

The attempt to dispense with dogma and to minimize creeds has never been successful. As has been indicated, there has never been a nontheological period in the history of the Church. Even when the Church has been held together only by a common life in the Spirit, a creed has always been implicit. The endeavor to have no creed but the Bible is successful only so long as there is common agreement as to what the Bible teaches. In the long run, organizational necessities demonstrate the need for creeds, and organizational integrity requires some kind of creedal subscription. The attempt to minimize creeds and to magnify Christianity without dogma runs aground either on the theological nature of Christian faith or on the nature of man, who is body as well as spirit, and who cannot get along without organizational structure.

The attempt to assert intentionally or unintentionally the absolute authority of creeds is predicated upon particular views of truth, of man, and of community. The creedal absolutist is likely to believe that propositional statements are fully adequate vehicles for truth. He must also believe that men, at least some men, are both good enough and wise enough, at least in certain situations, to know the truth in a final and definitive way. He is also likely to believe that community can exist only on the basis of full agreement as to truth propositionally stated. Over against the creedal absolutist, there is a considerable body of Christians who insist that, however useful and indispensable propositional statements may be as the embodiment of truth, the ultimate and final embodiment of the wisdom of God is the Person of Jesus Christ. Man's apprehension of the Word of God is never ultimate and final, for every man's theology is limited by his finiteness and his sin. Finally, the Christian community existed prior to the formulation of Christian faith in exact and precise creeds. None of this means that creeds are not indispensable pointers to the wisdom of God and necessary boundaries for Christian living, but it does reject every effort to absolutize a human achievement as idolatry and as, in the end, destructive of community. When creeds have been made absolute, someone always rises to protest in the name of the Word of God, which stands in judgment on every human word.

The awareness that every creed is a human achievement and subject to limitation by man's finiteness and sinfulness is the source of a truly Christian liberalism. The Church has the task not simply of the reformation of the world but also of the reformation of itself. Every human achievement in creed as well as elsewhere must be continually reformed by the Christian community's apprehension of the Word of God in Jesus Christ.

It remains to be noticed again that creeds do not receive their authority merely through the fiat of ecclesiastical authority. H. E. W. Turner has pointed out the importance of the common-sense wisdom of the Christian community, which in the long run is sounder than the action of church councils or the judgment of scholars.[7] Creeds become authoritative when they become the common-sense wisdom, the consensus of the Christian community. The final authority of a creed is the witness of the Holy Spirit in the life of the Church, an authority that in its deepest dimensions is always personal.

[7] *The Pattern of Christian Truth* by H. E. W. Turner (London: A. R. Mowbray & Co., Ltd., 1954), p. 498.

THE BIBLE

Theology and "creed making" are as old as the Christian community itself. Precise, fixed, official creeds did not appear until the third and fourth centuries, but the process that culminated in them had its beginning in the historical credos (Deuteronomy 26:5–9 and 6:21–25) and declaratory affirmations (Deuteronomy 6:4–5 and I Kings 18:39) of the Old Testament. It was continued in Jesus' self-interpretation and in the reflection of his disciples upon his significance for them and for the world.

There are no precisely defined and officially authorized creeds in the New Testament. Yet the Church of the New Testament did preach, sing, pray, exorcise, and bear witness. In these activities the content of the faith became more or less fixed in creed-like formulas. These formulas can be detected, sometimes by their introduction—as when Paul expressly stated that he is handing on that which has been delivered to him in I Corinthians 15:3–7—and sometimes by their formal style. Clearly the Church possessed a recognized body of teaching that was beginning to become fixed in stereotyped formulas.

There is no one creedal pattern in the New Testament formulas, even in the affirmations concerning Jesus. The Christological formulas, which are the most common type, range from charismatic cries, Jesus is Lord or Jesus is the Christ, to careful theological reflection as in Romans 1:1–4, which contains the rudiments of the fully developed Christology of Chalcedon. In addition to the Christological confessions, there are also in the New Testament two-article formulas confessing both God and Christ and three-article formulas affirming Father, Son, and Holy Ghost. These various formulas exist side by side and contemporaneously. In the third century the trinitarian formulas largely replaced the single-article and the two-article formulas, partly due to the influence of Baptismal rite and partly due to the implicit trinitarianism of the New Testament documents.

An important illustration of the theological reflection that finally issued in fixed creeds is seen in the sermons in Acts. These contain an outline of the faith that was commonly held, especially as applied to missionary situations.

Numerous situations in the life of the Church called for creed-like formulas and contributed to the development of fixed statements of the Christian faith. Among these situations were Preaching (Acts 2–3), Teaching (I Corinthians 15:3–7), Worship (Philippians 2:6–11), Baptism (Acts 8:36–38), Exorcism (Acts 3:6, Mark 1:24), Confession (I Timothy 6:12–16), Martyrdom (Acts 7:54–56), and Polemics (I John 4:2).

Cullmann, Oscar, *The Earliest Christian Confessions*, tr. by J. K. S. Reid (London: Lutterworth Press, 1949). Chapter 2 discusses situations that led to creed development. Chapters 3 and 4 argue for priority of Christological formulas.

Dodd, C. H., *The Apostolic Preaching and Its Developments* (London: Hodder & Stoughton, Ltd., 1936).

Kelly, J. N. D., *Early Christian Creeds*, 3rd ed. (London: Longmans, Green and Co., 1972).

Stauffer, Ethelbert, *New Testament Theology* (London: SCM Press, Ltd., 1955, Part III—"The Creeds of the Primitive Church"). Appendix iii gives criteria for recognizing creedal formulas in the New Testament.

Von Rad, Gerhard, *Theologie des Alten Testaments*, Vol. I (München: Chr. Kaiser Verlag, 1960).

Wright, G. E., *God Who Acts* (London: SCM Press, 1952).

A HISTORICAL CREDO

Deuteronomy 26:5–9 —". . .'A wandering Aramean was my father; and he went down into Egypt and sojourned there, few in number; and there he became a nation, great, mighty, and populous. And the Egyptians treated us harshly, and afflicted us, and laid upon us hard bondage. Then we cried to the Lord the God of our fathers, and the Lord heard our voice, and saw our affliction, our toil, and our oppression; and the Lord brought us out of Egypt with a mighty hand and an outstretched arm, with great terror, with signs and wonders; and he brought us into this place and gave us this land . . .' "

DECLARATORY AFFIRMATIONS

Deuteronomy 6:4–5–"Hear, O Israel: The Lord our God is one Lord; and you shall love the Lord your God with all your heart, and with all your soul, and with all your might."

1 Kings 18:39–. . . "The Lord, he is God; the Lord, he is God."

CHRISTOLOGICAL CONFESSIONS

Mark 8:29–And he asked them, "But who do you say that I am?" Peter answered him, "You are the Christ."

1 Corinthians 12:3–Therefore I want you to understand that no one speaking by the Spirit of God ever says "Jesus be cursed!" and no one can say "Jesus is Lord" except by the Holy Spirit.

Romans 10:9–. . . if you confess with your lips that Jesus is Lord and believe in your heart that God raised him from the dead, you will be saved.

Acts 2:36–"Let all the house of Israel therefore know assuredly that God has made him both Lord and Christ, this Jesus whom you crucified."

Romans 1:3–4–The gospel concerning his Son, who was descended from David according to the flesh and designated Son of God in power according to the Spirit of holiness by his resurrection from the dead, Jesus Christ our Lord.

1 Timothy 3:16–Great indeed, we confess, is the mystery of our religion:

He was manifested in the flesh, vindicated in the Spirit, seen by angels, preached among the nations, believed on in the world, taken up in glory.

A LITURGICAL CONFESSION

Philippians 2:6–11–. . . . who, though he was in the form of God, did not count equality with God a thing to be grasped, but emptied himself, taking the form of a servant, being born in the likeness of men. And being found in human form he humbled himself and became obedient unto death, even death on a cross. Therefore God has highly exalted him and bestowed on him the name which is above every name, that at the name of Jesus every knee should bow, in heaven and on earth and under the earth, and every tongue confess that Jesus Christ is Lord, to the glory of God the Father.

A SUMMARY OF FAITH FOR TEACHING OR PREACHING

*I Corinthians 15:3–7–*For I delivered to you as of first importance what I also received, that Christ died for our sins in accordance with the scriptures, that he was buried, that he was raised on the third day in accordance with the scriptures, and that he appeared to Cephas, then to the twelve. Then he appeared to more than five hundred brethren at one time, most of whom are still alive, though some have fallen asleep. Then he appeared to James, then to all the apostles.

A BINITARIAN CONFESSION

I Corinthians 8:6–. . . . yet for us there is one God, the Father, from whom are all things and for whom we exist, and one Lord, Jesus Christ, through whom are all things and through whom we exist. *Cf.* Romans 4:24, I Timothy 6:13 ff., I Timothy 2:5 ff., II Timothy 4:1.

TRINITARIAN AFFIRMATIONS

Matthew 28:19–"Go therefore and make disciples of all nations, baptizing them in the name of the Father and of the Son and of the Holy Spirit."

*II Corinthians 13:14–*The grace of the Lord Jesus Christ and the love of God and the fellowship of the Holy Spirit be with you all.

THE PAULINE KERYGMA[1]

The prophecies are fulfilled, and the new Age is inaugurated by the coming of Christ.

He was born of the seed of David.

He died according to the Scriptures, to deliver us out of the present evil age.

He was buried.

He rose on the third day according to the Scriptures.

He is exalted at the right hand of God, as Son of God and Lord of quick and dead.

He will come again as Judge and Saviour of men.

SECOND-CENTURY CREEDAL DEVELOPMENTS

IGNATIUS OF ANTIOCH (c. 107)

There is abundant evidence of the consolidation of Christian faith into precise, stereotyped summaries in the writings of the Apostolic Fathers, especially Ignatius. While these summaries of faith reflect the needs of the Church in instruction, worship, and preaching, there is nothing to indicate a fixed, official creed. This summary of the faith in Ignatius's Letter to the Trallians 9:1–2 is typical and reveals the Church's concern with Docetism, the doctrine that the human, historical life of Jesus was unreal. The date of Ignatius's Letters may be as early as A.D. 107, though some scholars date them in the time of the Emperor Hadrian, A.D. 117–138.

Be deaf, therefore, whenever anyone speaks to you apart from Jesus Christ, who is of the stock of David,

[1] As compiled by C. H. Dodd from the Pauline epistles. *The Apostolic Preaching and Its Developments*, by C. H. Dodd, p. 17. Used by permission.

who is of Mary, who was truly born, ate and drank, was truly persecuted under Pontius Pilate, was truly crucified and died in the sight of beings of heaven, of earth and the underworld, who was also truly raised from the dead. . . .

Corwin, Virginia, *St. Ignatius and Christianity in Antioch* (New Haven: Yale University Press, 1960).

Lightfoot, J. B., *The Apostolic Fathers* (London: The Macmillan Co., 1889), Part II, Vol. II, pp. 173–74; for Greek text.

EPISTULA APOSTOLORUM (c. 150)

This very early creedal summary of Christian faith appears in *Epistula Apostolorum* (or *Dialogues of Jesus with His Disciples after the Resurrection*). The date of this document is around the middle of the second century. It may therefore antedate Tertullian and Irenaeus. The place of origin is Asia Minor or Egypt.

> In the Father, the Ruler of the Universe,
> And in Jesus Christ, our Redeemer,
> In the Holy Spirit, the Paraclete,
> In the Holy Church,
> And in the Forgiveness of Sins.

Altaner, Berthold, *Patrology* (Freiburg: Herder, 1950).

Babcock, F. J., *The History of the Creeds* (London: S. P. C. K., 1930).

Kelly, J. N. D., *Early Christian Creeds*, 3rd ed. (London: Longmans, Green and Co., 1972).

Quasten, J., *Patrology* (Westminster, Md.: Newman Press, 1950).

Schmidt, Carl, *Gespräche Jesu mit seinen Jüngern nach der Auferstehung* (*Texte und Untersuchungen*, 43, ed. by Gebhardt-Harnack-Schmidt, Leipzig-Berlin, 1919). Contains critical text and scholarly commentary.

THE WITNESS OF JUSTIN MARTYR
(c. 165)

A creed-like formula that approaches a personal confession of faith is attributed to Justin Martyr in the account of his martyrdom. The date is probably 165.

> We worship the God of the Christians, whom we consider One from the beginning, the creator and maker of all creation, visible and invisible.
>
> And the Lord Jesus Christ, the Servant of God, who had also been proclaimed beforehand by the prophets as about to be present with the race of men, the herald of salvation and teacher of good instructions.

Kelly, *op. cit.*

Lietzmann, Hans, *The Founding of the Church Universal,* tr. by B. L. Woolf (New York: Charles Scribner's Sons, 1938).

——, "Symbolstudien," *Zeitschrift für die neutestamentliche Wissenschaft,* 1927, Vol. 26, p. 92.

The Ante-Nicene Fathers, ed. by Alexander Roberts and James Donaldson (New York: The Christian Literature Company, 1885), Vol. I, pp. 305–6.

PROFESSION OF THE PRESBYTERS OF
SMYRNA (c. 180)

The Presbyters who condemned Noetus at Smyrna about A.D. 180 professed their faith in a form that has been preserved by Hippolytus.

> We also know in truth one God, we know Christ, we know the Son, suffering as he suffered, dying as he died, and risen on the third day, and abiding at the right hand of the Father, and coming to judge the living and the dead. And in saying this we say what has been handed down to us.

Babcock, *op. cit.*
Kelly, *op. cit.*

Lietzmann, Hans, *The Founding of the Church Universal*, p. 142.

Migne, J. P., *Patrologia Graeca*, Vol. X, p. 805 (Greek text).

The Ante-Nicene Fathers, Vol. V, pp. 223 ff. (Hippolytus: *Against Heresy of One Noetus*).

DÊR BALYZEH PAPYRUS
(c. 200 OR LATER)

A papyrus discovered in 1907 contains a very interesting creed, the exact use of which is unknown. It has been dated as early as the last of the second century; but Kelly, following F. E. Brightman, concludes that nothing really warrants a date before the middle of the fourth century.

Confesses the faith . . .
I believe in God the Father Almighty [*pantokratora*]
And in his only begotten Son,
Our Lord, Jesus Christ,
And in the Holy Spirit,
And in the resurrection of the flesh
In the holy catholic Church.

Altaner, *op. cit.*

Kelly, *op. cit.*

Quasten, *op. cit.*

Roberts, C. H., and Dom B. Capelle, *An Early Euchologium, the Dêr Balyzeh Papyrus* (Louvain: 1949). Enlarged and re-edited. (Greek text translated above.)

Schermann, Th., *Der Liturgische Papyrus von Dêr Balyzeh* (Leipzig: 1910). (*Texte und Untersuchungen*, p. 36.)

RULES OF FAITH (c. 200)

Summaries of Christian faith, known as Rules of Faith, became common in the second half of the second century. They were fixed neither in words nor in theological affirmations. Tertullian, whose precise, legal mind would certainly have been inclined to fixed forms, gives the Rule of Faith in three different forms. Insofar as the Rule was fixed, it served as a standard of the faith, while its flexibility allowed for theological creativity and adaptation to local needs. The Rules of Faith served the Church by providing a basis for catechetical instruction and a guide for the interpretation of Scripture. They also provided theological material for defense against the heretics.

Sources: The selection from Irenaeus is taken from *The Ante-Nicene Fathers*, Alexander Roberts and James Donaldson, editors (New York: the Christian Literature Company, 1885), Vol. I, pp. 330–31; and the Rule of Faith of Tertullian from *Tertullian's Treatise Against Praxeas*, edited and translated by Ernest Evans (London: S. P. C. K., 1949), pp. 131–32.

Kelly, J. N. D., *Early Christian Creeds*, 3rd ed. (London: Longmans, Green and Co., 1972).
Turner, H. E. W., *The Pattern of Christian Truth* (London: A. R. Mowbray & Co., 1954).
Van Den Eynde, Damien, *Les Normes de l'Enseignement Chrétien dans la littérature patristique des trois premiers siècles* (Paris: Gabalda & Fils, *editeurs*, 1933).

IRENAEUS (c. 190)

The Church, though dispersed throughout the whole world, even to the ends of the earth, has received from the apostles and their disciples this faith: [She believes] in one God, the Father Almighty, Maker of heaven, and earth, and the sea, and all things that are in them; and in one Christ Jesus, the Son of God, who became incarnate for our salvation; and in the Holy Spirit, who proclaimed through the prophets the dispensations of God, and the advents, and the birth from a virgin, and the passion, and the resurrection from the dead, and the ascension into heaven in the flesh of the beloved Christ Jesus, our Lord, and His [future] manifestation from heaven in the glory of the Father "to gather all things in one," and to raise up anew all flesh of the whole human race, in order that to Christ Jesus, our Lord, and God, and Saviour, and King, according to the will of the invisible Father, "every knee should bow, of things in heaven, and things in earth, and things under the earth, and that every tongue should confess" to Him, and that He should execute just judgment towards all; that He may send "spiritual wickednesses," and the angels who transgressed and became apostates, together with the ungodly, and unrighteous, and wicked, and profane among men, into everlasting fire; but may, in the exercise of His grace, confer immortality on the righteous, and holy, and those who have kept His commandments, and have persevered in His love, some from the beginning [of their Christian course], and others from [the date of] their repentance, and may surround them with everlasting glory. (*Against Heresies* I, x, 1.)

TERTULLIAN (c. 200)

We however as always, the more so now as better equipped through the Paraclete, that leader into all truth, believe (as these do) in one only God, yet subject to this dispensation (which is our word for "economy") that the one only God has also a Son, his Word who has proceeded from himself, by whom all things were made and without whom nothing has been made: that this [Son] was sent by the Father into the virgin and was born of her both man and God, Son of man and Son of God, and was named Jesus Christ: that he suffered, died, and was buried, according to the scriptures, and, having been raised up by the Father and taken back into heaven, sits at the right hand of the Father and will come to judge the quick and the dead: and that thereafter he, according to his promise, sent from the Father the Holy Spirit the Paraclete, the sanctifier of the faith of those who believe in the Father and the Son and the Holy Spirit. That this Rule has come down from the beginning of the Gospel, even before all former heretics, not to speak of Praxeas of yesterday, will be proved as well by the comparative lateness of all heretics as by the very novelty of Praxeas of yesterday. (*Against Praxeas*, 2.)

THE ROMAN SYMBOL AND THE APOSTLES' CREED

The Apostles' Creed, according to legend, was composed by the Apostles on the tenth day after the Ascension under the inspiration of the Holy Spirit. The legend no doubt added prestige to the creed, but it was effectively exposed as legendary by Lorenzo Valla and subsequent scholars. The creed does have a legitimate claim to its title on the basis of the fact that all of its articles are to be found in the theological formulas that were current around A.D. 100.

The ancestry of the Apostles' Creed can be traced to a creed that developed at Rome about the end of the second century. The origin of this creed is not clear; but its early form is likely preserved in the Interrogatory Creed of Hippolytus's Apostolic Tradition (c. 215), the creed submitted by Marcellus to Julius I (340), and Rufinus's Commentary on the Apostles' Creed (c. 404), which was based on the baptismal creed of his own church, Aquileia, but in which he is careful to point out divergences from the Roman Creed.

INTERROGATORY CREED OF HIPPOLYTUS (c. 215)

Do you believe in God the Father All Governing [*pantokratora*]?

Do you believe in Christ Jesus, the Son of God, Who was begotten by the Holy Spirit from the Virgin Mary, Who was crucified under Pontius Pilate, and died (and was buried) and rose the third day living from the dead, and ascended into the heavens, and sat down on the right hand of the Father, and will come to judge the living and the dead?

Do you believe in the Holy Spirit, in the holy Church, and (in the resurrection of the body [*sarkos*])?

CREED OF MARCELLUS (340)

I believe in God, All Governing [*pantokratora*]; And in Christ Jesus His only begotten Son, our Lord, who was begotten of the Holy Spirit and the Virgin Mary, who was crucified under Pontius Pilate and buried, who rose from the dead on the third day, ascending to the heavens and taking his seat at the Father's right hand, whence He shall come to judge both living and dead;

And [I believe] in the Holy Spirit, the holy Church, the forgiveness of sins, the resurrection of the body [*sarkos*], life everlasting.

CREED OF RUFINUS (AQUILEIA) (c. 404)

I believe in God the Father almighty, invisible and impassable;

And in Christ Jesus, His only Son, our Lord, who was born by the Holy Spirit from Mary the Virgin, crucified under Pontius Pilate and buried. He descended to hell. On the third day He rose again from the dead, He ascended to heaven, where He sits at the Father's right hand and from whence He will come to judge both living and dead;
And [I believe] in the Holy Spirit, the holy Church, the forgiveness of sins, the resurrection of this flesh [*carnis*].

In the three centuries following the emergence of the old Roman Symbol numerous creeds developed in the area that was under Roman influence. While these creeds bear the marks of local influence, they have so strong a resemblance to the Roman Symbol that they can be called daughter creeds.

The date and place of the origin of the present form of the Apostles' Creed cannot be fixed with precision. There is considerable evidence for a date late in the sixth or seventh century somewhere in southwest France. The earliest appearance of the *Textus Receptus* of the Apostles' Creed is found in *De singulis libris canonicis scarapsus* of Priminius. The date of the *scarapsus* is somewhere between 710–24. This creed, which owed much to Rome, was finally adopted by Rome and became the common creed of Western Christendom. At the Council of Florence the Eastern representatives declared that they knew nothing of an Apostles' Creed.

TEXTUS RECEPTUS (c. 700)

I believe in God the Father almighty, creator of heaven and earth;
And in Jesus Christ, His only Son, our Lord, Who was conceived by the Holy Spirit, born of the Virgin Mary, suffered under Pontius Pilate, was crucified, dead and buried. He descended to hell, on the third day rose again from the dead, ascended to heaven, sits at the right hand of God the Father almighty, thence He will come to judge the living and the dead;

I believe in the Holy Spirit, the holy catholic Church, the communion of saints, the forgiveness of sins, the resurrection of the body [*carnis*], and the life everlasting. Amen.

AN AFRICAN VARIANT (c. 400)

A creed that was apparently used in Hippo can be reconstructed from Augustine's sermon on the Rendition of the Creed. It presents some interesting variations that are characteristic of African creeds.

We believe in God the Father Almighty, Creator of all things, Ruler of the ages, immortal and invisible.

We believe in Jesus Christ his Son, our Lord, born of the Holy Spirit from the Virgin Mary, who was crucified under Pontius Pilate, dead and buried, on the third day he arose from the dead, ascended to heaven, and sits at the right hand of God the Father, thence he shall come to judge the living and the dead.

We believe in the Holy Spirit, the forgiveness of sins, the resurrection of the body [*carnis*], the life everlasting through the holy catholic Church.

Badcock, F. J., *The History of the Creeds* (London: S. P. C. K., 1930).

Burn, A. E., *An Introduction to the Creeds* (London: Methuen & Co., 1899).

Caspari, C. P., *Alte und neue Quellen zur Geschichte des Taufsymbols und der Glaubensregel* (Christiana: 1879).

Easton, Burton Scott, *The Apostolic Tradition of Hippolytus* (Cambridge: Cambridge University Press, 1934).

Hahn, A. and G. L., *Bibliothek der Symbole und Glaubensregeln der alten Kirche*, 3rd ed. (Breslau: 1897).

Harnack, A., "The Apostles' Creed," *New Schaff Herzog Encyclopedia of Religious Knowledge*.

Holland, D. Larrimore, "The Earliest Text of the Old Roman Symbol: A Debate with Hans Lietzmann and J. N. D. Kelly," *Church History*, Vol. 34, No. 3, Sept. 1965, pp. 262–281.

Kattenbusch, F., *Das Apostolische Symbol* (Leipzig: 1894).

Kelly, J. N. D., *Early Christian Creeds,* 3rd ed. (London: Longmans, Green and Co., 1972).

——, *Rufinus, A Commentary on the Apostles' Creed,* Vol. 20 of *Ancient Christian Writers* (Westminster, Md.: The Newman Press, 1955; and London: Longmans, Green & Co., 1955).

Lietzmann, Hans, "Symbolstudien," *Zeitschrift für die neutestamentliche Wissenschaft,* 1927, Vol. 26, p. 81. (Text of Interrogatory Creed of Hippolytus.)

——, "Creeds," *Encyclopedia Britannica,* 1957.

McGiffert, A. C., *The Apostles' Creed* (New York: Charles Scribner's Sons, 1902). (Emphasizes role of polemics in development of creed.)

Migne, J. P., *Patrologia Graeca,* Vol. 42, pp. 385–88. (Text of Marcellus's Creed is found in Epiphanius: *Against Heresies,* LXXII.)

——, *Patrologia Latina,* Vol. LXXXIX, pp. 1029 ff. (*De singulis libris canonicis scarapsus* quotes Apostles' Creed in its received form.)

——, *op. cit.,* Vol. XXXVIII, pp. 1072 ff. (Augustine's sermon on Rendition of the Creed [Hippo].)

EASTERN CREEDS

In the East no one creed achieved the dominant influence of the Roman Symbol in the West. This is no doubt related to the fact that no church in the East had the influence of Rome in the West.

The early history of Eastern creeds is obscure. Some have argued that they have as their source the Roman Symbol. Others see the Eastern creed as the source of the Roman creed. Still others think there was some original formula from which both Eastern and Western creeds developed. A simpler explanation than any of the above is the supposition that many Eastern creeds developed in church centers with a similarity of pattern and theology but with no common ancestor.

Hans Lietzmann constructed a hypothetical creed as the source of Oriental creedal development. Even if this creed has only existed in the scholars' study, it is a shrewd approximation to what the original Eastern creed would have been if it had existed.

The Eastern creeds are more elaborately theological than the Western, and they are more concerned to place the drama of redemption in a cosmic setting.

Kelly, J. N. D., *Early Christian Creeds,* 3rd ed. (London: Longmans, Green and Co., 1972).

Lietzmann, Hans, *The Founding of the Church Universal,* tr. by B. L. Woolf (New York: Charles Scribner's Sons, 1950), Chap. 4.

——, "Symbolstudien," *Zeitschrift für die neutestamentliche Wissenschaft,* 1922, Vol. 1, p. 23 (text of Lietzmann's Oriental Creed).

Opitz, H. G., ed., *Athanasius Werke* (Berlin and Leipzig: De Gruyter, 1934), Vol. III, 1, p. 43 (Letter of Eusebius containing creed).

ORIENTAL CREED (LIETZMANN)

I believe in one God, the Father All Governing [*pantokratora*] the creator of all things visible and invisible.

And in one Lord Jesus Christ, the only-begotten Son of God, who was begotten from the Father before all the ages [*pro pantōn tōn aiōnōn*], through whom all things came into being, who [for our salvation] became man [*enanthrōpēsanta*], suffered, and rose on the third day, and ascended into the heavens, and will come [again] to judge the living and the dead.

And in the Holy Spirit.

CREED OF CAESAREA (EUSEBIUS)
(325)

We believe in one God, the Father All Governing [*pantokratora*], Creator [*poiētēn*] of everything visible and invisible.

And in one Lord Jesus Christ, the Word [*logos*] of God, God from God, Light from Light, Life from Life, the only-begotten Son, the first born of all creation, begotten of the Father before all time [*pro pantōn tōn aiōnōn*], by whom also everything came into being, who for our salvation became incarnate and lived among men. He suffered, and rose the third day, and ascended to the Father, and will come again in glory to judge the living and the dead.

We believe also in one Holy Spirit.

THE CREED OF NICAEA (325)

Creedal developments entered a new stage at Nicaea when an ecumenical council adopted a creed that was to be a test for orthodoxy and was to be authoritative for the whole Church. There were earlier indications of this type of development, as the Councils of Antioch (268 and 325) had prepared synodical statements and the local creeds had been regarded as containing the catholic faith. Nevertheless, Nicaea is sufficiently different from anything that had gone before to represent a new epoch in creed-making.

The occasion was the dispute concerning the theology of Arius, which raised in acute form the question of the real meaning and significance of Jesus Christ. The Christian community had been accustomed to regard him as God as well as man. Arian theology forced the Christian Church to say in what sense he was God.

Arius insisted that the Word or Son was a creature, that he was made by God, that he had a beginning, and that he was subject to change. This means, as Athanasius pointed out, that the Son does not have full and accurate knowledge of the Father. In Jesus Christ, man is not really confronted by God.

The Nicene Creed insisted that God has fully come into human history in Jesus Christ. It sought to make this clear through certain key phrases in the creed: "That is, of the essence of the Father"; "True God from true God"; "Begotten, not created"; "Of one essence [reality] with the Father." This last phrase was decisive, but it was the subject of considerable controversy. It was not Biblical, and it had been used in other theological contexts that placed it under suspicion.

For fifty years after Nicaea, the Church debated the affirmation, "Of one essence with the Father." Various alternatives were tried: "Exact image of the Godhead" (Second Creed of Antioch, 341); "Like the Father who begot Him according to the Scriptures" (Dated Creed, Fourth of Sirmium); "Like the Father in all things" (Dated Creed, Fourth of Sirmium); "Of like essence with the Father" (Ancyra, 358); "Unlike the Father" (the teaching of Aetius and Eunomius and, by implication, of the Second Creed of Sirmium, 357). In the end, the Christian community affirmed the declaration of Nicaea, "Of one essence [reality] with the Father," as the only affirmation that did justice to its conviction that it had been confronted by nothing less than God himself in Jesus Christ.

Theologically, the assertion that the Son is only like God undermined the Christian community's conviction about the finality of Jesus Christ. The claim that he was like God presupposed some standard to determine whether he was like God and the extent to which he was like God. It furthermore left open the possibility that someone else more like God might appear. Christianity would be only one of many possible religions. If God himself is incarnate in Jesus Christ, then this is the final Word. There is nothing further to be said.

The cultural significance of the Nicene theology is revealed in the disposition of the political Imperialists to be Arians. Imperialism as a political strategy was more compatible with the notion that Jesus Christ is something less than the full and absolute Word of God.

Texts of Creed

Opitz, H. G., ed., *Athanasius Werke,* Vol. III, 1 (Berlin and Leipzig: De Gruyter, 1934), pp. 44–45, 51–52 (Eusebius's Letter).

Schwartz, Eduard, ed., *Acta Conciliorum Oecumenicorum,* Vol. II, I, ii (Berlin: 1922), pp. 79, 127 (Acts of Council of Chalcedon).

General Introductions

Bethune-Baker, J. F., *An Introduction to the Early History of Christian Doctrine* (London: Methuen & Co., Ltd., 1929).

Hardy, Edward Rochie, ed., *Christology of the Later Fathers,* Vol. III of *The Library of Christian Classics* (Philadelphia: The Westminster Press, 1954).

Holland, D. Larrimore, "The Creeds of Nicea and Constantinople Reexamined," *Church History,* Vol. 38, No. 2, June 1969, pp. 248–261.

Kelly, J. N. D., *Early Christian Creeds,* 3rd ed. (London: Longmans, Green and Co., 1972).

Theological Significance

Baillie, Donald, *God Was in Christ* (New York: Charles Scribner's Sons, 1948) (especially Chapter III).

Tillich, Paul, *A History of Christian Thought,* recorded and edited by Peter H. John (New York: 1956).

Cultural Significance

Cochrane, Charles N., *Christianity and Classical Culture* (Oxford: The Clarendon Press, 1940).

Williams, George Huntston, "Christology and Church-State Relations in the Fourth Century." *Church History,* Vol. XX, No. 3, pp. 3–33; No. 4, pp. 3–25.

THE CREED OF NICAEA (325)

(CREED OF 318 FATHERS)

We believe in one God, the Father All Governing [*pantokratora*], creator [*poiētēn*] of all things visible and invisible;

And in one Lord Jesus Christ, the Son of God, begotten of the Father as only begotten, that is, from the essence [reality] of the Father, [*ek tēs ousias tou patros*], God from God, Light from Light, true God from true God, begotten not created [*poiēthenta*], of the same essence [reality] as the Father [*homoousion tō patri*], through whom all things came into being, both in heaven and in earth; Who for us men and for our salvation came down and was incarnate, becoming human [*enanthrōpēsanta*]. He suffered and the third day he rose, and ascended into the heavens. And he will come to judge both the living and the dead.

And [we believe] in the Holy Spirit.

But, those who say, Once he was not, or he was not before his generation, or he came to be out of nothing, or who assert that he, the Son of God, is of a different *hypostasis* or *ousia*, or that he is a creature, or changeable, or mutable, the Catholic and Apostolic Church anathematizes them.

THE CONSTANTINOPOLITAN CREED
(*381*)

(CREED OF 150 FATHERS)

The Constantinopolitan Creed, popularly known as the Nicene Creed, has since the Council of Chalcedon (451) been associated with the Council of Constantinople (381). The exact records of the Council (Constantinople, 381) do not contain the creed, and it was not popularly used before Chalcedon. For these and other reasons many scholars have concluded that the creed actually had no relation to the Council. This conclusion, however, is difficult to relate to the acceptance of the creed at Chalcedon as in some sense the work of the Council of Constantinople. Recent studies, including those of Schwartz and Kelly, conclude that the creed is properly called the Creed of the 150 Fathers of Constantinople, though the details of this Council's work on the creed remain obscure.

The creed is Nicene in that it affirms the theology of

Nicaea. It goes beyond Nicaea in that it affirms the full deity of the Holy Spirit, but in Biblical language rather than with the Nicene *"homoousios."* The clause "who with the Father and the Son is together worshiped and together glorified" leaves no doubt as to the authentic deity of the Holy Spirit. "From the Holy Spirit and the Virgin Mary" has been traditionally regarded as a refutation of Apollinarianism. The Council did condemn Apollinarianism, and the clause does contain the material for the refutation of Apollinarianism; but whether the clause was specifically added for this purpose is not clear.

The creed is suited to liturgy and may have largely developed in the liturgy of the Church. In any case, it was very early employed as a baptismal creed and was used in the liturgy of the Eucharist from the sixth century. After Chalcedon it became the most universally accepted of all the creeds.

In the West the original text "who proceeds from the Father" was altered to read "from the Father and the Son." This alteration is rooted in the theology of the Western Church, in particular the theology of Augustine. The procession from the Son was vigorously affirmed by the Council at Toledo in 589 and gradually was added to the creed, though it was not accepted as part of the creed at Rome until a number of centuries had passed.

Harnack, A., "Constantinopolitan Creed," *The New Schaff Herzog Encyclopedia of Religious Knowledge.*

Hort, F. J. A., *Two Dissertations* (Cambridge: The Macmillan Co., 1876).

Kelly, J. N. D., *Early Christian Creeds,* 3rd ed. (London: Longmans, Green and Co., 1972).

Schwartz, Eduard, ed., *Acta Conciliorum Oecumenicorum,* II, I, ii (Berlin: 1922), pp. 80, 128 (for Greek texts).

———, *"Das Nicaenum und das Constantinopolitanum auf der Synode von Chalcedon,"* *Zeitschrift für die neutestamentliche Wissenschaft,* xxv, 1926.

THE CONSTANTINOPOLITAN CREED
(CREED OF 150 FATHERS)

We believe in one God, the Father All Governing [*pantokratora*], creator [*poiētēn*] of heaven and earth, of all things visible and invisible;

And in one Lord Jesus Christ, the only-begotten Son of God, begotten from the Father before all time [*pro pantōn tōn aiōnōn*], Light from Light, true God from true God, begotten not created [*poiēthenta*], of the same essence [reality] as the Father [*homoousion tō patri*], through Whom all things came into being, Who for us men and because of our salvation came down from heaven, and was incarnate by the Holy Spirit and the Virgin Mary and became human [*enanthrōpēsanta*]. He was crucified for us under Pontius Pilate, and suffered and was buried, and rose on the third day, according to the Scriptures, and ascended to heaven, and sits on the right hand of the Father, and will come again with glory to judge the living and dead. His Kingdom shall have no end [*telos*].

And in the Holy Spirit, the Lord and life-giver, Who proceeds from the Father, Who is worshiped and glorified together with the Father and Son, Who spoke through the prophets; and in one, holy, catholic, and apostolic Church. We confess one baptism for the remission of sins. We look forward to the resurrection of the dead and the life of the world to come. Amen.

THE DEFINITION OF CHALCEDON
(451)

Nicaea settled the question as to whether the Son or the Logos was truly God, but the question of the person of Jesus Christ remained. In what sense was he truly man? How was he both God and man?

Various answers were given. Apollinarianism solved the problem by truncating the manhood. It was the conviction of the Church that he was truly man, and the Church rejected Apollinarianism. Nestorianism (though not necessarily Nestorius) solved the problem by endangering the unity of the person. Again the Church was convinced that Jesus Christ in his humanity and his divinity was truly one person. Another attempted answer, Eutychianism, absorbed the human into the divine. The doctrine of the person of Jesus Christ was not isolated from but involved in the whole range of theology, the doctrines of salvation, of the sacraments, and of history. Furthermore, the Christological controversy was not abstract theology but was intimately related to the social issues and culture of the day. A doctrine of the person of Christ, for example, that did not take seriously the historic life of Jesus would not likely take history in general very seriously.

The Christological settlement at Chalcedon illustrates the catholicity of the theology of the ancient church. Three major schools of theology had been involved in the Christological controversies and were represented at Chalcedon: Alexandria, Antioch, and Western Christianity. The final result could have been produced by none of these schools of thought alone. Chalcedon was truly catholic in the very great degree in which it was the result of the shared theological wisdom of the Church.

While the Definition of Chalcedon did not fully satisfy the Church of the fifth century or the Church since then, its critics have never been able to produce a definition that in the judgment of the Church improves upon Chalcedon. In spite of all the nontheological factors involved in the Christological controversies, the Church devoted its theological gifts to the problem with a singleness of interest that is hard to duplicate and with a catholicity that helped to keep the discussion in balance. Chalcedon is the place in "the history of Christian thought where the New Testament compound was explicated in exact balance so as to discourage the four favorite ways by which the divine and human 'energies' of the Christ event are commonly misconstrued."[1]

Source: Translation by Professor Albert C. Outler is based on text in *Acta Conciliorum Oecumenicorum*, Vol. II, II, i (Berlin: 1922), pp. 129–30.

Bindley, T. H., *The Oecumenical Documents of the Faith*, 4th ed., ed. by F. W. Green (London: Methuen & Co., Ltd., 1950).

Grillmeier, Aloys, S. J., and Bacht, Heinrich, S. J., *Das Konzil von Chalkedon*, Vols. I–III (Würzburg: Echter-Verlag, 1953).

Hardy, Edward Rochie, ed., *Christology of the Later Fathers*, Vol. III of *Library of Christian Classics* (Philadelphia: Westminster Press, 1954).

Sellers, R. V., *The Council of Chalcedon, A Historical and Doctrinal Survey* (London: S. P. C. K., 1953).

THE DEFINITION OF CHALCEDON

Following, then, the holy fathers, we unite in teaching all men to confess the one and only Son, our Lord Jesus Christ. This selfsame one is perfect [*teleion*] both in deity [*theotēti*] and also in human-ness [*anthrōpotēti*]; this selfsame one is also actually [*alēthōs*] God and actually man, with a rational soul [*psychēs*

[1] Albert C. Outler, "Jesus Christ as Divine-Human Savior." *Christian Century*, May 3, 1961.

logikēs] and a body. He is of the same reality as God [*homoousion tō patri*] as far as his deity is concerned and of the same reality as we are ourselves [*homoousion hēmin*] as far as his human-ness is concerned; thus like us in all respects, sin only excepted. Before time began [*pro aiōnōn*] he was begotten of the Father, in respect of his deity, and now in these "last days," for us and on behalf of our salvation, this selfsame one was born of Mary the virgin, who is God-bearer [*theotokos*] in respect of his human-ness [*anthrōpotēta*].

[We also teach] that we apprehend [*gnōridzomenon*] this one and only Christ—Son, Lord, only-begotten—in two natures [*duo physesin*]; [and we do this] without confusing the two natures [*asunkutōs*], without transmuting one nature into the other [*atreptōs*], without dividing them into two separate categories [*adiairetōs*], without contrasting them according to area or function [*achōristōs*]. The distinctiveness of each nature is not nullified by the union. Instead, the "properties" [*idiotētos*] of each nature are conserved and both natures concur [*suntrechousēs*] in one "person" [*prosōpon*] and in one *hypostasis*. They are not divided or cut into two *prosōpa*, but are together the one and only and only-begotten Logos of God, the Lord Jesus Christ. Thus have the prophets of old testified; thus the Lord Jesus Christ himself taught us; thus the Symbol of the Fathers [N] has handed down [*paradedōke*] to us.

THE COUNCIL OF ORANGE (529)

The doctrine of man came to the forefront of the Church's attention in the theology of Augustine (354–430) and in his controversy with Pelagius. The controversy centered upon the extent of the impairment of the human will and person by Adam's sin and the role of divine grace in the restoration of man. The controversy was resolved for the time being at the Council of Orange (Arausiacum) in 529 when Caesarius took advantage of a church dedication to defend himself against the Semi-Pelagians. The Council affirmed that man's free will has been so weakened by sin that he can of himself neither believe in God nor love him. Grace is necessary for man's restoration, and this grace is tied, though not exclusively, to baptism. Double predestination is repudiated and irresistible grace is omitted. Orange represents the victory of a moderate Augustinianism.

Source: Translation based on text in H. Denzinger, *Enchiridion Symbolorum* (Friburg: Herder, 1955), pp. 85-92. Translated by Ross Mackenzie. Rom. 5:12 translation by J. Patout Burns, S.J. (tr. and ed.), *Theological Anthropology* (in *Sources of Early Christian Thought*, ed. Wm. G. Rusch; Philadelphia: Fortress, 1981), p. 113.

Hefele, Charles J., *A History of the Councils of the Church*, tr. by William R. Clark, Vol. IV (Edinburgh: T. & T. Clark, 1895).

Schaff, Philip, *History of the Christian Church*, Vol. III (New York: Charles Scribner's Sons, 1914).

Seeberg, R., *Textbook of the History of Doctrine*, tr. by C. E. Hay (Philadelphia: Luther Pub. Soc., 1905).

Warfield, B. B., *Studies in Tertullian and Augustine* (New York: Oxford University Press, 1930).

THE COUNCIL OF ORANGE (529)

Canon 1. If anyone denies that it is the whole man, that is, both body and soul, that was "changed for the worse" through the offense of Adam's sin, but believes that the freedom of the soul remains unimpaired and that only the body is subject to corruption, he is deceived by the error of Pelagius and contradicts the scripture which says, "The soul that sinneth, the same shall die" (Ezek. 18:20); and, "Know you not, that to whom you yield yourselves servants to obey, his servants you are whom you obey?" (Rom. 6:16); and, "For by whom a man is overcome, of the same also he is the slave" (II Pet. 2:19).

Canon 2. If anyone asserts that Adam's sin affected him alone and not his descendants also, or at least if he declares that it is only the death of the body which is the punishment for sin, and not also that sin, which is the death of the soul, passed through one man to the whole human race, he does injustice to God and contradicts the Apostle, who says, "Through one person sin entered the world and through sin death, and thus it passed to all [men], in whom all have sinned" (Rom. 5:12).

Canon 3. If anyone says that the grace of God can be conferred as a result of human prayer, but that it is not grace itself which makes us pray to God, he contradicts the prophet Isaiah, or the Apostle who says the same thing, "I was found by them, that did not seek me: I appeared openly to them that asked not after me" (Rom. 10:20; cf. Isa. 65:1).

Canon 4. If anyone maintains that God awaits our will to be cleansed from sin, but does not confess that even our will to be cleansed comes to us through the infusion and working of the Holy Spirit, he resists the Holy Spirit himself who says through Solomon, "The will is prepared by the Lord" (Prov. 8:35, LXX), and the salutary word of the Apostle, "It is God who worketh in you both to will and to accomplish" (Phil. 2:13).

Canon 5. If anyone says that not only the increase of faith but also its beginning and the very desire for faith, by which we believe in Him who justifies the ungodly and come to the regeneration of holy baptism —if anyone says that this belongs to us by nature and not by a gift of grace, that is, by the inspiration of the Holy Spirit amending our will and turning it from unbelief to faith and from godlessness to godliness, it is proof that he is opposed to the teaching of the Apostles, for blessed Paul says, "Being confident of this very thing, that He, who hath begun a good work in you, will perfect it unto the day of Christ Jesus" (Phil. 1:6). And again, "Unto you it is given for Christ, not only to believe in Him, but also to suffer for Him" (Phil. 1:29). And again, "By grace you are saved through faith, and that not of yourselves, for it is the gift of God" (Eph. 2:8). For those who state that the faith by which we believe in God is natural make all who are separated from the Church of Christ by definition in some measure believers.

Canon 6. If anyone says that God has mercy upon us when, apart from his grace, we believe, will, desire, strive, labor, pray, watch, study, seek, ask, or knock, but does not confess that it is by the infusion and inspiration of the Holy Spirit within us that we have the faith, the will, or the strength to do all these things as we ought; or if anyone makes the assistance of grace depend on the humility or obedience of man and does not agree that it is a gift of grace itself that we are obedient and humble, he contradicts the Apostle who says, "What hast thou that thou hast not received?" (I Cor. 4:7), and, "By the grace of God, I am what I am" (I Cor. 15:10).

Canon 7. If anyone affirms that we can form any right opinion or make any right choice which relates to the salvation of eternal life, as is expedient for us, or that we can be saved, that is, assent to the preaching of the gospel through our natural powers without the illumination and inspiration of the Holy Spirit, who makes all men gladly assent to and believe in the truth, he is led astray by a heretical spirit, and does not understand the voice of God who says in the Gospel, "Without me you can do nothing" (John 15:5), and the word of the Apostle, "Not that we are sufficient to think any thing of ourselves, as of ourselves; but our sufficiency is from God" (II Cor. 3:5).

Canon 8. If anyone maintains that some are able to come to the grace of baptism by mercy but others through free will, which has manifestly been corrupted in all those who have been born after the transgression of the first man, it is proof that he has no place in the true faith. For he denies that the free will of all men has been weakened through the sin of the first man, or at least holds that it has been affected in such a way that some have still the ability to seek the mystery of eternal salvation by themselves without the revelation of God. The Lord himself shows how contradictory this is by declaring that no one is able to come to him "except the Father draw him" (John 6:44), as he also says to Peter, "Blessed art thou, Simon Bar-Jonah: because flesh and blood hath not revealed it to thee, but my Father who is in heaven" (Matt. 16:17), and as the Apostle says, "No man can say, the Lord Jesus, but by the Holy Ghost" (I Cor. 12:3).

Canon 9. Concerning the succor of God. It is a mark of divine favor when we are of a right purpose and keep our feet from hypocrisy and unrighteousness; for as often as we do good, God is at work in us and with us, in order that we may so do.

Canon 10. Concerning the succor of God. The succor of God is to be ever sought by the regenerate and converted also, so that they may be able to come to a successful end or persevere in good works.

Canon 11. Concerning the duty to pray. None would make any true prayer to the Lord had he not received from him the object of his prayer, as it is written, "Of thy own have we given thee" (I Chr. 29:14).

Canon 12. Of what sort we are whom God loves.

God loves us for what we shall be by his gift, and not by our own deserving.

Canon 13. Concerning the restoration of free will. The freedom of will that was destroyed [*infirmatum*] in the first man can be restored only by the grace of baptism, for what is lost can be returned only by the one who was able to give it. Hence the Truth itself declares: "If the Son makes you free, you will be free indeed" (John 8:36).

Canon 14. No mean wretch is freed from his sorrowful state, however great it be, save the one who is anticipated [*praevenitur*] by the mercy of God, as the Psalmist says, "Let thy compassion come speedily to meet us" (Ps. 79:8), and again, "My God in his steadfast love will meet me" (Ps. 59:10).

Canon 15. Adam was changed, but for the worse, through his own iniquity from what God made him. Through the grace of God the believer is changed, but for the better, from what his iniquity has done for him. The one, therefore, was the change brought about by the first sinner; the other, according to the Psalmist, is the change of the right hand of the Most High (Ps. 77:10).

Canon 16. No man shall be honored by his seeming attainment, as though it were not a gift, or suppose that he has received it because a missive from without stated it in writing or in speech. For the Apostle speaks thus, "If justification were through the law, then Christ died to no purpose" (Gal. 2:21); and "When he ascended on high he led a host of captives, and he gave gifts to men" (Eph. 4:8; *cf.* Ps. 68:18). It is from this source that any man has what he does; but whoever denies that he has it from this source either does not truly have it, or else "even what he has will be taken away" (Matt. 25:29).

Canon 17. Concerning Christian courage. The courage of the Gentiles is produced by simple greed, but the courage of Christians by the love of God which "has been poured into our hearts" not by freedom of will from our own side but "through the Holy Spirit which has been given to us" (Rom. 5:5).

Canon 18. That grace is not preceded by merit. Recompense is due to good works if they are performed; but grace, to which we have no claim, precedes [*praevenit*] them, to enable them to be done.

Canon 19. That a man can be saved only when God shows mercy. Human nature, even though it remained in that sound state in which it was created, could by no means save itself, without the assistance of the Creator; hence since man cannot safeguard his salvation without the grace of God, which is a gift, how will he be able to restore what he has lost without the grace of God?

Canon 20. That a man can do no good without God. God does much that is good in a man that the man does not do; but a man does nothing good for which God is not responsible, so as to let him do it.

Canon 21. Concerning nature and grace. As the Apostle most truly says to those who would be justified by the law and have fallen from grace, "If justification were through the law, then Christ died to no purpose" (Gal. 2:21), so it is most truly declared to those who imagine that grace, which faith in Christ advocates and lays hold of, is nature: "If justification were through nature, then Christ died to no purpose." Now there was indeed the law, but it did not justify, and there was indeed nature, but it did not justify. Not in vain did Christ therefore die, so that the law might be fulfilled by him who said, "I have not come to abolish the law, but to fulfil it" (Matt. 5:17), and that the nature which had been destroyed by Adam might be restored by him who said that he had come "to seek and to save the lost" (Luke 19:10).

Canon 22. Concerning those things that belong to man. No man has anything of his own but untruth and sin. But if a man has any truth or righteousness, it is from that fountain for which we must thirst in this desert, so that we may be refreshed from it as by drops of water and not faint on the way.

Canon 23. Concerning the will of God and of man. Men do their own will and not the will of God when they do what displeases him; but when they follow their own will and comply with the will of God, however willingly they do so, yet it is his will by which what they will is both prepared and instructed.

Canon 24. Concerning the branches of the vine. The branches on the vine do not give life to the vine, but receive life from it; thus the vine is related to its branches in such a way that it supplies them with what they need to live, and does not take this from them. Thus it is to the advantage of the disciples, not Christ, both to have Christ abiding in them and to abide in Christ. For if the vine is cut down another can shoot up from the live root; but one who is cut off from the vine cannot live without the root (John 15:5 ff.).

Canon 25. Concerning the love with which we love God. It is wholly a gift of God to love God. He who loves, even though he is not loved, allowed himself to be loved. We are loved, even when we displease him, so that we might have the means to please him. For the Spirit, whom we love with the Father and the Son, has poured into our hearts the love of the Father and the Son (Rom. 5:5).

Conclusion. And thus according to the passages of holy scripture quoted above or the interpretations of the ancient Fathers we must, under the blessing of God, preach and believe as follows. The sin of the first man has so impaired and weakened free will that no one thereafter can either love God as he ought or believe in God or do good for God's sake, unless the grace of divine mercy has preceded him. We therefore believe that the glorious faith which was given to Abel the righteous, and Noah, and Abraham, and Isaac, and Jacob, and to all the saints of old, and which the Apostle Paul commends in extolling them (Heb. 11), was not given through natural goodness as it was before to Adam, but was bestowed by the grace of God. And we know and also believe that

even after the coming of our Lord this grace is not
to be found in the free will of all who desire to be
baptized, but is bestowed by the kindness of Christ,
as has already been frequently stated and as the Apostle Paul declares, "Unto you it is given for Christ,
not only to believe in him, but also to suffer for him"
(Phil. 1:29). And again, "He who hath begun a
good work in you will perfect it unto the day of
Christ Jesus" (Phil. 1:6). And again, "By grace you
are saved through faith, and that not of yourselves,
for it is the gift of God" (Eph. 2:8). And as the
Apostle says of himself, "I have obtained mercy to
be faithful" (I Cor. 7:25, I Tim. 1:13). He did not
say "because I was faithful," but "to be faithful."
And again, "What hast thou that thou hast not received?" (I Cor. 4:7). And again, "Every best gift,
and every perfect gift, is from above, coming down
from the Father of lights" (Jas. 1:17). And again,
"A man cannot receive any thing, unless it be given
him from heaven" (John 3:27). There are innumerable passages of holy scripture which can be quoted
to prove the case for grace, but they have been omitted for the sake of brevity, because further examples
will not really be of use where few are deemed insufficient.

According to the catholic faith we also believe that
after grace has been received through baptism, all
baptized persons have the ability and responsibility,
if they desire to labor faithfully, to perform with the
aid and cooperation of Christ what is of essential importance in regard to the salvation of their soul. We
not only do not believe that any are foreordained to
evil by power of God, but even state with utter abhor-
rence that if there are those who want to believe so
evil a thing, they are anathema. We also believe and
confess to our benefit that in every good work it is
not we who take the initiative and are then assisted
through the mercy of God, but God himself first in-
spires in us both faith in him and love for him without
any previous good works of our own that deserve

reward, so that we may both faithfully seek the sacrament of baptism, and after baptism be able by his help to do what is pleasing to him. We must therefore most evidently believe that the praiseworthy faith of the thief whom the Lord called to his home in paradise, and of Cornelius the centurion, to whom the angel of the Lord was sent, and of Zacchaeus, who was worthy to receive the Lord himself, was not a natural endowment but a gift of God's kindness.

THE SECOND COUNCIL OF CONSTANTINOPLE (553)

The Council of Chalcedon did not end the Christological argument. The Alexandrians were dissatisfied. Their grievances were the omission of the formula "one incarnate nature of the divine Logos" and of the "hypostatic union" and of the confession "out of Two." The inclusion of the phrase "in two natures" after the union confirmed them in their worst suspicions. The more extreme opponents of Chalcedon were called Monophysites, because of their insistence upon one nature.

The Fifth Ecumenical Council was called by Justinian, who wanted the theological issue settled. The Council did not intend to repudiate Chalcedon, but rather to interpret it in such a way as to relieve some of the objections. The anathemas very well summarized its action. It condemned conspicuous representatives of the theology of Antioch: Theodore of Mopsuestia, the anti-Cyrillian writing of Theodoret of Cyrus, and the letter of Ibas to Marius, the Persian. It gave approval to the "hypostatic union" that was so important to the Alexandrians, and it endorsed the controversial, liturgical affirmation "that our Lord Jesus Christ who was crucified in the flesh is True God." It found the formula "one incarnate nature of the divine Logos" implied in Chalcedonian definition. The Council made possible an Alexandrian interpretation of Chalcedon, but it did not reject the Chalcedonian definition.

Hefele, Charles J., *A History of the Councils of the Church,* tr. by William R. Clark (Edinburgh: T. & T. Clark, 1895). Greek text, translation and commentary.

Sellers, R. V., *The Council of Chalcedon, A History and Doctrinal Survey* (London: S. P. C. K., 1953).

THE ANATHEMAS OF THE SECOND COUNCIL OF CONSTANTINOPLE (553)

I.

If anyone does not confess that the Father and the Son and the Holy Spirit are one nature or essence [reality], one power or authority, worshipped as a trinity of the same essence [reality], one deity in three hypostases or persons, let him be anathema. For there is one God and Father, of whom are all things, and one Lord Jesus Christ, through whom are all things, and one Holy Spirit, in whom are all things.

II.

If anyone does not confess that God the Word was twice begotten, the first before all time from the Father, non-temporal and bodiless, the other in the last days when he came down from the heavens and was incarnate by the holy, glorious, *theotokos,* ever-virgin Mary, and born of her, let him be anathema.

III.

If anyone says that God the Word who performed miracles is one and Christ who suffered is another, or says that God the Word was together with Christ who came from woman, or that [the Word] was in him as one [person] is in another, but is not one and the same, our Lord Jesus Christ, the Word of God, incarnate and become human, and that the wonders and the suffering which he voluntarily endured in flesh were [not] of the same [person], let him be anathema.

IV.

If anyone says that the union of the Word of God with man was only according to grace or function or dignity or equality of honor or authority or relation or effect or power or according to his good pleasure, as though God the Word was pleased with man, or approved of him, as the raving Theodosius says; or that the union exists according to similarity of name, by which the Nestorians call God the Word Jesus and Christ, designating the man separately as Christ and as Son, speaking thus clearly of two persons, but when it comes to his honor, dignity, and worship, pretend to say that there is one person, one Son and one Christ, by a single designation; and if he does not acknowledge, as the holy Fathers have taught, that the union of God is made with the flesh animated by a reasonable and intelligent soul, and that such union is according to synthesis or hypostasis, and that therefore there is only one person, the Lord Jesus Christ, one of the holy Trinity—let him be anathema. As the word "union" has many meanings, the followers of the impiety of Apollinaris and Eutyches, assuming the disappearance of the natures, affirm a union by confusion. On the other hand the followers of Theodore and of Nestorius rejoicing in the division of the natures, introduce only a union of relation. But the holy Church of God, rejecting equally the impiety of both heresies, recognises the union of God the Word with the flesh according to synthesis, that is according to hypostasis. For in the mystery of Christ the union according to synthesis preserves the [two natures] which have combined without confusion and without separation.

V.

If anyone understands the expression—one hypostasis of our Lord Jesus Christ—so that it means the union of many hypostases, and if he attempts thus to

introduce into the mystery of Christ two hypostases,
or two persons, and, after having introduced two persons, speaks of one person according to dignity, honour or worship, as Theodore and Nestorius insanely
have written; and if anyone slanders the holy synod
of Chalcedon, as though it had used this expression
[one hypostasis] in this impious sense, and does not
confess that the Word of God is united with the flesh
hypostatically, and that therefore there is but one
hypostasis or one person, and that the holy synod of
Chalcedon has professed in this sense the one hypostasis of our Lord Jesus Christ; let him be anathema.
For the Holy Trinity, when God the Word was incarnate, was not increased by the addition of a person
or hypostasis.

VI.

If anyone says that the holy, glorious, and ever-
virgin Mary is called *Theotokos* by misuse of language and not truly, or by analogy, believing that only
a mere man was born of her and that God the Word
was not incarnate of her, but that the incarnation of
God the Word resulted only from the fact that he
united himself to that man who was born [of her]; if
anyone slanders the Holy Synod of Chalcedon as
though it had asserted the Virgin to be *Theotokos* according to the impious sense of Theodore; or if anyone shall call her manbearer [*anthrōpotokos*] or
Christbearer [*Christokos*], as if Christ were not
God, and shall not confess that she is truly God-
bearer [*Theotokos*], because God the Word who before all time was begotten of the Father was in these
last days incarnate of her, and if anyone shall not
confess that in this pious sense the holy Synod of
Chalcedon confessed her to be Godbearer [*Theotokos*]: let him be anathema.

VII.

If anyone using the expression, "in two natures,"
does not confess that our one Lord Jesus Christ is
made known in the deity and in the manhood, in or-

der to indicate by that expression a difference of the natures of which the ineffable union took place without confusion, [a union] in which neither the nature of the Word has changed into that of the flesh, nor that of the flesh into that of the Word (for each remained what it was by nature, even when the union by hypostasis had taken place); but shall take the expression with regard to the mystery of Christ in a sense so as to divide the parties, [let him be anathema]. Or [if anyone] recognizing the number of natures in the same our one Lord Jesus Christ, God the Word incarnate, does not take in contemplation only the difference of the natures which compose him, which difference is not destroyed by the union between them—for one is composed of the two and the two are in one—but shall make use of the number [two] to divide the natures or to make of them persons properly so called, let him be anathema.

VIII.

If anyone confesses that the union took place out of two natures or speaks of the one incarnate nature of God the Word and does not understand those expressions as the holy Fathers have taught, that out of the divine and human natures, when union by hypostasis took place, one Christ was formed; but from these expressions tries to introduce one nature or essence of the Godhead and manhood of Christ; let him be anathema. For in saying that the only-begotten Word was united by hypostasis [personally] we do not mean that there was a mutual confusion of natures, but rather we understand that the Word was united to the flesh, each [nature] remaining what it was. Therefore there is one Christ, God and man, of the same essence [reality] with the Father as touching his Godhead, and of the same essence [reality] with us as touching his manhood. Therefore the Church of God equally rejects and anathematizes those who divide or cut a part or who introduce confusion into the mystery of the divine dispensation of Christ.

IX.

If anyone says that Christ ought to be worshipped in his two natures, in the sense that he introduces two adorations, the one peculiar to God the Word and the other peculiar to the man; or if anyone by destroying the flesh, or by confusing the Godhead and the humanity, or by contriving one nature or essence of those which were united and so worships Christ, and does not with one adoration worship God the Word incarnate with his own flesh, as the Church of God has received from the beginning; let him be anathema.

X.

If anyone does not confess that our Lord Jesus Christ who was crucified in the flesh is true God and the Lord of Glory and one of the Holy Trinity; let him be anathema.

XI.

If anyone does not anathematize Arius, Eunomius, Macedonius, Apollinaris, Nestorius, Eutyches and Origen, together with their impious, godless writings, and all the other heretics already condemned and anathematized by the holy catholic and apostolic Church, and by the aforementioned four Holy Synods and all those who have held and hold or who in their godlessness persist in holding to the end the same opinion as those heretics just mentioned; let him be anathema.

• • • •

THE THIRD COUNCIL OF CONSTANTINOPLE (681)

The theological controversy that occasioned the Sixth Ecumenical Council was monothelitism, the doctrine that in the Person of Jesus Christ there is only one will. While the advocates of monothelitism denied the implication, it was apparent that such a doctrine bordered on monophysitism and endangered a fully adequate doctrine of the humanity of Jesus Christ.

The Council reaffirmed the Definition of Chalcedon and then added its interpretation of Chalcedon, which is given below.

Source: Translation is taken from Edward Rochie Hardy, *Christology of the Later Fathers*, Vol. III of *Library of Christian Classics* (Philadelphia: The Westminster Press, 1954), pp. 383–84. Used by permission.

Every, George, *The Byzantine Patriarchate* (London: S. P. C. K., 1947), Chap. 5.

Sellers, R. V., *The Council of Chalcedon, A History and Doctrinal Survey* (London: S. P. C. K., 1953).

THE STATEMENT OF FAITH OF THE THIRD COUNCIL OF CONSTANTINOPLE
(SIXTH ECUMENICAL)

We also proclaim two natural willings or wills in him and two natural operations, without separation, without change, without partition, without confusion, according to the teaching of the holy Fathers—and two natural wills not contrary [to each other], God forbid, as the impious heretics have said [they would be], but his human will following, and not resisting or opposing, but rather subject to his divine and all-powerful will. For it was proper for the will of the flesh to be moved [naturally], yet to be subject to the divine will, according to the all-wise Athanasius. For as his flesh is called and is the flesh of God the Word, so also the natural will of his flesh is called and is God the Word's own will, as he himself says: "I came down from heaven, not to do my own will, but the will of the Father who sent me," calling the will of the flesh his own, as also the flesh had become his own. For in the same manner that his all-holy and spotless ensouled flesh, though divinized, was not de-

stroyed, but remained in its own law and principle[1]
so also his human will, divinized, was not destroyed,
but rather preserved, as Gregory the divine says: "His
will, as conceived of in his character as the Saviour,
is not contrary to God, [being] wholly divinized."
We also glorify two natural operations in the same
our Lord Jesus Christ, our true God, without separation, without change, without partition, without confusion, that is, a divine operation and a human operation, as the divine preacher Leo most clearly says:
"For each form does what is proper to it, in communion with the other; the Word, that is, performing what
belongs to the Word, and the flesh carrying out what
belongs to the flesh." We will not therefore grant
[the existence of] one natural operation of God and
the creature, lest we should either raise up into the
divine nature what is created, or bring down the pre-
eminence of the divine nature into the place suitable
for things that are made. For we recognize the wonders and the sufferings as of one and the same [per-
son], according to the difference[2] of the natures of
which he is and in which he has his being, as the elo-
quent Cyril said.

Preserving therefore in every way the unconfused
and undivided, we set forth the whole [confession]
in brief; believing our Lord Jesus Christ, our true God,
to be one of the holy Trinity even after the taking of
flesh, we declare that his two natures shine forth in
his one *hypostasis,* in which he displayed both the
wonders and the sufferings through the whole course
of his dispensation,[3] not in phantasm but truly, the
difference of nature being recognized in the same one
hypostasis by the fact that each nature wills and works
what is proper to it, in communion with the other. On
this principle we glorify two natural wills and opera-

---

[1] *Horos* and *logos*—boundary and rule.
[2] *Kat' allo kai allo* (neuter)—a difference of two elements, but
not of two persons, which would call for the masculine.
[3] I.e., his earthly life—literally, "His dispensatory conduct."

tions combining with each other for the salvation of the human race.

THE IMAGE CONTROVERSY

The Seventh Ecumenical Council dealt with the use of images in the life and worship of the Church. Among the factors involved in the controversy that led up to and influenced the Council were the politics of the empire, the influence and the wealth of the monks, the pressure of the Moslem and Jewish polemic against idolatry, and the superstition of much popular religion. Theologically, the image controversy was a continuation of the Christological debates of the earlier councils. Each side argued its case, at least in part, on Christological premises.

The Seventh Ecumenical Council (787), which nullified the Council of 753, was accepted by the Eastern Orthodox Churches and the Roman Catholic Church. It is not accepted by Protestants. In the eighth century it was opposed by the Carolingian Church and by the Synod of Frankfort, 794, though the issue was confused by faulty translation. The *Caroline Books,* written in opposition to image-worship and taking their name from Charlemagne, became a source of early Protestant polemic against Roman Catholic practices of the sixteenth century.

Source: *The Nicene and Post-Nicene Fathers,* Second Series, Vol. XIV (New York: Charles Scribner's Sons, 1900), pp. 544, 550.

Bevan, E. R., *Holy Images* (London: G. Allen & Unwin, 1940).

Kondakov, N., *The Russian Ikon* (Oxford: Oxford University Press, 1927).

Martin, E. J., *A History of the Iconoclastic Controversy* (London: S. P. C. K., 1930).

Ouspensky, L., and Lossky, V.: *The Meaning of Ikons* (Boston: Boston Book and Art Shop, 1952).

Zernov, Nicolas, *Eastern Christendom* (London: Weidenfeld and Nicolson, 1961).

THE SYNOD OF CONSTANTINOPLE (HIERIA)
(753)

When, however, they are blamed for undertaking to depict the divine nature of Christ, which should not be depicted, they take refuge in the excuse: We represent only the flesh of Christ which we have seen and handled. But that is a Nestorian error. For it should be considered that that flesh was also the flesh of God the Word, without any separation, perfectly assumed by the divine nature and made wholly divine. How could it now be separated and represented apart? So is it with the human soul of Christ which mediates between the Godhead of the Son and the dullness of the flesh. As the human flesh is at the same time flesh of God the Word, so is the human soul also soul of God the Word, and both at the same time, the soul being deified as well as the body, and the Godhead remained undivided even in the separation of the soul from the body in his voluntary passion. For where the soul of Christ is, there is also his Godhead; and where the body of Christ is, there too is his Godhead. If then in his passion the divinity remained inseparable from these, how do the fools venture to separate the flesh from the Godhead, and represent it by itself as the image of a mere man? They fall into the abyss of impiety, since they separate the flesh from the Godhead, ascribe to it a subsistence of its own, a personality of its own, which they depict, and thus introduce a fourth person into the Trinity. Moreover, they represent as not being made divine, that which has been made divine by being assumed by the Godhead.

Whoever, then, makes an image of Christ, either depicts the Godhead which cannot be depicted, and mingles it with the manhood (like the Monophysites), or he represents the body of Christ as not made divine and separate and as a person apart, like the Nestorians.

The only admissible figure of the humanity of Christ, however, is bread and wine in the holy Supper. This and no other form, this and no other type, has he chosen to represent his incarnation. . . .

COUNCIL OF NICAEA (787)

SEVENTH ECUMENICAL

To make our confession short, we keep unchanged all the ecclesiastical traditions handed down to us, whether in writing or verbally, one of which is the making of pictorial representations, agreeable to the history of the preaching of the Gospel, a tradition useful in many respects, but especially in this, that so the incarnation of the Word of God is shewn forth as real and not merely phantastic, for these have mutual indications and without doubt have also mutual significations.

We, therefore, following the royal pathway and the divinely inspired authority of our Holy Fathers and the traditions of the Catholic Church (for, as we all know, the Holy Spirit indwells her), define with all certitude and accuracy that just as the figure of the precious and life-giving Cross, so also the venerable and holy images, as well in painting and mosaic as of other fit materials, should be set forth in the holy churches of God, and on the sacred vessels and on the vestments and on hangings and in pictures both in houses and by the wayside, to wit, the figure of our Lord God and Saviour Jesus Christ, of our spotless Lady, the Mother of God, of the honourable Angels, of all Saints and of all pious people. For by so much more frequently as they are seen in artistic representation, by so much more readily are men lifted up to the memory of their prototypes, and to a longing after them; and to these should be given due salutation and honourable reverence [ἀσπασμὸν καὶ τιμητικὴν προσκύνησιν], not indeed that true worship of faith [λατρείαν] which pertains alone to the divine nature; but to these, as to the figure of the precious and life-giving Cross and to the Book of the Gospels and to the other holy objects, incense and lights may be offered according to ancient pious custom. For the honour which is paid to the image passes on to that which the image represents, and he who reveres the image reveres in it the subject represented. . . .

FOURTH LATERAN COUNCIL (1215)

(THE DOCTRINE OF MEDIEVAL CATHOLICISM)

The Fourth Lateran Council was the greatest of the medieval councils. It was called by the greatest of the medieval popes, Innocent III, to plan for the "regaining of the Holy Land and the reform of the whole Church."

Canon I is a very comprehensive and exact summary of the theology of Medieval Catholicism. In the canon the word "transubstantiation" receives official approval and the power of the priest is emphasized. Canon XXI is important because it requires all those who have reached the age of reason to confess once a year to a parish priest.

Denzinger, H., *Enchiridion Symbolorum*, ed. by Rahner, C., S.J. (Friburg: Herder, 1955). (Translation based on this text.) Translated by Ross Mackenzie.

Schroeder, Rev. H. J., O.P., *Disciplinary Decrees of the General Councils, Text, Translation and Commentary* (St. Louis, Mo.: B. Herder Book Co., 1937).

FOURTH LATERAN COUNCIL (1215)
Canon I.

We firmly believe and openly confess that there is only one true God, eternal, beyond measure and unchangeable, incomprehensible, omnipotent and ineffable, the Father, the Son, and the Holy Spirit: Three persons but a single essence, substance, or nature that is wholly one; the Father proceeding from none, the Son proceeding from the Father alone, and the Holy Spirit from both in like manner; without beginning and having no end for ever: the Father begetting, the Son being begotten, and the Holy Spirit proceeding; having the same substance, the same equality, the same omnipotence, and the same eternity; the one principle of the universe; the Creator of all things visible and invisible, spiritual and corporeal; who from the very beginning of time by His omnipotent power created out of nothing both the spiritual beings and the corporeal, that is to say the angelic beings and those of the earth, and thereafter human beings, who, as it were, partake of both, being composed of spirit and body. The Devil and other wicked spirits were created by God good by nature, but they became evil of their own accord. Man, however, sinned at the prompting of the Devil. This Holy Trinity, undivided in regard to its essence which is common to all, but distinct in regard to the attributes of the persons, gave the doctrine of salvation to the human race in due process of time, first through Moses and the holy prophets and their other servants.

And finally the only-begotten Son of God, Jesus Christ, made flesh by the Trinity in all its persons together, conceived of Mary, ever Virgin, with the cooperation of the Holy Spirit, made true man, composed of a rational soul and human flesh, one person in two natures, showed the way to life with greater clarity. Though immortal and impassible in His divinity He yet became subject to suffering and death in His humanity; nay more, He suffered and died for the salvation of the human race on the wood of the cross, descended into hell, rose from the dead, and ascended into heaven. But He descended in the soul, and rose in the flesh, and ascended alike in both. He will come at the end of time, and will judge the living and the dead, and will reward every man according to his works, both the reprobate and the elect. These will all arise in their own bodies which they now have, that they may receive their reward according to whether their works were good or evil, in the latter case unending punishment with the Devil, in the former eternal glory with Christ.

There is one universal church of believers outside which there is no salvation at all for any. In this church the priest and sacrifice is the same Jesus Christ Himself, whose body and blood are truly contained in the sacrament of the altar under the figures of bread and wine, the bread having been transubstantiated into His body and the wine into His blood by divine power, so that, to accomplish the mystery of our union, we may receive of Him what He has received of us. And none can effect this sacrament except the priest who has been rightly ordained in accordance with the keys of the church which Jesus Christ Himself granted to the Apostles and their successors. The sacrament of baptism is celebrated in water by prayer to God and each person of the Trinity separately, that is to say, the Father, the Son, and the Holy Spirit. Duly conferred on both infants and adults by any one at all in the form appointed by the church, it promotes our salvation. And if after receiving baptism, anyone should fall into sin, he can always be restored through true repentance. Not only virgins and those practicing continence merit the attainment of eternal blessedness, but married persons also, who are acceptable to God through true faith and good works.

CANON XXI.

All believers of both sexes shall after coming to the age of discretion faithfully confess all their sins at least once a year in private to their own priest, and strive to fulfil to the best of their ability the penance imposed upon them. They shall reverently receive at least at Easter the sacrament of the Eucharist, unless on the advice of their own priest they believe that they should temporarily abstain for some good reason. Otherwise, they are to be prohibited access to the church while alive and be denied Christian burial when they are dead. Therefore, let this beneficial rule be frequently made public in churches, so that no one in the blindness of his ignorance may find a shadow of excuse. If anyone should want for good reason to confess his sins to another priest, let him first seek and obtain permission from his own priest, since otherwise the other cannot loose or bind him.

Let the priest be discreet and cautious, so that he may pour wine and oil into the wounds of the injured person like a skilled physician, diligently inquiring into the circumstances both of the sinner and of the sin, so that he may wisely understand what advice he should give him and what remedy he should apply, trying different tests to heal the patient.

Let him guard with greatest care against exposing the sinner even slightly by word or sign or in any other way. But if he should need wiser advice, let him ask for it cautiously, without any mention of the person, for if anyone dares to reveal a sin uncovered to him in the place of confession, we decree that he not only be deposed from the office of priest but also be dispatched to a monastery of strict discipline to do penance for the rest of his life.

COUNCIL OF FLORENCE (1438-45)

(THE DOCTRINE OF THE SEVEN SACRAMENTS)

The Council of Florence, which dealt with the division between the Greek and Latin Churches, also gave expression to significant teaching on the sacraments. The Council met with the representatives of the Armenian Church, and as a result a decree was published that contained important instruction concerning the sacraments. This brief statement is a summary of the doctrine of the sacraments as it developed in medieval theology and is based on the teaching of Thomas Aquinas.

Source: Translation based on text in Denzinger, H., *Enchiridion Symbolorum*, ed. by Rahner, C., S.J. (Freiburg: Herder, 1955), pp. 253–54.

COUNCIL OF FLORENCE, 1438–45

(THE DOCTRINE OF THE SEVEN SACRAMENTS)

. . . To make it more easy to instruct Armenians of the present day as well as those to come, we summarize the true nature of the sacraments of the Church in the following brief formula.

There are seven sacraments of the New Law, *viz.* baptism, confirmation, the eucharist, penance, extreme unction, orders, and marriage. These are quite different from the sacraments of the Old Law, which did not cause grace, but foreshadowed the grace that was to be bestowed solely through the passion of Christ. Our sacraments, however, not only contain grace, but also confer it on those who receive them worthily. The first five have been ordained for the spiritual per-

fection of every individual in himself, the last two for
the government and increase of the whole Church.
Through baptism we are spiritually reborn; through
confirmation we grow in grace and are strengthened
in faith. Having been regenerated and strengthened,
we are sustained by the divine food of the eucharist.
But if we become sick in soul through sin, we are
healed spiritually through penance, and healed spiritually as well as physically, in proportion as it benefits
the soul, through extreme unction. Through orders the
Church is governed and grows spiritually, while
through marriage it grows physically.

Three elements are involved in the full administration of all these sacraments, *viz.* things as the matter,
words as the form, and the person of the minister
performing the sacrament with the intention of doing
what the Church does. If any one of these is lacking,
the sacrament is not effected. There are three of the
sacraments, baptism, confirmation, and orders, which
imprint on the soul an indelible character, i.e. a kind
of spiritual seal distinct from the others. They are not,
therefore, to be received more than once by the same
individual. The rest, however, do not imprint a character and may be performed more than once.

LUTHERAN CONFESSIONS

The Reformation ushered in a new era in creed-making.
Protestant insistence upon the supreme authority of the
Bible meant that no creed is infallible or of final authority.
One consequence was a creedal multiplicity that had not
existed since the third and fourth centuries. Because the

Reformation involved a dispute within the Christian community as to the nature of Christian faith, more comprehensive statements of the faith were demanded than had hitherto been needed. The Reformation creeds emphasize in particular those issues that were especially in conflict, such as the doctrines of grace, faith, justification, the church and sacraments.

The Lutheran confessions were written over a brief period of time in a rather small geographical area. All of the documents that were incorporated in the Book of Concord, with the exception of the Formula of Concord, were written between 1529 and 1537. Moreover, these confessions were composed on German soil by Martin Luther and Philip Melanchthon. This gives to the Lutheran confessions a unity and an authority that is in contrast to the diverse Reformed confessions.

The Lutheran confessions reflect Luther's emphasis upon Justification by Faith Alone, the experience of salvation and the correction of abuses in the life of the Church. The creeds reassert the Nicene and Chalcedonian theology of the Ancient Catholic Church. The Book of Concord opens with the Apostles', the Nicene, and the Athanasian creeds. The assumption is that the faith of these confessions is a continuation of the faith of the Holy Catholic Church. The creeds naturally emphasize the doctrines that were at issue in the struggle to reform the Church according to what was regarded by Luther as the Biblical norm.

During the years following Luther's death (1546), theological conflicts increasingly plagued his followers. The Book of Concord, which was published in 1580, fifty years after the presentation of the Augsburg Confession to Charles V, sought to resolve these conflicts. The Formula of Concord, which is composed of the Epitome of the Articles in Dispute and the Solid Declaration of Some Articles of the Augsburg Confession, deals with these disputes and seeks to resolve them in terms of the authentic teachings of Martin Luther.

The Book of Concord contained the following docu-

ments: The Three Universal or Ecumenical Creeds—
Apostles', Nicene, and Athanasian,
The Augsburg Confession (1530)
Apology of the Augsburg Confession (1531)
The Smalcald Articles (1537)
Treatise on the Power and Primacy of the Pope (1537)
The Small Catechism of Dr. Martin Luther (1529)
The Large Catechism of Dr. Martin Luther (1529)
The Formula of Concord (1577).

Allbeck, Willard Dow, *Studies in the Lutheran Confessions* (Philadelphia: Muhlenberg Press, 1952).

Bente, F., *Concordia Triglotta* (Minneapolis, Minn.: The Mott Press, 1955). Offset lithograph reproduction of 1921 edition.

Brunstäd, Friedrich, *Theologie der lutherischen Bekenntnis Schriften* (C. Bertelsmann Verlag, 1951).

Jacobs, H. E., *The Book of Concord* (Philadelphia, Pa.: United Lutheran Publication House, 1882–83).

Neve, J. L., *Introduction to the Symbolical Books of the Lutheran Church,* 2nd Edition (Columbus: Lutheran Book Concern, 1926).

Schlink, Edmund, *Theology of the Lutheran Confessions* (Philadelphia: Muhlenberg Press, 1961).

Tappert, T. G., editor, *The Book of Concord* (Philadelphia: Muhlenberg Press, 1959). Excellent critical and contemporary translations.

THE AUGSBURG CONFESSION (1530)

The Augsburg Confession was prepared by Philip Melanchthon for presentation to Charles V at the Diet of Augsburg, 1530. Charles was free at this time to turn his attention to the religious controversy, and the situation was critical for the Protestants. Melanchthon had a twofold task. He had to establish the integrity of the Christian faith of the Protestants, and he had to justify their corrections of abuses in the life of the Church. On the one hand, the Lutherans suffered from misrepresentation at the hands of Eck and others, and on the other hand they were easily associated with more radical reformers. The first part of the

Confession deals with matters of faith and draws on the
Schwabach Articles, which had been written by *Wittenberg
theologians*. The second half deals with church abuses and
makes use of the Torgau Articles, which had been written
in preparation for the Augsburg Diet.

The tone of the Augsburg Confession is moderate and
conservative. It passes in silence a number of disputed
points. Nevertheless, it states very clearly the fundamental
Lutheran doctrines, especially Justification by Faith Alone.

The Augsburg Confession, in part because of its historical significance and in part because of its intrinsic merit,
became the most influential of all the Lutheran creeds.

Source: *The Book of Concord* translated and edited by
Theodore G. Tappert (Philadelphia: Muhlenberg Press,
1959), pp. 23–96. Translation based on German text.

THE AUGSBURG CONFESSION

*A Confession of Faith Presented in Augsburg by
certain Princes and Cities to His Imperial Majesty
Charles V in the Year 1530*

PSALM 119:46
*"I will also speak of thy testimonies before kings,
and shall not be put to shame."*

PREFACE

Most serene, most mighty, invincible Emperor, most
gracious Lord:

A short time ago Your Imperial Majesty graciously
summoned a diet of the empire to convene here in
Augsburg. In the summons Your Majesty indicated
an earnest desire to deliberate concerning matters pertaining to the Turk, that traditional foe of ours and
of the Christian religion, and how with continuing
help he might effectively be resisted. The desire was
also expressed for deliberation on what might be done
about the dissension concerning our holy faith and the
Christian religion, and to this end it was proposed to
employ all diligence amicably and charitably to hear,
understand, and weigh the judgments, opinions, and
beliefs of the several parties among us, to unite the

same in agreement on one Christian truth, to put aside whatever may not have been rightly interpreted or treated by either side, to have all of us embrace and adhere to a single, true religion and live together in unity and in one fellowship and church, even as we are all enlisted under one Christ. Inasmuch as we, the undersigned elector and princes and our associates, have been summoned for these purposes, together with other electors, princes, and estates, we have complied with the command and can say without boasting that we were among the first to arrive.

In connection with the matter pertaining to the faith and in conformity with the imperial summons, Your Imperial Majesty also graciously and earnestly requested that each of the electors, princes, and estates should commit to writing and present, in German and Latin, his judgments, opinions, and beliefs with reference to the said errors, dissensions, and abuses. Accordingly, after due deliberation and counsel, it was decided last Wednesday that, in keeping with Your Majesty's wish, we should present our case in German and Latin today (Friday). Wherefore, in dutiful obedience to Your Imperial Majesty, we offer and present a confession of our pastors' and preachers' teaching and of our own faith, setting forth how and in what manner, on the basis of the Holy Scriptures, these things are preached, taught, communicated, and embraced in our lands, principalities, dominions, cities, and territories.

If the other electors, princes, and estates also submit a similar written statement of their judgments and opinions, in Latin and German, we are prepared, in obedience to Your Imperial Majesty, our most gracious lord, to discuss with them and their associates, in so far as this can honorably be done, such practical and equitable ways as may restore unity. Thus the matters at issue between us may be presented in writing on both sides, they may be discussed amicably and charitably, our differences may be reconciled, and we may be united in one, true religion, even as we are all under one Christ and should confess and contend for Christ. All of this is in accord with Your Imperial Majesty's aforementioned summons. That it may be done according to divine truth we invoke almighty God in deepest humility and implore him to bestow his grace to this end. Amen.

If, however, our lords, friends, and associates who represent the electors, princes, and estates of the other party do not comply with the procedure intended by Your Imperial Majesty's summons, if no amicable and charitable negotiations take place between us, and if no results are attained, nevertheless we on our part shall not omit doing anything, in so far as God and conscience allow, that may serve the cause of Christian unity. Of this Your Imperial Majesty, our aforementioned friends (the electors, princes, and estates), and every lover of the Christian religion who is concerned about these questions will be graciously and sufficiently assured from what follows in the confession which we and our associates submit.

In the past Your Imperial Majesty graciously gave assurance to the electors, princes, and estates of the empire, especially in a public instruction at the diet in Spires in 1526, that for reasons there stated Your Imperial Majesty was not disposed to render decisions in matters pertaining to our holy faith but would diligently urge it upon the pope to call a council. Again, by means of a written instruction at the last diet in Spires a year ago, the electors, princes, and estates of the empire were, among other things, informed and notified by Your Imperial Majesty's viceroy (His Royal Majesty of Hungary and Bohemia, etc.) and by Your Imperial Majesty's orator and appointed commissioners, that Your Imperial Majesty's viceroy, administrators, and councilors of the imperial government (together with the absent electors, princes, and representatives of the estates) who were assembled at the diet convened in Ratisbon had considered the proposal concerning a general council and acknowledged that it would be profitable to have such a council called.

Since the relations between Your Imperial Majesty and the pope were improving and were progressing toward a good, Christian understanding, Your Imperial Majesty was sure that the pope would not refuse to call a general council, and so Your Imperial Majesty graciously offered to promote and bring about the calling of such a general council by the pope, along with Your Imperial Majesty, at the earliest opportunity and to allow no hindrance to be put in the way.

If the outcome should be such as we mentioned above, we offer in full obedience, even beyond what is required, to participate in such a general, free, and Christian council as the electors, princes, and estates have with the highest and best motives requested in all the diets of the empire which have been held during Your Imperial Majesty's reign. We have at various times made our protestations and appeals concerning these most weighty matters, and have done so in legal form and procedure. To these we declare our continuing adherence, and we shall not be turned aside from our position by these or any following negotiations (unless the matters in dissension are finally heard, amicably weighed, charitably settled, and brought to Christian concord in accordance with Your Imperial Majesty's summons) as we herewith publicly witness and assert. This is our confession and that of our associates, and it is specifically stated, article by article, in what follows.

ARTICLES OF FAITH AND DOCTRINE

I. [*God*][1]

We unanimously hold and teach, in accordance with the decree of the Council of Nicaea, that there is one divine essence, which is called and which is truly God, and that there are three persons in this one divine essence, equal in power and alike eternal: God the Father, God the Son, God the Holy Spirit. All three

---

he titles of some articles, here enclosed in square brackets, re inserted in and after 1533.

are one divine essence, eternal, without division, without end, of infinite power, wisdom, and goodness, one creator and preserver of all things visible and invisible. The word "person" is to be understood as the Fathers employed the term in this connection, not as a part or a property of another but as that which exists of itself.

Therefore all the heresies which are contrary to this article are rejected. Among these are the heresy of the Manichaeans, who assert that there are two gods, one good and one evil; also that of the Valentinians, Arians, Eunomians, Mohammedans, and others like them; also that of the Samosatenes, old and new, who hold that there is only one person and sophistically assert that the other two, the Word and the Holy Spirit, are not necessarily distinct persons but that the Word signifies a physical word or voice and that the Holy Spirit is a movement induced in creatures.

II. [*Original Sin*]

It is also taught among us that since the fall of Adam all men who are born according to the course of nature are conceived and born in sin. That is, all men are full of evil lust and inclinations from their mothers' wombs and are unable by nature to have true fear of God and true faith in God. Moreover, this inborn sickness and hereditary sin is truly sin and condemns to the eternal wrath of God all those who are not born again through Baptism and the Holy Spirit.

Rejected in this connection are the Pelagians and others who deny that original sin is sin, for they hold that natural man is made righteous by his own powers, thus disparaging the sufferings and merit of Christ.

III. [*The Son of God*]

It is also taught among us that God the Son became man, born of the Virgin Mary, and that the two natures, divine and human, are so inseparably united in one person that there is one Christ, true God and true man, who was truly born, suffered, was crucified, died, and was buried in order to be a sacrifice not only for original sin but also for all other sins and to propitiate God's wrath. The same Christ also descended into hell, truly rose from the dead on the third day, ascended into heaven, and sits on the right hand of God, that he may eternally rule and have dominion over all creatures, that through the Holy Spirit he may sanctify, purify, strengthen, and comfort all who believe in him, that he may bestow on them life and every grace and blessing, and that he may protect and defend them against the devil and against sin. The same Lord Christ will return openly to judge the living and the dead, as stated in the Apostles' Creed.

IV. [*Justification*]

It is also taught among us that we cannot obtain forgiveness of sin and righteousness before God by our own merits, works, or satisfactions, but that we receive forgiveness of sin and become righteous before God by grace, for Christ's sake, through faith, when we believe that Christ suffered for us and that for his sake our sin is forgiven and righteousness and eternal life are given to us. For God will regard and reckon this faith as righteousness, as Paul says in Romans 3:21–26 and 4:5.

V. [*The Office of the Ministry*]

To obtain such faith God instituted the office of the ministry, that is, provided the Gospel and the sacraments. Through these, as through means, he gives the Holy Spirit, who works faith, when and where he pleases, in those who hear the Gospel. And the Gospel teaches that we have a gracious God, not by our own merits but by the merit of Christ, when we believe this.

Condemned are the Anabaptists and others who teach that the Holy Spirit comes to us through our own preparations, thoughts, and works without the external word of the Gospel.

VI. [*The New Obedience*]

It is also taught among us that such faith should produce good fruits and good works and that we must do all such good works as God has commanded, but we should do them for God's sake and not place our trust in them as if thereby to merit favor before God. For we receive forgiveness of sin and righteousness through faith in Christ, as Christ himself says, "So you also, when you have done all that is commanded you, say, 'We are unworthy servants'" (Luke 17:10). The Fathers also teach thus, for Ambrose says, "It is ordained of God that whoever believes in Christ shall be saved, and he shall have forgiveness of sins, not through works but through faith alone, without merit."

VII. [*The Church*]

It is also taught among us that one holy Christian church will be and remain forever. This is the assembly of all believers among whom the Gospel is preached in its purity and the holy sacraments are administered according to the Gospel. For it is sufficient for the true unity of the Christian church that the Gospel be preached in conformity with a pure understanding of it and that the sacraments be administered in accordance with the divine Word. It is not necessary for the true unity of the Christian church that ceremonies, instituted by men, should be observed uniformly in all places. It is as Paul says in Eph. 4:4, 5, "There is one body and one Spirit, just as you were called to the one hope that belongs to your call, one Lord, one faith, one baptism."

VIII. [*What the Church Is*]

Again, although the Christian church, properly speaking, is nothing else than the assembly of all believers and saints, yet because in this life many false Christians, hypocrites, and even open sinners remain among the godly, the sacraments are efficacious even if the priests who administer them are wicked men, for as Christ himself indicated, "The Pharisees sit on Moses' seat" (Matt. 23:2).

Accordingly the Donatists and all others who hold contrary views are condemned.

IX. Baptism

It is taught among us that Baptism is necessary and that grace is offered through it. Children, too, should be baptized, for in Baptism they are committed to God and become acceptable to him.

On this account the Anabaptists who teach that infant Baptism is not right are rejected.

X. *The Holy Supper of Our Lord*

It is taught among us that the true body and blood of Christ are really present in the Supper of our Lord under the form of bread and wine and are there distributed and received. The contrary doctrine is therefore rejected.

XI. *Confession*

It is taught among us that private absolution should be retained and not allowed to fall into disuse. However, in confession it is not necessary to enumerate all trespasses and sins, for this is impossible. Ps. 19:12, "Who can discern his errors?"

XII. *Repentance*

It is taught among us that those who sin after Baptism receive forgiveness of sin whenever they come to repentance, and absolution should not be denied them by the church. Properly speaking, true repentance is nothing else than to have contrition and sorrow, or terror, on account of sin, and yet at the same time to believe the Gospel and absolution (namely, that sin has been forgiven and grace has been obtained through Christ), and this faith will comfort the heart and again set it at rest. Amendment of life and the forsaking of sin should then follow, for these must be the fruits of repentance, as John says, "Bear fruit that befits repentance" (Matt. 3:8).

Rejected here are those who teach that persons who have once become godly cannot fall again.

Condemned on the other hand are the Novatians who denied absolution to such as had sinned after Baptism.

Rejected also are those who teach that forgiveness of sin is not obtained through faith but through the satisfactions made by man.

XIII. *The Use of the Sacraments*

It is taught among us that the sacraments were instituted not only to be signs by which people might be identified outwardly as Christians, but that they are signs and testimonies of God's will toward us for the purpose of awakening and strengthening our faith. For this reason they require faith, and they are rightly used when they are received in faith and for the purpose of strengthening faith.

XIV. *Order in the Church*

It is taught among us that nobody should publicly teach or preach or administer the sacraments in the church without a regular call.

XV. *Church Usages*

With regard to church usages that have been established by men, it is taught among us that those usages are to be observed which may be observed without sin and which contribute to peace and good order in the church, among them being certain holy days, festivals, and the like. Yet we accompany these observances with instruction so that consciences may not be burdened by the notion that such things are necessary for salvation. Moreover it is taught that all ordinances and traditions instituted by men for the purpose of propitiating God and earning grace are contrary to the Gospel and the teaching about faith in Christ. Accordingly monastic vows and other traditions concerning distinctions of foods, days, etc., by which it is intended to earn grace and make satisfaction for sin, are useless and contrary to the Gospel.

XVI. *Civil Government*

It is taught among us that all government in the world and all established rule and laws were instituted and ordained by God for the sake of good order, and that Christians may without sin occupy civil offices or serve as princes and judges, render decisions and pass sentence according to imperial and other existing laws, punish evildoers with the sword, engage in just wars, serve as soldiers, buy and sell, take required oaths, possess property, be married, etc.

Condemned here are the Anabaptists who teach that none of the things indicated above is Christian.

Also condemned are those who teach that Christian perfection requires the forsaking of house and home, wife and child, and the renunciation of such activities as are mentioned above. Actually, true perfection consists alone of proper fear of God and real faith in God, for the Gospel does not teach an outward and temporal but an inward and eternal mode of existence and righteousness of the heart. The Gospel does not overthrow civil authority, the state, and marriage but requires that all these be kept as true orders of God and that everyone, each according to his own calling, manifest Christian love and genuine good works in his station of life. Accordingly Christians are obliged to be subject to civil authority and obey its commands and laws in all that can be done without sin. But when commands of the civil authority cannot be obeyed without sin, we must obey God rather than men (Acts 5:29).

XVII. [*The Return of Christ to Judgment*]

It is also taught among us that our Lord Jesus Christ will return on the last day for judgment and will raise up all the dead, to give eternal life and everlasting joy to believers and the elect but to condemn ungodly men and the devil to hell and eternal punishment.

Rejected, therefore, are the Anabaptists who teach that the devil and condemned men will not suffer eternal pain and torment.

Rejected, too, are certain Jewish opinions which are even now making an appearance and which teach that, before the resurrection of the dead, saints and godly men will possess a worldly kingdom and annihilate all the godless.

XVIII. *Freedom of the Will*

It is also taught among us that man possesses some measure of freedom of the will which enables him to live an outwardly honorable life and to make choices among the things that reason comprehends. But without the grace, help, and activity of the Holy Spirit man is not capable of making himself acceptable to God, of fearing God and believing in God with his whole heart, or of expelling inborn evil lusts from his heart. This is accomplished by the Holy Spirit, who is given through the Word of God, for Paul says in I Cor. 2:14, "Natural man does not receive the gifts of the Spirit of God."

In order that it may be evident that this teaching is no novelty, the clear words of Augustine on free will are here quoted from the third book of his *Hypognosticon:* "We concede that all men have a free will, for all have a natural, innate understanding and reason. However, this does not enable them to act in matters pertaining to God (such as loving God with their whole heart or fearing him), for it is only in the outward acts of this life that they have freedom to choose good or evil. By good I mean what they are capable of by nature: whether or not to labor in the fields, whether or not to eat or drink or visit a friend, whether to dress or undress, whether to build a house, take a wife, engage in a trade, or do whatever else may be good and profitable. None of these is or exists without God, but all things are from him and through him. On the other hand, by his own choice man can also undertake evil, as when he wills to kneel before an idol, commit murder, etc."

XIX. The Cause of Sin

It is taught among us that although almighty God has created and still preserves nature, yet sin is caused in all wicked men and despisers of God by the perverted will. This is the will of the devil and of all ungodly men; as soon as God withdraws his support, the will turns away from God to evil. It is as Christ says in John 8:44, "When the devil lies, he speaks according to his own nature."

XX. Faith and Good Works

Our teachers have been falsely accused of forbidding good works. Their writings on the Ten Commandments, and other writings as well, show that they have given good and profitable accounts and instructions concerning true Christian estates and works. About these little was taught in former times, when for the most part sermons were concerned with childish and useless works like rosaries, the cult of saints, monasticism, pilgrimages, appointed fasts, holy days, brotherhoods, etc. Our opponents no longer praise these useless works so highly as they once did, and they have also learned to speak now of faith, about which they did not preach at all in former times. They do not teach now that we become righteous before God by our works alone, but they add faith in Christ and say that faith and works make us righteous before God. This teaching may offer a little more comfort than the teaching that we are to rely solely on our works.

Since the teaching about faith, which is the chief article in the Christian life, has been neglected so long (as all must admit) while nothing but works was preached everywhere, our people have been instructed as follows:

We begin by teaching that our works cannot reconcile us with God or obtain grace for us, for this happens only through faith, that is, when we believe that our sins are forgiven for Christ's sake, who alone is the mediator who reconciles the Father. Whoever imagines that he can accomplish this by works, or that he can merit grace, despises Christ and seeks his own way to God, contrary to the Gospel.

This teaching about faith is plainly and clearly treated by Paul in many passages, especially in Eph. 2:8, 9, "For by grace you have been saved through faith; and this is not your own doing, it is the gift of God—not because of works, lest any man should boast," etc.

That no new interpretation is here introduced can be demonstrated from Augustine, who discusses this question thoroughly and teaches the same thing, namely, that we obtain grace and are justified before

God through faith in Christ and not through works. His whole book, *De spiritu et litera,* proves this.

Although this teaching is held in great contempt among untried people, yet it is a matter of experience that weak and terrified consciences find it most comforting and salutary. The conscience cannot come to rest and peace through works, but only through faith, that is, when it is assured and knows that for Christ's sake it has a gracious God, as Paul says in Rom. 5:1, "Since we are justified by faith, we have peace with God."

In former times this comfort was not heard in preaching, but poor consciences were driven to rely on their own efforts, and all sorts of works were undertaken. Some were driven by their conscience into monasteries in the hope that there they might merit grace through monastic life. Others devised other works for the purpose of earning grace and making satisfaction for sins. Many of them discovered that they did not obtain peace by such means. It was therefore necessary to preach this doctrine about faith in Christ and diligently to apply it in order that men may know that the grace of God is appropriated without merits, through faith alone.

Instruction is also given among us to show that the faith here spoken of is not that possessed by the devil and the ungodly, who also believe the history of Christ's suffering and his resurrection from the dead, but we mean such true faith as believes that we receive grace and forgiveness of sin through Christ.

Whoever knows that in Christ he has a gracious God, truly knows God, calls upon him, and is not, like the heathen, without God. For the devil and the ungodly do not believe this article concerning the forgiveness of sin, and so they are at enmity with God, cannot call upon him, and have no hope of receiving good from him. Therefore, as has just been indicated, the Scriptures speak of faith but do not mean by it such knowledge as the devil and ungodly men possess. Heb. 11:1 teaches about faith in such a way as to make it clear that faith is not merely a knowledge of historical events but is a confidence in God and in the fulfillment of his promises. Augustine also reminds us that we should understand the word "faith" in the Scriptures to mean confidence in God, assurance that God is gracious to us, and not merely such a knowledge of historical events as the devil also possesses.

It is also taught among us that good works should and must be done, not that we are to rely on them to earn grace but that we may do God's will and glorify him. It is always faith alone that apprehends grace and forgiveness of sin. When through faith the Holy Spirit is given, the heart is moved to do good works. Before that, when it is without the Holy Spirit, the heart is too weak. Moreover, it is in the power of the devil, who drives poor human beings into many sins. We see this in the philosophers who undertook to lead honorable and blameless lives; they failed to accomplish this, and instead fell into many great and open sins. This is what happens when a man is without true faith and the Holy Spirit and governs himself by his own human strength alone.

Consequently this teaching concerning faith is not to be accused of forbidding good works but is rather to be praised for teaching that good works are to be done and for offering help as to how they may be done. For without faith and without Christ human nature and human strength are much too weak to do good works, call upon God, have patience in suffering, love one's neighbor, diligently engage in callings which are commanded, render obedience, avoid evil lusts, etc. Such great and genuine works cannot be done without the help of Christ, as he himself says in John 15:5, "Apart from me you can do nothing."

XXI. The Cult of Saints

It is also taught among us that saints should be kept in remembrance so that our faith may be strengthened when we see what grace they received and how they were sustained by faith. Moreover, their good works are to be an example for us, each of us in his own calling. So His Imperial Majesty may in salutary and godly fashion imitate the example of David in making war on the Turk, for both are incumbents of a royal office which demands the defense and protection of their subjects.

However, it cannot be proved from the Scriptures that we are to invoke saints or seek help from them. "For there is one mediator between God and men, Christ Jesus" (I Tim. 2:5), who is the only saviour, the only highpriest, advocate, and intercessor before God (Rom. 8:34). He alone has promised to hear our prayers. Moreover, according to the Scriptures, the highest form of divine service is sincerely to seek and call upon this same Jesus Christ in every time of need. "If anyone sins, we have an advocate with the Father, Jesus Christ the righteous" (I John 2:1).

This is just about a summary of the doctrines that are preached and taught in our churches for proper Christian instruction, the consolation of consciences, and the amendment of believers. Certainly we should not wish to put our own souls and consciences in grave peril before God by misusing his name or Word, nor should we wish to bequeath to our children and posterity any other teaching than that which agrees with the pure Word of God and Christian truth. Since this teaching is grounded clearly on the Holy Scriptures and is not contrary or opposed to that of the universal Christian church, or even of the Roman church (in so far as the latter's teaching is reflected in the writings of the Fathers), we think that our opponents cannot disagree with us in the articles set forth above. Therefore, those who presume to reject, avoid, and separate from our churches as if our teaching were heretical, act in an unkind and hasty fashion, contrary to all Christian unity and love, and do so without any solid basis of divine command or Scripture. The dispute and dissension are concerned chiefly with various traditions and abuses. Since, then, there is nothing unfounded or defective in the principal articles and since this our confession is seen to be godly and Christian, the bishops should in all fairness act more leniently, even if there were some defect among us in regard to traditions, although we hope to offer firm grounds and reasons why we have changed certain traditions and abuses.

ARTICLES ABOUT MATTERS IN DISPUTE, IN WHICH AN ACCOUNT IS GIVEN OF THE ABUSES WHICH HAVE BEEN CORRECTED

From the above it is manifest that nothing is taught in our churches concerning articles of faith that is contrary to the Holy Scriptures or what is common to the Christian church. However, inasmuch as some abuses have been corrected (some of the abuses having crept in over the years and others of them having been introduced with violence), we are obliged by our circumstances to give an account of them and to indicate our reasons for permitting changes in these cases in order that Your Imperial Majesty may perceive that we have not acted in an unchristian and frivolous manner but have been compelled by God's command (which is rightly to be regarded as above all custom) to allow such changes.

XXII. Both Kinds in the Sacrament

Among us both kinds are given to laymen in the sacrament. The reason is that there is a clear command and order of Christ, "Drink of it, all of you" (Matt. 26:27). Concerning the chalice Christ here commands with clear words that all should drink of it.

In order that no one might question these words and interpret them as if they apply only to priests, Paul shows in I Cor. 11:20 ff. that the whole assembly of the congregation in Corinth received both kinds. This usage continued in the church for a long time, as can be demonstrated from history and from writings of the Fathers. In several places Cyprian mentions that the cup was given to laymen in his time. St. Jerome also states that the priests who administered the sacrament distributed the blood of Christ to the people. Pope Gelasius himself ordered that the sacrament was not to be divided. Not a single canon can be found which requires the reception of only one kind. Nobody knows when or through whom this custom of receiving only one kind was introduced, although Cardinal Cusanus mentions when the use was approved. It is evident that such a custom, introduced contrary to God's command and also contrary to the ancient canons, is unjust. Accordingly it is not proper to burden the consciences of those who desire to observe the sacrament according to Christ's institution or to compel them to act contrary to the arrangement of our Lord Christ. Because the division of the sacrament is contrary to the institution of Christ, the customary carrying about of the sacrament in processions is also omitted by us.

XXIII. The Marriage of Priests

Among all people, both of high and of low degree, there has been loud complaint throughout the world concerning the flagrant immorality and the dissolute life of priests who were not able to remain continent and who went so far as to engage in abominable vices. In order to avoid such unbecoming offense, adultery, and other lechery, some of our priests have entered the married state. They have given as their reason that they have been impelled and moved to take this step by the great distress of their consciences, especially since the Scriptures clearly assert that the estate of marriage was instituted by the Lord God to avoid immorality, for Paul says, "Because of the temptation to immorality, each man should have his own wife" (I Cor. 7:3), and again, "It is better to marry than to be aflame with passion" (I Cor. 7:9). Moreover, when Christ said in Matt. 19:11, "Not all men can receive this precept," he indicated that few people have the gift of living in celibacy, and he certainly knew man's nature. God created man as male and female according to Gen. 1:27. Experience has made it all too manifest whether or not it lies in human power and ability to improve or change the creation of God, the supreme Majesty, by means of human resolutions or vows without a special gift or grace of God. What good has resulted? What honest and chaste manner of life, what Christian, upright, and honorable sort of conduct has resulted in many cases? It is well known what terrible torment and frightful disturbance of conscience many have experienced on their death-beds on this account, and many have themselves acknowledged this. Since God's Word and command cannot be altered by any human vows or laws, our priests and other clergy have taken wives to themselves for these and other reasons and causes.

It can be demonstrated from history and from the writings of the Fathers that it was customary for priests and deacons to marry in the Christian church of former times. Paul therefore said in I Tim. 3:2, "A bishop must be above reproach, married only once." It was only four hundred years ago that the priests in Germany were compelled by force to take the vows of celibacy. At that time there was such serious and strong resistance that an archbishop of Mayence who had published the new papal decree was almost killed during an uprising of the entire body of priests. The decree concerning celibacy was at once enforced so hastily and indecently that the pope at the time not only forbade future marriages of priests but also broke up the marriages which were of long standing. This was of course not only contrary to all divine, natural, and civil law, but was also utterly opposed and contrary to the canons which the popes had themselves made and to the decisions of the most renowned counciis.

Many devout and intelligent people in high station have expressed similar opinions and the misgiving that such enforced celibacy and such prohibition of marriage (which God himself instituted and left free to man) never produced any good but rather gave occasion for many great and evil vices and much scandal. As his biography shows, even one of the popes, Pius II, often said and allowed himself to be quoted as say-

ing that while there may well have been some reasons
for prohibiting the marriage of clergymen, there were
now more important, better, and weightier reasons for
permitting them to be married. There is no doubt that
Pope Pius, as a prudent and intelligent man, made
this statement because of grave misgivings.

In loyalty to Your Imperial Majesty we therefore
feel confident that, as a most renowned Christian emperor, Your Majesty will graciously take into account
the fact that, in these last times of which the Scriptures
prophesy, the world is growing worse and men are
becoming weaker and more infirm.

Therefore it is most necessary, profitable, and Christian to recognize this fact in order that the prohibition
of marriage may not cause worse and more disgrace-
ful lewdness and vice to prevail in German lands. No
one is able to alter or arrange such matters in a better
or wiser way than God himself, who instituted marriage to aid human infirmity and prevent unchastity.

The old canons also state that it is sometimes necessary to relax severity and rigor for the sake of human weakness and to prevent and avoid greater offense.

In this case relaxation would certainly be both Christian and very necessary. How would the marriage of
priests and the clergy, and especially of the pastors and
others who are to minister to the church, be of disadvantage to the Christian church as a whole? If this
hard prohibition of marriage is to continue longer,
there may be a shortage of priests and pastors in the
future.

As we have observed, the assertion that priests and
clergymen may marry is based on God's Word and
command. Besides, history demonstrates both that
priests were married and that the vow of celibacy has
been the cause of so much frightful and unchristian
offense, so much adultery, and such terrible, shocking
immorality and abominable vice that even some honest
men among the cathedral clergy and some of the
courtiers in Rome have often acknowledged this and

have complained that such vices among the clergy would, on account of their abomination and prevalence, arouse the wrath of God. It is therefore deplorable that Christian marriage has not only been forbidden but has in many places been swiftly punished, as if it were a great crime, in spite of the fact that in the Holy Scriptures God commanded that marriage be held in honor. Marriage has also been highly praised in the imperial laws and in all states in which there have been laws and justice. Only in our time does one begin to persecute innocent people simply because they are married—and especially priests, who above all others should be spared—although this is done contrary not only to divine law but also to canon law. In I Tim. 4:1, 3 the apostle Paul calls the teaching that forbids marriage a doctrine of the devil. Christ himself asserts that the devil is a murderer from the beginning (John 8:44). These two statements fit together well, for it must be a doctrine of the devil to forbid marriage and then to be so bold as to maintain such a teaching with the shedding of blood.

However, just as no human law can alter or abolish a command of God, neither can any vow alter a command of God. St. Cyprian therefore offered the counsel that women who were unable to keep their vows of chastity should marry. He wrote in his eleventh letter, "If they are unwilling or unable to keep their chastity, it is better for them to marry than to fall into the fire through their lusts, and they should see to it that they do not give their brothers and sisters occasion for offense."

In addition, all the canons show great leniency and fairness toward those who have made vows in their youth—and most of the priests and monks entered into their estates ignorantly when they were young.

XXIV. The Mass

We are unjustly accused of having abolished the Mass. Without boasting, it is manifest that the Mass is observed among us with greater devotion and more earnestness than among our opponents. Moreover, the

people are instructed often and with great diligence
concerning the holy sacrament, why it was instituted,
and how it is to be used (namely, as a comfort for
terrified consciences) in order that the people may be
drawn to the Communion and Mass. The people are
also given instruction about other false teachings concerning the sacrament. Meanwhile no conspicuous
changes have been made in the public ceremonies of
the Mass, except that in certain places German hymns
are sung in addition to the Latin responses for the instruction and exercise of the people. After all, the chief
purpose of all ceremonies is to teach the people what
they need to know about Christ.

Before our time, however, the Mass came to be mis-
used in many ways, as is well known, by turning it
into a sort of fair, by buying and selling it, and by
observing it in almost all churches for a monetary consideration. Such abuses were often condemned by
learned and devout men even before our time. Then
when our preachers preached about these things and
the priests were reminded of the terrible responsibility which should properly concern every Christian
(namely, that whoever uses the sacrament unworthily
is guilty of the body and blood of Christ), such mer-
cenary Masses and private Masses, which had hitherto
been held under compulsion for the sake of revenues
and stipends, were discontinued in our churches.

At the same time the abominable error was condemned according to which it was taught that our
Lord Christ had by his death made satisfaction only
for original sin, and had instituted the Mass as a sacrifice for other sins. This transformed the Mass into a
sacrifice for the living and the dead, a sacrifice by
means of which sin was taken away and God was
reconciled. Thereupon followed a debate as to whether
one Mass held for many people merited as much as a
special Mass held for an individual. Out of this grew
the countless multiplication of Masses, by the performance of which men expected to get everything they

needed from God. Meanwhile faith in Christ and true service of God were forgotten.

Demanded without doubt by the necessity of such circumstances, instruction was given so that our people might know how the sacrament is to be used rightly. They were taught, first of all, that the Scriptures show in many places that there is no sacrifice for original sin, or for any other sin, except the one death of Christ. For it is written in the Epistle to the Hebrews that Christ offered himself once and by this offering made satisfaction for all sin. It is an unprecedented novelty in church doctrine that Christ's death should have made satisfaction only for original sin and not for other sins as well. Accordingly it is to be hoped that everyone will understand that this error is not unjustly condemned.

In the second place, St. Paul taught that we obtain grace before God through faith and not through works. Manifestly contrary to this teaching is the misuse of the Mass by those who think that grace is obtained through the performance of this work, for it is well known that the Mass is used to remove sin and obtain grace and all sorts of benefits from God, not only for the priest himself but also for the whole world and for others, both living and dead.

In the third place, the holy sacrament was not instituted to make provision for a sacrifice for sin—for the sacrifice has already taken place—but to awaken our faith and comfort our consciences when we perceive that through the sacrament grace and forgiveness of sin are promised us by Christ. Accordingly the sacrament requires faith, and without faith it is used in vain.

Inasmuch, then, as the Mass is not a sacrifice to remove the sins of others, whether living or dead, but should be a Communion in which the priest and others receive the sacrament for themselves, it is observed among us in the following manner: On holy days, and at other times when communicants are present, Mass is held and those who desire it are communicated.

Thus the Mass is preserved among us in its proper use, the use which was formerly observed in the church and which can be proved by St. Paul's statement in I Cor. 11:20 ff. and by many statements of the Fathers. For Chrysostom reports how the priest stood every day, inviting some to Communion and forbidding others to approach. The ancient canons also indicate that one man officiated and communicated the other priests and deacons, for the words of the Nicene canon read, "After the priests the deacons shall receive the sacrament in order from the bishop or priest."

Since, therefore, no novelty has been introduced which did not exist in the church from ancient times, and since no conspicuous change has been made in the public ceremonies of the Mass except that other unnecessary Masses which were held in addition to the parochial Mass, probably through abuse, have been discontinued, this manner of holding Mass ought not in fairness be condemned as heretical or unchristian. In times past, even in large churches where there were many people, Mass was not held on every day that the people assembled, for according to the Tripartite History, Book 9, on Wednesday and Friday the Scriptures were read and expounded in Alexandria, and otherwise these services were held without Mass.

XXV. *Confession*

Confession has not been abolished by the preachers on our side. The custom has been retained among us of not administering the sacrament to those who have not previously been examined and absolved. At the same time the people are carefully instructed concerning the consolation of the Word of absolution so that they may esteem absolution as a great and precious thing. It is not the voice or word of the man who speaks it, but it is the Word of God, who forgives sin, for it is spoken in God's stead and by God's command. We teach with great diligence about this command and power of keys and how comforting and necessary it is for terrified consciences. We also teach that God requires us to believe this absolution as much as if we heard God's voice from heaven, that we should joyfully comfort ourselves with absolution, and that we should know that through such faith we obtain forgiveness of sins. In former times the preachers who taught much about confession never mentioned a word concerning these necessary matters but only tormented consciences with long enumerations of sins, with satisfactions, with indulgences, with pilgrimages and the like. Many of our opponents themselves acknowledge that we have written about and treated of true Christian repentance in a more fitting fashion than had been done for a long time.

Concerning confession we teach that no one should be compelled to recount sins in detail, for this is impossible. As the psalmist says, "Who can discern his errors?" Jeremiah also says, "The heart is desperately corrupt; who can understand it?" Our wretched human nature is so deeply submerged in sins that it is unable to perceive or know them all, and if we were to be absolved only from those which we can enumerate we would be helped but little. On this account there is no need to compel people to give a detailed account of their sins. That this was also the view of the Fathers can be seen in Dist. I, *De poenitentia*, where these words of Chrysostom are quoted: "I do not say that you should expose yourself in public or should accuse yourself before others, but obey the prophet who says, 'Show your way to the Lord.' Therefore confess to the Lord God, the true judge, in your prayer, telling him of your sins not with your tongue but in your conscience." Here it can be clearly seen that Chrysostom does not require a detailed enumeration of sins. The marginal note in *De poenitentia*, Dist. 5, also teaches that such confession is not commanded by the Scriptures but was instituted by the church. Yet the preachers on our side diligently teach that confession is to be retained for the sake of absolution (which is its chief and most important part), for the consolation of terrified consciences, and also for other reasons.

XXVI. *The Distinction of Foods*

In former times men taught, preached, and wrote that distinctions among foods and similar traditions which had been instituted by men serve to earn grace and make satisfaction for sin. For this reason new fasts, new ceremonies, new orders, and the like were invented daily, and were ardently and urgently promoted, as if these were a necessary service of God by means of which grace would be earned if they were observed and a great sin committed if they were omitted. Many harmful errors in the church have resulted from this.

In the first place, the grace of Christ and the teaching concerning faith are thereby obscured, and yet the Gospel earnestly urges them upon us and strongly insists that we regard the merit of Christ as something great and precious and know that faith in Christ is to be esteemed far above all works. On this account St. Paul contended mightily against the law of Moses and against human tradition so that we should learn that we do not become good in God's sight by our works but that it is only through faith in Christ that we obtain grace for Christ's sake. This teaching has been almost completely extinguished by those who have taught that grace is to be earned by prescribed fasts, distinctions among foods, vestments, etc.

In the second place, such traditions have also obscured the commands of God, for these traditions were exalted far above God's commands. This also was regarded as Christian life: whoever observed festivals in this way, prayed in this way, fasted in this way, and dressed in this way was said to live a spiritual and Christian life. On the other hand, other necessary good works were considered secular and unspiritual: the works which everybody is obliged to do according to his calling—for example, that a husband should labor to support his wife and children and bring them up in the fear of God, that a wife should bear children and care for them, that a prince and magistrates should govern land and people, etc. Such works, commanded by God, were to be regarded as secular and imperfect, while traditions were to be given the glamorous title of alone being holy and perfect works. Accordingly there was no end or limit to the making of such traditions.

In the third place, such traditions have turned out to be a grievous burden to consciences, for it was not possible to keep all the traditions, and yet the people were of the opinion that they were a necessary service of God. Gerson writes that many fell into despair on this account, and some even committed suicide, because they had not heard anything of the consolation of the grace of Christ. We can see in the writings of the summists and canonists how consciences have been confused, for they undertook to collate the traditions and sought mitigations to relieve consciences, but they were so occupied with such efforts that they neglected all wholesome Christian teachings about more important things, such as faith, consolation in severe trials, and the like. Many devout and learned people before our time have also complained that such traditions caused so much strife in the church that godly people were thereby hindered from coming to a right knowledge of Christ. Gerson and others have complained bitterly about this. In fact, Augustine was also displeased that consciences were burdened with so many traditions, and he taught in this connection that they were not to be considered necessary observances.

Our teachers have not taught concerning these matters out of malice or contempt of spiritual authority, but dire need has compelled them to give instruction about the aforementioned errors which have arisen from a wrong estimation of tradition. The Gospel demands that the teaching about faith should and must be emphasized in the church, but this teaching cannot be understood if it is supposed that grace is earned through self-chosen works.

It is therefore taught that grace cannot be earned, God cannot be reconciled, and sin cannot be atoned for by observing the said human traditions. Accordingly they should not be made into a necessary service of God. Reasons for this shall be cited from the Scriptures. In Matt. 15:1–20 Christ defends the apostles for not observing the customary traditions, and he adds, "In vain do they worship me, teaching as doctrines the precepts of men" (Matt. 15:9). Since he calls them vain service, they must not be necessary. Thereupon Christ says, "Not what goes into the mouth defiles a man." Paul also says in Rom. 14:17, "The kingdom of God does not mean food and drink," and in Col. 2:16 he says, "Let no one pass judgment on you in questions of food and drink or with regard to a festival," etc. In Acts 15:10, 11 Peter says, "Why do you make trial of God by putting a yoke upon the neck of the disciples which neither our fathers nor we have been able to bear? But we believe that we shall be saved through the grace of the Lord Jesus, just as they will." Here Peter forbids the burdening of consciences with additional outward ceremonies, whether of Moses or of another. In I Tim. 4:1, 3 such prohibitions as forbid food or marriage are called a doctrine of the devil, for it is diametrically opposed to the Gospel to institute or practice such works for the purpose of earning forgiveness of sin or with the notion that nobody is a Christian unless he performs such services.

Although our teachers are, like Jovinian, accused of forbidding mortification and discipline, their writings reveal something quite different. They have always taught concerning the holy cross that Christians are obliged to suffer, and this is true and real rather than invented mortification.

They also teach that everybody is under obligation to conduct himself, with reference to such bodily exercise as fasting and other discipline, so that he does not give occasion to sin, but not as if he earned grace by such works. Such bodily exercise should not be limited to certain specified days but should be practiced continually. Christ speaks of this in Luke 21:34, "Take heed to yourselves lest your hearts be weighed down with dissipation," and again, "This kind of demon cannot be driven out by anything but fasting and prayer." Paul said that he pommeled his body and subdued it, and by this he indicated that it is not the purpose of mortification to merit grace but to keep the body in such a condition that one can perform the duties required by one's calling. Thus fasting in itself is not rejected, but what is rejected is making a necessary service of fasts on prescribed days and with specified foods, for this confuses consciences.

We on our part also retain many ceremonies and traditions (such as the liturgy of the Mass and various canticles, festivals, and the like) which serve to preserve order in the church. At the same time, however, the people are instructed that such outward forms of service do not make us righteous before God and that they are to be observed without burdening consciences, which is to say that it is not a sin to omit them if this is done without causing scandal. The ancient Fathers maintained such liberty with respect to outward ceremonies, for in the East they kept Easter at a time different from that in Rome. When some regarded this difference as divisive of the church, they were admonished by others that it was not necessary to maintain uniformity in such customs. Irenaeus said, "Disagreement in fasting does not destroy unity in faith," and there is a statement in Dist. 12 that such disagreement in human ordinances is not in conflict with the unity of Christendom. Moreover, the Tripartite History, Book 9, gathers many examples of dissimilar church usages and adds the profitable Christian observation, "It was not the intention of the apostles to institute holy days but to teach faith and love."

XXVII. Monastic Vows

In discussing monastic vows it is necessary to begin by considering what opinions have hitherto been held concerning them, what kind of life was lived in the monasteries, and how many of the daily observances in them were contrary not only to the Word of God but also to papal canons. In the days of St. Augustine monastic life was voluntary. Later, when true discipline and doctrine had become corrupted, monastic vows were invented, and the attempt was made to restore discipline by means of these vows as if in a well-conceived prison.

In addition to monastic vows many other requirements were imposed, and such fetters and burdens were laid on many before they had attained an appropriate age.

Many persons also entered monastic life ignorantly, for although they were not too young, they had not sufficiently appreciated or understood their strength. All of those who were thus ensnared and entangled were pressed and compelled to remain, in spite of the fact that even the papal canons might have set many of them free. The practice was stricter in women's convents than in those of men, though it would have been seemly to show more consideration to women as the weaker sex. Such severity and rigor displeased many devout people in the past, for they must have seen that both boys and girls were thrust into monasteries to provide for their maintenance. They must also have seen what evils came from this arrangement, what scandals and burdened consciences resulted. Many people complained that in such a momentous matter the canons were not strictly adhered to. Besides, monastic vows gained such a reputation, as is well known, that many monks with even a little understanding were displeased.

It was claimed that monastic vows were equal to Baptism, and that by monastic life one could earn forgiveness of sin and justification before God. What is more, they added that monastic life not only earned righteousness and godliness, but also that by means of this life both the precepts and the counsels included in the Gospel were kept, and so monastic vows were praised more highly than Baptism. They also claimed that more merit could be obtained by monastic life than by all other states of life instituted by God—whether the office of pastor and preacher, of ruler, prince, lord, or the like, all of whom serve in their appointed calling according to God's Word and command without invented spirituality. None of these things can be denied, for they are found in their own books.

Furthermore, those who were thus ensnared and inveigled into a monastery learned little about Christ. Formerly the monasteries had conducted schools of Holy Scripture and other branches of learning which are profitable to the Christian church, so that pastors and bishops were taken from monasteries. But now the picture is changed. In former times people gathered and adopted monastic life for the purpose of learning the Scriptures, but now it is claimed that monastic life is of such a nature that thereby God's grace and righteousness before God are earned. In fact, it is called a state of perfection and is regarded as far superior to the other estates instituted by God. All this is mentioned, without misrepresentation, in order that one may better grasp and understand what our teachers teach and preach.

For one thing, it is taught among us with regard to those who desire to marry that all those who are not suited for celibacy have the power, right, and authority to marry, for vows cannot nullify God's order and command. God's command in I Cor. 7:2 reads, "Because of the temptation to immorality, each man should have his own wife and each woman her own husband." It is not alone God's command that urges, drives, and compels us to do this, but God's creation and order also direct all to marriage who are not endowed with the gift of virginity by a special act of God. This appears from God's own words in Gen. 2:18, "It is not good that the man should be alone; I will make him a helper fit for him."

What objection may be raised to this? No matter how much one extols the vow and the obligation, no matter how highly one exalts them, it is still impossible to abrogate God's command. Learned men say that a vow made contrary to papal canons is not binding. How much less must be their obligation, lawfulness, and power when they are contrary to God's command!

If there were no reasons which allowed annulment of the obligation of a vow, the popes could not have dispensed and released men from such obligation, for no man has the right to cancel an obligation which is derived from divine law. Consequently the popes were well aware that some amelioration ought to be exercised in connection with this obligation and have often given dispensations, as in the case of the king of Aragon and many others. If dispensations were granted for the maintenance of temporal interests, how much more should dispensations be granted for necessities of men's souls!

Why, then, do our opponents insist so strongly that vows must be kept without first ascertaining whether a vow is of the proper sort? For a vow must involve what is possible and voluntary and must be uncoerced. Yet it is commonly known to what an extent perpetual chastity lies within human power and ability, and there are few, whether men or women, who have taken monastic vows of themselves, willingly, and after due consideration. Before they came to a right understanding they were persuaded to take monastic vows, and sometimes they have been compelled and forced to do so. Accordingly it is not right to argue so rashly and insistently about the obligation of vows inasmuch as it is generally conceded that it belongs to the very nature and character of a vow that it should be voluntary and should be assumed only after due consideration and counsel.

Several canons and papal regulations annul vows that are made under the age of fifteen years. They hold that before this age one does not possess sufficient understanding to determine or arrange the order of one's whole future life. Another canon concedes still more years to human frailty, for it prohibits the taking of monastic vows before the eighteenth year. On the basis of this provision most monastics have excuse and reason for leaving their monasteries inasmuch as a majority of them entered the cloister in their childhood, before attaining such age.

Finally, although the breaking of monastic vows might be censured, it would not follow that the marriage of those who broke them should be dissolved. For St. Augustine says in his *Nuptiarum,* Question 27, Chapter I, that such a marriage should not be dissolved, and St. Augustine is no inconsiderable authority in the Christian church, even though some have subsequently differed from him.

Although God's command concerning marriage frees and releases many from monastic vows, our teachers offer still more reasons why monastic vows are null and void. For all service of God that is chosen and instituted by men to obtain righteousness and God's grace without the command and authority of God is opposed to God and the holy Gospel and contrary to God's command. So Christ himself says in Matt. 15:9, "In vain do they worship me, teaching as doctrines the precepts of men." St. Paul also teaches everywhere that one is not to seek for righteousness in the precepts and services invented by men but that righteousness and godliness in God's sight come from faith and trust when we believe that God receives us into his favor for the sake of Christ, his only Son.

It is quite evident that the monks have taught and preached that their invented spiritual life makes satisfaction for sin and obtains God's grace and righteousness. What is this but to diminish the glory and honor of the grace of Christ and deny the righteousness of faith? It follows from this that the customary vows were an improper and false service of God. Therefore they are not binding, for an ungodly vow, made contrary to God's command, is null and void. Even the canons teach that an oath should not be an obligation to sin.

St. Paul says in Gal. 5:4, "You are severed from Christ, you who would be justified by the law; you have fallen away from grace." In the same way, those who would be justified by vows are severed from

Christ and have fallen away from God's grace, for they rob Christ, who alone justifies, of his honor and bestow this honor on their vows and monastic life.

One cannot deny that the monks have taught and preached that they were justified and earned forgiveness of sins by their vows and their monastic life and observances. In fact, they have invented a still more indecent and absurd claim, namely, that they could apply their good works to others. If one were inclined to count up all these claims for the purpose of casting them into their teeth, how many items could be assembled which the monks themselves are now ashamed of and wish had never occurred! Besides all this, they persuaded the people that the invented spiritual estate of the orders was Christian perfection. Certainly this is exaltation of works as a means of attaining justification. Now, it is no small offense in the Christian church that the people should be presented with such a service of God, invented by men without the command of God, and should be taught that such a service would make men good and righteous before God. For righteousness of faith, which should be emphasized above all else in the Christian church, is obscured when man's eyes are dazzled with this curious angelic spirituality and sham of poverty, humility, and chastity.

Besides, the commands of God and true and proper service of God are obscured when people are told that monks alone are in a state of perfection. For this is Christian perfection: that we fear God honestly with our whole hearts, and yet have sincere confidence, faith, and trust that for Christ's sake we have a gracious, merciful God; that we may and should ask and pray God for those things of which we have need, and confidently expect help from him in every affliction connected with our particular calling and station in life; and that meanwhile we do good works for others and diligently attend to our calling. True perfection and right service of God consist of these things and not of mendicancy or wearing a black or gray cowl, etc. However, the common people, hearing the state of celibacy praised above all measure, draw many harmful conclusions from such false exaltation of monastic life, for it follows that their consciences are troubled because they are married. When the common man hears that only mendicants are perfect, he is uncertain whether he can keep his possessions and engage in business without sin. When the people hear that it is only a counsel not to take revenge, it is natural that some should conclude that it is not sinful to take revenge outside of the exercise of their office. Still others think that it is not right at all for Christians, even in the government, to avenge wrong.

Many instances are also recorded of men who forsook wife and child, and also their civil office, to take shelter in a monastery. This, they said, is fleeing from the world and seeking a life more pleasing to God than the other. They were unable to understand that one is to serve God by observing the commands God has given and not by keeping the commands invented by men. That is a good and perfect state of life which has God's command to support it; on the other hand, that is a dangerous state of life which does not have God's command behind it. About such matters it was necessary to give the people proper instruction.

In former times Gerson censured the error of the monks concerning perfection and indicated that it was an innovation of his time to speak of monastic life as a state of perfection.

Thus there are many godless opinions and errors associated with monastic vows: that they justify and render men righteous before God, that they constitute Christian perfection, that they are the means of fulfilling both evangelical counsels and precepts, and that they furnish the works of supererogation which we are not obligated to render to God. Inasmuch as all these things are false, useless, and invented, monastic vows are null and void.

XXVIII. The Power of Bishops

Many and various things have been written in former times about the power of bishops, and some have improperly confused the power of bishops with the temporal sword. Out of this careless confusion many serious wars, tumults, and uprisings have resulted because the bishops, under pretext of the power given them by Christ, have not only introduced new forms of worship and burdened consciences with reserved cases and violent use of the ban, but have also presumed to set up and depose kings and emperors according to their pleasure. Such outrage has long since been condemned by learned and devout people in Christendom. On this account our teachers have been compelled, for the sake of comforting consciences, to point out the difference between spiritual and temporal power, sword, and authority, and they have taught that because of God's command both authorities and powers are to be honored and esteemed with all reverence as the two highest gifts of God on earth.

Our teachers assert that according to the Gospel the power of keys or the power of bishops is a power and command of God to preach the Gospel, to forgive and retain sins, and to administer and distribute the sacraments. For Christ sent out the apostles with this command, "As the Father has sent me, even so I send you. Receive the Holy Spirit. If you forgive the sins of any, they are forgiven; if you retain the sins of any, they are retained" (John 20:21–23).

This power of keys or of bishops is used and exercised only by teaching and preaching the Word of God and by administering the sacraments (to many persons or to individuals, depending on one's calling). In this way are imparted not bodily but eternal things and gifts, namely, eternal rightousness, the Holy Spirit, and eternal life. These gifts cannot be obtained except through the office of preaching and of administering the holy sacraments, for St. Paul says, "The gospel is the power of God for salvation to everyone who has faith." Inasmuch as the power of the church or of bishops bestows eternal gifts and is used and exercised only through the office of preaching, it does not interfere at all with government or temporal authority. Temporal authority is concerned with matters altogether different from the Gospel. Temporal power does not protect the soul, but with the sword and physical penalties it protects body and goods from the power of others.

Therefore, the two authorities, the spiritual and the temporal, are not to be mingled or confused, for the spiritual power has its commission to preach the Gospel and administer the sacraments. Hence it should not invade the function of the other, should not set up and depose kings, should not annul temporal laws or undermine obedience to government, should not make or prescribe to the temporal power laws concerning worldly matters. Christ himself said, "My kingship is not of this world," and again, "Who made me a judge or divider over you?" Paul also wrote in Phil. 3:20, "Our commonwealth is in heaven," and in II Cor. 10:4, 5, "The weapons of our warfare are not worldly but have divine power to destroy strongholds and every proud obstacle to the knowledge of God."

Thus our teachers distinguish the two authorities and the functions of the two powers, directing that both be held in honor as the highest gifts of God on earth.

In cases where bishops possess temporal authority and the sword, they possess it not as bishops by divine right, but by human, imperial right, bestowed by Roman emperors and kings for the temporal administration of their lands. Such authority has nothing at all to do with the office of the Gospel.

According to divine right, therefore, it is the office of the bishop to preach the Gospel, forgive sins, judge doctrine and condemn doctrine that is contrary to the Gospel, and exclude from the Christian community the ungodly whose wicked conduct is manifest. All this is to be done not by human power but by God's Word alone. On this account parish ministers and churches are bound to be obedient to the bishops according to the saying of Christ in Luke 10:16, "He who hears you hears me." On the other hand, if they teach, introduce, or institute anything contrary to the Gospel, we have God's command not to be obedient in such cases, for Christ says in Matt. 7:15, "Beware of false prophets." St. Paul also writes in Gal. 1:8, "Even if we, or an angel from heaven, should preach to you a gospel contrary to that which we preached to you, let him be accursed," and in II Cor. 13:8, "We cannot do anything against the truth, but only for the truth." Again Paul refers to "the authority which the Lord has given me for building up and not for tearing down." Canon law requires the same in Part II, Question 7, in the chapters "Sacerdotes" and "Oves."

St. Augustine also writes in his reply to the letters of Petilian that one should not obey even regularly elected bishops if they err or if they teach or command something contrary to the divine Holy Scriptures.

Whatever other power and jurisdiction bishops may have in various matters (for example, in matrimonial cases and in tithes), they have these by virtue of human right. However, when bishops are negligent in the performance of such duties, the princes are obliged, whether they like to or not, to administer justice to their subjects for the sake of peace and to prevent discord and great disorder in their lands.

Besides, there is dispute as to whether bishops have the power to introduce ceremonies in the church or establish regulations concerning foods, holy days, and the different orders of the clergy. Those who attribute such power to bishops cite Christ's saying in John 16:12, 13, "I have yet many things to say to you, but you cannot bear them now. When the Spirit of truth comes, he will guide you into all the truth." They also cite the example in Acts 15:20, 29, where the eating of blood and what is strangled was forbidden. Besides, they appeal to the fact that the Sabbath was changed to Sunday—contrary, as they say, to the Ten Commandments. No case is appealed to and urged so insistently as the change of the Sabbath, for thereby they wish to maintain that the power of the church is indeed great because the church has dispensed from and altered part of the Ten Commandments.

Concerning this question our teachers assert that bishops do not have power to institute or establish anything contrary to the Gospel, as has been indicated above and as is taught by canon law throughout the whole of the ninth Distinction. It is patently contrary to God's command and Word to make laws out of opinions or to require that they be observed in order to make satisfaction for sins and obtain grace, for the glory of Christ's merit is blasphemed when we presume to earn grace by such ordinances. It is also apparent that because of this notion human ordinances have multiplied beyond calculation while the teaching concerning faith and righteousness of faith has almost been suppressed. Almost every day new holy days and new fasts have been prescribed, new ceremonies and new venerations of saints have been instituted in order that by such works grace and everything good might be earned from God.

Again, those who institute human ordinances also act contrary to God's command when they attach sin to foods, days, and similar things and burden Christendom with the bondage of the law, as if in order to earn God's grace there had to be a service of God among Christians like the Levitical service, and as if God had commanded the apostles and bishops to institute it, as some have written. It is quite believable that some bishops were misled by the example of the law of Moses. The result was that countless regulations came into being—for example, that it is a mortal sin to do manual work on holy days (even when it does not give offense to others), that it is a mortal sin to omit the seven hours, that some foods defile the conscience, that fasting is a work by which God is reconciled, that in a reserved case sin is not forgiven unless forgiveness is secured from the person for whom the case is reserved, in spite of the fact that canon law says nothing of the reservation of guilt but speaks only about the reservation of ecclesiastical penalties.

Where did the bishops get the right and power to impose such requirements on Christendom to ensnare men's consciences? In Acts 15:10 St. Peter forbids putting a yoke on the neck of the disciples. And St. Paul said in II Cor. 10:8 that authority was given for building up and not for tearing down. Why, then, do they multiply sins with such requirements?

Yet there are clear passages of divine Scripture which forbid the establishment of such regulations for the purpose of earning God's grace or as if they were necessary for salvation. Thus St. Paul says in Col. 2:16, "Let no one pass judgment on you in questions of food and drink or with regard to a festival or a new moon or a sabbath. These are only a shadow of what is to come; but the substance belongs to Christ." Again in Col. 2:20–23, "If with Christ you died to the regulations of the world, why do you live as if you still belonged to the world? Why do you submit to regulations, 'Do not handle, Do not taste, Do not touch' (referring to things which all perish as they are used), according to human precepts and doctrines? These have an appearance of wisdom." In Tit. 1:14 St. Paul also forbids giving heed to Jewish myths or to commands of men who reject the truth.

Christ himself says concerning those who urge human ordinances on people, "Let them alone; they are blind guides" (Matt. 15:14). He rejects such service of God and says, "Every plant which my heavenly Father has not planted will be rooted up" (Matt. 15:13).

If, then, bishops have the power to burden the churches with countless requirements and thus ensnare consciences, why does the divine Scripture so frequently forbid the making and keeping of human regulations? Why does it call them doctrines of the devil? Is it possible that the Holy Spirit warned against them for nothing?

Inasmuch as such regulations as have been instituted

as necessary to propitiate God and merit grace are contrary to the Gospel, it is not at all proper for the bishops to require such services of God. It is necessary to preserve the teaching of Christian liberty in Christendom, namely, that bondage to the law is not necessary for justification, as St. Paul writes in Gal. 5:1, "For freedom Christ has set us free; stand fast, therefore, and do not submit again to a yoke of slavery." For the chief article of the Gospel must be maintained, namely, that we obtain the grace of God through faith in Christ without our merits; we do not merit it by services of God instituted by men.

What are we to say, then, about Sunday and other similar church ordinances and ceremonies? To this our teachers reply that bishops or pastors may make regulations so that everything in the churches is done in good order, but not as a means of obtaining God's grace or making satisfaction for sins, nor in order to bind men's consciences by considering these things necessary services of God and counting it a sin to omit their observance even when this is done without offense. So St. Paul directed in I Cor. 11:5 that women should cover their heads in the assembly. He also directed that in the assembly preachers should not all speak at once, but one after another, in order.

It is proper for the Christian assembly to keep such ordinances for the sake of love and peace, to be obedient to the bishops and parish ministers in such matters, and to observe the regulations in such a way that one does not give offense to another and so that there may be no disorder or unbecoming conduct in the church. However, consciences should not be burdened by contending that such things are necessary for salvation or that it is a sin to omit them, even when no offense is given to others, just as no one would say that a woman commits a sin if without offense to others she goes out with uncovered head.

Of like character is the observance of Sunday, Easter, Pentecost, and similar holy days and usages. Those who consider the appointment of Sunday in place of the Sabbath as a necessary institution are very much mistaken, for the Holy Scriptures have abrogated the Sabbath and teach that after the revelation of the Gospel all ceremonies of the old law may be omitted. Nevertheless, because it was necessary to appoint a certain day so that the people might know when they ought to assemble, the Christian church appointed Sunday for this purpose, and it was the more inclined and pleased to do this in order that the people might have an example of Christian liberty and might know that the keeping neither of the Sabbath nor of any other day is necessary.

There are many faulty discussions of the transformation of the law, of the ceremonies of the New Testament, and of the change of the Sabbath, all of which have arisen from the false and erroneous opinion that in Christendom one must have services of God like the Levitical or Jewish services and that Christ commanded the apostles and bishops to devise new ceremonies which would be necessary for salvation. Such errors were introduced into Christendom when the righteousness of faith was no longer taught and preached with clarity and purity. Some argue that although Sunday must not be kept as of divine obligation, it must nevertheless be kept as almost of divine obligation, and they prescribe the kind and amount of work that may be done on the day of rest. What are such discussions but snares of conscience? For although they undertake to lighten and mitigate human regulations, yet there can be no moderation or mitigation as long as the opinion remains and prevails that their observance is necessary. And this opinion will remain as long as there is no understanding of the righteousness of faith and Christian liberty.

The apostles directed that one should abstain from blood and from what is strangled. Who observes this prohibition now? Those who do not observe it commit no sin, for the apostles did not wish to burden consciences with such bondage but forbade such eating for a time to avoid offense. One must pay attention to the chief article of Christian doctrine, and this is not abrogated by the decree.

Scarcely any of the ancient canons are observed according to the letter, and many of the regulations fall into disuse from day to day even among those who observe such ordinances most jealously. It is impossible to give counsel or help to consciences unless this mitigation is practiced, that one recognizes that such rules are not to be deemed necessary and that disregard of them does not injure consciences.

The bishops might easily retain the obedience of men if they did not insist on the observance of regulations which cannot be kept without sin. Now, however, they administer the sacrament in one kind and prohibit administration in both kinds. Again, they forbid clergymen to marry and admit no one to the ministry unless he first swears an oath that he will not preach this doctrine, although there is no doubt that it is in accord with the holy Gospel. Our churches do not ask that the bishops should restore peace and unity at the expense of their honor and dignity (though it is incumbent on the bishops to do this, too, in case of need), but they ask only that the bishops relax certain unreasonable burdens which did not exist in the church in former times and which were introduced contrary to the custom of the universal Christian church. Perhaps there was some reason for introducing them, but they are not adapted to our times. Nor can it be denied that some regulations were adopted from want of understanding. Accordingly the bishops ought to be so gracious as to temper these regulations inasmuch as such changes do not destroy the unity of Christian churches. For many regulations devised by men have with the passing of time fallen into disuse and are not obligatory, as papal law itself testifies. If, however, this is impossible and they cannot be persuaded to mitigate or abrogate human regulations which are not to be observed without sin, we are bound to follow the apostolic rule which commands us to obey God rather than men.

St. Peter forbids the bishops to exercise lordship as if they had power to coerce the churches according to their will. It is not our intention to find ways of reducing the bishops' power, but we desire and pray that they may not coerce our consciences to sin. If they are unwilling to do this and ignore our petition, let them consider how they will answer for it in God's sight, inasmuch as by their obstinacy they offer occasion for division and schism, which they should in truth help to prevent.

[Conclusion]

These are the chief articles that are regarded as controversial. Although we could have mentioned many more abuses and wrongs, to avoid prolixity and undue length we have indicated only the principal ones. The others can readily be weighed in the light of these. In the past there have been grave complaints about indulgences, pilgrimages, and misuse of the ban. Parish ministers also had endless quarrels with monks about the hearing of confessions, about burials, about sermons on special occasions, and about countless other matters. All these things we have discreetly passed over for the common good in order that the chief points at issue may better be perceived.

It must not be thought that anything has been said or introduced out of hatred or for the purpose of injuring anybody, but we have related only matters which we have considered it necessary to adduce and mention in order that it may be made very clear that we have introduced nothing, either in doctrine or in ceremonies, that is contrary to Holy Scripture or the universal Christian church. For it is manifest and evident (to speak without boasting) that we have diligently and with God's help prevented any new and godless teaching from creeping into our churches and gaining the upper hand in them.

In keeping with the summons, we have desired to present the above articles as a declaration of our confession and the teaching of our preachers. If anyone should consider that it is lacking in some respect, we are ready to present further information on the basis of the divine Holy Scripture.

Your Imperial Majesty's most obedient servants:

> JOHN, *duke of Saxony, elector*
> GEORGE, *margrave of Bran-denburg*
> ERNEST, *duke of Lüneburg*
> PHILIP, *landgrave of Hesse*
> JOHN FREDERICK, *duke of Saxony*
> FRANCIS, *duke of Lüneburg*
> WOLFGANG, *prince of Anhalt*
> *Mayor and council of Nu-remberg*
> *Mayor and council of Reut-lingen*

THE SMALL CATECHISM (1529)

Luther's Small Catechism grew out of his great concern for theological literacy among Christian people. Traditional Christian instruction had been based upon an exposition of the Apostles' Creed, the Decalogue, and the Lord's Prayer, to which were added other themes such as the Seven Deadly Sins, the Sacraments, and the House Table. Luther kept the traditional exposition of the Creed, the Decalogue, and the Lord's Prayer, to which he added an exposition of Baptism, Confession, the Sacrament of the Altar, and also Morning and Evening Prayers, Grace at Table, and Table of Duties.

Luther first asked some of his colleagues to prepare a catechism but finally took over the task himself. He had prepared himself for this work by preaching on the material covered in the catechism, which was first published in 1529. It was highly esteemed by the people and was called in the Formula of Concord "The Layman's Bible." It became a part of many church orders and was incorporated into The Book of Concord.

Source: The translation used here is taken from *The Book of Concord*, translated and edited by Theodore G.

Tappert (Philadelphia: Muhlenberg Press, 1959). Used by permission.

THE SMALL CATECHISM
of Dr. Martin Luther
for Ordinary Pastors and Preachers

[PREFACE]

Grace, mercy, and peace in Jesus Christ, our Lord, from Martin Luther to all faithful, godly pastors and preachers.

The deplorable conditions which I recently encountered when I was a visitor constrained me to prepare this brief and simple catechism or statement of Christian teaching. Good God, what wretchedness I beheld! The common people, especially those who live in the country, have no knowledge whatever of Christian teaching, and unfortunately many pastors are quite incompetent and unfitted for teaching. Although the people are supposed to be Christian, are baptized, and receive the holy sacrament, they do not know the Lord's Prayer, the Creed, or the Ten Commandments, they live as if they were pigs and irrational beasts, and now that the Gospel has been restored they have mastered the fine art of abusing liberty.

How will you bishops answer for it before Christ that you have so shamefully neglected the people and paid no attention at all to the duties of your office? May you escape punishment for this! You withhold the cup in the Lord's Supper and insist on the observance of human laws, yet you do not take the slightest interest in teaching the people the Lord's Prayer, the Creed, the Ten Commandments, or a single part of the Word of God. Woe to you forever!

I therefore beg of you for God's sake, my beloved brethren who are pastors and preachers, that you take the duties of your office seriously, that you have pity on the people who are entrusted to your care, and that you help me to teach the catechism to the people, especially those who are young. Let those who lack the qualifications to do better at least take this booklet and these forms and read them to the people word for word in this manner:

In the first place, the preacher should take the utmost care to avoid changes or variations in the text and wording of the Ten Commandments, the Creed, the Lord's Prayer, the sacraments, etc. On the contrary, he should adopt one form, adhere to it, and use it repeatedly year after year. Young and inexperienced people must be instructed on the basis of a uniform, fixed text and form. They are easily confused if a teacher employs one form now and another form—perhaps with the intention of making improvements—later on. In this way all the time and labor will be lost.

This was well understood by our good fathers, who were accustomed to use the same form in teaching the Lord's Prayer, the Creed, and the Ten Commandments. We, too, should teach these things to the young and unlearned in such a way that we do not alter a single syllable or recite the catechism differently from year to year. Choose the form that pleases you, therefore, and adhere to it henceforth. When you preach to intelligent and educated people, you are at liberty to exhibit your learning and to discuss these topics from different angles and in such a variety of ways as you may be capable of. But when you are teaching the young, adhere to a fixed and unchanging form and method. Begin by teaching them the Ten Commandments, the Creed, the Lord's Prayer, etc., following the text word for word so that the young may repeat these things after you and retain them in their memory.

If any refuse to receive your instructions, tell them that they deny Christ and are no Christians. They should not be admitted to the sacrament, be accepted as sponsors in Baptism, or be allowed to participate in any Christian privileges. On the contrary, they should be turned over to the pope and his officials, and even to the devil himself. In addition, parents and employers should refuse to furnish them with food and drink and should notify them that the prince is disposed to banish such rude people from his land.

Although we cannot and should not compel anyone to believe, we should nevertheless insist that the people learn to know how to distinguish between right and wrong according to the standards of those among whom they live and make their living. For anyone who desires to reside in a city is bound to know and observe the laws under whose protection he lives, no matter whether he is a believer or, at heart, a scoundrel or knave.

In the second place, after the people have become familiar with the text, teach them what it means. For this purpose, take the explanations in this booklet, or choose any other brief and fixed explanations which you may prefer, and adhere to them without changing a single syllable, as stated above with reference to the text. Moreover, allow yourself ample time, for it is not necessary to take up all the parts at once. They can be presented one at a time. When the learners have a proper understanding of the First Commandment, proceed to the Second Commandment, and so on. Otherwise they will be so overwhelmed that they will hardly remember anything at all.

In the third place, after you have thus taught this brief catechism, take up a large catechism so that the people may have a richer and fuller understanding. Expound every commandment, petition, and part, pointing out their respective obligations, benefits, dangers, advantages, and disadvantages, as you will find all of this treated at length in the many books written for this purpose. Lay the greatest weight on those commandments or other parts which seem to require special attention among the people where you are. For example, the Seventh Commandment, which treats of stealing, must be emphasized when instructing laborers and shopkeepers, and even farmers and servants, for many of these are guilty of dishonesty and thievery. So, too, the Fourth Commandment must be stressed when instructing children and the common people in order that they may be encouraged to be orderly, faithful, obedient, and peaceful. Always adduce many examples from the Scriptures to show how God punished and blessed.

You should also take pains to urge governing authorities and parents to rule wisely and educate their children. They must be shown that they are obliged to do so, and that they are guilty of damnable sin if they do not do so, for by such neglect they undermine and lay waste both the kingdom of God and the kingdom of the world and are the worst enemies of God and man. Make very plain to them the shocking evils they introduce when they refuse their aid in the training of children to become pastors, preachers, notaries, etc., and tell them that God will inflict awful punishments on them for these sins. It is necessary to preach about such things. The extent to which parents and governing authorities sin in this respect is beyond telling. The devil also has a horrible purpose in mind.

Finally, now that the people are freed from the tyranny of the pope, they are unwilling to receive the sacrament and they treat it with contempt. Here, too, there is need of exhortation, but with this understanding: No one is to be compelled to believe or to receive the sacrament, no law is to be made concerning it, and no time or place should be appointed for it. We should so preach that, of their own accord and without any law, the people will desire the sacrament and, as it were, compel us pastors to administer it to them. This can be done by telling them: It is to be feared that anyone who does not desire to receive the sacrament at least three or four times a year despises the sacrament and is no Christian, just as he is no Christian who does not hear and believe the Gospel. Christ did not say, "Omit this," or "Despise this," but he said, "Do this, as often as you drink it," etc. Surely he wishes that this be done and not that it be omitted and despised. *"Do* this," he said.

He who does not highly esteem the sacrament suggests thereby that he has no sin, no flesh, no devil, no world, no death, no hell. That is to say, he believes in none of these, although he is deeply immersed in them and is held captive by the devil. On the other hand, he suggests that he needs no grace, no life, no paradise, no heaven, no Christ, no God, nothing good at all. For if he believed that he was involved in so much that is evil and was in need of so much that is good, he would not neglect the sacrament in which aid is afforded against such evil and in which such good is bestowed. It is not necessary to compel him by any law to receive the sacrament, for he will hasten to it of his own accord, he will feel constrained to receive it, he will insist that you administer it to him.

Accordingly you are not to make a law of this, as the pope has done. All you need to do is clearly to set forth the advantage and disadvantage, the benefit and loss, the blessing and danger connected with this sacrament. Then the people will come of their own accord and without compulsion on your part. But if they refuse to come, let them be, and tell them that those who do not feel and acknowledge their great need and God's gracious help belong to the devil. If you do not give such admonitions, or if you adopt odious laws on the subject, it is your own fault if the people treat the sacrament with contempt. How can they be other than negligent if you fail to do your duty and remain silent. So it is up to you, dear pastor and preacher! Our office has become something different from what it was under the pope. It is now a ministry of grace and salvation. It subjects us to greater burdens and labors, dangers and temptations, with little reward or gratitude from the world. But Christ himself will be our reward if we labor faithfully. The Father of all grace grant it! To him be praise and thanks forever, through Christ, our Lord. Amen.

[I]

THE TEN COMMANDMENTS

*in the plain form in which the head of the family
shall teach it to his household*

THE FIRST

"You shall have no other gods."

What does this mean?

Answer: We should fear, love, and trust in God above all things.

THE SECOND

"You shall not take the name of the Lord your God in vain."

What does this mean?

Answer: We should fear and love God, and so we should not use his name to curse, swear, practice magic, lie, or deceive, but in every time of need call upon him, pray to him, praise him, and give him thanks.

THE THIRD

"Remember the Sabbath day, to keep it holy."

What does this mean?

Answer: We should fear and love God, and so we should not despise his Word and the preaching of the same, but deem it holy and gladly hear and learn it.

THE FOURTH

"Honor your father and your mother."

What does this mean?

Answer: We should fear and love God, and so we should not despise our parents and superiors, nor provoke them to anger, but honor, serve, obey, love, and esteem them.

THE FIFTH

"You shall not kill."

What does this mean?

Answer: We should fear and love God, and so we should not endanger our neighbor's life, nor cause him any harm, but help and befriend him in every necessity of life.

THE SIXTH

"You shall not commit adultery."

What does this mean?

Answer: We should fear and love God, and so we should lead a chaste and pure life in word and deed, each one loving and honoring his wife or her husband.

THE SEVENTH

"You shall not steal."

What does this mean?

Answer: We should fear and love God, and so we should not rob our neighbor of his money or property, nor bring them into our possession by dishonest trade or by dealing in shoddy wares, but help him to improve and protect his income and property.

THE EIGHTH

"You shall not bear false witness against your neighbor."

What does this mean?

Answer: We should fear and love God, and so we should not tell lies about our neighbor, nor betray, slander, or defame him, but should apologize for him, speak well of him, and interpret charitably all that he does.

THE NINTH

You shall not covet your neighbor's house."

What does this mean?

Answer: We should fear and love God, and so we should not seek by craftiness to gain possession of our neighbor's inheritance or home, nor to obtain them under pretext of legal right, but be of service and help to him so that he may keep what is his.

THE TENTH

"You shall not covet your neighbor's wife, or his manservant, or his maidservant, or his ox, or his ass, or anything that is your neighbor's."

What does this mean?

Answer: We should fear and love God, and so we should not abduct, estrange, or entice away our neighbor's wife, servants, or cattle, but encourage them to remain and discharge their duty to him.

[CONCLUSION]

What does God declare concerning all these commandments?

Answer: He says, "I the Lord your God am a jealous God, visiting the iniquity of the fathers upon the children to the third and the fourth generation of those who hate me, but showing steadfast love to thousands of those who love me and keep my commandments."

What does this mean?

Answer: God threatens to punish all who transgress these commandments. We should therefore fear his wrath and not disobey these commandments. On the other hand, he promises grace and every blessing to all who keep them. We should therefore love him, trust in him, and cheerfully do what he has commanded.

[II]

The Creed

in the plain form in which the head of the family shall teach it to his household

THE FIRST ARTICLE: CREATION

"I believe in God, the Father almighty, maker of heaven and earth."

What does this mean?

Answer: I believe that God has created me and all that exists; that he has given me and still sustains my body and soul, all my limbs and senses, my reason and all the faculties of my mind, together with food and clothing, house and home, family and property; that he provides me daily and abundantly with all the necessities of life, protects me from all danger, and preserves me from all evil. All this he does out of his pure, fatherly, and divine goodness and mercy, without any merit or worthiness on my part. For all of this I am bound to thank, praise, serve, and obey him. This is most certainly true.

THE SECOND ARTICLE: REDEMPTION

"And in Jesus Christ, his only son, our Lord: who was conceived by the Holy Spirit, born of the virgin Mary, suffered under Pontius Pilate, was crucified, dead, and buried: he descended into hell, the third day he rose from the dead, he ascended into heaven, and is seated on the right hand of God, the Father almighty, whence he shall come to judge the living and the dead."

What does this mean?

Answer: I believe that Jesus Christ, true God, begotten of the Father from eternity, and also true man, born of the virgin Mary, is my Lord, who has redeemed me, a lost and condemned creature, delivered me and freed me from all sins, from death, and from the power of the devil, not with silver and gold but with his holy and precious blood and with his innocent sufferings and death, in order that I may be his, live under him in his kingdom, and serve him in everlasting righteousness, innocence, and blessedness, even as he is risen from the dead and lives and reigns to all eternity. This is most certainly true.

THE THIRD ARTICLE: SANCTIFICATON

"I believe in the Holy Spirit, the holy Christian church, the communion of saints, the forgiveness of sins, the resurrection of the body, and the life everlasting. Amen."

What does this mean?

Answer: I believe that by my own reason or strength I cannot believe in Jesus Christ, my Lord, or come to him. But the Holy Spirit has called me through the Gospel, enlightened me with his gifts, and sanctified and preserved me in true faith, just as he calls, gathers, enlightens, and sanctifies the whole Christian church on earth and preserves it in union with Jesus Christ in the one true faith. In this Christian church he daily and abundantly forgives all my sins, and the sins of all believers, and on the last day he will raise me and all the dead and will grant eternal life to me and to all who believe in Christ. This is most certainly true.

[III]

THE LORD'S PRAYER

in the plain form in which the head of the family shall teach it to his household
[INTRODUCTION]
"Our Father who art in Heaven."
What does this mean?
Answer: Here God would encourage us to believe that he is truly our Father and we are truly his children in order that we may approach him boldly and confidently in prayer, even as beloved children approach their dear father.

THE FIRST PETITION
"Hallowed be thy name."
What does this mean?
Answer: To be sure, God's name is holy in itself, but we pray in this petition that it may also be holy for us.
How is this done?
Answer: When the Word of God is taught clearly and purely and we, as children of God, lead holy lives in accordance with it. Help us to do this, dear Father in heaven! But whoever teaches and lives otherwise than as the Word of God teaches, profanes the name of God among us. From this preserve us, heavenly Father!

THE SECOND PETITION
"Thy kingdom come."
What does this mean?
Answer: To be sure, the kingdom of God comes of itself, without our prayer, but we pray in this petition that it may also come to us.
How is this done?
Answer: When the heavenly Father gives us his Holy Spirit so that by his grace we may believe his

holy Word and live a godly life, both here in time and hereafter forever.

THE THIRD PETITION

"Thy will be done, on earth as it is in heaven."

What does this mean?

Answer: To be sure, the good and gracious will of God is done without our prayer, but we pray in this petition that it may also be done by us.

How is this done?

Answer: When God curbs and destroys every evil counsel and purpose of the devil, of the world, and of our flesh which would hinder us from hallowing his name and prevent the coming of his kingdom, and when he strengthens us and keeps us steadfast in his Word and in faith even to the end. This is his good and gracious will.

THE FOURTH PETITION

"Give us this day our daily bread."

What does this mean?

Answer: To be sure, God provides daily bread, even to the wicked, without our prayer, but we pray in this petition that God may make us aware of his gifts and enable us to receive our daily bread with thanksgiving.

What is meant by daily bread?

Answer: Everything required to satisfy our bodily needs, such as food and clothing, house and home, fields and flocks, money and property; a pious spouse and good children, trustworthy servants, godly and faithful rulers, good government; seasonable weather, peace and health, order and honor; true friends, faithful neighbors, and the like.

THE FIFTH PETITION

"And forgive us our debts, as we also have forgiven our debtors."

What does this mean?

Answer: We pray in this petition that our heavenly Father may not look upon our sins, and on their account deny our prayers, for we neither merit nor deserve those things for which we pray. Although we sin daily and deserve nothing but punishment, we nevertheless pray that God may grant us all things by his grace. And assuredly we on our part will heartily forgive and cheerfully do good to those who may sin against us.

THE SIXTH PETITION

"And lead us not into temptation."

What does this mean?

Answer: God tempts no one to sin, but we pray in this petition that God may so guard and preserve us that the devil, the world, and our flesh may not deceive us or mislead us into unbelief, despair, and other great and shameful sins, but that, although we may be so tempted, we may finally prevail and gain the victory.

THE SEVENTH PETITION

"But deliver us from evil."

What does this mean?

Answer: We pray in this petition, as in a summary, that our Father in heaven may deliver us from all manner of evil, whether it affect body or soul, property or reputation, and that at last, when the hour of death comes, he may grant us a blessed end and graciously take us from this world of sorrow to himself in heaven.

[CONCLUSION]

"Amen."

What does this mean?

Answer: It means that I should be assured that such petitions are acceptable to our heavenly Father and are heard by him, for he himself commanded us to pray like this and promised to hear us. "Amen, amen" means "Yes, yes, it shall be so."

[IV]

THE SACRAMENT OF HOLY BAPTISM

in the plain form in which the head of the family shall teach it to his household

FIRST

What is Baptism?

Answer: Baptism is not merely water, but it is water used according to God's command and connected with God's Word.

What is this Word of God?

Answer: As recorded in Matthew 28:19, our Lord Christ said, "Go therefore and make disciples of all nations, baptizing them in the name of the Father and of the Son and of the Holy Spirit."

SECOND

What gifts or benefits does Baptism bestow?

Answer: It effects forgiveness of sins, delivers from death and the devil, and grants eternal salvation to all who believe, as the Word and promise of God declare.

What is this Word and promise of God?

Answer: As recorded in Mark 16:16, our Lord Christ said, "He who believes and is baptized will be saved; but he who does not believe will be condemned."

THIRD

How can water produce such great effects?

Answer: It is not the water that produces these effects, but the Word of God connected with the water, and our faith which relies on the Word of God connected with the water. For without the Word of God the water is merely water and no Baptism. But when connected with the Word of God it is a Baptism, that is, a gracious water of life and a washing of regeneration in the Holy Spirit, as St. Paul wrote to Titus (3:5-8), "He saved us by the washing of regeneration and renewal in the Holy Spirit, which he poured out upon us richly through Jesus Christ our Saviour, so that we might be justified by his grace and become heirs in hope of eternal life. The saying is sure."

FOURTH

What does such baptizing with water signify?

Answer: It signifies that the old Adam in us, together with all sins and evil lusts, should be drowned by daily sorrow and repentance and be put to death, and that the new man should come forth daily and rise up, cleansed and righteous, to live forever in God's presence.

Where is this written?

Answer: In Romans 6:4, St. Paul wrote, "We were buried therefore with him by baptism into death, so that as Christ was raised from the dead by the glory of the Father, we too might walk in newness of life."

[V]

[CONFESSION AND ABSOLUTION]

How Plain People Are to Be Taught to Confess

What is confession?

Answer: Confession consists of two parts. One is that we confess our sins. The other is that we receive absolution or forgiveness from the confessor as from God himself, by no means doubting but firmly believing that our sins are thereby forgiven before God in heaven.

What sins should we confess?

Answer: Before God we should acknowledge that we are guilty of all manner of sins, even those of which we are not aware, as we do in the Lord's Prayer. Before the confessor, however, we should confess only those sins of which we have knowledge and which trouble us.

What are such sins?

Answer: Reflect on your condition in the light of the Ten Commandments: whether you are a father or mother, a son or daughter, a master or servant; whether you have been disobedient, unfaithful, lazy, ill-tempered, or quarrelsome; whether you have harmed anyone by word or deed; and whether you have stolen, neglected, or wasted anything, or done other evil.

Please give me a brief form of confession.

Answer: You should say to the confessor: "Dear Pastor, please hear my confession and declare that my sins are forgiven for God's sake."

"Proceed."

"I, a poor sinner, confess before God that I am guilty of all sins. In particular I confess in your presence that, as a manservant or maidservant, etc., I am unfaithful to my master, for here and there I have not done what I was told. I have made my master angry, caused him to curse, neglected to do my duty, and caused him to suffer loss. I have also been immodest in word and deed. I have quarreled with my equals. I have grumbled and sworn at my mistress, etc. For all this I am sorry and pray for grace. I mean to do better."

A master or mistress may say: "In particular I confess in your presence that I have not been faithful in training my children, servants, and wife to the glory of God. I have cursed. I have set a bad example by my immodest language and actions. I have injured my neighbor by speaking evil of him, overcharging him, giving him inferior goods and short measure." Masters and mistresses should add whatever else they have done contrary to God's commandments and to their action in life, etc.

If, however, anyone does not feel that his conscience is burdened by such or by greater sins, he should not worry, nor should he search for and invent other sins, for this would turn confession into torture; he should simply mention one or two sins of which he is aware. For example, "In particular I confess that I once cursed. On one occasion I also spoke indecently. And I neglected this or that," etc. Let this suffice.

If you have knowledge of no sin at all (which is quite unlikely), you should mention none in particular, but receive forgiveness upon the general confession which you make to God in the presence of the confessor.

Then the confessor shall say: "God be merciful to you and strengthen your faith. Amen."

Again he shall say: "Do you believe that the forgiveness I declare is the forgiveness of God?"

Answer: "Yes, I do."

Then he shall say: "Be it done for you as you have believed. According to the command of our Lord Jesus Christ, I forgive you your sins in the name of the Father and of the Son and of the Holy Spirit. Amen. Go in peace."

A confessor will know additional passages of the Scriptures with which to comfort and to strengthen the faith of those whose consciences are heavily burdened or who are distressed and sorely tried. This is intended simply as an ordinary form of confession for plain people.

[VI]

THE SACRAMENT OF THE ALTAR

in the plain form in which the head of the family shall teach it to his household

What is the Sacrament of the Altar?

Answer: Instituted by Christ himself, it is the true body and blood of our Lord Jesus Christ, under the bread and wine, given to us Christians to eat and to drink.

Where is this written?

Answer: The holy evangelists Matthew, Mark, and Luke, and also St. Paul, write thus: "Our Lord Jesus Christ, on the night when he was betrayed, took bread, and when he had given thanks, he broke it, and gave it to the disciples and said, 'Take, eat; this is my body which is given for you. Do this in remembrance of me.' In the same way also he took the cup, after supper, and when he had given thanks he gave it to them, saying, 'Drink of it, all of you. This cup is the new covenant in my blood, which is poured out for many for the forgiveness of sins. Do this, as often as you drink it, in remembrance of me.' "

What is the benefit of such eating and drinking?

Answer: We are told in the words "for you" and "for the forgiveness of sins." By these words the forgiveness of sins, life, and salvation are given to us in the sacrament, for where there is forgiveness of sins, there are also life and salvation.

How can bodily eating and drinking produce such great effects?

Answer: The eating and drinking do not in themselves produce them, but the words "for you" and "for the forgiveness of sins." These words, when accompanied by the bodily eating and drinking, are the chief thing in the sacrament, and he who believes these words has what they say and declare: the forgiveness of sins.

Who, then, receives this sacrament worthily?

Answer: Fasting and bodily preparation are a good external discipline, but he is truly worthy and well prepared who believes these words: "for you" and "for the forgiveness of sins." On the other hand, he who does not believe these words, or doubts them, is unworthy and unprepared, for the words "for you" require truly believing hearts.

[VII]

[Morning and Evening Prayers]

How the head of the family shall teach his household to say morning and evening prayers

In the morning, when you rise, make the sign of the cross and say, "In the name of God, the Father, the Son, and the Holy Spirit. Amen."

Then, kneeling or standing, say the Apostles' Creed and the Lord's Prayer. Then you may say this prayer:

"I give Thee thanks, heavenly Father, through thy dear Son Jesus Christ, that Thou hast protected me through the night from all harm and danger. I beseech Thee to keep me this day, too, from all sin and evil, that in all my thoughts, words, and deeds I may please Thee. Into thy hands I commend my body and soul and all that is mine. Let thy holy angel have charge of me, that the wicked one may have no power over me. Amen."

After singing a hymn (possibly a hymn on the Ten Commandments) or whatever your devotion may suggest, you should go to your work joyfully.

In the evening, when you retire, make the sign of the cross and say, "In the name of God, the Father, the Son, and the Holy Spirit. Amen."

Then, kneeling or standing, say the Apostles' Creed and the Lord's Prayer. Then you may say this prayer:

"I give Thee thanks, heavenly Father, through thy dear Son Jesus Christ, that Thou hast this day graciously protected me. I beseech Thee to forgive all my sin and the wrong which I have done. Graciously protect me during the coming night. Into thy hands I commend my body and soul and all that is mine. Let thy holy angels have charge of me, that the wicked one may have no power over me. Amen."

Then quickly lie down and sleep in peace.

[VIII]

[GRACE AT TABLE]

How the head of the family shall teach his household to offer blessing and thanksgiving at table

[BLESSING BEFORE EATING]

When the children and the whole household gather at the table, they should reverently fold their hands and say:

"The eyes of all look to Thee, O Lord, and Thou givest them their food in due season. Thou openest thy hand; Thou satisfieth the desire of every living thing."

(It is to be observed that "satisfying the desire of every living thing" means that all creatures receive enough to eat to make them joyful and of good cheer. Greed and anxiety about food prevent such satisfaction.)

Then the Lord's Prayer should be said, and afterwards this prayer:

"Lord God, heavenly Father, bless us, and these thy gifts which of thy bountiful goodness Thou hast bestowed on us, through Jesus Christ our Lord. Amen."

[THANKSGIVING AFTER EATING]

After eating, likewise, they should fold their hands reverently and say:

"O give thanks to the Lord, for he is good; for his steadfast love endures forever. He gives to the beasts their food, and to the young ravens which cry. His delight is not in the strength of the horse, nor his pleasure in the legs of a man; but the Lord takes pleasure in those who fear him, in those who hope in his steadfast love."

Then the Lord's Prayer should be said, and afterwards this prayer:

"We give Thee thanks, Lord God, our Father, for all thy benefits, through Jesus Christ our Lord, who lives and reigns forever. Amen."

[IX]

TABLE OF DUTIES

consisting of certain passages of the Scriptures, selected for various estates and conditions of men, by which they may be admonished to do their respective duties

[OMITTED]

REFORMED CREEDS

The designation "Reformed" refers to those Reformation churches that have their source in the work of Zwingli and Calvin. In one sense all Reformation churches are Reformed, but the term is applied more strictly to the churches that are related to Zwingli and Calvin because they were more radical in the reform of the Church according to the Word of God than were the Lutherans.

Reformed Protestantism has been prolific in the production of creeds. More than sixty creeds would qualify as Reformed, though no number can be exact since the boundaries that distinguish Reformed creeds have never been precisely fixed. The Reformed creeds were produced over a wide geographical area and over a very considerable period of time. Hence the Reformed creeds exhibit a variety that is the nemesis of all those who would write *the* theology of *the* Reformed confessions. All that is possible in this regard is a study in comparative symbols or an introduction to the theology of Reformed confessions.

The great variety of Reformed confessions is not simply an accident of history and geography but is rooted in Reformed theology, which was vigorously opposed to all idolatry, including the idolatry of creeds. All creeds are subordinate to the Word of God, and no one creed can presume to be *the* creed. Hence the Reformed theologians found safety in many creeds. Bullinger and Judae are said to have signed the First Helvetic Confession with this comment:

> We wish in no way to prescribe for all churches through these articles a single rule of faith. For we acknowledge no other rule of faith than Holy Scrip-

ture. We agree with whoever agrees with this, although he uses different expressions from our Confession. For we should have regard for the fact itself and for the truth, not for the words. We grant to everyone the freedom to use his own expressions which are suitable for his church and will make use of this freedom ourselves, at the same time defending the true sense of this Confession against distortions.[1]

Reformed creeds prior to 1650 include the following:
Zwingli's Sixty-Seven Articles of Religion (1523)
The Ten Conclusions of Berne (1528)
The Confession to Charles V (Zwingli, 1530)
The Confession to Francis I (Zwingli, 1531)
The Tetrapolitan Confession (1530)
Confession of Basel (1534)
First Helvetic Confession (1536)
Calvin's Catechisms (1537 and 1541)
Confession of Geneva (1537)
The Zurich Consensus (1549)
Gallican Confession (1559)
The Scots Confession (1560)
The Belgic Confession (1561)
The Heidelberg Catechism (1563)
The Second Helvetic Confession (1566)
The Canons of Dort (1619)
The Westminster Confession of Faith and Catechisms (1643–47)

Barth, Peter, *Opera Selecta, Joannis Calvini* (München: Chr. Kaiser, 1926).

Cochrane, A. C., ed., *Reformed Confessions of the 16th Century* (Philadelphia: Westminster Press, 1966).

Dunlop, William, *A Collection of Confessions of Faith, Catechisms, Directories, Books of Discipline, etc., of Public Authority in the Church of Scotland* (Edinburgh: 1719, 1722).

Hall, Peter, *The Harmony of Protestant Confessions* (London: John F. Shaw, 1842). The origin of the *Harmony* was the desire to meet the objection that Protestants were

[1] *Creeds of Christendom* by Philip Schaff, Vol. I (New York: Harper & Bros., 1877), pp. 389–90.

divided and to exhibit the same unity of confession as the Lutherans did in the *Book of Concord*. Plans for one confession fell through, and the compilation of a harmony was taken as a substitute. The task was intrusted to Beza, Daneau, and Salnar. See introduction to Hall's *Harmony* for further details. For role of Beza see *Théodore de Bèze* by Paul-F. Geisendorf (Geneva: Labor et Fides, 1949) pp. 337 ff.

Heppe, Heinrich, *Ursprung und Geschichte der Bezeichnungen "reformierte" und "lutherische" Kirche* (Gotha: 1859).

Müller, E. F. K., *Bekenntnisschriften der reformierten Kirche* (Leipzig: 1903).

Niemeyer, H. A., *Collectio Confessionum in Ecclesiis Reformatis* (Lipsiae: Iulii Klinkhardti, 1840).

Niesel, Wilhelm, *Bekenntnisschriften und Kirchenordnungen der nach Gottes Wort reformierten Kirche* (Zürich: Evangelischer Verlag, A. G. Zollikon, 1938).

Schaff, Philip, *Creeds of Christendom* (New York: Harper & Brothers, 1877).

THE TEN CONCLUSIONS OF BERNE
(1528)

The early Protestants in Switzerland delighted in disputations with their Catholic adversaries. In these disputations (e.g., Basel, 1524; Rive, 1535; Lausanne, 1536) the issues at stake in the Protestant revolt were set forth with singular clarity. The Ten Conclusions, written by Berthold Haller and Francis Kolb and revised by Zwingli, are typical and were debated at Berne in 1528.

Source: German and Latin texts may be found in *Creeds of Christendom* by Philip Schaff (New York: Harper & Bros., 1919), Vol. III, pp. 208–10.

THE TEN CONCLUSIONS

1. The holy Christian Church, whose only Head is Christ, is born of the Word of God, and abides in the same, and listens not to the voice of a stranger.

2. The Church of Christ makes no laws or com-

mandments apart from the Word of God; hence all human traditions are not binding upon us except so far as they are grounded upon or prescribed in the Word of God.

3. Christ is the only wisdom, righteousness, redemption, and satisfaction for the sins of the whole world. For this reason it is a denial of Christ to confess any other means of salvation or satisfaction for sin.

4. It cannot be shown from Holy Scripture that the body and blood of Christ are substantially and corporeally received in the bread of the Eucharist.

5. The mass, as it is now celebrated, in which Christ is offered to God the Father for the sins of the living and the dead is contrary to Scripture, a blasphemy against the most holy sacrifice, passion, and death of Christ and on account of its abuse, an abomination to God.

6. As Christ alone died for us, so he is also to be adored as the only Mediator and Advocate between God the Father and us. For this reason it is contrary to the basis of the Word of God to direct worship to be offered to other mediators beyond the present life.

7. Scripture does not tell us there is any place beyond this life in which souls are purged. Therefore all services for the dead, vigils, masses, processions, anniversaries, lights, candles, and other such things are vain.

8. It is contrary to the Word of God, contained in the books of the Old and New Testaments, to make images for use in worship. For this reason they are to be abolished, if they are set up as objects of worship.

9. Marriage is not forbidden in Scripture to any class of men, but is commanded and permitted to all in order to avoid fornication and unchastity.

10. Since according to Scripture an open fornicator must be excommunicated, it follows that fornication or impure celibacy are more pernicious to the clergy than to any other class on account of the scandal.

THE SECOND HELVETIC CONFESSION
(1566)

(CONFESSION AND SIMPLE EXPOSITION OF THE TRUE FAITH AND CATHOLIC ARTICLES OF THE PURE CHRISTIAN RELIGION.)

This confession was first written in 1561 as a personal confession and testament of Heinrich Bullinger, Zwingli's successor in Zurich. It was made public in 1566 when Frederick III of the Palatinate, needing to justify his Reformed faith, asked Bullinger to provide an exposition of the faith. At the same time the Swiss churches felt a need for a common confession. Frederick was highly pleased with Bullinger's Confession and the Swiss churches ratified it with a few minor changes. It was published in Zurich, March 12, 1566.

The Second Helvetic Confession appeared when the Reformed Churches were established and had reached theological maturity but before they came under the dominating influence of scholasticism. It is moderate in tone, catholic in outlook, and closely related to Christian experience. In this it is similar to the Scots Confession of 1560. On the other hand it lacks the precision of the Belgic or Westminster Confessions. One interesting aspect of the creed is the attention that is given to worship, church order, especially the ministry, and the ordering of life in marriage.

The Second Helvetic Confession was widely accepted and can justly claim to be the most universal of Reformed creeds.

Source: The translation printed here is a revision of the English translation found in *Creeds of Christendom* by Philip Schaff (New York: Harper & Bros., 1922). The revision is based upon the Latin text in *Bekenntnisschriften und Kirchenordnungen*, edited by W. Niesel (Zürich: Evangelischer Verlag, A. G. Zollikon), pp. 219–75.

Courvoisier, Jaques, *La Confession Helvétique Postérieure, Cahiers Théologiques de l'Actualité Protestante* (Paris: Éditions Delachaux & Niestl, S. A., 1944).

Hildebrandt, Walter, and Zimmerman, Rudolph, *Bedeutung und Geschichte des Zweiten Helvetischen Bekenntnisses* (Zürich: Zwingli Verlag, 1938).

——, *Das Zweite Helvetische Bekenntnis* (Zürich: Zwingli Verlag, 1938).

A SIMPLE CONFESSION AND EXPOSITION OF THE ORTHODOX FAITH

THE SECOND HELVETIC CONFESSION,
(1566)

CHAPTER I.—OF THE HOLY SCRIPTURE BEING THE TRUE WORD OF GOD.

(*CANONICAL SCRIPTURE*) We believe and confess the Canonical Scriptures of the holy prophets and apostles of both Testaments to be the true Word of God, and to have sufficient authority of themselves, not of men. For God himself spake to the fathers, prophets, apostles, and still speaks to us through the Holy Scriptures.

And in this Holy Scripture, the universal Church of Christ has all things fully expounded which belong to a saving faith, and also to the framing of a life acceptable to God; and in this respect it is expressly commanded of God that nothing be either put to or taken from the same (Deut. iv. 2; Rev. xxii. 18, 19).

(*SCRIPTURE TEACHES FULLY ALL GODLINESS*) We judge, therefore, that from these Scriptures are to be taken true wisdom and godliness, the reformation and government of churches; as also instruction in all duties of piety; and, to be short, the confirmation of doctrines, and the confutation of all errors, with all exhortations; according to that word of the Apostle, 'All Scripture is inspired by God and profitable for teaching, for reproof,' etc. (2 Tim. iii. 16, 17). Again, 'I am writing these instructions for

you,' says the Apostle of Timothy, 'so that you may
know how one ought to behave in the household of
God,' etc. (1 Tim. iii. 14, 15). (*SCRIPTURE IS THE
WORD OF GOD*) Again, the selfsame Apostle to the
Thessalonians: 'When,' says he, 'you received the
Word of God which you heard from us, you accepted
it, not as the word of men but as what it really is, the
Word of God,' etc. (1 Thess. ii. 13). For the Lord
himself has said in the Gospel, 'It is not you who speak,
but the Spirit of your Father speaking through you;'
therefore 'he who hears you hears me, and he who rejects me rejects him who sent me,' (Matt. x. 20; Luke
x. 16; John xiii. 20).

(*THE PREACHING OF THE WORD OF GOD
IS THE WORD OF GOD*) Wherefore when this Word
of God is now preached in the church by preachers
lawfully called, we believe that the very Word of God
is preached, and received of the faithful; and that
neither any other Word of God is to be feigned nor
to be expected from heaven: and that now the Word
itself which is preached is to be regarded, not the
minister that preaches; who, although he be evil and a
sinner, nevertheless the Word of God abides true and
good.

Neither do we think that therefore the outward
preaching is to be thought as fruitless because the instruction in true religion depends on the inward illumination of the Spirit, or because it is written 'And no
longer shall each man teach his neighbour . . . for
they shall all know me' (Jer. xxxi. 34), and 'Neither
he who plants nor he who waters is anything, but only
God who gives the growth,' (1 Cor. iii. 7). For albeit
'No one can come to me unless the Father who sent
me draws him' (John vi. 44), and unless he is inwardly
lightened by the Holy Spirit, yet we know undoubtedly
that it is the will of God that his word should be
preached even outwardly. God could indeed, by his
Holy Spirit, or by the ministry of an angel, without
the ministry of St. Peter, have taught Cornelius in the

Acts; but, nevertheless, he refers him to Peter, of whom the angel speaking says, 'He shall tell you what you ought to do' (Acts x. 6).

(*INWARD ILLUMINATION DOES NOT ELIMI-NATE EXTERNAL PREACHING*) For he that illuminates inwardly by giving men the Holy Spirit, the self-same, by way of commandment, said unto his disciples, 'Go into all the world, and preach the Gospel to the whole creation' (Mark xvi. 15). And so Paul preached the Word outwardly to Lydia, a purple-seller among the Philippians; but the Lord inwardly opened the woman's heart (Acts xvi. 14). And the same Paul, upon an elegant gradation, fitly placed in the tenth chapter to the Romans, at last infers, 'So faith comes from what is heard, and what is heard comes by the preaching of Christ' (Rom. x. 14–17).

We know, in the meantime, that God can illuminate whom and when he will, even without the external ministry, which is a thing appertaining to his power; but we speak of the usual way of instructing men, delivered unto us from God, both by commandment and examples.

(*HERESIES*) We therefore detest all the heresies of Artemon, the Manichaeans, the Valentinians, of Cerdon, and the Marcionites, who denied that the Scriptures proceeded from the Holy Spirit; or else received not, or interpolated and corrupted, some of them.

(*APOCRYPHA*) And yet we do not deny that certain books of the Old Testament were by the ancient authors called *Apocryphal,* and by others *Ecclesiastical;* to wit, such as they would have to be read in the churches, but not alleged to avouch or confirm the authority of faith by them. As also Augustine, in his *De Civitate Dei,* book xviii., chapter 38, makes mention that 'in the books of the Kings, the names and books of certain prophets are reckoned;' but he adds that 'they are not in the canon,' and that 'those books which we have suffice unto godliness.'

CHAPTER II.—OF INTERPRETING THE HOLY
SCRIPTURES: AND OF FATHERS, COUNCILS,
AND TRADITIONS.

(*THE TRUE INTERPRETATION OF SCRIP-
TURE*) The Apostle Peter has said that 'no prophecy
of Scripture is a matter of one's own interpretation'
(2 Pet. i. 20). Therefore we do not allow all kinds
of exposition. Whereupon we do not acknowledge that
which they call the instinct of the Church of Rome
for the true and natural interpretation of the Scriptures; which, forsooth, the defenders of the Romish
Church do strive to force all men simply to receive;
but we acknowledge only that interpretation of Scriptures for orthodox and genuine which, being taken
from the Scriptures themselves (that is, from the spirit
of that tongue in which they were written, they being
also weighed according to the circumstances and expounded according to the proportion of places, either
of like or of unlike, also of more and plainer), accords with the rule of faith and charity, and makes
notably for God's glory and man's salvation.

(*INTERPRETATIONS OF THE HOLY FA-
THERS*) Wherefore we do not despise the interpretations of the holy Greek and Latin fathers, nor reject
their disputations and treatises as far as they agree
with the Scriptures; but we do modestly dissent from
them when they are found to set down things differing
from, or altogether contrary to, the Scriptures. Neither
do we think that we do them any wrong in this matter;
seeing that they all, with one consent, will not have
their writings matched with the Canonical Scriptures,
but bid us allow of them so far forth as they either
agree with them or disagree.

(*COUNCILS*) And in the same order we also place
the decrees and canons of councils.

Wherefore we suffer not ourselves, in controversies
about religion or matters of faith, to be pressed with
the bare testimonies of fathers or decrees of councils;

much less with received customs, or with a large number of those who share the same opinion. (*WHO IS THE JUDGE?*) Therefore, in controversies of religion or matters of faith, we cannot admit any other judge than God himself, pronouncing by the Holy Scriptures what is true, what is false, what is to be followed, or what to be avoided. So we do not rest but in the judgment of spiritual men, drawn from the Word of God. Certainly Jeremiah and other prophets did vehemently condemn the assemblies of priests gathered against the law of God; and diligently forewarned us that we should not hear the fathers, or tread in their path who, walking in their own inventions, swerved from the law of God (Ezek. xx. 18).

(*TRADITIONS OF MEN*) We do likewise reject human traditions, which, although they be set out with goodly titles, as though they were divine and apostolical, delivered to the Church by the lively voice of the apostles, and, as it were, by the hands of apostolical men, by means of bishops succeeding in their room, yet, being compared with the Scriptures, disagree with them; and that by their disagreement bewray themselves in no wise to be apostolical. For as the apostles did not disagree among themselves in doctrine, so the apostles' scholars did not set forth things contrary to the apostles. Nay, it were blasphemous to avouch that the apostles, by lively voice, delivered things contrary to their writings. Paul affirms expressly that he taught the same things in all churches (1 Cor. iv. 17). And, again, 'For we write you nothing but what you can read and understand' (2 Cor. i. 13). Also, in another place, he witnesses that he and his disciples—to wit, apostolic men—walked in the same way, and jointly by the same Spirit did all things (2 Cor. xii. 18). The Jews also, in time past, had their traditions of elders; but these traditions were severely confuted by the Lord, showing that the keeping of them hinders God's law, and that God is in vain worshiped of such (Matt. xv. 8, 9; Mark vii. 6, 7).

CHAPTER III.—OF GOD; THE UNITY AND THE
TRINITY.

. . . .

CHAPTER IV.—OF IDOLS; OR OF IMAGES OF GOD,
OF CHRIST, AND OF THE SAINTS.

. . . .

CHAPTER V.—OF THE ADORATION, WORSHIP,
AND INVOCATION OF GOD THROUGH THE ONLY
MEDIATOR JESUS CHRIST.

. . . .

CHAPTER VI.—OF THE PROVIDENCE OF GOD.

. . . .

CHAPTER VII.—OF THE CREATION OF ALL
THINGS; OF ANGELS, THE DEVIL, AND MAN.

. . . .

CHAPTER VIII.—OF MAN'S FALL; SIN, AND THE
CAUSE OF SIN.

. . . .

CHAPTER IX.—OF FREE WILL, AND SO OF
MAN'S POWER AND ABILITY.

. . . .

CHAPTER X.—OF THE PREDESTINATION OF GOD
AND THE ELECTION OF THE SAINTS.

(*GOD HAS ELECTED US OUT OF GRACE*)
God has from the beginning freely, and of his pure
grace, without any respect of men, predestinated or
elected the saints, whom he will save in Christ, according to the saying of the apostle, 'He chose us in
him before the foundation of the world' (Eph. i. 4);
and again, 'Who saved us and called us with a holy
calling, not in virtue of our works, but in virtue of his
own purpose and the grace which he gave us in Christ
Jesus ages ago, and now has manifested through the
appearing of our Savior Christ Jesus' (2 Tim. i. 9, 10).

(*WE ARE ELECTED OR PREDESTINED IN
CHRIST*) Therefore, though not for any merit of ours,
yet not without a means, but in Christ, and for Christ,

did God choose us; and they who are now ingrafted into Christ by faith, the same also were elected. But such as are without Christ were rejected, according to the saying of the apostle, 'Examine yourselves, to see whether you are holding to your faith. Test yourselves. Do you not realize that Jesus Christ is in you? —unless indeed you fail to meet the test!' (2 Cor. xiii. 5).

(*WE ARE ELECTED TO A SURE END*) To conclude, the saints are chosen in Christ by God unto a sure end, which end the apostle declares when he says, 'He chose us in him, that we should be holy and blameless before him. He destined us in love to be his sons through Jesus Christ . . . to the praise of his glorious grace' (Eph. i. 4–6).

(*WE ARE TO HAVE A GOOD HOPE FOR ALL*) And although God knows who are his, and now and then mention is made of the small number of the elect, yet we must hope well of all, and not rashly judge any man to be a reprobate: for Paul says to the Philippians, 'I thank my God in all my remembrance of you' (now he speaks of the whole Church of the Philippians), 'thankful for your partnership in the Gospel . . . And I am sure that he who began a good work in you will bring it to completion at the day of Jesus Christ' (Phil. i. 3–7).

(*WHETHER FEW ARE ELECT*) And when the Lord was asked whether there were few that should be saved, he does not answer and tell them that few or many should be saved or damned, but rather he exhorts every man to 'strive to enter by the narrow door' (Luke xiii. 24): as if he should say, It is not for you curiously to inquire of these matters, but rather to endeavor that you may enter into heaven by the strait way.

(*WHAT IN THE PRESENT CASE IS TO BE CONDEMNED*) Wherefore we do not allow of the wicked speeches of some who say, Few are chosen, and seeing I know not whether I am in the number of these few, I will not defraud my nature of her desires.

Others there are who say, If I be predestinated and chosen of God, nothing can hinder me from salvation, which is already certainly appointed for me, whatsoever I do at any time; but if I be in the number of the reprobate, no faith or repentance will help me, seeing the decree of God cannot be changed: therefore all teachings and admonitions are to no purpose. Now the saying of the apostle contradicts these men: 'The Lord's servant must be an apt teacher . . . correcting his opponents with gentleness. God may perhaps grant that they will repent that they . . . may escape from the snare of the devil, after being captured by him to do his will' (2 Tim. ii. 24–26).

(*ADMONITIONS NOT USELESS BECAUSE SALVATION PROCEEDS FROM ELECTION*) Besides, Augustine also teaches, that both the grace of free election and predestination, and also wholesome admonitions and doctrines, are to be preached (*Lib. de Bono Preserverantiae,* cap. 14).

(*WHETHER WE ARE ELECTED*) We therefore condemn those who seek otherwise than in Christ whether they be chosen of eternity, and what God has decreed of them before all eternity. For men must hear the Gospel preached, and believe it. If thou believest, and art in Christ, thou mayest undoubtedly hold that thou art elected. For the Father has revealed unto us in Christ his eternal sentence of predestination, as we even now showed out of the apostle, in 2 Tim. i. 9, 10. This is therefore above all to be taught and well weighed, what great love of the Father toward us in Christ is revealed. We must hear what the Lord does daily preach unto us in his Gospel: how he calls and says, 'Come to me all who labor and are heavy-laden, and I will give you rest' (Matt. xi. 28); and 'God so loved the world, that he gave his only Son, that whoever believes in him should not perish, but have eternal life' (John iii. 16); also, 'It is not the will of my Father who is in heaven that one of these little ones should perish' (Matt. xviii. 14).

Let Christ, therefore, be our looking-glass, in whom

we may behold our predestination. We shall have a most evident and sure testimony that we are written in the Book of Life if we communicate with Christ, and he be ours, and we be his, by a true faith. (*TEMPTATION IN REGARD TO PREDESTINATION*) Let this comfort us in our temptation touching predestination, than which there is none more dangerous, that the promises of God are general to the faithful; in that he says, 'Ask, and it will be given you . . . for everyone who asks receives' (Luke xi. 9, 10). And, to conclude, we pray, with the whole Church of God, 'Our Father who art in heaven' (Matt. vi. 9); and in baptism, we are ingrafted into the body of Christ, and we are fed in his Church, oftentimes, with his flesh and blood, unto everlasting life. Thereby, being strengthened, we are commanded to 'work out our salvation with fear and trembling,' according to that precept of Paul, in Phil. ii. 12.

CHAPTER XI.—OF JESUS CHRIST, BEING TRUE GOD AND MAN, AND THE ONLY SAVIOUR OF THE WORLD.

. . . .

CHAPTER XII.—OF THE LAW OF GOD.

. . . .

CHAPTER XIII.—OF THE GOSPEL OF JESUS CHRIST: ALSO OF THE PROMISES: OF THE SPIRIT AND OF THE LETTER.

. . . .

CHAPTER XIV.—OF REPENTANCE, AND THE CONVERSION OF MAN.

. . . .

CHAPTER XV.—OF THE TRUE JUSTIFICATION OF THE FAITHFUL.

. . . .

CHAPTER XVI.—OF FAITH AND GOOD WORKS: OF THEIR REWARD: AND OF MAN'S MERIT.

. . . .

CHAPTER XVII.—OF THE CATHOLIC AND HOLY
CHURCH OF GOD, AND OF THE ONE ONLY HEAD
OF THE CHURCH.

(*THE CHURCH HAS ALWAYS EXISTED AND
IT WILL ALWAYS EXIST*) Forasmuch as God from
the beginning would have men to be saved, and to
come to the knowledge of the truth (1 Tim. ii. 4),
therefore it is necessary that there always should have
been, and should be at this day, and to the end of the
world, a Church—(*WHAT IS THE CHURCH?*) that
is, a company of the faithful called and gathered out
of the world; a communion (I say) of all saints, that
is, of them who truly know and rightly worship and
serve the true God, in Jesus Christ the Saviour, by the
word and the Holy Spirit, and who by faith are partakers of all those good graces which are freely
offered through Christ. (*CITIZENS OF ONE COM-
MONWEALTH*) These all are citizens of one and the
same city, living under one Lord, under the same laws,
and in the same fellowship of all good things; for the
apostle calls them 'fellow citizens with the saints and
members of the household of God' (Eph. ii. 19);
terming the faithful upon the earth saints (1 Cor. iv.
1), who are sanctified by the blood of the Son of God.
Of these is that article of our Creed wholly to be understood, 'I believe in the holy Catholic Church, the
communion of saints.'

(*ONLY ONE CHURCH IN ALL TIMES*) And,
seeing that there is always but 'one God, and there is
one mediator between God and men, the man Christ
Jesus' (1 Tim. ii. 5); also, one Shepherd of the whole
flock, one Head of this body, and, to conclude, one
Spirit, one salvation, one faith, one Testament, or
Covenant,—it follows necessarily that there is but one
Church, (*CHURCH 'CATHOLIC'*) which we therefore call CATHOLIC because it is universal, spread
abroad through all the parts and quarters of the world,
and reaches unto all times, and is not limited within
the compass either of time or place. Here, therefore,

we must condemn the Donatists, who pinned up the Church within the corners of Africa; neither do we assent to the Roman clergy, who vaunt that the Church of Rome alone is in a manner Catholic.

(*PARTS OR FORMS OF THE CHURCH*) The Church is divided by some into divers parts or sorts; not that it is rent and divided from itself, but rather distinguished in respect of the diversity of the members that are in it. (*MILITANT AND TRIUMPHANT*) One part thereof they make to be the Church Militant, the other the Church Triumphant. The Militant wars still on earth, and fights against the flesh, the world, and the prince of this world, the devil; against sin and against death. The other, being already set at liberty, is now in heaven, and triumphs over all those things overcome, and rejoices before the Lord. Yet these two churches have, notwithstanding, a communion and fellowship between themselves.

(*THE PARTICULAR CHURCH*) Moreover, the Church Militant upon the earth has evermore had many particular churches, which must all, notwithstanding, be referred to the unity of the Catholic Church. This Militant Church was otherwise ordered and governed before the Law, among the patriarchs; otherwise under Moses, by the Law; and otherwise of Christ, by the Gospel. (*THE TWO PEOPLES*) There are but two sorts of people, for the most part, mentioned; to wit, the Israelites and the Gentiles; or they who, of the Jews and Gentiles, were gathered to make a Church. There are also two Testaments, the Old and the New. (*ONE AND SAME CHURCH FOR THE OLD PEOPLE AND THE NEW*) Yet both these sorts of people have had, and still have, one fellowship, one salvation, in one and the same Messiah; in whom, as members of one body, they are all joined together under one head, and by one faith are all partakers of one and the same spiritual meat and drink. Yet here we do acknowledge a diversity of times, and a diversity in the pledges and signs of Christ promised and exhibited; and that now, the ceremonies being abolished, the light shines unto us more clearly, our gifts and graces are more abundant, and our liberty is more full and ample.

(*THE CHURCH AS TEMPLE OF THE LIVING GOD*) This holy Church of God is called 'the temple of the living God' (2 Cor. vi. 16), 'built of living and spiritual stones' (1 Peter ii. 5), 'founded upon a rock' (Matt. xvi. 18), 'which cannot be moved' (1 Cor. iii. 11). (*THE CHURCH DOES NOT ERR*) Whereupon it is called 'the pillar and bulwark of the truth' (1 Tim. iii. 15), that does not err, so long as it relies upon the rock Christ, and upon the foundation of the prophets and apostles. And no marvel if it do err, so often as it forsakes him who is the alone truth. (*THE CHURCH AS BRIDE AND VIRGIN*) This Church is also called a virgin (2 Cor. xi. 2), and 'the bride of Christ' (Cant. iv. 8), and 'his beloved' (Cant. v. 16). For the apostle says, 'I betrothed you to Christ to present you as a pure bride to her one husband' (2 Cor. xi. 2). (*THE CHURCH AS FLOCK OF SHEEP*) The Church is called 'a flock of sheep under one shepherd,' even Christ (Ezek. xxxiv. 22, 23, and John x. 16); (*THE CHURCH AS THE BODY*) also, 'the body of Christ' (Col. i. 24), because the faithful are the lively members of Christ, having him for their head.

(*CHRIST THE SOLE HEAD OF THE CHURCH*) It is the head which has the pre-eminence in the body, and from whence the whole body receives life; by whose spirit it is governed in all things; of whom, also, it receives increase, that it may grow up. Also, there is but one head to the body, which has agreement with the body; and therefore the Church cannot have any other head besides Christ. For as the Church is a spiritual body, so must it needs have a spiritual head like unto itself. Neither can it be governed by any other spirit than by the Spirit of Christ. Wherefore Paul says, 'He is the head of the body, the church; he is the beginning, the firstborn from the dead, that in everything he might be preëminent'

(Col. i. 18). And in another place, 'Christ,' saith he, 'is the head of the church, his body, and is himself its Savior' (Eph. v. 23). And again, he is 'the head over all things for the church, which is his body, the fulness of him who fills all in all' (Eph. i. 22, 23). Again, 'We are to grow up in every way into him who is the head, into Christ, from whom the whole body, joined and knit together, makes bodily growth' (Eph. iv. 15, 16). And therefore we do not allow of the doctrine of the Romish prelates, who would make the Pope the general pastor and supreme head of the Church Militant here on earth, and the very vicar of Jesus Christ, who has (as they say) all fullness of power and sovereign authority in the Church. (*CHRIST THE ONLY PASTOR OF THE CHURCH*) For we hold and teach that Christ our Lord is, and remains still, the only universal pastor, and highest bishop, before God his Father; and that in the Church he performs all the duties of a pastor or bishop, even to the world's end; (*VICAR*) and therefore stands not in need of any other to supply his room. For he is said to have a substitute, who is absent; but Christ is present with his Church, and is the head that gives life thereunto. (*NO PRIMATE IN THE CHURCH*) He did straitly forbid his apostles and their successors all superiority or dominion in the Church. They, therefore, that by gainsaying set themselves against so manifest a truth, and bring another kind of government into the Church, who sees not that they are to be counted in the number of them of whom the apostles of Christ prophesied? as in Peter, 2 Epist. ii. 1, and Paul, Acts xx. 29; 2 Cor. xi. 13; 2 Thess. ii. 8, 9, and in many other places.

(*NO DISORDER IN THE CHURCH*) Now, by taking away the Romish head we do not bring any confusion or disorder into the Church. For we teach that the government of the Church which the apostles handed down is sufficient to keep the Church in due order; which, from the beginning, while as yet it wanted such a Romish head as is now pretended to keep it in order, was not disordered or full of confusion. The Romish head doth maintain indeed his tyranny and corruption which have been brought into the Church; but in the meantime he hinders, resists, and, with all the might he can make, cuts off the right and lawful reformation of the Church.

(*DISSENT AND STRIFE IN THE CHURCH*)
They object against us that there have been great strifes and dissensions in our churches since they did sever themselves from the Church of Rome; and that therefore they cannot be true churches. As though there were never in the Church of Rome any sects, any contentions and quarrels; and that, in matters of religion, maintained not so much in the schools as in the holy Chairs, even in the audience of the people. We know that the apostle said, 'God is not a God of confusion but of peace' (1 Cor. xiv. 33), and, 'While there is jealousy and strife among you, are you not of the flesh?' (1 Cor. iii. 3, 4). Yet may we not deny that God was in that Church planted by the apostle; and that the Apostolic Church was a true Church, howsoever there were strifes and dissensions in it. The Apostle Paul reprehended Peter, an apostle (Gal. ii. 11), and Barnabas fell at variance with Paul (Acts xv. 39). Great contention arose in the Church of Antioch between them that preached one and the same Christ, as Luke records in the Acts of the Apostles, chap. xv. 2. And there have at all times been great contentions in the Church, and the most excellent doctors of the Church have, about no small matters, differed in opinion; yet so as, in the meantime, the Church ceased not to be the Church for all these contentions. For thus it pleases God to use the dissensions that arise in the Church, to the glory of his name, to the setting forth of the truth, and to the end that such as are not approved might be manifest (1 Cor. xi. 19).

(*NOTES OR SIGNS OF THE TRUE CHURCH*)
Now, as we acknowledge no other head of the Church than Christ, so do we not acknowledge every church

to be the true Church which vaunts herself so to be;
but we teach that to the true Church indeed in which
the marks and tokens of the true Church are to be
found. Firstly and chiefly, the' lawful and sincere
preaching of the word of God as it is left unto us in
the writings of the prophets and the apostles, which
do all seem to lead us unto Christ, who in the Gospel
has said, 'My sheep hear my voice, and I know them,
and they follow me; and I give unto them eternal life.
A stranger they will not follow, but they will flee from
him, for they do not know the voice of strangers'
(John x. 5, 27, 28).

And they that are such in the Church of God have
all but one faith and one spirit; and therefore they
worship but one God, and him alone they serve in
spirit and in truth, loving him with all their hearts and
with all their strength, praying unto him alone through
Jesus Christ, the only Mediator and Intercessor; and
they seek not life or justice but only in Christ, and
by faith in him; because they do acknowledge Christ
the only head and foundation of his Church, and,
being surely founded on him, do daily repair themselves by repentance, and do with patience bear the
cross laid upon them; and, besides, by unfeigned love
joining themselves to all the members of Christ, do
thereby declare themselves to be the disciples of
Christ, by continuing in the bond of peace and holy
unity. They do withal communicate in the sacraments
ordained by Christ, and delivered unto us by his apostles, using them in no other manner than as they received them from the Lord himself. That saying of
the Apostle Paul is well known to all, 'I received from
the Lord what I also delivered to you' (1 Cor. xi. 23).
For which cause we condemn all such churches, as
strangers from the true Church of Christ, which are
not such as we have heard they ought to be, howsoever, in the meantime, they brag of the succession of
bishops, of unity, and of antiquity. Moreover, we have
in charge from the apostles of Christ 'to shun the
worship of idols' (1 Cor. x. 14; 1 John v. 21), and

'to come out of Babylon,' and to have no fellowship with her, unless we mean to be partakers with her of all God's plagues laid upon her (Rev. xviii. 4; 2 Cor. vi. 17).

(*OUTSIDE THE CHURCH OF GOD THERE IS NO SALVATION*) But as for communicating with the true Church of Christ, we so highly esteem it that we say plainly that none can live before God who do not communicate with the true Church of God, but separate themselves from the same. For as without the ark of Noah there was no escaping when the world perished in the flood; even so do we believe that without Christ, who in the Church offers himself to be enjoyed of the elect, there can be no certain salvation: and therefore we teach that such as would be saved must in no wise separate themselves from the true Church of Christ.

(*CHURCH IS NOT BOUND TO ITS SIGNS*) But as yet we do not so strictly shut up the Church within those marks before mentioned, as thereby to exclude all those out of the Church who either do not participate of the sacraments (not willingly, nor upon contempt; but who, being constrained by necessity, do against their will abstain from them, or else do want them), or in whom faith does sometimes fail, though not quite decay, nor altogether die: or in whom some slips and errors of infirmity may be found. For we know that God had some friends in the world that were not of the commonwealth of Israel. We know what befell the people of God in the captivity of Babylon, where they were without their sacrifices seventy years. We know what happened to St. Peter, who denied his Master, and what is wont daily to happen among the faithful and chosen of God who go astray and are full of infirmities. We know, moreover, what manner of churches the churches in Galatia and Corinth were in the apostles' time: in which St. Paul condemns many and heinous crimes; yet he calls them holy churches of Christ (1 Cor. i. 2; Gal. i. 2).

(*THE CHURCH APPEARS AT TIMES TO BE EXTINCT*) Yea, and it happens sometimes that God in his just judgment suffers the truth of his Word, and the Catholic faith, and his own true worship, to be so obscured and defaced that the Church seems almost quite razed out, and not so much as a face of a Church to remain; as we see fell out in the days of Elijah (1 Kings xix. 10, 14), and at other times. And yet, in the meantime, the Lord has in this world, even in this darkness, his true worshippers, and those not a few, but even seven thousand and more (1 Kings xix. 18; Rev. vii. 4, 9). For the apostle cries, 'God's firm foundation stands, bearing this seal, "The Lord knows those who are his,"' etc. (2 Tim. ii. 19).

Whereupon the Church of God may be termed invisible; not that the men whereof it consists are invisible, but because, being hidden from our sight, and known only unto God, it cannot be discerned by the judgment of man.

(*NOT ALL WHO ARE IN THE CHURCH ARE OF THE CHURCH*) Again, not all that are reckoned in the number of the Church are saints, and lively and true members of the Church. For there are many hypocrites, who outwardly do hear the word of God, and publicly receive the sacraments, and do seem to pray unto God alone through Christ, to confess Christ to be their only righteousness, and to worship God, and to exercise the duties of charity to the brethren, and for a while through patience to endure in troubles and calamities. And yet they are altogether destitute of the inward illumination of the Spirit of God, of faith and sincerity of heart, and of perseverance or continuance to the end. And these men are, for the most part, at length laid open in their true character. For the Apostle John says, 'They went out from us, but they were not of us; for if they had been of us, they would have continued with us' (1 John ii. 19). Yet these men, while they do pretend religion, are accounted to be in the Church, although they are not of the Church: even as traitors in a commonwealth, before they be detected, are accounted in the number of good citizens; and as the cockle and darnel and chaff are found among the wheat; and as wens and swellings are in a perfect body, when they are rather diseases and deformities than true members of the body. And therefore the Church is very well compared to a drag-net, which draws up fishes of all sorts; and to a field, wherein is found both darnel and good corn (Matt. xiii. 26, 47). (*WE MUST NOT JUDGE RASHLY OR PREMATURELY*) Hence we must be very careful not to judge rashly before the time, nor to exclude, and cast off or cut away, those whom the Lord would not have excluded nor cut off, or whom, without some damage to the Church, we cannot separate from it. Again, we must be very vigilant lest the godly, falling fast asleep, the wicked grow stronger, and do some mischief in the Church.

(*UNITY OF CHURCH DOES NOT CONSIST IN EXTERNAL RITES*) Furthermore, we teach that great care is to be taken wherein especially the truth and unity of the Church consists, lest we either rashly breed or nourish schisms in the Church. It consists not in outward rites and ceremonies, but rather in the truth and unity of the Catholic faith. This Catholic faith is not taught us by the ordinances or laws of men, but by the holy Scriptures, a compendious and short sum whereof is the Apostles' Creed. And, therefore, we read in the ancient writers that there were manifold diversities of ceremonies, but that those were always free; neither did any man think that the unity of the Church was thereby broken or dissolved. We say, then, that the true unity of the Church does consist in several points of doctrine, in the true and uniform preaching of the Gospel, and in such rites as the Lord himself has expressly set down. And here we urge that saying of the apostle very earnestly, 'Let those of us who are mature be thus minded; and if in any thing you are otherwise minded, God will reveal that also to you. Only let us hold true to what we have attained' (Phil. iii. 15, 16).

CHAPTER XVIII.—OF THE MINISTERS OF THE
CHURCH, THEIR INSTITUTION AND OFFICES.

(*GOD USES MINISTERS IN THE BUILDING
OF THE CHURCH*) God has always used his ministers for the gathering or erecting of a Church to himself, and for the governing and preservation of the
same; and still he does, and always will, use them so
long as the Church remains on earth. Therefore, the
first beginning, institution, and office of the ministers
is a most ancient ordinance of God himself, not a new
device appointed by men. (*INSTITUTION AND ORI-
GIN OF THE MINISTRY*) True it is that God can,
by his power, without any means, take unto himself a
Church from among men; but he had rather deal with
men by the ministry of men. Therefore ministers are
to be considered, not as ministers by themselves alone,
but as the ministers of God, by whose means God
does work the salvation of mankind. (*THE MINIS-
TRY MUST NOT BE DEPRECIATED*) For which
cause we give counsel to beware that we do not so
attribute the things appertaining to our conversion and
instruction unto the secret virtue of the Holy Spirit
as to make void the ecclesiastical ministry. For it
behooves us always to have in mind the words of the
apostle, 'How are they to believe in him of whom
they have not heard? And how are they to hear without a preacher? So faith comes from what is heard,
and what is heard comes by the preaching of Christ'
(Rom. x. 14, 17). And that also which the Lord says,
in the Gospel, 'Truly, truly, I say to you, he who receives any one whom I send receives me; and he who
receives me receives him who sent me' (John xiii.
20). Likewise what a man of Macedonia, appearing
in a vision to Paul, being then in Asia, said unto him:
'Come over to Macedonia and help us' (Acts xvi. 9).
And in another place the same apostle says, 'We are
fellow workmen for God; you are God's field, God's
building' (1 Cor. iii. 9).

Yet, on the other side, we must take heed that we
do not attribute too much to the ministers and minis-

try; herein remembering also the words of our Lord in the Gospel, 'No one can come to me unless the Father who sent me draws him' (John vi. 44), and the words of the apostle, 'What then is Apollos? What is Paul? Servants through whom you believed, as the Lord assigned to each. So neither he who plants nor he who waters is anything, but only God who gives the growth' (1 Cor. iii. 5, 7). (*GOD INFLUENCES THE HEART*) Therefore let us believe that God does teach us by his word, outwardly through his ministers, and does inwardly move and persuade the hearts of his elect unto belief by his Holy Spirit; and that therefore we ought to render all the glory of this whole benefit unto God. But we have spoken of this matter in the First Chapter of this our Declaration.

(*WHO THE MINISTERS ARE AND OF WHAT SORT WHOM GOD HAS GIVEN TO THE WORLD*) God has used for his ministers, even from the beginning of the world, the best and most eminent men in the world (for, although some of them were inexperienced in worldly wisdom or philosophy, yet surely in true divinity they were most excellent) — namely, the patriarchs, to whom he spake very often by his angels. For the patriarchs were the prophets or teachers of their age, whom God, for this purpose, would have to live many years, that they might be, as it were, fathers and lights of the world. They were followed by Moses and the prophets renowned throughout all the world.

(*CHRIST THE TEACHER*) Then, after all these, our heavenly Father sent his only-begotten Son, the most perfect teacher of the world; in whom is hidden the wisdom of God, and from whom we derive that most holy, simple and perfect doctrine of the Gospel. For he chose unto himself disciples, whom he made apostles; and they, going out into the whole world, gathered together churches in all places by the preaching of the Gospel. And afterward they ordained pastors and teachers in all churches, by the commandment of Christ; who, by such as succeeded them, has

taught and governed the Church unto this day. Therefore, as God gave unto his ancient people the patriarchs, together with Moses and the prophets, so also
to his people under the new covenant he sent his only-
begotten Son, and, with him, the apostles and teachers
of this Church.

(*MINISTERS OF THE NEW TESTAMENT*)
Furthermore, the ministers of the new people are
termed by divers names; for they are called apostles,
prophets, evangelists, bishops, elders, pastors, and
teachers (1 Cor. xii. 28; Eph. vi. 11). (*APOSTLES*)
The apostles remained in no certain place, but gathered together divers churches throughout the whole
world; which churches, when they were once established, there ceased to be any more apostles, and in
their places were particular pastors appointed in
every Church. (*PROPHETS*) The prophets, in old
time, did foresee and foretell things to come; and, besides, did interpret the Scriptures; and such are found
some among us at this day. (*EVANGELISTS*) They
were called evangelists, who were the penmen of the
history of the Gospel, and were also preachers of the
Gospel of Christ; as the Apostle Paul gives in charge
unto Timothy, 'do the work of an evangelist' (2 Tim.
iv. 5). (*BISHOPS*) Bishops are the overseers and
watchmen of the Church, who distribute food and
other necessities to the Church. (*PRESBYTERS*) The
elders are the ancients and, as it were, the senators
and fathers of the Church, governing it with wholesome counsel. (*PASTORS*) The pastors both keep
the Lord's flock, and also provide things necessary for
it. (*TEACHERS*) The teachers do instruct, and teach
the true faith and godliness. Therefore the Church
ministers that now are may be called bishops, elders,
pastors, and teachers.

(*ORDERS OF THE PAPISTS*) But in process
of time there were many more names of ministers
brought into the Church. For some were created patriarchs, others archbishops, others suffragans; also,
metropolitans, archdeacons, deacons, subdeacons, aco-

lytes, exorcists, choristers, porters, and I know not what others, as cardinals, provosts, and priors; abbots, greater and lesser; orders, higher and lower. But touching all these, we little heed what they have been in times past, or what they are now; it is sufficient for us that, so much as concerns ministers, we have the doctrine of the apostles.

(*MONKS*) We, therefore, knowing certainly that monks, and the orders or sects of them, are instituted neither by Christ nor by his apostles, we teach that they are so far from being profitable that they are pernicious and hurtful unto the Church of God. For, although in former times they were tolerable (when they lived solitarily, getting their livings with their own hands, and were burdensome to none, but did in all places obey their pastors, even as laymen), yet what kind of men they be now all the world sees and perceives. They pretend I know not what vows; but they lead a life altogether disagreeing from their vows: so that the very best of them may justly be numbered among those of whom the apostle speaks: 'We hear that some of you are living in idleness, mere busybodies, not doing any work' etc. (2 Thess. iii. 11). Therefore, we have no such in our churches; and we teach that they should not be allowed in the churches of Christ.

(*CALLING AND ELECTION OF MINISTERS*) Furthermore, no man ought to usurp the honor of the ecclesiastical ministry; that is to say, greedily to pluck it to himself by bribes, or any evil shifts, or of his own accord. But let the ministers of the Church be called and chosen by a lawful and ecclesiastical election and vocation; that is to say, let them be chosen religiously by the Church, and that in due order, without any tumult, seditions, or contention. Not every one that will should be elected, but such men as are fit and have sufficient learning, especially in the Scriptures, and godly eloquence, and wise simplicity; to conclude, such men as are of good report for moderation and honesty of life, according to that apostolic rule which St. Paul gives in the 1st Epistle to Timothy iii. 2–7, and to Titus i. 7–9. (*ORDINATION*) And those who are chosen let them be ordained by the elders with public prayer, and laying on of hands. We do here, therefore, condemn all those who run of their own accord, being neither chosen, sent, nor ordained. We do also utterly disallow unfit ministers, and such as are not furnished with gifts requisite for a pastor.

In the mean time we are not ignorant that the innocent simplicity of certain pastors in the primitive Church did sometimes more profit the Church than the manifold, exquisite, and nice learning of some others that were over-lofty and high-minded. And for this cause we also, at this day, do not reject the honest simplicity of certain men, who yet are not destitute of all knowledge and learning.

(*PRIESTHOOD OF ALL BELIEVERS*) The apostles of Christ do term all those who believe in Christ 'priests;' not in regard to their ministry, but because that all the faithful, being made kings and priests, may, through Christ, offer up spiritual sacrifices unto God (Exod. xix. 6; 1 Pet. ii. 5, 9; Rev. i. 6). The ministry, then, and the priesthood are things far different one from the other. For the priesthood, as we said even now, is common to all Christians; not so is the ministry. And we have not taken away the ministry of the Church because we have thrust the popish priesthood out of the Church of Christ. (*PRIESTS AND PRIESTHOOD*) For surely in the new covenant of Christ there is no longer any such priesthood as was in the ancient Church of the Jews; which had an external anointing, holy garments, and very many ceremonies which were figures and types of Christ, who, by his coming, fulfilled and abolished them (Heb. ix. 10, 11). And he himself remains the only priest forever; and we do not communicate the name of priest to any of the ministers, lest we should detract any thing from Christ. For the Lord himself has not appointed in the Church any priests of the

New Testament, who, having received authority from the suffragan, may offer up the host every day, that is, the very flesh and the very blood of our Savior, for the quick and the dead; but ministers, who may teach and administer the sacraments. (*THE NA-TURE OF THE MINISTERS OF THE NEW TES-TAMENT*) Paul declares plainly and shortly what we are to think of the ministers of the New Testament, or of the Church of Christ, and what we must attribute unto them: 'This is how one should regard us, as servants of Christ and stewards of the mysteries of God' (1 Cor. iv. 1). So that the apostle wants us to esteem ministers as ministers. Now the apostle calls them ὑπηρέτας, as it were under-rowers, who have an eye only to their pilot; that is to say, men that live not unto themselves, nor according to their own will, but for others—to wit, their masters, at whose commandment and beck they ought to be. For the minister of the Church is commanded wholly, and in all parts of his duty, not to please himself; but to execute that only which he has received in commandment from his Lord. And in this place it is expressly declared who is our Master, even Christ; to whom the ministers are in subjection in all the functions of their ministry. (*MINISTERS AS STEWARDS OF THE MYSTER-IES OF GOD*) He adds further that the ministers of the Church are 'servants and stewards of the mysteries of God' (1 Cor. iv. 1). Now the mysteries of God Paul in many places, and especially in Eph. iii. 4, does call 'the gospel of Christ.' And the sacraments of Christ are also called mysteries by the ancient writers. Therefore for this purpose are the ministers of the Church called—namely, to preach the Gospel of Christ unto the faithful, and to administer the sacraments. We read, also, in another place in the Gospel, of 'the faithful and wise steward,' whom 'his master will set over his household, to give them their portion of food at the proper time' (Luke xii. 42). Again, in another place of the Gospel, a man goes into a strange country, and, leaving his house, gives unto his servants authority therein, commits to them his substance, and appoints every man his work (Matt. xxv. 14).

(*THE POWER OF MINISTERS OF THE CHURCH*) This is now a fit place to speak somewhat also of the power and office of the ministers of the Church. And concerning their power some have disputed over busily, and would bring all things, even the very greatest, under their jurisdiction; and that against the commandment of God, who forbade unto his disciples all dominion, and highly commended humility (Luke xxii. 26; Matt. xviii. 3). Indeed, there is one kind of power which is mere and absolute power, called the power of right. According to this power all things in the whole world are subject to Christ, who is Lord of all: even as he himself witnesses, saying, 'All authority in heaven and on earth has been given to me' (Matt. xxviii. 18), and again, 'I am the first and the last, and behold I am alive for evermore, and I have the keys of Death and Hades' (Rev. i. 17, 18); also, 'He has the key of David, which opens and no one shall shut, who shuts and no one opens' (Rev. iii. 7).

(*THE LORD RESERVES TRUE POWER FOR HIMSELF*) This power the Lord reserves to himself, and does not transfer it to any other, that he might sit idly by, and look on his ministers while they wrought. For Isaiah says, 'I will place on his shoulder the key of the house of David' (Isa. xxii. 22), and again, 'the government will be upon his shoulders' (Isa. ix. 6). For he does not lay the government on other men's shoulders, but does still keep and use his own power, thereby governing all things. (*POWER OF THE OFFICE AND OF THE MINISTER*) Furthermore, there is another power, that of office, or ministerial power, limited by him who has full and absolute power and authority. And this is more like a service than a dominion. (*KEYS*) For we see that a master does give unto the steward of his house authority and power over his house, and for that cause delivers him the keys, that he may admit or exclude such as his master will have admitted or excluded. According to this power does the minister, by his office, that which the Lord has commanded him to do; and the Lord does ratify and confirm that which he does, and will have the deeds of his ministers to be acknowledged and esteemed by his own deeds. Unto which end are those speeches in the Gospel: 'I will give you the keys of the kingdom of heaven, and whatever you bind on earth shall be bound in heaven, and whatever you loose on earth shall be loosed in heaven' (Matt. xvi. 19). Again, 'If you forgive the sins of any, they are forgiven; if you retain the sins of any, they are retained' (John xx. 23). But if the minister deal not in all things as the Lord has commanded him, but pass the limits and bounds of faith, then the Lord does make void that which he has done. Wherefore the ecclesiastical power of the ministers of the Church is that function whereby they do indeed govern the Church of God, but yet so do all things in the Church as he has prescribed in his Word: which thing being so done, the faithful do esteem them as done of the Lord himself. But touching the keys we have spoken somewhat before.

(*POWER OF MINISTERS IS ONE AND EQUAL IN ALL*) Now the power, or function, that is given to the ministers of the Church is the same and alike in all. Certainly, in the beginning, the bishops or elders did, with a common consent and labor, govern the Church; no man lifted up himself above another, none usurped greater power or authority over his fellow-bishops. For they remembered the words of the Lord, 'Let the leader among you become as one who serves' (Luke xxii. 26); they kept themselves by humility, and did mutually aid one another in the government and preservation of the Church. (*FOR MAINTENANCE OF ORDER*) Notwithstanding, for order's sake, some one of the ministers called the assembly together, propounded unto the assembly the matters to be consulted of, gathered together the voices or sentences of the rest, and, to be brief, as much as lay in him, provided that there might arise no confusion.

So did St. Peter, as we read in the Acts of the Apostles, xi. 4–18, who yet for all that neither was above the rest, nor had greater authority than the rest. Very true, therefore, is that saying of Cyprian the martyr, in his book *De Simplicitate Clericorum:* 'The same doubtless were the rest of the apostles that Peter was, having an equal fellowship with him both in honor and power: but the beginning hereof proceedeth from unity, to signify unto us that there is but one Church.' (*WHEN AND HOW ONE WAS PLACED BEFORE THE OTHERS*) St. Jerome, also, in his commentary upon the Epistle of Paul to Titus, has a saying not much unlike this: 'Before that, by the instigation of the devil, there arose parties in religion, the churches were governed by the common advice of the elders; but after that every one thought that whom he had baptized were his own, and not Christ's, it was decreed that one of the elders should be chosen, and set over the rest, who should have the care of the whole Church laid upon him, and by whose means all schisms should be removed.' Yet Jerome does not avouch this as an order set down of God; for straightway he adds, 'Even as the elders knew, by the continual custom of the Church, that they were subject to him that is set over them, so the bishops must know that they are above the elders rather by custom than by the prescript rule of God's truth, and that they ought to have the government of the Church in common with them.' Thus far Jerome. Now, therefore, no man can forbid by any right that we may return to the old appointment of God, and rather receive that than the custom devised by men.

(*THE DUTIES OF THE MINISTER*) The offices of the ministers are divers; yet, notwithstanding, most men do restrain them to two, in which all the rest are comprehended: to the teaching of the Gospel of Christ, and to the lawful administration of the sacraments. For it is the duty of the ministers to gather together a holy assembly, therein to expound the Word of God, and also to apply the general doctrine to the state and use of the Church; to the end that the doctrine which they teach may profit the hearers, and may build up the faithful. The ministers' duty, I say, is to teach the unlearned, and to exhort; yea, and to urge them to go forward in the way of the Lord who do stand still, or linger and go slowly on: moreover, to comfort and to strengthen those which are faint-hearted, and to arm them against the manifold temptations of Satan; to rebuke offenders; to bring them home that go astray; to raise them that are fallen; to convince the gainsayers; to chase away the wolf from the Lord's flock; to rebuke wickedness and wicked men wisely and severely; not to wink at nor to pass over great wickedness. And, besides, to administer the sacraments, and to commend the right use of them, and to prepare all men by wholesome doctrine to receive them; to keep together all the faithful in a holy unity; and to check schisms. To conclude, to catechise the ignorant, to commend the necessity of the poor to the Church, to visit and instruct those that are sick, or entangled with divers temptations, and so keep them in the way of life. Besides all this, to provide diligently that there be public prayers and supplications made in time of necessity, together with fastings, that is, a holy abstinency, and most carefully to look to those things which belong to the tranquillity, peace, and safety of the Church.

And to the end that the minister may perform all these things the better, and with more ease, it is required of him that he be one that fears God, prays diligently, gives himself much to the reading of the Scripture, and, in all things, and in all times, is watchful, and does show forth a good example unto all men of holiness of life.

(*DISCIPLINE*) And seeing that there must be discipline in the Church, and that, among the ancient Fathers, excommunication was in use, and there were ecclesiastical judgments among the people of God, wherein this discipline was exercised by godly men; it belongs also to the minister's duty, for the edifying of the Church, to manage this discipline, according to the condition of the time and public estate, and according to necessity. Where this rule is always to be maintained, 'all things should be done decently and in order' (1 Cor. xiv. 40), without any oppression or tumult. For the apostle witnesses, that authority was given to him by the Lord 'for building up and not for destroying' (2 Cor. x. 8). And the Lord himself forbade the weeds to be plucked up in the Lord's field, because there would be danger lest the wheat also be plucked up with it (Matt. xiii. 29).

(*EVEN EVIL MINISTERS SHOULD BE HEARD*) But as for the error of the Donatists, we do here utterly detest it; who esteem the doctrine and administration of the sacraments to be either effectual or not effectual, according to the good or evil life of the ministers. For we know that the voice of Christ is to be heard, though it be out of the mouths of evil ministers; forasmuch as the Lord himself said, 'Practice and observe whatever they tell you, but not what they do' (Matt. xxiii. 3). We know that the sacraments are sanctified by the institution, and through the word of Christ; and that they are effectual to the godly, although they be administered by ungodly ministers. Of which matter Augustine, that blessed servant of God, did reason diversely out of the Scriptures against the Donatists. (*SYNODS*) Yet, notwithstanding there ought to be a discipline among the ministers—for there should be intelligent inquiry in the synods touching the life and doctrine of the ministers—those that offend should be rebuked of the elders, and be brought into the way, if they be not past recovery; or else be deposed, and, as wolves, be driven from the Lord's flock by the true pastors if they be incurable. For, if they be false teachers, they are in no wise to be tolerated. Neither do we disallow of general councils, if that they be taken up according to the example of the apostles, to the salvation of the Church, and not to the destruction thereof.

(*THE WORKER IS WORTHY OF HIS REWARD*) The faithful ministers also are worthy (as good workmen) of their reward; neither do they offend when they receive a stipend, and all things that be necessary for themselves and their family. For the apostle shows that these things are for just cause given by the Church, and received by the ministers, in 1 Cor. ix. 14, and in 1 Tim. v. 17, 18, and in other places also.

The Anabaptists likewise are confuted by this apostolical doctrine, who condemn and rail upon those ministers who live upon the ministry.

CHAPTER XIX.—OF THE SACRAMENTS OF THE CHURCH OF CHRIST.

(*THE SACRAMENTS ARE ADDED TO THE WORD AND WHAT SACRAMENTS ARE*) God even from the beginning added unto the preaching of the Word his sacraments, or sacramental signs, in his Church. And to this does the holy Scripture plainly testify. Sacraments are mystical symbols, or holy rites, or sacred actions, ordained by God himself, consisting of his Word, of outward signs, and of things signified: whereby he keeps in continual memory, and recalls to mind, in his Church, his great benefits bestowed upon man; and whereby he seals up his promises, and outwardly represents, and, as it were, offers unto our sight those things which inwardly he performs unto us, and therewithal strengthens and increases our faith through the working of God's Spirit in our hearts; lastly, whereby he does separate us from all other people and religions, and consecrates and binds us wholly unto himself, and gives us to understand what he requires of us.

(*THE SACRAMENTS OF THE OLD AND NEW TESTAMENTS*) These sacraments are either of the Old People or of the New. The sacraments of the Old were Circumcision, and the Paschal Lamb, which was offered up; under which name, reference is made to the sacrifices which were in use from the beginning of the world.

(*THE NUMBER OF THE SACRAMENTS OF THE NEW PEOPLE*) The sacraments of the New People are Baptism and the Supper of the Lord. Some there are who reckon seven sacraments of the New Church. Of which number we grant that Repentance, Matrimony, and the Ordination of ministers (we mean not the popish, but the apostolical ordination) are very profitable, but no sacraments. As for confirmation and extreme unction, they are mere devices of men, which the Church may very well spare, without any damage or inconvenience at all; and, therefore, we have them not in our churches, because there are certain things in them which we can by no means allow of. As for that merchandise which the Romish prelates use in ministering their sacraments, we utterly abhor it.

(*THE AUTHOR OF THE SACRAMENTS*) The author and institutor of all sacraments is not any man, but God alone; for man can by no means ordain sacraments; because they belong to the worship of God, and it is not for man to appoint and prescribe a service of God, but to embrace and retain that which is taught unto him by the Lord. Besides, the sacramental signs have God's promises annexed to them, which necessarily require faith: now faith stays itself only upon the Word of God; and the Word of God resembles writings or letters, the sacraments to seals, which the Lord alone sets to his own letters. (*CHRIST STILL WORKS IN SACRAMENTS*) And as God is the author of the sacraments, so he continually works in that Church where they are rightly used; so that the faithful, when they receive them from the ministers, do know that God works in his own ordinance, and therefore they receive them as from the hand of God; and the minister's faults (if there be any thing notorious in them) cannot hurt them, seeing they do acknowledge the goodness of the sacraments to depend upon the ordinance of the Lord. (*A DIFFERENCE BETWEEN THE AUTHOR AND THE MINISTER*

OF SACRAMENTS) For which cause they put a difference, in the administration of the sacraments, between the Lord himself and his minister; confessing that the substance of the sacraments is given them by the Lord, and the outward signs by the ministers of the Lord.

(*THE ESSENCE AND CHIEF THING IN THE SACRAMENTS*) But the principal thing, which in all sacraments is offered by the Lord, and chiefly regarded by the godly of all ages (which some have called the the substance and matter of the sacraments), is Christ our Saviour—that only sacrifice (Heb. x. 12); and that Lamb of God slain from the foundation of the world (Rev. xiii. 8); that rock, also, of which all our fathers drank (1 Cor. x. 4), by whom all the elect are circumcised with the circumcision made without hands, through the Holy Spirit (Col. ii. 11, 12), and are washed from all their sins (Rev. i. 5), and are nourished with the very body and blood of Christ unto eternal life (John vi. 54).

(*THE SIMILARITY AND DIFFERENCE IN THE SACRAMENTS OF OLD AND NEW PEOPLES*) Now, in respect of that which is the chief thing, and the very matter and substance of the sacraments, the sacraments of both covenants are equal. For Christ, the only Mediator and Saviour of the faithful, is the chief thing and substance in them both: one and the same God is author of them both: they were given unto both churches as signs and seals of the grace and promises of God; which should call to mind and renew the memory of God's great benefits to them, and should distinguish the faithful from all the religions in the world; lastly, which should be received spiritually by faith, and should bind the receivers unto the Church, and admonish them of their duty. In these, I say, and such like things, the sacraments of both churches are not unequal, although in the outward signs they are diverse.

And, indeed, we do yet put a greater difference between them: for ours are more firm and durable, as those which are not to be changed to the end of the world. Again, ours testify that the substance and promise is already fulfilled and performed in Christ, whereas the other did only signify that they should be fulfilled. And again, ours are more simple, and nothing so painful. nothing so sumptuous, nor so full of ceremonies. Moreover, they belong to a greater people, that is dispersed through the face of the whole earth; and because they are more excellent, and do by the Spirit of God stir up in us a greater measure of faith, therefore a more plentiful measure of the spirit does follow them.

(*OUR SACRAMENTS SUCCEED THE OLD WHICH ARE ABROGATED*) But now, since Christ the true Messiah is exhibited unto us, and the abundance of grace is poured forth upon the people of the New Testament, the sacraments of the Old Law are surely abrogated and have ceased; and in their stead the sacraments of the New Testament are placed— namely, for Circumcision, Baptism; and for the Paschal Lamb and sacrifices, the Supper of the Lord.

(*IN WHAT THE SACRAMENTS CONSIST*) And as in the old Church the sacraments consisted of the word, the sign, and the thing signified; so even at this day they are composed, as it were, of the same parts.

(*THE CONSECRATION OF SACRAMENTS*) For the Word of God makes them sacraments, which before were none: for they are consecrated by the Word, and declared to be sanctified by him who first ordained them. To sanctify or consecrate a thing is to dedicate it unto God, and unto holy uses; that is, to take it from the common and ordinary use, and to appoint it to some holy use. For the signs in the sacraments are drawn from common use, things external and visible. As in Baptism, the outward sign is the element of water, and that visible washing which is done by the minister; but the thing signified is regeneration and the cleansing from sins. Likewise, in the Lord's Supper, the outward sign is bread and wine, taken from things commonly used for meat and drink;

but the thing signified is the body of Christ which was given, and his blood which was shed for us, or the communion of the body and blood of the Lord. Wherefore, the water, bread, and wine, considered in their own nature, and out of this holy use and institution of the Lord, are only that which they are called, and which we find them to be. But let the Word of God be added to them, together with invocation upon his holy name, and the renewing of their first institution and sanctification, and then these signs are consecrated, and declared to be sanctified by Christ. For Christ's first institution and consecration of the sacraments stands yet in force in the Church of God, in such sort that they who celebrate the sacraments no otherwise than the Lord himself from the beginning has appointed, have still, even to this day, the use and benefit of that first and most excellent consecration. And for this cause, in the administration of the sacraments, the very words of Christ are repeated.

(*SIGNS TAKE NAME OF THING SIGNIFIED*) And as we learn out of the Word of God that these signs were appointed unto another end and use than the common one, therefore we teach that they now, in this their holy use, do take upon them the names of things signified, and are not still called bare water, bread, or wine; but that the water is called 'the washing of regeneration and renewal' (Tit. iii. 5), and the bread and wine 'the body of Christ' (1 Cor. x. 16), or the pledges and sacraments of his body and blood. Not that the signs are turned into the things signified, or cease to be that which in their own nature they are (for then they could not be sacraments, which should consist only of the thing signified, and have no signs); (*SACRAMENTAL UNION*) but therefore do the signs bear the names of things, because they are mystical tokens of holy things, and because the signs and the things signified are sacramentally joined together; joined together, I say, or united by a mystical signification, and by the purpose and will of him who first instituted them. For the water, bread, and wine are not common, but holy signs. And he that instituted water in Baptism did not institute it with that mind and purpose that the faithful should only be dipped in the water of Baptism; and he which commanded the bread to be eaten and the wine to be drunk in the Supper did not mean that the faithful should only receive bread and wine without any further mystery, as they eat bread at home in their houses; but that they should spiritually be partakers of the things signified, and by faith be truly purged from their sins, and be partakers of Christ also.

(*SECTS*) And, therefore, we cannot allow of them who attribute the consecration of the sacraments to I know not what syllables; to the rehearsal of certain words pronounced by him that is consecrated, and that has an intent of consecrating; or to some other accidental things, which are not left unto us either by the word, or by the example, of Christ or his apostles. We do also mislike the doctrine of those that speak no otherwise of the sacraments than of common signs, not sanctified, nor effectual. We condemn them also who, because of the invisible things, do despise the visible, and think the signs superfluous, because they do already enjoy the things themselves; such were the Messalians, as it is recorded. (*IN THE SACRA-MENTS THE SIGN AND THE PROMISE ARE NOT BOUND TO EACH OTHER*) We do disallow their doctrine also who teach that grace and the things signified are to be so tied to and included in the signs that whatsoever do outwardly receive the signs must needs inwardly participate in the grace, and in the things signified, what manner of men soever they be.

Notwithstanding, as we esteem not the goodness of the sacraments by the worthiness or unworthiness of the ministers, so likewise we do not weigh them by the condition of the receivers. For we know that the goodness of the sacraments does depend upon the faithfulness, or truth, and the mere goodness of God. For even as God's Word remains the true Word of God (wherein not merely bare words are uttered when it is preached, but therewithal the things signified or announced by the words are offered of God), although the wicked and unbelievers hear and understand the words, yet enjoy not the things signified, because they receive them not by a true faith; even so the sacraments, consisting of the Word, the signs, and the things signified, continue true and perfect sacraments, not only because they signify holy things, but also because God offers the things signified, howsoever the unbelievers receive not the things which are offered. This comes to pass, not by any fault in God, the author and offerer of them, but by the fault of men, who do receive them without faith, and unlawfully, whose faithlessness does not nullify the faithfulness of God (Rom. iii. 3).

(*THE END FOR WHICH SACRAMENTS INSTITUTED*) Now, forasmuch as in the beginning, where we showed what the sacraments were, we did also, by the way, set down to what end they were ordained, it will not be necessary to trouble ourselves with repeating any thing which has been already handled. Next, therefore, in order, it remains to speak severally of the sacraments of the Christian Church.

CHAPTER XX.—OF HOLY BAPTISM.

(*THE INSTITUTION OF BAPTISM*) Baptism was instituted and consecrated by God; and the first that baptized was John, who dipped Christ in the water in Jordan. From him it came to the apostles, who also did baptize with water. The Lord, in plain words, commanded them to preach the Gospel and to baptize 'in the name of the Father and of the Son and of the Holy Spirit' (Matt. xxviii. 19). And Peter also, when divers demanded of him what they ought to do, said to them, in the Acts, 'Be baptized every one of you in the name of Jesus Christ for the forgiveness of your sins; and you shall receive the gift of the Holy Spirit' (Acts ii. 38). Hence baptism is called by some a sign of initiation for God's people, whereby the elect of God are consecrated unto God.

(*ONE BAPTISM*) There is but one baptism in the

Church of God; for it is sufficient to be once baptized or consecrated unto God. For baptism once received does continue all a man's life, and is a perpetual sealing of our adoption unto us. (*WHAT IT MEANS TO BE BAPTIZED*) For to be baptized in the name of Christ is to be enrolled, entered, and received into the covenant and family, and so into the inheritance, of the sons of God; yea, and in this life to be called after the name of God; that is to say, to be called a son of God; to be purged also from the filthiness of sins, and to be endued with the manifold grace of God, in order to lead a new and innocent life. Baptism, therefore, does call to mind and keep in remembrance the great benefit of God performed to mankind. For we are all born in the pollution of sin and are the children of wrath. But God, who is rich in mercy, does freely purge us from our sins by the blood of his Son, and in him does adopt us to be his sons, and by a holy covenant does join us to himself, and does enrich us with divers gifts, that we might live a new life. All these things are sealed up unto us in baptism. For inwardly we are regenerated, purified, and renewed of God through the Holy Spirit; and outwardly we receive the sealing of most notable gifts by the water, by which also those great benefits are represented, and, as it were, set before our eyes to be looked upon. (*BAPTISM WITH WATER*) And therefore are we baptized, that is, washed or sprinkled with visible water. For the water makes clean that which is filthy, and refreshes and cools the bodies that fail and faint. And the grace of God deals in like manner with the soul; and that invisibly and spiritually.

(*THE OBLIGATION OF BAPTISM*) Moreover, by the sacrament of baptism God does separate us from all other religions and nations, and does consecrate us a peculiar people to himself. We, therefore, by being baptized, do confess our faith, and are bound to give unto God obedience, mortification of the flesh, and newness of life; yea, and we are soldiers enlisted for the holy warfare of Christ, that all our life long we should fight against the world, Satan, and our own flesh. Moreover, we are baptized into one body of the Church, that we might well agree with all the members of the Church in the same religion and mutual duties.

(*THE FORM OF BAPTISM*) We believe that the most perfect form of baptism is that by which Christ was baptized, and which the apostles did use. Those things, therefore, which by man's device were added afterwards and used in the Church we do not consider necessary to the perfection of baptism. Of this kind is exorcism, the use of lights, oil, salt, spittle, and such other things; as, namely, that baptism is twice every year consecrated with divers ceremonies. But we believe that the baptism of the Church, which is but one, was sanctified in God's first institution of it, and is consecrated by the Word, and is now of full force, by the first blessing of God upon it.

(*MINISTER OF BAPTISM*) We teach that baptism should not be ministered in the Church by women or midwives. For Paul secludes women from ecclesiastical callings; but baptism belongs to ecclesiastical offices.

(*ANABAPTISTS*) We condemn the Anabaptists, who deny that young infants, born of faithful parents, are to be baptized. For, according to the doctrine of the Gospel, 'to such belongs the kingdom of God' (Luke xviii. 16), and they are written in the covenant of God (Acts iii. 25). Why, then, should not the sign of the covenant of God be given to them? Why should they not be consecrated by holy baptism, who are God's peculiar people and are in the Church of God? We condemn also the Anabaptists in the rest of those peculiar opinions which they hold against the Word of God. We therefore are not Anabaptists, neither do we agree with them in any point that is theirs.

CHAPTER XXI.—OF THE HOLY SUPPER OF THE LORD.

(*THE SUPPER OF THE LORD*) The Supper of the Lord (which is called the Lord's Table, and the Eucharist, that is, a Thanksgiving) is, therefore, com-

monly called a supper, because it was instituted by
Christ at his last supper, and does as yet represent the
same, and because in it the faithful are spiritually fed
and given drink. (*THE AUTHOR AND CONSE-
CRATOR OF SUPPER*) For the author of the Supper
of the Lord is not an angel or man, but the very Son of
God, our Lord Jesus Christ, who did first of all consecrate it to his Church. And the same blessing and
consecration does still remain among all those who
celebrate no other but that very Supper, which the
Lord did institute, and at that do recite the words of
the Supper of the Lord, and in all things look unto
the one Christ by a true faith; at whose hands, as it
were, they do receive that which they do receive by
the ministry of the ministers of the Church.

(*MEMORIAL OF BENEFITS OF GOD*) The
Lord, by this sacred rite, would have that great benefit
to be kept in fresh remembrance which he procured
for mankind; to wit, that by giving up his body to death
and shedding his blood he has forgiven us all our sins,
and redeemed us from eternal death and the power
of the devil, and now feeds us with his flesh, and gives
us his blood to drink: which things, being apprehended
spiritually by a true faith, do nourish us up to life
everlasting. And this so great a benefit is renewed so
oft as the Supper is celebrated. For the Lord said, 'Do
this in remembrance of me' (Luke xxii. 19).

By this holy Supper also it is sealed unto us, that
the very body of Christ was truly given up for us,
and his blood shed for the remission of our sins, lest
our faith might somewhat waver. (*THE SIGN AND
THING SIGNIFIED*) And this is outwardly represented unto us by the minister in the sacrament, after
a visible manner, and, as it were, laid before our eyes
to be seen, which is inwardly in the soul invisibly performed by the Holy Spirit. Outwardly, bread is offered
by the minister, and the words of the Lord are heard:
'Take, eat; this is my body;' and, 'Drink of it, all of
you; for this is my blood' (Matt. xxvi. 26–28; Luke
xxii. 17–20). Therefore the faithful do receive that

which is given by the ministers of the Lord, and do eat the bread of the Lord, and do drink of the Lord's cup. And at the same time inwardly, by the working of Christ through the Holy Spirit, they receive also the flesh and blood of the Lord, and do feed on them unto life eternal. For the flesh and blood of Christ is true meat and drink unto life eternal; yea, Christ himself, in that he was delivered for us, and is our Saviour, is that special thing and substance of the Supper; and therefore we suffer nothing to be put in his place.

But that it may the better and more plainly be understood how the flesh and blood of Christ are the meat and drink of the faithful, and are received by the faithful unto life eternal, we will add, moreover, these few things:

Eating is of divers sorts. (1) There is a corporeal eating, whereby meat is taken into a man's mouth, chewed with the teeth, swallowed down, and digested. After this manner did the Capernaites in times past think that they should eat the flesh of the Lord; but they are confuted by him (John vi. 30–63). For as the flesh of Christ could not be eaten bodily, without great wickedness and cruelty, so is it not food for the body, as all men do confess. We therefore disallow that canon in the Pope's decrees, *Ego Berengarius* (*De Consecrat. Dist.* 2). For neither did godly antiquity believe, neither yet do we believe, that the body of Christ can be eaten corporeally and essentially, with a bodily mouth.

(*SPIRITUAL EATING OF THE LORD*) (2) There is also a *spiritual* eating of Christ's body; not such a one whereby it may be thought that the very meat is changed into the spirit, but whereby (the Lord's body and blood remaining in their own essence and property) those things are spiritually communicated unto us, not after a corporeal, but after a spiritual manner, through the Holy Spirit, who does apply and bestow upon us those things (to wit, remission of sins, deliverance, and life eternal) which are prepared for us by the flesh and blood of our Lord, sacrificed for us; so that Christ does now live in us, as we live in him; and does cause us to apprehend him by true faith to this end, that he may become unto us such a spiritual meat and drink, that is to say, our life. (*CHRIST AS OUR FOOD SUSTAINS US IN LIFE*) For even as corporeal meat and drink do not only refresh and strengthen our bodies, but also do keep them in life; even so the flesh of Christ delivered for us, and his blood shed for us, do not only refresh and strengthen our souls, but also do preserve them alive, not so far as they be corporeally eaten and drunken, but so far as they are communicated unto us spiritually by the Spirit of God, the Lord saying, 'The bread which I shall give for the life of the world is my flesh' (John vi. 51): also it is the spirit that gives life: 'the flesh' (to wit, corporeally eaten) 'is of no avail; the words that I have spoken to you are spirit and life' (John vi. 63). (*CHRIST EATEN AND RE-CEIVED BY FAITH*) And as we must by eating receive the meat into our bodies, to the end that it may work in us, and show its efficacy in us (because, while it is without us, it profiteth us not at all); even so it is necessary that we receive Christ by faith, that he may be made ours, and that he live in us, and we in him. For he says, 'I am the bread of life; he who comes to me shall not hunger, and he who believes in me shall never thirst' (John vi. 35); and also, 'He who eats me will live because of me . . . he abides in me, and I in him' (John vi. 57, 56).

(*SPIRITUAL FOOD*) From all this it appears manifestly, that by spiritual meat we mean not any imaginary thing, but the very body of our Lord Jesus, given to us; which yet is received by the faithful not corporeally, but spiritually by faith: in which point we do wholly follow the doctrine of our Lord and Saviour Christ, in the 6th chapter of John. (*EATING NEC-ESSARY TO SALVATION*) And this eating of the flesh and drinking of the blood of the Lord is so necessary to salvation that without it no man can be saved.

But this spiritual eating and drinking takes place also without the Supper of the Lord, even so often as, and wheresoever, a man does believe in Christ. To which purpose that sentence of St. Augustine does happily belong, 'Why dost thou prepare thy teeth and belly? Believe, and thou hast eaten.'

(*SACRAMENTAL EATING OF THE LORD*) (3) Besides that former spiritual eating, there is a *sacramental* eating of the body of the Lord; whereby the believer not only is partaker, spiritually and internally, of the true body and blood of the Lord, but also, by coming to the Table of the Lord, does outwardly receive the visible sacrament of the body and blood of the Lord. True it is, that by faith the believer did before receive the food that gives life, and still receives the same; but yet, when he receives the sacrament, he receives something more. For he goes on in continual communication of the body and blood of the Lord, and his faith is daily more and more kindled, more strengthened and refreshed, by the spiritual nourishment. For while we live, faith has continual increasings; and he that outwardly does receive the sacrament with a true faith, the same does not only receive the sign, but also does enjoy (as we said) the thing itself. Moreover, the same does obey the Lord's institution and commandment, and with a joyful mind gives thanks for his redemption and that of all mankind, and makes a faithful remembrance of the Lord's death, and does witness the same before the Church, of which body he is a member. This also is sealed to those who receive the sacrament, that the body of the Lord was given, and his blood shed, not only for men in general, but particularly for every faithful communicant, whose meat and drink he is, to life eternal.

(*UNBELIEVERS TAKE THE SACRAMENT TO THEIR JUDGMENT*) But as for him that without faith comes to this Holy Table of the Lord, he is made partaker of the outward sacrament only; but the matter of the sacrament, from whence comes life unto salvation, he receives not at all; and such men do unworthily eat of the Lord's Table. 'Whoever eats the bread or drinks the cup of the Lord in an unworthy manner will be guilty of profaning the body and blood of the Lord, and eats and drinks judgment upon himself' (1 Cor. xi. 26–29). For when they do not approach with true faith, they do despite unto the death of Christ, and therefore eat and drink condemnation to themselves.

(*PRESENCE OF CHRIST IN SUPPER*) We do not, therefore, so join the body of the Lord and his blood with the bread and wine, as though we thought that the bread is the body of Christ, more than after a sacramental manner; or that the body of Christ does lie hid corporeally under the bread, so that it ought to be worshiped under the form of bread; or yet that whosoever he be who receives the sign, receives also the thing itself. The body of Christ is in the heavens, at the right hand of his Father; and therefore our hearts are to be lifted up on high, and not to be fixed on the bread, neither is the Lord to be worshiped in the bread. Yet the Lord is not absent from his Church when she celebrates the Supper. The sun, being absent from us in the heavens, is yet, notwithstanding, present among us effectually: how much more Christ, the Sun of Righteousness, though in body he be absent from us in the heavens, yet is present among us, not corporeally, but spiritually, by his lively operation, and so as he himself promised, in his Last Supper, to be present among us (John xiv. xv. and xvi.). Whereupon it follows that we have not the Supper without Christ, and yet that we may have meanwhile an unbloody and mystical supper, even as all antiquity called it.

(*OTHER PURPOSES OF THE SUPPER*) Moreover, we are admonished, in the celebration of the Supper of the Lord, to be mindful of the body whereof we are members; and that, therefore, we should be at concord with our brethren, that we live holily, and not pollute ourselves with wickedness and strange religions; but, persevering in the true faith to the end of our life, give diligence to excel in holiness of life.

(*PREPARATION FOR THE SUPPER*) It is therefore very requisite that, purposing to come to the Supper of the Lord, we do examine ourselves, according to the commandment of the apostle; first, with what faith we are indued, whether we believe that Christ is come to save sinners and to call them to repentance, and whether each man believes that he is in the number of them that are delivered by Christ and saved; and whether he has purposed to change this wicked life, to live holily, and to persevere through God's assistance, in the true religion, and in concord with his brethren, and to give worthy thanks to God for his delivery.

(*THE OBSERVANCE OF SUPPER WITH BOTH BREAD AND WINE*) We think that rite, manner, or form of the Supper to be the most simple and excellent which comes nearest to the first institution of the Lord and to the apostles' doctrine: which does consist in declaring the Word of God, in godly prayers, in the action itself that the Lord used, and the repeating of it; in the eating of the Lord's body and drinking of his blood; in the wholesome remembrance of the Lord's death, and faithful giving of thanks; and in a holy fellowship in the union of the body of the Church.

We therefore disallow those who have taken from the faithful one part of the sacrament, to wit, the Lord's cup. For these do very grievously offend against the institution of the Lord, who says, 'Drink ye *all* of this' (Matt. xxvi. 27); which he did not so plainly say of the bread.

What manner of mass it was that the fathers used, whether it were tolerable or intolerable, we do not now dispute. But this we say freely, that the mass which is now used throughout the Roman Church is quite abolished out of our churches for many and just causes, which, for brevity's sake, we will not now particularly recite. Truly we could not approve of it, because they have changed a most wholesome action into a vain spectacle; also because the mass is made a meritorious matter, and is said for money; likewise because in it the priest is said to make the very body of the Lord, and to offer the same really, even for the remission of the sins of the quick and the dead. Add this also, that they do it for the honor, worship, and reverence of the saints in heaven (and for the relief of souls in purgatory), etc.

CHAPTER XXII.—OF HOLY AND ECCLESIASTICAL MEETINGS.

(*WHAT ONE IS TO DO IN WORSHIP*) Although it be lawful for all men privately at home to read the Holy Scriptures, and by instruction to edify one another in the true religion, yet that the Word of God may be lawfully preached to the people, and prayers and supplications publicly made, also that the sacraments may be lawfully administered, and that collections may be made for the poor, and to defray all necessary charges, or to supply the wants of the Church, it is very needful that there should be holy meetings and ecclesiastical assemblies. For it is manifest that, in the apostolic and primitive Church, there were such assemblies, frequented of godly men. (*THE WORSHIP OF GOD MUST NOT BE NEGLECTED*) So many, then, as do despise them, and separate themselves from them, they despise true religion, and are to be urged by the pastors and godly magistrates to abstain from stubbornly absenting themselves from sacred assemblies. (*WORSHIP IS PUBLIC*) Now, ecclesiastical assemblies must not be hidden and secret, but public and common; except persecution by the enemies of Christ and the Church will not suffer them to be public; for we know what manner of assemblies the primitive Church had formerly in secret corners, being under the tyranny of Roman emperors. (*WORTHY PLACE OF WORSHIP*) But let those places where the faithful meet together be decent, and in all respects fit for God's Church. Therefore, let houses be chosen for that purpose, or churches, that are large and fair, so that they be purged from all such things as do not beseem the

Church. And let all things be ordered as is most meet for comeliness, necessity, and godly decency, that nothing be wanting which is requisite for rites and orders, and the necessary uses of the Church.

(*MODESTY AND HUMILITY SHOULD GOVERN IN WORSHIP*) And as we believe that God does not dwell in temples made with hands, so we know that by reason of the Word of God, and holy exercises therein celebrated, places dedicated to God and his worship are not profane, but holy; and that therefore such as are conversant in them ought to behave themselves reverently and modestly, as they who are in a sacred place, in the presence of God and his holy angels. (*THE TRUE ORNAMENTS OF THE TEMPLE*) All excess of apparel, therefore, is to be abandoned in churches and places where Christians meet for prayer, together with all pride and whatsoever else does not beseem Christian humility, discipline, and modesty. For the true ornament of churches does not consist in ivory, gold, and precious stones, but in the sobriety, godliness, and virtues of those who are in the Church. 'Let all things be done decently and in order' in the church (1 Cor. xiv. 40). To conclude, 'Let things be done for edification' (ver. 26). (*WORSHIP IN THE COMMON LANGUAGE*) Therefore, let all strange tongues keep silence in the holy assemblies, and let all things be uttered in the common tongue, which is understood of all men in the company.

CHAPTER XXIII.—OF THE PRAYERS OF THE CHURCH, OF SINGING, AND OF CANONICAL HOURS.

(*COMMON LANGUAGE*) True it is that a man may lawfully pray privately in any tongue that he does understand; but public prayers ought, in the holy assemblies, to be made in the common tongue, or such a language as is known to all. (*PRAYER*) Let all the prayers of the faithful be poured forth to God alone, through the mediation of Christ only, out of a true faith and pure love. As for invocation of saints, or using them as intercessors to entreat for us, the priesthood of our Lord Christ and true religion will not permit us. Prayer must be made for the magistracy, for kings, and all that are placed in authority, for ministers of the Church, and for all necessities of churches; and especially in any calamity of the Church prayer must be made, both privately and publicly, without ceasing.

(*FREE PRAYER*) Moreover, we must pray willingly, and not by constraint, nor for any reward; neither must we superstitiously tie prayer to any place, as though it were not lawful to pray but in the church. There is no necessity that public prayers should be in form and time the same or alike in all churches. Let all churches use their liberty. Socrates, in his *History*, says, 'In any country or nation whatsoever, you shall not find two churches which do wholly agree in prayer' (*Hist. ecclesiast*. V. 22, 57). The authors of this difference, I think, were those who had the government of the churches in several ages. But if any do agree, it deserves great commendation, and is to be imitated by others.

(*THE MANNER OF PUBLIC PRAYER*) Besides this, there must be a mean and measure, as in every other thing, so also in public prayers, that they be not over-long and tedious. Let, therefore, most time be given to the teaching of the Gospel in such holy assemblies; and let there be diligent heed taken that the people in the assemblies be not wearied with over-long prayers, so that, when the preaching of the gospel should be heard, they, through wearisomeness, either desire to go forth themselves or to have the assembly wholly dismissed. For unto such the sermons seem to be overlong which otherwise are brief enough. Yea, and the preachers ought to keep a mean.

(*SINGING*) Likewise the singing in sacred assemblies ought to be moderated where it is in use. That song which they call the Gregorian Chant has many gross things in it; wherefore it is upon good cause rejected by our Church, and most other Reformed churches. If there be any churches which have faithful prayer in good manner, without any singing, they are not therefore to be condemned, for all churches have not the advantage and opportunity of sacred music. And certain it is by testimonies of antiquity that, as the custom of singing is very ancient in the Eastern churches, so it was long ere it was received in the Western churches.

(*CANONICAL HOURS*) In ancient times there were no such things as canonical hours; that is, fixed prayers framed for certain hours in the day, and therein chanted or often repeated, as the Papists' manner is: which may be proved by many of their lessons, appointed in their hours, and divers other arguments. Moreover, they have many absurd things (of which I say no more) that are well omitted by our churches and replaced by matters more wholesome for the universal Church of God.

CHAPTER XXIV.—OF HOLIDAYS, FASTS, AND CHOICE OF MEATS.

(*THE TIME NECESSARY FOR WORSHIP*) Although religion be not tied unto time, yet can it not be planted and exercised without a due dividing and allotting-out of time. Every Church, therefore, does choose unto itself a certain time for public prayers, and for the preaching of the Gospel, and for the celebration of the sacraments; and it is not lawful for any one to overthrow this appointment of the Church at his own pleasure. For except some due time and leisure were allotted to the outward exercise of religion, without doubt men would be quite drawn from it by their own affairs.

(*THE LORD'S DAY*) In regard hereof, we see that in the ancient churches there were not only certain set hours in the week appointed for meetings, but that also the Lord's Day itself, ever since the apostles' time, was consecrated to religious exercises and to a holy rest; which also is now very well observed by our churches, for the worship of God and the increase of charity. (*SUPERSTITION*) Yet herein we give no place unto the Jewish observation of the day, or to any superstitions. For we do not account one day to be holier than another, nor think that mere rest is of itself acceptable to God. Besides, we do celebrate and keep the Lord's Day, and not the Jewish Sabbath, and that with a free observation.

(*THE FESTIVALS OF CHRIST AND THE SAINTS*) Moreover, if the churches do religiously celebrate the memory of the Lord's Nativity, Circumcision, Passion, Resurrection, and of his Ascension into heaven, and the sending of the Holy Spirit upon his disciples, according to Christian liberty, we do very well approve of it. But as for festival days, ordained for men or saints departed, we cannot allow of them. For, indeed, festival days must be referred to the first table of the law, and belong peculiarly unto God. To conclude, those festival days which are appointed for saints, and abrogated by us, have in them many gross things, unprofitable and not to be tolerated. In the mean time, we confess that the remembrance of saints, in due time and place, may be to good use and profit commended unto the people in sermons, and the holy examples of holy men set before their eyes to be imitated by all.

(*FASTING*) Now, the more sharply the Church of Christ does condemn surfeiting, drunkenness, and all kinds of lusts and intemperance, so much the more earnestly does it commend unto us Christian fasting. For fasting is nothing else than the abstinence and temperance of the godly, and a watching and chastising of our flesh, taken up for present necessity, whereby we are humbled before God, and withdraw from the flesh those things with which it is cherished, to the end that it may the more willingly and easily obey the Spirit. Wherefore they do not fast at all that have no regard for those things, but imagine that they fast if they stuff their bellies once a day, and for a set or prescribed time do abstain from certain meats, thinking that by this very work wrought they please

God and acquire merit. Fasting is a help of the prayers of the saints and all virtues; but the fasts wherein the Jews fasted from meat, and not from wickedness, pleased God nothing at all, as we may see in the books of the Prophets.

(*PUBLIC AND PRIVATE FASTING*) Now, fasting is either public or private. In olden times they celebrated public fasts in troublesome times and in the affliction of the Church; wherein they abstained altogether from meat till the evening, and bestowed all that time in holy prayers, the worship of God, and repentance. These differed little from mournings and lamentations; and of these there is often mention made in the Prophets, and especially in the 2nd chapter of Joel. Such a fast should be kept at this day, when the Church is in distress. Private fasts are used by every one of us, according as every one feels the spirit weakened in him; for so he withdraws that which might cherish and strengthen the flesh.

(*NATURE OF FASTING*) All fasts ought to proceed from a free and willing spirit, and such a one as is truly humbled, and not framed to win applause and the liking of men, much less to the end that a man might merit righteousness by them. But let every one fast to this end, that he may deprive the flesh of that which would cherish it, and that he may the more zealously serve God.

(*LENT*) The fast of Lent has testimony of antiquity, but none out of the apostles' writings; and therefore ought not, nor can not, be imposed on the faithful. It is certain that in old time there were divers manners and uses of this fast; whereupon Irenaeus, a most ancient writer, says, 'Some think that this fast should be observed one day only, others two days, but others more, and some forty days. This diversity in keeping this fast began not in our times, but long before us; by those, as I suppose, who, not simply holding that which was delivered them from the beginning, fell shortly after into another custom, either through negligence or ignorance' (Fragm. 3, ed.

Stieren, I. 824 f.). Moreover, Socrates, the historian, says, 'Because no ancient record is found concerning this matter, I think the apostles left this to every man's own judgment, that every one might work that which is good, without fear or constraint' (*Hist. ecclesiast.* V. 22, 40).

(*CHOICE OF FOOD*) Now, as concerning the choice of meats, we suppose that, in fasting, all things should be denied to the flesh whereby the flesh is made more lusty, wherein it does most immoderately delight, and whereby it is most of all pampered, whether they be fish, spices, dainties, or excellent wines. Otherwise we know that all the creatures of God were made for the use and service of men. All things which God made are good (Gen. i. 31), and are to be used in the fear of God, and with due moderation, without putting any difference between them. For the apostle says, 'To the pure all things are pure' (Tit. i. 15), and also, 'Eat whatever is sold in the meat market without raising any question on the ground of conscience' (1 Cor. x. 25). The same apostle calls the doctrine of those who teach to abstain from meats 'the doctrine of demons;' for that 'God created foods to be received with thanksgiving by those who believe and know the truth. For everything created by God is good, and nothing is to be rejected if it is received with thanksgiving' (1 Tim. iv. 1, 3, 4). The same apostle, in the Epistle to the Colossians, reproves those who, by an overmuch abstinence, will get unto themselves a reputation for holiness (Col. ii. 20–23). (*SECTS*) Therefore we do altogether disapprove of the Tatians and the Encratites, and all the disciples of Eustathius (of Sebaste), against whom the Gangrian Synod was assembled.

CHAPTER XXV.—OF CATECHISING, OF COMFORTING AND VISITING THE SICK.

(*TEACHING THE YOUTH IN GODLINESS*) The Lord enjoined his ancient people to take great care and diligence in instructing the youth well, even from their infancy; and, moreover, commanded expressly in his Law that they should teach them, and declare the mystery of the sacraments unto them. Now, forasmuch as is evident by the writings of the evangelists and apostles, that God has no less care of the youth of his new people, seeing he says, 'Let the children come to me; for to such belongs the kingdom of heaven' (Matt. xix. 14), therefore the pastors of the churches do very wisely who do diligently and betimes catechise their youth, laying the first grounds of faith, and faithfully teaching the rudiments of our religion, by expounding the Ten Commandments, the Apostles' Creed, the Lord's Prayer, and the doctrine of the sacraments, with other like principles and chief heads of our religion. And here let the Church perform her faithfulness and diligence in bringing the children to be catechised, as being desirous and glad to have her children well instructed.

(*THE VISITATION OF THE SICK*) Seeing that men do never lie open to more grievous temptations than when they are exercised with infirmities, or else are sick and brought low by diseases, it behooves the pastors of the churches to be never more vigilant and careful for the safety of the flock than in such diseases and infirmities. Therefore let them visit the sick betimes, and let them be quickly sent for by the sick, if the matter shall so require; let them comfort and confirm them in the true faith; finally, let them strengthen them against the dangerous suggestions of Satan. In like manner, let them pray with the sick person at home in his house; and, if need be, let them make prayers for the sick in the public meeting; and let them be careful that they have a happy passage out of this life. As for Popish visiting with the extreme unction, we have said before that we do not like it, because it has many absurd things in it, and such as are not approved by the canonical Scriptures.

CHAPTER XXVI.—OF THE BURIAL OF THE
FAITHFUL, AND OF THE CARE WHICH IS TO BE
HAD FOR SUCH AS ARE DEAD; OF PURGATORY,
AND THE APPEARING OF SPIRITS.

(*THE BURIAL OF THE BODY*) The Scripture
directs that the bodies of the faithful, as being temples
of the Holy Spirit, which we truly believe shall rise
again at the last day, should be honorably, without
any superstition, committed to the earth; and, besides, that we should make honorable mention of those
who died in the Lord, and perform all duties of love
to those they leave behind, as their widows and fatherless children. Other care for the dead we do not en-
join. Therefore, we do greatly disapprove of the
Cynics, who neglected the bodies of the dead, or did
carelessly and disdainfully cast them into the earth,
never speaking so much as a good word of the deceased, nor any whit regarding those whom they left
behind them.

(*THE CARE FOR THE DEAD*) Again, we disapprove of those who are too much and preposterously
officious to the dead; who, like the heathen, do greatly
lament and bewail their dead (although we do not
censure that moderate mourning which the apostle
does allow [1 Thess. iv. 13], since it is unnatural not
to be touched with sorrow); and who do sacrifice for
the dead, and mumble certain prayers, not without
their penny for their pains; thinking by these prayers
to deliver their friends from torments, wherein, being
wrapped by death, they suppose they may be rid of
them again by such lamentable songs.

(*THE STATE OF THE SOUL WHEN SEPA-
RATED FROM THE BODY*) For we believe that the
faithful, after bodily death, do go directly unto Christ,
and, therefore, do not stand in need of helps or prayers
for the dead, or any other such duty of them that are
alive. In like manner, we believe that the unbelievers
are cast headlong into hell, from whence there is no
return opened to the wicked by any offices of those
who live.

(*PURGATORY*) But as touching that which some teach concerning the fire of purgatory, it is directly contrary to the Christian faith ('I believe in the forgiveness of sins, and the life everlasting'), and to the absolute purgation of sins made by Christ, and to these sayings of Christ our Lord: 'Truly, truly, I say to you, he who hears my word and believes him who sent me, has eternal life; he does not come into judgment, but has passed from death to life' (John v. 24). Again, 'He who has bathed does not need to wash, except for his feet, but he is clean all over, and you are clean' (John xiii. 10).

(*THE APPARITION OF SPIRITS*) Now, that which is recorded of the spirits or souls of the dead sometimes appearing to them that are alive, and craving certain duties of them whereby they may be set free: we count those apparitions among the delusions, crafts, and deceits of the Devil, who, as he can transform himself into an angel of light, so he labors tooth and nail either to overthrow the true faith, or else to call it into doubt. The Lord, in the Old Testament, forbade us to inquire the truth of the dead, and to have any thing to do with spirits (Deut. xviii. 10, 11). And to the glutton, being bound in torments, as the truth of the Gospel does declare, is denied any return to his brethren on earth; the oracle of God pronouncing and saying, 'They have Moses and the prophets, neither will they be convinced if some one should rise from the dead' (Luke xvi. 29, 31).

CHAPTER XXVII.—OF RITES, CEREMONIES, AND THINGS INDIFFERENT.

(*CEREMONIES AND RITES*) Unto the ancient people were given in old time certain ceremonies, as a kind of schooling to those who were kept under the law, as under a schoolmaster or tutor. But Christ, the deliverer, being once come and the law taken away, we who believe are no more under the law (Rom. vi. 14), and the ceremonies have vanished out of use. And the apostles were so far from retaining them, or repairing them, in the Church of Christ, that they witnessed plainly that they would not lay any burden upon the Church (Acts xv. 28). Wherefore we should seem to bring in and set up Judaism again if we should multiply ceremonies or rites in the Church according to the manner of the Jewish Church. And thus we are not of their judgment who would have the Church of Christ bound by many and divers rites, as it were by a certain schooling. For if the apostles would not thrust upon the Christian people the ceremonies and rites which were appointed by God, who is there, I pray you, that is well in his wits, that will thrust upon it the inventions devised by man? The greater the heap of ceremonies in the Church, so much the more is taken, not only from Christian liberty, but also from Christ, and from faith in him; while the people seek those things in ceremonies which they should seek in the only Son of God, Jesus Christ, through faith. Wherefore a few moderate and simple rites, that are not contrary to the Word of God, do suffice the godly.

(*DIVERSITY OF RITES*) And in that there is found diversity of rites in the churches, let no man say, therefore, that the churches do not agree. Socrates says, in his Church History, 'It were not possible to set down in writing all the ceremonies of the churches which are observed throughout cities and countries. No religion does keep every where the same ceremonies, although they admit and receive one and the selfsame doctrine touching them; for even they who have one and the selfsame faith do disagree among themselves about ceremonies' (*Hist. ecclesiast.* V. 22, 30, 62). This much says Socrates; and we, at this day, having diversities in the celebration of the Lord's Supper, and in certain other things, in our churches, yet we do not disagree in doctrine and faith; neither is the unity and society of our churches rent asunder. For the churches have always used their liberty in such rites, as being things indifferent; which we also do at this day.

(*THINGS INDIFFERENT*) But yet, notwithstanding, we admonish men to take heed that they count not among things indifferent such as are not indeed indifferent; as some used to count the mass and the use of images in the Church for things indifferent. 'That is indifferent' (says Jerome to Augustine) 'which is neither good nor evil; so that, whether you do it or do it not, you are never the more just or unjust thereby.' Therefore, when things indifferent are wrested to the confession of faith, they cease to be free; as Paul does show that it is lawful for a man to eat flesh if no man do admonish him that it was offered to idols (1 Cor. x. 27, 28); for then it is unlawful, because he that eats it does seem to approve idolatry by eating of it (1 Cor. viii. 10).

CHAPTER XXVIII.—OF THE POSSESSIONS OF THE CHURCH, AND THE RIGHT USE OF THEM.

(*THE POSSESSIONS OF THE CHURCH AND THEIR PROPER USE*) The Church of Christ has riches through the bountifulness of princes, and the liberality of the faithful, who have given their goods to the Church. For the Church has need of such goods; and has had goods from ancient time for the maintenance of things necessary for the Church. Now, the true use of the ecclesiastical goods was, and now is, to maintain learning in schools and in holy assemblies, with all the service, rites, and buildings of the Church; finally, to maintain teachers, scholars, and ministers, with other necessary things, and chiefly for the succor and relief of the poor. (*MANAGEMENT*) But for the lawful dispensing of these ecclesiastical goods let men be chosen that fear God; wise men, and such as are of good report in the government of their families.

(*THE MISUSE OF THE CHURCH'S POSSESSIONS*) But if the goods of the Church, by injury of the time, and the boldness, ignorance, or covetousness of some, be turned to any abuse, let them be restored again, by godly and wise men, unto their holy use; for they must not connive at so impious an abuse.

Therefore, we teach that schools and colleges, whereinto corruption is crept in doctrine, in the service of God, and in manners, must be reformed; and that there provision should be made, piously, faithfully, and wisely, for the relief of the poor.

CHAPTER XXIX.—OF SINGLE LIFE, MARRIAGE, AND HOUSEHOLD GOVERNMENT.

(*CELIBACY*) Such as have the gift of chastity given unto them from above, so that they can with the heart or whole mind be pure and continent, and not be grievously burned with lust, let them serve the Lord in that calling, as long as they shall feel themselves endued with that heavenly gift; and let them not lift up themselves above others, but let them serve the Lord daily in simplicity and humility. For such are more apt for attending to heavenly things than they who are distracted with the private affairs of a family. But if, again, the gift be taken away, and they feel a continual burning, let them call to mind the words of the apostle, 'It is better to marry than to be aflame' (1 Cor. vii. 9).

(*MARRIAGE*) For wedlock (which is the medicine of incontinency, and continency itself) was ordained by the Lord God himself, who blessed it most bountifully, and willed man and woman to cleave one to the other inseparably, and to live together in great concord (Gen. ii. 24; Matt. xiv. 5, 6). Whereupon we know the apostle said, 'Let marriage be held in honor among all, and let the marriage bed be undefiled' (Heb. xiii. 4). And again, 'If a girl marries, she does not sin' (1 Cor. vii. 28). (*SECTS*) We therefore condemn polygamy, and those who condemn second marriages.

(*HOW MARRIAGES ARE ESTABLISHED*) We teach that marriages ought to be contracted lawfully, in the fear of the Lord, and not against the laws which forbid certain degrees to join in matrimony, lest the marriages should be incestuous. Let marriages be made with consent of the parents, or such as are instead of parents; and for that end especially for which the Lord ordained marriages. And let them be confirmed publicly in the Church, with prayer and blessing. Moreover, let them be kept holy, with peace, faithfulness, dutifulness, love, and purity of the persons coupled together. Therefore let them take heed of brawlings, debates, lusts, and adulteries. Let lawful judgments and holy judges be established in the Church, who may maintain marriages, and may repress all dishonesty and shamefulness, and before whom controversies in matrimony may be decided and ended.

(*THE REARING OF CHILDREN*) Let children also be brought up by the parents in the fear of the Lord; and let parents provide for their children, remembering the saying of the apostle, 'If anyone does not provide for his relatives, he has disowned the faith and is worse than an unbeliever' (1 Tim. v. 8). But especially let them teach their children honest arts and occupations, whereby they may maintain themselves. Let them keep them from idleness, and plant in them a true confidence in God in all these things; lest they, through distrust, or overmuch careless security, or filthy covetousness, wax loose, and in the end come to no good.

Now, it is most certain that those works which parents do in true faith, by the duties of marriage, and government of their families, are, before God, holy and good works indeed, and do please God no less than prayers, fastings, and alms-deeds. For so the apostle has taught in his epistles, especially in those to Timothy and Titus. And with the same apostle we account the doctrine of such as forbid marriage, or do openly dispraise or secretly discredit it as not holy or clean, among the 'doctrine of demons' (1 Tim. iv. 1).

And we do detest unclean single life, licentious lusts, and fornications, both open and secret, and the continency of dissembling hypocrites, when they are, of all men, most incontinent. All these God will judge. We do not disallow riches, nor despise rich men, if they be godly and use their riches well; but we reprove the sect of the Apostolicals, etc.

CHAPTER XXX.—OF THE MAGISTRACY.

(*THE MAGISTRATE IS FROM GOD*) The magistracy, of what sort so ever it be, is ordained of God himself, for the peace and quietness of mankind; and so that he should have the chief place in the world. If the magistrate be an adversary to the Church, he may hinder and disturb it very much; but if he be a friend and a member of the Church, he is a most useful and excellent member thereof; he may profit it very much, and finally may help and further it very excellently.

(*THE DUTY OF THE MAGISTRATE*) The chief duty of the civil magistrate is to procure and maintain peace and public tranquillity: which, doubtless, he shall never do more happily than when he shall be truly seasoned with the fear of God and true religion —namely, when he shall, after the example of the most holy kings and princes of the people of the Lord, advance the preaching of the truth, and the pure and sincere faith, and shall root out lies and all superstition, with all impiety and idolatry, and shall defend the Church of God. For indeed we teach that the care of religion does chiefly appertain to the holy magistrate.

Let him, therefore, hold the Word of God in his hands, and look that nothing be taught contrary thereunto. In like manner, let him govern the people, committed to him of God, with good laws, made according to the Word of God in his hands, and look that nothing be taught contrary thereunto. Let him hold them in discipline and in duty and in obedience. Let him exercise judgment by judging uprightly: let him not respect any man's person, or receive bribes. Let him protect widows, fatherless children, and those that be afflicted, against wrong; let him repress, yea, and cut off, such as are unjust, whether in deceit or by violence. 'For he does not bear the sword in vain' (Rom. xiii.

4). Therefore let him draw forth this sword of God against all malefactors, seditious persons, thieves, murderers, oppressors, blasphemers, perjured persons, and all those whom God has commanded him to punish or even to execute. Let him suppress stubborn heretics (who are heretics indeed), who cease not to blaspheme the majesty of God, and to trouble the Church, yea, and finally to destroy it.

(*WAR*) And if it be necessary to preserve the safety of the people by war, let him do it in the name of God; provided he have first sought peace by all means possible, and can save his subjects in no way but by war. And while the magistrate does these things in faith, he serves God with those works which are good, and shall receive a blessing from the Lord.

We condemn the Anabaptists, who, as they deny that a Christian man should bear the office of a magistrate, deny also that any man can justly be put to death by the magistrate, or that the magistrate may make war, or that oaths should be administered by the magistrate, and such like things.

(*THE DUTY OF SUBJECTS*) For as God will work the safety of his people by the magistrate, whom it is given to be, as it were, a father of the world, so all subjects are commanded to acknowledge this benefit of God in the magistrate. Therefore let them honor and reverence the magistrate as the minister of God; let them love him, favor him, and pray for him as their father; and let them obey all his just and equal commandments. Finally, let them pay all customs and tributes, and all other duties of the like sort, faithfully and willingly. And if the common safety of the country and justice require it, and the magistrate do of necessity make war, let them even lay down their life, and spend their blood for the common safety and defense of the magistrate; and that in the name of God, willingly, valiantly, and cheerfully. For he that opposes himself against the magistrate does provoke the wrath of God against him.

(SECTS AND SEDITIONS) We condemn, therefore, all who hold in contempt magistrates, rebels, enemies of the commonwealth, seditious villains, and, in a word, all such as do either openly or closely refuse to perform those duties which they owe.

The Conclusion.—We beseech God, our most merciful Father in heaven, that he will bless the rulers of the people, and us, and his whole people, through Jesus Christ, our only Lord and Saviour; to whom be praise and glory and thanksgiving, both now and forever. Amen.

THE WESTMINSTER CONFESSION (1646)

The Westminster Confession was written by the Assembly that met in Westminster Abbey during the Puritan Revolution. Representatives of the Church of Scotland met with the Assembly as commissioners of their government, which had signed the Solemn League and Convenant. The Confession, completed in 1646, was produced a full century after the Reformation was established on the Continent and represents the precision and comprehensiveness of a fully developed theology. It is the product of numerous theological traditions: native British Augustinianism, Puritan Covenant theology, the Reformed theology of the Rhineland, and Calvinism. Some members of the Assembly had participated in the Synod of Dort. The influence of the Irish Articles in the composition of the Confession is obvious and considerable, though other Reformed Confessions were also used. While members of the Assembly were careful to keep the Confession in the mainstream of Reformed theology, the Confession did effectively stifle the liberal Calvinism of Saumur, which was represented in the Assembly, and of Arminius.

The Confession and Catechisms were adopted by Presbyterians in Scotland and England and became the dominant standards of Presbyterianism in the English-speaking world. The Confession was adopted with modifications by Congregationalists in England and New England, and it was the basis of the Baptist creeds, the London Confession,

1677, 1688, and the Philadelphia Confession of Faith, 1742.

Source: The text printed here is taken from *Creeds of Christendom* by Philip Schaff, Vol. III (New York: Harper & Bros., 1877), pp. 600–73. Scripture references are omitted.

Carruthers, S. W., *The Westminster Confession of Faith* (Manchester: R. Ackman & Son, 1937) critical text.

Hetherington, W. M., *History of the Westminster Assembly of Divines* (New York: Anson D. F. Randolph & Co., 1890).

Mitchell, A. F., and Struthers, John, *Minutes of the Sessions of the Westminster Assembly* (London: Wm. Blackwood & Sons, 1874).

Mitchell, A. F., *The Westminster Assembly, Its History and Standards* (London: James Nisbet & Co., 1883).

Warfield, B. B., *The Westminster Assembly and Its Work* (New York: Oxford University Press, 1931).

THE WESTMINSTER CONFESSION OF FAITH (1646)

CHAPTER I.
Of the Holy Scripture.

I. Although the light of nature, and the works of creation and providence, do so far manifest the goodness, wisdom, and power of God, as to leave men inexcusable; yet are they not sufficient to give that knowledge of God, and of his will, which is necessary unto salvation; therefore it pleased the Lord, at sundry times, and in divers manners, to reveal himself, and to declare that his will unto his Church; and afterwards, for the better preserving and propagating of the truth, and for the more sure establishment and comfort of the Church against the corruption of the flesh, and the malice of Satan and of the world, to commit the same wholly unto writing; which maketh the holy Scripture to be most necessary; those former ways of God's revealing his will unto his people being now ceased.

II. Under the name of holy Scripture, or the Word

of God written, are now contained all the Books of the Old and New Testament, which are these:

OF THE OLD TESTAMENT.

Genesis.	*Ecclesiastes.*
Exodus.	*The Song of Songs.*
Leviticus.	*Isaiah.*
Numbers.	*Jeremiah.*
Deuteronomy.	*Lamentations.*
Joshua.	*Ezekiel.*
Judges.	*Daniel.*
Ruth.	*Hosea.*
I. Samuel.	*Joel.*
II. Samuel.	*Amos.*
I. Kings.	*Obadiah.*
II. Kings.	*Jonah.*
I. Chronicles.	*Micah.*
II. Chronicles.	*Nahum.*
Ezra.	*Habakkuk.*
Nehemiah.	*Zephaniah.*
Esther.	*Haggai.*
Job.	*Zechariah.*
Psalms.	*Malachi.*
Proverbs.	

OF THE NEW TESTAMENT.

The Gospels according to
  Matthew.
  Mark.
  Luke.
  John.
The Acts of the Apostles.
Paul's Epistles to the Romans.
Corinthians I.
Corinthians II.
Galatians.
Ephesians.
Philippians.
Colossians.
Thessalonians I.

Thessalonians II.
To Timothy I.
To Timothy II.
To Titus.
To Philemon.
The Epistle to the Hebrews.
The Epistle of James.
The First and Second Epistles of Peter.
The First, Second, and Third Epistles of John.
The Epistle of Jude.
The Revelation.

All which are given by inspiration of God, to be the rule of faith and life.

III. The books commonly called Apocrypha, not being of divine inspiration, are no part of the Canon of the Scripture; and therefore are of no authority in the Church of God, nor to be any otherwise approved, or made use of, than other human writings.

IV. The authority of the holy Scripture, for which it ought to be believed and obeyed, dependeth not upon the testimony of any man or church, but wholly upon God (who is truth itself), the Author thereof; and therefore it is to be received, because it is the Word of God.

V. We may be moved and induced by the testimony of the Church to an high and reverent esteem of the holy Scripture; and the heavenliness of the matter, the efficacy of the doctrine, the majesty of the style, the consent of all the parts, the scope of the whole (which is to give all glory to God), the full discovery it makes of the only way of man's salvation, the many other incomparable excellencies, and the entire perfection thereof, are arguments whereby it doth abundantly evidence itself to be the Word of God; yet, notwithstanding, our full persuasion and assurance of the infallible truth, and divine authority thereof, is from the inward work of the Holy Spirit, bearing witness by and with the Word in our hearts.

VI. The whole counsel of God, concerning all things necessary for his own glory, man's salvation, faith, and life, is either expressly set down in Scripture, or by good and necessary consequence may be deduced from Scripture: unto which nothing at any time is to be added, whether by new revelations of the Spirit, or traditions of men. Nevertheless we acknowledge the inward illumination of the Spirit of God to be necessary for the saving understanding of such things as are revealed in the Word; and that there are some circumstances concerning the worship of God, and government of the Church, common to human actions and societies, which are to be ordered by the light of nature and Christian prudence, according to the general rules of the Word, which are always to be observed.

VII. All things in Scripture are not alike plain in themselves, nor alike clear unto all; yet those things which are necessary to be known, believed, and observed, for salvation, are so clearly propounded and opened in some place of Scripture or other, that not only the learned, but the unlearned, in a due use of the ordinary means, may attain unto a sufficient understanding of them.

VIII. The Old Testament in Hebrew (which was the native language of the people of God of old), and the New Testament in Greek (which at the time of the writing of it was most generally known to the nations), being immediately inspired by God, and by his singular care and providence kept pure in all ages, are therefore authentical; so as in all controversies of religion the Church is finally to appeal unto them. But because these original tongues are not known to all the people of God who have right unto, and interest in the Scriptures, and are commanded, in the fear of God, to read and search them, therefore they are to be translated into the vulgar language of every nation unto which they come, that the Word of God dwelling plentifully in all, they may worship him in an acceptable manner, and, through patience and comfort of the Scriptures, may have hope.

IX. The infallible rule of interpretation of Scripture is the Scripture itself; and therefore, when there is a question about the true and full sense of any Scripture (which is not manifold, but one), it must be searched and known by other places that speak more clearly.

X. The Supreme Judge, by which all controversies of religion are to be determined, and all decrees of councils, opinions of ancient writers, doctrines of men, and private spirits, are to be examined, and in whose sentence we are to rest, can be no other but the Holy Spirit speaking in the Scripture.

CHAPTER II

Of God, and of the Holy Trinity.

I. There is but one only living and true God, who is infinite in being and perfection, a most pure spirit, invisible, without body, parts, or passions, immutable, immense, eternal, incomprehensible, almighty, most wise, most holy, most free, most absolute, working all things according to the counsel of his own immutable and most righteous will, for his own glory; most loving, gracious, merciful, long-suffering, abundant in goodness and truth, forgiving iniquity, transgression, and sin; the rewarder of them that diligently seek him; and withal most just and terrible in his judgments; hating all sin, and who will by no means clear the guilty.

II. God hath all life, glory, goodness, blessedness, in and of himself; and is alone in and unto himself all-sufficient, not standing in need of any creatures which he hath made, nor deriving any glory from them, but only manifesting his own glory in, by, unto, and upon them: he is the alone foundation of all being, of whom, through whom, and to whom are all things; and hath most sovereign dominion over them, to do by them, for them, or upon them whatsoever himself pleaseth. In his sight all things are open and manifest; his knowledge is infinite, infallible, and independent upon the creature; so as nothing is to him contingent or uncertain. He is most holy in all his counsels, in all his works, and in all his commands. To him is due from angels and men, and every other creature, whatsoever worship, service, or obedience, he is pleased to require of them.

III. In the unity of the Godhead there be three persons, of one substance, power, and eternity: God the Father, God the Son, and God the Holy Ghost. The Father is of none, neither begotten nor proceeding; the Son is eternally begotten of the Father; the Holy Ghost eternally proceeding from the Father and the Son.

CHAPTER III.
Of God's Eternal Decree.

I. God from all eternity did, by the most wise and holy counsel of his own will, freely and unchangeably ordain whatsoever comes to pass; yet so as thereby neither is God the author of sin, nor is violence offered to the will of the creatures, nor is the liberty or contingency of second causes taken away, but rather established.

II. Although God knows whatsoever may or can come to pass upon all supposed conditions, yet hath he not decreed any thing because he foresaw it as future, or as that which would come to pass upon such conditions.

III. By the decree of God, for the manifestation of his glory, some men and angels are predestinated unto everlasting life, and others foreordained to everlasting death.

IV. These angels and men, thus predestinated and foreordained, are particularly and unchangeably designed; and their number is so certain and definite that it can not be either increased or diminished.

V. Those of mankind that are predestinated unto life, God, before the foundation of the world was laid, according to his eternal and immutable purpose, and the secret counsel and good pleasure of his will, hath chosen in Christ, unto everlasting glory, out of his mere free grace and love, without any foresight of faith or good works, or perseverance in either of them, or any other thing in the creature, as conditions, or causes moving him thereunto; and all to the praise of his glorious grace.

VI. As God hath appointed the elect unto glory, so hath he, by the eternal and most free purpose of his will, foreordained all the means thereunto. Wherefore they who are elected, being fallen in Adam, are redeemed by Christ, are effectually called unto faith in Christ by his Spirit working in due season; are justified, adopted, sanctified, and kept by his power through faith unto salvation. Neither are any other redeemed by Christ, effectually called, justified, adopted, sanctified, and saved, but the elect only.

VII. The rest of mankind God was pleased, according to the unsearchable counsel of his own will, whereby he extendeth or withholdeth mercy as he pleaseth, for the glory of his sovereign power over his creatures, to pass by, and to ordain them to dishonor and wrath for their sin, to the praise of his glorious justice.

VIII. The doctrine of this high mystery of predestination is to be handled with special prudence and care, that men attending the will of God revealed in his Word, and yielding obedience thereunto, may, from the certainty of their effectual vocation, be assured of their eternal election. So shall this doctrine afford matter of praise, reverence, and admiration of God; and of humility, diligence, and abundant consolation to all that sincerely obey the gospel.

CHAPTER IV.
Of Creation.

I. It pleased God the Father, Son, and Holy Ghost, for the manifestation of the glory of his eternal power, wisdom, and goodness, in the beginning, to create or make of nothing the world, and all things therein, whether visible or invisible, in the space of six days, and all very good.

II. After God had made all other creatures, he created man, male and female, with reasonable and immortal souls, endued with knowledge, righteousness, and true holiness, after his own image, having the law of God written in their hearts, and power to fulfill it; and yet under a possibility of transgressing, being left to the liberty of their own will, which was subject unto change. Beside this law written in their hearts, they received a command not to eat of the tree of the knowledge of good and evil; which while they kept they were happy in their communion with God, and had dominion over the creatures.

CHAPTER V.
Of Providence.

I. God, the great Creator of all things, doth uphold, direct, dispose, and govern all creatures, actions, and things, from the greatest even to the least, by his most wise and holy providence, according to his infallible foreknowledge and the free and immutable counsel of his own will, to the praise of the glory of his wisdom, power, justice, goodness, and mercy.

II. Although in relation to the foreknowledge and decree of God, the first cause, all things come to pass immutably and infallibly, yet by the same providence he ordereth them to fall out, according to the nature of second causes, either necessarily, freely, or contingently.

III. God, in his ordinary providence, maketh use of means, yet is free to work without, above, and against them, at his pleasure.

IV. The almighty power, unsearchable wisdom, and infinite goodness of God so far manifest themselves in his providence that it extendeth itself even to the first fall, and all other sins of angels and men, and that not by a bare permission, but such as hath joined with it a most wise and powerful bounding, and otherwise ordering and governing of them, in a manifold dispensation, to his own holy ends; yet so as the sinfulness thereof proceedeth only from the creature, and not from God; who, being most holy and righteous, neither is nor can be the author or approver of sin.

V. The most wise, righteous, and gracious God doth oftentimes leave for a season his own children to manifold temptations and the corruption of their own hearts, to chastise them for their former sins, or to discover unto them the hidden strength of corruption and deceitfulness of their hearts, that they may be humbled; and to raise them to a more close and constant dependence for their support unto himself, and to make them more watchful against all future occasions of sin, and for sundry other just and holy ends.

VI. As for those wicked and ungodly men whom God, as a righteous judge, for former sins, doth blind and harden, from them he not only withholdeth his grace, whereby they might have been enlightened in their understandings and wrought upon in their hearts, but sometimes also withdraweth the gifts which they had, and exposeth them to such objects as their corruption makes occasion of sin; and withal, gives them over to their own lusts, the temptations of the world, and the power of Satan; whereby it comes to pass that they harden themselves, even under those means which God useth for the softening of others.

VII. As the providence of God doth, in general, reach to all creatures, so, after a most special manner, it taketh care of his Church, and disposeth all things to the good thereof.

CHAPTER VI.

Of the Fall of Man, of Sin, and of the Punishment thereof.

I. Our first parents, being seduced by the subtilty and temptation of Satan, sinned in eating the forbidden fruit. This their sin God was pleased, according to his wise and holy counsel, to permit, having purposed to order it to his own glory.

II. By this sin they fell from their original righteousness and communion with God, and so became dead in sin, and wholly defiled in all the faculties and parts of soul and body.

III. They being the root of all mankind, the guilt of this sin was imputed, and the same death in sin and corrupted nature conveyed to all their posterity descending from them by ordinary generation.

IV. From this original corruption, whereby we are utterly indisposed, disabled, and made opposite to all good, and wholly inclined to all evil, do proceed all actual transgressions.

V. This corruption of nature, during this life, doth remain in those that are regenerated; and although it be through Christ pardoned and mortified, yet both itself and all the motions thereof are truly and properly sin.

VI. Every sin, both original 'and actual, being a transgression of the righteous law of God, and contrary thereunto, doth, in its own nature, bring guilt upon the sinner, whereby he is bound over to the wrath of God and curse of the law, and so made subject to death, with all miseries spiritual, temporal, and eternal.

CHAPTER VII.
Of God's Covenant with Man.

I. The distance between God and the creature is so great that although reasonable creatures do owe obedience unto him as their Creator, yet they could never have any fruition of him as their blessedness and reward but by some voluntary condescension on God's part, which he hath been pleased to express by way of covenant.

II. The first covenant made with man was a covenant of works, wherein life was promised to Adam, and in him to his posterity, upon condition of perfect and personal obedience.

III. Man by his fall having made himself incapable of life by that covenant, the Lord was pleased to make a second, commonly called the covenant of grace: wherein he freely offered unto sinners life and salvation by Jesus Christ, requiring of them faith in him that they may be saved, and promising to give unto all those that are ordained unto life his Holy Spirit, to make them willing and able to believe.

IV. This covenant of grace is frequently set forth in the Scripture by the name of a testament, in reference to the death of Jesus Christ the testator, and to the everlasting inheritance, with all things belonging to it, therein bequeathed.

V. This covenant was differently administered in the time of the law and in the time of the gospel: under the law it was administered by promises, prophecies, sacrifices, circumcision, the paschal lamb, and other types and ordinances delivered to the people of the Jews, all foresignifying Christ to come, which were for that time sufficient and efficacious, through the operation of the Spirit, to instruct and build up the elect in faith in the promised Messiah, by whom they had full remission of sins and eternal salvation; and is called the Old Testament.

VI. Under the gospel, when Christ the substance was exhibited, the ordinances in which this covenant is dispensed are the preaching of the word and the administration of the sacraments of Baptism and the Lord's Supper; which, though fewer in number, and administered with more simplicity and less outward glory, yet in them it is held forth in more fullness, evidence, and spiritual efficacy, to all nations, both Jews and Gentiles; and is called the New Testament. There are not, therefore, two covenants of grace differing in substance, but one and the same under various dispensations.

CHAPTER VIII.
Of Christ the Mediator.

I. It pleased God, in his eternal purpose, to choose and ordain the Lord Jesus, his only-begotten Son, to be the Mediator between God and man, the Prophet, Priest, and King; the Head and Saviour of his Church, the Heir of all things, and Judge of the world; unto whom he did, from all eternity, give a people to be his seed, and to be by him in time redeemed, called, justified, sanctified, and glorified.

II. The Son of God, the second person in the Trinity, being very and eternal God, of one substance, and equal with the Father, did, when the fullness of time was come, take upon him man's nature, with all the essential properties and common infirmities thereof, yet without sin: being conceived by the power of the Holy Ghost in the womb of the Virgin Mary, of her substance. So that two whole, perfect, and distinct natures, the Godhead and the manhood, were inseparably joined together in one person, without conversion, composition, or confusion. Which person is very God and very man, yet one Christ, the only mediator between God and man.

III. The Lord Jesus, in his human nature thus united to the divine, was sanctified and anointed with the Holy Spirit above measure; having in him all the treasures of wisdom and knowledge, in whom it pleased the Father that all fullness should dwell; to the end that, being holy, harmless, undefiled, and full of grace and truth, he might be thoroughly furnished to execute the office of a mediator and surety. Which office he took not unto himself, but was thereunto called by his Father, who put all power and judgment into his hand, and gave him commandment to execute the same.

IV. This office the Lord Jesus did most willingly undertake, which, that he might discharge, he was made under the law, and did perfectly fulfill it; endured most grievous torments immediately in his soul, and most painful sufferings in his body; was crucified, and died; was buried, and remained under the power of death, yet saw no corruption. On the third day he arose from the dead, with the same body in which he suffered; with which also he ascended into heaven, and there sitteth at the right hand of his Father, making intercession; and shall return to judge men and angels at the end of the world.

V. The Lord Jesus, by his perfect obedience and sacrifice of himself, which he through the eternal Spirit once offered up unto God, hath fully satisfied the justice of his Father, and purchased not only reconciliation, but an everlasting inheritance in the kingdom of heaven, for all those whom the Father hath given unto him.

VI. Although the work of redemption was not actually wrought by Christ till after his incarnation, yet the virtue, efficacy, and benefits thereof were communicated unto the elect, in all ages successively, from the beginning of the world, in and by those promises, types, and sacrifices, wherein he was revealed, and signified to be the seed of the woman which should bruise the serpent's head, and the lamb slain from the beginning of the world, being yesterday and to-day the same and forever.

VII. Christ, in the work of mediation, acteth according to both natures; by each nature doing that which is proper to itself; yet, by reason of the unity of the person, that which is proper to one nature is sometimes, in Scripture, attributed to the person denominated by the other nature.

VIII. To all those for whom Christ hath purchased redemption he doth certainly and effectually apply and communicate the same; making intercession for them, and revealing unto them, in and by the Word, the mysteries of salvation; effectually persuading them by his Spirit to believe and obey; and governing their hearts by his Word and Spirit; overcoming all their enemies by his almighty power and wisdom, in such manner and ways as are most consonant to his wonderful and unsearchable dispensation.

CHAPTER IX.

Of Free-will.

I. God hath endued the will of man with that natural liberty, that is neither forced nor by any absolute necessity of nature determined to good or evil.

II. Man, in his state of innocency, had freedom and power to will and to do that which is good and well-pleasing to God, but yet mutably, so that he might fall from it.

III. Man, by his fall into a state of sin, hath wholly lost all ability of will to any spiritual good accompanying salvation; so as a natural man, being altogether averse from that good, and dead in sin, is not able, by his own strength, to convert himself, or to prepare himself thereunto.

IV. When God converts a sinner, and translates him into the state of grace, he freeth him from his natural bondage under sin, and by his grace alone enables him freely to will and to do that which is spiritually good; yet so as that, by reason of his remaining corruption, he doth not perfectly, nor only, will that which is good, but doth also will that which is evil.

V. The will of man is made perfectly and immutably free to good alone, in the state of glory only.

CHAPTER X.
Of Effectual Calling.

I. All those whom God hath predestinated unto life, and those only, he is pleased, in his appointed and accepted time, effectually to call, by his Word and Spirit, out of that state of sin and death, in which they are by nature, to grace and salvation by Jesus Christ; enlightening their minds, spiritually and savingly, to understand the things of God; taking away their heart of stone, and giving unto them an heart of flesh; renewing their wills, and by his almighty power determining them to that which is good, and effectually drawing them to Jesus Christ; yet so as they come most freely, being made willing by his grace.

II. This effectual call is of God's free and special grace alone, not from any thing at all foreseen in man; who is altogether passive therein, until, being quickened and renewed by the Holy Spirit, he is thereby enabled to answer this call, and to embrace the grace offered and conveyed in it.

III. Elect infants, dying in infancy, are regenerated and saved by Christ through the Spirit, who worketh when, and where, and how he pleaseth. So also are all other elect persons, who are incapable of being outwardly called by the ministry of the Word.

IV. Others, not elected, although they may be called by the ministry of the Word, and may have some common operations of the Spirit, yet they never truly come unto Christ, and therefore can not be saved: much less can men, not professing the Christian religion, be saved in any other way whatsoever, be they never so diligent to frame their lives according to the light of nature and the law of that religion they do profess; and to assert and maintain that they may is very pernicious, and to be detested.

CHAPTER XI.
Of Justification.

I. Those whom God effectually calleth he also freely justifieth; not by infusing righteousness into them, but by pardoning their sins, and by accounting and accepting their persons as righteous: not for any thing wrought in them, or done by them, but for Christ's sake alone; nor by imputing faith itself, the act of believing, or any other evangelical obedience to them, as their righteousness; but by imputing the obedience and satisfaction of Christ unto them, they receiving and resting on him and his righteousness by faith; which faith they have not of themselves, it is the gift of God.

II. Faith, thus receiving and resting on Christ and his righteousness, is the alone instrument of justification; yet is it not alone in the person justified, but is ever accompanied with all other saving graces, and is no dead faith, but worketh by love.

III. Christ, by his obedience and death, did fully discharge the debt of all those that are thus justified, and did make a proper, real, and full satisfaction to his Father's justice in their behalf. Yet inasmuch as he was given by the Father for them, and his obedience and satisfaction accepted in their stead, and both freely, not for anything in them, their justification is only of free grace; that both the exact justice and rich grace of God might be glorified in the justification of sinners.

IV. God did, from all eternity, decree to justify all the elect, and Christ did, in the fullness of time, die for their sins, and rise again for their justification: nevertheless, they are not justified until the Holy Spirit doth, in due time, actually apply Christ unto them.

V. God doth continue to forgive the sins of those that are justified; and although they can never fall from the state of justification, yet they may by their sins fall under God's fatherly displeasure, and not have the light of his countenance restored unto them, until they humble themselves, confess their sins, beg pardon, and renew their faith and repentance.

VI. The justification of believers under the Old Testament was, in all these respects, one and the same with the justification of believers under the New Testament.

CHAPTER XII.
Of Adoption.

All those that are justified God vouchsafeth, in and for his only Son Jesus Christ, to make partakers of the grace of adoption; by which they are taken into the number, and enjoy the liberties and privileges of the children of God; have his name put upon them; receive the Spirit of adoption; have access to the throne of grace with boldness; are enabled to cry, Abba, Father; are pitied, protected, provided for, and chastened by him as by a father; yet never cast off, but sealed to the day of redemption, and inherit the promises, as heirs of everlasting salvation.

CHAPTER XIII.
Of Sanctification.

I. They who are effectually called and regenerated, having a new heart and a new spirit created in them, are further sanctified, really and personally, through the virtue of Christ's death and resurrection, by his Word and Spirit dwelling in them; the dominion of the whole body of sin is destroyed, and the several lusts thereof are more and more weakened and mortified, and they more and more quickened and strengthened, in all saving graces, to the practice of true holiness, without which no man shall see the Lord.

II. This sanctification is throughout in the whole man, yet imperfect in this life; there abideth still some remnants of corruption in every part, whence ariseth a continual and irreconcilable war, the flesh lusting against the spirit, and the spirit against the flesh.

III. In which war, although the remaining corruption for a time may much prevail, yet, through the continual supply of strength from the sanctifying Spirit of Christ, the regenerate part doth overcome;

and so the saints grow in grace, perfecting holiness in the fear of God.

CHAPTER XIV.
Of Saving Faith.

I. The grace of faith, whereby the elect are enabled to believe to the saving of their souls, is the work of the Spirit of Christ in their hearts, and is ordinarily wrought by the ministry of the Word; by which also, and by the administration of the sacraments and prayer, it is increased and strengthened.

II. By this faith a Christian believeth to be true whatsoever is revealed in the Word, for the authority of God himself speaking therein; and acteth differently upon that which each particular passage thereof containeth; yielding obedience to the commands, trembling at the threatenings, and embracing the promises of God for this life and that which is to come. But the principal acts of saving faith are accepting, receiving, and resting upon Christ alone for justification, sanctification, and eternal life, by virtue of the covenant of grace.

III. This faith is different in degrees, weak or strong; may be often and many ways assailed and weakened, but gets the victory; growing up in many to the attainment of a full assurance through Christ, who is both the author and finisher of our faith.

CHAPTER XV.
Of Repentance unto Life.

I. Repentance unto life is an evangelical grace, the doctrine whereof is to be preached by every minister of the gospel, as well as that of faith in Christ.

II. By it a sinner, out of the sight and sense, not only of the danger, but also of the filthiness and odiousness of his sins, as contrary to the holy nature and righteous law of God, and upon the apprehension of his mercy in Christ to such as are penitent, so grieves for and hates his sins as to turn from them all unto God, purposing and endeavoring to walk with him in all the ways of his commandments.

III. Although repentance be not to be rested in as

any satisfaction for sin, or any cause of the pardon thereof, which is the act of God's free grace in Christ; yet is it of such necessity to all sinners that none may expect pardon without it.

IV. As there is no sin so small but it deserves damnation, so there is no sin so great that it can bring damnation upon those who truly repent.

V. Men ought not to content themselves with a general repentance, but it is every man's duty to endeavor to repent of his particular sins particularly.

VI. As every man is bound to make private confession of his sins to God, praying for the pardon thereof, upon which, and the forsaking of them, he shall find mercy; so he that scandalizeth his brother, or the Church of Christ, ought to be willing, by a private or public confession and sorrow for his sin, to declare his repentance to those that are offended, who are thereupon to be reconciled to him, and in love to receive him.

CHAPTER XVI.
Of Good Works.

I. Good works are only such as God hath commanded in his holy Word, and not such as, without the warrant thereof, are devised by men out of blind zeal, or upon any pretense of good intention.

II. These good works, done in obedience to God's commandments, are the fruits and evidences of a true and lively faith; and by them believers manifest their thankfulness, strengthen their assurance, edify their brethren, adorn the profession of the gospel, stop the mouths of the adversaries, and glorify God, whose workmanship they are, created in Christ Jesus thereunto, that, having their fruit unto holiness, they may have the end, eternal life.

III. Their ability to do good works is not at all of themselves, but wholly from the Spirit of Christ. And that they may be enabled thereunto, besides the graces they have already received, there is required an actual influence of the same Holy Spirit to work in them to will and to do of his good pleasure; yet are they not hereupon to grow negligent, as if they were not bound to perform any duty unless upon a special motion of the Spirit; but they ought to be diligent in stirring up the grace of God that is in them.

IV. They who in their obedience attain to the greatest height which is possible in this life, are so far from being able to supererogate and to do more than God requires, as that they fall short of much which in duty they are bound to do.

V. We can not, by our best works, merit pardon of sin, or eternal life at the hand of God, by reason of the great disproportion that is between them and the glory to come, and the infinite distance that is between us and God, whom by them we can neither profit nor satisfy for the debt of our former sins; but when we have done all we can, we have done but our duty, and are unprofitable servants; and because, as they are good, they proceed from his Spirit; and as they are wrought by us, they are defiled and mixed with so much weakness and imperfection that they can not endure the severity of God's judgment.

VI. Yet notwithstanding, the persons of believers being accepted through Christ, their good works also are accepted in him, not as though they were in this life wholly unblamable and unreprovable in God's sight; but that he, looking upon them in his Son, is pleased to accept and reward that which is sincere, although accompanied with many weaknesses and imperfections.

VII. Works done by unregenerate men, although for the matter of them they may be things which God commands, and of good use both to themselves and others; yet because they proceed not from a heart purified by faith, nor are done in a right manner, according to the Word, nor to a right end, the glory of God; they are therefore sinful, and can not please God, or make a man meet to receive grace from God. And yet their neglect of them is more sinful and displeasing unto God.

CHAPTER XVII.
Of the Perseverance of the Saints.

I. They whom God hath accepted in his Beloved, effectually called and sanctified by his Spirit, can neither totally nor finally fall away from the state of grace; but shall certainly persevere therein to the end, and be eternally saved.

II. This perseverance of the saints depends, not upon their own free-will, but upon the immutability of the decree of election, flowing from the free and unchangeable love of God the Father; upon the efficacy of the merit and intercession of Jesus Christ; the abiding of the Spirit and of the seed of God within them; and the nature of the covenant of grace: from all which ariseth also the certainty and infallibility thereof.

III. Nevertheless they may, through the temptations of Satan and of the world, the prevalency of corruption remaining in them, and the neglect of the means of their preservation, fall into grievous sins; and for a time continue therein: whereby they incur God's displeasure, and grieve his Holy Spirit; come to be deprived of some measure of their graces and comforts; have their hearts hardened, and their consciences wounded; hurt and scandalize others, and bring temporal judgments upon themselves.

CHAPTER XVIII.
Of the Assurance of Grace and Salvation.

I. Although hypocrites and other unregenerate men may vainly deceive themselves with false hopes and carnal presumptions of being in the favor of God and estate of salvation, which hope of theirs shall perish: yet such as truly believe in the Lord Jesus, and love him in sincerity, endeavoring to walk in all good conscience before him, may in this life be certainly assured that they are in a state of grace, and may rejoice in the hope of the glory of God, which hope shall never make them ashamed.

II. This certainty is not a bare conjectural and probable persuasion, grounded upon a fallible hope; but an infallible assurance of faith, founded upon the divine truth of the promises of salvation, the inward evidence of those graces unto which these promises are made, the testimony of the Spirit of adoption witnessing with our spirits that we are the children of God: which Spirit is the earnest of our inheritance, whereby we are sealed to the day of redemption.

III. This infallible assurance doth not so belong to the essence of faith, but that a true believer may wait long, and conflict with many difficulties before he be partaker of it: yet, being enabled by the Spirit to know the things which are freely given him of God, he may, without extraordinary revelation, in the right use of ordinary means, attain thereunto. And therefore it is the duty of every one to give all diligence to make his calling and election sure; that thereby his heart may be enlarged in peace and joy in the Holy Ghost, in love and thankfulness to God, and in strength and cheerfulness in the duties of obedience, the proper fruits of this assurance: so far is it from inclining men to looseness.

IV. True believers may have the assurance of their salvation divers ways shaken, diminished, and intermitted; as, by negligence in preserving of it; by falling into some special sin, which woundeth the conscience, and grieveth the Spirit; by some sudden or vehement temptation; by God's withdrawing the light of his countenance, and suffering even such as fear him to walk in darkness and to have no light: yet are they never utterly destitute of that seed of God, and life of faith, that love of Christ and the brethren, that sincerity of heart and conscience of duty, out of which, by the operation of the Spirit, this assurance may in due time be revived, and by the which, in the mean time, they are supported from utter despair.

CHAPTER XIX.
Of the Law of God.

I. God gave to Adam a law, as a covenant of works, by which he bound him and all his posterity to personal, entire, exact, and perpetual obedience; promised life upon the fulfilling, and threatened death upon the breach of it; and endued him with power and ability to keep it.

II. This law, after his fall, continued to be a perfect rule of righteousness; and, as such, was delivered by God upon mount Sinai in ten commandments, and written in two tables; the first four commandments containing our duty towards God, and the other six our duty to man.

III. Beside this law, commonly called moral, God was pleased to give to the people of Israel, as a Church under age, ceremonial laws, containing several typical ordinances, partly of worship, prefiguring Christ, his graces, actions, sufferings, and benefits; and partly holding forth divers instructions of moral duties. All which ceremonial laws are now abrogated under the New Testament.

IV. To them also, as a body politic, he gave sundry judicial laws, which expired together with the state of that people, not obliging any other, now, further than the general equity thereof may require.

V. The moral law doth forever bind all, as well justified persons as others, to the obedience thereof; and that not only in regard of the matter contained in it, but also in respect of the authority of God the Creator who gave it. Neither doth Christ in the gospel any way dissolve, but much strengthen, this obligation.

VI. Although true believers be not under the law as a covenant of works, to be thereby justified or condemned; yet is it of great use to them, as well as to others; in that, as a rule of life, informing them of the will of God and their duty, it directs and binds them to walk accordingly; discovering also the sinful pollutions of their nature, hearts, and lives; so as, examining themselves thereby, they may come to further conviction of, humiliation for, and hatred against sin; together with a clearer sight of the need they have of Christ, and the perfection of his obedience. It is likewise of use to the regenerate, to restrain their corruptions, in that it forbids sin; and the threatenings of it serve to show what even their sins deserve, and what afflictions in this life they may expect for them, although freed from the curse thereof threatened in the law. The promises of it, in like manner, show them God's approbation of obedience, and what blessings they may expect upon the performance thereof; although not as due to them by the law as a covenant of words: so as a man's doing good, and refraining from evil, because the law encourageth to the one, and deterreth from the other, is no evidence of his being under the law, and not under grace.

VII. Neither are the forementioned uses of the law contrary to the grace of the gospel, but do sweetly comply with it: the Spirit of Christ subduing and enabling the will of man to do that freely and cheerfully which the will of God, revealed in the law, requireth to be done.

CHAPTER XX.
Of Christian Liberty, and Liberty of Conscience.

I. The liberty which Christ hath purchased for believers under the gospel consists in their freedom from the guilt of sin, the condemning wrath of God, the curse of the moral law; and in their being delivered from this present evil world, bondage to Satan, and dominion of sin, from the evil of afflictions, the sting of death, the victory of the grave, and everlasting damnation; as also in their free access to God, and their yielding obedience unto him, not out of slavish fear, but a child-like love and willing mind. All which were common also to believers under the law; but under the New Testament the liberty of Christians is further enlarged in their freedom from the yoke of the ceremonial law, to which the Jewish Church was subjected; and in greater boldness of access to the throne of grace, and in fuller communications of the free Spirit of God, than believers under the law did ordinarily partake of.

II. God alone is Lord of the conscience, and hath left it free from the doctrines and commandments of men which are in any thing contrary to his Word, or beside it in matters of faith or worship. So that to believe such doctrines, or to obey such commands out of conscience, is to betray true liberty of conscience; and the requiring of an implicit faith, and an absolute and blind obedience, is to destroy liberty of conscience, and reason also.

III. They who, upon pretense of Christian liberty, do practice any sin, or cherish any lust, do thereby destroy the end of Christian liberty; which is, that, being delivered out of the hands of our enemies, we might serve the Lord without fear, in holiness and righteousness before him, all the days of our life.

IV. And because the power which God hath ordained, and the liberty which Christ hath purchased, are not intended by God to destroy, but mutually to uphold and preserve one another; they who, upon pretense of Christian liberty, shall oppose any lawful power, or the lawful exercise of it, whether it be civil or ecclesiastical, resist the ordinance of God. And for their publishing of such opinions, or maintaining of such practices, as are contrary to the light of nature, or to the known principles of Christianity, whether concerning faith, worship, or conversation; or to the power of godliness; or such erroneous opinions or practices, as, either in their own nature, or in the manner of publishing or maintaining them, are destructive to the external peace and order which Christ hath established in the Church; they may lawfully be called to account, and proceeded against by the censures of the Church, and by the power of the Civil Magistrate.

CHAPTER XXI.
Of Religious Worship and the Sabbath-day.

I. The light of nature showeth that there is a God, who hath lordship and sovereignty over all; is good, and doeth good unto all; and is therefore to be feared, loved, praised, called upon, trusted in, and served with all the heart, and with all the soul, and with all the might. But the acceptable way of worshiping the true God is instituted by himself, and so limited to his own revealed will, that he may not be worshiped according to the imaginations and devices of men, or the suggestions of Satan, under any visible representations or any other way not prescribed in the Holy Scripture.

II. Religious worship is to be given to God, the Father, Son, and Holy Ghost; and to him alone: not to angels, saints, or any other creature: and since the fall, not without a Mediator; nor in the mediation of any other but of Christ alone.

III. Prayer with thanksgiving, being one special part of religious worship, is by God required of all men; and that it may be accepted, it is to be made in the name of the Son, by the help of his Spirit, according to his will, with understanding, reverence, humility, fervency, faith, love, and perseverance; and, if vocal, in a known tongue.

IV. Prayer is to be made for things lawful, and for all sorts of men living, or that shall live hereafter; but not for the dead, nor for those of whom it may be known that they have sinned the sin unto death.

V. The reading of the Scriptures with godly fear; the sound preaching; and conscionable hearing of the Word, in obedience unto God with understanding, faith, and reverence; singing of psalms with grace in the heart; as, also, the due administration and worthy receiving of the sacraments instituted by Christ; are all parts of the ordinary religious worship of God: besides religious oaths, vows, solemn fastings, and thanksgivings upon several occasions; which are, in their several times and seasons, to be used in an holy and religious manner.

VI. Neither prayer, nor any other part of religious worship, is now under the gospel, either tied unto or made more acceptable by any place in which it is performed, or towards which it is directed: but God is to be worshiped every where in spirit and truth; as in private families daily, and in secret each one by himself, so more solemnly in the public assemblies, which are not carelessly or willfully to be neglected or forsaken, when God, by his Word or providence, calleth thereunto.

VII. As it is of the law of nature, that, in general, a due proportion of time be set apart for the worship of God; so, in his Word, by a positive, moral, and perpetual commandment, binding all men in all ages, he hath particularly appointed one day in seven for a Sabbath, to be kept holy unto him: which, from the beginning of the world to the resurrection of Christ, was the last day of the week; and, from the resurrection of Christ, was changed into the first day of the week, which in Scripture is called the Lord's day, and is to be continued to the end of the world, as the Christian Sabbath.

VIII. This Sabbath is then kept holy unto the Lord, when men, after a due preparing of their hearts, and ordering of their common affairs beforehand, do not only observe an holy rest all the day from their own works, words, and thoughts, about their worldly employments and recreations; but also are taken up the whole time in the public and private exercises of his worship, and in the duties of necessity and mercy.

CHAPTER XXII.
Of Lawful Oaths and Vows.

I. A lawful oath is a part of religious worship, wherein, upon just occasion, the person swearing solemnly calleth God to witness what he asserteth or promiseth; and to judge him according to the truth or falsehood of what he sweareth.

II. The name of God only is that by which men ought to swear, and therein it is to be used with all holy fear and reverence; therefore to swear vainly or rashly by that glorious and dreadful name, or to swear at all by any other thing, is sinful, and to be abhorred. Yet as, in matters of weight and moment, an oath is warranted by the Word of God, under the New Testament, as well as under the Old, so a lawful oath, being imposed by lawful authority, in such matters ought to be taken.

III. Whosoever taketh an oath ought duly to consider the weightiness of so solemn an act, and therein to avouch nothing but what he is fully persuaded is the truth. Neither may any man bind himself by oath to any thing but what is good and just, and what he believeth so to be, and what he is able and resolved to perform. Yet it is a sin to refuse an oath touching any thing that is good and just, being imposed by lawful authority.

IV. An oath is to be taken in the plain and common sense of the words, without equivocation or mental reservation. It can not oblige to sin; but in any thing not sinful, being taken, it binds to performance, although to a man's own hurt: nor is it to be violated, although made to heretics or infidels.

V. A vow is of the like nature with a promissory oath, and ought to be made with the like religious care, and to be performed with the like faithfulness.

VI. It is not to be made to any creature, but to God alone: and that it may be accepted, it is to be made voluntarily, out of faith and conscience of duty, in way of thankfulness for mercy received, or for the obtaining of what we want; whereby we more strictly bind ourselves to necessary duties, or to other things, so far and so long as they may fitly conduce thereunto.

VII. No man may vow to do any thing forbidden in the Word of God, or what would hinder any duty therein commanded, or which is not in his own power, and for the performance whereof he hath no promise or ability from God. In which respect, popish monastical vows of perpetual single life, professed poverty, and regular obedience, are so far from being degrees of higher perfection, that they are superstitious and sinful snares, in which no Christian may entangle himself.

CHAPTER XXIII.
Of the Civil Magistrate.

I. God, the Supreme Lord and King of all the world, hath ordained civil magistrates to be under him, over the people, for his own glory and the public good, and to this end hath armed them with the power of the sword, for the defense and encouragement of them that are good, and for the punishment of evil-doers.

II. It is lawful for Christians to accept and execute the office of a magistrate when called thereunto; in the managing whereof, as they ought especially to maintain piety, justice, and peace, according to the wholesome laws of each commonwealth, so, for that end, they may lawfully, now under the New Testament, wage war upon just and necessary occasion.

III. The civil magistrate may not assume to himself the administration of the Word and Sacraments, or the power of the keys of the kingdom of heaven: yet he hath authority, and it is his duty to take order, that unity and peace be preserved in the Church, that the truth of God be kept pure and entire, that all blasphemies and heresies be suppressed, all corruptions and abuses in worship and discipline prevented or reformed, and all the ordinances of God duly settled, administered, and observed. For the better effecting whereof he hath power to call synods, to be present at them, and to provide that whatsoever is transacted in them be according to the mind of God.

IV. It is the duty of people to pray for magistrates, to honor their persons, to pay them tribute and other dues, to obey their lawful commands, and to be subject to their authority, for conscience' sake. Infidelity or difference in religion doth not make void the magistrate's just and legal authority, nor free the people from their due obedience to him: from which ecclesiastical persons are not exempted; much less hath the Pope any power or jurisdiction over them in their dominions, or over any of their people; and least of all to deprive them of their dominions or lives, if he shall judge them to be heretics, or upon any other pretense whatsoever.

CHAPTER XXIV.
Of Marriage and Divorce.

I. Marriage is to be between one man and one woman: neither is it lawful for any man to have more than one wife, nor for any woman to have more than one husband at the same time.

II. Marriage was ordained for the mutual help of husband and wife; for the increase of mankind with a legitimate issue, and of the church with an holy seed; and for preventing of uncleanness.

III. It is lawful for all sorts of people to marry who are able with judgment to give their consent. Yet it is the duty of Christians to marry only in the Lord. And, therefore, such as profess the true reformed religion should not marry with infidels, Papists, or other idolaters: neither should such as are godly be unequally yoked, by marrying with such as are notoriously wicked in their life, or maintain damnable heresies.

IV. Marriage ought not to be within the degrees of consanguinity or affinity forbidden in the Word; nor can such incestuous marriages ever be made lawful by any law of man, or consent of parties, so as those persons may live together, as man and wife. The man may not marry any of his wife's kindred nearer in blood than he may of his own, nor the woman of her husband's kindred nearer in blood than of her own.

V. Adultery or fornication, committed after a contract, being detected before marriage, giveth just occasion to the innocent party to dissolve that contract. In the case of adultery after marriage, it is lawful for the innocent party to sue out a divorce, and after the divorce to marry another, as if the offending party were dead.

VI. Although the corruption of man be such as is apt to study arguments, unduly to put asunder those whom God hath joined together in marriage; yet nothing but adultery, or such willful desertion as can no way be remedied by the Church or civil magistrate, is cause sufficient of dissolving the bond of marriage; wherein a public and orderly course of proceeding is to be observed; and the persons concerned in it, not left to their own wills and discretion in their own case.

CHAPTER XXV.
Of the Church.

I. The catholic or universal Church, which is invisible, consists of the whole number of the elect, that have been, are, or shall be gathered into one, under Christ the head thereof; and is the spouse, the body, the fullness of him that filleth all in all.

II. The visible Church, which is also catholic or universal under the gospel (not confined to one nation as before under the law) consists of all those, throughout the world, that profess the true religion, and of their children; and is the kingdom of the Lord Jesus Christ, the house and family of God, out of which there is no ordinary possibility of salvation.

III. Unto this catholic visible Church Christ hath given the ministry, oracles, and ordinances of God, for the gathering and perfecting of the saints, in this life, to the end of the world: and doth by his own presence and Spirit, according to his promise, make them effectual thereunto.

IV. This catholic Church hath been sometimes more, sometimes less visible. And particular churches, which are members thereof, are more or less pure, according as the doctrine of the gospel is taught and embraced, ordinances administered, and public worship performed more or less purely in them.

V. The purest churches under heaven are subject both to mixture and error; and some have so degenerated as to become no churches of Christ, but synagogues of Satan. Nevertheless, there shall be always a Church on earth to worship God according to his will.

VI. There is no other head of the Church but the Lord Jesus Christ: nor can the Pope of Rome, in any sense be head thereof; but is that Antichrist, that man of sin and son of perdition, that exalteth himself in the Church against Christ, and all that is called God.

CHAPTER XXVI.
Of the Communion of Saints.

I. All saints that are united to Jesus Christ their head, by his Spirit and by faith, have fellowship with him in his graces, sufferings, death, resurrection, and glory: and being united to one another in love, they have communion in each other's gifts and graces, and are obliged to the performance of such duties, public and private, as do conduce to their mutual good, both in the inward and outward man.

II. Saints, by profession, are bound to maintain an holy fellowship and communion in the worship of God, and in performing such other spiritual services as tend to their mutual edification; as also in relieving each other in outward things, according to their several abilities and necessities. Which communion, as God offereth opportunity, is to be extended unto all those who, in every place, call upon the name of the Lord Jesus.

III. This communion which the saints have with Christ, doth not make them in anywise partakers of the substance of his Godhead, or to be equal with Christ in any respect: either of which to affirm is impious and blasphemous. Nor doth their communion one with another, as saints, take away or infringe the title or propriety which each man hath in his goods and possessions.

CHAPTER XXVII.
Of the Sacraments.

I. Sacraments are holy signs and seals of the covenant of grace, immediately instituted by God, to represent Christ and his benefits, and to confirm our interest in him: as also to put a visible difference between those that belong unto the Church and the rest of the world; and solemnly to engage them to the service of God in Christ, according to his Word.

II. There is in every sacrament a spiritual relation or sacramental union, between the sign and the thing signified; whence it comes to pass that the names and the effects of the one are attributed to the other.

III. The grace which is exhibited in or by the sacraments, rightly used, is not conferred by any power in them; neither doth the efficacy of a sacrament depend upon the piety or intention of him that doth administer it, but upon the work of the Spirit, and the word of institution, which contains, together with a precept authorizing the use thereof, a promise of benefit to worthy receivers.

IV. There be only two sacraments ordained by Christ our Lord in the gospel, that is to say, Baptism and the Supper of the Lord: neither of which may be dispensed by any but by a minister of the Word lawfully ordained.

V. The sacraments of the Old Testament, in regard of the spiritual things thereby signified and exhibited, were, for substance, the same with those of the New.

CHAPTER XXVIII.

Of Baptism.

I. Baptism is a sacrament of the New Testament, ordained by Jesus Christ, not only for the solemn admission of the party baptized into the visible Church, but also to be unto him a sign and seal of the covenant of grace, of his ingrafting into Christ, of regeneration, of remission of sins, and of his giving up unto God, through Jesus Christ, to walk in newness of life: which sacrament is, by Christ's own appointment, to be continued in his Church until the end of the world.

II. The outward element to be used in this sacrament is water, wherewith the party is to be baptized in the name of the Father, and of the Son, and of the Holy Ghost, by a minister of the gospel lawfully called thereunto.

III. Dipping of the person into the water is not necessary; but baptism is rightly administered by pouring or sprinkling water upon the person.

IV. Not only those that do actually profess faith in and obedience unto Christ, but also the infants of one or both believing parents are to be baptized.

V. Although it be a great sin to contemn or neglect this ordinance, yet grace and salvation are not so inseparably annexed unto it, as that no person can be regenerated or saved without it, or that all that are baptized are undoubtedly regenerated.

VI. The efficacy of baptism is not tied to that moment of time wherein it is administered; yet, notwithstanding, by the right use of this ordinance the grace promised is not only offered, but really exhibited and conferred by the Holy Ghost, to such (whether of age or infants) as that grace belongeth unto, according to the counsel of God's own will, in his appointed time.

VII. The sacrament of baptism is but once to be administered to any person.

CHAPTER XXIX.
Of the Lord's Supper.

I. Our Lord Jesus, in the night wherein he was betrayed, instituted the sacrament of his body and blood, called the Lord's Supper, to be observed in his Church, unto the end of the world; for the perpetual remembrance of the sacrifice of himself in his death, the sealing all benefits thereof unto true believers, their spiritual nourishment and growth in him, their further engagement in, and to all duties which they owe unto him; and to be a bond and pledge of their communion with him, and with each other, as members of his mystical body.

II. In this sacrament Christ is not offered up to his Father, nor any real sacrifice made at all for remission of sins of the quick or dead, but only a commemoration of that one offering up of himself, by himself, upon the cross, once for all, and a spiritual oblation of all possible praise unto God for the same; so that the Popish sacrifice of the mass, as they call it, is most abominably injurious to Christ's one only sacrifice, the alone propitiation for all the sins of the elect.

III. The Lord Jesus hath, in this ordinance, appointed his ministers to declare his word of institution to the people, to pray, and bless the elements of bread and wine, and thereby to set them apart from a common to an holy use; and to take and break the bread, to take the cup, and (they communicating also themselves) to give both to the communicants; but to none who are not then present in the congregation.

IV. Private masses, or receiving this sacrament by

a priest, or any other, alone; as likewise the denial of the cup to the people; worshiping the elements, the lifting them up, or carrying them about for adoration, and the reserving them for any pretended religious use, are all contrary to the nature of this sacrament, and to the institution of Christ.

V. The outward elements in this sacrament, duly set apart to the uses ordained by Christ, have such relation to him crucified, as that truly, yet sacramentally only, they are sometimes called by the name of the things they represent, to wit, the body and blood of Christ; albeit, in substance and nature, they still remain truly, and only, bread and wine, as they were before.

VI. That doctrine which maintains a change of the substance of bread and wine, into the substance of Christ's body and blood (commonly called transubstantiation) by consecration of a priest, or by any other way, is repugnant, not to Scripture alone, but even to common-sense and reason; overthroweth the nature of the sacrament; and hath been, and is the cause of manifold superstitions, yea, of gross idolatries.

VII. Worthy receivers, outwardly partaking of the visible elements in this sacrament, do then also inwardly by faith, really and indeed, yet not carnally and corporally, but spiritually, receive and feed upon Christ crucified, and all benefits of his death: the body and blood of Christ being then not corporally or carnally in, with, or under the bread and wine; yet as really, but spiritually, present to the faith of believers in that ordinance, as the elements themselves are, to their outward senses.

VIII. Although ignorant and wicked men receive the outward elements in this sacrament, yet they receive not the thing signified thereby; but by their unworthy coming thereunto are guilty of the body and blood of the Lord, to their own damnation. Wherefore all ignorant and ungodly persons, as they are unfit to enjoy communion with him, so are they unworthy of the Lord's table, and can not, without great sin against

Christ, while they remain such, partake of these holy mysteries, or be admitted thereunto.

CHAPTER XXX.
Of Church Censures.

I. The Lord Jesus, as king and head of his Church, hath therein appointed a government in the hand of Church officers, distinct from the civil magistrate.

II. To these officers the keys of the kingdom of heaven are committed, by virtue whereof they have power respectively to retain and remit sins, to shut that kingdom against the impenitent, both by the Word and censures; and to open it unto penitent sinners, by the ministry of the gospel, and by absolution from censures, as occasion shall require.

III. Church censures are necessary for the reclaiming and gaining of offending brethren; for deterring of others from the like offenses; for purging out of that leaven which might infect the whole lump; for vindicating the honor of Christ, and the holy profession of the gospel; and for preventing the wrath of God, which might justly fall upon the Church, if they should suffer his covenant, and the seals thereof, to be profaned by notorious and obstinate offenders.

IV. For the better attaining of these ends, the officers of the Church are to proceed by admonition, suspension from the Sacrament of the Lord's Supper for a season, and by excommunication from the Church, according to the nature of the crime and demerit of the person.

CHAPTER XXXI.
Of Synods and Councils.

I. For the better government and further edification of the Church, there ought to be such assemblies as are commonly called synods or councils.

II. As magistrates may lawfully call a synod of ministers and other fit persons to consult and advise with about matters of religion; so, if magistrates be open enemies to the Church, the ministers of Christ, of themselves, by virtue of their office, or they, with other fit persons, upon delegation from their churches, may meet together in such assemblies.

III. It belongeth to synods and councils, ministerially, to determine controversies of faith, and cases of conscience; to set down rules and directions for the better ordering of the public worship of God, and government of his Church; to receive complaints in cases of maladministration, and authoritatively to determine the same: which decrees and determinations, if consonant to the Word of God, are to be received with reverence and submission, not only for their agreement with the Word, but also for the power whereby they are made, as being an ordinance of God, appointed thereunto in his Word.

IV. All synods or councils since the apostles' times, whether general or particular, may err, and many have erred; therefore they are not to be made the rule of faith or practice, but to be used as a help in both.

V. Synods and councils are to handle or conclude nothing but that which is ecclesiastical: and are not to intermeddle with civil affairs which concern the commonwealth, unless by way of humble petition in cases extraordinary; or by way of advice for satisfaction of conscience, if they be thereunto required by the civil magistrate.

CHAPTER XXXII.
Of the State of Men after Death, and of the Resurrection of the Dead.

I. The bodies of men, after death, return to dust, and see corruption; but their souls (which neither die nor sleep), having an immortal subsistence, immediately return to God who gave them. The souls of the righteous, being then made perfect in holiness, are received into the highest heavens, where they behold the face of God in light and glory, waiting for the full redemption of their bodies: and the souls of the wicked are cast into hell, where they remain in torments and utter darkness, reserved to the judgment of the great day. Besides these two places for souls separated from their bodies, the Scripture acknowledgeth none.

II. At the last day, such as are found alive shall not die, but be changed; and all the dead shall be raised up with the self-same bodies, and none other, although with different qualities, which shall be united again to their souls forever.

III. The bodies of the unjust shall, by the power of Christ, be raised to dishonor; the bodies of the just, by his Spirit, unto honor, and be made conformable to his own glorious body.

CHAPTER XXXIII.

Of the Last Judgment.

I. God hath appointed a day wherein he will judge the world in righteousness by Jesus Christ, to whom all power and judgment is given of the Father. In which day, not only the apostate angels shall be judged, but likewise all persons, that have lived upon earth, shall appear before the tribunal of Christ, to give an account of their thoughts, words, and deeds; and to receive according to what they have done in the body, whether good or evil.

II. The end of God's appointing this day, is for the manifestation of the glory of his mercy in the eternal salvation of the elect; and of his justice in the damnation of the reprobate, who are wicked and disobedient. For then shall the righteous go into everlasting life, and receive that fullness of joy and refreshing which shall come from the presence of the Lord: but the wicked, who know not God, and obey not the gospel of Jesus Christ, shall be cast into eternal torments, and be punished with everlasting destruction from the presence of the Lord, and from the glory of his power.

III. As Christ would have us to be certainly persuaded that there shall be a day of judgment, both to deter all men from sin, and for the greater consolation of the godly in their adversity: so will he have that day unknown to men, that they may shake off all carnal security, and be always watchful, because they know not at what hour the Lord will come; and may

be ever prepared to say, Come, Lord Jesus, come
quickly. Amen.

> *Charles Herle, Prolocutor.*
> *Cornelius Burges, Assessor.*
> *Herbert Palmer, Assessor.*
> *Henry Robroughe, Scriba.*
> *Adoniram Byfield, Scriba.*

THE ENGLISH REFORMATION

THE EDWARDIAN HOMILIES (1547)

One of the first acts of the Reformation under Edward
VI was the issuance of Twelve Homilies by the Council of
Regency. Such a series had been proposed by Cranmer to
the Convocation as early as 1542, but it had not been authorized. The first five homilies expound Christian doctrine,
and the last seven are concerned with the moral life of the
Christian. The Homilies were to be read in local churches
as the "true setting forth and pure declaring of God's
word."

Thomas Cranmer is credited with the homilies that are
reproduced here. The homily "Of the Salvation of Mankind" has been described as one of the finest pieces of
theological writing in the English language. "A Fruitful Exhortation to the Reading and Knowledge of Holy Scripture"
is a clear presentation of one of the dominant themes of
the English Reformation, which made the Bible the book
of the common man. The homilies on faith and good works
are unusually perceptive statements of the basic doctrines
of the Reformation.

Source: The homilies here reprinted are taken from
Certain Sermons or Homilies, Appointed to be read in

churches in the time of the late Queen Elizabeth of famous memory (Oxford: Oxford University Press, 1832).

Bromiley, G., *Thomas Cranmer, Theologian* (New York: Oxford University Press, 1956).

Hughes, Philip, *The Reformation in England* (New York: The Macmillan Co., 1950–1954), Vol. II.

Ridley, J., *Thomas Cranmer* (New York: Oxford University Press, 1962).

Rupp, E. Gordon, *Studies in the Making of the English Protestant Tradition* (Cambridge: Cambridge University Press, 1947).

A FRUITFUL EXHORTATION TO THE READING AND KNOWLEDGE OF HOLY SCRIPTURE.

Unto a Christian man there can be nothing either more necessary or profitable, than the knowledge of holy scripture, forasmuch as in it is contained God's true word, setting forth his glory, and also man's duty. And there is no truth nor doctrine necessary for our justification and everlasting salvation, but that is, or may be drawn out of that fountain and well of truth. Therefore as many as be desirous to enter into the right and perfect way unto God, must apply their minds to know holy scripture; without the which, they can neither sufficiently know God and his will, neither their office and duty. And as drink is pleasant to them that be dry, and meat to them that be hungry; so is the reading, hearing, searching, and studying of holy scripture, to them that be desirous to know God, or themselves, and to do his will. And their stomachs only do loathe and abhor the heavenly knowledge and food of God's word, that be so drowned in worldly vanities, that they neither savour God, nor any godliness: for that is the cause why they desire such vanities, rather than the true knowledge of God. As they that are sick of an ague, whatsoever they eat and drink, though it be never so pleasant, yet it is as bitter to them as wormwood; not for the bitterness of the meat, but for the corrupt and bitter humour that is in their own tongue and mouth: even so is the sweetness of God's word bitter, not of itself, but only unto them that have their minds corrupted with long custom of sin and love of this world. Therefore forsaking the corrupt judgment of fleshly men, which care not but for their carcase; let us reverently hear and read holy scriptures, which is the food of the soul. Let us diligently search for the well of life in the books of the New and Old Testament, and not run to the stinking puddles of men's traditions, devised by men's imagination, for our justification and salvation. For in holy scripture is fully contained what we ought to do, and what to eschew, what to believe, what to love, and what to look for at God's hands at length. In these books we shall find the Father from whom, the Son by whom, and the Holy Ghost in whom, all things have their being and keeping up; and these three persons to be but one God, and one substance. In these books we may learn to know ourselves, how vile and miserable we be, and also to know God, how good he is of himself, and how he maketh us and all creatures partakers of his goodness. We may learn also in these books to know God's will and pleasure, as much as, for this present time, is convenient for us to know. And, as the great clerk and godly preacher, St. John Chrysostom saith, whatsoever is required to salvation of man, is fully contained in the scripture of God. He that is ignorant may there learn and have knowledge. He that is hardhearted, and an obstinate sinner, shall there find everlasting torments, prepared of God's justice, to make him afraid, and to mollify or soften him. He that is oppressed with misery in this world shall there find relief in the promises of everlasting life, to his great consolation and comfort. He that is wounded by the Devil unto death shall find there medicine whereby he may be restored again unto health; if it shall require to teach any truth, or reprove false doctrine, to rebuke any vice, to commend any virtue, to give good counsel, to comfort or to exhort, or to do any other thing requisite for our salvation, all those things, saith St. Chrysostom, we may learn plentifully of the scripture. There is, saith Fulgentius, abundantly enough, both for men to eat, and children to suck. There is whatsoever is meet for all ages, and for all degrees and sorts of men. These books therefore ought to be much in our hands, in our eyes, in our ears, in our mouths, but most of all in our hearts. For the scripture of God is the heavenly meat of our souls; the hearing and keeping of it maketh us blessed, sanctifieth us, and maketh us holy; it turneth our souls, it is a light lantern to our feet; it is a sure, steadfast, and everlasting instrument of salvation; it giveth wisdom to the humble and lowly hearts; it comforteth, maketh glad, cheereth, and cherisheth our conscience: it is a more excellent jewel or treasure than any gold or precious stone; it is more sweet than honey or honey-comb; it is called the best part, which Mary did choose, for it hath in it everlasting comfort. The words of holy scripture be called words of everlasting life: for they be God's instrument, ordained for the same purpose. They have power to turn (convert) through God's promise, and they be effectual through God's assistance, and (being received in a faithful heart) they have ever an heavenly spiritual working in them: they are lively, quick, and mighty in operation, and "sharper than any two-edged sword, and entereth through, even unto the dividing asunder of the soul and the spirit, of the joints and the marrow." Christ calleth him a wise builder, that buildeth upon his word, upon his sure and substantial foundation. By this word of God we shall be judged: for "the word that I speak," saith Christ, "is it, that shall judge in the last day." He that keepeth the word of Christ, is promised the love and favour of God, and that he shall be the dwelling-place or temple of the blessed Trinity. This word whosoever is diligent to read, and in his heart to print that he readeth, the great affection to the transitory things of this world shall be minished in him, and the great desire of heavenly things (that be therein promised of God) shall increase in him. And there is nothing that so much strengtheneth our faith and trust in God, that so much keepeth up innocency and pureness of the heart, and also of outward godly life and conversation, as continual reading and recording of God's word. For that thing, which (by continual use of reading of holy scripture, and diligent searching of the same) is deeply imprinted and graven in the heart, at length turneth almost into nature. And moreover, the effect and virtue of God's word is to illuminate the ignorant, and to give more light unto them that faithfully and diligently read it, to comfort their hearts, and to encourage them to perform that, which of God is commanded. It teacheth patience in all adversity, in prosperity humbleness; what honour is due unto God, what mercy and charity to our neighbour. It giveth good counsel in all doubtful things. It sheweth of whom we shall look for aid and help in all perils, and that God is the only giver of victory in all battles and temptations of our enemies, bodily and ghostly. And in reading of God's word, he most profiteth not always that is most ready in turning of the book, or in saying of it without the book; but he that is most turned into it, that is most inspired with the Holy Ghost, most in his heart and life altered and changed into that thing which he readeth; he that is daily less and less proud, less wrathful, less covetous, and less desirous of worldly and vain pleasures; he that daily (forsaking his old vicious life) increaseth in virtue more and more. And, to be short, there is nothing that more maintaineth godliness of the mind, and driveth away ungodliness, than doth the continual reading or hearing of God's word, if it be joined with a godly mind, and a good affection to know and follow God's will. For without a single eye, pure intent, and good mind, nothing is allowed for good before God. And, on the other side, nothing more darkeneth Christ and the glory of God, nor bringeth in more blindness and all kinds of vices, than doth the ignorance of God's word.

*The Second Part of the Sermon of the Knowledge
of Holy Scripture.*

In the first part of this sermon, which exhorteth to the knowledge of holy scripture, was declared wherefore the knowledge of the same is necessary and profitable to all men, and that by the true knowledge and understanding of scripture, the most necessary points of our duty towards God and our neighbours are also known. Now as concerning the same matter you shall hear what followeth. If we profess Christ, why be we not ashamed to be ignorant in his doctrine? seeing that every man is ashamed to be ignorant in that learning which he professeth. That man is ashamed to be called a philosopher which readeth not the books of philosophy, and to be called a lawyer, an astronomer, or a physician, that is ignorant in the books of law, astronomy, and physic. How can any man then say that he professeth Christ and his religion, if he will not apply himself (as far forth as he can or may conveniently) to read and hear, and so to know the books of Christ's gospel and doctrine? Although other sciences be good, and to be learned, yet no man can deny but this is the chief, and passeth all other incomparably. What excuse shall we therefore make, at the last day before Christ, that delight to read or hear men's fantasies and inventions, more than his most holy Gospel? and will find no time to do that which chiefly, above all things, we should do, and will rather read other things than that, for the which we ought rather to leave reading of all other things. Let us therefore apply ourselves, as far forth as we can have time and leisure, to know God's word, by diligent hearing and reading thereof, as many as profess God, and have faith and trust in him. But they that have no good affection to God's word (to colour this their fault) allege commonly two vain and feigned excuses. Some go about to excuse them by their own frailness and fearfulness, saying, that they dare not read holy scripture, lest through their ignorance they should fall into any error. Other pretend that the difficulty to understand it and the hardness thereof is so great, that it is meet to be read only of clerks and learned men.

As touching the first: Ignorance of God's word is the cause of all error, as Christ himself affirmed to the Sadducees, saying, that "they erred, because they knew not the scripture." How should they then eschew error, that will be still ignorant? And how should they come out of ignorance, that will not read nor hear that thing which should give them knowledge? He that now hath most knowledge, was at the first ignorant; yet he forbare not to read, for fear he should fall into error: but he diligently read, lest he should remain in ignorance, and through ignorance in error. And if you will not know the truth of God (a thing most necessary for you) lest you fall into error; by the same reason you may then lie still, and never go, lest, if you go, you fall into the mire; nor eat any good meat, lest you take a surfeit; nor sow your corn, nor labour in your occupation, nor use your merchandise, for fear you lose your seed, your labour, your stock, and so by that reason it should be best for you to live idly, and never to take in hand to do any manner of good thing, lest peradventure some evil thing may chance thereof. And if you be afraid to fall into error by reading of holy scripture, I shall shew you how you may read it without danger of error. Read it humbly with a meek and lowly heart, to the intent you may glorify God, and not yourself, with the knowledge of it: and read it not without daily praying to God, that he would direct your reading to good effect; and take upon you to expound it no further than you can plainly understand it. For, as St. Augustine saith, the knowledge of holy scripture is a great, large, and a high place; but the door is very low, so that the high and arrogant man cannot run in; but he must stoop low, and humble himself, that shall enter into it. Presumption and arrogancy is the mother of all error; and humility needeth to fear no error. For humility will only search to know the truth; it will search, and will bring together one place with another, and where it cannot find out the meaning, it will pray, it will ask of other that know, and will not presumptuously and rashly define any thing which it knoweth not. Therefore the humble man may search any truth boldly in the scripture, without any danger of error. And if he be ignorant, he ought the more to read and to search holy scripture, to bring him out of ignorance. I say not nay, but a man may prosper with only hearing; but he may much more prosper with both hearing and reading. This have I said as touching the fear to read, through ignorance of the person.

And concerning the hardness of scripture; he that is so weak that he is not able to brook strong meat, yet he may suck the sweet and tender milk, and defer the rest until he wax stronger, and come to more knowledge. For God receiveth the learned and unlearned, and casteth away none, but is indifferent unto all. And the scripture is full, as well of low valleys, plain ways, and easy for every man to use and to walk in; as also of high hills and mountains, which few men can climb unto. And whosoever giveth his mind to holy scriptures with diligent study and burning desire, it cannot be, saith St. Chrysostom, that he should be left without help. For either God Almighty will send him some godly doctor to teach him, as he did to instruct Eunuchus, a nobleman of Ethiope, and treasurer unto queen Candace, who having affection to read the scripture, (although he understood it not,) yet for the desire that he had unto God's word, God sent his apostle Philip to declare unto him the true sense of the scripture that he read; or else, if we lack a learned man to instruct and teach us, yet God himself from above will give light unto our minds, and teach us those things which are necessary for us, and wherein we be ignorant. And in another place Chrysostom saith, that man's human and worldly wisdom or science needeth not to the understanding of scripture, but the revelation of the Holy Ghost, who inspireth the true meaning unto them, that with humility and diligence do search therefore. "He that asketh shall have, and he that seeketh shall find, and he that knocketh shall have the door open." If we read once, twice, or thrice, and understand not, let us not cease so, but still continue reading, praying, asking of other, and so by still knocking, at the last the door shall be opened; as St. Augustin saith, Although many things in the scripture be spoken in obscure mysteries, yet there is nothing spoken under dark mysteries in one place, but the selfsame thing in other places is spoken more familiarly and plainly, to the capacity both of learned and unlearned. And those things in the scripture that be plain to understand, and necessary for salvation, every man's duty is to learn them, to print them in memory, and effectually to exercise them. And as for the dark mysteries, to be contented to be ignorant in them, until such time as it shall please God to open those things unto him. In the mean season, if he lack either aptness or opportunity, God will not impute it to his folly: but yet it behoveth not, that such as be apt should set aside reading, because some other be unapt to read; nevertheless, for the hardness of such places, the reading of the whole ought not to be set apart. And briefly to conclude, as St. Augustin saith, by the scripture all men be amended, weak men be strengthened, and strong men be comforted. So that surely none be enemies to the reading of God's word, but such as either be so ignorant, that they know not how wholesome a thing it is; or else be so sick, that they hate the most comfortable medicine that should heal them; or so ungodly, that they would wish the people still to continue in blindness and ignorance of God.

Thus we have briefly touched some part of the commodities of God's holy word, which is one of God's chief and principal benefits, given and declared to mankind here in earth. Let us thank God heartily for this his great and special gift, beneficial favour, and fatherly providence; let us be glad to receive this precious gift of our heavenly father; let us hear, read, and know these holy rules, injunctions, and statutes of our Christian religion, and upon that we have made profession to God at our baptism; let us with fear and reverence lay up, in the chest of our hearts, these necessary and fruitful lessons; let us night and day muse, and have meditation and contemplation in them; let us ruminate, and, as it were, chew the cud, that we may have the sweet juice, spiritual effect, marrow, honey, kernel, taste, comfort, and consolation of them; let us stay, quiet, and certify our consciences, with the most infallible certainty, truth, and perpetual assurance of them: let us pray to God (the only author of these heavenly studies) that we may speak, think, believe, live, and depart hence, according to the wholesome doctrine and verities of them. And, by that means, in this world we shall have God's defence, favour, and grace, with the unspeakable solace of peace, and quietness of conscience; and after this miserable life we shall enjoy the endless bliss and glory of heaven: which he grant us all, that died for us all, Jesus Christ, to whom, with the Father and the Holy Ghost, be all honour and glory, both now and everlastingly. Amen.

A SERMON OF THE SALVATION OF MANKIND,
BY ONLY CHRIST OUR SAVIOUR, FROM SIN AND
DEATH EVERLASTING.

Because all men be sinners and offenders against God, and breakers of his law and commandments, therefore can no man by his own acts, works, and deeds (seem they never so good) be justified, and made righteous before God: But every man of necessity is constrained to seek for another righteousness or justification, to be received at God's own hands, that is to say, the forgiveness of his sins and trespasses, in such things as he hath offended. And this justification or righteousness, which we so receive of God's mercy and Christ's merits, embraced by faith, is taken, accepted, and allowed of God, for our perfect and full justification. For the more full understanding hereof, it is our parts and duties ever to remember the great mercy of God, how that (all the world being wrapped in sin by breaking of the law) God sent his only son our saviour Christ, into this world, to fulfil the law for us, and, by shedding of his most precious blood, to make a sacrifice and satisfaction, or (as it may be called) amends to his Father for our sins, to assuage his wrath and indignation conceived against us for the same.

Insomuch that infants, being baptized and dying in their infancy, are by this sacrifice washed from their sins, brought to God's favour, and made his children, and inheritors of his kingdom of heaven. And they, which in act or deed do sin after their baptism, when they turn again to God unfeignedly, they are likewise washed by this sacrifice from their sins, in such sort, that there remaineth not any spot of sin, that shall be imputed to their damnation. This is that justification or righteousness which St. Paul speaketh of, when he saith, "No man is justified by the works of the law, but freely by faith in Jesus Christ." And again he saith, "We believe in Jesu Christ, that we be justified freely by the faith of Christ, and not by the works of the law, because that no man shall be justified by the works of the law." And although this justification be free unto us, yet it cometh not so freely unto us, that there is no ransom paid therefore at all. But here may man's reason be astonied, reasoning after this fashion: if a ransom be paid for our redemption, then is it not given us freely. For a prisoner that paid his ransom is not let go freely; for if he go freely, then he goeth without ransom: for what is it else to go freely, than to be set at liberty without paying of ransom? This reason is satisfied by the great wisdom of God in this mystery of our redemption, who hath so tempered his justice and mercy together, that he would neither by his justice condemn us unto the everlasting captivity of the devil, and his prison of hell, remediless for ever without mercy, nor by his mercy deliver us clearly, without justice, or payment of a just ransom: but with his endless mercy he joined his most upright and equal justice. His great mercy he shewed unto us in delivering us from our former captivity, without requiring of any ransom to be paid, or amends to be made upon our parts, which thing by us had been impossible to be done. And whereas it lay not in us that to do, he provided a ransom for us, that was, the most precious body and blood of his own most dear and best beloved son Jesu Christ, who, besides this ransom, fulfilled the law for us perfectly. And so the justice of God and his mercy did embrace together, and fulfilled the mystery of our redemption. And of this justice and mercy of God, knit together, speaketh St. Paul in the third chapter to the Romans, "All have offended, and have need of the glory of God; but are justified freely by his grace, by redemption which is in Jesu Christ, whom God hath set forth to us for a reconciler and peace-maker, through faith in his blood, to shew his righteousness." And in the tenth chapter, "Christ is the end of the law, unto righteousness, to every man that believeth." And in the eighth chapter, "That which was impossible by the law, inasmuch as it was weak by the flesh, God sending his own son in the similitude of sinful flesh, by sin damned sin in the flesh, that the righteousness of the law might be fulfilled in us, which walk not after the flesh, but after the Spirit." In these foresaid places, the apostle toucheth specially three things, which must go together in our justification. Upon God's part, his great mercy and grace; upon Christ's part, justice, that is, the satisfaction of God's justice, or the price of our redemption, by the offering of his body, and shedding of his blood, with fulfilling of the law perfectly and throughly; and upon our part, true and lively faith in the merits of Jesus Christ, which yet is not ours, but by God's working in us: so that in our justification, is not only God's mercy and grace, but also his justice, which the apostle calleth the justice of God, and it consisteth in paying our ransom, and fulfilling of the law: and so the grace of God doth not shut out the justice of God in our justification, but only shutteth out the justice of man, that is to say, the justice of our works, as to be merits of deserving our justification. And therefore St. Paul declareth here nothing upon the behalf of man concerning his justification, but only a true and lively faith, which nevertheless is the gift of God, and not man's only work, without God. And yet that faith doth not shut out repentance, hope, love, dread, and the fear of God, to be joined with faith in every man that is justified; but it shutteth them out from the office of justifying. So that, although they be all present together in him that is justified, yet they justify not altogether. Nor the faith also doth not shut out the justice of our good works, necessarily to be done afterwards of duty towards God; (for we are most bounden to serve God, in doing good deeds, commanded by him in his holy scripture, all the days of our life;) but it excludeth them, so that we may not do them to this intent, to be made good by doing of them. For all the good works that we can do be unperfect, and therefore not able to deserve our justification: but our justification doth come freely by the mere mercy of God, and of so great and free mercy, that, whereas all the world was not able of theirselves to pay any part towards their ransom, it pleased our heavenly Father of his infinite mercy, without any our desert or deserving, to prepare for us the most precious jewels of Christ's body and blood, whereby our ransom might be fully paid, the law fulfilled, and his justice fully satisfied. So that Christ is now the righteousness of all them that truly do believe in him. He for them paid their ransom by his death. He for them fulfilled the law in his life. So that now in him, and by him, every true Christian man may be called a fulfiller of the law; forasmuch as that which their infirmity lacked, Christ's justice hath supplied.

The Second Part of the Sermon of Salvation.

Ye have heard, of whom all men ought to seek their justification and righteousness, and how also this righteousness cometh unto men by Christ's death and merits: ye heard also, how that three things are required to the obtaining of our righteousness, that is, God's mercy, Christ's justice, and a true and lively faith, out of the which faith springeth good works. Also before was declared at large, that no man can be justified by his own good works, that no man fulfilleth the law, according to the full request of the law.

And St. Paul in his Epistle to the Galatians proveth the same, saying thus: "If there had been any law given, which could have justified, verily righteousness should have been by the law." And again he saith, "If righteousness be by the law, then Christ died in vain." And again he saith, "You that are justified by the law are fallen away from grace." And furthermore, he writeth to the Ephesians on this wise, "By grace are ye saved through faith, and that not of yourselves, for it is the gift of God, and not of works, lest any man should glory." And, to be short, the sum of all Paul's disputation is this; that if justice come of works, then it cometh not of grace; and if it come of grace, then it cometh not of works. And to this end tendeth all the prophets, as St. Peter saith in the tenth of the Acts: "Of Christ all the prophets," saith St. Peter, "do witness, that through his name, all they that believe in him shall receive the remission of sins." And after this wise to be justified only by this true and lively faith in Christ, speaketh all the old and ancient authors, both Greeks and Latins; of whom I will specially rehearse three, Hilary, Basil, and Ambrose. St. Hilary saith these words plainly in the ninth canon upon Matthew; "Faith only justifieth." And St. Basil, a Greek author, writeth thus; "This is a perfect and whole rejoicing in God, when a man advanceth not himself for his own righteousness, but knowledgeth himself to lack true justice and righteousness, and to be justified by the only faith in Christ. And Paul," saith he, "doth glory in the contempt of his own righteousness, and that he looketh for the righteousness of God by faith."

These be the very words of St. Basil; and St. Ambrose, a Latin author, saith these words; "This is the ordinance of God, that they which believe in Christ should be saved without works, by faith only, freely receiving remission of their sins." Consider diligently these words, without works, by faith only, freely we receive remission of our sins. What can be spoken more plainly, than to say, that freely without works, by faith only, we obtain remission of our sins? These and other like sentences, that we be justified by faith only, freely, and without works, we do read ofttimes in the most and best ancient writers: as, beside Hilary, Basil, and St. Ambrose, before rehearsed, we read the same in Origen, St. Chrysostom, St. Cyprian, St. Augustin, Prosper, Œcumenius, Photius, Bernardus, Anselm, and many other authors, Greek and Latin. Nevertheless, this sentence, that we be justified by faith only, is not so meant of them, that the said justifying faith is alone in man, without true repentance, hope, charity, dread, and the fear of God, at any time and season. Nor when they say, that we be justified freely, they mean not that we should or might afterwards be idle, and that nothing should be required on our parts afterward: neither they mean not so to be justified without good words, that we should do no good works at all, like as shall be more expressed at large hereafter. But this saying, that we be justified by faith only, freely, and without works, is spoken for to take away clearly all merit of our works, as being unable to deserve our justification at God's hands, and thereby most plainly to express the weakness of man, and the goodness of God; the great infirmity of ourselves, and the might and power of God; the imperfectness of our own works, and the most abundant grace of our saviour Christ; and therefore wholly to ascribe the merit and deserving of our justification unto Christ only, and his most precious bloodshedding. This faith the holy scripture teacheth us; this is the strong rock and foundation of Christian religion; this doctrine all old and ancient authors of Christ's church do approve; this doctrine advanceth and setteth forth the true glory of Christ, and beateth down the vain-glory of man; this whosoever denieth, is not to be accounted for a Christian man, nor for a setter-forth of Christ's glory; but for an adversary to Christ and his gospel, and for a setter-forth of men's vain-glory. And although this doctrine be never so true, (as it is most true indeed,) that we be justified freely, without all merit of our own good works, (as St. Paul doth express it,) and freely, by this lively and perfect faith in Christ only, (as the ancient authors use to speak it,) yet this true doctrine must be also truly understood, and most plainly declared, lest carnal men should take unjustly occasion thereby to live carnally, after the appetite and will of the world, the flesh, and the devil. And because no man should err by mistaking of this doctrine, I shall plainly and shortly so declare the right understanding of the same, that no man shall justly think that he may thereby take any occasion of carnal liberty, to follow the desires of the flesh, or that thereby any kind of sin shall be committed, or any ungodly living the more used.

First, you shall understand, that in our justification by Christ it is not all one thing, the office of God unto man, and the office of man unto God. Justification is not the office of man, but of God; for man cannot make himself righteous by his own works, neither in part, nor in the whole; for that were the greatest arrogancy and presumption of man that Antichrist could set up against God, to affirm that a man might by his own works take away and purge his own sins, and so justify himself. But justification is the office of God only, and is not a thing which we render unto him, but which we receive of him; not which we give to him, but which we take of him, by his free mercy, and by the only merits of his most dearly beloved son, our only redeemer, saviour, and justifier, Jesus Christ: so that the true understanding of this doctrine, we be justified freely by faith without works, or that we be justified by faith in Christ only, is not, that this our own act to believe in Christ, or this our faith in Christ, which is within us, doth justify us, and deserve our justification unto us; (for that were to count ourselves to be justified by some act or virtue that is within ourselves;) but the true understanding and meaning thereof is, that although we hear God's word, and believe it; although we have faith, hope, charity, repentance, dread, and fear of God within us, and do never so many works thereunto; yet we must renounce the merit of all our said virtues, of faith, hope, charity, and all other virtues and good deeds, which we either have done, shall do, or can do, as things that be far too weak and insufficient, and unperfect, to deserve remission of our sins, and our justification; and therefore we must trust only in God's mercy, and that sacrifice which our high priest and saviour Christ Jesus, the son of God, once offered for us upon the cross, to obtain thereby God's grace and remission, as well of our original sin in baptism, as of all actual sin committed by us after our baptism, if we truly repent, and turn unfeignedly to him again. So that, as St. John Baptist, although he were never so virtuous and godly a man, yet in this matter of forgiving of sin, he did put the people from him, and appointed them unto Christ, saying thus unto them, "Behold, yonder is the lamb of God, which taketh away the sins of the world;" even so, as great and as godly a virtue as the lively faith is, yet it putteth us from itself, and remitteth or appointeth us unto Christ, for to have only by him remission of our sins, or justification. So that our faith in Christ (as it were) saith unto us thus: It is not I that take away your sins, but it is Christ only; and to him only I send you for that purpose, forsaking therein all your good virtues, words, thoughts, and works, and only putting your trust in Christ.

The Third Part of the Sermon of Salvation.

It hath been manifestly declared unto you, that no man can fulfil the law of God; and therefore by the law all men are condemned: whereupon it followeth necessarily, that some other thing should be required for our salvation than the law; and that is, a true and a lively faith in Christ; bringing forth good works, and a life according to God's commandments. And also you heard the ancient authors' minds of this saying, Faith in Christ only justifieth man, so plainly declared, that you see, that the very true meaning of this proposition or saying, We be justified by faith in Christ only (according to the meaning of the old ancient authors) is this: We put our faith in Christ, that we be justified by him only, that we be justified by God's free mercy, and the merits of our Saviour Christ only, and by no virtue or good works of our own that is in us, or that we can be able to have, or to do, for to deserve the same; Christ himself only being the cause meritorious thereof.

Here you perceive many words to be used to avoid contention in words with them that delight to brawl about words, and also to shew the true meaning to avoid evil taking and misunderstanding; and yet peradventure all will not serve with them that be contentious; but contenders will ever forge matters of contention, even when they have none occasion thereto. Notwithstanding, such be the less to be passed upon, so that the rest may profit, which will be more desirous to know the truth, than (when it is plain enough) to contend about it, and with contentious and captious cavillation, to obscure and darken it. Truth it is, that our own works do not justify us, to speak properly of our justification; that is to say, our works do not merit or deserve remission of our sins, and make us, of unjust, just before God: but God of his own mercy, through the only merits and deservings of his son Jesus Christ, doth justify us. Nevertheless, because faith doth directly send us to Christ for remission of our sins, and that, by faith given us of God, we embrace the promise of God's mercy, and of the remission of our sins, (which thing none other of our virtues or works properly doth,) therefore scripture useth to say, that faith without works doth justify. And forasmuch that it is all one sentence in effect, to say, faith without works, and only faith, doth justify us; therefore the old ancient fathers of the church from time to time have uttered our justification with this speech; Only faith justifieth us; meaning none other thing than St. Paul meant, when he said, "Faith without works justifieth us." And because all this is brought to pass through the only merits and deservings of our saviour Christ, and not through our merits, or through the merit of any virtue that we have within us, or of any work that cometh from us; therefore, in that respect of merit and deserving, we forsake, as it were, altogether again, faith, works, and all other virtues. For our own imperfection is so great, through the corruption of original sin, that all is unperfect that is within us, faith, charity, hope, dread, thoughts, words, and works, and therefore not apt to merit and deserve any part of our justification for us. And this form of speaking use we, in the humbling of ourselves to God, and to give all the glory to our saviour Christ, which is best worthy to have it.

Here you have heard the office of God in our justification, and how we receive it of him freely, by his mercy, without our deserts, through true and lively faith. Now you shall hear the office and duty of a Christian man unto God, what we ought on our part to render unto God again for his great mercy and goodness. Our office is, not to pass the time of this present life unfruitfully and idly, after that we are baptized or justified, not caring how few good works we do, to the glory of God, and profit of our neighbours: much less is it our office, after that we be once made Christ's members, to live contrary to the same; making ourselves members of the devil, walking after his enticements, and after the suggestions of the world and the flesh, whereby we know that we do serve the world and the devil, and not God. For that faith which bringeth forth (without repentance) either evil works, or no good works, is not a right, pure, and lively faith, but a dead, devilish, counterfeit, and feigned faith, as St. Paul and St. James call it. For even the devils know and believe that Christ was born of a virgin; that he fasted forty days and forty nights without meat and drink; that he wrought all kind of miracles, declaring himself very God: they believe also, that Christ for our sakes suffered most painful death, to redeem us from everlasting death, and that he rose again from death the third day: they believe that he ascended into heaven, and that he sitteth on the right hand of the Father, and at the last end of this world shall come again, and judge both the quick and the dead. These articles of our faith the devils believe, and so they believe all things that be written in the New and Old Testament to be true: and yet for all this faith they be but devils, remaining still in their damnable estate, lacking the very true Christian faith. For the right and true Christian faith is, not only to believe that holy scripture, and all the foresaid articles of our faith are true; but also to have a sure trust and confidence in God's merciful promises, to be saved from everlasting damnation by Christ: whereof doth follow a loving heart to obey his commandments. And this true Christian faith neither any devil hath, nor yet any man, which in the outward profession of his mouth, and in his outward receiving of the sacraments, in coming to the church, and in all other outward appearances, seemeth to be a Christian man, and yet in his living and deeds sheweth the contrary. For how can a man have this true faith, this sure trust and confidence in God, that by the merits of Christ his sins be forgiven, and he reconciled to the favour of God, and to be partaker of the kingdom of heaven by Christ, when he liveth ungodly, and denieth Christ in his deeds? Surely no such ungodly man can have this faith and trust in God. For as they know Christ to be the only saviour of the world; so they know also that wicked men shall not enjoy the kingdom of God. They know that God hateth unrighteousness; that he will destroy all those that speak untruly; that those which have done good works (which cannot be done without a lively faith in Christ) shall come forth into the resurrection of life, and those that have done evil shall come unto the resurrection of judgment. Very well they know also, that to them that be contentious, and to them that will not be obedient unto the truth, but will obey unrighteousness, shall come indignation, wrath, and affliction, etc. Therefore, to conclude, considering the infinite benefits of God, shewed and given unto us mercifully without our deserts, who hath not only created us of nothing, and from a piece of vile clay, of his infinite goodness hath exalted us, as touching our soul, unto his own similitude and likeness; but also, whereas we were condemned to hell and death everlasting, hath given his own natural son, being God eternal, immortal, and equal unto himself in power and glory, to be incarnated, and to take our mortal nature upon him, with the infirmities of the same, and in the same nature to suffer most shameful and painful death for our offences, to the intent to justify us, and to restore us to life everlasting: so making us also his dear children, brethren unto his only son our saviour Christ, and inheritors for ever with him of his eternal kingdom of heaven.

These great and merciful benefits of God, if they be well considered, do neither minister unto us occasion to be idle, and to live without doing any good works, neither yet stirreth us up by any means to do evil things; but contrariwise, if we be not desperate persons, and our hearts harder than stones, they move us to render ourselves unto God wholly, with all our will, hearts, might, and power, to serve him in all good deeds, obeying his commandments during our lives, to seek in all things his glory and honour, not our sensual pleasures and vain-glory; evermore dreading willingly to offend such a merciful God and loving redeemer, in word, thought, or deed. And the said benefits of God, deeply considered, move us for his sake also to be ever ready to give ourselves to our neighbours, and, as much as lieth in us, to study with all our endeavour to do good to every man. These be the fruits of true faith, to do good as much as lieth in us to every man, and, above all things, and in all things, to advance the glory of God, of whom only we have our sanctification, justification, salvation, and redemption: to whom be ever glory, praise, and honour, world without end. Amen.

A SHORT DECLARATION OF THE TRUE, LIVELY, AND CHRISTIAN FAITH.

The first coming unto God, good Christian people, is through faith, whereby (as it is declared in the last sermon) we be justified before God. And lest any man should be deceived, for lack of right understanding thereof, it is diligently to be noted, that faith is taken in the scripture two manner of ways. There is one faith, which in scripture is called a dead faith, which bringeth forth no good works; but is idle, barren, and unfruitful. And this faith, by the holy apostle St. James, is compared to the faith of devils, which believe God to be true and just, and tremble for fear; yet they do nothing well but all evil. And such a manner of faith have the wicked and naughty Christian people, "which confess God," as St. Paul saith, "in their mouth," but "deny him in their deeds, being abominable, and without the right faith, and to all good works reprovable." And this faith is a persuasion and belief in man's heart, whereby he knoweth that there is a God, and agreeth unto all truth of God's most holy word, contained in the holy scripture. So that it consisteth only in believing in the word of God, that it is true. And this is not properly called faith. But as he that readeth Caesar's Commentaries, believing the same to be true, hath thereby a knowledge of Caesar's life and notable acts, because he believeth the history of Caesar: yet it is not properly said, that he believeth in Caesar, of whom he looketh for no help nor benefit. Even so, he that believeth that all that is spoken of God in the Bible is true, and yet liveth so ungodly, that he cannot look to enjoy the promises and benefits of God; although it may be said, that such a man hath a faith and belief to the words of God; yet it is not properly said that he believeth in God, or hath such a faith and trust in God, whereby he may surely look for grace, mercy, and everlasting life at God's hand, but rather for indignation and punishment, according to the merits of his wicked life. For as it is written in a book, intituled to be of Didymus Alexandrinus, "Forasmuch as faith without works is dead, it is not now faith, as a dead man is not a man." This dead faith therefore is not the sure and substantial faith which saveth sinners. Another faith there is in scripture, which is not, as the foresaid faith, idle, unfruitful, and dead, but worketh by charity, (as St. Paul declareth, Gal. v.) which as the other vain faith is called a dead faith, so may this be called a quick or lively faith. And this is not only the common belief of the articles of our faith, but it is also a true trust and confidence of the mercy of God through our Lord Jesus Christ, and a steadfast hope of all good things to be received at God's hand: and that although we, through infirmity, or temptation of our ghostly enemy, do fall from him by sin; yet if we return again unto him by true repentance, that he will forgive and forget our offences for his son's sake, our saviour Jesus Christ, and will make us inheritors with him of his everlasting kingdom; and that in the mean time, until that kingdom come, he will be our protector and defender in all perils and dangers, whatsoever do chance: and that though sometime he doth send us sharp adversity, yet that evermore he will be a loving Father unto us, correcting us for our sin, but not withdrawing his mercy finally from us, if we trust in him, and commit ourselves wholly unto him, hang only upon him, and call upon him, ready to obey and serve him. This is the true, lively, and unfeigned Christian faith, and is not in the mouth and outward profession only, but it liveth, and stirreth inwardly in the heart. And this faith is not without hope and trust in God, nor without the love of God and of our neighbours, nor without the fear of God, nor without the

desire to hear God's word, and to follow the same
in eschewing evil, and doing gladly all good works.

This faith, as St. Paul describeth it, "is the sure
ground and foundation of the benefits which we ought
to look for," and trust to receive of God a certificate
and sure looking for them, although they yet sensibly
appear not unto us. And after he saith, "He that
cometh to God, must believe, both that he is, and that
he is a merciful rewarder of well-doers." And nothing
commendeth good men unto God so much as this assured faith and trust in him. Of this faith three things
are specially to be noted.

First, that this faith doth not lie dead in the heart,
but is lively and fruitful in bringing forth good works.
Second, that without it can no good works be done,
that shall be acceptable and pleasant to God. Third,
what manner of good works they be that this faith
doth bring forth.

For the first, as the light cannot be hid, but will
shew forth itself at one place or other; so a true faith
cannot be kept secret; but when occasion is offered,
it will break out, and shew itself by good works. And
as the living body of a man ever exerciseth such things
as belong to a natural and living body, for nourishment and preservation of the same, as it hath need,
opportunity, and occasion; even so the soul that hath
a lively faith in it will be doing alway some good work,
which shall declare that it is living, and will not be
unoccupied. Therefore, when men hear in the scriptures so high commendations of faith, that it maketh
us to please God, to live with God, and to be the
children of God; if then they phantasy that they be
set at liberty from doing all good works, and may
live as they list, they trifle with God, and deceive
themselves. And it is a manifest token that they be
far from having the true and lively faith, and also
far from knowledge what true faith meaneth. For
the very sure and lively Christian faith is, not only to
believe all things of God which are contained in holy
scripture, but also is an earnest trust and confidence

in God, that he doth regard us, and that he is careful over us, as the father is over the child whom he doth love, and that he will be merciful unto us for his only son's sake, and that we have our saviour Christ our perpetual advocate and priest, in whose only merits, oblation, and suffering, we do trust that our offences be continually washed and purged, whensoever we, repenting truly, do return to him with our whole heart, steadfastly determining with ourselves, through his grace, to obey and serve him in keeping his commandments, and never to turn back again to sin. Such is the true faith that the scripture doth so much commend, the which, when it seeth and considereth what God hath done for us, is also moved, through continual assistance of the Spirit of God, to serve and please him, to keep his favour, to fear his displeasure, to continue his obedient children, shewing thankfulness again by observing or keeping his commandments, and that freely, for true love chiefly, and not for dread of punishment, or love of temporal reward, considering how clearly, without deservings, we have received his mercy and pardon freely.

This true faith will shew forth itself, and cannot long be idle: for as it is written, "The just man doth live by his faith." He never sleepeth, nor is idle, when he would wake and be well occupied. And God by his prophet Jeremy saith, that "he is a happy and blessed man, which hath faith and confidence in God." For he is like a tree set by the water-side, and spreadeth his roots abroad toward the moisture, and feareth not heat when it cometh; his leaf will be green, and will not cease to bring forth his fruit: even so, faithful men, putting away all fear of adversity, will shew forth the fruit of their good works, as occasion is offered to do them.

The Second Part of the Sermon of Faith.

YE have heard in the first part of this sermon, that there be two kinds of faith, a dead and an unfruitful faith, and a faith lively, that worketh by charity: the first, to be unprofitable; the second, necessary for the obtaining of our salvation: the which faith hath charity always joined unto it, and is fruitful, and bringeth forth all good works. Now as concerning the same matter, you shall hear what followeth. The wise man saith, "He that believeth in God will hearken unto his commandments." For if we do not shew ourselves faithful in our conversation, the faith which we pretend to have is but a feigned faith: because the true Christian faith is manifestly shewed by good living, and not by words only, as St. Augustin saith, "Good living cannot be separated from true faith, which worketh by love." And St. Chrysostom saith, "Faith of itself is full of good works: as soon as a man doth believe, he shall be garnished with them." How plentiful, this faith is of good works, and how it maketh the work of one man more acceptable to God than of another, St. Paul teacheth at large in the eleventh chapter to the Hebrews, saying, that "faith made the oblation of Abel better than the oblation of Cain." This made Noe to "build the ark." This made Abraham to "forsake his country, and all his friends, and to go into a far country," there to dwell among strangers. So did also Isaac and Jacob, depending or hanging only of the help and trust that they had in God. And when they came to the country which God promised them, they would build no cities, towns, nor houses; but lived like strangers in tents, that might every day be removed. Their trust was so much in God, that they set but little by any worldly thing, for that God had prepared for them better dwelling-places in heaven, of his own foundation and building. This faith made Abraham ready at God's commandment to offer his own son and heir Isaac, whom he loved so well, and by whom he was promised to have innumerable issue, among the which, one should be born, in "whom all nations should be blessed," trusting so much in God, that though he were slain, yet that God was able by his omnipotent power to raise him from death, and perform his promise. He mistrusted not the promise of God, although unto his reason every thing seemed contrary. He believed verily that God would not forsake him in dearth and famine that was in the country. And in all other dangers that he was brought unto, he trusted ever that God should be his God, and his protector and defender, whatsoever he saw to the contrary. This faith wrought so in the heart of Moses, that he "refused to be taken for king Pharao his daughter's son, and to have great inheritance in Egypt, thinking it better with the people of God to have affliction and sorrow," than with naughty men in sin to live pleasantly for a time. "By faith he cared not for the threatening of king Pharao:" for his trust was so in God, that he passed not of the felicity of this world, but looked for the reward to come in heaven; setting his heart upon the invisible God, as if he had seen him ever present before his eyes. "By faith the children of Israel passed through the Red sea. By faith the walls of Jericho fell down without stroke," and many other wonderful miracles have been wrought. In all good men that heretofore have been, faith hath brought forth their good works, and obtained the promises of God. "Faith hath stopped the lions' mouths: faith hath quenched the force of fire: faith hath escaped the sword's edges: faith hath given weak men strength, victory in battle, overthrown the armies of infidels, raised the dead to life:" faith hath made good men to take adversity in good part; some have been "mocked and whipped, bound and cast in prison; some have lost all their goods, and lived in great poverty; some have wandered in mountains, hills, and wilderness: some have been racked, some slain, some stoned, some sawn, some rent in pieces, some beheaded, some brent without mercy, and would not be delivered, because they looked to rise again to a better state."

All these fathers, martyrs, and other holy men, whom St. Paul spake of, had their faith surely fixed in God, when all the world was against them. They did not only know God to be the lord, maker, and governor of all men in the world; but also they had a special confidence and trust, that he was and would be their God, their comforter, aider, helper, maintainer, and defender. This is the Christian faith, which these holy men had, and we also ought to have. And although they were not named Christian men, yet was it a Christian faith that they had; for they looked for all benefits of God the father, through the merits of his son Jesu Christ, as we now do. This difference is between them and us, that they looked when Christ should come, and we be in the time when he is come. Therefore, saith St. Augustin, "The time is altered and changed, but not the faith." For we have both one faith in one Christ. "The same Holy Ghost also that we have, had they," saith St. Paul. For as the Holy Ghost doth teach us to trust in God, and to call upon him as our Father, so did he teach them to say, as it is written, "Thou, Lord, art our father and redeemer; and thy name is without beginning, and everlasting." God gave them then grace to be his children, as he doth us now. But now, by the coming of our saviour Christ we have received more abundantly the Spirit of God in our hearts, whereby we may conceive a greater faith, and a surer trust, than many of them had. But in effect they and we be all one: we have the same faith that they had in God, and they the same that we have. And St. Paul so much extolleth their faith, because we should no less, but rather more, give ourselves wholly unto Christ, both in profession and living, now when Christ is come, than the old fathers did before his coming. And by all the declaration of St. Paul, it is evident, that the true, lively, and Christian faith is no dead, vain, or unfruitful thing, but a thing of perfect virtue, of wonderful operation or working, and strength, bringing forth all good motions and good works.

All holy scripture agreeably beareth witness, that a true lively faith in Christ doth bring forth good works; and therefore every man must examine and try himself diligently, to know whether he have the same true lively faith in his heart unfeignedly, nor not; which he shall know by the fruits thereof. Many that professed the faith of Christ were in this error, that they thought they knew God, and believed in him, when in their life they declared the contrary. . . .

The Third Part of the Sermon of Faith.

YOU have heard in the second part of this sermon, that no man should think that he hath that lively faith which scripture commandeth, when he liveth not obediently to God's laws; for all good works spring out of that faith: and also it hath been declared unto you by examples, that faith maketh men steadfast, quiet, and patient in all affliction. Now as concerning the same matter, you shall hear what followeth. A man may soon deceive himself, and think in his own phantasy that he by faith knoweth God, loveth him, feareth him, and belongeth to him, when in very deed he doth nothing less. For the trial of all these things is a very godly and Christian life. He that feeleth his heart set to seek God's honour, and studieth to know the will and commandments of God, and to frame himself thereunto, and leadeth not his life after the desire of his own flesh, to serve the devil by sin, but setteth his mind to serve God for his own sake, and for his sake also to love all his neighbours, whether they be friends or adversaries, doing good to every man, as opportunity serveth, and willingly hurting no man: such a man may well rejoice in God, perceiving by the trade of his life, that he unfeignedly hath the right knowledge of God, a lively faith, a steadfast hope, a true and unfeigned love, and fear of God. But he that casteth away the yoke of God's commandments from his neck, and giveth himself to live without true repentance, after his own sensual mind and pleasure, not regarding to know God's word, and much less to live according thereunto; such a man clearly deceiveth himself, and seeth not his own heart, if he thinketh that he either knoweth God, loveth him, feareth him, or trusteth in him. Some peradventure phantasy in themselves that they belong to God, although they live in sin, and so they come to the church, and shew themselves as God's dear children. But St. John saith plainly, "If we say that we have any company with God, and walk in darkness, we do lie." Other do vainly think that they know and love God, although they pass not of the commandments. But St. John saith clearly, "He that saith, I know God, and keepeth not his commandments, he is a liar." Some falsely persuade themselves, that they love God, when they hate their neighbours. But St. John saith manifestly, "If any man say, I love God, and yet hateth his brother, he is a liar. He that saith that he is in the light, and hateth his brother, he is still in darkness. He that loveth his brother dwelleth in the light; but he that hateth his brother is in darkness, and walketh in darkness, and knoweth not whither he goeth: for darkness hath blinded his eyes." And moreover he saith, "Hereby we manifestly know the children of God from the children of the devil. He that doth not righteously is not the child of God, nor he that hateth his brother." Deceive not yourselves, therefore, thinking that you have faith in God, or that you love God, or do trust in him, or do fear him, when you live in sin: for then your ungodly and sinful life declareth the contrary, whatsoever you say or think. It pertaineth to a Christian man to have this true Christian faith, and to try himself whether he hath it or no, and to know what belongeth to it, and how it doth work in him. It is not the world that we can trust to; the world, and all that is therein, is but vanity. It is God that must be our defence and protection against all temptation of wickedness and sin, errors, superstition, idolatry, and all evil. If all the world were on our side, and God against us, what could the world avail us? Therefore let us set our whole faith and trust in God, and neither the world, the devil, nor all the power of them shall prevail against us. Let us therefore, good Christian people, try and examine our faith, what it is: let us not flatter ourselves, but look upon our works, and so judge of our faith what it is. Christ himself speaketh of this matter, and saith, "The tree is known by the fruit." Therefore let us do good works, and thereby declare our faith to be the lively Christian faith. Let us, by such virtues as ought to spring out of faith, shew our election to be sure and stable, as St. Peter teacheth, "Endeavour yourselves to make your calling and election certain by good works." And also he saith, "Minister or declare in your faith virtue, in virtue knowledge, in knowledge temperance, in temperance patience, in patience godliness, in godliness brotherly charity, in brotherly charity love:" so shall we shew indeed that we have the very lively Christian faith, and may so both certify our conscience the better that we be in the right faith, and also by these means confirm other men. If these fruits do not follow, we do but mock with God, deceive ourselves, and also other men. Well may we bear the name of Christian men, but we do lack the true faith that doth belong thereunto: for true faith doth ever bring forth good works, as St. James saith: "Shew me thy faith by thy deeds." Thy deeds and works must be an open testimonial of thy faith: otherwise thy faith, being without good works, is but the devil's faith, the faith of the wicked, a phantasy of faith, and not a true Christian faith. And like as the devils and evil people be nothing the better for their counterfeit faith, but it is unto them the more cause of damnation: so they that be Christians, and have received knowledge of God, and of Christ's merits, and yet of a set purpose do live idly, without good works, thinking the name of a naked faith to be either sufficient for them, or else setting their minds upon vain pleasures of this world, do live in sin without repentance, not uttering the fruits that do belong to such an high profession; upon such presumptuous persons, and wilful sinners, must needs remain the great vengeance of God, and eternal punishment in hell, prepared for the unjust and wicked livers. Therefore as you profess the name of Christ, good Christian people, let no such phantasy and imagination of faith at any time beguile you; but be sure of your faith, try it by your living, look upon the fruits that cometh of it, mark the increase of love and charity by it towards God and your neighbour, and so shall you perceive it to be a true lively faith. If you feel and perceive such a faith in you, rejoice in it; and be diligent to maintain it, and keep it still in you; let it be daily increasing, and more and more by well working, and so shall you be sure that you shall please God by this faith; and at the length, as other faithful men have done before, so shall you, when his will is, come to him, and receive "the end and final reward of your faith" as St. Peter nameth it, "the salvation of your souls:" The which God grant us, that hath promised the same unto his faithful; to whom be all honour and glory, world without end. Amen.

A SERMON OF GOOD WORKS ANNEXED UNTO FAITH.

In the last sermon was declared unto you, what the lively and true faith of a Christian man is; that it causeth not a man to be idle, but to be occupied in bringing forth good works, as occasion serveth.

Now, by God's grace, shall be declared the second thing that before was noted of faith; that without it can no good work be done, accepted, and pleasant unto God; For as a branch cannot bear fruit of itself, saith our saviour Christ, except it abide in the vine; so cannot you, except you abide in me. I am the vine, and you be the branches: he that abideth in me, and I in him, he bringeth forth much fruit: for without me you can do nothing. And St. Paul proveth, that Enoch had faith, because he pleased God; For without faith, saith he, it is not possible to please God. And again, to the Romans he saith, Whatsoever work is done without faith, it is sin. Faith giveth life to the soul; and they be as much dead to God that lack faith, as they be to the world whose bodies lack souls. Without faith, all that is done of us is but dead before God, although the work seem never so gay and glorious before man. Even as the picture graven or painted is but a dead representation of the thing itself, and is without life, or any manner of moving; so be the works of all unfaithful persons before God: they do appear to be lively works, and indeed they be but dead, not availing to the everlasting life: they be but shadows and shews of lively and good things, and not good and lively things indeed: for true faith doth give life to the works, and out of such faith come good works, that be very good works indeed; and without faith no work is good before God, as saith St. Augustin. We must set no good works before faith, nor think that before faith a man may do any good works; for such works, although they seem unto men to be praiseworthy, yet indeed they be but vain, and not allowed before God. They be as the course of an horse that runneth out of the way, which taketh great labour, but to no purpose. Let no man, therefore, saith he, reckon upon his good works before his faith; whereas faith was not, good works were not. The intent, saith he, maketh the good works; but faith must guide and order the intent of man. And Christ saith, "If thine eye be naught, thy whole body is full of darkness." The eye doth signify the intent, saith St. Augustin, wherewith a man doth a thing: so that he which doth not his good works with a godly intent, and a true faith that worketh by love, the whole body beside, that is to say, all the whole number of his works is dark, and there is no light in them. For good deeds be not measured by the facts themselves, and so discerned from vices; but by the ends and intents, for the which they were done. If a heathen man clothe the naked, feed the hungry, and do such other like works; yet, because he doth them not in faith for the honour and love of God, they be but dead, vain, and fruitless works to him. Faith it is that doth commend the work to God: for, as St. Augustin saith, whether thou wilt or no, that work, that cometh not of faith, is naught; where the faith of Christ is not the foundation, there is no good work, what building soever we make. There is one work, in the which be all good works, that is faith, which worketh by charity: if thou have it, thou hast the ground of all good works; for the virtues of strength, wisdom, temperance, and justice, be all referred unto this same faith. Without this faith we have not them, but only the names and shadows of them; as St. Augustin saith, All the life of them that lack the true faith is sin, and nothing is good without him that is the author of goodness: where he is not, there is but feigned virtue, although it be in the best works. . . .

The Second Part of the Sermon of Good Works.

OF three things which were in the former sermon especially noted of lively faith, two be declared unto you, the first was, that faith is never idle, without good works when occasion serveth: the second, that good works acceptable to God cannot be done without faith. Now to go forward to the third part, that is, what manner of works they be which spring out of true faith, and lead faithful men unto everlasting life. This cannot be known so well as by our saviour Christ himself, who was asked of a certain great man the same question; "What works shall I do," said a prince, "to come to everlasting life?" To whom Jesus answered, "If thou wilt come to everlasting life, keep the commandments." But the prince, not satisfied herewith, asked farther, Which commandments? The scribes and Pharisees had made so many of their own laws and traditions, to bring men to heaven, besides God's commandments, that this man was in doubt whether he should come to heaven by those laws and traditions, or by the law of God; and therefore he asked Christ, which commandments he meant. Whereunto Christ made him a plain answer, rehearsing the commandments of God, saying, Thou shalt not kill, Thou shalt not commit adultery, Thou shalt not steal, Thou shalt not bear false witness, Honour thy father and thy mother, and Love thy neighbour as thyself. By which words Christ declared, that the laws of God be the very way that doth lead to everlasting life, and not the traditions and laws of men. So that this is to be taken for a most true lesson taught by Christ's own mouth, that the works of the moral commandments of God be the very true works of faith, which lead to the blessed life to come. . . .

The Third Part of the Sermon of Good Works.

THAT all men might rightly judge of good works, it hath been declared in the second part of this sermon, what kind of good works they be that God would have his people to walk in, namely, such as he hath commanded in his holy scripture, and not such works as men have studied out of their own brain, of a blind zeal and devotion, without the word of God: and by mistaking the nature of good works, man hath most highly displeased God, and hath gone from his will and commandments. So that thus you have heard how much the world, from the beginning until Christ's time, was ever ready to fall from the commandments of God, and to seek other means to honour and serve him, after a devotion found out of their own heads; and how they did set up their own traditions as high or above God's commandments; which hath happened also in our times (the more it is to be lamented) no less than it did among the Jews, . . .

Such hath been the corrupt inclination of man, ever superstitiously given to make new honouring of God of his own head, and then to have more affection and devotion to keep that, than to search out God's holy commandments, and to keep them. And furthermore, to take God's commandments for men's commandments, and men's commandments for God's commandments, yea, and for the highest and most perfect and holy of all God's commandments. And so was all confused, that scant well learned men, and but a small number of them knew, or at the least would know, and durst affirm the truth, to separate or sever God's commandments from the commandments of men. Whereupon did grow much error, superstition, idolatry, vain religion, overthwart judgment, great contention, with all ungodly living.

Wherefore, as you have any zeal to the right and pure honouring of God, as you have any regard to your own souls, and to the life that is to come, which is both without pain, and without end, apply yourselves chiefly above all things to read and hear God's word, mark diligently therein what his will is you shall do, and with all your endeavour apply yourselves to follow the same. First, you must have an assured faith in God, and give yourselves wholly unto him, love him in prosperity and adversity, and dread to offend him evermore: then, for his sake, love all men, friends and foes, because they be his creation and image, and redeemed by Christ, as ye are. Cast in your minds, how you may do good unto all men unto your powers, and hurt no man. Obey all your superiors and governors; serve your masters faithfully and diligently, as well in their absence as in their presence, not for dread of punishment only, but for conscience sake, knowing that you are bound so to do by God's commandments. Disobey not your fathers and mothers, but honour them, help them, and please them to your power. Oppress not, kill not, beat not, neither slander nor hate any man; but love all men, speak well of all men, help and succour every man as you may, yea, even your enemies that hate you, that speak evil of you, and that do hurt you. Take no man's goods, nor covet your neighbour's goods wrongfully; but content yourselves with that which ye get truly; and also bestow your own goods charitably, as need and case requireth. Flee all idolatry, witchcraft, and perjury; commit no manner of adultery, fornication, or other unchasteness, in will nor in deed, with any other man's wife, widow, or maid, or otherwise. And travailing continually (during this life) thus in keeping the commandments of God, (wherein standeth the pure, principal, and right honour of God, and which wrought in faith, God hath ordained to be the right trade and path-way unto heaven,) you shall not fail, as Christ hath promised, to come to that blessed and everlasting life, where you shall live in glory and joy with God for ever: to whom be praise, honour, and empery, for ever and ever. Amen.

THE THIRTY-NINE ARTICLES (1563)

The Thirty-Nine Articles are rooted in the various creedal statements of the English Reformation during the reign of Henry VIII and are a revision of the Forty-Two Articles of 1553, which were largely the work of Archbishop Cranmer. They were promulgated in 1563 by the Convocation as part of the Elizabethan Settlement. The authorized English text was adopted by the Convocation in 1571.

The Articles are not as comprehensive as many of the Continental creeds. Neither do they have the full authority that was given to the creeds in Lutheran and Reformed churches. They are moderate in theological expression and are designed to provide a minimal basis for a comprehensive, national church that sought to preserve both the Catholic and Protestant traditions.

Source: The text reprinted here is taken from *Creeds of Christendom* by Philip Schaff, Vol. III (New York: Harper & Bros., 1877), pp. 487–514.

Bicknell, E. J., *A Theological Introduction to the Thirty-Nine Articles of the Church of England,* 3rd ed., revised by H. J. Carpenter (London: Longmans, Green & Co., 1955).

THE THIRTY-NINE ARTICLES OF RELIGION

(According to the American Revision, 1801)

I.   *Of Faith in the Holy Trinity.*

There is but one living and true God, everlasting, without body, parts, or passions; of infinite power, wisdom, and goodness; the Maker, and Preserver of all things both visible and invisible. And in unity of this Godhead there be three Persons, of one substance, power, and eternity: the Father, the Son, and the Holy Ghost.

II. *Of the Word or Son of God, which was made very Man.*

The Son, which is the Word of the Father, begotten from everlasting of the Father, the very and eternal God, and of one substance with the Father, took Man's nature in the womb of the blessed Virgin, of her substance: so that two whole and perfect Natures, that is to say, the Godhead and Manhood, were joined together in one Person, never to be divided, whereof is one Christ, very God, and very Man; who truly suffered, was crucified, dead, and buried, to reconcile his Father to us, and to be a sacrifice, not only for original guilt, but also for actual sins of men.

III. *Of the going down of Christ into Hell.*

As Christ died for us, and was buried, so also is it to be believed that he went down into Hell.

IV. *Of the Resurrection of Christ.*

Christ did truly rise again from death, and took again his body, with flesh, bones, and all things appertaining to the perfection of Man's nature; wherewith he ascended into Heaven, and there sitteth, until he return to judge all Men at the last day.

V. *Of the Holy Ghost.*

The Holy Ghost, proceeding from the Father and the Son, is of one substance, majesty, and glory, with the Father and the Son, very and eternal God.

VI. *Of the Sufficiency of the Holy Scriptures for Salvation.*

Holy Scripture containeth all things necessary to salvation: so that whatsoever is not read therein, nor may be proved thereby, is not to be required of any man, that it should be believed as an article of the Faith, or be thought requisite or necessary to salvation.

In the name of the Holy Scripture we do understand those canonical Books of the Old and New

Testament, of whose authority was never any doubt in the Church.

OF THE NAMES AND NUMBER OF THE CANONICAL BOOKS.

Genesis,
Exodus,
Leviticus,
Numbers,
Deuteronomy,
Joshua,
Judges,
Ruth,
The First Book of Samuel,
The Second Book of Samuel,
The First Book of Kings,
The Second Book of Kings,
The First Book of Chronicles,
The Second Book of Chronicles,
The First Book of Esdras,
The Second Book of Esdras,
The Book of Esther,
The Book of Job,
The Psalms,
The Proverbs,
Ecclesiastes or Preacher,
Cantica, or Songs of Solomon,
Four Prophets the greater,
Twelve Prophets the less.

And the other Books (as Hierome saith) the Church doth read for example of life and instruction of manners: but yet doth it not apply to them to establish any doctrine: such are these following:

The Third Book of Esdras,
The Fourth Book of Esdras,
The Book of Tobias,
The Book of Judith,
The rest of the Book of Esther,
The Book of Wisdom,

Jesus the Son of Sirach,
Baruch the Prophet,
The Song of the Three Children,
The Story of Susanna,
Of Bel and the Dragon,
The Prayer of Manasses,
The First Book of Maccabees,
The Second Book of Maccabees.

All the Books of the New Testament, as they are commonly received, we do receive, and account them Canonical.

VII. *Of the Old Testament.*

The Old Testament is not contrary to the New: for both in the Old and New Testament everlasting life is offered to Mankind by Christ, who is the only Mediator between God and Man, being both God and Man. Wherefore they are not to be heard, which feign that the old Fathers did look only for transitory promises. Although the Law given from God by Moses, as touching Ceremonies and Rites, do not bind Christian men, nor the Civil precepts thereof ought of necessity to be received in any commonwealth; yet notwithstanding, no Christian man whatsoever is free from the obedience of the Commandments which are called Moral.

VIII. *Of the Creeds.*

The Nicene Creed, and that which is commonly called the Apostles' Creed, ought thoroughly to be received and believed: for they may be proved by most certain warrants of Holy Scripture. [The English Edition of 1571 included the Athanasian Creed.]

IX. *Of Original or Birth-Sin.*

Original sin standeth not in the following of Adam (as the Pelagians do vainly talk); but it is the fault and corruption of the Nature of every man, that naturally is engendered of the offspring of Adam; whereby man is very far gone from original righteousness, and is of his own nature inclined to evil, so that the flesh lusteth always contrary to the spirit; and therefore in every person born into this world, it de-

serveth God's wrath and damnation. And this infec-
tion of nature doth remain, yea in them that are regenerated; whereby the lust of the flesh, called in Greek
φρόνημα σαρκὸς (which some do expound the wisdom,
some sensuality, some the affection, some the desire,
of the flesh), is not subject to the Law of God. And
although there is no condemnation for them that believe and are baptized; yet the Apostle doth confess,
that concupiscence and lust hath of itself the nature
of sin.

X. *Of Free-Will.*

The condition of Man after the fall of Adam is
such, that he can not turn and prepare himself, by
his own natural strength and good works, to faith, and
calling upon God. Wherefore we have no power to do
good works pleasant and acceptable to God, without
the grace of God by Christ preventing us, that we
may have a good will, and working with us, when we
have that good will.

XI. *Of the Justification of Man.*

We are accounted righteousness before God, only
for the merit of our Lord and Saviour Jesus Christ
by Faith, and not for our own works or deservings.
Wherefore, that we are justified by Faith only, is a
most wholesome Doctrine, and very full of comfort,
as more largely is expressed in the Homily of Justification.

XII. *Of Good Works.*

Albeit that Good Works, which are the fruits of
Faith, and follow after Justification, can not put away
our sins, and endure the severity of God's judgment;
yet are they pleasing and acceptable to God in Christ,
and do spring out necessarily of a true and lively
Faith; insomuch that by them a lively Faith may be
as evidently known as a tree discerned by the fruit.

XIII. *Of Works before Justification.*

Works done before the grace of Christ, and the
Inspiration of his Spirit, are not pleasant to God, forasmuch as they spring not of faith in Jesus Christ;

neither do they make men meet to receive grace, or (as the School-authors say) deserve grace of congruity: yea rather, for that they are not done as God hath willed and commanded them to be done, we doubt not but they have the nature of sin.

XIV. *Of Works of Supererogation.*

Voluntary Works besides, over and above, God's Commandments, which they call Works of Supererogation, can not be taught without arrogancy and impiety: for by them men do declare, that they do not only render unto God as much as they are bound to do, but that they do more for his sake, than of bounden duty is required: whereas Christ saith plainly, When ye have done all that are commanded to you, say, We are unprofitable servants.

XV. *Of Christ alone without Sin.*

Christ in the truth of our nature was made like unto us in all things, sin only except, from which he was clearly void, both in his flesh, and in his spirit. He came to be the Lamb without spot, who, by sacrifice of himself once made, should take away the sins of the world; and sin (as Saint John saith) was not in him. But all we the rest, although baptized, and born again in Christ, yet offend in many things; and if we say we have no sin, we deceive ourselves, and the truth is not in us.

XVI. *Of Sin after Baptism.*

Not every deadly sin willingly committed after Baptism is sin against the Holy Ghost, and unpardonable. Wherefore the grant of repentance is not to be denied to such as fall into sin after Baptism. After we have received the Holy Ghost, we may depart from grace given, and fall into sin, and by the grace of God we may arise again, and amend our lives. And therefore they are to be condemned, which say, they can no more sin as long as they live here, or deny the place of forgiveness to such as truly repent.

XVII.   *Of Predestination and Election.*

Predestination to Life is the everlasting purpose of God, whereby (before the foundations of the world were laid) he hath constantly decreed by his counsel secret to us, to deliver from curse and damnation those whom he hath chosen in Christ out of mankind, and to bring them by Christ to everlasting salvation, as vessels made to honour. Wherefore, they which be endued with so excellent a benefit of God, be called according to God's purpose by his Spirit working in due season: they through Grace obey the calling: they be justified freely: they be made sons of God by adoption: they be made like the image of his only-begotten Son Jesus Christ: they walk religiously in good works, and at length, by God's mercy, they attain to everlasting felicity.

As the godly consideration of Predestination, and our Election in Christ, is full of sweet, pleasant, and unspeakable comfort to godly persons, and such as feel in themselves the working of the Spirit of Christ, mortifying the works of the flesh, and their earthly members, and drawing up their mind to high and heavenly things, as well because it doth greatly establish and confirm their faith of eternal Salvation to be enjoyed through Christ, as because it doth fervently kindle their love towards God: So, for curious and carnal persons, lacking the Spirit of Christ, to have continually before their eyes the sentence of God's Predestination, is a most dangerous downfall, whereby the Devil doth thrust them either into desperation, or into wretchlessness of most unclean living, no less perilous than desperation.

Furthermore, we must receive God's promises in such wise, as they be generally set forth to us in Holy Scripture; and, in our doings, that Will of God is to be followed, which we have expressly declared unto us in the Word of God.

XVIII. *Of obtaining eternal Salvation only by the Name of Christ.*

They also are to be had accursed that presume to say, That every man shall be saved by the Law or Sect which he professeth, so that he be diligent to frame his life according to that Law, and the light of Nature. For Holy Scripture doth set out unto us only the Name of Jesus Christ, whereby men must be saved.

XIX. *Of the Church.*

The visible Church of Christ is a congregation of faithful men, in the which the pure Word of God is preached, and the Sacraments be duly ministered according to Christ's ordinance, in all those things that of necessity are requisite to the same.

As the Church of Jerusalem, Alexandria, and Antioch, have erred; so also the Church of Rome hath erred, not only in their living and manner of Ceremonies, but also in matters of Faith.

XX. *Of the Authority of the Church.*

The Church hath power to decree Rites or Ceremonies, and authority in Controversies of Faith: and yet it is not lawful for the Church to ordain any thing that is contrary to God's Word written, neither may it so expound one place of Scripture, that it be repugnant to another. Wherefore, although the Church be a witness and a keeper of Holy Writ, yet, as it ought not to decree any thing against the same, so besides the same ought it not to enforce any thing to be believed for necessity of Salvation.

XXI. *Of the Authority of General Councils.*
[From the English Edition of 1571. Omitted in the American Revision of 1801.]

General Counsels may not be gathered together without the commaundement and wyll of princes. And when they be gathered together (forasmuche as they be an assemblie of men, whereof all be not gouerned with the spirite and word of God) they may erre, and sometyme haue erred, euen in thinges parteynyng unto God. Wherfore, thinges ordayned by them as neces-

sary to saluation, haue neyther strength nor aucthoritie, unlesse it may be declared that they be taken out
of holy Scripture.

XXII.   *Of Purgatory.*

The Romish Doctrine concerning Purgatory, Pardons, Worshipping and Adoration, as well of Images
as of Relics, and also Invocation of Saints, is a fond
thing, vainly invented, and grounded upon no war-
ranty of Scripture, but rather repugnant to the Word
of God.

XXIII.   *Of Ministering in the Congregation.*

It is not lawful for any man to take upon him the
office of public preaching, or ministering the Sacraments in the Congregation, before he be lawfully
called, and sent to execute the same. And those we
ought to judge lawfully called and sent, which be
chosen and called to this work by men who have public authority given unto them in the Congregation, to
call and send Ministers into the Lord's vineyard.

XXIV.   *Of Speaking in the Congregation in such a Tongue as the people understandeth.*

It is a thing plainly repugnant to the Word of God,
and the custom of the Primitive Church, to have
public Prayer in the Church, or to minister the Sacraments, in a tongue not understanded of the people.

XXV.   *Of the Sacraments.*

Sacraments ordained of Christ be not only badges
or tokens of Christian men's profession, but rather
they be certain sure witnesses, and effectual signs of
grace, and God's good will towards us, by the which
he doth work invisibly in us, and doth not only
quicken, but also strengthen and confirm our Faith in
him.

There are two Sacraments ordained of Christ our
Lord in the Gospel, that is to say, Baptism, and the
Supper of the Lord.

Those five commonly called Sacraments, that is to
say, Confirmation, Penance, Orders, Matrimony, and
Extreme Unction, are not to be counted for Sacra-

ments of the Gospel, being such as have grown partly of the corrupt following of the Apostles, partly are states of life allowed in the Scriptures; but yet have not like nature of Sacraments with Baptism, and the Lord's Supper, for that they have not any visible sign or ceremony ordained of God.

The Sacraments were not ordained of Christ to be gazed upon, or to be carried about, but that we should duly use them. And in such only as worthily receive the same, they have a wholesome effect or operation: but they that receive them unworthily, purchase to themselves damnation, as Saint Paul saith.

XXVI. *Of the Unworthiness of the Ministers, which hinders not the effect of the Sacraments.*

Although in the visible Church the evil be ever mingled with the good, and sometimes the evil have chief authority in the Ministration of the Word and Sacraments, yet forasmuch as they do not the same in their own name, but in Christ's, and do minister by his commission and authority, we may use their Ministry, both in hearing the Word of God, and in receiving the Sacraments. Neither is the effect of Christ's ordinance taken away by their wickedness, nor the grace of God's gifts diminished from such as by faith, and rightly, do receive the Sacraments ministered unto them; which be effectual, because of Christ's institution and promise, although they be ministered by evil men.

Nevertheless, it appertaineth to the discipline of the Church, that inquiry be made of evil Ministers, and that they be accused by those that have knowledge of their offences; and finally, being found guilty, by just judgment be deposed.

XXVII. *Of Baptism.*

Baptism is not only a sign of profession, and mark of difference, whereby Christian men are discerned from others that be not christened, but it is also a sign of Regeneration or New-Birth, whereby, as by an instrument, they that receive Baptism rightly are grafted into the Church; the promises of the forgiveness of sin, and of our adoption to be the sons of God by the Holy Ghost, are visibly signed and sealed; Faith is confirmed, and Grace increased by virtue of prayer unto God.

The Baptism of young Children is in any wise to be retained in the Church, as most agreeable with the institution of Christ.

XXVIII. *Of the Lord's Supper.*

The Supper of the Lord is not only a sign of the love that Christians ought to have among themselves one to another; but rather it is a Sacrament of our Redemption by Christ's death: insomuch that to such as rightly, worthily, and with faith, receive the same, the Bread which we break is a partaking of the Body of Christ; and likewise the Cup of Blessing is a partaking of the Blood of Christ.

Transubstantiation (or the change of the substance of Bread and Wine) in the Supper of the Lord, can not be proved by Holy Writ; but is repugnant to the plain words of Scripture, overthroweth the nature of a Sacrament, and hath given occasion to many superstitions.

The Body of Christ is given, taken, and eaten, in the Supper, only after an heavenly and spiritual manner. And the mean whereby the Body of Christ is received and eaten in the Supper, is Faith.

The Sacrament of the Lord's Supper was not by Christ's ordinance reserved, carried about, lifted up, or worshiped.

XXIX. *Of the Wicked, which eat not the Body of Christ in the use of the Lord's Supper.*

The Wicked, and such as be void of a lively faith, although they do carnally and visibly press with their teeth (as Saint Augustine saith) the Sacrament of the Body and Blood of Christ; yet in no wise are they partakers of Christ: but rather, to their condemnation, do eat and drink the sign or Sacrament of so great a thing.

XXX. *Of both Kinds.*

The Cup of the Lord is not to be denied to the Lay-people: for both the parts of the Lord's Sacrament, by Christ's ordinance and commandment, ought to be ministered to all Christian men alike.

XXXI. *Of the one Oblation of Christ finished upon the Cross.*

The Offering of Christ once made is that perfect redemption, propitiation, and satisfaction, for all the sins of the whole world, both original and actual; and there is none other satisfaction for sin, but that alone. Wherefore the sacrifices of Masses, in the which it was commonly said that the Priest did offer Christ for the quick and the dead, to have remission of pain or guilt, were blasphemous fables, and dangerous deceits.

XXXII. *Of the Marriage of Priests.*

Bishops, Priests, and Deacons, are not commanded by God's Law, either to vow the estate of single life, or to abstain from marriage: therefore it is lawful for them, as for all other Christian men, to marry at their own discretion, as they shall judge the same to serve better to godliness.

XXXIII. *Of excommunicate Persons, how they are to be avoided.*

That person which by open denunciation of the Church is rightly cut off from the unity of the Church, and excommunicated, ought to be taken of the whole multitude of the faithful, as a Heathen and Publican, until he be openly reconciled by penance, and received into the Church by a judge that hath authority there-unto.

XXXIV. *Of the Traditions of the Church.*

It is not necessary that Traditions and Ceremonies be in all places one, or utterly like; for at all times they have been divers, and may be changed according to the diversity of countries, times, and men's manners, so that nothing be ordained against God's Word.

Whosoever, through his private judgment, willingly and purposely, doth openly break the Traditions and

Ceremonies of the Church, which be not repugnant to the Word of God, and be ordained and approved by common authority, ought to be rebuked openly (that others may fear to do the like), as he that offendeth against the common order of the Church, and hurteth the authority of the Magistrate, and woundeth the consciences of the weak brethren.

Every particular or national Church hath authority to ordain, change, and abolish, Ceremonies or Rites of the Church ordained only by man's authority, so that all things be done to edifying.

XXXV. *Of the Homilies.*

The Second Book of Homilies, the several titles whereof we have joined under this Article, doth contain a godly and wholesome Doctrine, and necessary for these times, as doth the former Book of Homilies, which were set forth in the time of Edward the Sixth; and therefore we judge them to be read in Churches by the Ministers, diligently and distinctly, that they may be understanded of the people.

Of the Names of the Homilies.

1. Of the right Use of the Church.
2. Against Peril of Idolatry.
3. Of repairing and keeping clean of Churches.
4. Of good Works: first of Fasting.
5. Against Gluttony and Drunkenness.
6. Against Excess of Apparel.
7. Of Prayer.
8. Of the Place and Time of Prayer.
9. That Common Prayers and Sacraments ought to be ministered in a known tongue.
10. Of the reverend Estimation of God's Word.
11. Of Alms-doing.
12. Of the Nativity of Christ.
13. Of the Passion of Christ.
14. Of the Resurrection of Christ.
15. Of the worthy receiving of the Sacrament of the Body and Blood of Christ.
16. Of the Gifts of the Holy Ghost.

17. For the Rogation-days.
18. Of the State of Matrimony.
19. Of Repentance.
20. Against Idleness.
21. Against Rebellion.

[This Article is received in this Church, so far as it declares the Books of Homilies to be an explication of Christian doctrine, and instructive in piety and morals. But all references to the constitution and laws of England are considered as inapplicable to the circumstances of this Church; which also suspends the order for the reading of said Homilies in churches, until a revision of them may be conveniently made, for the clearing of them, as well from obsolete words and phrases, as from the local references.][1]

XXXVI. *Of Consecration of Bishops and Ministers.*

The Book of Consecration of Bishops,[2] and Ordering of Priests and Deacons, as set forth by the General Convention of this Church in 1792,[3] doth contain all things necessary to such Consecration and Ordering; neither hath it any thing that, of itself, is superstitious and ungodly. And, therefore, whosoever are consecrated or ordered according to said Form, we decree all such to be rightly, orderly, and lawfully consecrated and ordered.

XXXVII. *Of the Power of the Civil Magistrates.*

The Power of the Civil Magistrate extendeth to all men, as well Clergy as Laity, in all things temporal; but hath no authority in things purely spiritual. And we hold it to be the duty of all men who are professors of the Gospel, to pay respectful obedience to the Civil Authority, regularly and legitimately constituted.

---

[1] American Revision, 1801.
[2] English Edition of 1571 reads "Archbyshops, and Byshops."
[3] English Edition of 1571 reads "lately set foorth in the time of Edwarde the sixt, and confyrmed at the same tyme by aucthoritie of Parliament."

XXXVII. *Of the ciuill Magistrates.*
[English Edition of 1571]

The Queenes Maiestie hath the cheefe power in this Realme of Englande, and other her dominions, unto whom the cheefe gouernment of all estates of this Realme, whether they be Ecclesiasticall or Ciuile, in all causes doth apparteine, and is not, nor ought to be subiect to any forraigne iurisdiction.

Where we attribute to the Queenes Maiestie the cheefe gouernment, by whiche titles we understande the mindes of some slanderous folkes to be offended: we geue not to our princes the ministring either of God's word, or of Sacraments, the which thing the iniunctions also lately set forth by Elizabeth our Queene, doth most plainlie testifie: But that only prerogatiue whiche we see to haue ben geuen alwayes to all godly Princes in holy Scriptures by God him selfe, that is, that they should rule all estates and degrees committed to their charge by God, whether they be Ecclesiasticall or Temporall, and restraine with the ciuill sworde the stubberne and euyll doers.

The bishop of Rome hath no iurisdiction in this Realme of Englande.

The lawes of the Realme may punishe Christian men with death, for heynous and greeuous offences.

It is lawful for Christian men, at the commaundement of the Magistrate, to weare weapons, and serue in the warres.

XXXVIII. *Of Christian Men's Goods, which are not common.*

The Riches and Goods of Christians are not common, as touching the right, title, and possession of the same; as certain Anabaptists do falsely boast. Notwithstanding, every man ought, of such things as he possesseth, liberally to give alms to the poor, according to his ability.

XXXIX. *Of a Christian Man's Oath.*

As we confess that vain and rash Swearing is forbidden Christian men by our Lord Jesus Christ, and

James his Apostle, so we judge, that Christian Religion doth not prohibit, but that a man may swear when the Magistrate requireth, in a cause of faith and charity, so it be done according to the Prophets' teaching, in justice, judgment, and truth.

ANABAPTIST CONFESSIONS

The Radical Reformers were disappointed with the reform of Luther and of Zwingli, and with all the established Protestant Churches. They were united in their opposition to a church that was officially related to the state. They wanted a reformation of the roots and branches. The Radical or Left Wing of Reformation contained such a variety of theologies that generalizations are impossible. One study of church-type in the "Left Wing of the Reformation" distinguishes four types: 1. Anabaptists (including Swiss Brethren, South German Brethren, Hutterites, Dutch Mennonites); 2. Anti-Trinitarians; 3. Spiritualizers; 4. revolutionary prophets.[1]

The Anabaptists are represented in this collection by the Schleitheim Confession and the Dordrecht Confession of Faith. The Schleitheim Confession originated in a meeting of the Swiss Brethren on February 24, 1527. It was widely circulated among the Anabaptists and was the subject of refutation by both Zwingli and Calvin. The author was Michael Sattler, who was to pay for his conviction, in May 1527, with his life. The Confession is not a comprehensive statement of Christian faith, but it does emphasize the beliefs and practices that distinguished the Anabaptists from

[1] *The Anabaptist View of the Church* by Franklin Littell, 2nd ed. (Boston: Starr King Press, 1958).

the Protestantism that became dominant in Zurich and Geneva. It gives clear expression of the intense concern of the Anabaptists for the Church as a disciplined community.

Source: The translations reprinted here are taken by permission of the publisher from *The Doctrines of The Mennonites* by John C. Wenger (Scottdale, Pa.: Mennonite Publishing House, 1952), pp. 71–85.

Bainton, Roland, *The Reformation of the Sixteenth Century* (Boston: Beacon Press, 1952).

Horsch, John, *The Mennonites In Europe*, Rev. Edition (Scottdale, Pa.: Mennonite Publishing House, 1950).

Littell, Franklin H., *The Anabaptist View of the Church*, 2nd ed. (Boston: Starr King Press, 1956).

Wenger, John C., "The Schleitheim Confession of Faith," *The Mennonite Quarterly Review*, Vol. 19, No. 4, Oct. 1945, pp. 243–53.

Williams, George and Mergal, Angel, editors, *Spiritual and Anabaptist Writers*, Library of Christian Classics, Vol. XXV (Philadelphia: Westminster Press, 1957).

THE SCHLEITHEIM CONFESSION

(1527)

Brotherly Union of a Number of Children of God Concerning Seven Articles

May joy, peace and mercy from our Father through the atonement of the blood of Christ Jesus, together with the gifts of the Spirit—who is sent from the Father to all believers for their strength and comfort and for their perseverance in all tribulation until the end, Amen—be to all those who love God, who are the children of light, and who are scattered everywhere as it has been ordained of God our Father, where they are with one mind assembled together in one God and Father of us all: Grace and peace of heart be with you all, Amen.

Beloved brethren and sisters in the Lord: First and supremely we are always concerned for your consolation and the assurance of your conscience (which was previously misled)[1] so that you may not always remain foreigners to us and by right almost completely excluded, but that you may turn again to the true implanted members of Christ, who have been armed through patience and knowledge of themselves, and have therefore again been united with us in the strength of a godly Christian spirit and zeal for God.

It is also apparent with what cunning the devil has turned us aside, so that he might destroy and bring to an end the work of God which in mercy and grace has been partly begun in us. But Christ, the true Shepherd of our souls, Who has begun this in us, will certainly direct the same and teach [us] to His honor and our salvation, Amen.

Dear brethren and sisters, we who have been assembled in the Lord at Schleitheim on the Border, make known in points and articles to all who love God that as concerns us we are of one mind to abide in the Lord as God's obedient children, [His] sons and daughters, we who have been and shall be separated from the world in everything, [and] completely at peace. To God alone be praise and glory without the contradiction of any brethren. In this we have perceived the oneness of the Spirit of our Father and of our common Christ with us. For the Lord is the Lord of peace and not of quarreling, as Paul points out. That you may understand in what articles this has been formulated you should observe and note [the following].

A very great offense has been introduced by certain false brethren among us, so that some have turned aside from the faith, in the way they intend to practice and observe the freedom of the Spirit and of Christ. But such have missed the truth and to their condemnation are given over to the lasciviousness and self-indulgence of the flesh. They think faith and love may

[1] The words in brackets are inserted by the translator to clarify the text. The words in parentheses are a part of the original text. [J.C.W.]

do and permit everything, and nothing will harm them nor condemn them, since they are believers.

Observe, you who are God's members in Christ Jesus, that faith in the heavenly Father through Jesus Christ does not take such form. It does not produce and result in such things as these false brethren and sisters do and teach. Guard yourselves and be warned of such people, for they do not serve our Father, but their father, the devil.

But you are not that way. For they that are Christ's have crucified the flesh with its passions and lusts. You understand me well and [know] the brethren whom we mean. Separate yourselves from them for they are perverted. Petition the Lord that they may have the knowledge which leads to repentance, and [pray] for us that we may have constancy to persevere in the way which we have espoused, for the honor of God and of Christ, His Son, Amen.

The articles which we discussed and on which we were of one mind are these: 1. Baptism; 2. The Ban [Excommunication]; 3. Breaking of Bread; 4. Separation from the Abomination; 5. Pastors in the Church; 6. The Sword; and 7. The Oath.

First. Observe concerning baptism: Baptism shall be given to all those who have learned repentance and amendment of life, and who believe truly that their sins are taken away by Christ, and to all those who walk in the resurrection of Jesus Christ, and wish to be buried with Him in death, so that they may be resurrected with Him, and to all those who with this significance request it [baptism] of us and demand it for themselves. This excludes all infant baptism, the highest and chief abomination of the pope. In this you have the foundation and testimony of the apostles. Matt. 28, Mark 16, Acts 2, 8, 16, 19. This we wish to hold simply, yet firmly and with assurance.

Second. We are agreed as follows on the ban: The ban shall be employed with all those who have given themselves to the Lord, to walk in His commandments, and with all those who are baptized into the one body of Christ and who are called brethren or sisters, and yet who slip sometimes and fall into error and sin, being inadvertently overtaken. The same shall be admonished twice in secret and the third time openly disciplined or banned according to the command of Christ. Matt. 18. But this shall be done according to the regulation of the Spirit (Matt. 5) before the breaking of bread, so that we may break and eat one bread, with one mind and in one love, and may drink of one cup.

Third. In the breaking of bread we are of one mind and are agreed [as follows]: All those who wish to break one bread in remembrance of the broken body of Christ, and all who wish to drink of one drink as a remembrance of the shed blood of Christ, shall be united beforehand by baptism in one body of Christ which is the church of God and whose Head is Christ. For as Paul points out we cannot at the same time be partakers of the Lord's table and the table of devils; we cannot at the same time drink the cup of the Lord and the cup of the devil. That is, all those who have fellowship with the dead works of darkness have no part in the light. Therefore all who follow the devil and the world have no part with those who are called unto God out of the world. All who lie in evil have no part in the good.

Therefore it is and must be [thus]: Whoever has not been called by one God to one faith, to one baptism, to one Spirit, to one body, with all the children of God's church, cannot be made [into] one bread with them, as indeed must be done if one is truly to break bread according to the command of Christ.

Fourth. We are agreed [as follows] on separation: A separation shall be made from the evil and from the wickedness which the devil planted in the world; in this manner, simply that we shall not have fellowship with them [the wicked] and not run with them in the multitude of their abominations. This is the way it is: Since all who do not walk in the obedience of faith, and have not united themselves with God so that they wish to do His will, are a great abomination before God, it is not possible for anything to grow or issue from them except abominable things. For truly all creatures are in but two classes, good and bad, believing and unbelieving, darkness and light, the world and those who [have come] out of the world, God's temple and idols, Christ and Belial; and none can have part with the other.

To us then the command of the Lord is clear when He calls upon us to be separate from the evil and thus He will be our God and we shall be His sons and daughters.

He further admonishes us to withdraw from Babylon and the earthly Egypt that we may not be partakers of the pain and suffering which the Lord will bring upon them.

From this we should learn that everything which is not united with our God and Christ cannot be other than an abomination which we should shun and flee from. By this is meant all popish and antipopish works and church services, meetings and church attendance,[2] drinking houses, civic affairs, the commitments [made in] unbelief and other things of that kind, which are highly regarded by the world and yet are carried on in flat contradiction to the command of God, in accordance with all the unrighteousness which is in the world. From all these things we shall be separated and have no part with them for they are nothing but an abomination, and they are the cause of our being hated before our Christ Jesus, Who has set us free

---

[2] This severe judgment on the state churches must be understood in the light of sixteenth century conditions. The state clergymen were in many cases careless and carnal men. All citizens in a given province were considered members of the state church because they had been made Christians ("christened") by infant baptism. Also, in 1527 Zurich had begun to use capital punishment on the Swiss Brethren, with the full approval of the state church leaders. Sattler himself was burned at the stake less than three months after the Schleitheim conference.

from the slavery of the flesh and fitted us for the service of God through the Spirit Whom He has given us.

Therefore there will also unquestionably fall from us the unchristian, devilish weapons of force—such as sword, armor and the like, and all their use [either] for friends or against one's enemies—by virtue of the word of Christ, Resist not [him that is] evil.

Fifth. We are agreed as follows on pastors in the church of God: The pastor in the church of God shall, as Paul has prescribed, be one who out-and-out has a good report of those who are outside the faith. This office shall be to read, to admonish and teach, to warn, to discipline, to ban in the church, to lead out in prayer for the advancement of all the brethren and sisters, to lift up the bread when it is to be broken, and in all things to see to the care of the body of Christ, in order that it may be built up and developed, and the mouth of the slanderer be stopped.

This one moreover shall be supported of the church which has chosen him, wherein he may be in need, so that he who serves the Gospel may live of the Gospel as the Lord has ordained. But if a pastor should do something requiring discipline, he shall not be dealt with except [on the testimony of] two or three witnesses. And when they sin they shall be disciplined before all in order that the others may fear.

But should it happen that through the cross this pastor should be banished or led to the Lord [through martyrdom] another shall be ordained in his place in the same hour so that God's little flock and people may not be destroyed.

Sixth. We are agreed as follows concerning the sword: The sword is ordained of God outside the perfection of Christ. It punishes and puts to death the wicked, and guards and protects the good. In the Law the sword was ordained for the punishment of the wicked and for their death, and the same [sword] is [now] ordained to be used by the worldly magistrates.

In the perfection of Christ, however, only the ban

is used for a warning and for the excommunication of the one who has sinned, without putting the flesh to death—simply the warning and the command to sin no more.

Now it will be asked by many who do not recognize [this as] the will of Christ for us, whether a Christian may or should employ the sword against the wicked for the defence and protection of the good, or for the sake of love.

Our reply is unanimously as follows: Christ teaches and commands us to learn of Him, for He is meek and lowly in heart and so shall we find rest to our souls. Also Christ says to the heathenish woman who was taken in adultery, not that one should stone her according to the law of His Father (and yet He says, As the Father has commanded me, thus I do), but in mercy and forgiveness and warning, to sin no more. Such [an attitude] we also ought to take completely according to the rule of the ban.

Secondly, it will be asked concerning the sword, whether a Christian shall pass sentence in worldly disputes and strife such as unbelievers have with one another. This is our united answer. Christ did not wish to decide or pass judgment between brother and brother in the case of the inheritance, but refused to do so. Therefore we should do likewise.

Thirdly, it will be asked concerning the sword, Shall one be a magistrate if one should be chosen as such? The answer is as follows: They wished to make Christ king, but He fled and did not view it as the arrangement of His Father. Thus shall we do as He did, and follow Him, and so shall we not walk in darkness. For He Himself says, He who wishes to come after me, let him deny himself and take up his cross and follow me. Also, He Himself forbids [employment of] the force of the sword saying, The worldly princes lord it over them, etc., but not so shall it be with you. Further, Paul says, Whom God did foreknow He also did predestinate to be conformed to the image of His Son, etc. Also Peter says, Christ has suffered (not ruled) and left us an example, that ye should follow His steps.

Finally it will be observed that it is not appropriate for a Christian to serve as a magistrate because of these points: The government magistracy is according to the flesh, but the Christians' is according to the Spirit; their houses and dwelling remain in this world, but the Christians' are in heaven; their citizenship is in this world, but the Christians' citizenship is in heaven; the weapons of their conflict and war are carnal and against the flesh only, but the Christians' weapons are spiritual, against the fortification of the devil. The worldlings are armed with steel and iron, but the Christians are armed with the armor of God, with truth, righteousness, peace, faith, salvation and the Word of God. In brief, as is the mind of Christ toward us, so shall the mind of the members of the body of Christ be through Him in all things, that there may be no schism in the body through which it would be destroyed. For every kingdom divided against itself will be destroyed. Now since Christ is as it is written of Him, His members must also be the same, that His body may remain complete and united to its own advancement and upbuilding.

Seventh. We are agreed as follows concerning the oath: The oath is a confirmation among those who are quarreling or making promises. In the Law it is commanded to be performed in God's Name, but only in truth, not falsely. Christ, who teaches the perfection of the Law, prohibits all swearing to His [followers], whether true or false—neither by heaven, nor by the earth, nor by Jerusalem, nor by our head— and that for the reason which He shortly thereafter gives, For you are not able to make one hair white or black. So you see it is for this reason that all swearing is forbidden: we cannot fulfill that which we promise when we swear, for we cannot change [even] the very least thing on us.

Now there are some who do not give credence to the simple command of God, but object with this question: Well now, did not God swear to Abraham by Himself (since He was God) when He promised him that He would be with him and that He would be his God if he would keep His commandments,—why then should I not also swear when I promise to someone? Answer: Hear what the Scripture says: God, since He wished more abundantly to show unto the heirs the immutability of His counsel, inserted an oath, that by two immutable things (in which it is impossible for God to lie) we might have a strong consolation. Observe the meaning of this Scripture: What God forbids you to do, He has power to do, for every thing is possible for Him. God swore an oath to Abraham, says the Scripture, so that He might show that His counsel is immutable. That is, no one can withstand nor thwart His will; therefore He can keep His oath. But we can do nothing, as is said above by Christ, to keep or perform [our oaths]: therefore we shall not swear at all [*nichts schweren*].

Then others further say as follows: It is not forbidden of God to swear in the New Testament, when it is actually commanded in the Old, but it is forbidden only to swear by heaven, earth, Jerusalem and our head. Answer: Hear the Scripture, He who swears by heaven swears by God's throne and by Him who sitteth thereon. Observe: it is forbidden to swear by heaven, which is only the throne of God: how much more is it forbidden [to swear] by God Himself! Ye fools and blind, which is greater, the throne or Him that sitteth thereon?

Further some say, Because evil is now [in the world, and] because man needs God for [the establishment of] the truth, so did the apostles Peter and Paul also swear. Answer: Peter and Paul only testify of that which God promised to Abraham with the oath. They themselves promise nothing, as the example indicates clearly. Testifying and swearing are two different things. For when a person swears he is in the first place promising future things, as Christ was promised to Abraham Whom we a long time afterwards received. But when a person bears testimony he is testifying about the present, whether it is good or evil, as Simeon spoke to Mary about Christ and testified, Behold this [child] is set for the fall and rising of many in Israel, and for a sign which shall be spoken against.

Christ also taught us along the same line when He said, Let your communication be Yea, yea; Nay, nay; for whatsoever is more than these cometh of evil. He says, Your speech or word shall be yea and nay. [However] when one does not wish to understand, he remains closed to the meaning. Christ is simply Yea and Nay, and all those who seek Him simply will understand His Word. Amen.

Dear brethren and sisters in the Lord: These are the articles of certain brethren who had heretofore been in error and who had failed to agree in the true understanding, so that many weaker consciences were perplexed, causing the Name of God to be greatly slandered. Therefore there has been a great need for us to become of one mind in the Lord, which has come to pass. To God be praise and glory!

Now since you have so well understood the will of God which has been made known by us, it will be necessary for you to achieve perseveringly, without interruption, the known will of God. For you know well what the servant who sinned knowingly heard as his recompense.

Everything which you have unwittingly done and confessed as evil doing is forgiven you through the believing prayer which is offered by us in our meeting for all our shortcomings and guilt. [This state is yours] through the gracious forgiveness of God and through the blood of Jesus Christ. Amen.

Keep watch on all who do not walk according to the simplicity of the divine truth which is stated in this letter from [the decisions of] our meeting, so that everyone among us will be governed by the rule of the ban and henceforth the entry of false brethren and sisters among us may be prevented.

Eliminate from you that which is evil and the Lord will be your God and you will be His sons and daughters.

Dear brethren, keep in mind what Paul admonishes Timothy when he says, The grace of God that bringeth salvation hath appeared to all men, teaching us that, denying ungodliness and worldly lusts, we should live soberly, righteously, and godly, in this present world; looking for that blessed hope, and the glorious appearing of the great God and our Saviour Jesus Christ; Who gave Himself for us, that He might redeem us from all iniquity, and purify unto Himself a people of His own, zealous of good works. Think on this and exercise yourselves therein and the God of peace will be with you.

May the Name of God be hallowed eternally and highly praised, Amen. May the Lord give you His peace, Amen.

The Acts of Schleitheim on the Border [Canton Schaffhausen, Switzerland], on Matthias' [Day],[3] Anno MDXXVII.

THE DORDRECHT CONFESSION (1632)

The Dordrecht Confession was adopted by Mennonites at Dordrecht on April 21, 1632. It represents the mature development of Anabaptist thought and is valued by present-day Mennonites. It is a comprehensive statement of belief and it also gives expression to the distinctive church order and practice of the Mennonites.

THE DORDRECHT CONFESSION (1632)

Article I

OF GOD AND THE CREATION OF ALL THINGS

Whereas it is declared, that "without faith it is impossible to please God" (Heb. 11:6), and that "he that cometh to God must believe that He is, and that

[3] February 24.

He is a rewarder of them that diligently seek Him," therefore we confess with the mouth and believe with the heart, together with all the pious, according to the Holy Scriptures, that there is one eternal, almighty, and incomprehensible God, Father, Son, and the Holy Ghost, and none more and none other, before whom no God existed, neither will exist after Him. For from Him, through Him, and in Him are all things. To Him be blessing, praise, and honor, for ever and ever. Gen. 17:1; Deut. 6:4; Isaiah 46:9; I John 5:7.

In this one God, who "worketh all in all," we believe. Him we confess as the Creator of all things, visible and invisible; who in six days created and prepared "heaven and earth, and the sea, and all things that are therein." And we further believe, that this God still governs and preserves the same, together with all His works, through His wisdom, His might, and the "word of His power." Gen. 5:1, 2; Acts 14:15; I Cor. 12:6; Heb. 1:3.

When He had finished His works and, according to His good pleasure, had ordained and prepared each of them, so that they were right and good according to their nature, being, and quality, He created the first man, Adam, the father of all of us, gave him a body formed "of the dust of the ground, and breathed into his nostrils the breath of life," so that he "became a living soul," created by God "in His own image and likeness," in "righteousness and true holiness" unto eternal life. He also gave him a place above all other creatures and endowed him with many high and excellent gifts, put him into the garden of Eden, and gave him a commandment and an interdiction. Thereupon He took a rib from the said Adam, made a woman out of it, brought her to him, and gave her to him as a helpmate and housewife. Consequently He has caused, that from this first man, Adam, all men who "dwell on the face of the earth," have been begotten and have descended. Gen. 1:27; 2:7, 15–17, 22; 5:1; Acts 17:26.

Article II
OF THE FALL OF MAN

We believe and confess, that, according to the purport of the Holy Scriptures, our first parents, Adam and Eve, did not long remain in the happy state in which they were created; but did, after being seduced by the deceit and subtilty of the serpent, and envy of the devil, violate the high command of God, and became disobedient to their Creator; through which disobedience "sin entered into the world, and death by sin;" so that "death passed upon all men, for that all have sinned," and thereby incurred the wrath of God and condemnation. For which reason our first parents were, by God, driven out of Paradise, to cultivate the earth, to maintain themselves thereon in sorrow, and to "eat their bread in the sweat of their face," until they "returned to the ground, from which they were taken." And that they did, therefore, through this one sin, so far apostatize, depart, and estrange themselves from God, that they could neither help themselves, nor be helped by any of their descendants, nor by angels, nor by any other creature in heaven or on earth, nor be redeemed, or reconciled to God; but would have had to be lost forever, had not God, who pitied His creatures, in mercy, interposed in their behalf and made provision for their restoration. Gen. 3:6, 23; Rom. 5:12–19; Ps. 47:8, 9; Rev. 5:3; John 3:16.

Article III
OF THE RESTORATION OF MAN THROUGH THE PROMISE OF THE COMING OF CHRIST

Regarding the Restoration of our first parents and their descendants, we believe and confess: That God, not withstanding their fall, transgression and sin, and although they had no power to help themselves, He was nevertheless not willing that they should be cast off entirely, or be eternally lost; but again called them unto Him, comforted them, and showed them that there were yet means with Him for their reconciliation; namely, the immaculate Lamb, the Son of God; who "was fore-ordained" to this purpose "before the foundation of the world," and who was promised to them and all their descendants, while they (our first parents) were yet in paradise, for their comfort, redemption, and salvation; yea, who was given to them thenceforward, through faith, as their own; after which all the pious patriarchs, to whom this promise was often renewed, longed and searched, beholding it through faith at a distance, and expecting its fulfillment—expecting that He (the Son of God), would, at His coming, again redeem and deliver the fallen race of man from their sins, their guilt, and unrighteousness. John 1:29; 11:27; I Pet. 1:18, 19; Gen. 3:15; I John 2:1, 2; 3:8; Gal. 4:4, 5.

Article IV

OF THE ADVENT OF CHRIST INTO THIS WORLD, AND THE REASON OF HIS COMING

We believe and confess further: That "when the fulness of the time was come," after which all the pious patriarchs so ardently longed, and which they so anxiously awaited—the previously promised Messiah, Redeemer, and Saviour, proceeded from God, being sent by Him, and according to the prediction of the prophets and the testimony of the evangelists, came into the world, yea, into the flesh—, so that the Word itself thus became flesh and man; and that He was conceived by the Virgin Mary (who was espoused to a man named Joseph, of the house of David), and that she bare Him as her first-born son at Bethlehem, "wrapped Him in swaddling clothes, and laid Him in a manger." John 4:25; 16:28; I Tim. 3:16; Matt. 1:21; John 1:14; Luke 2:7.

Further we believe and confess, that this is the same One, "whose goings forth have been from of old, from everlasting;" who has "neither beginning of days, nor end of life." Of whom it is testified, that He is "Alpha and Omega, the beginning and the end, the first and the last." That this is also He—and none other—who was chosen, promised, and sent; who came into the world; and who is God's only, first, and proper Son;

who was before John the Baptist, before Abraham, before the world; yea, who was David's Lord, and who was God of the "whole earth," "the first-born of every creature;" who was sent into the world, and Himself delivered up the body prepared for Him, as "an offering and a sacrifice to God for a sweet smelling savour;" yea, for the comfort, redemption, and salvation of all—of the human race. Micah 5:2; Heb. 7:3; Rev. 1:8; John 3:16; Rom. 8:32; Col. 1:15; Heb. 10:5.

But how, or in what manner, this worthy body was prepared, or how the Word became flesh, and He Himself man, we content ourselves with the declaration which the worthy evangelists have given and left in their description thereof; according to which we confess with all the saints, that He is the Son of the living God, in whom exist all our hope, comfort, redemption, and salvation, and which we are to seek in no one else. Luke 1:31–35; John 20:31.

Further, we believe and confess by authority of scripture, that when He had ended His course, and "finished" the work for which He was sent into the world, He was, by the providence of God, delivered into the hands of the unrighteous; suffered under the judge, Pontius Pilate, was crucified, died, was buried, rose again from the dead on the third day, and ascended into heaven, where He now sits at the right hand of the Majesty of God on high; from whence He will come again to judge the living and dead. Luke 23:1, 52, 53; 24:5, 6, 51.

Thus we believe the Son of God died—"tasted death for every man," shed His precious blood, and thereby bruised the head of the serpent, destroyed the works of the devil, "blotted out the hand-writing," and purchased redemption for the whole human race; and thus He became the source of eternal salvation to all who from the time of Adam to the end of the world, shall have believed in Him, and obeyed Him. Gen. 3:15; I John 3:8; Col. 2:14; Rom. 5:18.

Article V

OF THE LAW OF CHRIST, WHICH IS THE HOLY GOSPEL, OR THE NEW TESTAMENT

We also believe and confess, that Christ, before His ascension, established and instituted His New Testament and left it to His followers, to be and remain an everlasting testament, which He confirmed and sealed with His own precious blood; and which He has so highly commended to them, that neither men or angels may change it, neither take therefrom nor add thereto. Jer. 31:31; Heb. 9:15–17; Matt. 26:28; Gal. 1:8; I Tim. 6:3–5; Rev. 22:18, 19; Matt. 5:18; Luke 21:33.

And that He has caused this Testament (in which the whole counsel and will of His heavenly Father, so far as these are necessary to the salvation of man, are comprehended), to be proclaimed, in His name, through His beloved apostles, messengers, and servants (whom He chose and sent into all the world for this purpose)—to all nations, people and tongues; these apostles preaching repentance and remission of sins; and that He, in said Testament, caused it to be declared, that all men without distinction, if they are obedient, through faith, follow, fulfill and live according to the precepts of the same, are His children and rightful heirs; having thus excluded none from the precious inheritance of eternal salvation, except the unbelieving and disobedient, the headstrong and unconverted; who despise such salvation; and thus by their own actions incur guilt by refusing the same, and "judge themselves unworthy of everlasting life." Mark 16:15; Luke 24:46, 47; Rom. 8:17; Acts 13:46.

Article VI

OF REPENTANCE AND AMENDMENT OF LIFE

We believe and confess, that, as the "imagination of man's heart is evil from his youth," and consequently inclined to all unrighteousness, sin, and wickedness, that, therefore, the first doctrine of the precious New Testament of the Son of God is, Repentance and amendment of life. Gen. 8:21; Mark 1:15.

Therefore those who have ears to hear, and hearts to understand, must "bring forth fruits meet for repentance," amend their lives, believe the Gospel, "depart from evil and do good," desist from wrong and cease from sinning, "put off the old man with his deeds and put on the new man," which after God is created in "righteousness and true holiness." For neither *Baptism, Supper, nor church-fellowship,* nor any other external ceremony, can, without faith, the new birth, and a change or renewal of life, help, or qualify us, that we may please God, or receive any consolation or promise of salvation from Him. Luke 3:8; Eph. 4:22–24; Col. 3:9, 10.

But on the contrary, we must go to God "with a sincere heart in full assurance of faith," and believe in Jesus Christ, as the Scriptures speak and testify of Him. Through which faith we obtain the pardon of our sins, become sanctified, justified, and children of God; yea, partakers of His mind, nature and image, as we are born again of God through His incorruptible seed from above. Heb. 10:21, 22; John 7:38; II Pet. 1:4.

Article VII
OF HOLY BAPTISM

Regarding baptism, we confess that all penitent believers, who through faith, the new birth and renewal of the Holy Ghost, have become united with God, and whose names are recorded in heaven, must, on such Scriptural confession of their faith, and renewal of life, according to the command and doctrine of Christ, and the example and custom of the apostles, be baptized with water in the ever adorable name of the Father, and of the Son, and of the Holy Ghost, to the burying of their sins, and thus to become incorporated into the communion of the saints; whereupon they must learn to observe all things whatsoever the Son of God taught, left on record, and commanded His followers to do. Matt. 3:15; 28:19, 20; Mark 16:15, 16; Acts 2:38; 8:12, 38; 9:18; 10:47; 16:33; Rom. 6:3, 4; Col. 2:12.

Article VIII
OF THE CHURCH OF CHRIST

We believe in and confess a visible Church of God, consisting of those, who, as before remarked, have truly repented, and rightly believed; who are rightly baptized, united with God in heaven, and incorporated into the communion of the saints on earth. I Cor. 12:13.

And these, we confess, are a "chosen generation, a royal priesthood, an holy nation," who have the testimony that they are the "bride" of Christ; yea, that they are children and heirs of eternal life—a "habitation of God through the Spirit," built on the foundation of the apostles and prophets, of which "Christ Himself is the chief cornerstone"—the foundation on which His church is built. John 3:29; Matt. 16:18; Eph. 2:19–21; Tit. 3:7; I Pet. 1:18, 19; 2:9.

This church of the living God, which He has purchased and redeemed through His own precious blood, and with which He will be—according to His own promise—for her comfort and protection, "always, even unto the end of the world;" yea, will dwell and walk with her, and preserve her, that no "winds" nor "floods," yea, not even the "gates of hell shall prevail against her"—may be known by her evangelical faith, doctrine, love, and godly conversation; also by her pure walk and practice, and her observance of the true ordinances of Christ, which He has strictly enjoined on His followers. Matt. 7:25; 16:18; 28:20; II Cor. 6:16.

Article IX
OF THE ELECTION, AND OFFICES OF TEACHERS, DEACONS, AND DEACONESSES, IN THE CHURCH

Regarding the offices, and election of persons to the same, in the church, we believe and confess: That, as the church cannot exist and prosper, nor continue in its structure, without offices and regulations, that therefore the Lord Jesus has Himself (as a father in his house), appointed and prescribed His offices and ordinances, and has given commandments concerning the same, as to how each one should walk therein, give heed to His own work and calling, and do it as it becomes Him to do. Eph. 4:11, 12.

For He Himself, as the faithful and great Shepherd, and Bishop of our souls, was sent into the world, not to wound, to break, or destroy the souls of men, but to heal them; to seek that which is lost, and to pull down the hedges and partition wall, so as to make out of many one; thus collecting out of Jews and heathen, yea, out of all nations, a church in His name; for which (so that no one might go astray or be lost) He laid down His own life, and thus procured for them salvation, made them free and redeemed them, to which blessing no one could help them, or be of service in obtaining it. I Pet. 2:25; Matt. 18:11; Eph. 2:13, 14; John 10:9, 11, 15.

And that He, besides this, left His church before His departure, provided with faithful ministers, apostles, evangelists, pastors, and teachers, whom He had chosen by prayer and supplication through the Holy Spirit, so that they might govern the church, feed His flock, watch over, maintain, and care for the same: yea, do all things as He left them an example, taught them, and commanded them to do; and likewise to teach the church to observe all things whatsoever He commanded them. Eph. 4:11, 12; Luke 6:12, 13; 10:1; Matt. 28:20.

Also that the apostles were afterwards, as faithful followers of Christ and leaders of the church, diligent in these matters, namely, in choosing through prayer and supplication to God, brethren who were to provide all the churches in the cities and circuits, with bishops, pastors, and leaders, and to ordain to these offices such men as took "heed unto themselves and unto the doctrine," and also unto the flock; who were sound in the faith, pious in their life and conversation, and who had—as well within the church as "without" —a good reputation and a good report; so that they might be a light and example in all godliness and good works; might worthily administer the Lord's ordinances—baptism and supper—and that they (the brethren sent by the apostles) might also, at all places, where such were to be had, appoint faithful men as elders, who were able to teach others, confirm them in the name of the Lord "with the laying on of hands," and who (the elders) were to take care of all things of which the church stood in need; so that they, as faithful servants, might well "occupy" their Lord's money, gain thereby, and thus "save themselves and those who hear them." I Tim. 3:1; 4:14–16; Acts 1:23, 24; Tit. 1:5; Luke 19:13.

That they should also take good care (particularly each one of the charge over which he had the oversight), that all the circuits should be well provided with deacons, who should have the care and oversight of the poor, and who were to receive gifts and alms, and again faithfully to distribute them among the poor saints who were in need, and this is in all honesty, as is becoming. Acts 6:3–6.

Also that honorable old widows should be chosen as deaconesses, who, besides the deacons are to visit, comfort, and take care of the poor, the weak, afflicted, and the needy, as also to visit, comfort and take care of widows and orphans; and further to assist in taking care of any matters in the church that properly come within their sphere, according to their ability. I Tim. 5:9, 10; Rom. 16:1, 2.

And as it further regards the deacons, that they (particularly if they are fit persons, and chosen and ordained thereto by the church), may also in aid and relief of the bishops, exhort the church (being, as already remarked, chosen thereto), and thus assist in word and doctrine; so that each one may serve the other from love, with the gift which he has received from the Lord; so that through the common service and assistance of each member, according to his ability, the body of Christ may be edified, and the Lord's vineyard and church be preserved in its growth and structure. II Tim. 2:2.

Article X
OF THE LORD'S SUPPER

We also believe in and observe the breaking of bread, or the Lord's Supper, as the Lord Jesus instituted the same (with bread and wine) before His sufferings, and also observed and ate it with the apostles, and also commanded it to be observed to His remembrance, as also the apostles subsequently taught and observed the same in the church, and commanded it to be observed by believers in commemoration of the death and sufferings of the Lord—the breaking of His worthy body and the shedding of His precious blood —for the whole human race. So is the observance of this sacrament also to remind us of the benefit of the said death and sufferings of Christ, namely, the redemption and eternal salvation which He purchased thereby, and the great love thus shown to sinful man; whereby we are earnestly exhorted also to love one another—to love our neighbor—to forgive and absolve him—even as Christ has done unto us—and also to endeavor to maintain and keep alive the union and communion which we have with God, and amongst one another; which is thus shown and represented to us by the aforesaid breaking of bread. Matt. 26:26; Mark 14:22; Luke 22:19, 20; Acts 2:42, 46; I Cor. 10:16; 11:23–26.

Article XI
OF THE WASHING OF THE SAINTS' FEET

We also confess a washing of the feet of the saints, as the Lord Jesus did not only institute and command the same, but did also Himself wash the feet of the apostles, although He was their Lord and Master; thereby giving an example that they also should wash one another's feet, and thus do to one another as He did to them; which they also afterwards taught believers to observe, and all this is a sign of true humiliation; but yet more particularly as a sign to remind us of the true washing—the washing and purification of the soul in the blood of Christ. John 13:4–17; I Tim. 5:9, 10.

Article XII
OF MATRIMONY

We also confess that there is in the church of God an "honorable" state of matrimony between two believers of the different sexes, as God first instituted the same in paradise between Adam and Eve, and as the Lord Jesus reformed it by removing all abuses which had crept into it, and restoring it to its first order. Gen. 1:27; 2:18, 21–24.

In this manner the Apostle Paul also taught and permitted matrimony in the church, leaving it to each one's own choice to enter into matrimony with any person who would unite with him in such state, provided that it was done "in the Lord," according to the primitive order; the words "in the Lord," to be understood, according to our opinion, that just as the patriarchs had to marry amongst their own kindred or generation, so there is also no other liberty allowed to believers under the New Testament dispensation, than to marry among the "chosen generation," or the spiritual kindred of Christ; that is, to such—and none others—as are already, previous to their marriage, united to the church in heart and soul, have received the same baptism, belong to the same church, are of the same faith and doctrine, and lead the same course of life, with themselves. I Cor. 7:39; 9:5; Gen. 24:4; 28:6, 7; Num. 36:6–9.

Such are then, as already remarked, united by God and the church according to the primitive order, and this is then called, "Marrying in the Lord." I Cor. 7:39.

Article XIII
OF THE OFFICE OF CIVIL GOVERNMENT

We also believe and confess, that God has instituted civil government, for the punishment of the wicked and the protection of the pious; and also further, for the purpose of governing the world, countries and cities; and also to preserve its subjects in good order and under good regulations. Wherefore we are not permitted to despise, revile, or resist the same, but are to acknowledge it as a minister of God and be subject and obedient to it, in all things that do not militate against the law, will, and commandments of God; yea, "to be ready to every good work;" also faithfully to pay it custom, tax, and tribute; thus giving it what is its due; as Jesus Christ taught, did Himself, and commanded His followers to do. That we are also to pray to the Lord earnestly for the government and its welfare, and in behalf of our country, so that we may live under its protection, maintain ourselves, and "lead a quiet and peaceable life in all godliness and honesty." And further, that the Lord would recompense them (our rulers), here and in eternity, for all the benefits, liberties, and favors which we enjoy under their laudable administration. Rom. 13:1–7; Titus 3:1, 2; I Pet. 2:17; Matt. 17:27; 22:20, 21; I Tim. 2:1, 2.

Article XIV
OF DEFENSE BY FORCE

Regarding revenge, whereby we resist our enemies with the sword, we believe and confess that the Lord Jesus has forbidden His disciples and followers all revenge and resistance, and has thereby commanded them not to "return evil for evil, nor railing for railing;" but to "put up the sword into the sheath," or, as the prophet foretold, "beat them into ploughshares." Matt. 5:39, 44; Rom. 12:14; I Pet. 3:9; Isa. 2:4; Micah 4:3.

From this we see, that, according to the example, life, and doctrine of Christ, we are not to do wrong, or cause offense or vexation to anyone; but to seek the welfare and salvation of all men; also, if necessity should require it, to flee, for the Lord's sake, from one city or country to another, and suffer the "spoiling of our goods," rather than give occasion of offense to anyone; and if we are struck in our "right cheek, rather to turn the other also," than revenge ourselves, or return the blow. Matt. 5:39; 10:23; Rom. 12:19.

And that we are, besides this, also to pray for our

enemies, comfort and feed them, when they are hungry or thirsty, and thus by well-doing convince them and overcome the evil with good. Rom. 12:20, 21.

Finally, that we are to do good in all respects, "commending ourselves to every man's conscience in the sight of God," and according to the law of Christ, do nothing to others that we would not wish them to do unto us. II Cor. 4:2; Matt. 7:12; Luke 6:31.

Article XV
OF THE SWEARING OF OATHS

Regarding the swearing of oaths, we believe and confess that the Lord Jesus has dissuaded His followers from and forbidden them the same; that is, that He commanded them to "swear not at all;" but that their "Yea" should be "yea," and their "Nay, nay." From which we understand that all oaths, high and low, are forbidden; and that instead of them we are to confirm all our promises and covenants, declarations and testimonies of all matters, merely with "Yea that is yea," and "Nay that is nay;" and that we are to perform and fulfill at all times, and in all things, to every one, every promise and obligation to which we thus affirm, as faithfully as if we had confirmed it by the most solemn oath. And if we thus do, we have the confidence that no one—not even government itself—will have just cause to require more of us. Matt. 5:34–37; Jas. 5:12; II Cor. 1:17.

Article XVI
OF THE ECCLESIASTICAL BAN OR EXCOMMUNI-
CATION FROM THE CHURCH

We also believe in and acknowledge the ban, or excommunication, a separation or spiritual correction by the church, for the amendment, and not for the destruction, of offenders; so that what is pure may be separated from that which is impure. That is, if a person, after having been enlightened, and received the knowledge of the truth, and has been received into the communion of the saints, does willfully, or out of presumption, sin against God, or commit some other "sin unto death," thereby falling into such unfruitful works of darkness, that he becomes separated from God, and is debarred from His Kingdom—that such an one—when his works are become manifest, and sufficiently known to the church—cannot remain in the "congregation of the righteous;" but must, as an offensive member and open sinner, be excluded from the church, "rebuked before all," and "purged out as a leaven," and thus remain until his amendment, as an example and warning to others, and also that the church may be kept pure from such "spots" and "blemishes;" so that not for the want of this, the name of the Lord be blasphemed, the church dishonored, and a stumblingblock thrown in the way of those "without," and finally, that the offender may not be condemned with the world, but that he may again be convinced of the error of his ways, and brought to repentance and amendment of life. Isa. 59:2; I Cor. 5:5, 6, 12; I Tim. 5:20; II Cor. 13:10.

Regarding the brotherly admonition, as also the instruction of the erring, we are to "give all diligence" to watch over them, and exhort them in all meekness to the amendment of their ways (Jas. 5:19, 20); and in case any should remain obstinate and unconverted, to reprove them as the case may require. In short, the church must "put away from among herself him that is wicked," whether it be in doctrine or life.

Article XVII

OF THE SHUNNING OF THOSE WHO ARE EXPELLED

As regards the withdrawing from, or the shunning of, those who are expelled, we believe and confess, that if any one, whether it be through a wicked life or perverse doctrine—is so far fallen as to be separated from God, and consequently rebuked by, and expelled from, the church, he must also, according to the doctrine of Christ and His apostles, be shunned and avoided by all the members of the church (particularly by those to whom his misdeeds are known), whether it be in eating or drinking, or other such like social matters. In short, that we are to have nothing to do with him; so that we may not become defiled by intercourse with him, and partakers of his sins; but that he may be made ashamed, be affected in his mind, convinced in his conscience, and thereby induced to amend his ways. I Cor. 5:9–11; Rom. 16:17; II Thess. 3:14; Tit. 3:10, 11.

That nevertheless, as well in shunning as in reproving such offender, such moderation and Christian discretion be used, that such shunning and reproof may not be conducive to his ruin, but be serviceable to his amendment. For should he be in need, hungry, thirsty, naked, sick or visited by some other affliction, we are in duty bound, according to the doctrine and practice of Christ and His apostles, to render him aid and assistance, as necessity may require; otherwise the shunning of him might be rather conducive to his ruin than to his amendment. I Thess. 5:14.

Therefore we must not treat such offenders as enemies, but exhort them as brethren, in order thereby to bring them to a knowledge of their sins and to repentance; so that they may again become reconciled to God and the church, and be received and admitted into the same—thus exercising love towards them, as is becoming. II Thess. 3:15.

Article XVIII

OF THE RESURRECTION OF THE DEAD AND THE LAST JUDGMENT

Regarding the resurrection of the dead, we confess with the mouth, and believe with the heart, that according to the Scriptures all men who shall have died or "fallen asleep," will, through the incomprehensible power of God, at the day of judgment, be "raised up" and made alive; and that these, together with all those who then remain alive, and who shall be "changed in a moment, in the twinkling of an eye, at the last trump," shall "appear before the judgment seat of Christ," where the good shall be separated from the evil, and where "every one shall receive the things done in his body, according to that he hath done, whether it be good or bad"; and that the good or pious shall then further, as the blessed of their Father, be received by Christ into eternal life, where they shall receive that joy which "eye hath not seen, nor ear heard, nor hath entered into the heart of man." Yea, where they shall reign and triumph with Christ for ever and ever. Matt. 22:30–32; 25:31; Dan. 12:2; Job 19:25, 26; John 5:28, 29; I Cor. 15:51, 52; I Thess. 4:13.

And that, on the contrary, the wicked or impious, shall, as the accursed of God, be cast into "outer darkness;" yea, into eternal, hellish torments; "where their worm dieth not, and the fire is not quenched;" and where—according to Holy Scripture—they can expect no comfort nor redemption throughout eternity. Isa. 66:24; Matt. 25:46; Mark 9:46; Rev. 14:10, 11.

May the Lord through His grace make us all fit and worthy, that no such calamity may befall any of us; but that we may be diligent, and so take heed to ourselves, that we may be found of Him in peace, without spot, and blameless. Amen.

PROTESTANT SCHOLASTICISM

THE HELVETIC CONSENSUS FORMULA
(1675)

Following the initial enthusiasm of the Reformation, Protestant theology entered into a scholastic period. Scholasticism placed a very great emphasis upon logic and rhetoric, upon sharp and clear definitions as a means to truth and as a way of eliminating theological controversy. It was also a method of defense against the theology of Roman Catholicism, but this was secondary to the internal development of the theology itself.

The clearest expression of scholasticism in Reformed

theology is found in the Helvetic Consensus Formula, which was written by John Henry Heidegger of Zurich at the request of the Swiss Diet. The Consensus deals especially with the theology of Saumur, a liberalized Calvinism. It is best known for its contention that the Hebrew vowel points were inspired. The creed was used in Switzerland for half a century and then fell into disuse.

Source: Text printed here is taken from *Outlines of Theology* by Archibald Alexander Hodge (New York: A. C. Armstrong and Son, 1897), pp. 656–63. Latin text may be found in *Collectio Confessionum*, edited by H. A. Niemeyer, (Lipsiae: Iulii Klinkhardti, 1840), pp. 729–39.

Dillenberger, John, *Protestant Thought and Natural Science* (Garden City, New York: Doubleday & Co., 1960), for a discussion of Scholasticism.

Geiger, Max, *Die Basler Kirche und Theologie im Zeitalter der Hochorthodoxie* (Zurich: 1952).

Good, James I., *History of the Swiss Reformed Church Since the Reformation* (Philadelphia: Publication and Sunday School Board of the Reformed Church in the United States, 1913).

Pelikan, J., *From Luther to Kierkegaard* (St. Louis: Concordia Publishing House, 1950, for a discussion of Scholasticism.

Schaff, *Creeds of Christendom* (New York: Harper & Bros., 1877).

FORM OF AGREEMENT OF THE HELVETIC REFORMED CHURCHES RESPECTING THE DOCTRINE OF UNIVERSAL GRACE, THE DOCTRINES CONNECTED THEREWITH, AND SOME OTHER POINTS

Canons

I. God, the Supreme Judge, not only took care to have His word, which is the "power of God unto salvation to every one that believeth" (Rom. i. 16), committed to writing by Moses, the Prophets, and the Apostles, but has also watched and cherished it with paternal care ever since it was written up to the present time, so that it could not be corrupted by craft of Satan or fraud of man. Therefore the Church justly ascribes it to His singular grace and goodness that she has, and will have to the end of the world, a "sure word of prophecy" and "Holy Scriptures" (2 Tim. iii. 15), from which, though heaven and earth perish, "one jot or one tittle shall in no wise pass" (Matt. v. 18).

II. But, in particular, the Hebrew Original of the Old Testament, which we have received and to this day do retain as handed down by the Jewish Church, unto whom formerly "were committed the oracles of God" (Rom. iii. 2), is, not only in its consonants, but in its vowels—either the vowel points themselves, or at least the power of the points—not only in its matter, but in its words, inspired of God, thus forming, together with the Original of the New Testament, the sole and complete rule of our faith and life; and to its standard, as to a Lydian stone, all extant versions, oriental and occidental, ought to be applied, and wherever they differ, be conformed.

III. Therefore we can by no means approve the opinion of those who declare that the *text* which the Hebrew Original exhibits was determined by man's will alone, and do not scruple at all to remodel a Hebrew reading which they consider unsuitable, and amend it from the Greek Versions of the LXX and others, the Samaritan Pentateuch, the Chaldee Targums, or even from other sources, yea, sometimes from their own reason alone; and furthermore, they do not acknowledge any other reading to be genuine except that which can be educed by the critical power of the human judgment from the collation of editions with each other and with the various readings of the Hebrew Original itself—which, they maintain, has been corrupted in various ways; and finally, they affirm that besides the Hebrew edition of the present time, there are in the Versions of the ancient interpreters which differ from our Hebrew context other Hebrew Originals, since these Versions are also indicative of ancient Hebrew Originals differing from each other. Thus they bring the foundation of our faith and its inviolable authority into perilous hazard.

IV. Before the foundation of the world God purposed in Christ Jesus, our Lord, an eternal purpose (Eph. iii. 11), in which, from the mere good pleasure of His own will, without any prevision of the merit of works or of faith, unto the praise of His glorious grace, out of the human race lying in the same mass of corruption and of common blood, and, therefore, corrupted by sin, *He elected a certain and definite number* to be led, in time, unto salvation by Christ, their Surety and sole Mediator, and on account of His merit, by the mighty power of the regenerating Holy Spirit, to be effectually called, regenerated, and gifted with faith and repentance. So, indeed, God, determining to illustrate His glory, decreed to create man perfect, in the first place, then, permit him to fall, and at length pity some of the fallen, and therefore elect those, but leave the rest in the corrupt mass, and finally give them over to eternal destruction.

V. In that gracious decree of Divine Election, moreover, Christ himself is also included, not as the meritorious cause, or foundation anterior to Election itself, but as being Himself also elect (I Peter ii. 4, 6), foreknown before the foundation of the world, and accordingly, as the first requisite of the execution of the decree of Election, chosen Mediator, and our first born Brother, whose precious merit God determined to use for the purpose of conferring, without detriment to His own justice, salvation upon us. For the Holy Scriptures not only declare that Election was made according to the mere good pleasure of the Divine counsel and will (Eph. i. 5, 9; Matt. xi. 26), but also make the appointment and giving of Christ, our Mediator, to proceed from the *strenuous love* of God the Father toward the world of the elect.

VI. Wherefore we can not give suffrage to the opinion of those who teach:—(1) that God, moved by philanthropy, or a sort of special love for the fallen human race, to *previous election*, did, in a kind of conditioned willing—willingness—first moving of pity, as they call it—inefficacious desire—purpose the salvation of all and each, at least, conditionally, i.e., if they would believe; (2) that He appointed Christ Mediator for all and each of the fallen; and (3) that, at length, certain ones whom He regarded, not simply as sinners in the first Adam, but as redeemed in the second Adam, He *elected,* i.e., He determined to graciously bestow on these, in time, the saving gift of faith; and in this sole act Election properly so called is complete. For these and all other kindred teachings are in no wise insignificant deviations from the form of sound words respecting Divine Election; because the Scriptures do not extend unto all and each God's purpose of showing mercy to man, but restrict it to the elect alone, the reprobate being excluded, even by name, as Esau, whom God hated with an eternal hatred (Rom. ix. 10–13). The same Holy Scriptures testify that the counsel and the will of God change not, but stand immovable, and God in the heavens *doeth* whatsoever he will (Ps. cxv. 3; Isa. xlvi. 10); for God is infinitely removed from all that human imperfection which characterizes inefficacious affections and desires, rashness, repentance, and change of purpose. The appointment, also, of Christ, as Mediator, equally with the salvation of those who were given to Him for a possession and an inheritance that can not be taken away, proceeds from one and the same Election, and does not underly Election as its foundation.

VII. As all His works were known unto God from eternity (Acts xv. 18), so in time, according to His infinite power, wisdom, and goodness, He made man, the glory and end of His works, in His own image, and, therefore, upright, wise, and just. Him, thus constituted, He put under the Covenant of Works, and in this Covenant freely promised him communion with God, favor, and life, if indeed he acted in obedience to His will.

VIII. Moreover that promise annexed to the Covenant of Works was not a continuation only of earthly life and happiness, but the possession especially of life eternal and celestial, a life, namely, of both body and soul in heaven—if indeed man ran the course of perfect obedience—with unspeakable joy in communion with God. For not only did the Tree of Life prefigure this very thing unto Adam, but the power of the law, which, being fulfilled by Christ, who went under it in our stead, awards to us no other than celestial life in Christ who kept the righteousness of the law (Rom. ii. 26), manifestly proves the same, as also the opposite threatening of death both temporal and eternal.

IX. Wherefore we can not assent to the opinion of those who deny that a reward of *heavenly* bliss was proffered to Adam on condition of obedience to God, and do not admit that the promise of the Covenant of Works was any thing more than a promise of perpetual life abounding in every kind of good that can be suited to the body and soul of man in a state of *perfect* nature, and the enjoyment thereof in an *earthly* Paradise. For this also is contrary to the sound sense of the Divine Word, and weakens the power (*potestas*) of the law in itself considered.

X. As however, God entered into the Covenant of Works not only with Adam for himself, but also, in him as the head and root (*stirps*), with the whole human race, who would, by virtue of the blessing of the nature derived from him, inherit also the same perfection, provided he continued therein; so Adam by his mournful fall, not only for himself, but also for the whole human race that would be born of bloods and the will of the flesh, sinned and lost the benefits promised in the Covenant. We hold, therefore, that the sin of Adam is imputed by the mysterious and just judgment of God to all his posterity. For the Apostle testifies that *in Adam all sinned, by one man's disobedience many were made sinners* (Rom. v. 12, 19), and *in Adam all die* (1 Cor. xv. 21, 22). But there appears no way in which hereditary corruption could fall, as a spiritual death, upon the whole human race by the just judgment of God, unless some sin (*delictum*) of that race preceded, incurring (*inducens*) the penalty (*reatum,* guilt) of that death. For God, the supremely just Judge of all the earth, punishes none but the guilty.

XI. For a double reason, therefore, man, because of sin (*post peccatum*) is by nature, and hence from his birth, before committing any actual sin, exposed to God's wrath and curse; first, on account of the transgression and disobedience which he committed in the loins of Adam; and, secondly, on account of the consequent hereditary corruption implanted in his very conception, whereby his whole nature is depraved and spiritually dead; so that original sin may rightly be regarded as twofold, viz., *imputed sin* and *inherent hereditary sin*.

XII. Accordingly we can not, without harm to Divine truth, give assent to those who deny that Adam represented his posterity by appointment of God, and that his sin is imputed, therefore, *immediately* to his posterity; and under the term *imputation mediate and consequent* not only destroy the imputation of the first sin, but also expose the doctrine (*assertio*) of hereditary corruption to great danger.

XIII. As Christ was from eternity elected the Head, Prince, and Lord (*Haeres*) of all who, in time, are saved by His grace, so also, in time, He was made Surety of the New Covenant only for those who, by the eternal Election, were given to Him as His own people (*populus peculii*), His seed and inheritance. For according to the determinate counsel of the Father and His own intention, He encountered dreadful death instead of the elect alone, restored only these into the bosom of the Father's grace, and these only he reconciled to God, the offended Father, and delivered from the curse of the law. For our Jesus saves *His people* from their sins (Matt. i. 21), who gave His life a ransom for *many sheep* (Matt. xx. 28; John x. 15), His own, who hear His voice (John x. 27, 28),

and for these only He also intercedes, as a divinely
appointed Priest, and not for the world (John xvii. 9).
Accordingly in the death of Christ, only the elect, who
in time are made new creatures (2 Cor. v. 17), and
for whom Christ in His death was substituted as an
expiatory sacrifice, are regarded as having died with
Him and as being justified from sin; and thus, with
the counsel of the Father who gave to Christ none but
the elect to be redeemed, and also with the working
of the Holy Spirit, who sanctifies and seals unto a living hope of eternal life none but the elect, the will of
Christ who died so agrees and amicably conspires in
perfect harmony, that the sphere of the Father's election (*Patris eligentis*), the Son's redemption (*Filii redi-
mentis*), and the Spirit's sanctification (*Spiritus S.
sanctificantis*) is one and the same (*aequalis pateat*).

XIV. This very thing further appears in this also,
that Christ merited for those in whose stead He died
the *means of salvation,* especially the regenerating
Spirit and the heavenly gift of faith, as well as salvation itself, and actually confers these upon them. For
the Scriptures testify that Christ, the Lord, came *to
save the lost sheep of the house of Israel* (Matt. xv.
24) and sends the same Holy Spirit, the fount of regeneration, as His own (John xvi. 7, 8); that among
the better promises of the New Covenant of which He
was made Mediator and Surety this one is pre-eminent,
that He will write His law, i.e., the law of faith, *in
the hearts of his people* (Heb. viii. 10); that *whatsoever the Father has given to Christ will come to Him,*
by faith, surely; and finally, that we are *chosen in
Christ to be holy and without blame,* and, moreover,
children by Him (Eph. i. 4, 5); but our being holy
and children of God proceeds only from faith and
the Spirit of regeneration.

XV. But *by the obedience of his death* Christ instead of the elect so satisfied God the Father, that in
the estimate, nevertheless, of His vicarious righteousness and of that obedience, all of that which He rendered to the law, as its just servant, during the whole

course of His life, whether by doing or by suffering, ought to be called obedience. For Christ's life, according to the Apostle's testimony (Philip. ii. 7, 8), was nothing but a continuous emptying of self, submission and humiliation, descending step by step to the very lowest extreme, even the death of the Cross; and the Spirit of God plainly declares that Christ in our stead satisfied the law and Divine justice by His most holy life, and makes that ransom with which God has redeemed us to consist not in His sufferings only, but in His whole life conformed to the law. The Spirit, however, ascribes our redemption to the death, or the blood, of Christ, in no other sense than that it was consummated by sufferings; and from that last terminating and grandest act derives a name (*denominationem facit*) indeed, but in such a way as by no means to separate the life preceding from His death.

XVI. Since all these things are entirely so, surely we can not approve the contrary doctrine of those who affirm that of His own intention, by His own counsel and that of the Father who sent Him, Christ died for all and each upon the impossible condition, provided they believe; that He obtained for all a salvation, which, nevertheless, is not applied to all, and by His death merited salvation and faith for no one individually and certainly (*proprie et actu*), but only removed the obstacles of Divine justice, and acquired for the Father the liberty of entering into a new covenant of grace with all men; and finally, they so separate the active and passive righteousness of Christ, as to assert that He claims His *active* righteousness for himself as His own, but gives and imputes only His *passive* righteousness to the elect. All these opinions, and all that are like these, are contrary to the plain Scriptures and the glory of Christ, who is *Author and Finisher* of our faith and salvation; they make His cross of none effect, and under the appearance of augmenting His merit, they really diminish it.

XVII. The call unto salvation was suited to its *due time* (1 Tim. ii. 6); since by God's will it was at one

time more restricted, at another, more extended and
general, but never absolutely universal. For, indeed,
in the Old Testament God *showed His word unto Jacob, His statutes and His judgments unto Israel; He
dealt not so with any nation* (Ps. cxlvii. 19, 20). In
the New Testament, peace being made in the blood of
Christ and the inner wall of partition broken down,
God so extended the limits (*pomoeria*) of Gospel
preaching and the external call, that there is no longer
any *difference between the Jew and the Greek; for
the same Lord over all is rich unto all that call upon
Him* (Rom. x. 12). But not even thus is the call universal; for Christ testifies that *many are called* (Matt.
xx. 16), not all; and when Paul and Timothy essayed
to go into Bithynia to preach the Gospel, *the Spirit
suffered them not* (Acts xvi. 7); and there have been
and there are to-day, as experience testifies, innumerable myriads of men to whom Christ is not known
even by rumor.

XVIII. Meanwhile God *left not himself without
witness* (Acts xiv. 17) unto those whom He refused to
call by His Word unto salvation. For He divided unto
them the spectacle of the heavens and the stars (Deut.
iv. 19), and *that which may be known of God,* even
from the works of nature and Providence, *He hath
showed unto them* (Rom. i. 19), for the purpose of
attesting His long suffering. Yet it is not to be affirmed
that the works of nature and Divine Providence were
means (*organa*), sufficient of themselves and fulfilling
the function of the external call, whereby He would
reveal unto them the mystery of the good pleasure or
mercy of God in Christ. For the Apostle immediately
adds (Rom. i. 20), "The invisible things of Him from
the creation are clearly seen, being understood by the
things that are made, even *His eternal power and
Godhead;*" not His hidden good pleasure in Christ,
and not even to the end that thence they might learn
the mystery of salvation through Christ, but that they
might be *without excuse,* because they did not use
aright the knowledge that was left them, but *when*

they knew God, they glorified Him not as God, neither were thankful. Wherefore also Christ glorifies God, His Father, because *He had hidden these things from the wise and the prudent, and revealed them unto babes* (Matt. xi. 25); and the Apostle teaches, moreover, that God has made known unto us the mystery of His will according to His good pleasure which He hath purposed in Himself (*in Christo*), (Eph. i. 9).

XIX. Likewise the external call itself, which is made by the preaching of the Gospel, is on the part of God also, who calls, earnest and sincere. For in His Word He unfolds earnestly and most truly, not, indeed, His secret intention respecting the salvation or destruction of each individual, but what belongs to our duty, and what remains for us if we do or neglect this duty. Clearly it is the will of God who calls, that they who are called come to Him and not neglect so great salvation, and so He promises eternal life also in good earnest, to those who come to Him by faith; for, as the Apostle declares, "it is a faithful saying:—For if we be dead with Him, we shall also live with Him; if we suffer, we shall also reign with Him; if we deny Him, He also will deny us; if we believe not, yet He abideth faithful; He can not deny Himself." Nor in regard to those who do not obey the call is this will inefficacious; for God always attains that which He intends in His will (*quod volens intendit*), even the demonstration of duty, and following this, either the salvation of the elect who do their duty, or the inexcusableness of the rest who neglect the duty set before them. Surely the spiritual man in no way secures (*conciliat*) the internal purpose of God to produce faith (*conceptum Dei internum, fidei analogum*) along with the externally proffered, or written Word of God. Moreover, because God approved every verity which flows from His counsel, therefore it is rightly said to be His will, that *all who see the Son and believe on Him may have everlasting life* (John vi. 40). Although these "all" are the elect alone, and God formed no plan of universal salvation without any selection of persons, and Christ therefore died not for every one but for the elect only who were given to Him; yet He intends this in any case to be universally true, which follows from His special and definite purpose. But that, by God's will, the elect alone believe in the external call thus universally proffered, while the reprobate are hardened, proceeds solely from the discriminating grace of God: election by the same grace to them that believe; but their own native wickedness to the reprobate who remain in sin, and after their hardness and impenitent heart treasure up unto themselves wrath against the day of wrath, and revelation of the righteous judgment of God (Rom. ii. 5).

XX. Accordingly we have no doubt that they err who hold that the call unto salvation is disclosed not by the preaching of the Gospel solely, but even by the works of nature and Providence without any further proclamation; adding, that the call unto salvation is so indefinite and universal that there is no mortal who is not, at least objectively, as they say, sufficiently called either *mediately,* namely, in that God will further bestow the light of grace on him who rightly uses the light of nature, or *immediately,* unto Christ and salvation; and finally denying that the external call can be said to be serious and true, or the candor and sincerity of God be defended, without asserting the absolute universality of grace. For such doctrines are contrary to the Holy Scriptures and the experience of all ages, and manifestly confound nature with grace, that which may be known of God with His hidden wisdom, the light of reason, in fine, with the light of Divine Revelation.

XXI. They who are called unto salvation through the preaching of the Gospel can neither believe nor obey the call, unless they are raised up out of spiritual death by that very power whereby God commanded the light to shine out of darkness, and God shines into their hearts with the soul-swaying grace of His Spirit, to give *the light of the knowledge of the glory of God in the face of Jesus Christ* (2 Cor. iv. 6). *For the natural man receiveth not the things of the Spirit of God; for they are foolishness unto him: neither can he know them, because they are spiritually discerned* (1 Cor. ii. 14); and this utter inability the Scripture demonstrates by so many direct testimonies and under so many emblems that scarcely in any other point is it surer (*locupletior*). This inability *may*, indeed, be called *moral* even in so far as it pertains to a moral subject or object; but it *ought* at the same time to be also called *natural*, inasmuch as man by nature, and so by the law of his formation in the womb, and hence from his birth, is *the child of disobedience* (Eph. ii. 2); and has that inability so innate (*congenitam*) that it can be shaken off in no way except by the omnipotent heart-turning grace of the Holy Spirit.

XXII. We hold therefore that they speak with too little accuracy and not without danger, who call this inability to believe *moral* inability, and do not hold it to be *natural*, adding that man in whatever condition he may be placed is able to believe if he will, and that faith in some way or other, indeed, is self-originated; and yet the Apostle most distinctly calls it the gift of God (Eph. ii. 8).

XXIII. There are two ways in which God, the just Judge, has promised justification: either by one's own works or deeds in the law; or by the obedience or righteousness of another, even of Christ our Surety, imputed by grace to him that believes in the Gospel. The former is the method of justifying man perfect; but the latter, of justifying man a sinner and corrupt. In accordance with these two ways of justification the Scripture establishes two covenants: the Covenant of Works, entered into with Adam and with each one of his descendants in him, but made void by sin; and the Covenant of Grace, made with only the elect in Christ, the second Adam, eternal, and liable to no abrogation, as the former.

XXIV. But this later Covenant of Grace according to the diversity of times had also different dispensations. For when the Apostle speaks of the dispensation

of the fullness of times, i.e., the administration of the
last time, he very clearly indicates that there had been
another dispensation and administration for the times
which the προθεσμίαν (Gal. iv. 2), or appointed time.
Yet in each dispensation of the Covenant of Grace the
elect have not been saved in any other way than by
the *Angel of his presence* (Is. lxiii. 9), *the Lamb slain
from the foundation of the world* (Rev. xiii. 8), Christ
Jesus, through the knowledge of that just Servant and
faith in Him and in the Father and His Spirit. For
Christ is *the same yesterday, to-day, and forever* (Heb.
xiii. 8); and by His grace we believe that we are saved
(*servari*) in the same manner as the Fathers also were
saved (*salvati sunt*) and in both Testaments these statutes remain immutable: "Blessed are all they that put
their trust in Him," the Son (Ps. ii. 12); "He that believeth in Him is not condemned, but he that believeth
not is condemned already" (John iii. 18); "Ye believe in God," even the Father, "believe also in me"
(John xiv. 1). But if, moreover, the sainted Fathers believed in Christ as their Goël, it follows that they also
believed in the Holy Spirit, without whom no one can
call Jesus Lord. Truly so many are the clearest exhibi-
tions of this faith of the Fathers and of the necessity
thereof in either Covenant, that they can not escape
any one unless he wills it. But though this saving
knowledge of Christ and the Holy Trinity was necessarily derived, according to the dispensation of that
time, both from the promise and from shadows and
figures and enigmas, with greater difficulty (*operosius*)
than now in the New Testament; yet it was a true
knowledge, and, in proportion to the measure of Divine Revelation, was sufficient to procure for the elect,
by help of God's grace, salvation and peace of conscience.

XXV. We disapprove therefore of the doctrine of
those who fabricate for us three Covenants, the Natural, the Legal, and the Gospel Covenant, different in
their whole nature and pith; and in explaining these
and assigning their differences, so intricately entangle

themselves that they obscure not a little, or even impair, the nucleus of solid truth and piety; nor do they hesitate at all, with regard to the necessity, under the Old Testament dispensation, of knowledge of Christ and faith in Him and His satisfaction and in the whole sacred Trinity, to theologize much too loosely and not without danger.

XXVI. Finally, both unto us, to whom in the Church, which is God's house, has been entrusted the dispensation for the present, and unto all our Nazarenes, and unto those who under the will and direction of God will at any time succeed us in our charge, in order to prevent the fearful enkindling of dissensions with which the Church of God in different places is disturbed (*infestatur*) in terrible ways, *we earnestly wish* (*volumus,* will) *this to be a law:—*

That in this corruption of the world, with the Apostle of the Gentiles as our faithful monitor, *we all keep faithfully that which is committed to our trust, avoiding profane and vain babblings* (1 Tim. vi. 20); and religiously guard the purity and simplicity of that knowledge which is according to piety, constantly clinging to that beautiful pair, Charity and Faith, unstained.

Moreover, in order that no one may be induced to propose either publicly or privately some doubtful or new dogma of faith hitherto unheard of in our churches, and contrary to God's Word, to our Helvetic Confession, our Symbolical Books, and to the Canons of the Synod of Dort, and not proved and sanctioned in a public assembly of brothers according to the Word of God, let it also be a law:—

That we not only hand down sincerely in accordance with the Divine Word, the especial necessity of the sanctification of the Lord's Day, but also impressively inculcate it and importunately urge its observation; and, in fine, that in our churches and schools, as often as occasion demands, we unanimously and faithfully hold, teach, and assert the truth of the Canons herein recorded, truth deduced from the indubitable Word of God.

The very God of peace in truth sanctify us wholly, and preserve our whole spirit and soul and body blameless unto the coming of our Lord Jesus Christ! to whom, with the Father and the Holy Spirit be eternal honor, praise and glory. AMEN!

THESES THEOLOGICAE
OF ROBERT BARCLAY (1675)

The faith of the Quakers was formulated by Robert Barclay, who had come to his Quaker convictions from the background of Scottish Presbyterianism. The *Theses Theologicae*, which served as a basis for his Apology, first appeared in 1675. In a preface introducing the *Theses* to doctors, professors, and students of divinity, Barclay disparages "school divinity, (which taketh up almost a man's whole lifetime to learn,) brings not a whit nearer to God, either makes any man less wicked, or more righteous than he was." The dominant theology of the time had been expressed in the *Westminster Confession*, from which Barclay's *Theses* differ significantly. Barclay himself, however, has been accused of stating the Quaker faith in too "orthodox" a fashion and in terms of a Calvinistic dualism.

Source: Text printed here is taken from *An Apology for the True Christian Divinity being an Explanation and Vindication of the Principles and Doctrines of the People Called Quakers* by Robert Barclay (New York: Samuel Wood and Sons, 1832), pp. 1–14. Scripture references are omitted and italics eliminated.

Braithwaite, William C., *The Second Period of Quaker-ism* (Second Edition prepared by Henry J. Cadbury) (Cambridge: Cambridge University Press, 1961).

Eeg-Olofsson, Leif, *The Conception of the Inner Light in Robert Barclay's Theology* (Lund: C. W. K. Gleerup, 1954).

King, Rachel Hadley, *George Fox and the Light Within* (Philadelphia: Friends Book Store, 1940).

THESES THEOLOGICAE
OF ROBERT BARCLAY (1675)

The First Proposition.
CONCERNING THE TRUE FOUNDATION OF KNOWLEDGE.

Seeing the height of all happiness is placed in the true knowledge of God ('This is life eternal, to know thee the only true God, and Jesus Christ whom thou hast sent'), the true and right understanding of this foundation and ground of knowledge, is that which is most necessary to be known and believed in the first place.

The Second Proposition.
CONCERNING IMMEDIATE REVELATION.

Seeing 'no man knoweth the Father but the Son, and he to whom the Son revealeth him'; and seeing 'the revelation of the Son is in and by the Spirit'; therefore the testimony of the Spirit is that alone by which the true knowledge of God hath been, is, and can be only revealed; who as, by the moving of his own Spirit, he converted the chaos of this world into that wonderful order wherein it was in the beginning, and created man a living soul, to rule and govern it, so by the revelation of the same Spirit he hath manifested himself all along unto the sons of men, both patriarchs, prophets, and apostles; which revelations of God by the Spirit, whether by outward voices, and appearances, dreams, or inward objective manifestations in the heart, were of old the formal object of their faith, and remain yet so to be; since the object of the saints' faith is the same in all ages, though set forth under divers administrations. Moreover, these divine inward revelations, which we make absolutely necessary for the building up of true faith, neither do nor can ever contradict the outward testimony of the Scriptures, or right and sound reason. Yet from hence it will not follow that these divine revelations are to be subjected to the examination, either of the outward testimony of the Scriptures or of the natural reason of man, as to a more noble or certain rule or touchstone; for this divine revelation and inward illumination is that which is evident and clear of itself, forcing, by its own evidence and clearness, the well-disposed understanding to assent, irresistibly moving the same thereunto; even as the common principles of natural truths move and incline the mind to a natural assent: as, that the whole is greater than its part; that two contradictory sayings can not be both true, nor both false: which is also manifest, according to our adversaries' principle, who (supposing the possibility of inward divine revelations) will nevertheless confess with us that neither Scripture nor sound reason will contradict it: and yet it will not follow, according to them, that the Scripture or sound reason should be subjected to the examination of the divine revelations in the heart.

The Third Proposition.

CONCERNING THE SCRIPTURES.

From these revelations of the Spirit of God to the saints have proceeded the Scriptures of truth, which contain: 1. A faithful historical account of the actings of God's people in divers ages, with many singular and remarkable providences attending them. 2. A prophetical account of several things, whereof some are already past, and some yet to come. 3. A full and ample account of all the chief principles of the doctrine of Christ, held forth in divers precious declarations, exhortations, and sentences, which, by the moving of God's Spirit, were at several times, and upon sundry occasions, spoken and written unto some churches and their pastors: nevertheless, because they are only a declaration of the fountain, and not the fountain itself, therefore they are not to be esteemed the principal ground of all truth and knowledge, nor yet the adequate primary rule of faith and manners. Nevertheless, as that which giveth a true and faithful testimony of the first foundation, they are and may be esteemed a secondary rule, subordinate to the Spirit, from which they have all their excellency and certainty; for as by the inward testimony of the Spirit we do alone truly know them, so they testify that the Spirit is that guide by which the saints are led into all truth: therefore, according to the Scriptures, the Spirit is the first and principal leader. And seeing we do therefore receive and believe the Scriptures, because they proceeded from the Spirit; therefore also the Spirit is more originally and principally the rule, according to that received maxim in the schools, *Propter quod unumquodque est tale, illud ipsum est magis tale.* Englished thus: 'That for which a thing is such, that thing itself is more such.'

The Fourth Proposition.
CONCERNING THE CONDITION OF MAN IN THE FALL.

All Adam's posterity (or mankind) both Jews and Gentiles, as to the first Adam, or earthly man, is fallen, degenerated, and dead, deprived of the sensation or feeling of this inward testimony or seed of God, and is subject unto the power, nature, and seed of the Serpent, which he sows in men's hearts, while they abide in this natural and corrupted state; from whence it comes that not their words and deeds only, but all their imaginations are evil perpetually in the sight of God, as proceeding from this depraved and wicked seed. Man, therefore, as he is in this state, can know nothing aright; yea, his thoughts and conceptions concerning God and things spiritual, until he be disjoined from this evil seed, and united to the Divine Light, are unprofitable both to himself and others: Hence are rejected the Socinian and Pelagian errors, in exalting a natural light; as also of the Papists, and most

Protestants, who affirm that man, without the true grace of God, may be a true minister of the gospel. Nevertheless, this seed is not imputed to infants, until by transgression they actually join themselves therewith; for they are by nature the children of wrath, who walk according to the power of the prince of the air.

The Fifth and Sixth Propositions.

CONCERNING THE UNIVERSAL REDEMPTION BY CHRIST, AND ALSO THE SAVING AND SPIRITUAL LIGHT, WHEREWITH EVERY MAN IS ENLIGHTENED.

The Fifth Proposition.

God, out of his infinite love, 'who delighteth not in the death of a sinner, but that all should live and be saved, hath so loved the world that he hath given his only Son a Light, that whosoever believeth in him should be saved; who enlighteneth every man that cometh into the world, and maketh manifest all things that are reprovable, and teacheth all temperance, righteousness, and godliness': and this Light enlighteneth the hearts of all in a day, in order to salvation, if not resisted: nor is it less universal than the seed of sin, being the purchase of his death, who tasted death for every man; 'for as in Adam all die, even so in Christ shall all be made alive.'

The Sixth Proposition.

According to which principle (or hypothesis), all the objections against the universality of Christ's death are easily solved; neither is it needful to recur to the ministry of angels, and those other miraculous means which, they say, God makes use of, to manifest the doctrine and history of Christ's passion unto such, who (living in those places of the world where the outward preaching of the gospel is unknown) have well improved the first and common grace; for hence it well follows, that as some of the old philosophers might have been saved, so also may now some (who by providence are cast into those remote parts of the world where the knowledge of the history is wanting) be made partakers of the divine mystery, if they receive and resist not that grace, 'a manifestation whereof is given to every man to profit withal.' This certain doctrine then being received (to wit) that there is an evangelical and saving light and grace in all, the universality of the love and mercy of God towards mankind (both in the death of his beloved Son, the Lord Jesus Christ, and in the manifestation of the light in the heart) is established and confirmed against all the objections of such as deny it. Therefore 'Christ hath tasted death for every man': not only for all kinds of men, as some vainly talk, but for every one, of all kinds; the benefit of whose offering is not only extended to such, who have the distinct outward knowledge of his death and sufferings, as the same is declared in the Scriptures, but even unto those who are necessarily excluded from the benefit of this knowledge by some inevitable accident; which knowledge we willingly confess to be very profitable and comfortable, but not absolutely needful unto such, from whom God himself hath withheld it; yet they may be made partakers of the mystery of his death (though ignorant of the history) if they suffer his seed and light (enlightening their hearts) to take place; (in which light communion with the Father and Son is enjoyed) so as of wicked men to become holy, and lovers of that power by those inward and secret touches they feel themselves turned from the evil to the good, and learn 'to do to others as they would be done by'; in which Christ himself affirms all to be included. As they then have falsely and erroneously taught who have denied Christ to have died for all men, so neither have they sufficiently taught the truth, who, affirming him to have died for all, have added the absolute necessity of the outward knowledge, thereof in order to the obtaining its saving effect; among whom the Remonstrants of Holland have been chiefly wanting, and many other asserters of Universal Redemption, in that they have not placed the extent of this salvation in that divine and evangelical principle of light and life wherewith Christ hath enlightened every man that comes into the world, which is excellently and evidently held forth in these Scriptures: Gen. vi. 3; Deut. xxx. 14; John i. 7–9; Rom. x. 8; Titus ii. 11.

The Seventh Proposition.

CONCERNING JUSTIFICATION.

As many as resist not this light, but receive the same, in them is produced an holy, pure, and spiritual birth, bringing forth holiness, righteousness, purity, and all these other blessed fruits which are acceptable to God; by which holy birth (to wit, Jesus Christ formed within us, and working his works in us) as we are sanctified, so we are justified in the sight of God, according to the apostle's words, 'But ye are washed, but ye are sanctified, but ye are justified, in the name of the Lord Jesus, and by the Spirit of our God.' Therefore it is not by our works wrought in our will, nor yet by good works, considered as of themselves, but by Christ, who is both the gift and the giver, and the cause producing the effects in us; who, as he hath reconciled us while we were enemies, doth also in his wisdom save us, and justify us after this manner, as saith the same apostle elsewhere, 'According to his mercy he saved us, by the washing of regeneration, and the renewing of the Holy Ghost.'

The Eighth Proposition.

CONCERNING PERFECTION.

In whom this holy and pure birth is fully brought forth, the body of death and sin comes to be crucified and removed, and their hearts united and subjected unto the truth, so as not to obey any suggestion or temptation of the evil one, but to be free from actual sinning and transgressing of the law of God, and in that respect perfect. Yet doth this perfection still admit of a growth; and there remaineth a possibility of sinning where the mind doth not most diligently and watchfully attend unto the Lord.

The Ninth Proposition.

CONCERNING PERSEVERANCE, AND THE POS-
SIBILITY OF FALLING FROM GRACE.

Although this gift and inward grace of God be sufficient to work out salvation, yet in those in whom it is
resisted it both may and doth become their condemnation. Moreover, in whom it hath wrought in part,
to purify and sanctify them, in order to their further
perfection, by disobedience such may fall from it, and
turn it to wantonness, making shipwreck of faith; and
'after having tasted of the heavenly gift, and been
made partakers of the Holy Ghost, again fall away.'
Yet such an increase and stability in the truth may in
this life be attained, from which there can not be a
total apostasy.

The Tenth Proposition.

CONCERNING THE MINISTRY.

As by this gift, or light of God, all true knowledge
in things spiritual is received and revealed; so by the
same, as it is manifested and received in the heart, by
the strength and power thereof, every true minister of
the gospel is ordained, prepared, and supplied in the
work of the ministry; and by the leading, moving, and
drawing hereof ought every evangelist and Christian
pastor to be led and ordered in his labor and work of
the gospel, both as to the place where, as to the persons to whom, and as to the times when he is to minister. Moreover, those who have this authority may
and ought to preach the gospel, though without human
commission or literature; as, on the other hand, those
who want the authority of this divine gift, however
learned or authorized by the commissions of men and
churches, are to be esteemed but as deceivers, and not
true ministers of the gospel. Also, who have received
this holy and unspotted gift, 'as they have freely received, so are they freely to give,' without hire or bar-
gaining, far less to use it as a trade to get money by
it: yet if God hath called any from their employments
or trades, by which they acquire their livelihood, it
may be lawful for such (according to the liberty

which they feel given them in the Lord) to receive such temporals (to wit, what may be needful to them for meat and clothing) as are freely given them by those to whom they have communicated spirituals.

The Eleventh Proposition.
CONCERNING WORSHIP.

All true and acceptable worship to God is offered in the inward and immediate moving and drawing of his own Spirit, which is neither limited to places, times, or persons; for though we be to worship him always, in that we are to fear before him, yet as to the outward signification thereof in prayers, praises, or preachings, we ought not to do it where and when we will, but where and when we are moved thereunto by the secret inspirations of his Spirit in our hearts, which God heareth and accepteth of, and is never wanting to move us thereunto, when need is, of which he himself is the alone proper judge. All other worship, then, both praises, prayers, and preachings, which man sets about in his own will, and at his own appointment, which he can both begin and end at his pleasure, do or leave undone, as himself sees meet, whether they be a prescribed form, as a liturgy, or prayers conceived extemporarily, by the natural strength and faculty of the mind, they are all but superstitions, will-worship, and abominable idolatry in the sight of God; which are to be denied, rejected, and separated from, in this day of his spiritual arising: however it might have pleased him (who winked at the times of ignorance, with respect to the simplicity and integrity of some, and of his own innocent seed, which lay as it were buried in the hearts of men, under the mass of superstition) to blow upon the dead and dry bones, and to raise some breathings, and answer them, and that until the day should more clearly dawn and break forth.

The Twelfth Proposition.
CONCERNING BAPTISM.

As there is one Lord and one faith, so there is 'one baptism; which is not the putting away the filth of the flesh, but the answer of a good conscience before God, by the resurrection of Jesus Christ.' And this baptism is a pure and spiritual thing, to wit, the baptism of the spirit and fire, by which we are buried with him, that, being washed and purged from our sins, we may 'walk in newness of life'; of which the baptism of John was a figure, which was commanded for a time, and not to continue forever. As to the baptism of infants, it is a mere human tradition, for which neither precept nor practice is to be found in all the Scripture.

The Thirteenth Proposition.

CONCERNING THE COMMUNION, OR PARTICI-
PATION OF THE BODY AND BLOOD OF CHRIST.

The communion of the body and blood of Christ is inward and spiritual, which is the participation of his flesh and blood, by which the inward man is daily nourished in the hearts of those in whom Christ dwells; of which things the breaking of bread by Christ with his disciples was a figure, which they even used in the church for a time, who had received the substance, for the cause of the weak; even as 'abstaining from things strangled, and from blood; the washing one another's feet, and the anointing of the sick with oil'; all which are commanded with no less authority and solemnity than the former; yet seeing they are but the shadows of better things, they cease in such as have obtained the substance.

The Fourteenth Proposition.

CONCERNING THE POWER OF THE CIVIL
MAGISTRATE, IN MATTERS PURELY RELI-
GIOUS, AND PERTAINING TO THE CONSCIENCE.

Since God hath assumed to himself the power and dominion of the conscience, who alone can rightly instruct and govern it, therefore it is not lawful for any whatsoever, by virtue of any authority or principality they bear in the government of this world, to force the consciences of others; and therefore all killing, banishing, fining, imprisoning, and other such things, which men are afflicted with, for the alone exercise of their conscience, or difference in worship or opinion, proceedeth from the spirit of Cain, the murderer, and is contrary to the truth; provided always that no man, under the pretense of conscience, prejudice his neighbor in his life or estate, or do any thing destructive to, or inconsistent with human society; in which case the law is for the transgressor, and justice to be administered upon all, without respect of persons.

The Fifteenth Proposition.

CONCERNING SALUTATIONS AND RECREATIONS, ETC.

Seeing the chief end of all religion is to redeem man from the spirit and vain conversation of this world, and to lead into inward communion with God, before whom, if we fear always, we are accounted happy; therefore all the vain customs and habits thereof, both in word and deed, are to be rejected and forsaken by those who come to this fear; such as the taking off the hat to a man, the bowings and cringings of the body, and such other salutations of that kind, with all the foolish and superstitious formalities attending them; all which man has invented in his degenerate state, to feed his pride in the vain pomp and glory of this world; as also the unprofitable plays, frivolous recreations, sportings and gamings which are invented to pass away the precious time, and divert the mind from the witness of God in the heart, and from the living sense of his fear, and from that evangelical Spirit wherewith Christians ought to be leavened, and which leads into sobriety, gravity, and godly fear; in which, as we abide, the blessing of the Lord is felt to attend us in those actions in which we are necessarily engaged, in order to the taking care for the sustenance of the outward man.

BAPTIST CREEDS

THE NEW HAMPSHIRE CONFESSION
(1833)

The New Hampshire Baptist Convention appointed a committee on June 24, 1830, to prepare a statement of faith, which was published by the Board of the Convention in 1833. The confession reflects the moderate Calvinism of the time. Its publication, in 1853, with some revision by J. Newton Brown, editorial secretary of the American Baptist Publication Society, gave it wide distribution. Unlike earlier Baptist confessions, it is silent on the doctrine of the universal Church; and this has made it especially attractive to those who emphasized the local congregation and to the Landmark Baptist movement.

Source: The text printed here is taken from *Baptist Confessions of Faith* by William L. Lumpkin (Valley Forge, Pa.: Judson Press, 1959), pp. 361–67. The text is also found in *Baptist Confessions of Faith* by W. J. McGlothin (Philadelphia: American Baptist Publication Society, 1911), pp. 301–7.

Stealey, Sydnor L., editor, *A Baptist Treasury* (New York: Thomas Y. Crowell Co., 1958).

Torbet, R. G., *A History of the Baptists* (Philadelphia: Judson Press, 1950).

DECLARATION OF FAITH.
i. Of the Scriptures.

We believe [that][1] the Holy Bible was written by

[1] Additions made by J. Newton Brown in 1853 are enclosed in brackets.

men divinely inspired, and is a perfect treasure of
heavenly instruction; that it has God for its author,
salvation for its end, and truth, without any mixture
of error, for its matter; that it reveals the principles
by which God will judge us; and therefore is, and
shall remain to the end of the world, the true centre
of Christian union, and the supreme standard by
which all human conduct, creeds, and opinions should
be tried.

ii. Of the True God.

[We believe] That there is one, and only one, living
and true God, [an infinite, intelligent Spirit,] whose
name is JEHOVAH, the Maker and Supreme Ruler
of heaven and earth; inexpressibly glorious in holiness;
[and] worthy of all possible honor, confidence, and
love; revealed under the personal and relative distinctions of the Father, the Son, and the Holy Spirit; equal
in every divine perfection, and executing distinct but
harmonious offices in the great work of redemption.

iii. Of the Fall of Man.

[We believe] That man was created in a state of
holiness, under the law of his Maker; but by voluntary
transgression fell from that holy and happy state; in
consequence of which all mankind are now sinners,
not by constraint but choice, being by nature utterly
void of that holiness required by the law of God,
wholly given to the gratification of the world, of Satan, and of their own sinful passions, therefore under
just condemnation to eternal ruin, without defense or
excuse.

iv. Of the Way of Salvation.

[We believe] That the salvation of sinners is wholly
of grace; through the Mediatorial Offices of the Son
of God, who [by the appointment of the Father,
freely] took upon him our nature, yet without sin;
honored the [divine] law by his personal obedience,
and made atonement for our sins by his death; being
risen from the dead he is now enthroned in heaven;
and uniting in his wonderful person the tenderest sympathies with divine perfections, [he] is every way

qualified to be a suitable, a compassionate, and an all-sufficient Saviour.

v. Of Justification.

[We believe] That the great Gospel blessing which Christ of his fulness bestows on such as believe in Him, is Justification; that Justification consists in the pardon of sin and the promise of eternal life, on principles of righteousness; that it is bestowed not in consideration of any works of righteousness which we have done, but solely through His own redemption and righteousness, [by virtue of which faith his perfect righteousness is freely imputed to us of God;] that it brings us into a state of most blessed peace and favor with God, and secures every other blessing needful for time and eternity.

vi. Of the Freeness of Salvation.

[We believe] That the blessings of salvation are made free to all by the Gospel; that it is the immediate duty of all to accept them by a cordial, [penitent,] and obedient faith; and that nothing prevents the salvation of the greatest sinner on earth except his own [inherent depravity and] voluntary refusal to submit to the Lord Jesus Christ, which refusal will subject him to an aggravated condemnation.

vii. Of grace in Regeneration.

[We believe] That in order to be saved, we must be regenerated or born again; that regeneration consists in giving a holy disposition to the mind; and is effected in a manner above our comprehension or calculation, by the power of the Holy Spirit, [in connection with divine truth,] so as to secure our voluntary obedience to the Gospel; and that its proper evidence is found in the holy fruit which we bring forth to the glory of God.

viii. Of Repentance and Faith.
[This article added in 1853.]

We believe that Repentance and Faith are sacred duties, and also inseparable graces, wrought in our souls by the regenerating Spirit of God; whereby being deeply convinced of our guilt, danger, and helplessness, and of the way of salvation by Christ, we turn to God with unfeigned contrition, confession, and supplication for mercy; at the same time heartily receiving the Lord Jesus Christ as our Prophet, Priest, and King, and relying on him alone as the only and all-sufficient Saviour.

ix. Of God's Purpose of Grace.

[We believe] That Election is the gracious purpose of God, according to which he [graciously] regenerates, sanctifies, and saves sinners; that being perfectly consistent with the free agency of man, it comprehends all the means in connection with the end; that it is a most glorious display of God's sovereign goodness, being infinitely [free,] wise, holy, and unchangeable; that it utterly excludes boasting, and promotes humility, [love,] prayer, praise, trust in God, and active imitation of his free mercy; that it encourages the use of means in the highest degree; that it is ascertained by its effects in all who [truly] believe the gospel; [that it] is the foundation of Christian assurance; and that to ascertain it with regard to ourselves, demands and deserves our utmost diligence.

x. Of Sanctification.
[Added in 1853.]

We believe that Sanctification is the process by which, according to the will of God, we are made partakers of his holiness; that it is a progressive work; that it is begun in regeneration; and that it is carried on in the hearts of believers by the presence and power of the Holy Spirit, the Sealer and Comforter, in the continual use of the appointed means—especially the Word of God, self-examination, self-denial, watchfulness and prayer.

xi. Of the Perseverance of Saints.

[We believe] That such only are real believers as endure unto the end; that their persevering attachment to Christ is the grand mark which distinguishes them from mere professors; that a special Providence watches over their welfare; and [that] they are kept by the power of God through faith unto salvation.

xii. [Of the] Harmony of the Law and the Gospel.

[We believe] That the Law of God is the eternal and unchangeable rule of his moral government; that it is holy, just, and good; and that the inability which the Scriptures ascribe to fallen men to fulfill its precepts, arises entirely from their love of sin; to deliver them from which, and to restore them through a Mediator to unfeigned obedience to the holy law, is one great end of the Gospel, and of the means of grace connected with the establishment of the visible Church.

xiii. Of a Gospel Church.

[We believe] That a visible Church of Christ is a congregation of baptized believers, associated by covenant in the faith and fellowship of the Gospel; observing the ordinances of Christ; governed by his laws; and exercising the gifts, rights, and privileges invested in them by his word; that its only proper officers are Bishops or Pastors, and Deacons, whose qualifications, claims, and duties are defined in the Epistles to Timothy and Titus.

xiv. Of Baptism and the Lord's Supper.

[We believe] That Christian Baptism is the immersion of a believer in water, in the name of the Father [and] Son, and Spirit, to show forth in a solemn and beautiful emblem, our faith in a crucified, buried, and risen Saviour, with its purifying power; that it is prerequisite to the privileges of a church relation; and to the Lord's Supper, in which the members of the church, by the [sacred] use of bread and wine, are to commemorate together the dying love of Christ; preceded always by solemn self-examination.

xv. Of the Christian Sabbath.

[We believe] That the first day of the week is the Lord's-Day, or Christian Sabbath; and is to be kept sacred to religious purposes, by abstaining from all secular labor and [sinful] recreations; by the devout observance of all the means of grace, both private and public; and by preparation for that rest which remaineth for the people of God.

xvi. Of Civil Government.

[We believe] That civil government is of divine appointment, for the interests and good order of human society; and that magistrates are to be prayed for, conscientiously honored, and obeyed, except [only] in things opposed to the will of our Lord Jesus Christ, who is the only Lord of the conscience, and the Prince of the kings of the earth.

xvii. Of the Righteous and the Wicked.

[We believe] That there is a radical and essential difference between the righteous and the wicked; that such only as through faith are justified in the name of the Lord Jesus, and sanctified by the Spirit of our God, are truly righteous in his esteem; while all such as continue in impenitence and unbelief are in his sight wicked, and under the curse; and this distinction holds among men both in and after death.

xviii. Of the World to Come.

[We believe] That the end of this world is approaching: that at the last day, Christ will descend from heaven, and raise the dead from the grave to final retribution; that a solemn separation will then take place; that the wicked will be adjudged to endless punishment, and the righteous to endless joy; and that this judgment will fix forever the final state of men in heaven or hell, on principles of righteousness.

ABSTRACT OF PRINCIPLES (1859)

This statement of faith was adopted by the Southern Baptist Seminary, Louisville, Kentucky in 1859 and by Southeastern Baptist Theological Seminary in 1950. It will be noted that Article XIV affirms the Church universal as well as the local church. In this it has precedent in the Second London Confession of 1677 and the Philadelphia Confession of 1742. It is a Baptist interpretation of the Westminster Confession, and it has great influence.

Source: *Southeastern Baptist Theological Seminary Bulletin, Tenth Catalog,* May 1961, Vol. 10, No. 3, pp. 74–76.

ABSTRACT OF PRINCIPLES (1859)

I. *The Scriptures.*

The Scriptures of the Old and New Testaments were given by inspiration of God, and are the only sufficient, certain and authoritative rule of all saving knowledge, faith and obedience.

II. *God.*

There is but one God, the Maker, Preserver and Ruler of all things, having in and of himself, all perfections, and being infinite in them all; and to Him all creatures owe the highest love, reverence and obedience.

III. *The Trinity.*

God is revealed to us as Father, Son and Holy Spirit each with distinct personal attributes, but without division of nature, essence or being.

IV. *Providence.*

God from eternity decrees or permits all things that come to pass, and perpetually upholds, directs and governs all creatures and all events; yet so as not in any wise to be the author or approver of sin nor to destroy the free will and responsibility of intelligent creatures.

V. *Election.*

Election is God's eternal choice of some persons unto everlasting life—not because of foreseen merit in them, but of His mere mercy in Christ—in consequence of which choice they are called, justified and glorified.

VI. *The Fall of Man.*

God originally created man in His own image, and free from sin; but through the temptation of Satan, he transgressed the command of God, and fell from his original holiness and righteousness; whereby his posterity inherit a nature corrupt and wholly opposed to God and His law, are under condemnation, and as soon as they are capable of moral action, become actual transgressors.

VII. *The Mediator.*

Jesus Christ, the only begotten Son of God, is the divinely appointed mediator between God and man. Having taken upon Himself human nature, yet without sin, He perfectly fulfilled the law, suffered and died upon the cross for the salvation of sinners. He was buried, and rose again the third day, and ascended to His Father, at whose right hand He ever liveth to make intercession for His people. He is the only Mediator, the Prophet, Priest and King of the Church, and Sovereign of the Universe.

VIII. *Regeneration.*

Regeneration is a change of heart, wrought by the Holy Spirit, who quickeneth the dead in trespasses and sins, enlightening their minds spiritually and savingly to understand the Word of God, and renewing their whole nature, so that they love and practice holiness. It is a work of God's free and special grace alone.

IX. *Repentance.*

Repentance is an evangelical grace, wherein a person being, by the Holy Spirit, made sensible of the manifold evil of his sin, humbleth himself for it, with godly sorrow, detestation of it, and self-abhorrence, with a purpose and endeavor to walk before God so as to please Him in all things.

X. *Faith.*

Saving faith is the belief, on God's authority, of whatsoever is revealed in His Word concerning Christ; accepting and resting upon Him alone for justification and eternal life. It is wrought in the heart by the Holy Spirit, and is accompanied by all other saving graces, and leads to a life of holiness.

XI. *Justification.*

Justification is God's gracious and full acquittal of sinners, who believe in Christ, from all sin, through the satisfaction that Christ has made; not for anything wrought in them or done by them; but on account of the obedience and satisfaction of Christ, they receiving and resting on Him and His righteousness by faith.

XII. Sanctification.

Those who have been regenerated are also sanctified, by God's word and Spirit dwelling in them. This sanctification is progressive through the supply of Divine strength, which all saints seek to obtain, pressing after a heavenly life in cordial obedience to all Christ's commands.

XIII. Perseverance of the Saints.

Those whom God hath accepted in the Beloved, and sanctified by His Spirit, will never totally nor finally fall away from the state of grace, but shall certainly persevere to the end; and though they may fall, through neglect and temptation, into sin, whereby they grieve the Spirit, impair their graces and comforts, bring reproach on the Church, and temporal judgments on themselves, yet they shall be renewed again unto repentance, and be kept by the power of God through faith unto salvation.

XIV. The Church.

The Lord Jesus is the Head of the Church, which is composed of all His true disciples, and in Him is invested supremely all power for its government. According to His commandment, Christians are to associate themselves into particular societies or churches; and to each of these churches He hath given needful authority for administering that order, discipline and worship which He hath appointed. The regular officers of a Church are Bishops or Elders, and Deacons.

XV. Baptism.

Baptism is an ordinance of the Lord Jesus, obligatory upon every believer, wherein he is immersed in water in the name of the Father, and of the Son, and of the Holy Spirit, as a sign of his fellowship with the death and resurrection of Christ, of remission of sins, and of his giving himself up to God, to live and walk in newness of life. It is prerequisite to church fellowship, and to participation in the Lord's Supper.

XVI. The Lord's Supper.

The Lord's Supper is an ordinance of Jesus Christ to be administered with the elements of bread and wine, and to be observed by His churches till the end of the world. It is in no sense a sacrifice, but is designed to commemmorate His death, to confirm the faith and other graces of Christians, and to be a bond, pledge and renewal of their communion with Him, and of their church fellowship.

XVII. The Lord's Day.

The Lord's day is a Christian institution for regular observance, and should be employed in exercises of worship and spiritual devotion, both public and private, resting from worldly employments and amusements, works of necessity and mercy only excepted.

XVIII. Liberty of Conscience.

God alone is Lord of the conscience; and He hath left it free from the doctrines and commandments of men, which are in anything contrary to His word, or not contained in it. Civil magistrates being ordained of God, subjection in all lawful things commanded by them ought to be yielded by us in the Lord, not only for wrath, but also for conscience sake.

XIX. The Resurrection.

The bodies of men after death return to dust, but their spirits return immediately to God—the righteous to rest with Him; the wicked, to be reserved under darkness to the judgment. At the last day, the bodies of all the dead, both just and unjust will be raised.

XX. The Judgment.

God hath appointed a day, wherein He will judge the world by Jesus Christ, when everyone shall receive according to his deeds: the wicked shall go into everlasting punishment; the righteous, into everlasting life.

STATEMENT OF BAPTIST FAITH AND MESSAGE

(SOUTHERN BAPTIST CONVENTION, 1925)

In 1925, amid the evolution and modernist controversies, the Southern Baptist Convention issued a statement on Baptist faith and message. This statement had been prepared by an able committee including E. Y. Mullins, W. J. McGlothlin, and E. C. Dargan. The basis of the statement was the New Hampshire Confession, which, with some modifications and omissions, substantially remains in the 1925 statement. Paragraphs 16 through 25 were added. The Confession has a preface that explains the role of a creed among Baptists, and is a significant illustration of creedal modification in the face of the pressures of the evolutionist and modernist controversies. The insertion of the doctrine of the Virgin Birth in Paragraph 4 and the modification of the statement on the creation of man in Paragraph 3 reflect the pressures and the creedal needs of the time.

The Confession has no binding authority, but it is widely used and exercises a very great influence.

Source: *Annual of the Southern Baptist Convention, 1925*, pp. 71–76.

REPORT OF COMMITTEE ON BAPTIST FAITH AND MESSAGE
(*Southern Baptist Convention, 1925*)

Your committee beg leave to report as follows:

Your committee recognize that they were appointed "to consider the advisability of issuing another statement of the Baptist Faith and Message, and to report at the next Convention."

In pursuance of the instructions of the Convention, and in consideration of the general denominational situation, your committee have decided to recommend the New Hampshire Confession of Faith, revised at certain points, and with some additional articles growing out of present needs, for approval by the Convention, in the event a statement of the Baptist faith and message is deemed necessary at this time.

The present occasion for a reaffirmation of Christian fundamentals is the prevalence of naturalism in the modern teaching and preaching of religion. Christianity is supernatural in its origin and history. We repudiate every theory of religion which denies the supernatural elements in our faith.

As introductory to the doctrinal articles, we recommend the adoption by the Convention of the following statement of the historic Baptist conception of the nature and function of confessions of faith in our religious and denominational life, believing that some such statements will clarify the atmosphere and remove some causes of misunderstanding, friction, and apprehension. Baptists approve and circulate confessions of faith with the following understanding, namely:

(1) That they constitute a consensus of opinion of some Baptist body, large or small, for the general instruction and guidance of our own people and others concerning those articles of the Christian faith which are most surely held among us. They are not intended to add anything to the simple conditions of salvation revealed in the New Testament, viz., repentance towards God and faith in Jesus Christ as Saviour and Lord.

(2) That we do not regard them as complete statements of our faith, having any quality of finality or infallibility. As in the past so in the future Baptists should hold themselves free to revise their statements of faith as may seem to them wise and expedient at any time.

(3) That any group of Baptists, large or small, have the inherent right to draw up for themselves and publish to the world a confession of their faith whenever they may think it advisable to do so.

(4) That the sole authority for faith and practice among Baptists is the Scriptures of the Old and New Testaments. Confessions are only guides in interpretation, having no authority over the conscience.

(5) That they are statements of religious convictions, drawn from the Scriptures, and are not to be used to hamper freedom of thought or investigation in other realms of life.

THE SCRIPTURES

1. We believe that the Holy Bible was written by men divinely inspired and is a perfect treasure of heavenly instruction; that it has God for its author, salvation for its end, and truth, without any mixture of

error, for its matter; that it reveals the principles by which God will judge us; and therefore is, and will remain to the end of the world, the true center of Christian union, and the supreme standard by which all human conduct, creeds and religious opinions should be tried.

GOD

2. There is one and only one living and true God, an intelligent, spiritual and personal Being, the Creator, Preserver and Ruler of the universe, infinite in holiness and all other perfections, to whom we owe the highest love, reverence and obedience. He is revealed to us as Father, Son and Holy Spirit, each with distinct personal attributes, but without division of nature, essence or being.

THE FALL OF MAN

3. Man was created by the special act of God, as recorded in Genesis. Gen. 1:27; Gen. 2:7. He was created in a state of holiness under the law of his maker, but, through the temptation of Satan he transgressed the command of God and fell from his original holiness and righteousness; whereby his posterity inherit a nature corrupt and in bondage to sin, are under condemnation, and as soon as they are capable of moral action, become actual transgressors.

THE WAY OF SALVATION

4. The salvation of sinners is wholly of grace, through the mediatorial office of the Son of God, who by the Holy Spirit was born of the Virgin Mary and took upon him our nature, yet without sin; honored the divine law by his personal obedience, and made atonement for our sins by his death. Being risen from the dead, he is now enthroned in heaven, and, uniting in his person the tenderest sympathies with divine perfections, he is in every way qualified to be a compassionate and all-sufficient Saviour.

JUSTIFICATION

5. Justification is God's gracious and full acquittal upon principles of righteousness of all sinners who be-

lieve in Christ. This blessing is bestowed, not in consideration of any works of righteousness which we have done, but through the redemption which is in and through Jesus Christ. It brings us into a state of most blessed peace and favor with God, and secures every other needed blessing.

THE FREENESS OF SALVATION

6. The blessings of salvation are made free to all by the Gospel. It is the duty of all to accept them by penitent and obedient faith. Nothing prevents the salvation of the greatest sinner except his own voluntary refusal to accept Jesus Christ as teacher, Saviour and Lord.

REGENERATION

7. Regeneration or the new birth is a change of heart wrought by the Holy Spirit, whereby we become partakers of the divine nature and a holy disposition is given, leading to the love and practice of righteousness. It is a work of God's free grace conditioned upon faith in Christ and made manifest by the fruit which we bring forth to the glory of God.

REPENTANCE AND FAITH

8. We believe that repentance and faith are sacred duties, and also inseparable graces, wrought in our souls by the regenerating Spirit of God; whereby being deeply convinced of our guilt, danger, and helplessness, and of the way of salvation by Christ, we turn to God with unfeigned contrition, confession, and supplication for mercy; at the same time heartily receiving the Lord Jesus Christ as our Prophet, Priest and King and relying on him alone as the only and all-sufficient Saviour.

GOD'S PURPOSE OF GRACE

9. Election is the gracious purpose of God, according to which he regenerates, sanctifies and saves sinners. It is perfectly consistent with the free agency of man, and comprehends all the means in connection with the end. It is a most gracious display of God's sovereign goodness, and is infinitely wise, holy and unchangeable. It excludes boasting and promotes humil-

ity. It encourages the use of means in the highest degree.

SANCTIFICATION

10. Sanctification is the process by which the regenerate gradually attain to moral and spiritual perfection through the presence and power of the Holy Spirit dwelling in their hearts. It continues throughout the earthly life, and is accomplished by the use of all the ordinary means of grace, and particularly by the Word of God.

PERSEVERANCE

11. All real believers endure to the end. Their continuance in well-doing is the mark which distinguishes them from mere professors. A special Providence cares for them, and they are kept by the power of God through faith unto salvation.

A GOSPEL CHURCH

12. A church of Christ is a congregation of baptized believers, associated by covenant in the faith and fellowship of the gospel; observing the ordinances of Christ, governed by his law, and exercising the gifts, rights and privileges invested in them by his word, and seeking to extend the Gospel to the ends of the earth. Its Scriptural officers are bishops or elders and deacons.

BAPTISM AND THE LORD'S SUPPER

13. Christian baptism is the immersion of a believer in water in the name of the Father, the Son and the Holy Spirit. The act is a symbol of our faith in a crucified, buried and risen Saviour. It is prerequisite to the privileges of a church relation and to the Lord's Supper, in which the members of the church, by the use of bread and wine, commemorate the dying love of Christ.

THE LORD'S DAY

14. The first day of the week is the Lord's day. It is a Christian institution for regular observance. It commemorates the resurrection of Christ from the dead, and should be employed in exercises of worship

and spiritual devotion, both public and private, and by refraining from worldly amusements, and resting from secular employments, works of necessity and mercy only excepted.

THE RIGHTEOUS AND THE WICKED

15. There is a radical and essential difference between the righteous and the wicked. Those only who are justified through the name of the Lord Jesus Christ and sanctified by the Holy Spirit are truly righteous in his sight. Those who continue in impenitence and unbelief are in his sight wicked and are under condemnation. This distinction between the righteous and the wicked holds in and after death, and will be made manifest at the judgment when final and everlasting awards are made to all men.

THE RESURRECTION

16. The Scriptures clearly teach that Jesus rose from the dead. His grave was emptied of its contents. He appeared to his disciples after his resurrection in many convincing manifestations. He now exists in his glorified body at God's right hand. There will be a resurrection of the righteous and the wicked. The bodies of the righteous will conform to the glorious spiritual body of Jesus.

THE RETURN OF THE LORD

17. The New Testament teaches in many places the visible and personal return of Jesus to this earth. "This same Jesus which is taken up from you into Heaven, shall so come in like manner as ye have seen him go into Heaven." The time of his coming is not revealed (Matt. 24:36). It is the duty of all believers to live in readiness for his coming and by diligence in good works to make manifest to all men the reality and power of their hope in Christ.

RELIGIOUS LIBERTY

18. God alone is Lord of the conscience, and he has left it free from the doctrines and commandments of men which are contrary to his word or not contained in it. Church and state should be separate. The

state owes to the church protection and full freedom in the pursuit of its spiritual ends. In providing for such freedom no ecclesiastical group or denomination should be favored by the state more than others. Civil government being ordained of God, it is the duty of Christians to render loyal obedience thereto in all things not contrary to the revealed will of God. The church should not resort to the civil power to carry on its work. The Gospel of Christ contemplates spiritual means alone for the pursuit of its ends. The state has no right to impose penalties for religious opinions of any kind. The state has no right to impose taxes for the support of any form of religion. A free church in a free state is the Christian ideal, and this implies the right of free and unhindered access to God on the part of all men, and the right to form and propagate opinions in the sphere of religion without interference by the civil power.

PEACE AND WAR

19. It is the duty of Christians to seek peace with all men on principles of righteousness. In accordance with the spirit and teachings of Christ they should do all in their power to put an end to war.

The true remedy for the war spirit is the pure gospel of our Lord. The supreme need of the world is the acceptance of his teachings in all the affairs of men and nations, and the practical application of his law of love.

We urge Christian people throughout the land to pray for the reign of the Prince of Peace, and to oppose everything likely to provoke war.

EDUCATION

20. Christianity is the religion of enlightenment and intelligence. In Jesus Christ are hidden all the treasures of wisdom and knowledge. All sound learning is therefore a part of our Christian heritage. The new birth opens all human faculties and creates a thirst for knowledge. An adequate system of schools is necessary to a complete spiritual program for Christ's people. The cause of education in the Kingdom of Christ

is co-ordinate with the causes of missions and general benevolence, and should receive along with these the liberal support of the churches.

SOCIAL SERVICE

21. Every Christian is under obligation to seek to make the will of Christ regnant in his own life and in human society; to oppose in the spirit of Christ every form of greed, selfishness and vice; to provide for the orphaned, the aged, the helpless, and the sick; to seek to bring industry, government and society as a whole under the sway of the principles of righteousness, truth and brotherly love; to promote these ends Christians should be ready to work with all men of good will in any good cause, always being careful to act in the spirit of love without compromising their loyalty to Christ and his truth. All means and methods used in social service for the amelioration of society and the establishment of righteousness among men must finally depend on the regeneration of the individual by the saving grace of God in Christ Jesus.

CO-OPERATION

22. Christ's people should, as occasion requires, organize such associations and conventions as may best secure co-operation for the great objects of the Kingdom of God. Such organizations have no authority over each other or over the churches. They are voluntary and advisory bodies designed to elicit, combine and direct the energies of our people in the most effective manner. Individual members of New Testament churches should co-operate with each other, and the churches themselves should co-operate with each other in carrying forward the missionary, educational and benevolent program for the extension of Christ's Kingdom. Christian unity in the New Testament sense is spiritual harmony and voluntary co-operation for common ends by various groups of Christ's people. It is permissible and desirable as between the various Christian denominations, when the end to be attained is itself justified, and when such co-operation involves no violation of conscience or compromise of loyalty to

Christ and his Word as revealed in the New Testament.

EVANGELISM AND MISSIONS

23. It is the duty of every Christian man and woman, and the duty of every church of Christ, to seek to extend the gospel to the ends of the earth. The new birth of man's spirit by God's Holy Spirit means the birth of love for others. Missionary effort on the part of all rests thus upon a spiritual necessity of the regenerate life. It is also expressly and repeatedly commanded in the teachings of Christ. It is the duty of every child of God to seek constantly to win the lost to Christ by personal effort and by all other methods sanctioned by the Gospel of Christ.

STEWARDSHIP

24. God is the source of all blessings, temporal and spiritual; all that we have and are we owe to him. We have a spiritual debtorship to the whole world, a holy trusteeship in the Gospel, and a binding stewardship in our possessions. We are therefore under obligation to serve him with our time, talents and material possessions; and should recognize all these as entrusted to us to use for the glory of God and helping others. Christians should cheerfully, regularly, systematically, proportionately, and liberally contribute of their means to advancing the Redeemer's cause on earth.

THE KINGDOM

25. The Kingdom of God is the reign of God in the heart and life of the individual in every human relationship, and in every form and institution of organized society. The chief means for promoting the Kingdom of God on earth are preaching the Gospel of Christ, and teaching the principles of righteousness contained therein. The Kingdom of God will be complete when every thought and will of man shall be brought into captivity to the will of Christ. And it is the duty of all Christ's people to pray and labor continually that his Kingdom may come and his will be done on earth as it is in heaven.

METHODISM

John Wesley's place in the evolution of Protestantism has been the subject of debate. He stands between Classic Protestantism and the Liberal Protestantism of the nineteenth century. Wesley's emphasis upon Christian experience, upon holiness, upon "an optimism of grace" gives a distinct character to his theology.

The Twenty-Five Articles of Religion are a revision of the Thirty-Nine Articles of the Church of England. The revision was made by John Wesley and was adopted by the Methodist Conference in Baltimore in 1784. The Twenty-Third Article, which acknowledges the United States as a sovereign and independent nation, was adopted in 1804.

"The Scripture Way of Salvation" is not one of the original four volumes of sermons that were given authoritative status in Methodism, but it is an excellent introduction to Wesley's theology, dealing with such important themes as the prevenience of grace, justification, and sanctification. The sermon was first published in 1765.

"The Minutes" grew out of conversations of John Wesley with a group of his colleagues on topics that were suggested by the exigencies of the revival. The conversations were summarized by Wesley at their conclusions in question-and-answer form. "The Minutes" served as doctrinal standards for the early Methodist societies.

Sources: "The Scripture Way of Salvation" and "Minutes of Some Late Conversations" are taken from *The Works of the Rev. John Wesley, A.M.* (Third American Complete and Standard Edition from the latest London edition) (New York: Carlton & Porter, 1831). "The Articles of Religion" have been compared with the text in *The*

Doctrines and Discipline of the Methodist Church (Nashville: The Methodist Publishing House, 1957), pp. 27–33. Variations and emendations in the text are indicated in *Doctrinal Standards of Methodism, Including the Methodist Episcopal Churches,* by Thomas B. Neely (New York: Fleming H. Revell, 1918).

Outler, Albert C., ed., *John Wesley,* a volume of *A Library of Protestant Thought* (New York: Oxford University Press, 1964).

Rupp, Gordon, *Methodism in Relation to Protestant Tradition* (London: Epworth, 1954).

Lee, Umphrey, *John Wesley and Modern Religion* (Nashville: Cokesbury Press, 1936).

THE ARTICLES OF RELIGION (1784)

I. Of Faith in the Holy Trinity.

There is but one living and true God, everlasting, without body or parts, of infinite power, wisdom, and goodness; the Maker and Preserver of all things, visible and invisible. And in unity of this Godhead there are three persons, of one substance, power, and eternity—the Father, the Son, and the Holy Ghost.

II. Of the Word, or Son of God, Who Was Made Very Man.

The Son, who is the Word of the Father, the very and eternal God, of one substance with the Father, took man's nature in the womb of the blessed Virgin; so that two whole and perfect natures—that is to say, the Godhead and manhood—were joined together in one person, never to be divided; whereof is one Christ, very God and very man, who truly suffered, was crucified, dead and buried, to reconcile his Father to us, and to be a sacrifice, not only for original guilt, but also for the actual sins of men.

III. Of the Resurrection of Christ.

Christ did truly rise again from the dead, and took again his body, with all things appertaining to the perfection of man's nature, wherewith he ascended into heaven, and there sitteth until he return to judge all men at the last day.

IV. Of the Holy Ghost.

The Holy Ghost, proceeding from the Father and the Son, is of one substance, majesty, and glory with the Father and the Son, very and eternal God.

V. Of the Sufficiency of the Holy Scriptures for Salvation.

The Holy Scriptures contain all things necessary to salvation; so that whatsoever is not read therein, nor may be proved thereby, is not to be required of any man that it should be believed as an article of faith, or be thought requisite or necessary to salvation. In the name of the Holy Scripture we do understand those canonical books of the Old and New Testament of whose authority was never any doubt in the Church. The names of the canonical books are—

Genesis, Exodus, Leviticus, Numbers, Deuteronomy, Joshua, Judges, Ruth, The First Book of Samuel, The Second Book of Samuel, The First Book of Kings, The Second Book of Kings, The First Book of Chronicles, The Second Book of Chronicles, The Book of Ezra, The Book of Nehemiah, The Book of Esther, The Book of Job, The Psalms, The Proverbs, Ecclesiastes or the Preacher, Cantica or Songs of Solomon, Four Prophets the greater, Twelve Prophets the less.

All the books of the New Testament, as they are commonly received, we do receive and account canonical.

VI. Of the Old Testament.

The Old Testament is not contrary to the New; for both in the Old and New Testament everlasting life is offered to mankind by Christ, who is the only Mediator between God and man, being both God and man. Wherefore they are not to be heard who feign that the old fathers did look only for transitory promises. Although the law given from God by Moses, as touching ceremonies and rites, doth not bind Christians, nor ought the civil precepts thereof of necessity be received in any commonwealth, yet, notwithstanding, no Christian whatsoever is free from the obedience of the commandments which are called moral.

VII. Of Original or Birth Sin.

Original sin standeth not in the following of Adam (as the Pelagians do vainly talk), but it is the corruption of the nature of every man, that naturally is engendered of the offspring of Adam, whereby man is very far gone from original righteousness, and of his own nature inclined to evil, and that continually.

VIII. Of Free Will.

The condition of man after the fall of Adam is such that he can not turn and prepare himself, by his own natural strength and works, to faith and calling upon God; wherefore we have no power to do good works, pleasant and acceptable to God, without the grace of God by Christ preventing us, that we may have a good will, and working with us, when we have that good will.

IX. Of the Justification of Man.

We are accounted righteous before God only for the merit of our Lord and Saviour Jesus Christ by faith, and not for our own works or deservings. Wherefore, that we are justified by faith only is a most wholesome doctrine, and very full of comfort.

X. Of Good Works.

Although good works, which are the fruits of faith, and follow after justification, can not put away our sins, and endure the severity of God's judgments; yet are they pleasing and acceptable to God in Christ, and spring out of a true and lively faith, insomuch that by them a lively faith may be as evidently known as a tree is discerned by its fruit.

XI. Of Works of Supererogation.

Voluntary works—besides, over, and above God's commandments—which are called works of supererogation, can not be taught without arrogancy and impiety. For by them men do declare that they do not only render unto God as much as they are bound to do, but that they do more for his sake than of bounden duty is required: whereas Christ saith plainly, When ye have done all that is commanded you, say, We are unprofitable servants.

XII. Of Sin after Justification.

Not every sin willingly committed after justification is the sin against the Holy Spirit, and unpardonable. Wherefore, the grant of repentance is not to be denied to such as fall into sin after justification: after we have received the Holy Spirit, we may depart from grace given, and fall into sin, and, by the grace of God, rise again and amend our lives. And therefore they are to be condemned who say they can no more sin as long as they live here; or deny the place of forgiveness to such as truly repent.

XIII. Of the Church.

The visible Church of Christ is a congregation of faithful men, in which the pure Word of God is preached, and the Sacraments duly administered, according to Christ's ordinance, in all those things that of necessity are requisite to the same.

XIV. Of Purgatory.

The Romish doctrine concerning purgatory, pardon, worshiping, and adoration, as well of images as of relics, and also invocation of saints, is a fond thing, vainly invented, and grounded upon no warrant of Scripture, but repugnant to the Word of God.

XV. Of Speaking in the Congregation in Such a Tongue as the People Understand.

It is a thing plainly repugnant to the Word of God, and the custom of the primitive Church, to have public prayer in the church, or to minister the Sacraments, in a tongue not understood by the people.

XVI. Of the Sacraments.

Sacraments ordained of Christ are not only badges or tokens of Christian men's profession, but rather they are certain signs of grace, and God's good will toward us, by the which he doth work invisibly in us, and doth not only quicken, but also strengthen and confirm our faith in him.

There are two sacraments ordained of Christ our Lord in the Gospel; that is to say, Baptism and the Supper of the Lord.

Those five commonly called sacraments, that is to

say, confirmation, penance, orders, matrimony, and extreme unction, are not to be counted for Sacraments of the Gospel, being such as have partly grown out of the *corrupt* following of the apostles; and partly are states of life allowed in the Scriptures, but yet have not the like nature of Baptism and the Lord's Supper, because they have not any visible sign or ceremony ordained of God.

The sacraments were not ordained of Christ to be gazed upon, or to be carried about, but that we should duly use them. And in such only as worthily receive the same they have a wholesome effect or operation; but they that receive them unworthily purchase to themselves condemnation, as St. Paul saith, 1 Cor. xi. 29.

XVII. *Of Baptism.*

Baptism is not only a sign of profession, and mark of difference, whereby Christians are distinguished from others that are not baptized; but it is also a sign of regeneration, or the new birth. The baptism of young children is to be retained in the Church.

XVIII. *Of the Lord's Supper.*

The Supper of the Lord is not only a sign of the love that Christians ought to have among themselves one to another, but rather is a sacrament of our redemption by Christ's death; insomuch that, to such as rightly, worthily, and with faith receive the same, the bread which we break is a partaking of the body of Christ; and likewise the cup of blessing is a partaking of the blood of Christ.

Transubstantiation, or the change of the substance of bread and wine in the Supper of our Lord, can not be proved by Holy Writ, but is repugnant to the plain words of Scripture, overthroweth the nature of a sacrament, and hath given occasion to many superstitions.

The body of Christ is given, taken, and eaten in the Supper only after a heavenly and spiritual manner. And the means whereby the body of Christ is received and eaten in the Supper is faith.

The sacrament of the Lord's Supper was not by

Christ's ordinance reserved, carried about, lifted up, or worshiped.

XIX. Of Both Kinds.

The cup of the Lord is not to be denied to the lay people; for both the parts of the Lord's Supper, by Christ's ordinance and commandment, ought to be administered to all Christians alike.

XX. Of the One Oblation of Christ, Finished upon the Cross.

The offering of Christ, once made, is that perfect redemption, propitiation, and satisfaction for all the sins of the whole world, both original and actual; and there is none other satisfaction for sin but that alone. Wherefore the sacrifice of masses, in the which it is commonly said that the priest doth offer Christ for the quick and the dead, to have remission of pain or guilt, is a blasphemous fable and dangerous deceit.

XXI. Of the Marriage of Ministers.

The ministers of Christ are not commanded by God's law either to vow the estate of single life or to abstain from marriage; therefore it is lawful for them, as for all other Christians, to marry at their own discretion, as they shall judge the same to serve best to godliness.

XXII. Of the Rites and Ceremonies of Churches.

It is not necessary that rites and ceremonies should in all places be the same, or exactly alike; for they have been always different, and may be changed according to the diversity of countries, times, and men's manners, so that nothing be ordained against God's Word. Whosoever, through his private judgment, willingly and purposely doth openly break the rites and ceremonies of the Church to which he belongeth, which are not repugnant to the Word of God, and are ordained and approved by common authority, ought to be rebuked openly (that others may fear to do the like), as one that offendeth against the common order of the Church, and woundeth the consciences of weak brethren.

Every particular Church may ordain, change, or

abolish rites and ceremonies, so that all things may be done to edification.

XXIII. Of the Rulers of the United States of America.

The President, the Congress, the General Assemblies, the Governors, and the Councils of State, *as the delegates of the people,* are the rulers of the United States of America, according to the division of power made to them by the Constitution of the United States, and by the Constitutions of their respective States. And the said States are a sovereign and independent nation, and ought not to be subject to any foreign jurisdiction.

XXIV. Of Christian Men's Goods.

The riches and goods of Christians are not common, as touching the right, title, and possession of the same, as some do falsely boast. Notwithstanding, every man ought, of such things as he possesseth, liberally to give alms to the poor, according to his ability.

XXV. Of a Christian Man's Oath.

As we confess that vain and rash swearing is forbidden Christian men by our Lord Jesus Christ and James his apostle, so we judge that the Christian religion doth not prohibit but that a man may swear when the magistrate requireth, in a cause of faith and charity, so it be done according to the prophet's teaching, in justice, judgment, and truth.

THE SCRIPTURE WAY OF SALVATION (1765)

"Ye are saved through faith," Eph. ii, 8.

1. Nothing can be more intricate, complex, and hard to be understood, than religion, as it has been often described. And this is not only true concerning the religion of the heathens, even many of the wisest of them, but concerning the religion of those also who were, in some sense, Christians; yea, and men of great name in the Christian world; men who seemed to be pillars thereof. Yet how easy to be understood, how plain and simple a thing is the genuine religion of

Jesus Christ; provided only that we take it in its native form, just as it is described in the oracles of God! It is exactly suited, by the wise Creator and Governor of the world, to the weak understanding and narrow capacity of man in his present state. How observable is this, both with regard to the end it proposes, and the means to attain that end! The end is, in one word, salvation; the means to attain it, faith.

2. It is easily discerned, that these two little words, I mean faith and salvation, include the substance of all the Bible, the marrow, as it were, of the whole Scripture. So much the more should we take all possible care to avoid all mistake concerning them, and to form a true and accurate judgment concerning both the one and the other.

3. Let us then seriously inquire,

    I. What is salvation?

    II. What is that faith whereby we are saved? And,

    III. How are we saved by it?

I. 1. And, first, let us inquire, What is salvation? The salvation which is here spoken of, is not what is frequently understood by that word, the going to heaven, eternal happiness. It is not the soul's going to paradise, termed by our Lord, "Abraham's bosom." It is not a blessing which lies on the other side death; or, as we usually speak, in the other world. The very words of the text itself put this beyond all question: *"ye are saved."* It is not something at a distance; it is a present thing; a blessing which, through the free mercy of God, ye are now in possession of. Nay, the words may be rendered, and that with equal propriety, "Ye *have been* saved:" So that the salvation which is here spoken of might be extended to the entire work of God, from the first dawning of grace in the soul, till it is consummated in glory.

2. If we take this in its utmost extent, it will include all that is wrought in the soul by what is frequently termed, "natural conscience," but more properly, "preventing grace;"—all the drawings of the Father; the desires after God, which, if we yield to them, in-

crease more and more;—all that light wherewith the
Son of God "enlighteneth every one that cometh into
the world;" showing every man, "to do justly, to love
mercy, and to walk humbly with his God;"—all the convictions which his Spirit, from time to time, works in
every child of man; although, it is true, the generality
of men stifle them as soon as possible, and after a
while forget, or at least deny, that they ever had them
at all.

3. But we are at present concerned only with that
salvation which the apostle is directly speaking of. And
this consists of two general parts, justification and
sanctification.

Justification is another word for pardon. It is the
forgiveness of all our sins; and, what is necessarily
implied therein, our acceptance with God. The price
whereby this hath been procured for us, (commonly
termed the meritorious cause of our justification,) is
the blood and righteousness of Christ; or, to express
it a little more clearly, all that Christ hath done and
suffered for us, till he "poured out his soul for the
transgressors." The immediate effects of justification
are, the peace of God, a "peace that passeth all understanding," and a "rejoicing in hope of the glory of
God," "with joy unspeakable and full of glory."

4. And at the same time that we are justified, yea, in
that very moment, sanctification begins. In that instant
we are born again, born from above, born of the
Spirit: there is a *real* as well as a *relative* change.
We are inwardly renewed by the power of God. We
feel "the love of God shed abroad in our heart, by
the Holy Ghost which is given unto us," producing
love to all mankind, and more especially to the children of God; expelling the love of the world, the love
of pleasure, of ease, of honour, of money; together
with pride, anger, self will, and every other evil temper; in a word, changing the earthly, sensual, devilish
mind, into "the mind which was in Christ Jesus."

5. How naturally do those who experience such a
change, imagine that all sin is gone; that it is utterly

rooted out of their heart, and has no more any place therein? How easily do they draw that inference, "I *feel* no sin; therefore I *have* none: it does not *stir;* therefore it does not *exist:* it has no *motion;* therefore it has no *being*."

6. But it is seldom long before they are undeceived, finding sin was only suspended, not destroyed. Temptations return, and sin revives; showing it was but stunned before, not dead. They now feel two principles in themselves, plainly contrary to each other; "the flesh lusting against the Spirit;" nature opposing the grace of God. They cannot deny, that, although they still feel power to believe in Christ, and to love God; and, although his "Spirit [still] witnesses with their spirits that they are children of God;" yet they feel in themselves sometimes pride or self will, sometimes anger or unbelief. They find one or more of these frequently *stirring* in their heart, though not *conquering;* yea, perhaps, "thrusting sore at them that they may fall;" but the Lord is their help.

7. How exactly did Macarius, fourteen hundred years ago, describe the present experience of the children of God! "The unskilful," [or the unexperienced,] "when grace operates, presently imagine they have no more sin. Whereas they that have discretion cannot deny, that even we who have the grace of God may be molested again.—For we have often had instances of some among the brethren, who have experienced such grace as to affirm that they had no sin in them; and yet, after all, when they thought themselves entirely freed from it, the corruption that lurked within was stirred up anew, and they were well nigh burned up."

8. From the time of our being born again the gradual work of sanctification takes place. We are enabled, "by the Spirit," to "mortify the deeds of the body," of our evil nature; and as we are more and more dead to sin, we are more and more alive to God. We go on from grace to grace, while we are careful to "abstain from all appearance of evil," and are "zealous of good works," as we have opportunity of doing good to all

men; while we walk in all his ordinances blameless, therein worshipping him in spirit and in truth; while we take up our cross, and deny ourselves every pleasure that does not lead us to God.

9. It is thus that we wait for entire sanctification; for a full salvation from all our sins,—from pride, self will, anger, unbelief; or, as the apostle expresses it, "go unto perfection." But what is perfection? The word has various senses: here it means perfect love. It is love excluding sin; love filling the heart, taking up the whole capacity of the soul. It is love "rejoicing evermore, praying without ceasing, in every thing giving thanks."

II. But what is that faith through which we are saved? This is the second point to be considered.

1. Faith in general is defined by the apostle, πραγματων ελεγχος ου βλεπομένων: *an evidence,* a divine *evidence and conviction* [the word means both] *of things not seen;* not visible, not perceivable either by sight, or by any other of the external senses. It implies both a supernatural *evidence* of God, and of the things of God, a kind of spiritual *light* exhibited to the soul, and a supernatural *sight* or perception thereof. Accordingly the Scripture speaks of God's giving sometimes light, sometimes a power of discerning it. So St. Paul, "God, who commanded light to shine out of darkness, hath shined in our hearts, to give us the light of the knowledge of the glory of God in the face of Jesus Christ." And elsewhere the same apostle speaks of "the eyes of [our] understanding being opened." By this two fold operation of the Holy Spirit, having the eyes of our soul both *opened* and *enlightened,* we see the things which the natural "eye hath not seen, neither the ear heard." We have a prospect of the invisible things of God; we see the *spiritual world,* which is all round about us, and yet no more discerned by our natural faculties, than if it had no being: and we see the *eternal world;* piercing through the veil which hangs between time and eternity. Clouds and darkness then rest upon it no more,

but we already see the glory which shall be revealed.

2. Taking the word in a more particular sense, faith is a divine *evidence* and *conviction*, not only that "God was in Christ, reconciling the world unto himself," but also that Christ loved *me*, and gave himself for *me*. It is by this faith (whether we term it the *essence*, or rather a *property* thereof) that we *receive Christ;* that we receive him in all his offices, as our Prophet, Priest, and King. It is by this that he is "made of God unto us wisdom, and righteousness, and sanctification, and redemption."

3. "But is this the *faith of assurance*, or *faith of adherence?*" The Scripture mentions no such distinction. The apostle says, "There is one faith, and one hope of our calling;" one Christian, saving faith; "as there is one Lord," in whom we believe, and "one God and Father of us all." And it is certain, this faith necessarily implies an *assurance* (which is here only another word for *evidence*, it being hard to tell the difference between them) that Christ loved me, and gave himself for me. For "he that believeth," with the true living faith, "hath the witness in himself:" "The Spirit witnesseth with his spirit, that he is a child of God." "Because he is a son, God hath sent forth the Spirit of his Son into his heart, crying, Abba, Father;" giving him an assurance that he is so, and a childlike confidence in him. But let it be observed that, in the very nature of the thing, the assurance goes before the confidence. For a man cannot have a childlike confidence in God till he knows he is a child of God. Therefore confidence, trust, reliance, adherence, or whatever else it be called, is not the first, as some have supposed, but the second branch or act of faith.

4. It is by this faith we are saved, justified, and sanctified; taking that word in its highest sense. But how are we justified and sanctified by faith? This is our third head of inquiry. And this being the main point in question, and a point of no ordinary importance, it will not be improper to give it a more distinct and particular consideration.

III. 1. And, first, How are we justified by faith? In what sense is this to be understood? I answer, faith is the condition, and the only condition of justification. It is the *condition:* none is justified but he that believes: without faith no man is justified. And it is the *only condition:* this alone is sufficient for justification. Every one that believes is justified, whatever else he has or has not. In other words: no man is justified till he believes; every man, when he believes, is justified.

2. "But does not God command us to repent also? Yea, and to 'bring forth fruits meet for repentance?' To cease, for instance, from doing evil, and learn to do well? And is not both the one and the other of the utmost necessity, insomuch that if we willingly neglect either, we cannot reasonably expect to be justified at all? But if this be so, how can it be said that faith is the only condition of justification?"

God does undoubtedly command us both to repent, and to bring forth fruits meet for repentance; which if we willingly neglect, we cannot reasonably expect to be justified at all: therefore both repentance, and fruits meet for repentance, are, in some sense, necessary to justification. But they are not necessary in the *same sense* with faith, nor in the *same degree.* Not in the *same degree;* for those fruits are only necessary *conditionally;* if there be time and opportunity for them. Otherwise a man may be justified without them, as was the *thief* upon the cross; (if we may call him so; for a late writer has discovered that he was no thief, but a very honest and respectable person!) but he cannot be justified without faith; this is impossible. Likewise, let a man have ever so much repentance, or ever so many of the fruits meet for repentance, yet all this does not at all avail; he is not justified till he believes. But the moment he believes, with or without those fruits, yea, with more or less repentance, he is justified.—Not in the *same sense;* for repentance and its fruits are only *remotely* necessary; necessary in order to faith; whereas faith is *immediately* and *directly* necessary to justification. It remains, that faith is the only condition, which is *immediately* and *proximately* necessary to justification.

3. "But do you believe we are sanctified by faith? We know you believe that we are justified by faith; but do not you believe, and accordingly teach, that we are sanctified by our works?" So it has been roundly and vehemently affirmed for these five and twenty years: but I have constantly declared just the contrary; and that in all manner of ways. I have continually testified in private and in public, that we are sanctified as well as justified by faith. And indeed the one of those great truths does exceedingly illustrate the other. Exactly as we are justified by faith, so are we sanctified by faith. Faith is the condition, and the only condition of sanctification, exactly as it is of justification. It is the *condition:* none is sanctified but he that believes; without faith no man is sanctified. And it is the *only condition:* this alone is sufficient for sanctification. Every one that believes is sanctified, whatever else he has or has not. In other words, no man is sanctified till he believes: every man when he believes is sanctified.

4. "But is there not a repentance consequent upon, as well as a repentance previous to, justification? And is it not incumbent on all that are justified to be 'zealous of good works?' Yea, are not these so necessary, that if a man willingly neglect them he cannot reasonably expect that he shall ever be sanctified in the full sense; that is, perfected in love? Nay, can he grow at all in grace, in the loving knowledge of our Lord Jesus Christ? Yea, can he retain the grace which God has already given him? Can he continue in the faith which he has received, or in the favour of God? Do not you yourself allow all this, and continually assert it? But, if this be so, how can it be said, that faith is the only condition of sanctification?"

5. I do allow all this, and continually maintain it as the truth of God. I allow there is a repentance consequent upon, as well as a repentance previous to, justification. It is incumbent on all that are justified

to be zealous of good works. And these are so necessary, that if a man willingly neglect them he cannot reasonably expect that he shall ever be sanctified; he cannot grow in grace, in the image of God, the mind which was in Christ Jesus; nay, he cannot retain the grace he has received, he cannot continue in faith, or in the favour of God.

What is the inference we must draw herefrom? Why, that both repentance, rightly understood, and the practice of all good works,—works of piety, as well as works of mercy, (now properly so called, since they spring from faith), are, in some sense, necessary to sanctification.

6. I say, "repentance rightly understood;" for this must not be confounded with the former repentance. The repentance consequent upon justification, is widely different from that which is antecedent to it. This implies no guilt, no sense of condemnation, no consciousness of the wrath of God. It does not suppose any doubt of the favour of God, or any "fear that hath torment." It is properly a conviction, wrought by the Holy Ghost, of the *sin* which still *remains* in our heart; of the φρονημα σαρκος, *the carnal mind,* which "does still *remain,* (as our church speaks,) even in them that are regenerate;" although it does no longer *reign;* it has not now dominion over them. It is a conviction of our proneness to evil, of a heart bent to backsliding, of the still continuing tendency of the flesh to lust against the Spirit. Sometimes, unless we continually watch and pray, it lusteth to pride, sometimes to anger, sometimes to love of the world, love of ease, love of honour, or love of pleasure more than of God. It is a conviction of the tendency of our heart to self will, to atheism or idolatry, and above all, to unbelief, whereby, in a thousand ways, and under a thousand pretences, we are ever departing, more or less, from the living God.

7. With this conviction of the sin remaining in our hearts, there is joined a clear conviction of the sin remaining in our lives; still *cleaving* to all our words

and actions. In the best of these we now discern a mixture of evil, either in the spirit, the matter, or the manner of them; something that could not endure the righteous judgment of God, were he extreme to mark what is done amiss. Where we least suspected it, we find a taint of pride or self will, of unbelief or idolatry; so that we are now more ashamed of our best duties than formerly of our worst sins: and hence we cannot but feel, that these are so far from having any thing meritorious in them, yea, so far from being able to stand in sight of the divine justice, that for those also we should be guilty before God, were it not for the blood of the covenant.

8. Experience shows that, together with this conviction of sin *remaining* in our hearts, and *cleaving* to all our words and actions; as well as the guilt which on account thereof we should incur, were we not continually sprinkled with the atoning blood; one thing more is implied in this repentance: namely, a conviction of our helplessness, of our utter inability to think one good thought, or to form one good desire; and much more to speak one word aright, or to perform one good action, but through his free, almighty grace, first preventing us, and then accompanying us every moment.

9. "But what good works are those, the practice of which you affirm to be necessary to sanctification?" First, all works of piety; such as public prayer, family prayer, and praying in our closet; receiving the supper of the Lord; searching the Scriptures, by hearing, reading, meditating; and using such a measure of fasting or abstinence as our bodily health allows.

10. Secondly, all works of mercy, whether they relate to the bodies or souls of men; such as feeding the hungry, clothing the naked, entertaining the stranger, visiting those that are in prison, or sick, or variously afflicted; such as the endeavoring to instruct the ignorant, to awaken the stupid sinner, to quicken the lukewarm, to confirm the wavering, to comfort the feeble minded, to succour the tempted, or contribute

in any manner to the saving of souls from death. This is the repentance, and these the "fruits meet for repentance," which are necessary to full sanctification. This is the way wherein God hath appointed his children to wait for complete salvation.

11. Hence may appear the extreme mischievousness of that seemingly innocent opinion, That there is no sin in a believer; that all sin is destroyed, root and branch, the moment a man is justified. By totally preventing that repentance, it quite blocks up the way to sanctification: there is no place for repentance in him who believes there is no sin either in his life or heart: consequently there is no place for his being perfected in love, to which that repentance is indispensably necessary.

12. Hence it may likewise appear, that there is no possible danger in *thus* expecting full salvation. For suppose we were mistaken, suppose no such blessing ever was or can be attained, yet we lose nothing: nay, the very expectation quickens us in using all the talents which God has given us; yea, in improving them all; so that when our Lord cometh he will receive his own with increase.

13. But to return. Though it be allowed, that both this repentance and its fruits are necessary to full salvation; yet they are not necessary either in the same sense with faith, or in the same degree: not in the *same degree;*—for these fruits are only necessary *conditionally*, if there be time and opportunity for them; otherwise a man may be sanctified without them. But he cannot be sanctified without faith. Likewise, let a man have ever so much of this repentance, or ever so many good works, yet all this does not at all avail: he is not sanctified till he believes: but the moment he believes, with or without those fruits, yea, with more or less of this repentance, he is sanctified.—Not in the *same sense:*—for this repentance and these fruits are only *remotely* necessary, necessary in order to the continuance of his faith, as well as the increase of it; whereas faith is *immediately* and *directly* necessary to

sanctification. It remains, that faith is the only condition, which is *immediately* and *proximately* necessary to sanctification.

14. "But what is that faith whereby we are sanctified —saved from sin, and perfected in love?" It is a divine evidence and conviction, first, that God hath promised it in the holy Scripture. Till we are thoroughly satisfied of this, there is no moving one step farther. And one would imagine there needed not one word more to satisfy a reasonable man of this than the ancient promise, "Then will I circumcise thy heart and the heart of thy seed, to love the Lord thy God with all thy heart, and with all thy soul, and with all thy mind." How clearly does this express the being perfected in love! How strongly imply the being saved from all sin! For as long as love takes up the whole heart, what room is there for sin therein?

15. It is a divine evidence and conviction, secondly, that what God hath promised he is able to perform. Admitting, therefore, that "with men it is impossible" to "bring a clean thing out of an unclean," to purify the heart from all sin, and to fill it with all holiness; yet this creates no difficulty in the case, seeing "with God all things are possible." And surely no one ever imagined it was possible to any power less than that of the Almighty! But if God speaks, it shall be done. God saith, "Let there be light; and there [is] light!"

16. It is, thirdly, a divine evidence and conviction that he is able and willing to do it now. And why not? Is not a moment to him the same as a thousand years? He cannot want more time to accomplish whatever is his will. And he cannot want or stay for any more *worthiness* or *fitness* in the persons he is pleased to honour. We may therefore boldly say, at any point of time, "Now is the day of salvation!" "To day, if ye will hear his voice, harden not your hearts!" "Behold, all things are now ready, come unto the marriage!"

17. To this confidence, that God is both able and willing to sanctify us now, there needs to be added

one thing more,—a divine evidence and conviction, that he doeth it. In that hour it is done: God says to the inmost soul, "According to thy faith be it unto thee!" Then the soul is pure from every spot of sin; it is clean "from all unrighteousness." The believer then experiences the deep meaning of those solemn words, "If we walk in the light as he is in the light, we have fellowship one with another, and the blood of Jesus Christ his Son cleanseth us from all sin."

18. "But does God work this great work in the soul gradually or instantaneously?" Perhaps it may be gradually wrought in some; I mean in this sense,—they do not advert to the particular moment wherein sin ceases to be. But it is infinitely desirable, were it the will of God that it should be done instantaneously; that the Lord should destroy sin "by the breath of his mouth," in a moment, in the twinkling of an eye. And so he generally does; a plain fact, of which there is evidence enough to satisfy any unprejudiced person. *Thou* therefore look for it every moment! Look for it in the way above described; in all those *good works* whereunto thou art "created anew in Christ Jesus." There is then no danger: you can be no worse, if you are no better for that expectation. For were you to be disappointed of your hope, still you lose nothing. But you shall not be disappointed of your hope: it will come, and will not tarry. Look for it then every day, every hour, every moment! Why not this hour, this moment? Certainly you may look for it *now*, if you believe it is by faith. And by this token you may surely know whether you seek it by faith or by works. If by works, you want something to be done *first, before* you are sanctified. You think, I must first *be* or *do* thus or thus. Then you are seeking it by works unto this day. If you seek it by faith, you may expect it *as you are;* and if as you are, then expect it *now*. It is of importance to observe, that there is an inseparable connection between these three points,—Expect it *by faith,* Expect it *as you are,* and Expect it *now!* To deny one of them is to deny them all. To allow one, is to

allow them all. Do *you* believe we are sanctified by faith? Be true then to your principle; and look for this blessing just as you are, neither better nor worse; as a poor sinner that has still nothing to pay, nothing to plead, but "Christ *died*." And if you look for it as you are, then expect it *now*. Stay for nothing: why should you? Christ is ready; and he is all you want. He is waiting for you: he is at the door! Let your inmost soul cry out,

> "Come in, come in, thou heavenly guest!
>   Nor hence again remove;
> But sup with me, and let the feast
>   Be everlasting love."

MINUTES OF SOME LATE CONVERSATIONS BETWEEN THE REV. MESSRS. WESLEY AND OTHERS.

CONVERSATION I.
Monday, June 25th, 1744. (sic)

Q. 1. What is it to be justified?

A. To be pardoned and received into God's favour; into such a state, that, if we continue therein, we shall be finally saved.

Q. 2. Is faith the condition of justification?

A. Yes; for every one who believeth not is condemned; and every one who believes is justified.

Q. 3. But must not repentance, and works meet for repentance, go before this faith?

A. Without doubt; if by repentance you mean conviction of sin; and by works meet for repentance, obeying God as far as we can, forgiving our brother, leaving off from evil, doing good, and using his ordinances, according to the power we have received.

Q. 4. What is faith?

A. Faith in general is a divine, supernatural [evidence or conviction] of things not seen; that is, of past, future, or spiritual things: it is a spiritual sight of God and the things of God.

First. A sinner is convinced by the Holy Ghost,

"Christ loved me, and gave himself for me." This is that faith by which he is justified, or pardoned, the moment he receives it. Immediately the same Spirit bears witness, "Thou art pardoned; thou hast redemption in his blood." And this is saving faith, whereby the love of God is shed abroad in his heart.

Q. 5. Have all Christians this faith? May not a man be justified and not know it?

A. That all true Christians have such a faith as implies an assurance of God's love, appears from Romans viii, 15; Ephes. iv, 32; 2 Cor. xiii, 5; Heb. viii, 10; 1 John iv, 10, and 19. And that no man can be justified and not know it, appears farther from the nature of the thing: for faith after repentance is ease after pain, rest after toil, light after darkness. It appears also from the immediate, as well as distant, fruits thereof.

Q. 6. But may not a man go to heaven without it?

A. It does not appear from holy writ that a man who hears the Gospel can, (Mark xvi, 16,) whatever a Heathen may do: Romans ii, 14.

Q. 7. What are the immediate fruits of justifying faith?

A. Peace, joy, love, power over all outward sin, and power to keep down inward sin.

Q. 8. Does any one believe, who has not the witness in himself, or any longer than he sees, loves, obeys God?

A. We apprehend not; seeing God being the very essence of faith; love and obedience, the inseparable properties of it.

Q. 9. What sins are consistent with justifying faith?

A. No wilful sin. If a believer wilfully sins, he casts away his faith. Neither is it possible he should have justifying faith again, without previously repenting.

Q. 10. Must every believer come into a state of doubt, or fear, or darkness? Will he do so, unless by ignorance, or unfaithfulness? Does God otherwise withdraw himself?

A. It is certain, a believer need never again come into condemnation. It seems he need not come into a state of doubt, or fear, or darkness; and that (ordinarily at least) he will not, unless by ignorance or unfaithfulness. Yet it is true, that the first joy does seldom last long; that it is commonly followed by doubts and fears; and that God frequently permits great heaviness before any large manifestation of himself.

Q. 11. Are works necessary to the continuance of faith?

A. Without doubt; for a man may forfeit the free gift of God, either by sins of omission or commission.

Q. 12. Can faith be lost but for want of works?

A. It cannot but through disobedience.

Q. 13. How is faith "made perfect by works?"

A. The more we exert our faith, the more it is increased. "To him that hath shall be given."

Q. 14. St. Paul says, Abraham was not justified by works; St. James, he was justified by works. Do they not contradict each other?

A. No: (1) Because they do not speak of the same justification. St. Paul speaks of that justification which was when Abraham was seventy five years old, above twenty years before Isaac was born; St. James, of that justification which was when he offered up Isaac on the altar. (2) Because they do not speak of the same works; St. Paul speaking of works that precede faith; St. James, of works that spring from it.

Q. 15. In what sense is Adam's sin imputed to all mankind?

A. In Adam all die; that is, (1) Our bodies then became mortal. (2) Our souls died; that is, were disunited from God. And hence, (3) We are all born with a sinful, devilish nature. By reason whereof, (4) We are children of wrath, liable to death eternal: Rom. v, 18; Ephes. ii, 3.

Q. 16. In what sense is the righteousness of Christ imputed to all mankind, or to believers?

A. We do not find it expressly affirmed in Scripture, that God imputes the righteousness of Christ to any; although we do find that "faith is imputed" to us "for righteousness."

That text, "As by one man's disobedience all men were made sinners, so by the obedience of One, all were made righteous," we conceive means, By the merits of Christ, all men are cleared from the guilt of Adam's actual sin.

We conceive farther, that through the obedience and death of Christ, (1) The bodies of all men become immortal after the resurrection. (2) Their souls receive a capacity of spiritual life. And, (3) An actual spark or seed thereof. (4) All believers become children of grace, reconciled to God; and, (5) Made partakers of the divine nature.

Q. 17. Have we not then unawares leaned too much toward Calvinism?

A. We are afraid we have.

Q. 18. Have we not also leaned toward Antinomianism?

A. We are afraid we have.

Q. 19. What is Antinomianism?

A. The doctrine which makes void the law through faith.

Q. 20. What are the main pillars hereof?

A. (1) That Christ abolished the moral law.

(2) That therefore Christians are not obliged to observe it.

(3) That one branch of Christian liberty is, liberty from obeying the commandments of God.

(4) That it is bondage to do a thing because it is commanded, or forbear it because it is forbidden.

(5) That a believer is not obliged to use the ordinances of God, or to do good works.

(6) That a preacher ought not to exhort to good works; not unbelievers, because it is hurtful; not believers, because it is needless.

*On Tuesday morning, June 26th, was considered
the doctrine of Sanctification:*

Q. 1. What is it to be sanctified?

A. To be renewed in the image of God, in righteousness and true holiness.

Q. 2. Is faith the condition, or the instrument, of
sanctification?

A. It is both the condition and instrument of it.
When we begin to believe, then sanctification begins.
And as faith increases, holiness increases, till we are
created anew.

Q. 3. What is implied in being a perfect Christian?

A. The loving the Lord our God with all our heart,
and with all our mind, and soul, and strength; Deut.
vi, 5, xxx, 6; Ezek. xxxvi, 25–29.

Q. 4. Does this imply that all inward sin is taken
away?

A. Without doubt; or how could we be said to be
saved "from all our uncleannesses?" verse 29.

Q. 5. Can we know one who is thus saved? What
is a reasonable proof of it?

A. We cannot, without the miraculous discernment
of spirits, be infallibly certain of those who are thus
saved. But we apprehend, these would be the best
proofs which the nature of the thing admits: (1) If
we had sufficient evidence of their unblamable behaviour preceding. (2) If they gave a distinct account of
the time and manner wherein they were saved from
sin, and of the circumstances thereof, with such sound
speech as could not be reproved. And, (3) If, upon a
strict inquiry afterward from time to time, it appeared
that all their tempers, and words, and actions, were
holy and unreprovable.

Q. 6. How should we treat those who think they
have attained this?

A. Exhort them to forget the things that are behind, and to watch and pray always, that God may
search the ground of their hearts.

• • • •

Friday, August 2nd [1745] (sic)

Q. 20. Should we not have a care of depreciating justification, in order to exalt the state of full sanctification?

A. Undoubtedly we should beware of this; for one may insensibly slide into it.

Q. 21. How shall we effectually avoid it?

A. When we are going to speak of entire sanctification, let us first describe the blessings of a justified state, as strongly as possible.

Q. 22. Does not the truth of the Gospel lie very near both to Calvinism and Antinomianism?

A. Indeed it does; as it were, within a hair's breadth: so that it is altogether foolish and sinful, because we do not quite agree either with one or the other, to run from them as far as ever we can.

Q. 23. Wherein may we come to the very edge of Calvinism?

A. (1) In ascribing all good to the free grace of God. (2) In denying all natural free-will, and all power antecedent to grace. And (3) In excluding all merit from man; even for what he has or does by the grace of God.

Q. 24. Wherein may we come to the edge of Antinomianism?

A. (1) In exalting the merits and love of Christ. (2) In rejoicing evermore.

Q. 25. Does faith supersede (set aside the necessity of) holiness or good works?

A. In nowise. So far from it, that it implies both, as a cause does its effects.

About ten, we began to speak of Sanctification: with regard to which, it was inquired:

Q. 1. When does inward sanctification begin?

A. In the moment we are justified. The seed of every virtue is then sown in the soul. From that time the believer gradually dies to sin, and grows in grace. Yet sin remains in him; yea, the seed of all sin, till he is sanctified throughout in spirit, soul, and body.

Q. 2. What will become of a Heathen, a Papist,

a Church of England man, if he dies without being thus sanctified?

A. He cannot see the Lord. But none who seeks it sincerely shall or can die without it; though possibly he may not attain it, till the very article of death.

Q. 3. Is it ordinarily given till a little before death?

A. It is not, to those that expect it no sooner, nor consequently ask for it, at least, not in faith.

Q. 4. But ought we to expect it sooner?

A. Why not? For although we grant, (1) That the generality of believers whom we have hitherto known were not so sanctified till near death: (2) That few of those to whom St. Paul wrote his Epistles were so at the time he wrote: (3) Nor he himself at the time of writing his former Epistles: yet this does not prove that we may not today.

Q. 5. But would not one who was thus sanctified be incapable of worldly business?

A. He would be far more capable of it than ever, as going through all without distraction.

Q. 6. Would he be capable of marriage?

A. Why should he not?

Q. 7. Should we not beware of bearing hard on those who think they have attained?

A. We should. And the rather, because if they are faithful to the grace they have received, they are in no danger of perishing at last. No, not even if they remain in luminous faith, as some term it, for many months or years; perhaps till within a little time of their spirits returning to God.

Q. 8. In what manner should we preach entire sanctification?

A. Scarce at all to those who are not pressing forward. To those who are, always by way of promise; always drawing, rather than driving.

Q. 9. How should we wait for the fulfilling of this promise?

A. In universal obedience; in keeping all the commandments; in denying ourselves and taking up our cross daily. These are the general means which God hath ordained for our receiving his sanctifying grace. The particular are, prayer, searching the Scripture, communicating, and fasting.

. . . .

Conversation—Tuesday, May 13, 1746. (sic)

Q. 24. But do you consider, that we are under the covenant of grace, and that the covenant of works is now abolished?

A. All mankind were under the covenant of grace, from the very hour that the original promise was made. If by the covenant of works you mean, that of unsinning obedience made with Adam before the fall, no man but Adam was ever under that covenant; for it was abolished before Cain was born. Yet it is not so abolished, but that it will stand, in a measure, even to the end of the world; that is, If we "do this," we shall live; if not, we shall die eternally: if we do well, we shall live with God in glory; if evil, we shall die the second death. For every man shall be judged in that day, and rewarded "according to his works."

Q. 25. What means then, "To him that believeth, his faith is counted for righteousness?"

A. That God forgives him that is unrighteous as soon as he believes, accepting his faith instead of perfect righteousness. But then observe, universal righteousness follows, though it did not precede, faith.

Q. 26. But is faith thus "counted to us for righteousness," at whatsoever time we believe?

A. Yes. In whatsoever moment we believe, all our past sins vanish away: they are as though they had never been, and we stand clear in the sight of God.

Tuesday—ten o'clock

Q. 4. Wherein does our doctrine now differ from that we preached when at Oxford?

A. Chiefly in these two points: (1) We then knew nothing of that righteousness of faith, in justification; nor (2) Of the nature of faith itself, as implying consciousness of pardon.

Q. 5. May not some degree of the love of God go before a distinct sense of justification?

A. We believe it may.

Q. 6. Can any degree of sanctification or holiness?

A. Many degrees of outward holiness may; yea, and some degree of meekness, and several other tempers which would be branches of Christian holiness, but that they do not spring from Christian principles. For the abiding love of God cannot spring but from faith in a pardoning God. And no true Christian holiness can exist without that love of God for its foundation.

Q. 7. Is every man, as soon as he believes, a new creature, sanctified, pure in heart? Has he then a new heart? Does Christ dwell therein? And is he a temple of the Holy Ghost?

A. All these things may be affirmed of every believer, in a true sense. Let us not therefore contradict those who maintain it. Why should we contend about words?

Tuesday, June 16th, 1747. (sic)

Q. 1. Is justifying faith a divine assurance that Christ loved me, and gave himself for me?

A. We believe it is.

Q. 2. What is the judgment of most of the serious Dissenters concerning this?

A. They generally allow, that many believers have such an assurance; and, that it is to be desired and prayed for by all. But then they affirm, that this is the highest species or degree of faith; that it is not the common privilege of believers: consequently, they deny that this is justifying faith, or necessarily implied therein.

Wednesday, June 17th.

Q. 1. How much is allowed by our brethren who differ from us, with regard to entire sanctification?

A. They grant, (1) That every one must be entirely sanctified in the article of death.

(2) That, till then, a believer daily grows in grace, comes nearer and nearer to perfection.

(3) That we ought to be continually pressing after this, and to exhort all others so to do.

Q. 2. What do we allow them?

A. We grant, (1) That many of those who have died in the faith, yea, the greater part of those we have known, were not sanctified throughout, not made perfect in love, till a little before death.

(2) That the term, "sanctified," is continually applied by St. Paul to all that were justified, were true believers.

(3) That by this term alone, he rarely, if ever, means saved from all sin.

(4) That, consequently, it is not proper to use it in this sense, without adding the word "wholly, entirely," or the like.

(5) That the inspired writers almost continually speak of or to those who are justified; but very rarely, either of or to those who are wholly sanctified.

(6) That, consequently, it behooves us to speak in public almost continually of the state of justification; but, more rarely, in full and explicit terms, concerning entire sanctification.

Q. 3. What then is the point wherein we divide?

A. It is this: whether we should expect to be saved from all sin before the article of death.

• • • •

Q. 9. But how does it appear that this is to be done before the article of death?

A. First. From the very nature of a command, which is not given to the dead, but to the living. Therefore, "Thou shalt love God with all thy heart," cannot mean, Thou shalt do this when thou diest, but while thou livest.

Secondly. From express texts of Scripture: (1) "The grace of God that bringeth salvation hath appeared to all men, teaching us that, having renounced ungodliness and worldly lusts, we should live soberly, righteously, and godly, in this present world; looking for—the glorious appearing of our Saviour Jesus Christ; who gave himself for us, that he might redeem us from all iniquity, and purify unto himself a peculiar people, zealous of good works," Titus ii, 11–14. (2) "He hath raised up a horn of salvation for us,—to perform the mercy promised to our fathers; the oath which he sware to our father Abraham, that he would grant unto us, that we, being delivered out of the hand of our enemies, should serve him without fear, in holiness and righteousness before him, all the days of our life," Luke i, 69–75.

Q. 10. Is there any example in Scripture of persons who had attained to this?

A. Yes. St. John, and all those of whom he says in his First Epistle, "Herein is our love made perfect, that we may have confidence in the day of judgment: because as he is, so are we in this world," iv, 17.

Q. 11. But why are there not more examples of this kind recorded in the New Testament?

A. It does not become us to be peremptory in this matter. One reason might possibly be, because the Apostles wrote to the Church while it was in a state of infancy. Therefore they might mention such persons the more sparingly, lest they should give strong meat to babes.

Q. 12. Can you show one such example now? Where is he that is thus perfect?

A. To some who make this inquiry one might answer, "If I knew one here, I would not tell you. For you do not inquire out of love. You are like Herod. You only seek the young child to slay it."

But more directly we answer, there are numberless reasons why there should be few (if any indisputable) examples. What inconveniences would this bring on the person himself, set as a mark for all to shoot at! What a temptation would it be to others, not only to men who knew not God, but to believers themselves! How hardly would they refrain from idolizing such a person! And yet, how unprofitable to gainsayers! "For if they hear not Moses and the Prophets," Christ and his Apostles, "neither would they be persuaded, though one rose from the dead."

Q. 13. Suppose one had attained to this, would you advise him to speak of it?

A. Not to them who know not God. It would only provoke them to contradict and blaspheme: nor to any without some particular reason, without some particular good in view. And then they should have an especial care to avoid all appearance of boasting.

Q. 14. Is it a sin, not to believe those who say they have attained?

A. By no means, even though they said true. We ought not hastily to believe, but to suspend our judgment, till we have full and strong proof.

Q. 15. But are we not apt to have a secret distaste to any who say they are saved from all sin?

A. It is very possible we may, and that on several grounds; partly from a concern for the honour of God, and the good of souls, who may be hurt, yea, or turned out of the way, if these are not what they profess; partly from a kind of implicit envy at those who speak of higher attainments than our own; and partly from our slowness and unreadiness of heart to believe the works of God.

Q. 16. Does not the harshly preaching perfection tend to bring believers into a kind of bondage, or slavish fear?

A. It does; therefore we should always place it in the most amiable light, so that it may excite only hope, joy, and desire.

Q. 17. Why may we not continue in the joy of faith even till we are made perfect?

A. Why indeed! since holy grief does not quench this joy; since, even while we are under the cross, while we deeply partake of the sufferings of Christ, we may rejoice with joy unspeakable.

Q. 18. Do we not discourage believers from rejoicing evermore?

A. We ought not so to do. Let them all their life long rejoice unto God, so it be with reverence. And even if lightness or pride should mix with their joy, let us not strike at the joy itself, (this is the gift of

God,) but at that lightness or pride, that the evil may cease and the good remain.

Q. 19. Ought we to be anxiously careful about perfection, lest we should die before we have attained?

A. In no wise. We ought to be thus careful for nothing, neither spiritual nor temporal.

Q. 20. But ought we not to be troubled on account of the sinful nature which still remains in us?

A. It is good for us to have a deep sense of this, and to be much ashamed before the Lord: but this should only incite us the more earnestly to turn unto Christ every moment, and to draw light, and life, and strength from him, that we may go on conquering and to conquer. And, therefore, when the sense of our sin most abounds, the sense of his love should much more abound.

Q. 21. Will our joy or our trouble increase as we grow in grace?

A. Perhaps both. But without doubt our joy in the Lord will increase as our love increases.

Q. 22. Is not the teaching believers to be continually poring upon their inbred sin the ready way to make them forget that they were purged from their former sins?

A. We find by experience it is; or to make them undervalue and account it a little thing; whereas, indeed, (though there are still greater gifts behind,) this is inexpressibly great and glorious.

THE CAMBRIDGE PLATFORM (1648)

English Calvinists in the latter part of the sixteenth century and in the seventeenth century developed significant differences in ecclesiology. Congregationalists meeting in Cambridge, Massachusetts in 1648 and in London in 1658 were satisfied to accept the Westminster Confession of Faith; but they were not satisfied with Presbyterian polity. Neither were they satisfied with Brownism or Separatism. Many factors contributed to these ecclesiastical developments, but certainly some of the factors are inherent in the Calvinist theology itself with its emphasis upon the sovereignty of God and the disciplined life of the Church. The New England Calvinists were free to develop their own polity in their new country, and the Cambridge Platform reflects this experience. The chapters that bear most directly upon the doctrine of the Church are quoted here.

Source: The texts reprinted here are taken (with modernization of spelling) from *The Creeds and Platforms of Congregationalism* by Williston Walker (New York: Charles Scribner's Sons, 1893), pp. 203–10, 217–20, 221–24, 229–34. *Cf.* introduction in new edition by Douglas Horton, published by Pilgrim Press, 1961. Text may also be found in *The Results of Three Synods* (Boston, 1725). Also a modern and abridged text in *American Christianity*, edited by H. Shelton Smith, Robert T. Handy, and Lefferts A. Loetscher (New York: Charles Scribner's Sons, 1960).

THE CAMBRIDGE PLATFORM (1648)

Chap. I.

OF THE FORM OF CHURCH-GOVERNMENT; AND THAT IT IS ONE, IMMUTABLE, AND PRESCRIBED IN THE WORD OF GOD.

Ecclesiastical Polity or Church Government, or discipline is nothing else, but that Form and order that is to be observed in the Church of Christ upon earth, both for the Constitution of it, and all the Administrations that therein are to be performed.

2. Church-Government is Considered in a double respect either in regard of the parts of Government themselves, or necessary Circumstances thereof. . . .

3. The parts of Church-Government are all of them

exactly described in the word of God being parts or means of Instituted worship according to the second Commandment: and therefore to continue one and the same, unto the appearing of our Lord Jesus Christ as a kingdom that cannot be shaken, until he shall deliver it up unto God, even the Father. So that it is not left in the power of men, officers, Churches, or any state in the world to add, or diminish, or alter any thing in the least measure therein.

4. The necessary circumstances, as time and place &c belonging unto order and decency, are not so left unto men as that under pretence of them, they may thrust their own Inventions upon the Churches: Being Circumscribed in the word with many General limitations. . . .

Chap. II.

OF THE NATURE OF THE CATHOLIC CHURCH IN GENERAL, AND IN SPECIAL, OF A PARTICULAR VISIBLE CHURCH.

The Catholic Church, is the whole company of those that are elected, redeemed, and in time effectually called from the state of sin and death unto a state of Grace, and salvation in Jesus Christ.

2. This church is either Triumphant, or Militant. Triumphant, the number of them who are Glorified in heaven: Militant, the number of them who are conflicting with their enemies upon earth.

3. This Militant Church is to be considered as Invisible, and Visible. Invisible, in respect of their relation wherein they stand to Christ, as a body unto the head, being united unto him, by the spirit of God, and faith in their hearts: Visible, in respect of the profession of their faith, in their persons, and in particular Churches: and so there may be acknowledged an universal visible Church.

4. The members of the Militant visible Church, considered either as not yet in church-order, or as walking according to the church-order of the Gospel. In order, and so besides the spiritual union, and com-

munion, common to all believers, they enjoy more over an union and communion ecclesiastical-Political: So we deny an universal visible church.

5. The state the members of the Militant visible church walking in order, was either before the law, Oeconomical, that is in families; or under the law, National: or, since the coming of Christ, only congregational: (The term Independent, we approve not:) Therefore neither national, provincial, nor classical.

6. A Congregational-church, is by the institution of Christ a part of the Militant-visible-church, consisting of a company of Saints by calling, united into one body, by a holy covenant, for the public worship of God, and the mutual edification one of another, in the Fellowship of the Lord Jesus.

Chap. III.

OF THE MATTER OF THE VISIBLE CHURCH
BOTH IN RESPECT OF QUALITY AND QUANTITY.

The matter of a visible church are Saints by calling.

2. By Saints, we understand,

(1) Such, as have not only attained the knowledge of the principles of Religion, and are free from gross and open scandals, but also do together with the profession of their faith and Repentance, walk in blameless obedience to the word, so as that in charitable discretion they may be accounted Saints by calling, (though perhaps some or more of them be unsound, and hypocrites inwardly:) because the members of such particular churches are commonly by the holy ghost called Saints and faithful brethren in Christ, and sundry churches have been reproved for receiving, and suffering such persons to continue in fellowship amongst them, as have been offensive and scandalous: the name of God also by this means is Blasphemed: and the holy things of God defiled and Prophaned: the hearts of godly grieved: and the wicked themselves hardened: and helped forward to damnation: the example of such doth endanger the sanctity of others. A little Leaven Leaveneth the whole lump.

(2) The children of such, who are also holy.

3. The members of churches though orderly constituted, may in time degenerate, and grow corrupt and scandalous, which though they ought not to be tolerated in the church, yet their continuance therein, through the defect of the execution of discipline and Just censures, doth not immediately dissolve the being of the church, as appears in the church of Israel, and the churches of Galatia and Corinth, Pergamus, and Thyatira.

4. The matter of the Church in respect of its quantity ought not to be of greater number than may ordinarily meet together conveniently in one place: nor ordinarily fewer, than may conveniently carry on Church-work. . . .

5. Nor can it with reason be thought but that every church appointed and ordained by Christ, had a ministry ordained and appointed for the same: and yet plain it is, that there were no ordinary officers appointed by Christ for any other, than Congregational churches: Elders being appointed to feed, not all flocks, but the particular flock of God over which the holy Ghost had made them the overseers, and that flock they must attend, even the whole flock: and one Congregation being as much as any ordinary Elders can attend, therefore there is no greater Church than a Congregation, which may ordinarily meet in one place.

Chap. IV.

OF THE FORM OF A VISIBLE CHURCH AND OF CHURCH COVENANT.

Saints by Calling, must have a Visible-Political-Union amongst themselves, or else they are not yet a particular church: as those similitudes hold forth, which Scripture makes use of, to show the nature of particular Churches: As a Body, A building, or House, Hands, Eyes, Feet, and other members must be united, or else, remaining separate are not a body. Stones, Timber, though squared, hewn and polished, are not an house, until they are compacted and united: so

Saints or believers in judgment of charity, are not a church, unless Orderly knit together.

2. Particular churches cannot be distinguished one from another but by their forms. Ephesus is not Smyrna, and Pergamus Thyatira, but each one a distinct society of it self, having officers of their own, which had not the charge of others: Virtues of their own, for which others are not praised: Corruptions of their own, for which others are not blamed.

3. This Form is the Visible Covenant, Agreement, or consent whereby they give up themselves unto the Lord, to the observing of the ordinances of Christ together in the same society, which is usually called the Church-Covenant; For we see not otherwise how members can have Church-power one over another mutually.

The comparing of each particular church unto a City, and unto a Spouse, seemeth to conclude not only a Form, but that that Form, is by way of a Covenant.

The Covenant, as it was that which made the Family of Abraham and children of Israel to be a church and people unto God, so it is that which now makes the several societies of Gentile believers to be churches in these days.

4. This Voluntary Agreement, Consent or Covenant (for all these are here taken for the same): Although the more express and plain it is, the more fully it puts us in mind of our mutual duty, and stirreth us up to it, and leaveth less room for the questioning of the Truth of the Church-estate of a Company of professors, and the Truth of membership of particular persons: yet we conceive, the substance of it is kept, where there is a real Agreement and consent, of a company of faithful persons to meet constantly together in one Congregation, for the public worship of God, and their mutual edification: which real agreement and consent they do express by their constant practice in coming together for the public worship of God, and by their religious subjection unto the ordinances of God there: the rather, if we do con-

sider how Scripture covenants have been entered into, not only expressly by word of mouth, but by sacrifice; by hand writing, and seal; and also sometimes by silent consent, without any writing, or expression of words at all.

5. This form then being by mutual covenant, it followeth, it is not faith in the heart, nor the profession of that faith, nor cohabitation, nor Baptism; (1) Not faith in the heart? because that is invisible: (2) not a bare profession; because that declareth them no more to be members of one church than of another: (3) not Cohabitation; Atheists or Infidels may dwell together with believers: (4) not Baptism; because it presupposeth a church estate, as circumcision in the old Testament, which gave no being unto the church, the church being before it, and in the wilderness without it; seals presuppose a covenant already in being, one person is a complete subject of Baptism: but one person is incapable of being a church.

Chap. V.

OF THE FIRST SUBJECT OF CHURCH POWER OR, TO WHOM CHURCH POWER DOTH FIRST BELONG.

The first subject of church power, is either Supreme, or Subordinate, and Ministerial: The Supreme (by way of gift from the father) is the Lord Jesus Christ: The Ministerial, is either extraordinary; as the Apostles, Prophets, and Evangelists: or Ordinary; as every particular Congregational church.

2. Ordinary church power, is either the power of office that is such as is proper to the eldership: or, power of privilege, such as belongs unto the brotherhood. The latter is in the brethren formally, and immediately from Christ, that is, so as it may according to order be acted or exercised immediately by themselves: the former, is not in them formally or immediately, and therefore cannot be acted or exercised immediately by them, but is said to be in them, in that they design the persons unto office, who only are to act, or to exercise this power.

Chap. VI.

OF THE OFFICERS OF THE CHURCH, AND ESPECIALLY OF PASTORS AND TEACHERS.

A Church being a company of people combined together by covenant for the worship of God, it appeareth thereby, that there may be the essence and being of a church without any officers, seeing there is both the form and matter of a church, which is implied when it is said, the Apostles ordained elders in every church.

2. Nevertheless, though officers be not absolutely necessary, to the simple being of churches, when they be called: yet ordinarily to their calling they are, and to their well being: and therefore the Lord Jesus out of his tender compassion hath appointed, and ordained officers which he would not have done, if they had not been useful and needful for the church; yea, being Ascended into heaven, he received gifts for men, and gave gifts to men, whereof officers for the church are Justly accounted no small parts; they being to continue to the end of the world, and for the perfecting of all the Saints.

Chap. X.

OF THE POWER OF THE CHURCH, AND ITS PRESBYTERY.

Supreme and Lordly power over all the Churches upon earth, doth only belong unto Jesus Christ, who is King of the church, and the head thereof. He hath the Government upon his shoulders, and hath all power given to him, both in heaven and earth.

2. A Company of professed believers Ecclesiastically Confederate, as they are a church before they have officers, and without them; so even in that estate, subordinate Church-power under Christ delegated to them by him, doth belong to them, in such a manner as is before expressed. . . .

3. This Government of the church, is a mixed Government (and so hath been acknowledged long before the term of Independency was heard of:) In respect

of Christ, the head and King of the church, and the Sovereign power residing in him, and exercised by him, it is a Monarchy: In respect of the body, or Brotherhood of the church, and power from Christ granted unto them, it resembles a Democracy; in respect of the Presbytery and power committed to them, it is an Aristocracy.

4. The Sovereign power which is peculiar unto Christ, is exercised, I. In calling the church out of the world unto holy fellowship with himself. II. In instituting the ordinances of his worship, and appointing his ministers and officers for the dispensing of them. III. In giving laws for the ordering of all our ways, and the ways of his house. IV. In giving power and life to all his Institutions, and to his people by them. V. In protecting and delivering his church against and from all the enemies of their peace.

5. The power granted by Christ unto the body of the church and Brotherhood, is a prerogative or privilege which the church doth exercise: I. In Choosing their own officers, whether Elders, or Deacons. II. In admission of their own members and therefore, there is great reason they should have power to Remove any from their fellowship again. . . .

6. In case an Elder offend incorrigibly, the matter so requiring, as the church had power to call him to office, so they have power according to order (the counsel of other churches where it may be had) directing thereto to remove him from his Office: and being now but a member, in case he add contumacy to his sin, the Church that had power to receive him into their fellowship, hath also the same power to cast him out, that they have concerning any other member.

7. Church-government, or Rule, is placed by Christ in the officers of the church, who are therefore called Rulers, while they rule with God: yet in case of maladministration, they are subject to the power of the church, according as hath been said before. . . .

11. From the premises, namely, that the ordinary power of Government belonging only to the elders, power of privilege remaineth with the brotherhood, (as power of judgment in matters of censure, and power of liberty, in matters of liberty:) It followeth, that in an organic Church, and right administration; all church acts, proceed after the manner of a mixed administration, so as no church act can be consummated, or perfected without the consent of both.

Chap. XII.
OF ADMISSION OF MEMBERS INTO THE CHURCH.

The doors of the Churches of Christ upon earth, do not by God's appointment stand so wide open, that all sorts of people good or bad, may freely enter therein at their pleasure; but such as are admitted thereto, as members ought to be examined and tried first; whether they be fit and meet to be received into church-society, or not. The Eunuch of Ethiopia, before his admission was examined by Philip, whether he did believe on Jesus Christ with all his heart; the Angel of the church at Ephesus is commended, for trying such as said they were Apostles and were not. There is like reason for trying of them that profess themselves to be believers.

The officers are charged with the keeping of the doors of the Church, and therefore are in a special manner to make trial of the fitness of such who enter. Twelve Angels are set at the gates of the Temple, lest such as were Ceremonially unclean should enter thereinto.

2. The things which are requisite to be found in all church members, are, Repentance from sin, and faith in Jesus Christ. And therefore these are the things whereof men are to be examined, at their admission into the church and which then they must profess and hold forth in such sort, as may satisfy rational charity that the things are there indeed. . . .

3. The weakest measure of faith is to be accepted

in those that desire to be admitted into the church: because weak christians if sincere, have the substance of that faith, repentance and holiness which is required in church members: and such have most need of the ordinances for their confirmation and growth in grace. . . .

4. In case any through excessive fear, or other infirmity, be unable to make their personal relation of their spiritual estate in public, it is sufficient that the Elders having received private satisfaction, make relation thereof in public before the church, they testifying their assents thereunto; this being the way that tendeth most to edification. But whereas persons are of better abilities, there it is more expedient, that they make their relations, and confessions personally with their own mouth, as David professeth of himself.

5. A personal and public confession, and declaring of God's manner of working upon the soul, is both lawful, expedient, and useful, in sundry respects, and upon sundry grounds. . . .

7. The like trial is to be required from such members of the church, as were born in the same, or received their membership, and were baptized in their infancy, or minority, by virtue of the covenant of their parents, when being grown up unto years of discretion, they shall desire to be made partakers of the Lord's supper: unto which, because holy things must not be given unto the unworthy, therefore it is requisite, that these as well as others, should come to their trial and examination, and manifest their faith and repentance by an open profession thereof, before they are received to the Lord's supper, and otherwise not to be admitted there unto.

Yet these church-members that were so born, or received in their childhood, before they are capable of being made partakers of full communion, have many privileges which others (not church-members) have not: they are in covenant with God; have the seal thereof upon them, *viz.* Baptism; and so if not regenerated, yet are in a more hopeful way of attaining regenerating grace, and all the spiritual blessings both of the covenant and seal; they are also under Church-watch, and consequently subject, to the reprehensions, admonitions, and censures thereof, for their healing and amendment, as need shall require.

Chap. XV.
OF THE COMMUNION OF CHURCHES ONE WITH ANOTHER.

Although Churches be distinct, and therefore may not be confounded one with another: and equal, and therefore have not dominion one over another: yet all the churches ought to preserve Church-communion one with another, because they are all united unto Christ, not only as a mystical, but as a political head; whence is derived a communion suitable thereunto.

2. The communion of Churches is exercised sundry ways.

I. By way of mutual care in taking thought for one another's welfare.

II. By way of Consultation one with another, when we have occasion to require the judgment and counsel of other churches, touching any person, or cause wherewith they may be better acquainted than our selves. . . .

III. A third way then of communion of churches is by way of admonition, to wit, in case any public offence be found in a church, which they either discern not, or are slow in proceeding to use the means for the removing and healing of. . . .

IV. A fourth way of communion of churches, is by way of participation: the members of one church occasionally coming unto another, we willingly admit them to partake with us at the Lord's table, it being the seal of our communion not only with Christ, nor only with the members of our own church, but also with all the churches of the saints: in which regard, we refuse not to baptize their children presented to us, if either their own minister be absent, or such a fruit of holy fellowship be desired with us. In like case such churches as are furnished with more ministers than one, do willingly afford one of their own ministers to supply the place of an absent or sick minister of another church for a needful season.

V. A fifth way of Church-communion is, by way of recommendation when a member of one church hath occasion to reside in another church; if but for a season, we commend him to their watchful fellowship by letters of recommendation: but if he be called to settle his abode there, we commit him according to his desire, to the fellowship of their covenant, by letters of dismission.

VI. A sixth way of Church-communion, is in case of Need, to minister relief and succour one unto another: either of able members to furnish them with officers; or of outward support to the necessities of poorer churches; as did the churches of the Gentiles contribute liberally to the poor saints at Jerusalem.

3. When a company of believers purpose to gather into church fellowship, it is requisite for their safer proceeding, and the maintaining of the communion of churches, that they signify their intent unto the neighbour-churches, walking according unto the order of the Gospel, and desire their presence, and help, and right hand of fellowship which they ought readily to give unto them, when there is no just cause of excepting against their proceedings.

4. Besides these several ways of communion, there is also a way of propagation of churches; when a church shall grow too numerous, it is a way, and fit season, to propagate one Church out of another, by sending forth such of their members as are willing to remove, and to procure some officers to them, as may enter with them into church-estate amongst themselves: as Bees, when the hive is too full, issue forth by swarms, and are gathered into other hives, so the Churches of Christ may do the same upon like necessity; and therein hold forth to them the right hand of

fellowship, both in their gathering into a church; and in the ordination of their officers.

Chap. XVI.

Synods orderly assembled, and rightly proceeding according to the pattern, Acts 15, we acknowledge as the ordinance of Christ: and though not absolutely necessary to the being, yet many times, through the iniquity of men, and perverseness of times, necessary to the well-being of churches, for the establishment of truth, and peace therein.

3. Magistrates, have power to call a Synod, by calling to the Churches to send forth their Elders and other messengers, to counsel and assist them in matters of religion: but yet the constituting of a Synod, is a church act, and may be transacted by the churches, even when civil magistrates may be enemies to churches and to church assemblies.

4. It belongeth unto Synods and counsels, to debate and determine controversies of faith, and cases of conscience; to clear from the word holy directions for the holy worship of God, and good government of the church; to bear witness against mal-administration and Corruption in doctrine or manners in any particular Church, and to give directions for the reformation thereof: Not to exercise Church-censures in way of discipline, nor any other act of church-authority or jurisdiction: which that presidential Synod did forbear.

5. The Synod's directions and determinations, so far as consonant to the word of God, are to be received with reverence and submission; not only for their agreement therewith (which is the principal ground thereof, and without which they bind not at all:) but also secondarily, for the power whereby they are made, as being an ordinance of God appointed thereunto in his word.

6. Because it is difficult, if not impossible, for many churches to come altogether in one place, in all their members universally: therefore they may assemble by their delegates or messengers, as the church of Antioch

went not all to Jerusalem, but some select men for that purpose.

. . . .

CREEDS OF MODERN ROMAN CATHOLICISM

COUNCIL OF TRENT

The aftermath of Martin Luther's Ninety-Five Theses precipitated a widespread demand for a General Council. Two issues seemed to make such an assembly imperative. One was the general state of the Church and ecclesiastical practice. The other was the teaching and doctrine of the Church. Luther had raised his voice on both counts, but the doctrinal issue increasingly became the more important. Because of the political and ecclesiastical controversies and because of certain misgivings in Rome as to a General Council, the Council was not convened until December 13, 1545. It met with long interruptions until December 1563. The Protestants did not participate in the Council, though a few Protestants from Germany visited the Council in 1552, largely from political pressure.

The Council of Trent was the Roman Catholic answer to the Protestant Reformation, though it is too simple to interpret it as simply an answer to the Reformation. It did significantly limit the boundaries of the Church by excluding not only the Protestant position but other positions that had been permissible in Medieval Catholicism. The Council was also an answer, at least in part, to the desire for inner moral and spiritual renewal of the Church. Its legislation was concerned not simply with doctrine, but also with abuse. This Council was to shape the life of Roman Catholicism for a whole epoch, and its importance cannot be overestimated.

Source: Translation used here is by the Rev. H. J. Schroeder, O.P. and may be found in *Canons and Decrees of the Council of Trent* (St. Louis: B. Herder Book Co., 1941), pp. 15–23, 29–46, 51–55, 72–80, 144–46. Scripture references are omitted, but italics are retained.

Jedin, Hubert, *A History of the Council of Trent* (London: Thomas Nelson & Sons, 1957).

Tavard, George H., *Holy Writ or Holy Church* (London: Burns and Oates, 1959).

——, "The Catholic Reform in the Sixteenth Century," *Church History*, Vol. XXVI, 1957, pp. 275–88.

THE CANONS AND DECREES OF THE COUNCIL OF TRENT. A.D. 1563

THIRD SESSION,
celebrated on the fourth day of February, 1546.

DECREE CONCERNING THE SYMBOL OF FAITH

In the name of the holy and undivided Trinity, Father, Son, and Holy Ghost.

This holy, ecumenical and general Council of Trent, lawfully assembled in the Holy Ghost, the same three legates of the Apostolic See presiding, considering the magnitude of the matters to be dealt with, especially those comprised under the two heads, the extirpation of heresies and the reform of morals, for which purposes it was chiefly assembled, and recognizing with the Apostle that its *wrestling is not against flesh and blood, but against the spirits of wickedness in high places,* exhorts with the same Apostle each and all above all things to be *strengthened in the Lord and in the might of his power, in all things taking the shield of faith, wherewith they may be able to extinguish all the fiery darts of the most wicked one, and to take the helmet of the hope of salvation and the sword of the spirit, which is the word of God.* Wherefore, that this pious solicitude [of the council] may begin and continue by the grace of God, it ordains and decrees that before all else a confession of faith be set forth; following herein the examples of the Fathers, who in the more outstanding councils were accustomed at the beginning of their work to use this shield against heresies, with which alone they have at times drawn unbelievers to the faith, overcome heretics and confirmed the faithful. For this reason it has thought it well that the symbol of faith which the holy Roman Church uses as the cardinal principle wherein all who profess the faith of Christ necessarily agree and as the firm and sole foundation *against which the gates of hell shall never prevail,* be expressed in the same words in which it is read in all the churches, which is as follows: *I believe in one God the Father Almighty, creator of heaven and earth, of all things visible and invisible; and in one Lord Jesus Christ, the only begotten Son of God and born of the Father before all ages; God of God, light of light, true God of true God; begotten, not made, consubstantial with the Father, by whom all things were made; who for us men and for our salvation descended from heaven, and was incarnate by the Holy Ghost of the Virgin Mary, and was made man; crucified also for us under Pontius Pilate, he suffered and was buried; and he arose on the third day according to the Scriptures, and ascended into heaven, sits at the right hand of the Father; and again he will come with glory to judge the living and the dead; of whose kingdom there shall be no end; and in the Holy Ghost the Lord and giver of life, who proceeds from the Father and the Son; who with the Father and the Son together is adored and glorified; who spoke by the prophets; and in one holy Catholic and Apostolic Church. I confess one baptism for the remission of sins; and I look for the resurrection of the dead, and the life of the world to come. Amen.*

FOURTH SESSION,
celebrated on the eighth day of April, 1546.
DECREE CONCERNING THE CANONICAL
SCRIPTURES.

The holy, ecumenical and general Council of Trent, lawfully assembled in the Holy Ghost, the same three legates of the Apostolic See presiding, keeps this constantly in view, namely, that the purity of the Gospel may be preserved in the Church after the errors have been removed. This [Gospel], of old promised through the Prophets in the Holy Scriptures, our Lord Jesus Christ, the Son of God, promulgated first with His own mouth, and then commanded it to be preached by His Apostles to every creature as the source at once of all saving truth and rules of conduct. It also clearly perceives that these truths and rules are contained in the written books and in the unwritten traditions, which, received by the Apostles from the mouth of Christ Himself, or from the Apostles themselves, the Holy Ghost dictating, have come down to us, transmitted as it were from hand to hand. Following, then, the examples of the orthodox Fathers, it receives and venerates with a feeling of piety and reverence all the books both of the Old and New Testaments, since one God is the author of both; also the traditions, whether they relate to faith or to morals, as having been dictated either orally by Christ or by the Holy Ghost, and preserved in the Catholic Church in unbroken succession. It has thought it proper, moreover, to insert in this decree a list of the sacred books, lest a doubt might arise in the mind of someone as to which are the books received by this council. They are the following: of the Old Testament, the five books of Moses, namely, Genesis, Exodus, Leviticus, Numbers, Deuteronomy; Josue, Judges, Ruth, the four books of Kings, two of Paralipomenon, the first and second of Esdras, the latter of which is called Nehemias, Tobias, Judith, Esther, Job, the Davidic Psalter of 150 Psalms, Proverbs, Ecclesiastes, the Canticle of Canticles, Wisdom, Ecclesiasticus, Isaias, Jeremias, with Baruch, Ezechiel, Daniel, the twelve minor Prophets, namely, Osee, Joel, Amos, Abdias, Jonas, Micheas, Nahum, Habacuc, Sophonias, Aggeus, Zacharias, Malachias; two books of Machabees, the first and second. Of the New Testament, the four Gospels, according to Matthew, Mark, Luke and John; the Acts of the Apostles written by

Luke the Evangelist; fourteen Epistles of Paul the Apostle, to the Romans, two to the Corinthians, to the Galatians, to the Ephesians, to the Philippians, to the Colossians, two to the Thessalonians, two to Timothy, to Titus, to Philemon, to the Hebrews; two of Peter the Apostle, three of John the Apostle, one of James the Apostle, one of Jude the Apostle, and the Apocalypse of John the Apostle. If anyone does not accept as sacred and canonical the aforesaid books in their entirety and with all their parts, as they have been accustomed to be read in the Catholic Church and as they are contained in the old Latin Vulgate Edition, and knowingly and deliberately rejects the aforesaid traditions, let him be anathema. Let all understand, therefore, in what order and manner the council, after having laid the foundation of the confession of faith, will proceed, and who are the chief witnesses and supports to whom it will appeal in confirming dogmas and in restoring morals in the Church.

DECREE CONCERNING THE EDITION AND USE OF THE SACRED BOOKS.

Moreover, the same holy council considering that not a little advantage will accrue to the Church of God if it be made known which of all the Latin editions of the sacred books now in circulation is to be regarded as authentic, ordains and declares that the old Latin Vulgate Edition, which, in use for so many hundred years, has been approved by the Church, be in public lectures, disputations, sermons and expositions held as authentic, and that no one dare or presume under any pretext whatsoever to reject it.

Furthermore, to check unbridled spirits, it decrees that no one relying on his own judgment shall, in matters of faith and morals pertaining to the edification of Christian doctrine, distorting the Holy Scriptures in accordance with his own conceptions, presume to interpret them contrary to that sense which holy mother Church, to whom it belongs to judge of their true sense and interpretation, has held and holds, or even contrary to the unanimous teaching of the Fathers, even though such interpretations should never at any time be published. Those who act contrary to this shall be made known by the ordinaries and punished in accordance with the penalties prescribed by the law.

And wishing, as is proper, to impose a restraint in this matter on printers also, who, now without restraint, thinking what pleases them is permitted them, print without the permission of ecclesiastical superiors the books of the Holy Scriptures and the notes and commentaries thereon of all persons indiscriminately, often with the name of the press omitted, often also under a fictitious press-name, and what is worse, without the name of the author, and also indiscreetly have for sale such books printed elsewhere, [this council] decrees and ordains that in the future the Holy Scriptures, especially the old Vulgate Edition, be printed in the most correct manner possible, and that it shall not be lawful for anyone to print or to have printed any books whatsoever dealing with sacred doctrinal matters without the name of the author, or in the future to sell them, or even to have them in possession, unless they have first been examined and approved by the ordinary, under penalty of anathema and fine prescribed by the last Council of the Lateran. If they be regulars they must in addition to this examination and approval obtain permission also from their own superiors after these have examined the books in accordance with their own statutes. Those who lend or circulate them in manuscript before they have been examined and approved, shall be subject to the same penalties as the printers, and those who have them in their possession or read them, shall, unless they make known the authors, be themselves regarded as the authors. The approbation of such books, however, shall be given in writing and shall appear authentically at the beginning of the book, whether it be written or printed, and all this, that is, both the examination and approbation, shall be done gratuitously, so that what ought to be approved may be approved and what ought to be condemned may be condemned.

Furthermore, wishing to repress that boldness whereby the words and sentences of the Holy Scriptures are turned and twisted to all kinds of profane usages, namely, to things scurrilous, fabulous, vain to flatteries, detractions, superstitions, godless and diabolical incantations, divinations, the casting of lots and defamatory libels, to put an end to such irreverence and contempt, and that no one may in the future date use in any manner the words of Holy Scripture for these and similar purposes, it is commanded and enjoined that all people of this kind be restrained by the bishops as violators and profaners of the word of God, with the penalties of the law and other penalties that they may deem fit to impose.

FIFTH SESSION,

celebrated on the seventeenth day of June, 1546.

DECREE CONCERNING ORIGINAL SIN.

That our Catholic faith, *without which it is impossible to please God,* may, after the destruction of errors, remain integral and spotless in its purity, and that the Christian people may not be *carried about with every wind of doctrine,* since that old serpent, the everlasting enemy of the human race, has, among the many evils with which the Church of God is in our times disturbed, stirred up also not only new but also old dissensions concerning original sin and its remedy, the holy, ecumenical and general Council of Trent, lawfully assembled in the Holy Ghost, the same three legates of the Apostolic See presiding, wishing now to reclaim the erring and to strengthen the wavering, and following the testimonies of the Holy Scriptures, of the holy Fathers, of the most approved councils, as well as the judgment and unanimity of the Church herself, ordains, confesses and declares these things concerning original sin:

1. If anyone does not confess that the first man, Adam, when he transgressed the commandment of

God in paradise, immediately lost the holiness and justice in which he had been constituted, and through the offense of that prevarication incurred the wrath and indignation of God, and thus death with which God had previously threatened him, and, together with death, captivity under his power who thenceforth *had the empire of death, that is to say, the devil,* and that the entire Adam through that offense of prevarication was changed in body and soul for the worse, let him be anathema.

2. If anyone asserts that the transgression of Adam injured him alone and not his posterity, and that the holiness and justice which he received from God, which he lost, he lost for himself alone and not for us also; or that he, being defiled by the sin of disobedience, has transfused only death and the pains of the body into the whole human race, but not sin also, which is the death of the soul, let him be anathema, since he contradicts the Apostle who says: *By one man sin entered into the world and by sin death; and so death passed upon all men, in whom all have sinned.*

3. If anyone asserts that this sin of Adam, which in its origin is one, and by propagation, not by imitation, transfused into all, which is in each one as something that is his own, is taken away either by the forces of human nature or by a remedy other than the merit of the one mediator, our Lord Jesus Christ, who has reconciled us to God in his blood, *made unto us justice, sanctification and redemption;* or if he denies that that merit of Jesus Christ is applied both to adults and to infants by the sacrament of baptism rightly administered in the form of the Church, let him be anathema; *for there is no other name under heaven given to men, whereby we must be saved.* Whence that declaration: *Behold the Lamb of God, behold him who taketh away the sins of the world;* and that other: *As many of you as have been baptized, have put on Christ.*

4. If anyone denies that infants, newly born from their mothers' wombs, are to be baptized, even though

they be born of baptized parents, or says that they are indeed *baptized for the remission of sins,* but that they derive nothing of original sin from Adam which must be expiated by the laver of regeneration for the attainment of eternal life, whence it follows that in them the form of baptism for the remission of sins is to be understood not as true but as false, let him be anathema, for what the Apostle has said, *by one man sin entered into the world, and by sin death, and so death passed upon all men, in whom all have sinned,* is not to be understood otherwise than as the Catholic Church has everywhere and always understood it. For in virtue of this rule of faith handed down from the apostles, even infants who could not as yet commit any sin of themselves, are for this reason truly baptized for the remission of sins, in order that in them what they contracted by generation may be washed away by regeneration. For, *unless a man be born again of water and the Holy Ghost, he cannot enter into the kingdom of heaven.*

5. If anyone denies that by the grace of our Lord Jesus Christ which is conferred in baptism, the guilt of original sin is remitted, or says that the whole of that which belongs to the essence of sin is not taken away, but says that it is only canceled or not imputed, let him be anathema. For in those who are born again God hates nothing, because *there is no condemnation to those who are* truly *buried together with Christ by baptism unto death, who walk not according to the flesh,* but putting off the old man and putting on the new one who is created according to God, are made innocent, immaculate, pure, guiltless and beloved of God, *heirs indeed of God, joint heirs with Christ;* so that there is nothing whatever to hinder their entrance into heaven. But this holy council perceives and confesses that in the one baptized there remains concupiscence or an inclination to sin, which, since it is left for us to wrestle with, cannot injure those who do not acquiesce but resist manfully by the grace of Jesus Christ; indeed, he who shall have *striven lawfully*

shall be crowned. This concupiscence, which the Apostle sometimes calls sin, the holy council declares the Catholic Church has never understood to be called sin in the sense that it is truly and properly sin in those born again, but in the sense that it is of sin and inclines to sin. But if anyone is of the contrary opinion, let him be anathema.

This holy council declares, however, that it is not its intention to include in this decree, which deals with original sin, the blessed and immaculate Virgin Mary, the mother of God, but that the constitutions of Pope Sixtus IV, of happy memory, are to be observed under the penalties contained in those constitutions, which it renews.

SIXTH SESSION,

celebrated on the thirteenth day of January, 1547.

DECREE CONCERNING JUSTIFICATION.

Chapter I

THE IMPOTENCY OF NATURE AND OF

THE LAW TO JUSTIFY MAN.

The holy council declares first, that for a correct and clear understanding of the doctrine of justification, it is necessary that each one recognize and confess that since all men had lost innocence in the prevarication of Adam, having become unclean, and, as the Apostle says, *by nature children of wrath,* as has been set forth in the decree on original sin, they were so far *the servants of sin* and under the power of the devil and of death, that not only the Gentiles by the force of nature, but not even the Jews by the very letter of the law of Moses, were able to be liberated or to rise therefrom, though free will, weakened as it was in its powers and downward bent, was by no means extinguished in them.

Chapter II.

THE DISPENSATION AND MYSTERY OF

THE ADVENT OF CHRIST.

Whence it came to pass that the heavenly Father, *the Father of mercies and the God of all comfort, when the blessed fulness of the time was come,* sent to men Jesus Christ, His own Son, who had both before the law and during the time of the law been announced and promised to many of the holy fathers, *that he might redeem the Jews who were under the law,* and *that the Gentiles who followed not after justice* might attain to justice, and that all men might receive the adoption of sons. Him has God *proposed* as a propitiator *through faith in his blood for our sins, and not for our sins only, but also for those of the whole world.*

Chapter III.
WHO ARE JUSTIFIED THROUGH CHRIST.

But though *He died for all,* yet all do not receive the benefit of His death, but those only to whom the merit of His passion is communicated; because as truly as men would not be born unjust, if they were not born through propagation of the seed of Adam, since by that propagation they contract through him, when they are conceived, injustice as their own, so if they were not born again in Christ, they would never be justified, since in that new birth there is bestowed upon them, through the merit of His passion, the grace by which they are made just. For this benefit the Apostle exhorts us always *to give thanks to the Father, who hath made us worthy to be partakers of the lot of the saints in light, and hath delivered us from the power of darkness, and hath translated us into the kingdom of the Son of his love, in whom we have redemption and remission of sins.*

Chapter IV.
A BRIEF DESCRIPTION OF THE JUSTIFICATION OF THE SINNER AND ITS MODE IN THE STATE OF GRACE.

In which words is given a brief description of the justification of the sinner, as being a translation from that state in which man is born a child of the first Adam, to the state of grace and of the adoption of the sons of God through the second Adam, Jesus

Christ, our Saviour. This translation however cannot, since the promulgation of the Gospel, be effected except through the laver of regeneration or its desire, as it is written: *Unless a man be born again of water and the Holy Ghost, he cannot enter into the kingdom of God.*

Chapter V.
THE NECESSITY OF PREPARATION FOR JUSTIFICATION IN ADULTS, AND WHENCE IT PROCEEDS.

It is furthermore declared that in adults the beginning of that justification must proceed from the predisposing grace of God through Jesus Christ, that is, from His vocation, whereby, without any merits on their part, they are called; that they who by sin had been cut off from God, may be disposed through His quickening and helping grace to convert themselves to their own justification by freely assenting to and co-operating with that grace; so that, while God touches the heart of man through the illumination of the Holy Ghost, man himself neither does absolutely nothing while receiving that inspiration, since he can also reject it, nor yet is he able by his own free will and without the grace of God to move himself to justice in His sight. Hence, when it is said in the sacred writings: *Turn ye to me, and I will turn to you,* we are reminded of our liberty; and when we reply: *Convert us, O Lord, to thee, and we shall be converted,* we confess that we need the grace of God.

Chapter VI.
THE MANNER OF PREPARATION.

Now, they [the adults] are disposed to that justice when, aroused and aided by divine grace, receiving *faith by hearing,* they are moved freely toward God, believing to be true what has been divinely revealed and promised, especially that the sinner is justified by God *by his grace, through the redemption that is in Christ Jesus;* and when, understanding themselves to be sinners, they, by turning themselves from the fear

of divine justice, by which they are salutarily aroused,
to consider the mercy of God, are raised to hope,
trusting that God will be propitious to them for
Christ's sake; and they begin to love Him as the
fountain of all justice, and on that account are moved
against sin by a certain hatred and detestation, that is,
by that repentance that must be performed before
baptism; finally, when they resolve to receive baptism, to begin a new life and to keep the commandments of God. Of this disposition it is written: *He
that cometh to God, must believe that he is, and is a
rewarder to them that seek him;* and, *Be of good faith,
son, thy sins are forgiven thee;* and *The fear of the
Lord driveth out sin;* and, *Do penance, and be baptized every one of you in the name of Jesus Christ,
for the remission of your sins, and you shall receive
the gift of the Holy Ghost;* and, *Going, therefore,
teach ye all nations, baptizing them in the name of the
Father, and of the Son, and of the Holy Ghost, teaching them to observe all things whatsoever I have
commanded you;* finally, *Prepare your hearts unto the
Lord.*

Chapter VII.

IN WHAT THE JUSTIFICATION OF THE SINNER CONSISTS, AND WHAT ARE ITS CAUSES.

This disposition or preparation is followed by justification itself, which is not only a remission of sins
but also the sanctification and renewal of the inward
man through the voluntary reception of the grace and
gifts whereby an unjust man becomes just and from
being an enemy becomes a friend, that he may be *an
heir according to hope of life everlasting.* The causes
of this justification are: the final cause is the glory of
God and of Christ and life everlasting; the efficient
cause is the merciful God who *washes and sanctifies*
gratuitously, signing and anointing *with the holy
Spirit of promise, who is the pledge of our inheritance;*
the meritorious cause is His most beloved only begotten, our Lord Jesus Christ, who, *when we were
enemies, for the exceeding charity wherewith he loved*

us, merited for us justification by His most holy passion on the wood of the cross and made satisfaction for us to God the Father; the instrumental cause is the sacrament of baptism, which is the sacrament of faith, without which no man was ever justified; finally, the single formal cause is the justice of God, not that by which He Himself is just, but that by which He makes us just, that, namely, with which we being endowed by Him, are *renewed in the spirit of our mind,* and not only are we reputed but we are truly called and are just, receiving justice within us, each one according to his own measure, which the Holy Ghost distributes to everyone as He wills, and according to each one's disposition and co-operation. For though no one can be just except he to whom the merits of the passion of our Lord Jesus Christ are communicated, yet this takes place in the justification of the sinner, when by the merit of the most holy passion, *the charity of God is poured forth by the Holy Ghost in the hearts* of those who are justified and inheres in them; whence man through Jesus Christ, in whom he is ingrafted, receives in that justification, together with the remission of sins, all these infused at the same time, namely, faith, hope and charity. For faith, unless hope and charity be added to it, neither unites man perfectly with Christ nor makes him a living member of His body. For which reason it is most truly said that *faith without works is dead* and of no profit, and *in Christ Jesus neither circumcision availeth nor uncircumcision, but faith that worketh by charity.* This faith, conformably to Apostolic tradition, catechumens ask of the Church before the sacrament of baptism, when they ask for the faith that gives eternal life, which without hope and charity faith cannot give. Whence also they hear immediately the word of Christ: *If thou wilt enter into life, keep the commandments.* Wherefore, when receiving true and Christian justice, they are commanded, immediately on being born again, to preserve it pure and spotless, as *the first robe* given them through Christ Jesus in place of that which Adam by his disobedience lost for himself and for us, so that they may bear it before the tribunal of our Lord Jesus Christ and may have life eternal.

Chapter VIII.

HOW THE GRATUITOUS JUSTIFICATION OF THE SINNER BY FAITH IS TO BE UNDERSTOOD.

But when the Apostle says that man is justified by faith and freely, these words are to be understood in that sense in which the uninterrupted unanimity of the Catholic Church has held and expressed them, namely, that we are therefore said to be justified by faith, because faith is the beginning of human salvation, the foundation and root of all justification, *without which it is impossible to please God* and to come to the fellowship of His sons; and we are therefore said to be justified gratuitously, because none of those things that precede justification, whether faith or works, merit the grace of justification. For, *if by grace, it is not now by works, otherwise,* as the Apostle says, *grace is no more grace.*

Chapter IX.

AGAINST THE VAIN CONFIDENCE OF HERETICS.

But though it is necessary to believe that sins neither are remitted nor ever have been remitted except gratuitously by divine mercy for Christ's sake, yet it must not be said that sins are forgiven or have been forgiven to anyone who boasts of his confidence and certainty of the remission of his sins, resting on that alone, though among heretics and schismatics this vain and ungodly confidence may be and in our troubled times indeed is found and preached with untiring fury against the Catholic Church. Moreover, it must not be maintained, that they who are truly justified must needs, without any doubt whatever, convince themselves that they are justified, and that no one is absolved from sins and justified except he that believes with certainty that he is absolved and justified, and that absolution and justification are effected by this faith alone, as if he who does not believe this, doubts the promises of God and the efficacy of the death and resurrection of Christ. For as no pious person ought to doubt the mercy of God, the merit of Christ and the virtue and efficacy of the sacraments, so each one, when he considers himself and his own weakness and indisposition, may have fear and apprehension concerning his own grace, since no one can know with the certainty of faith, which cannot be subject to error, that he has obtained the grace of God.

Chapter X.

THE INCREASE OF THE JUSTIFICATION RECEIVED.

Having, therefore, been thus justified and made the friends and *domestics of God,* advancing *from virtue to virtue,* they are *renewed,* as the Apostle says, *day by day,* that is, *mortifying the members* of their flesh, and presenting them as instruments of justice unto sanctification, they, through the observance of the commandments of God and of the Church, faith co-operating with good works, increase in that justice received through the grace of Christ and are further justified, as it is written: *He that is just, let him be justified still;* and, *Be not afraid to be justified even to death;* and again, *Do you see that by works a man is justified, and not by faith only?* This increase of justice holy Church asks for when she prays: "Give unto us, O Lord, an increase of faith, hope and charity."

Chapter XI.

THE OBSERVANCE OF THE COMMANDMENTS AND THE NECESSITY AND POSSIBILITY THEREOF.

But no one, however much justified, should consider himself exempt from the observance of the commandments; no one should use that rash statement, once forbidden by the Fathers under anathema, that the observance of the commandments of God is impossible for one that is justified. For God does not command impossibilities, but by commanding admonishes thee to do what thou canst and to pray for what thou canst not, and aids thee that thou mayest be able. *His com-*

mandments are not heavy, and *his yoke is sweet and burden light*. For they who are the sons of God love Christ, but they who love Him, keep His commandments, as He Himself testifies; which, indeed, with the divine help they can do. For though during this mortal life, men, however holy and just, fall at times into at least light and daily sins, which are also called venial, they do not on that account cease to be just, for that petition of the just, *forgive us our trespasses*, is both humble and true; for which reason the just ought to feel themselves the more obliged to walk in the way of justice, for *being now freed from sin and made servants of God*, they are able, *living soberly, justly and godly*, to proceed onward through Jesus Christ, by whom they have access unto this grace. For God does not forsake those who have been once justified by His grace, unless He be first forsaken by them. Wherefore, no one ought to flatter himself with faith alone, thinking that by faith alone he is made an heir and will obtain the inheritance, even though *he suffer* not *with Christ, that he may be also glorified with him*. For even Christ Himself, as the Apostle says, *whereas he was the Son of God, he learned obedience by the things which he suffered, and being consummated, he became to all who obey him the cause of eternal salvation*. For which reason the same Apostle admonishes those justified, saying: *Know you not that they who run in the race, all run indeed, but one receiveth the prize? So run that you may obtain. I therefore so run, not as at an uncertainty; I so fight, not as one beating the air, but I chastise my body and bring it into subjection; lest perhaps when I have preached to others, I myself should become a castaway*. So also the prince of the Apostles, Peter: *Labor the more, that by good works you may make sure your calling and election. For doing these things, you shall not sin at any time*. From which it is clear that they are opposed to the orthodox teaching of religion who maintain that the just man sins, venially at least, in every good work; or, what is more intolerable, that he merits eternal punishment; and they also who assert that the just sin in all works, if, in order to arouse their sloth and to encourage themselves to run the race, they, in addition to this, that above all God may be glorified, have in view also the eternal reward, since it is written: *I have inclined my heart to do thy justifications on account of the reward;* and of Moses the Apostle says; that *he looked unto the reward.*

Chapter XII.

RASH PRESUMPTION OF PREDESTINATION IS TO BE AVOIDED.

No one, moreover, so long as he lives this mortal life, ought in regard to the sacred mystery of divine predestination, so far presume as to state with absolute certainty that he is among the number of the predestined, as if it were true that the one justified either cannot sin any more, or, if he does sin, that he ought to promise himself an assured repentance. For except by special revelation, it cannot be known whom God has chosen to Himself.

Chapter XIII.

THE GIFT OF PERSEVERANCE.

Similarly with regard to the gift of perseverance, of which it is written: *He that shall persevere to the end, he shall be saved,* which cannot be obtained from anyone except from Him who is able to make him stand who stands, that he may stand perseveringly, and to raise him who falls, let no one promise himself herein something as certain with an absolute certainty, though all ought to place and repose the firmest hope in God's help. For God, unless men themselves fail in His grace, as *he has begun a good work, so will he perfect it, working to will and to accomplish.* Nevertheless, let those who think themselves to stand, take heed lest they fall, and with fear and trembling work out their salvation, in labors, in watchings, in alms-deeds, in prayer, in fastings and chastity. For knowing that they are born again unto the hope of glory, and not as yet unto glory, they ought to fear for the combat that yet remains with the flesh, with the world and with the devil, in which they cannot be victorious unless they be with the grace of God obedient to the Apostle who says: *We are debtors, not to the flesh, to live according to the flesh; for if you live according to the flesh, you shall die, but if by the spirit you mortify the deeds of the flesh, you shall live.*

Chapter XIV.
THE FALLEN AND THEIR RESTORATION.

Those who through sin have forfeited the received grace of justification, can again be justified when, moved by God, they exert themselves to obtain through the sacrament of penance the recovery, by the merits of Christ, of the grace lost. For this manner of justification is restoration for those fallen, which the holy Fathers have aptly called a second plank after the shipwreck of grace lost. For on behalf of those who fall into sins after baptism, Christ Jesus instituted the sacrament of penance when He said: *Receive ye the Holy Ghost, whose sins you shall forgive, they are forgiven them, and whose sins you shall retain, they are retained.* Hence, it must be taught that the repentance of a Christian after his fall is very different from that at his baptism, and that it includes not only a determination to avoid sins and a hatred of them, or *a contrite and humble heart,* but also the sacramental confession of those sins, at least in desire, to be made in its season, and sacerdotal absolution, as well as satisfaction by fasts, alms, prayers and other devout exercises of the spiritual life, not indeed for the eternal punishment, which is, together with the guilt, remitted either by the sacrament or by the desire of the sacrament, but for the temporal punishment which, as the sacred writings teach, is not always wholly remitted, as is done in baptism, to those who, ungrateful to the grace of God which they have received, have grieved the Holy Ghost and have not feared to *violate the temple of God.* Of which repentance it is written: *Be mindful whence thou art fallen; do penance, and do the first works;* and again, *The sorrow that is accord-*

ing to God worketh penance, steadfast unto salvation; and again, *Do penance, and bring forth fruits worthy of penance.*

Chapter XV.
BY EVERY MORTAL SIN GRACE IS LOST, BUT NOT FAITH.

Against the subtle wits of some also, who *by pleasing speeches and good words seduce the hearts of the innocent*, it must be maintained that the grace of justification once received is lost not only by infidelity, whereby also faith itself is lost, but also by every other mortal sin, though in this case faith is not lost; thus defending the teaching of the divine law which excludes from the kingdom of God not only unbelievers, but also the faithful [who are] *fornicators, adulterers, effeminate, liers with mankind, thieves, covetous, drunkards, railers, extortioners,* and all others who commit deadly sins, from which with the help of divine grace they can refrain, and on account of which they are cut off from the grace of Christ.

Chapter XVI.
THE FRUITS OF JUSTIFICATION, THAT IS, THE MERIT OF GOOD WORKS, AND THE NATURE OF THAT MERIT.

Therefore, to men justified in this manner, whether they have preserved uninterruptedly the grace received or recovered it when lost, are to be pointed out the words of the Apostle: *Abound in every good work, knowing that your labor is not in vain in the Lord. For God is not unjust, that he should forget your work, and the love which you have shown in his name;* and, *Do not lose your confidence, which hath a great reward.* Hence, to those who work well *unto the end* and trust in God, eternal life is to be offered, both as a grace mercifully promised to the sons of God through Christ Jesus, and as a reward promised by God himself, to be faithfully given to their good works and merits. For this is the crown of justice which after his fight and course the Apostle declared was laid up for him, to be rendered to him by the just judge, and not only to him, but also to all that love his coming. For since Christ Jesus Himself, as the head into the members and the vine into the branches, continually infuses strength into those justified, which strength always precedes, accompanies and follows their good works, and without which they could not in any manner be pleasing and meritorious before God, we must believe that nothing further is wanting to those justified to prevent them from being considered to have, by those very works which have been done in God, fully satisfied the divine law according to the state of this life and to have truly merited eternal life, to be obtained in its [due] time, provided they depart [this life] in grace, since Christ our Saviour says: *If anyone shall drink of the water that I will give him, he shall not thirst forever; but it shall become in him a fountain of water springing up unto life everlasting.* Thus, neither is our own justice established as our own from ourselves, nor is the justice of God ignored or repudiated, for that justice which is called ours, because we are justified by its inherence in us, that same is [the justice] of God, because it is infused into us by God through the merit of Christ. Nor must this be omitted, that although in the sacred writings so much is attributed to good works, that even *he that shall give a drink of cold water to one of his least ones,* Christ promises, *shall not lose his reward;* and the Apostle testifies that, *That which is at present momentary and light of our tribulation, worketh for us above measure exceedingly an eternal weight of glory;* nevertheless, far be it that a Christian should either trust or glory in himself and not in the Lord, whose bounty toward all men is so great that He wishes the things that are His gifts to be their merits. And since *in many things we all offend,* each one ought to have before his eyes not only the mercy and goodness but also the severity and judgment [of God]; neither ought anyone to judge himself, even though he be not conscious to himself of anything; because the whole life of man is to be examined and judged not by the judgment of man but of God, *who will bring to light the hidden things of darkness, and will make manifest the counsels of the hearts, and then shall every man have praise from God,* who, as it is written, *will render to every man according to his works.*

After this Catholic doctrine on justification, which whosoever does not faithfully and firmly accept cannot be justified, it seemed good to the holy council to add these canons, that all may know not only what they must hold and follow, but also what to avoid and shun.

CANONS CONCERNING JUSTIFICATION.

Canon 1. If anyone says that man can be justified before God by his own works, whether done by his own natural powers or through the teaching of the law, without divine grace through Jesus Christ, let him be anathema.

Canon 2. If anyone says that divine grace through Christ Jesus is given for this only, that man may be able more easily to live justly and to merit eternal life, as if by free will without grace he is able to do both, though with hardship and difficulty, let him be anathema.

Canon 3. If anyone says that without the predisposing inspiration of the Holy Ghost and without His help, man can believe, hope, love or be repentant as he ought, so that the grace of justification may be bestowed upon him, let him be anathema.

Canon 4. If anyone says that man's free will moved and aroused by God, by assenting to God's call and action, in no way co-operates toward disposing and preparing itself to obtain the grace of justification, that it cannot refuse its assent if it wishes, but that, as something inanimate, it does nothing whatever and is merely passive, let him be anathema.

Canon 5. If anyone says that after the sin of Adam man's free will was lost and destroyed, or that it is a thing only in name, indeed a name without reality, a fiction introduced into the Church by Satan, let him be anathema.

Canon 6. If anyone says that it is not in man's power to make his ways evil, but that the works that are evil as well as those that are good God produces, not permissively only but also *proprie et per se,* so that the treason of Judas is no less His own proper work than the vocation of St. Paul, let him be anathema.

Canon 7. If anyone says that all works done before justification, in whatever manner they may be done, are truly sins, or merit the hatred of God; that the more earnestly one strives to dispose himself for grace, the more grievously he sins, let him be anathema.

Canon 8. If anyone says that the fear of hell, whereby, by grieving for sins, we flee to the mercy of God or abstain from sinning, is a sin or makes sinners worse, let him be anathema.

Canon 9. If anyone says that the sinner is justified by faith alone, meaning that nothing else is required to co-operate in order to obtain the grace of justification, and that it is not in any way necessary that he be prepared and disposed by the action of his own will, let him be anathema.

Canon 10. If anyone says that men are justified without the justice of Christ, whereby He merited for us, or by that justice are formally just, let him be anathema.

Canon 11. If anyone says that men are justified either by the sole imputation of the justice of Christ or by the sole remission of sins, to the exclusion of the grace and *the charity which is poured forth in their hearts by the Holy Ghost,* and remains in them, or also that the grace by which we are justified is only the good will of God, let him be anathema.

Canon 12. If anyone says that justifying faith is nothing else than confidence in divine mercy, which remits sins for Christ's sake, or that it is this confidence alone that justifies us, let him be anathema.

Canon 13. If anyone says that in order to obtain the remission of sins it is necessary for every man to believe with certainty and without any hesitation arising from his own weakness and indisposition that his sins are forgiven him, let him be anathema.

Canon 14. If anyone says that man is absolved from his sins and justified because he firmly believes that he is absolved and justified, or that no one is truly justified except him who believes himself justified, and that by this faith alone absolution and justification are effected, let him be anathema.

Canon 15. If anyone says that a man who is born again and justified is bound *ex fide* to believe that he is certainly in the number of the predestined, let him be anathema.

Canon 16. If anyone says that he will for certain, with an absolute and infallible certainty, have that great gift of perseverance even to the end, unless he shall have learned this by a special revelation, let him be anathema.

Canon 17. If anyone says that the grace of justification is shared by those only who are predestined to life, but that all others who are called are called indeed but receive not grace, as if they are by divine power predestined to evil, let him be anathema.

Canon 18. If anyone says that the commandments of God are, even for one that is justified and constituted in grace, impossible to observe, let him be anathema.

Canon 19. If anyone says that nothing besides faith is commanded in the Gospel, that other things are indifferent, neither commanded nor forbidden, but free; or that the ten commandments in no way pertain to Christians, let him be anathema.

Canon 20. If anyone says that a man who is justified and however perfect is not bound to observe the commandments of God and the Church, but only to believe, as if the Gospel were a bare and absolute promise of eternal life without the condition of observing the commandments, let him be anathema.

Canon 21. If anyone says that Christ Jesus was given by God to men as a redeemer in whom to trust, and not also as a legislator whom to obey, let him be anathema.

Canon 22. If anyone says that the one justified either can without the special help of God persevere in the justice received, or that with that help he cannot, let him be anathema.

Canon 23. If anyone says that a man once justified can sin no more, nor lose grace, and that therefore he that falls and sins was never truly justified; or on the contrary, that he can during his whole life avoid all sins, even those that are venial, except by a special privilége from God, as the Church holds in regard to the Blessed Virgin, let him be anathema.

Canon 24. If anyone says that the justice received is not preserved and also not increased before God through good works, but that those works are merely the fruits and signs of justification obtained, but not the cause of its increase, let him be anathema.

Canon 25. If anyone says that in every good work the just man sins at least venially, or, what is more intolerable, mortally, and hence merits eternal punishment, and that he is not damned for this reason only, because God does not impute these works unto damnation, let him be anathema.

Canon 26. If anyone says that the just ought not for the good works done in God to expect and hope for an eternal reward from God through His mercy and the merit of Jesus Christ, if by doing well and by keeping the divine commandments they persevere to the end, let him be anathema.

Canon 27. If anyone says that there is no mortal sin except that of unbelief, or that grace once received is not lost through any other sin however grievous and enormous except by that of unbelief, let him be anathema.

Canon 28. If anyone says that with the loss of grace through sin faith is also lost with it, or that the faith which remains is not a true faith, though it is not a living one, or that he who has faith without charity is not a Christian, let him be anathema.

Canon 29. If anyone says that he who has fallen after baptism cannot by the grace of God rise again, or that he can indeed recover again the lost justice but by faith alone without the sacrament of penance, contrary to what the holy Roman and Universal Church, instructed by Christ the Lord and His Apostles, has hitherto professed, observed and taught, let him be anathema.

Canon 30. If anyone says that after the reception of the grace of justification the guilt is so remitted and the debt of eternal punishment so blotted out to every repentant sinner, that no debt of temporal punishment remains to be discharged either in this world or in purgatory before the gates of heaven can be opened, let him be anathema.

Canon 31. If anyone says that the one justified sins when he performs good works with a view to an eternal reward, let him be anathema.

Canon 32. If anyone says that the good works of the one justified are in such manner the gifts of God that they are not also the good merits of him justified; or that the one justified by the good works that he performs by the grace of God and the merit of Jesus Christ, whose living member he is, does not truly merit an increase of grace, eternal life, and in case he dies in grace, the attainment of eternal life itself and also an increase of glory, let him be anathema.

Canon 33. If anyone says that the Catholic doctrine of justification as set forth by the holy council in the present decree, derogates in some respect from the glory of God or the merits of our Lord Jesus Christ, and does not rather illustrate the truth of our faith and no less the glory of God and of Christ Jesus, let him be anathema.

SEVENTH SESSION,
celebrated on the third day of March, 1547.
DECREE CONCERNING THE SACRAMENTS.
FOREWORD.

For the completion of the salutary doctrine on justification, which was promulgated with the unanimous consent of the Fathers in the last session, it has seemed proper to deal with the most holy sacraments of the Church, through which all true justice either begins, or being begun is increased, or being lost is restored. Wherefore, in order to destroy the errors and extirpate the heresies that in our stormy times are directed against the most holy sacraments, some of which are a revival of heresies long ago condemned by our Fathers, while others are of recent origin, all of which are exceedingly detrimental to the purity of the Catholic Church and the salvation of souls, the holy, ecumenical and general Council of Trent, lawfully assembled in the Holy Ghost, the same legates of the Apostolic See presiding, adhering to the teaching of the Holy Scriptures, to the Apostolic traditions, and to the unanimous teaching of other councils and of the Fathers, has thought it proper to establish and enact these present canons; hoping, with the help of the Holy Spirit, to publish later those that are wanting for the completion of the work begun.

CANONS ON THE SACRAMENTS IN GENERAL.

Canon 1. If anyone says that the sacraments of the New Law were not all instituted by our Lord Jesus Christ, or that there are more or less than seven, namely, baptism, confirmation, Eucharist, penance, extreme unction, order and matrimony, or that any one of these seven is not truly and intrinsically a sacrament, let him be anathema.

Canon 2. If anyone says that these sacraments of the New Law do not differ from the sacraments of the Old Law, except that the ceremonies are different and the external rites are different, let him be anathema.

Canon 3. If anyone says that these seven sacraments are so equal to each other that one is not for any reason more excellent than the other, let him be anathema.

Canon 4. If anyone says that the sacraments of the New Law are not necessary for salvation but are superfluous, and that without them or without the desire of them men obtain from God through faith alone the grace of justification, though all are not necessary for each one, let him be anathema.

Canon 5. If anyone says that these sacraments have been instituted for the nourishment of faith alone, let him be anathema.

Canon 6. If anyone says that the sacraments of the New Law do not contain the grace which they signify, or that they do not confer that grace on those who place no obstacles in its way, as though they are only outward signs of grace of justice received through faith and certain marks of Christian profession, whereby among men believers are distinguished from unbelievers, let him be anathema.

Canon 7. If anyone says that grace, so far as God's part is concerned, is not imparted through the sacraments always and to all men even if they receive them rightly, but only sometimes and to some persons, let him be anathema.

Canon 8. If anyone says that by the sacraments of the New Law grace is not conferred *ex opere operato*, but that faith alone in the divine promise is sufficient to obtain grace, let him be anathema.

Canon 9. If anyone says that in three sacraments, namely, baptism, confirmation and order, there is not imprinted on the soul a character, that is, a certain spiritual and indelible mark, by reason of which they cannot be repeated, let him be anathema.

Canon 10. If anyone says that all Christians have the power to administer the word and all the sacraments, let him be anathema.

Canon 11. If anyone says that in ministers, when they effect and confer the sacraments, there is not required at least the intention of doing what the Church does, let him be anathema.

Canon 12. If anyone says that a minister who is in mortal sin, though he observes all the essentials that pertain to the effecting or conferring of a sacrament, neither effects nor confers a sacrament, let him be anathema.

Canon 13. If anyone says that the received and approved rites of the Catholic Church, accustomed to be used in the administration of the sacraments, may be despised or omitted by the ministers without sin and at their pleasure, or may be changed by any pastor of the churches to other new ones, let him be anathema.

CANONS ON BAPTISM.

Canon 1. If anyone says that the baptism of John had the same effect as the baptism of Christ, let him be anathema.

Canon 2. If anyone says that true and natural water is not necessary for baptism and thus twists into some metaphor the words of our Lord Jesus Christ: *Unless a man be born again of water and the Holy Ghost,* let him be anathema.

Canon 3. If anyone says that in the Roman Church, which is the mother and mistress of all churches, there is not the true doctrine concerning the sacrament of baptism, let him be anathema.

Canon 4. If anyone says that the baptism which is given by heretics in the name of the Father, and of the Son, and of the Holy Ghost, with the intention of doing what the Church does, is not true baptism, let him be anathema.

Canon 5. If anyone says that baptism is optional, that is, not necessary for salvation, let him be anathema.

Canon 6. If anyone says that one baptized cannot, even if he wishes, lose grace, however much he may sin, unless he is unwilling to believe, let him be anathema.

Canon 7. If anyone says that those baptized are by baptism made debtors only to faith alone, but not to the observance of the whole law of Christ, let him be anathema.

Canon 8. If anyone says that those baptized are free from all the precepts of holy Church, whether written or unwritten, so that they are not bound to observe them unless they should wish to submit to them of their own accord, let him be anathema.

Canon 9. If anyone says that the remembrance of the baptism received is to be so impressed on men that they may understand that all the vows made after baptism are void in virtue of the promise already made in that baptism, as if by those vows they detracted from the faith which they professed and from the baptism itself, let him be anathema.

Canon 10. If anyone says that by the sole remembrance and the faith of the baptism received, all sins committed after baptism are either remitted or made venial, let him be anathema.

Canon 11. If anyone says that baptism, truly and rightly administered must be repeated in the one converted to repentance after having denied the faith of Christ among the infidels, let him be anathema.

Canon 12. If anyone says that no one is to be baptized except at that age at which Christ was baptized, or when on the point of death, let him be anathema.

Canon 13. If anyone says that children, because they have not the act of believing, are not after having received baptism to be numbered among the faithful, and that for this reason are to be rebaptized when they have reached the years of discretion; or that it is better that the baptism of such be omitted than that, while not believing by their own act, they should be baptized in the faith of the Church alone, let him be anathema.

Canon 14. If anyone says that those who have been thus baptized when children, are, when they have grown up, to be questioned whether they will ratify

what their sponsors promised in their name when they
were baptized, and in case they answer in the negative, are to be left to their own will; neither are they
to be compelled in the meantime to a Christian life
by any penalty other than exclusion from the reception of the Eucharist and the other sacraments, until
they repent, let him be anathema.

CANONS ON CONFIRMATION.

Canon 1. If anyone says that the confirmation of
those baptized is an empty ceremony and not a true
and proper sacrament; or that of old it was nothing
more than a sort of instruction, whereby those approaching adolescence gave an account of their faith
to the Church, let him be anathema.

Canon 2. If anyone says that those who ascribe any
power to the holy chrism of confirmation, offer in-
sults to the Holy Ghost, let him be anathema.

Canon 3. If anyone says that the ordinary minister
of holy confirmation is not the bishop alone, but any
simple priest, let him be anathema.

THIRTEENTH SESSION,

*which is the third under the Supreme Pontiff, Julius III
celebrated on the eleventh day of October, 1551.*

DECREE CONCERNING THE MOST HOLY
SACRAMENT OF THE EUCHARIST.

Chapter I.

THE REAL PRESENCE OF OUR LORD
JESUS CHRIST IN THE MOST HOLY
SACRAMENT OF THE EUCHARIST.

First of all, the holy council teaches and openly and
plainly professes that after the consecration of bread
and wine, our Lord Jesus Christ, true God and true
man, is truly, really and substantially contained in the
august sacrament of the Holy Eucharist under the appearance of those sensible things. For there is no
repugnance in this that our Saviour sits always at the
right hand of the Father in heaven according to the
natural mode of existing, and yet is in many other
places sacramentally present to us in His own sub-

stance by a manner of existence which, though we can scarcely express in words, yet with our understanding illumined by faith, we can conceive and ought most firmly to believe is possible to God. For thus all our forefathers, as many as were in the true Church of Christ and who treated of this most holy sacrament, have most openly professed that our Redeemer instituted this wonderful sacrament at the last supper, when, after blessing the bread and wine, He testified in clear and definite words that He gives them His own body and His own blood. Since these words, recorded by the holy Evangelists and afterwards repeated by St. Paul, embody that proper and clearest meaning in which they were understood by the Fathers, it is a most contemptible action on the part of some contentious and wicked men to twist them into fictitious and imaginary tropes by which the truth of the flesh and blood of Christ is denied, contrary to the universal sense of the Church, which, as *the pillar and ground of truth,* recognizing with a mind ever grateful and unforgetting this most excellent favor of Christ, has detested as satanical these untruths devised by impious men.

Chapter II.

THE REASON FOR THE INSTITUTION OF THIS MOST HOLY SACRAMENT.

Therefore, our Saviour, when about to depart from this world to the Father, instituted this sacrament, in which He poured forth, as it were, the riches of His divine love towards men, *making a remembrance of his wonderful works,* and commanded us in the participation of it to reverence His memory and *to show forth his death until he comes* to judge the world. But He wished that this sacrament should be received as the spiritual food of souls, whereby they may be nourished and strengthened, living by the life of Him who said: *He that eateth me, the same also shall live by me,* and as an antidote whereby we may be freed from daily faults and be preserved from mortal sins. He wished it furthermore to be a pledge of our future glory and everlasting happiness, and thus be a symbol of that one body of which He is the head and to which He wished us to be united as members by the closest bond of faith, hope and charity, that we might *all speak the same thing and there might be no schisms among us.*

Chapter III.
THE EXCELLENCE OF THE MOST HOLY EUCHARIST OVER THE OTHER SACRAMENTS.

The most Holy Eucharist has indeed this in common with the other sacraments, that it is a symbol of a sacred thing and a visible form of an invisible grace; but there is found in it this excellent and peculiar characteristic, that the other sacraments then first have the power of sanctifying when one uses them, while in the Eucharist there is the Author Himself of sanctity before it is used. For the Apostles had not yet received the Eucharist from the hands of the Lord, when He Himself told them that what He was giving them is His own body. This has always been the belief of the Church of God, that immediately after the consecration the true body and the true blood of our Lord, together with His soul and divinity exist under the form of bread and wine, the body under the form of bread and the blood under the form of wine *ex vi verborum;* but the same body also under the form of wine and the same blood under the form of bread and the soul under both, in virtue of that natural connection and concomitance whereby the parts of Christ the Lord, *who hath now risen from the dead, to die no more,* are mutually united; also the divinity on account of its admirable hypostatic union with His body and soul. Wherefore, it is very true that as much is contained under either form as under both. For Christ is whole and entire under the form of bread and under any part of that form; likewise the whole Christ is present under the form of wine and under all its parts.

Chapter IV.

TRANSUBSTANTIATION.

But since Christ our Redeemer declared that to be truly His own body which He offered under the form of bread, it has, therefore, always been a firm belief in the Church of God, and this holy council now declares it anew, that by the consecration of the bread and wine a change is brought about of the whole substance of the bread into the substance of the body of Christ our Lord, and of the whole substance of the wine into the substance of His blood. This change the holy Catholic Church properly and appropriately calls transubstantiation.

Chapter V.

THE WORSHIP AND VENERATION TO BE SHOWN TO THIS MOST HOLY SACRAMENT.

There is, therefore, no room for doubt that all the faithful of Christ may, in accordance with a custom always received in the Catholic Church, give to this most holy sacrament in veneration the worship of *latria,* which is due to the true God. Neither is it to be less adored for the reason that it was instituted by Christ the Lord in order to be received. For we believe that in it the same God is present of whom the eternal Father, when introducing Him into the world, says: *And let all the angels of God adore him;* whom the Magi, falling down, adores; who, finally, as the Scriptures testify, was adored by the Apostles in Galilee.

The holy council declares, moreover, that the custom that this sublime and venerable sacrament be celebrated with special veneration and solemnity every year on a fixed festival day, and that it be borne reverently and with honor in processions through the streets and public places, was very piously and religiously introduced into the Church of God. For it is most reasonable that some days be set aside as holy on which all Christians may with special and unusual demonstration testify that their minds are grateful to and mindful of their common Lord and Redeemer for so ineffable and truly divine a favor whereby the victory and triumph of His death are shown forth. And thus indeed did it behoove the victorious truth to celebrate a triumph over falsehood and heresy, that in the sight of so much splendor and in the midst of so great joy of the universal Church, her enemies may either vanish weakened and broken, or, overcome with shame and confounded, may at length repent.

Chapter VI.
THE RESERVATION OF THE SACRAMENT
OF THE HOLY EUCHARIST AND TAKING
IT TO THE SICK.

The custom of reserving the Holy Eucharist in a sacred place is so ancient that even the period of the Nicene Council recognized that usage. Moreover, the practice of carrying the Sacred Eucharist to the sick and of carefully reserving it for this purpose in churches, besides being exceedingly reasonable and appropriate, is also found enjoined in numerous councils and is a very ancient observance of the Catholic Church. Wherefore, this holy council decrees that this salutary and necessary custom be by all means retained.

Chapter VII.
THE PREPARATION TO BE EMPLOYED
THAT ONE MAY RECEIVE THE SACRED
EUCHARIST WORTHILY.

If it is unbecoming for anyone to approach any of the sacred functions except in a spirit of piety, assuredly, the more the holiness and divinity of this heavenly sacrament are understood by a Christian, the more diligently ought he to give heed lest he receive it without great reverence and holiness, especially when we read those terrifying words of the Apostle: *He that eateth and drinketh unworthily, eateth and drink-*

eth judgment to himself, not discerning the body of the Lord. Wherefore, he who would communicate, must recall to mind his precept: *Let a man prove himself*. Now, ecclesiastical usage declares that such an examination is necessary in order that no one conscious to himself of mortal sin, however contrite he may feel, ought to receive the Sacred Eucharist without previous sacramental confession. This the holy council has decreed to be invariably observed by all Christians, even by those priests on whom it may be incumbent by their office to celebrate, provided the opportunity of a confessor is not wanting to them. But if in an urgent necessity a priest should celebrate without previous confession, let him confess as soon as possible.

Chapter VIII.
ON THE USE OF THIS ADMIRABLE SACRAMENT.

As to the use of this holy sacrament, our Fathers have rightly and wisely distinguished three ways of receiving it. They have taught that some receive it sacramentally only, as sinners; others spiritually only, namely, those who eating in desire the heavenly bread set before them, are by a lively *faith which worketh by charity* made sensible of its fruit and usefulness; while the third class receives it both sacramentally and spiritually, and these are they who so prove and prepare themselves beforehand that they approach this divine table clothed with the wedding garment. As regards the reception of the sacrament, it has always been the custom in the Church of God that laics receive communion from priests, but that priests when celebrating communicate themselves, which custom ought with justice and reason to be retained as coming down from Apostolic tradition. Finally, the holy council with paternal affection admonishes, exhorts, prays and beseeches through the bowels of the mercy of our God, that each and all who bear the Christian name will now at last agree and be of one mind in this sign of unity, in this bond of charity, in this symbol of concord, and that, mindful of so great a majesty and such boundless love of our Lord Jesus Christ, who gave His own beloved soul as the price of our salvation and His own flesh to eat, they may believe and venerate these sacred mysteries of His body and blood with such constancy and firmness of faith, with such devotion of mind, with such piety and worship, that they may be able to receive frequently that supersubstantial bread and that it may truly be to them the life of the soul and the perpetual health of their mind; that being invigorated by its strength, they may be able after the journey of this miserable pilgrimage to arrive in their heavenly country, there to eat, without any veil, the same bread of angels which they now eat under sacred veils.

But since it is not enough to declare the truth unless errors be exposed and repudiated, it has seemed good to the holy council to subjoin these canons, so that, the Catholic doctrine being already known, all may understand also what are the heresies which they ought to guard against and avoid.

CANONS ON THE MOST HOLY SACRAMENT OF THE EUCHARIST.

Canon 1. If anyone denies that in the sacrament of the most Holy Eucharist are contained truly, really and substantially the body and blood together with the soul and divinity of our Lord Jesus Christ, and consequently the whole Christ, but says that He is in it only as in a sign, or figure or force, let him be anathema.

Canon 2. If anyone says that in the sacred and holy sacrament of the Eucharist the substance of the bread and wine remains conjointly with the body and blood of our Lord Jesus Christ, and denies that wonderful and singular change of the whole substance of the bread into the body and the whole substance of the wine into the blood, the appearances only of bread and wine remaining, which change the Catholic

Church most aptly calls transubstantiation, let him be anathema.

Canon 3. If anyone denies that in the venerable sacrament of the Eucharist the whole Christ is contained under each form and under every part of each form when separated, let him be anathema.

Canon 4. If anyone says that after the consecration is completed, the body and blood of our Lord Jesus Christ are not in the admirable sacrament of the Eucharist, but are there only *in usu,* while being taken and not before or after, and that in the hosts or consecrated particles which are reserved or which remain after communion, the true body of the Lord does not remain, let him be anathema.

Canon 5. If anyone says that the principal fruit of the most Holy Eucharist is the remission of sins, or that other effects do not result from it, let him be anathema.

Canon 6. If anyone says that in the holy sacrament of the Eucharist, Christ, the only begotten Son of God, is not to be adored with the worship of *latria,* also outwardly manifested, and is consequently neither to be venerated with a special festive solemnity, nor to be solemnly borne about in procession according to the laudable and universal rite and custom of holy Church, or is not to be set publicly before the people to be adored and that the adorers thereof are idolaters, let him be anathema.

Canon 7. If anyone says that it is not lawful that the Holy Eucharist be reserved in a sacred place, but immediately after consecration must necessarily be distributed among those present, or that it is not lawful that it be carried with honor to the sick, let him be anathema.

Canon 8. If anyone says that Christ received in the Eucharist is received spiritually only and not also sacramentally and really, let him be anathema.

Canon 9. If anyone denies that each and all of

Christ's faithful of both sexes are bound, when they have reached the years of discretion, to communicate every year at least at Easter, in accordance with the precept of holy mother Church, let him be anathema.

Canon 10. If anyone says that it is not lawful for the priest celebrating to communicate himself, let him be anathema.

Canon 11. If anyone says that faith alone is a sufficient preparation for receiving the sacrament of the most Holy Eucharist, let him be anathema. And lest so great a sacrament be received unworthily and hence unto death and condemnation, this holy council ordains and declares that sacramental confession, when a confessor can be had, must necessarily be made beforehand by those whose conscience is burdened with mortal sin, however contrite they may consider themselves. Moreover, if anyone shall presume to teach, preach or obstinately assert, or in public disputation defend the contrary, he shall be *eo ipso* excommunicated.

TWENTY-SECOND SESSION,

which is the sixth under the Supreme Pontiff, Pius IV, celebrated on the seventeenth day of September, 1562.

DOCTRINE CONCERNING THE SACRIFICE
OF THE MASS.

Chapter I.

THE INSTITUTION OF THE MOST HOLY
SACRIFICE OF THE MASS.

Since under the former Testament, according to the testimony of the Apostle Paul, there was no perfection because of the weakness of the Levitical priesthood, there was need, God the Father of mercies so ordaining, *that another priest should rise according to the order of Melchisedech,* our Lord Jesus Christ, who might perfect and lead to perfection as many as were to be sanctified. He, therefore, our God and Lord, though He was by His death about to offer Himself once upon the altar of the cross to God the Father that He might there accomplish an eternal redemption, nevertheless, that His priesthood might not come to an end with His death, at the last supper, on the night He was betrayed, that He might leave to His beloved spouse the Church a visible sacrifice, such as the nature of man requires, whereby that bloody sacrifice once to be accomplished on the cross might be represented, the memory thereof remain even to the end of the world, and its salutary effects applied to the remission of those sins which we daily commit, declaring Himself constituted *a priest forever according to the order of Melchisedech,* offered up to God the Father His own body and blood under the form of bread and wine, and under the forms of those same things gave to the Apostles, whom He then made priests of the New Testament, that they might partake, commanding them and their successors in the priesthood by these words to do likewise: *Do this in commemoration of me,* as the Catholic Church has always understood and taught. For having celebrated the ancient Passover which the multitude of the children of Israel sacrificed in memory of their departure from Egypt, He instituted a new Passover, namely, Himself, to be immolated under visible signs by the Church through the priests in memory of His own passage from this world to the Father, when by the shedding of His blood He redeemed and *delivered us from the power of darkness and translated us into his kingdom.* And this is indeed that clean oblation which cannot be defiled by any unworthiness or malice on the part of those who offer it; which the Lord foretold by Malachias was to be great among the Gentiles, and which the Apostle Paul has clearly indicated when he says, that they who are defiled by partaking of the table of devils cannot be partakers of the table of the Lord, understanding by table in each case the altar. It is, finally, that [sacrifice] which was prefigured by various types of sacrifices during the period of nature and of the law, which namely, comprises all the good things signified by them, as being the consummation and perfection of them all.

Chapter II.

THE SACRIFICE OF THE MASS IS PROPITIATORY BOTH FOR THE LIVING AND THE DEAD.

And inasmuch as in this divine sacrifice which is celebrated in the mass is contained and immolated in an unbloody manner the same Christ who once offered Himself in a bloody manner on the altar of the cross, the holy council teaches that this is truly propitiatory and has this effect, that if we, contrite and penitent, with sincere heart and upright faith, with fear and reverence, draw nigh to God, *we obtain mercy and find grace in seasonable aid.* For, appeased by this sacrifice, the Lord grants the grace and gift of penitence and pardons even the gravest crimes and sins. For the victim is one and the same, the same now offering by the ministry of priests who then offered Himself on the cross, the manner alone of offering being different. The fruits of that bloody sacrifice, it is well understood, are received most abundantly through this unbloody one, so far is the latter from derogating in any way from the former. Wherefore, according to the tradition of the Apostles, it is rightly offered not only for the sins, punishments, satisfactions and other necessities of the faithful who are living, but also for those departed in Christ but not yet fully purified.

THE CREED OF THE COUNCIL OF TRENT (1564)

The Creed of the Council of Trent is a summary of the doctrines of Trent. It was promulgated by Pope Pius IV in 1564. This creed is still in force and is a creedal test to which, upon demand, every faithful Catholic must subscribe.

Source: *The Church Teaches: Documents of the Church in English Translation* (St. Louis: B. Herder Book Co., 1955), pp. 6–8.

THE CREED OF THE COUNCIL OF TRENT
(1564)

I, N., with firm faith believe and profess each and every article contained in the Symbol of faith which the holy Roman Church uses; namely: [Constantino-politan Creed with Western additions].

I resolutely accept and embrace the apostolic and ecclesiastical traditions and the other practices and regulations of that same Church. In like manner I accept Sacred Scripture according to the meaning which has been held by holy Mother Church and which she now holds. It is her prerogative to pass judgment on the true meaning and interpretation of Sacred Scripture. And I will never accept or interpret it in a manner different from the unanimous agreement of the Fathers.

I also acknowledge that there are truly and properly seven sacraments of the New Law, instituted by Jesus Christ our Lord, and that they are necessary for the salvation of the human race, although it is not necessary for each individual to receive them all. I acknowledge that the seven sacraments are: baptism, confirmation, Eucharist, penance, extreme unction, holy orders, and matrimony; and that they confer grace; and that of the seven, baptism, confirmation, and holy orders cannot be repeated without committing a sacrilege. I also accept and acknowledge the customary and approved rites of the Catholic Church in the solemn administration of these sacraments. I embrace and accept each and every article on original sin and justification declared and defined in the most holy Council of Trent.

I likewise profess that in the Mass a true, proper, and propitiatory sacrifice is offered to God on behalf of the living and the dead, and that the body and blood together with the soul and divinity of our Lord

Jesus Christ is truly, really, and substantially present in the most holy sacrament of the Eucharist, and that there is a change of the whole substance of the bread into the body, and of the whole substance of the wine into blood; and this change the Catholic Church calls transubstantiation. I also profess that the whole and entire Christ and a true sacrament is received under each separate species.

I firmly hold that there is a purgatory, and that the souls detained there are helped by the prayers of the faithful. I likewise hold that the saints reigning together with Christ should be honored and invoked, that they offer prayers to God on our behalf, and that their relics should be venerated. I firmly assert that images of Christ, of the Mother of God ever Virgin, and of the other saints should be owned and kept, and that due honor and veneration should be given to them. I affirm that the power of indulgences was left in the keeping of the Church by Christ, and that the use of indulgences is very beneficial to Christians.

I acknowledge the holy, Catholic, and apostolic Roman Church as the mother and teacher of all churches; and I promise and swear true obedience to the Roman Pontiff, vicar of Christ and successor of Blessed Peter, Prince of the Apostles.

I unhesitatingly accept and profess all the doctrines (especially those concerning the primacy of the Roman Pontiff and his infallible teaching authority) handed down, defined, and explained by the sacred canons and ecumenical councils and especially those of this most holy Council of Trent (and by the ecumenical Vatican Council). And at the same time I condemn, reject, and anathematize everything that is contrary to those propositions, and all heresies without exception that have been condemned, rejected, and anathematized by the Church. I, N., promise, vow, and swear that, with God's help, I shall most constantly hold and profess this true Catholic faith, outside which no one can be saved and which I now freely profess and truly hold. With the help of God, I shall profess it whole and unblemished to my dying breath; and, to the best of my ability, I shall see to it that my subjects or those entrusted to me by virtue of my office hold it, teach it, and preach it. So help me God and his holy Gospel. [The words in parentheses in this paragraph were inserted into the Tridentine profession of faith by order of Pope Pius IX in a decree issued by the Holy Office, January 20, 1877 (*Acta Sanctae Sedis*, X [1877], pp. 71 ff.).]

THE DOGMA OF THE IMMACULATE CONCEPTION (1854)

The Dogma of the Immaculate Conception of the Virgin Mary was proclaimed by Pius IX in 1854. Pius IX was himself very devoted to Mary and had prepared the way for the dogma by inviting the opinions of the bishops of the Church in 1849. It is to be noted that the dogma is issued on the authority of the Pope and without the sanction of a council. It represents a stage in the growth of the doctrine of the papacy as well as of the doctrine of Mary.

Source: Translation printed here is by Rev. Dominic Unger. Copyright 1946 by St. Anthony's Guild, Paterson, N. J. Used by permission.

Congar, Yves, *Christ, Our Lady and The Church* (Westminster, Md.: Newman Press, 1957; London: Longmans, Green & Co., 1957).

Miegge, Giovanni, *The Virgin Mary* (London: The Lutterworth Press, 1955; Toronto: Ryerson Press, 1955).

O'Connor, Edward Dennis, editor, *The Dogma of the Immaculate Conception, History and Significance* (Notre Dame, Ind.: University of Notre Dame Press, 1958).

Palmer, Paul F., *Mary in the Documents of the Church* (Westminster, Md.: The Newman Press, 1952).

THE DOGMA OF THE IMMACULATE CONCEPTION

Ineffabilis Deus of Pope Pius IX

• • • •

All are aware with how much diligence this doctrine of the Immaculate Conception of the Mother of

God has been handed down, proposed and defended by the most outstanding religious orders, by the more celebrated theological academies, and by very eminent doctors in the science of divinity. All know, likewise, how anxious the bishops have been to profess openly and publicly, even in ecclesiastical assemblies, that the Most Holy Mother of God, the Virgin Mary, because of the merits of Christ our Lord, the Savior of mankind, which were foreseen, was never subject to original sin, but was entirely preserved free from the original stain, and therefore was redeemed in a more sublime manner.

Besides, we must note a fact, most grave and important indeed. Even the Council of Trent itself, when it gave out the dogmatic decree concerning original sin, following the testimonies of the Sacred Scriptures, of the Holy Fathers and of the very worthy Councils, decreed and defined that all men are born infected by original sin; nevertheless, it solemnly declared that it had no intention of including the Blessed and Immaculate Virgin Mary, the Mother of God, in this decree and in the very broad sweep of its definition. Indeed, considering the times and circumstances, the Fathers of Trent sufficiently insinuated by this declaration that the Blessed Virgin Mary was free from the original stain; and thus they clearly signified that nothing could be reasonably cited from the Sacred Writings, from Tradition, or from the authority of the Fathers, which would in any way be opposed to so great a prerogative of the Virgin.

And indeed, illustrious documents of venerable antiquity, of both the Eastern and Western Church, very forcefully testify that this doctrine of the Immaculate Conception of the Most Blessed Virgin, which was daily more and more splendidly explained, stated and confirmed by the highest authority, teaching, zeal, knowledge and wisdom of the Church, and which was disseminated among all peoples and nations of the Catholic world in a marvellous manner,—this doctrine always existed in the Church as a doctrine that has been received from our ancestors, and that has been stamped with the character of revealed doctrine. For the Church of Christ, watchful guardian that she is, and defender of the dogmas deposited with her, never changes anything, never diminishes anything, never adds anything to them; but with all diligence she treats the ancient documents faithfully and wisely; if they really are of ancient origin and if the faith of the Fathers has sown them, she strives to investigate and explain them in such a way that the ancient dogmas of heavenly doctrine will be made evident and clear, but will retain their full, integral and proper nature, and will grow only within their own genus; that is, within the same dogma, in the same sense and same meaning.

. . . .

And so, well aware of all these things and having considered them seriously, as soon as We, though unworthy, had been raised by a mysterious design of Providence to the exalted Chair of Peter and undertaken the government of the whole Church, We really had nothing more at heart than to accomplish all the wishes of the Church—a unique spiritual joy for Us— so that the honor of the Most Blessed Virgin might be increased and her prerogatives shine with a more resplendent light. This was in keeping with the deepest veneration, piety and affection We had toward the Holy Mother of God, the Virgin Mary, even from Our childhood days.

We desired, however, to proceed with great prudence. So We established a special congregation of Our Venerable Brethren, the Cardinals of the Holy Roman Church, illustrious for their piety, wisdom and knowledge of the sacred sciences. We also selected priests, both secular and regular, well-trained in the theological sciences, that they should most carefully consider all matters pertaining to the Immaculate Conception of the Virgin and make known to Us their opinion.

Although We knew what the mind of the bishops was from the petitions which We had received from them, that the Immaculate Conception of the Virgin be finally defined, nevertheless, on February 2, 1849, We sent an Encyclical Letter from Gaeta to all Our Venerable Brethren, the Bishops of the Catholic world, that they should offer prayers to God and then tell Us in writing what the piety and devotion of their faithful was in regard to the Immaculate Conception of the Mother of God, and especially what the bishops themselves thought about defining this doctrine and what their wishes were in regard to making known Our supreme judgment as solemnly as possible.

We were certainly filled with no slight consolation when the replies of Our Venerable Brethren came to Us. For, replying to Us with an incredible joyfulness, gladness and zeal, they not only again confirmed their own singular piety toward the Immaculate Conception of the Most Blessed Virgin, and that of the secular and religious clergy and of the faithful, but with one voice they even entreated Us to define with Our supreme judgment and authority the Immaculate Conception of the Virgin.

In the meantime We were indeed filled with no less joy when, after a diligent examination, Our Venerable Brethren, the Cardinals of the special congregation and the theologians chosen by Us as counsellors (whom We mentioned above), asked Us with the same alacrity and zeal for the definition of the Immaculate Conception of the Mother of God.

After these things had taken place, following the example of Our predecessors, and desiring to proceed properly and rightly, We announced and held a consistory, in which We addressed Our Brethren, the Cardinals of the Holy Roman Church. It was the greatest spiritual joy for Us when We heard them ask Us to promulgate the dogmatic definition of the Immaculate Conception of the Virgin Mother of God.

Therefore, having full trust in the Lord that the opportune time had come for defining the Immaculate Conception of the Virgin Mary, the Mother of God, which the Divine Words, the venerable tradition, the perpetual mind of the Church, the singular agreement of the Catholic bishops and of the faithful, and the signal acts and constitutions of Our predecessors wonderfully illustrate and proclaim; also having most diligently considered all things, and having poured forth to God diligent and heartfelt prayers, We thought that We should no longer delay in ratifying and defining by Our supreme authority the Immaculate Conception of the Virgin, and thus satisfy the most devout wishes of the Catholic world and Our own piety towards the Most Holy Virgin, and at the same time honor more and more the Only-begotten Son, Jesus Christ Our Lord in the Virgin, since whatever honor and praise are bestowed on the Mother redound to the Son.

Wherefore, in humility and fasting, We unceasingly offered Our private prayers as well as the public prayers of the Church to God the Father through His Son, that He would deign to direct and strengthen Our mind by the power of the Holy Spirit. We also implored the help of the entire heavenly host and with sighs invoked the Paraclete. So by His inspiration, for the honor of the Holy and Undivided Trinity, for the glory and adornment of the Virgin Mother of God, for the exaltation of the Catholic faith and for the increase of the Catholic religion, by the authority of Jesus Christ Our Lord, of the Blessed Apostles Peter and Paul, and by Our own, *We declare, pronounce and define that the Most Blessed Virgin Mary, at the first instant of her Conception was preserved immaculate from all stain of original sin, by the singular grace and privilege of the Omnipotent God, in virtue of the merits of Jesus Christ, the Savior of mankind, and that this doctrine was revealed by God, and therefore, must be believed firmly and constantly by all the faithful.*

• • • •

THE VATICAN COUNCIL (1870)
FIRST DOGMATIC CONSTITUTION ON
THE CHURCH OF CHRIST

The Vatican Council opened in Rome on December 8, 1869 at the call of Pius IX. The Council was a defense against the developments of the nineteenth century as well as an expression of the internal development of the Church's theology. Pius IX had already issued his Syllabus of Errors (1864), which was a vigorous repudiation of many of the intellectual, political, and social developments of the nineteenth century.

The work of the Council resulted in two dogmatic pronouncements. The first is the "Constitution on the Catholic Faith." It devotes a chapter to the doctrine of God as Creator and then expounds the doctrine of faith and reason in three chapters. The second dogmatic pronouncement is on the "Constitution on the Church of Christ" and concludes with the dogma of papal infallibility. In addition to defining the nature of papal infallibility, the Council also asserted that the power of the Roman Pontiff is immediate throughout the Church.

Source: *Petri Privilegium: Three Pastoral Letters to the Clergy of the Diocese*, by Henry Edward (Manning), Archbishop of Westminster (London: Longmans, Green & Co., 1871), pp. 192–203, 211–19.

Jedin, H., *The Ecumenical Councils* (Freiburg: Herder, 1960) (translation by Ernest Graf).

MacGregor, Geddes, *The Vatican Revolution* (Boston: Beacon Press, 1957).

FIRST DOGMATIC CONSTITUTION ON THE
CHURCH OF CHRIST.

*Published In The Fourth Session of The Holy
Œcumenical Council of The Vatican.*

PIUS BISHOP, SERVANT OF THE SERVANTS
OF GOD, WITH THE APPROVAL OF THE SACRED
COUNCIL, FOR AN EVERLASTING REMEM-
BRANCE.

The Eternal Pastor and Bishop of our souls, in order to continue for all time the life-giving work of His
Redemption, determined to build up the Holy Church,
wherein, as in the House of the living God, all who
believe might be united in the bond of one faith and
one charity. Wherefore, before He entered into His
glory, He prayed unto the Father, not for the Apostles only, but for those also who through their preaching should come to believe in Him, that all might be
one even as He the Son and the Father are one.[1] As
then He sent the Apostles whom He had chosen to
Himself from the world, as He Himself had been
sent by the Father: so He willed that there should
ever be pastors and teachers in His Church to the end
of the world. And in order that the Episcopate also
might be one and undivided, and that by means of a
closely united priesthood the multitude of the faithful
might be kept secure in the oneness of faith and communion, He set Blessed Peter over the rest of the
Apostles, and fixed in him the abiding principle of this
two-fold unity, and its visible foundation, in the
strength of which the everlasting temple should arise
and the Church in the firmness of that faith should
lift her majestic front to Heaven.[2] And seeing that the
gates of hell with daily increase of hatred are gathering their strength on every side to upheave the foundation laid by God's own hand, and so, if that might be,

[1] St. John xvii. 21.
[2] From Sermon iv. Chap. ii. of St. Leo the Great, A.D. 440,
Vol. i. p. 17 of edition of Ballerini, Venice, 1753: read in the
eighth lection on the Feast of St. Peter's Chair at Antioch,
February 22.

to overthrow the Church: We, therefore, for the preservation, safe-keeping, and increase of the Catholic
flock, with the approval of the Sacred Council, do
judge it to be necessary to propose to the belief and
acceptance of all the faithful, in accordance with the
ancient and constant faith of the universal Church, the
doctrine touching the institution, perpetuity, and nature of the sacred Apostolic Primacy, in which is
found the strength and solidity of the entire Church,
and at the same time to proscribe and condemn the
contrary errors, so hurtful to the flock of Christ.

CHAPTER I.

OF THE INSTITUTION OF THE APOSTOLIC PRIMACY IN BLESSED PETER.

We therefore teach and declare that, according to
the testimony of the Gospel, the primacy of jurisdiction over the universal Church of God was immediately and directly promised and given to Blessed Peter
the Apostle by Christ the Lord. For it was to Simon
alone, to whom He had already said: Thou shalt be
called Cephas,[3] that the Lord after the confession
made by him, saying: Thou art the Christ, the Son of
the living God, addressed these solemn words: Blessed
art thou, Simon Bar-Jona, because flesh and blood have
not revealed it to thee, but my Father who is in
Heaven. And I say to thee that thou art Peter; and
upon this rock I will build my Church, and the gates
of hell shall not prevail against it. And I will give to
thee the keys of the kingdom of Heaven. And whatsoever thou shalt bind upon earth, it shall be bound
also in heaven, and whatsoever thou shalt loose on
earth, it shall be loosed also in heaven.[4] And it was
upon Simon alone that Jesus after His resurrection bestowed the jurisdiction of Chief Pastor and Ruler over
all His fold in the words: Feed my lambs: feed my
sheep.[5] At open variance with this clear doctrine of
Holy Scripture as it has been ever understood by the

[3] St. John i. 42.
[4] St. Matthew xvi. 16–19.
[5] St. John xxi. 15–17.

Catholic Church are the perverse opinions of those who, while they distort the form of government established by Christ the Lord in His Church, deny that Peter in his single person, preferably to all the other Apostles, whether taken separately or together, was endowed by Christ with a true and proper primacy of jurisdiction; or of those who assert that the same primacy was not bestowed immediately and directly upon Blessed Peter himself, but upon the Church, and through the Church on Peter as her Minister.

If anyone, therefore, shall say that Blessed Peter the Apostle was not appointed the Prince of all the Apostles and the visible Head of the whole Church Militant; or that the same directly and immediately received from the same Our Lord Jesus Christ a primacy of honour only, and not of true and proper jurisdiction; let him be anathema.

CHAPTER II.

ON THE PERPETUITY OF THE PRIMACY OF BLESSED PETER IN THE ROMAN PONTIFFS.

That which the Prince of Shepherds and great Shepherd of the sheep, Jesus Christ our Lord, established in the person of the Blessed Apostle Peter to secure the perpetual welfare and lasting good of the Church, must, by the same institution, necessarily remain unceasingly in the Church; which, being founded upon the Rock, will stand firm to the end of the world. For none can doubt, and it is known to all ages, that the holy and Blessed Peter, the Prince and Chief of the Apostles, the pillar of the faith and foundation of the Catholic Church, received the keys of the kingdom from Our Lord Jesus Christ, the Saviour and Redeemer of mankind, and lives, presides, and judges, to this day and always in his successors the Bishops of the Holy See of Rome, which was founded by him, and consecrated by his blood.[6] Whence, whosoever

[6] From the Acts (session third) of the Third General Council of Ephesus, A.D. 431, Labbé's Councils, Vol. iii. p. 1154, Venice edition of 1728. See also letter of St. Peter Chrysologus to Eutyches, in life prefixed to his works, p. 13, Venice, 1750.

succeeds to Peter in this See, does by the institution of Christ Himself obtain the Primacy of Peter over the whole Church. The disposition made by Incarnate Truth therefore remains, and Blessed Peter, abiding through the strength of the Rock in the power that he received, has not abandoned the direction of the Church.[7] Wherefore it has at all times been necessary that every particular Church—that is to say, the faithful throughout the world—should agree with the Roman Church, on account of the greater authority of the princedom which this has received; that all being associated in the unity of that See whence the rights of communion spread to all, might grow together as members of one Head in the compact unity of the body.[8]

If, then, any should deny that it is by the institution of Christ the Lord, or by divine right, that Blessed Peter should have a perpetual line of successors in the Primacy over the Universal Church, or that the Roman Pontiff is the successor of Blessed Peter in this primacy; let him be anathema.

CHAPTER III.

ON THE POWER AND NATURE OF THE PRIMACY
OF THE ROMAN PONTIFF.

Wherefore, resting on plain testimonies of the Sacred Writings, and adhering to the plain and express decrees both of our predecessors, the Roman Pontiffs, and of the General Councils, We renew the definition of the Œcumenical Council of Florence, in virtue of which all the faithful of Christ must believe that the Holy Apostolic See and the Roman Pontiff possesses the primacy over the whole world, and that the Roman Pontiff is the successor of Blessed Peter, Prince of the Apostles, and is true Vicar of Christ, and Head of the whole Church, and Father and Teacher of all Christians; and that full power was given to him in

[7] From Sermon iii. Chap. iii. of St. Leo the Great, Vol. i. p. 12.
[8] From St. Irenaeus against Heresies, Book iii. Chap. iii. p. 175, Benedictine edition, Venice, 1734; and Acts of Synod of Aquileia, A.D. 381, Labbé's Councils, Vol. ii. p. 1185, Venice, 1728.

Blessed Peter to rule, feed, and govern the Universal Church by Jesus Christ our Lord: as is also contained in the acts of the General Councils and in the Sacred Canons.

Hence we teach and declare that by the appointment of our Lord the Roman Church possesses a superiority of ordinary power over all other Churches, and that this power of jurisdiction of the Roman Pontiff, which is truly episcopal, is immediate; to which all, of whatever rite and dignity, both pastors and faithful, both individually and collectively, are bound, by their duty of hierarchical subordination and true obedience, to submit, not only in matters which belong to faith and morals, but also in those that appertain to the discipline and government of the Church throughout the world, so that the Church of Christ may be one flock under one supreme pastor through the preservation of unity both of communion and of profession of the same faith with the Roman Pontiff. This is the teaching of Catholic truth, from which no one can deviate without loss of faith and of salvation.

But so far is this power of the Supreme Pontiff from being any prejudice to the ordinary and immediate power of episcopal jurisdiction, by which Bishops, who have been set by the Holy Ghost to succeed and hold the place of the Apostles,[9] feed and govern, each his own flock, as true Pastors, that this their episcopal authority is really asserted, strengthened, and protected by the supreme and universal Pastor; in accordance with the words of St. Gregory the Great: my honour is the honour of the whole Church. My honour is the firm strength of my brethren. I am truly honoured, when the honour due to each and all is not withheld.[10]

Further, from this supreme power possessed by the Roman Pontiff of governing the Universal Church, it

[9] From Chap. iv. of xxiii. session of Council of Trent, "Of the Ecclesiastical Hierarchy."
[10] From the letters of St. Gregory the Great, Book viii. 30, Vol. ii. p. 919, Benedictine edition, Paris, 1705.

follows that he has the right of free communication with the Pastors of the whole Church, and with their flocks, that these may be taught and ruled by him in the way of salvation. Wherefore we condemn and reject the opinions of those who hold that the communication between this supreme Head and the Pastors and their flocks can lawfully be impeded; or who make this communication subject to the will of the secular power, so as to maintain that whatever is done by the Apostolic See, or by its authority, for the government of the Church, cannot have force or value unless it be confirmed by the assent of the secular power. And since by the divine right of Apostolic primacy, the Roman Pontiff is placed over the Universal Church, we further teach and declare that he is the supreme judge of the faithful,[11] and that in all causes, the decision of which belongs to the Church, recourse may be had to his tribunal,[12] and that none may re-open the judgment of the Apostolic See, than whose authority there is no greater, nor can any lawfully review its judgment.[13] Wherefore they err from the right course who assert that it is lawful to appeal from the judgments of the Roman Pontiffs to an Œcumenical Council, as to an authority higher than that of the Roman Pontiff.

If then any shall say that the Roman Pontiff has the office merely of inspection or direction, and not full and supreme power of jurisdiction over the Universal Church, not only in things which belong to faith and morals, but also in those which relate to the discipline and government of the Church spread throughout the world; or assert that he possesses merely the principal part, and not all the fullness of this supreme power; or that this power which he enjoys is not ordinary and

[11] From a Brief of Pius VI, *Super soliditate,* of November 28, 1786.
[12] From the Acts of the Fourteenth General Council of Lyons, A.D. 1274, Labbé's Councils, Vol. xiv. p. 512.
[13] From Letter viii. of Pope Nicholas I, A.D. 858, to the Emperor Michael, in Labbé's Councils, Vol. ix. pp. 1339 and 1570.

immediate, both over each and all the Churches and over each and all the Pastors and the faithful; let him be anathema.

CHAPTER IV.

CONCERNING THE INFALLIBLE TEACHING OF THE ROMAN PONTIFF.

Moreover, that the supreme power of teaching is also included in the Apostolic primacy, which the Roman Pontiff, as the successor of Peter, Prince of the Apostles, possesses over the whole Church, this Holy See has always held, the perpetual practice of the Church confirms, and Œcumenical Councils also have declared, especially those in which the East with the West met in the union of faith and charity. For the Fathers of the Fourth Council of Constantinople, following in the footsteps of their predecessors, gave forth this solemn profession: The first condition of salvation is to keep the rule of the true faith. And because the sentence of our Lord Jesus Christ cannot be passed by, who said: Thou art Peter, and upon this Rock I will build my Church,[14] these things which have been said are approved by events, because in the Apostolic See the Catholic Religion and her holy and well-known doctrine has always been kept undefiled. Desiring, therefore, not to be in the least degree separated from the faith and doctrine of that See, we hope that we may deserve to be in the one communion, which the Apostolic See preaches, in which is the entire and true solidity of the Christian religion.[15] And, with the approval of the Second Council of Lyons, the Greeks professed that the Holy Roman Church enjoys supreme and full Primacy and preeminence over the whole Catholic Church, which it truly and humbly acknowledges that it has received with the plenitude of power from our Lord Himself in the person of blessed Peter, Prince or Head of the Apostles, whose successor

[14] St. Matthew xvi. 18.
[15] From the Formula of St. Hormisdas, subscribed by the Fathers of the Eighth General Council (Fourth of Constantinople), A.D. 869. Labbé's Councils, Vol. v. pp. 583, 622.

the Roman Pontiff is; and as the Apostolic See is
bound before all others to defend the truth of faith,
so also if any questions regarding faith shall arise,
they must be defined by its judgment.[16] Finally, the
Council of Florence defined:[17] That the Roman Pontiff is the true Vicar of Christ, and the Head of the
whole Church, and the Father and Teacher of all
Christians; and that to him in blessed Peter was delivered by our Lord Jesus Christ the full power of
feeding, ruling, and governing the whole Church.[18]

To satisfy this pastoral duty our predecessors ever
made unwearied efforts that the salutary doctrine of
Christ might be propagated among all the nations of
the earth, and with equal care watched that it might
be preserved genuine and pure where it had been received. Therefore the Bishops of the whole world, now
singly, now assembled in synod, following the long-
established custom of Churches,[19] and the form of the
ancient rule,[20] sent word to this Apostolic See of those
dangers especially which sprang up in matters of faith,
that there the losses of faith might be most effectually
repaired where the faith cannot fail.[21] And the Roman
Pontiffs, according to the exigencies of times and circumstances, sometimes assembling Œcumenical Councils, or asking for the mind of the Church scattered
throughout the world, sometimes by particular Synods,
sometimes using other helps which Divine Providence
supplied, defined as to be held those things which
with the help of God they had recognised as conformable with the Sacred Scriptures and Apostolic Tradi-

[16] From the Acts of the Fourteenth General Council (Second
of Lyons), A.D. 1274. Labbé, Vol. xiv. p. 512.
[17] From the Acts of the Seventeenth General Council of Florence, A.D. 1438. Labbé, Vol. xviii. p. 526.
[18] John xxi. 15–17.
[19] From a letter of St. Cyril of Alexandria to Pope St. Celestine
I, A.D. 422, Vol. vi. part ii. p. 36. Paris edition of 1638.
[20] From a Rescript of St. Innocent I to the Council of Milevis,
A.D. 402. Labbé, Vol. iii. p. 47.
[21] From a letter of St. Bernard to Pope Innocent II A.D. 1130.
Epist. 191, Vol. iv. p. 433. Paris edition of 1742.

tions. For the Holy Spirit was not promised to the successors of Peter that by His revelation they might make known new doctrine, but that by His assistance they might inviolably keep and faithfully expound the revelation or deposit of faith delivered through the Apostles. And indeed all the venerable Fathers have embraced and the holy orthodox Doctors have venerated and followed their Apostolic doctrine; knowing most fully that this See of holy Peter remains ever free from all blemish of error according to the divine promise of the Lord our Saviour made to the Prince of His disciples: I have prayed for thee that thy faith fail not, and, when thou art converted, confirm thy brethren.[22]

This gift, then, of truth and never-failing faith was conferred by Heaven upon Peter and his successors in this Chair, that they might perform their high office for the salvation of all; that the whole flock of Christ kept away by them from the poisonous food of error, might be nourished with the pasture of heavenly doctrine; that the occasion of schism being removed the whole Church might be kept one, and, resting on its foundation, might stand firm against the gates of hell.

But since in this very age, in which the salutary efficacy of the Apostolic office is most of all required, not a few are found who take away from its authority, we judge it altogether necessary solemnly to assert the prerogative which the only-begotten Son of God vouchsafed to join with the supreme pastoral office.

Therefore faithfully adhering to the tradition received from the beginning of the Christian faith, for the glory of God Our Saviour, the exaltation of the Catholic Religion, and the salvation of Christian people, the Sacred Council approving, We teach and define that it is a dogma divinely revealed: that the Roman Pontiff, when he speaks *ex cathedrâ,* that is, when in discharge of the office of Pastor and Doctor of all Christians, by virtue of his supreme Apostolic author-

[22] St. Luke xxii. 32. See also the Acts of the Sixth General Council, A.D. 680. Labbé, Vol. vii. p. 659.

ity he defines a doctrine regarding faith or morals to be held by the Universal Church, by the divine assistance promised to him in blessed Peter, is possessed of that infallibility with which the divine Redeemer willed that His Church should be endowed for defining doctrine regarding faith or morals: and that therefore such definitions of the Roman Pontiff are irreformable[23] of themselves, and not from the consent of the Church.

But if anyone—which may God avert—presume to contradict this Our definition; let him be anathema.

Given at Rome in Public Session solemnly held in the Vatican Basilica in the year of Our Lord One thousand eight hundred and seventy, on the eighteenth day of July, in the twenty-fifth year of our Pontificate.

In conformity with the original.

Joseph, Bishop of S. Polten,
Secretary to the Vatican Council.

THE DOGMA OF THE ASSUMPTION OF THE VIRGIN MARY (1950)

The promulgation of the Dogma of the Assumption of the Virgin Mary is a continuation of the dogmatic development of the doctrine of Mary. As in the case of the Dogma of the Immaculate Conception, it is important not only for the dogma of the Assumption but as an illustration of the dogmatic process. The dogma has a weak Biblical foundation, and there is no strong case for it in the ancient tradition of the church. Accordingly, the Bull emphasized the importance of the consensus of the Church at the present time and the theological suitability of the doctrine.

Source: Text is taken from *Munificentissimus Deus,* translated by the Rev. Joseph C. Fenton, S.T.D. (Washington: National Catholic Welfare Conference). Used by permission.

[23] I.e. in the words used by Pope Nicholas I note 13, and in the Synod of Quedlinburg, A.D. 1085, "it is allowed to none to revise its judgment, and to sit in judgment upon what it has judged." Labbé, Vol. xii. p. 679.

Congar, Yves, *Christ, Our Lady and the Church* (Westminster, Md.: Newman Press, 1957; also London: Longmans, Green & Co., 1957).

Bennett, V. and Winch, R., *The Assumption of Our Lady and Catholic Theology* (London: S.P.C.K., 1950).

Miegge, G., *The Virgin Mary* (London: Lutterworth Press, 1955; Toronto: Ryerson Press, 1955).

Palmer, Paul F., *Mary in the Documents of the Church* (Westminster, Md.: Newman Press, 1952).

Pelikan, J., *The Riddle of Roman Catholicism* (New York: Abingdon Press, 1959).

Roschini, *The Dogma of the Assumption* (Rome: 1950).

THE APOSTOLIC CONSTITUTION BY WHICH IS DEFINED THE DOGMA OF FAITH THAT MARY, THE VIRGIN MOTHER OF GOD, HAS BEEN ASSUMED INTO HEAVEN IN BODY AND SOUL

44. For which reason, after We have poured forth prayers of supplication again and again to God, and have invoked the light of the Spirit of Truth, for the glory of Almighty God Who has lavished His special affection upon the Virgin Mary, for the honor of her Son, the immortal King of the Ages and the Victor over sin and death, for the increase of the glory of that same august Mother, and for the joy and exultation of the entire Church; by the authority of Our Lord Jesus Christ, of the Blessed Apostles Peter and Paul, and by Our own authority, We pronounce, declare, and define it to be a divinely revealed dogma: that the Immaculate Mother of God, the ever Virgin Mary, having completed the course of her earthly life, was assumed body and soul into heavenly glory.

VATICAN COUNCIL II, 1962-1965
DOGMATIC CONSTITUTION ON THE CHURCH
(1964)

Vatican Council II, called by Pope John XXIII, is still being assessed theologically and ecclesiastically. There is no question, however, of its enduring significance. The Dogmatic Constitution on the Church was its most carefully prepared and important document.

Source: The excerpts reprinted here are taken from *The Documents of Vatican II*, Walter M. Abbott, S.J., general editor, and Very Rev. Msgr. Joseph Gallagher, translation editor, published by Guild Press, America Press, and Association Press, and copyrighted 1966 by The America Press. Used by permission. (Footnotes have been omitted.)

DOGMATIC CONSTITUTION
ON THE CHURCH
Chapter I
THE MYSTERY OF THE CHURCH

1. Christ is the light of all nations. Hence this most sacred Synod, which has been gathered in the Holy Spirit, eagerly desires to shed on all men that radiance of His which brightens the countenance of the Church. This it will do by proclaiming the gospel to every creature (cf. Mk. 16:15).

By her relationship with Christ, the Church is a kind of sacrament of intimate union with God, and of the unity of all mankind, that is, she is a sign and an instrument of such union and unity. For this reason, following in the path laid out by its predecessors, this Council wishes to set forth more precisely to the faithful and to the entire world the nature and encompassing mission of the Church. The conditions of this age lend special urgency to the Church's task of bringing all men to full union with Christ, since mankind today is joined together more closely than ever before by social, technical, and cultural bonds.

• • • •

8. Christ, the one Mediator, established and cease-lessly sustains here on earth His holy Church, the community of faith, hope, and charity, as a visible structure. Through her He communicates truth and grace to all. But the society furnished with hier-archical agencies and the Mystical Body of Christ are not to be considered as two realities, nor are the visible assembly and the spiritual community, nor the earthly Church and the Church enriched with heav-enly things. Rather they form one interlocked re-ality which is comprised of a divine and a human element. For this reason, by an excellent analogy, this reality is compared to the mystery of the incar-nate Word. Just as the assumed nature inseparably united to the divine Word serves Him as a living instrument of salvation, so, in a similar way, does the communal structure of the Church serve Christ's Spirit, who vivifies it by way of building up the body (cf. Eph. 4:16).

This is the unique Church of Christ which in the Creed we avow as one, holy, catholic, and apostolic. After His Resurrection our Savior handed her over to Peter to be shepherded (Jn. 21:17), commissioning him and the other apostles to propagate and govern her (cf. Mt. 28:18 ff.). Her He erected for all ages as "the pillar and mainstay of the truth" (1 Tim. 3:15). This Church, constituted and organized in the world as a society, subsists in the Catholic Church, which is governed by the successor of Peter and by the bishops in union with that successor, although many elements of sanctification and of truth can be found outside of her visible structure. These elements, however, as gifts properly belonging to the Church of Christ, possess an inner dynamism toward Catholic unity.

Just as Christ carried out the work of redemption

in poverty and under oppression, so the Church is called to follow the same path in communicating to men the fruits of salvation. Christ Jesus, "though He was by nature God . . . emptied himself, taking the nature of a slave" (Phil. 2:6), and "being rich, he became poor" (2 Cor. 8:9) for our sakes. Thus, although the Church needs human resources to carry out her mission, she is not set up to seek earthly glory, but to proclaim humility and self-sacrifice, even by her own example.

Christ was sent by the Father "to bring good news to the poor, to heal the contrite of heart" (Lk. 4:18), "to seek and to save what was lost" (Lk. 19:10). Similarly, the Church encompasses with love all those who are afflicted with human weakness. Indeed, she recognizes in the poor and the suffering the likeness of her poor and suffering Founder. She does all she can to relieve their need and in them she strives to serve Christ. While Christ, "holy, innocent, undefiled" (Heb. 7:26) knew nothing of sin (2 Cor. 5:21), but came to expiate only the sins of the people (cf. Heb. 2:17), the Church, embracing sinners in her bosom, is at the same time holy and always in need of being purified, and incessantly pursues the path of penance and renewal.

The Church, "like a pilgrim in a foreign land, presses forward amid the persecutions of the world and the consolations of God," announcing the cross and death of the Lord until He comes (cf. 1 Cor. 11:26). By the power of the risen Lord, she is given strength to overcome patiently and lovingly the afflictions and hardships which assail her from within and without, and to show forth in the world the mystery of the Lord in a faithful though shadowed way, until at the last it will be revealed in total splendor.

Chapter II

THE PEOPLE OF GOD

9. At all times and among every people, God has given welcome to whosoever fears Him and does what is right (cf. Acts 10:35). It has pleased God, however, to make men holy and save them not merely as individuals without any mutual bonds, but by making them into a single people, a people which acknowledges Him in truth and serves Him in holiness. He therefore chose the race of Israel as a people unto Himself. With it He set up a covenant. Step by step He taught this people by manifesting in its history both Himself and the decree of His will, and by making it holy unto Himself. All these things, however, were done by way of preparation and as a figure of that new and perfect covenant which was to be ratified in Christ, and of that more luminous revelation which was to be given through God's very Word made flesh.

• • • •

10. Christ the Lord, High Priest taken from among men (cf. Heb. 5:1–5), "made a kingdom and priests to God his Father" (Apoc. 1:6; cf. 5:9–10) out of this new people. The baptized, by regeneration and the anointing of the Holy Spirit, are consecrated into a spiritual house and a holy priesthood. Thus through all those works befitting Christian men they can offer spiritual sacrifices and proclaim the power of Him who has called them out of darkness into His marvelous light (cf. 1 Pet. 2:4–10). Therefore all the disciples of Christ, persevering in prayer and praising God (cf. Acts 2:42–47), should present themselves as living sacrifice, holy and pleasing to God (cf. Rom. 12:1). Everywhere on earth they must bear witness to Christ and give an answer to those who seek an account of that hope of eternal life which is in them (cf. 1 Pet. 3:15).

Though they differ from one another in essence and not only in degree, the common priesthood of the faithful and ministerial or hierarchical priesthood are nonetheless interrelated. Each of them in its own special way is a participation in the one priesthood of Christ. The ministerial priest, by the sacred power he enjoys, molds and rules the priestly people. Acting in the person of Christ, he brings about the Eucharistic Sacrifice, and offers it to God in the name of all the people. For their part, the faithful join in the offering of the Eucharist by virtue of their royal priesthood. They likewise exercise that priesthood by receiving the sacraments, by prayer and thanksgiving, by the witness of a holy life, and by self-denial and active charity.

• • • •

13. All men are called to belong to the new People of God. Wherefore this People, while remaining one and unique, is to be spread throughout the whole world and must exist in all ages, so that the purpose of God's will may be fulfilled. In the beginning God made human nature one. After His children were scattered, He decreed that they should at length be unified again (cf. Jn. 11:52). It was for this reason that God sent His Son, whom He appointed heir of all things (cf. Heb. 1:2), that He might be Teacher, King, and Priest of all, the Head of the new and universal people of the sons of God. For this God finally sent His Son's Spirit as Lord and Lifegiver. He it is who, on behalf of the whole Church and each and every one of those who believe, is the principle of their coming together and remaining together in the teaching of the apostles and in fellowship, in the breaking of bread and in prayers (cf. Acts 2:42, Greek text).

It follows that among all the nations of earth there is but one People of God, which takes its citizens from every race, making them citizens of a kingdom which is of a heavenly and not an earthly nature. For all the faithful scattered throughout the world are in communion with each other in the Holy

Spirit, so that "he who occupies the See of Rome knows the people of India are his members." Since the kingdom of Christ is not of this world (cf. Jn. 18:36), the Church or People of God takes nothing away from the temporal welfare of any people by establishing that kingdom. Rather does she foster and take to herself, insofar as they are good, the ability, resources, and customs of each people. Taking them to herself she purifies, strengthens, and ennobles them. The Church in this is mindful that she must harvest with that King to whom the nations were given for an inheritance (cf. Ps. 2:8) and into whose city they bring gifts and presents (cf. Ps. 71[72]:10; Is. 60:4–7; Apoc. 21:24). This characteristic of universality which adorns the People of God is a gift from the Lord Himself. By reason of it, the Catholic Church strives energetically and constantly to bring all humanity with all its riches back to Christ its Head in the unity of His Spirit.

In virtue of this catholicity each individual part of the Church contributes through its special gifts to the good of the other parts and of the whole Church. Thus through the common sharing of gifts and through the common effort to attain fullness in unity, the whole and each of the parts receive increase. Not only, then, is the People of God made up of different peoples but even in its inner structure it is composed of various ranks. This diversity among its members arises either by reason of their duties, as is the case with those who exercise the sacred ministry for the good of their brethren, or by reason of their situation and way of life, as is the case with those many who enter the religious state and, tending toward holiness by a narrower path, stimulate their brethren by their example.

Moreover, within the Church particular Churches hold a rightful place. These Churches retain their own traditions without in any way lessening the primacy of the Chair of Peter. This Chair presides over the whole assembly of charity and protects legitimate differences, while at the same time it sees that such differences do not hinder unity but rather contribute toward it. Finally, between all the parts of the Church there remains a bond of close communion with respect to spiritual riches, apostolic workers, and temporal resources. For the members of the People of God are called to share these goods, and to each of the Churches the words of the Apostle apply: "According to the gift that each has received, administer it to one another as good stewards of the manifold grace of God" (1 Pet. 4:10).

All men are called to be part of this catholic unity of the People of God, a unity which is harbinger of the universal peace it promotes. And there belong to it or are related to it in various ways, the Catholic faithful as well as all who believe in Christ, and indeed the whole of mankind. For all men are called to salvation by the grace of God.

14. This sacred Synod turns its attention first to the Catholic faithful. Basing itself upon sacred Scripture and tradition, it teaches that the Church, now sojourning on earth as an exile, is necessary for salvation. For Christ, made present to us in His Body, which is the Church, is the one Mediator and the unique Way of salvation. In explicit terms He Himself affirmed the necessity of faith and baptism (cf. Mk. 16:16; Jn. 3:5) and thereby affirmed also the necessity of the Church, for through baptism as through a door men enter the Church. Whosoever, therefore, knowing that the Catholic Church was made necessary by God through Jesus Christ, would refuse to enter her or to remain in her could not be saved.

They are fully incorporated into the society of the Church who, possessing the Spirit of Christ, accept her entire system and all the means of salvation given to her, and through union with her visible structure are joined to Christ, who rules her through the

Supreme Pontiff and the bishops. This joining is effected by the bonds of professed faith, of the sacraments, of ecclesiastical government, and of communion. He is not saved, however, who, though he is part of the body of the Church, does not persevere in charity. He remains indeed in the bosom of the Church, but, as it were, only in a "bodily" manner and not "in his heart." All the sons of the Church should remember that their exalted status is to be attributed not to their own merits but to the special grace of Christ. If they fail moreover to respond to that grace in thought, word, and deed, not only will they not be saved but they will be the more severely judged.

Catechumens who, moved by the Holy Spirit, seek with explicit intention to be incorporated into the Church are by that very intention joined to her. With love and solicitude Mother Church already embraces them as her own.

15. The Church recognizes that in many ways she is linked with those who, being baptized, are honored with the name of Christian, though they do not profess the faith in its entirety or do not preserve unity of communion with the successor of Peter. For there are many who honor sacred Scripture, taking it as a norm of belief and of action, and who show a true religious zeal. They lovingly believe in God the Father Almighty and in Christ, Son of God and Savior. They are consecrated by baptism, through which they are united with Christ. They also recognize and receive other sacraments within their own Churches or ecclesiastical communities. Many of them rejoice in the episcopate, celebrate the Holy Eucharist, and cultivate devotion toward the Virgin Mother of God. They also share with us in prayer and other spiritual benefits.

Likewise, we can say that in some real way they are joined with us in the Holy Spirit, for to them also He gives His gifts and graces, and is thereby operative among them with His sanctifying power. Some indeed He has strengthened to the extent of the shedding of their blood. In all of Christ's disciples the Spirit arouses the desire to be peacefully united, in the manner determined by Christ, as one flock under one shepherd, and He prompts them to pursue this goal. Mother Church never ceases to pray, hope, and work that they may gain this blessing. She exhorts her sons to purify and renew themselves so that the sign of Christ may shine more brightly over the face of the Church.

16. Finally, those who have not yet received the gospel are related in various ways to the People of God. In the first place there is the people to whom the covenants and the promises were given and from whom Christ was born according to the flesh (cf. Rom. 9:4–5). On account of their fathers, this people remains most dear to God, for God does not repent of the gifts He makes nor of the calls He issues (cf. Rom. 11:28–29).

But the plan of salvation also includes those who acknowledge the Creator. In the first place among these there are the Moslems, who, professing to hold the faith of Abraham, along with us adore the one and merciful God, who on the last day will judge mankind. Nor is God Himself far distant from those who in shadows and images seek the unknown God, for it is He who gives to all men life and breath and every other gift (cf. Acts 17:25–28), and who as Savior wills that all men be saved (cf. 1 Tim. 2:4).

Those also can attain to everlasting salvation who through no fault of their own do not know the gospel of Christ or His Church, yet sincerely seek God and, moved by grace, strive by their deeds to do His will as it is known to them through the dictates of conscience. Nor does divine Providence deny the help necessary for salvation to those who, without blame on their part, have not yet arrived at an explicit knowledge of God, but who strive to live a good life, thanks to His grace. Whatever goodness or truth is found among them is looked upon by the Church as a preparation for the gospel. She regards such qualities as given by Him who enlightens all men so that they may finally have life.

But rather often men, deceived by the Evil One, have become caught up in futile reasoning and have exchanged the truth of God for a lie, serving the creature rather than the Creator (cf. Rom. 1:21, 25). Or some there are who, living and dying in a world without God, are subject to utter hopelessness. Consequently, to promote the glory of God and procure the salvation of all such men, and mindful of the command of the Lord, "Preach the gospel to every creature" (Mk. 16:16), the Church painstakingly fosters her missionary work.

17. Just as the Son was sent by the Father, so He too sent the apostles (cf. Jn. 20:21), saying: "Go, therefore, and make disciples of all nations, baptizing them in the name of the Father and of the Son and of the Holy Spirit, teaching them to observe all that I have commanded you; and behold, I am with you all days even unto the consummation of the world" (Mt. 28:18–20).

The Church has received from the apostles as a task to be discharged even to the ends of the earth this solemn mandate of Christ to proclaim the saving truth (cf. Acts 1:8). Hence she makes the words of the Apostle her own: "Woe to me, if I do not preach the gospel" (1 Cor. 9:16), and continues unceasingly to send heralds of the gospel until such time as the infant churches are fully established and can themselves carry on the work of evangelizing. For the Church is compelled by the Holy Spirit to do her part towards the full realization of the will of God, who has established Christ as the source of salvation for the whole world. By the proclamation of the gospel, she prepares her hearers to receive and profess the faith, disposes them for baptism, snatches them from slavery of error, and incorporates them into Christ so that through charity they may grow up into full maturity in Christ.

Through her work, whatever good is in the minds and hearts of men, whatever good lies latent in the religious practices and cultures of diverse peoples, is not only saved from destruction but is also healed, ennobled, and perfected unto the glory of God, the confusion of the devil, and the happiness of man. The obligation of spreading the faith is imposed on every disciple of Christ, according to his ability. Though all the faithful can baptize, the priest alone can complete the building up of the Body in the Eucharistic Sacrifice. Thus are fulfilled the Words of God, spoken through His prophet: "From the rising of the sun even to the going down, my name is great among the Gentiles, and in every place there is sacrifice, and there is offered to my name a clean oblation" (Mal. 1:11). In this way the Church simultaneously prays and labors in order that the entire world may become the People of God, the Body of the Lord, and the Temple of the Holy Spirit, and that in Christ, the Head of all, there may be rendered to the Creator and Father of the Universe all honor and glory.

Chapter III

THE HIERARCHICAL STRUCTURE OF THE CHURCH, WITH SPECIAL REFERENCE TO THE EPISCOPATE

18. For the nurturing and constant growth of the People of God, Christ the Lord instituted in His Church a variety of ministries, which work for the good of the whole body. For those ministers who are endowed with sacred power are servants of their brethren, so that all who are of the People of God, and therefore enjoy a true Christian dignity, can work toward a common goal freely and in an orderly way, and arrive at salvation.

This most sacred Synod, following in the footsteps of the First Vatican Council, teaches and declares with that Council that Jesus Christ, the eternal Shepherd, established His holy Church by sending forth the apostles as He Himself had been sent by the Father (cf. Jn. 20:21). He willed that their successors, namely the bishops, should be shepherds in His Church even to the consummation of the world.

In order that the episcopate itself might be one and undivided, He placed blessed Peter over the other apostles, and instituted in him a permanent and visible source and foundation of unity of faith and fellowship. And all this teaching about the institution, the perpetuity, the force and reason for the sacred primacy of the Roman Pontiff and of his infallible teaching authority, this sacred Synod again proposes to be firmly believed by all the faithful.

Continuing in the same task of clarification begun by Vatican I, this Council has decided to declare and proclaim before all men its teaching concerning bishops, the successors of the apostles, who together with the successor of Peter, the Vicar of Christ and the visible Head of the whole Church, govern the house of the living God.

19. The Lord Jesus, after praying to the Father and calling to Himself those whom He desired, appointed twelve men who would stay in His company, and whom He would send to preach the kingdom of God (cf. Mk. 3:13–19; Mt. 10:1–42). These apostles (cf. Lk. 6:13) He formed after the manner of a college or a fixed group, over which He placed Peter, chosen from among them (cf. Jn. 21:15–17). He sent them first to the children of Israel and then to all nations (cf. Rom. 1:16), so that as sharers in His power they might make all peoples His disciples, sanctifying and governing them (cf. Mt. 28:16–20; Mk. 16:15; Lk. 24:45–48; Jn. 20:21–23). Thus they would spread His Church, and by ministering to it

under the guidance of the Lord, which shepherd it all days even to the consummation of the world (cf. Mt. 28:20).

They were fully confirmed in this mission on the day of Pentecost (cf. Acts 2:1–26) in accordance with the Lord's promise: "You shall receive power when the Holy Spirit comes upon you, and you shall be witnesses for me in Jerusalem and in all Judea and in Samaria and even to the very ends of the earth" (Acts 1:8). By everywhere preaching the gospel (cf. Mk 16:20), which was accepted by their hearers under the influence of the Holy Spirit, the apostles gathered together the universal Church, which the Lord established on the apostles and built upon blessed Peter, their chief, Christ Jesus Himself remaining the supreme cornerstone (cf. Apoc. 21:14; Mt. 16:18; Eph. 2:20).

20. That divine mission, entrusted by Christ to the apostles, will last until the end of the world (Mt. 28:20), since the gospel which was to be handed down by them is for all time the source of all life for the Church. For this reason the apostles took care to appoint successors in this hierarchically structured society.

For they not only had helpers in their ministry, but also, in order that the mission assigned to them might continue after their death, they passed on to their immediate cooperators, as a kind of testament, the duty of perfecting and consolidating the work begun by themselves, charging them to attend to the whole flock in which the Holy Spirit placed them to shepherd the Church of God (cf. Acts 20:28). They therefore appointed such men, and authorized the arrangement that, when these men should have died, other approved men would take up their ministry.

Among those various ministries which, as tradition witnesses, were exercised in the Church from the earliest times, the chief place belongs to the office of those who, appointed to the episcopate in a sequence running back to the beginning, are the ones who pass on the apostolic seed. Thus, as St. Irenaeus testifies, through those who were appointed bishops by the apostles, and through their successors down to our own time, the apostolic tradition is manifested and preserved throughout the world.

With their helpers, the priests and deacons, bishops have therefore taken up the service of the community, presiding in place of God over the flock whose shepherds they are, as teachers of doctrine, priests of sacred worship, and officers of good order. Just as the role that the Lord gave individually to Peter, the first among the apostles, is permanent and was meant to be transmitted to his successors, so also the apostles' office of nurturing the Church is permanent, and was meant to be exercised without interruption by the sacred order of bishops. Therefore, this sacred Synod teaches that by divine institution bishops have succeeded to the place of the apostles as shepherds of the Church, and that he who hears them, hears Christ, while he who rejects them, rejects Christ and Him who sent Christ (cf. Lk. 10:16).

21. In the bishops, therefore, for whom priests are assistants, our Lord Jesus Christ, the supreme High Priest, is present in the midst of those who believe. For sitting at the right hand of God the Father, He is not absent from the gathering of His high priests, but above all through their excellent service He is preaching the Word of God to all nations, and constantly administering the sacraments of faith to those who believe. By their paternal role (cf. 1 Cor. 4:15), He incorporates new members into His body by a heavenly regeneration, and finally by their wisdom and prudence He directs and guides the people of the New Testament in its pilgrimage toward eternal happiness.

These pastors, selected to shepherd the Lord's flock, are servants of Christ and stewards of the mysteries of God (cf. 1 Cor. 4:1). To them has been assigned the bearing of witness to the gospel of God's grace (cf. Rom. 15:16; Acts 20:24), and to the ministration of the Spirit and of God's glorious power to make men just (cf. 2 Cor. 3:8–9).

For the discharging of such great duties, the apostles were enriched by Christ with a special outpouring of the Holy Spirit, who came upon them (cf. Acts 1:8; 2:4; Jn. 20:22–23). This spiritual gift they passed on to their helpers by the imposition of hands (cf. 1 Tim. 4:14; 2 Tim. 1:6–7), and it has been transmitted down to us in episcopal consecration. This sacred Synod teaches that by episcopal consecration is conferred the fullness of the sacrament of orders, that fullness which in the Church's liturgical practice and in the language of the holy Fathers of the Church is undoubtedly called the high priesthood, the apex of the sacred ministry.

But episcopal consecration, together with the office of sanctifying, also confers the offices of teaching and of governing. (These, however, of their very nature, can be exercised only in hierarchical communion with the head and the members of the college.) For from tradition, which is expressed especially in liturgical rites and in the practice of the Church both of the East and of the West, it is clear that, by means of the imposition of hands and the words of consecration, the grace of the Holy Spirit is so conferred, and the sacred character so impressed, that bishops in an eminent and visible way undertake Christ's own role as Teacher, Shepherd, and High Priest, and that they act in His person. Therefore it devolves on the bishops to admit newly elected members into the episcopal body by means of the sacrament of orders.

22. Just as, by the Lord's will, St. Peter and the other apostles constituted one apostolic college, so in a similar way the Roman Pontiff as the successor of Peter, and the bishops as the successors of the

apostles are joined together. The collegial nature and meaning of the episcopal order found expression in the very ancient practice by which bishops appointed the world over were linked with one another and with the Bishop of Rome by the bonds of unity, charity, and peace; also, in the conciliar assemblies which made common judgments about more profound matters in decisions reflecting the views of many. The ecumenical councils held through the centuries clearly attest this collegial aspect. And it is suggested also in the practice, introduced in ancient times, of summoning several bishops to take part in the elevation of someone newly elected to the ministry of the high priesthood. Hence, one is constituted a member of the episcopal body by virtue of sacramental consecration and by hierarchical communion with the head and members of the body.

But the college or body of bishops has no authority unless it is simultaneously conceived of in terms of its head, the Roman Pontiff, Peter's successor, and without any lessening of his power of primacy over all, pastors as well as the general faithful. For in virtue of his office, that is, as Vicar of Christ and pastor of the whole Church, the Roman Pontiff has full, supreme, and universal power over the Church. And he can always exercise this power freely.

The order of bishops is the successor to the college of the apostles in teaching authority and pastoral rule; or, rather, in the episcopal order the apostolic body continues without a break. Together with its head, the Roman Pontiff, and never without this head, the episcopal order is the subject of supreme and full power over the universal Church. But this power can be exercised only with the consent of the Roman Pontiff. For our Lord made Simon Peter alone the rock and key-bearer of the Church (cf. Mt. 16:18–19), and appointed him shepherd of the whole flock (cf. Jn. 21:15 ff.).

It is definite, however, that the power of binding

and loosing, which was given to Peter (Mt. 16:19), was granted also to the college of apostles, joined with their head (Mt. 18:18; 28:16–20). This college, insofar as it is composed of many, expresses the variety and universality of the People of God, but insofar as it is assembled under one head, it expresses the unity of the flock of Christ. In it, the bishops, faithfully recognizing the primacy and pre-eminence of their head, exercise their own authority for the good of their own faithful, and indeed of the whole Church, with the Holy Spirit constantly strengthening its organic structure and inner harmony.

The supreme authority with which this college is empowered over the whole Church is exercised in a solemn way through an ecumenical council. A council is never ecumenical unless it is confirmed or at least accepted as such by the successor of Peter. It is the prerogative of the Roman Pontiff to convoke these councils, to preside over them, and to confirm them. The same collegiate power can be exercised in union with the Pope by the bishops living in all parts of the world, provided that the head of the college calls them to collegiate action, or at least so approves or freely accepts the united action of the dispersed bishops, that it is made a true collegiate act.

23. This collegial union is apparent also in the mutual relations of the individual bishops with particular churches and with the universal Church. The Roman Pontiff, as the successor of Peter, is the perpetual and visible source and foundation of the unity of the bishops and of the multitude of the faithful. The individual bishop, however, is the visible principle and foundation of unity in his particular church, fashioned after the model of the universal Church. In and from such individual churches there comes into being the one and only Catholic Church. For this reason each individual bishop represents his own church, but all of them together in union with the

Pope represent the entire Church joined in the bond of peace, love, and unity.

The individual bishops, who are placed in charge of particular churches, exercise their pastoral government over the portion of the People of God committed to their care, and not over other churches nor over the universal Church. But each of them, as a member of the episcopal college and a legitimate successor of the apostles, is obliged by Christ's decree and command to be solicitous for the whole Church.

This solicitude, though it is not exercised by an act of jurisdiction, contributes immensely to the welfare of the universal Church. For it is the duty of all bishops to promote and to safeguard the unity of faith and the discipline common to the whole Church, to instruct the faithful in love for the whole Mystical Body of Christ, especially for its poor and sorrowing members and for those who are suffering persecution for justice' sake (cf. Mt. 5:10), and, finally, to foster every activity which is common to the whole Church, especially efforts to spread the faith and make the light of full truth dawn on all men. For the rest, it is a sacred reality that by governing well their own church as a portion of the universal Church, they themselves are effectively contributing to the welfare of the whole Mystical Body, which is also the body of the churches.

The task of proclaiming the gospel everywhere on earth devolves on the body of pastors, to all of whom in common Christ gave His command, thereby imposing upon them a common duty, as Pope Celestine in his time reminded the Fathers of the Council of Ephesus. From this it follows that the individual bishops, insofar as the discharge of their duty permits, are obliged to enter into a community of effort among themselves and with the successor of Peter, upon whom was imposed in a special way the great duty of spreading the Christian name. With all their energy, therefore, they must supply to the missions both workers for the harvest and also spiritual and material aid, both directly and on their own account, as well as by arousing the ardent cooperation of the faithful. And finally, in a universal fellowship of charity, bishops should gladly extend their fraternal aid to other churches, especially to neighboring and more needy dioceses, in accordance with the venerable example of antiquity.

By divine Providence it has come about that various churches established in diverse places by the apostles and their successors have in the course of time coalesced into several groups, organically united, which, preserving the unity of faith and the unique divine constitution of the universal Church, enjoy their own discipline, their own liturgical usage, and their own theological and spiritual heritage. Some of these churches, notably the ancient patriarchal churches, as parent-stocks of the faith, so to speak, have begotten others as daughter churches. With these they are connected down to our own time by a close bond of charity in their sacramental life and in their mutual respect for rights and duties.

This variety of local churches with one common aspiration is particularly splendid evidence of the catholicity of the undivided Church. In like manner the episcopal bodies of today are in a position to render a manifold and fruitful assistance, so that this collegiate sense may be put into practical application.

• • • •

25. Among the principal duties of bishops, the preaching of the gospel occupies an eminent place. For bishops are preachers of the faith who lead new disciples to Christ. They are authentic teachers, that is, teachers endowed with the authority of Christ, who preach to the people committed to them the faith they must believe and put into practice. By the light of the Holy Spirit, they make that faith clear, bringing forth from the treasury of revelation new things and old (cf. Mt. 13:52), making faith

bear fruit and vigilantly warding off any errors which threaten their flock (cf. 2 Tim. 4:1–4).

Bishops, teaching in communion with the Roman Pontiff, are to be respected by all as witnesses to divine and Catholic truth. In matters of faith and morals, the bishops speak in the name of Christ and the faithful are to accept their teaching and adhere to it with a religious assent of soul. This religious submission of will and of mind must be shown in a special way to the authentic teaching authority of the Roman Pontiff, even when he is not speaking ex cathedra. That is, it must be shown in such a way that his supreme magisterium is acknowledged with reverence, the judgments made by him are sincerely adhered to, according to his manifest mind and will. His mind and will in the matter may be known chiefly either from the character of the documents, from his frequent repetition of the same doctrine, or from his manner of speaking.

Although the individual bishops do not enjoy the prerogative of infallibility, they can nevertheless proclaim Christ's doctrine infallibly. This is so, even when they are dispersed around the world, provided that while maintaining the bond of unity among themselves and with Peter's successor, and while teaching authentically on a matter of faith or morals, they concur in a single viewpoint as the one which must be held conclusively. This authority is even more clearly verified when, gathered together in an ecumenical council, they are teachers and judges of faith and morals for the universal Church. Their definitions must then be adhered to with the submission of faith.

This infallibility with which the divine Redeemer willed His Church to be endowed in defining a doctrine of faith and morals extends as far as extends the deposit of divine revelation, which must be religiously guarded and faithfully expounded. This is the infallibility which the Roman Pontiff, the head of the college of bishops, enjoys in virtue of his office, when, as the supreme shepherd and teacher of all the faithful, who confirms his brethren in their faith (cf. Lk. 22:32), he proclaims by a definitive act some doctrine of faith or morals. Therefore his definitions, of themselves, and not from the consent of the Church, are justly styled irreformable, for they are pronounced with the assistance of the Holy Spirit, an assistance promised to him in blessed Peter. Therefore they need no approval of others, nor do they allow an appeal to any other judgment. For then the Roman Pontiff is not pronouncing judgment as a private person. Rather, as the supreme teacher of the universal Church, as one in whom the charism of the infallibility of the Church herself is individually present, he is expounding or defending a doctrine of Catholic Faith.

The infallibility promised to the Church resides also in the body of bishops when that body exercises supreme teaching authority with the successor of Peter. To the resultant definitions the assent of the Church can never be wanting, on account of the activity of that same Holy Spirit, whereby the whole flock of Christ is preserved and progresses in unity of faith.

But when either the Roman Pontiff or the body of bishops together with him formulates a definition, they do so in accord with revelation itself. All are obliged to maintain and be ruled by this revelation, which, as written or preserved by tradition, is transmitted in its entirety through the legitimate succession of bishops and especially through the care of the Roman Pontiff himself.

Under the guiding light of the Spirit of truth, revelation is thus religiously preserved and faithfully expounded in the Church. The Roman Pontiff and the bishops, in conformity with their duty and as befits the gravity of the matter, strive painstakingly and by appropriate means to inquire properly into that revelation and to give apt expression to its contents. But they do not accept any new public revelation as part of the divine deposit of faith.

• • • •

29. At a lower level of the hierarchy are deacons, upon whom hands are imposed "not unto the priesthood, but unto a ministry of service." For strengthened by sacramental grace, in communion with the bishop and his group of priests, they serve the People of God in the ministry of the liturgy, of the word, and of charity. It is the duty of the deacon, to the extent that he has been authorized by competent authority, to administer baptism solemnly, to be custodian and dispenser of the Eucharist, to assist at and bless marriages in the name of the Church, to bring Viaticum to the dying, to read the sacred Scripture to the faithful, to instruct and exhort the people, to preside at the worship and prayer of the faithful, to administer sacramentals, and to officiate at funeral and burial services. Dedicated to duties of charity and of administration, let deacons be mindful of the admonition of Blessed Polycarp: "Be merciful, diligent, walking according to the truth of the Lord, who became the servant of all."

These duties, so very necessary for the life of the Church, can in many areas be fulfilled only with difficulty according to the prevailing discipline of the Latin Church. For this reason, the diaconate can in the future be restored as a proper and permanent rank of the hierarchy. It pertains to the competent territorial bodies of bishops, of one kind or another, to decide, with the approval of the Supreme Pontiff, whether and where it is opportune for such deacons to be appointed for the care of souls. With the consent of the Roman Pontiff, this diaconate will be able to be conferred upon men of more mature age, even upon those living in the married state. It may also be conferred upon suitable young men. For them, however, the law of celibacy must remain intact.

Chapter IV
THE LAITY

30. Having set forth the functions of the hierarchy, this holy Synod gladly turns its attention to the status of those faithful called the laity. Everything which has been said so far concerning the People of God applies equally to the laity, religious, and clergy. But there are certain things which pertain in a particular way to the laity, both men and women, by reason of their situation and mission. Because of the special circumstances of our time the foundations of these particularities must be examined more thoroughly.

For their sacred pastors know how much the laity contribute to the welfare of the entire Church. Pastors also know that they themselves were not meant by Christ to shoulder alone the entire saving mission of the Church toward the world. On the contrary, they understand that it is their noble duty so to shepherd the faithful and recognize their services and charismatic gifts that all according to their proper roles may cooperate in this common undertaking with one heart. For we must all "practice the truth in love, and so grow up in all things in him who is head, Christ. For from him the whole body (being closely joined and knit together through every joint of the system according to the functioning in due measure of each single part) derives its increase to the building up of itself in love" (Eph. 4:15–16).

31. The term laity is here understood to mean all the faithful except those in holy orders and those in a religious state sanctioned by the Church. These faithful are by baptism made one body with Christ and are established among the People of God. They are in their own way made sharers in the priestly, prophetic, and kingly functions of Christ. They carry out their own part in the mission of the whole Christian people with respect to the Church and the world.

A secular quality is proper and special to laymen.

It is true that those in holy orders can at times engage in secular activities, and even have a secular profession. But by reason of their particular vocation they are chiefly and professedly ordained to the sacred ministry. Similarly, by their state in life, religious give splendid and striking testimony that the world cannot be transfigured and offered to God without the spirit of the beatitudes.

But the laity, by their very vocation, seek the kingdom of God by engaging in temporal affairs and by ordering them according to the plan of God. They live in the world, that is, in each and in all of the secular professions and occupations. They live in the ordinary circumstances of family and social life, from which the very web of their existence is woven.

They are called there by God so that by exercising their proper function and being led by the spirit of the gospel they can work for the sanctification of the world from within, in the manner of leaven. In this way they can make Christ known to others, especially by the testimony of a life resplendent in faith, hope, and charity. The layman is closely involved in temporal affairs of every sort. It is therefore his special task to illumine and organize these affairs in such a way that they may always start out, develop, and persist according to Christ's mind, to the praise of the Creator and the Redeemer.

• • • •

33. The laity are gathered together in the People of God and make up the Body of Christ under one Head. Whoever they are, they are called upon, as living members, to expend all their energy for the growth of the Church and its continuous sanctification. For this very energy is a gift of the Creator and a blessing of the Redeemer.

The lay apostolate, however, is a participation in the saving mission of the Church itself. Through their baptism and confirmation, all are commissioned to that apostolate by the Lord Himself. Moreover, through the sacraments, especially the Holy Eucharist, there is communicated and nourished that charity toward God and man which is the soul of the entire apostolate. Now, the laity are called in a special way to make the Church present and operative in those places and circumstances where only through them can she become the salt of the earth. Thus every layman, by virtue of the very gifts bestowed upon him, is at the same time a witness and a living instrument of the mission of the Church herself, "according to the measure of Christ's bestowal" (Eph. 4:7).

Besides this apostolate, which pertains to absolutely every Christian, the laity can also be called in various ways to a more direct form of cooperation in the apostolate of the hierarchy. This was the case with certain men and women who assisted Paul the Apostle in the gospel, laboring much in the Lord (cf. Phil. 4:3; Rom. 16:3 ff.). Further, laymen have the capacity to be deputed by the hierarchy to exercise certain church functions for a spiritual purpose.

Upon all the laity, therefore, rests the noble duty of working to extend the divine plan of salvation ever increasingly to all men of each epoch and in every land. Consequently, let every opportunity be given them so that, according to their abilities and the needs of the times, they may zealously participate in the saving work of the Church.

34. Since the supreme and eternal Priest, Christ Jesus, wills to continue His witness and serve through the laity too, He vivifies them in His Spirit and unceasingly urges them on to every good and perfect work.

For besides intimately associating them with His life and His mission, Christ also gives them a share in His priestly function of offering spiritual worship for the glory of God and the salvation of men. For this reason the laity, dedicated to Christ and anointed by the Holy Spirit, are marvelously called and equipped to produce in themselves ever more abundant fruits of the Spirit. For all their works, prayers, and apostolic endeavors, their ordinary married and family life, their daily labor, their mental and physical relaxation, if carried out in the Spirit, and even the hardships of life, if patiently borne—all of these become spiritual sacrifices acceptable to God through Jesus Christ (cf. 1 Pet. 2:5). During the celebration of the Eucharist, these sacrifices are most lovingly offered to the Father along with the Lord's body. Thus, as worshipers whose every deed is holy, the laity consecrate the world itself to God.

. . . .

Chapter V
THE CALL OF THE WHOLE CHURCH TO HOLINESS

. . . .

Chapter VI
RELIGIOUS

. . . .

Chapter VII
THE ESCHATOLOGICAL NATURE OF THE PILGRIM CHURCH AND HER UNION WITH THE HEAVENLY CHURCH

. . . .

Chapter VIII
THE ROLE OF THE BLESSED VIRGIN MARY, MOTHER OF GOD, IN THE MYSTERY OF CHRIST AND THE CHURCH

I. Preface
II. The Role of the Blessed Virgin in the Economy of Salvation
III. The Blessed Virgin and the Church
IV. Devotion to the Blessed Virgin in the Church
V. Mary, a Sign of Sure Hope and of Solace for God's People in Pilgrimage

THE CONFESSION OF DOSITHEUS
(1672)

This creed was produced by a synod convened in Jerusalem in 1672 by Patriarch Dositheus. The occasion for the creed was the work of Cyril Lucaris, who had been elected Patriarch of Alexandria in 1602 and of Constantinople in 1621. Lucaris was strongly influenced by Protestantism and especially by Reformed theology. His Protestant predilections aroused not only the opposition of his own people but also the opposition of the Jesuits who were active in Constantinople. Lucaris was finally strangled by the Turks, who thought he was guilty of treason.

The Confession of Dositheus defines Orthodox theology over against Protestantism. It is the most important Orthodox confession of recent centuries, though it does not have the status of the early creeds.

Source: The text used here is taken from *The Acts and Decrees of the Synod of Jerusalem, sometimes called the Council of Bethlehem, holden under Dositheus, Patriarch of Jerusalem in 1672,* tr. by J. N. W. B. Robertson (London: Thomas Baker, 1899).

Bulgakov, Sergius, *The Orthodox Church* (London: The Centenary Press, 1935).

French, R. M., *The Eastern Orthodox Church* (London: Hutchinson House, 1951).

Hadjiantoniou, George A., *Protestant Patriarch* (Richmond: John Knox Press, 1961). (Contains a translation of *Confessio Fidei* of Cyril Lucaris.)

Zernov, N., *Eastern Christendom* (London: Weidenfeld and Nicolson, 1961).

THE CONFESSION OF DOSITHEUS.

Dositheus, by the mercy of God, Patriarch of Jerusalem, to those that ask and inquire concerning the faith and worship of the Greeks, that is of the Eastern Church, how forsooth it thinketh concerning the Orthodox faith, in the common name of all Christians subject to our Apostolic Throne, and of the Orthodox worshippers that are sojourning in this holy and great city of Jerusalem (with whom the whole Catholic Church agreeth in all that concerneth the faith) publisheth this concise Confession, for a testimony both before God and before man, with a sincere conscience, and devoid of all dissimulation.

Decree I.

We believe in one God, true, almighty, and infinite, the Father, the Son, and the Holy Spirit; the Father unbegotten; the Son begotten of the Father before the ages, and consubstantial with Him; and the Holy Spirit proceeding from the Father, and consubstantial with the Father and the Son. These three Persons in one essence we call the All-holy Trinity, —by all creation to be ever blessed, glorified, and adored.

Decree II.

We believe the Divine and Sacred Scriptures to be God-taught; and, therefore, we ought to believe the same without doubting; yet not otherwise than as the Catholic Church hath interpreted and delivered the same. For every foul heresy receiveth, indeed, the Divine Scriptures, but perversely interpreteth the same, using metaphors, and homonymies, and sophistries of man's wisdom, confounding what ought to be distinguished, and trifling with what ought not to be trifled with. For if (we were to receive the same) otherwise, each man holding every day a different sense concerning the same, the Catholic Church would not (as she doth) by the grace of Christ continue to be the Church until this day, holding the same doctrine of faith, and always identically and steadfastly believing, but would be rent into innumerable parties, and subject to heresies; neither would the Church be holy, the pillar and ground of the truth, without spot or wrinkle; but would be the Church of the malignant; as it is manifest that of the heretics undoubtedly is, and especially that of Calvin, who are not ashamed to learn from the Church, and then to wickedly repudiate her. Wherefore, the witness also of the Catholic Church is, we believe, not of inferior authority to that of the Divine Scriptures. For one and the same Holy Spirit being the author of both, it is quite the same to be taught by the Scriptures and by the Catholic Church. Moreover, when any man speaketh from himself he is liable to err, and to deceive, and be deceived; but the Catholic Church, as never having spoken, or speaking from herself, but from the Spirit of God—who being her teacher, she is ever unfailingly rich—it is impossible for her to in any wise err, or to at all deceive, or be deceived; but like the Divine Scriptures, is infallible, and hath perpetual authority.

Decree III.

We believe the most good God to have from eternity predestinated unto glory those whom He hath chosen, and to have consigned unto condemnation those whom He hath rejected; but not so that He would justify the one, and consign and condemn the other without cause. For that were contrary to the nature of God, who is the common Father of all, and no respecter of persons, and would have all men to be saved, and to come to the knowledge of the truth; but since He foreknew the one would make a right use of their free-will, and the other a wrong, He predestinated the one, or condemned the other. And we understand the use of free-will thus, that the Divine and illuminating grace, and which we call preventing grace, being, as a light to those in darkness, by the Divine goodness imparted to all, to those that are willing to obey this—for it is of use only to the willing, not to the unwilling—and co-operate with it, in what it requireth as necessary to salvation, there is consequently granted particular grace; which, co-operating with us, and enabling us, and making us perseverant in the love of God, that is to say, in performing those good things that God would have us to do, and which His preventing grace admonisheth us that we should do, justifieth us, and maketh us predestinated. But those who will not obey, and co-operate with grace; and, therefore, will not observe those things that God would have us perform, and that abuse in the service of Satan the free-will, which they have received of God to perform voluntarily what is good, are consigned to eternal condemnation.

But to say, as the most wicked heretics do—and as is contained in the Chapter answering hereto—that God, in predestinating, or condemning, had in no wise regard to the works of those predestinated, or condemned, we know to be profane and impious. For thus Scripture would be opposed to itself, since it promiseth the believer salvation through works, yet supposeth God to be its sole author, by His sole illuminating grace, which He bestoweth without preceding works, to shew to man the truth of divine things, and to teach him how he may co-operate therewith, if he will, and do what is good and acceptable, and so obtain salvation. He taketh not away the power to will—to will to obey, or not obey him.

But than to affirm that the Divine Will is thus solely and without cause the author of their condemnation, what greater calumny can be fixed upon God? and what greater injury and blasphemy can be offered to the Most High? For that the Deity is not tempted with evils, and that He equally willeth the salvation of all, since there is no respect of persons with Him, we do know; and that for those who through their own wicked choice, and their impenitent heart, have become vessels of dishonour, there is, as is just, decreed condemnation, we do confess. But of eternal punishment, of cruelty, of pitilessness, and of inhumanity, we never, never say God is the author, who telleth us that there is joy in heaven over one sinner that repenteth. Far be it from us, while we have our senses, thus to believe, or to think; and we do subject to an eternal anathema those who say and think such things, and esteem them to be worse than any infidels.

Decree IV.

We believe the tri-personal God, the Father, the Son, and the Holy Spirit to be the maker of all things visible and invisible; and the invisible are the angelic Powers, rational souls, and demons—though God made not the demons what they afterwards became by their own choice,—but the visible are heaven and what is under heaven. And because the Maker is good by nature, He made all things very good whatsoever He hath made, nor can He ever be the maker of evil. But if there be aught evil, that is to say, sin, come about contrarily to the Divine Will, in man or in demon,—for that evil is simply in nature, we do not acknowledge,—it is either of man, or of the devil. For it is a true and infallible rule, that God is in no wise the author of evil, nor can it at all by just reasoning be attributed to God.

Decree V.

We believe all things that are, whether visible or invisible, to be governed by the providence of God; but although God fore-knoweth evils, and permitteth them, yet in that they are evils, He is neither their contriver nor their author. But when such are come about, they may be over-ruled by the Supreme Goodness for something beneficial, not indeed as being their author, but as engrafting thereon something for the better. And we ought to adore, but not curiously pry into, Divine Providence in its ineffable and only partially revealed judgments. Albeit what is revealed to us in Divine Scripture concerning it as being conducive to eternal life, we ought honestly to search out, and then unhesitatingly to interpret the same agreeably to primary notions of God.

Decree VI.

We believe the first man created by God to have fallen in Paradise, when, disregarding the Divine commandment, he yielded to the deceitful counsel of the serpent. And hence hereditary sin flowed to his posterity; so that none is born after the flesh who beareth not this burden, and experienceth not the fruits thereof in this present world. But by these fruits and this burden we do not understand (actual) sin, such as impiety, blasphemy, murder, sodomy, adultery, fornication, enmity, and whatsoever else is by our depraved choice committed contrarily to the Divine Will, not from nature; for many both of the Forefathers and of the Prophets, and vast numbers of others, as well of those under the shadow (of the Law), as under the truth (of the Gospel), such as the divine Precursor, and especially the Mother of God the Word, the ever-virgin Mary, experienced not these, or such like faults; but only what the Divine Justice inflicted upon man as a punishment for the (original) transgression, such as sweats in labour, afflictions, bodily sicknesses, pains in child-bearing, and in fine, while on our pilgrimage, to live a laborious life, and lastly, bodily death.

Decree VII.

We believe the Son of God, Jesus Christ, to have emptied Himself, that is, to have taken into His own Person human flesh, being conceived of the Holy Spirit, in the womb of the ever-virgin Mary; and, becoming man, to have been born, without causing any pain or labour to His own Mother after the flesh, or injury to her virginity, to have suffered, to have been buried, to have risen again in glory on the third day, according to the Scriptures, to have ascended into the heavens, and to be seated at the right hand of God the Father. Whom also we look for to judge the living and the dead.

Decree VIII.

We believe our Lord Jesus Christ to be the only mediator, and that in giving Himself a ransom for all He hath through His own Blood made a reconciliation between God and man, and that Himself having a care for His own is advocate and propitiation for our sins. Albeit, in prayers and supplications unto Him, we say the Saints are intercessors, and, above all, the undefiled Mother of the very God the Word; the holy Angels too—whom we know to be set over us—the Apostles, Prophets, Martyrs, Pure Ones, and all whom He hath glorified as having served Him faithfully. With whom we reckon also the Bishops and Priests, as standing about the Altar of God, and righteous men eminent for virtue. For that we should pray one for another, and that the prayer of the righteous availeth much, and that God heareth the Saints rather than those who are steeped in sins, we learn from the Sacred Oracles. And not only are the Saints while on their pilgrimage regarded as mediators and intercessors for us with God, but especially after their death, when all reflective vision being done away, they behold clearly the Holy Trinity; in whose infinite light they know what concerneth us. For as we doubt not but that the Prophets while they were in a body with the perceptions of the senses knew what was done in heaven, and thereby foretold what was future; so also that the Angels, and the Saints become as Angels, know in the infinite light of God what concerneth us, we doubt not, but rather unhesitatingly believe and confess.

Decree IX.

We believe no one to be saved without faith. And by faith we mean the right notion that is in us concerning God and divine things, which, working by love, that is to say, by (observing) the Divine commandments, justifieth us with Christ; and without this (faith) it is impossible to please God.

Decree X.

We believe that what is called, or rather is, the Holy Catholic and Apostolic Church, and in which we have been taught to believe, containeth generally all the Faithful in Christ, who, that is to say, being still on their pilgrimage, have not yet reached their home in the Fatherland. But we do not in any wise confound this Church which is on its pilgrimage with that which is in the Fatherland, because it may be, as some of the heretics say, that the members of the two are sheep of God, the Chief Shepherd, and hallowed by the same Holy Spirit; for that is absurd and impossible, since the one is yet militant, and on its journey; and the other is triumphant, and settled in the Fatherland, and hath received the prize. Of which Catholic Church, since a mortal man cannot universally and perpetually be head, our Lord Jesus Christ Himself is head, and Himself holding the rudder is at the helm in the governing of the Church, through the Holy Fathers. And, therefore, over particular Churches, that are real Churches, and consist of real members (of the Catholic Church), the Holy Spirit hath appointed Bishops as leaders and shepherds, who being not at all by abuse, but properly, authorities and heads, look unto the Author and Finisher of our Salvation, and refer to Him what they do in their capacity of heads forsooth.

But forasmuch as among their other impieties, the Calvinists have fancied this also, that the simple Priest and the High Priest are perhaps the same; and that there is no necessity for High Priests, and that the Church may be governed by some Priests; and that not a High Priest (only), but a Priest also is able to ordain a Priest, and a number of Priests to ordain a High Priest; and affirm in lofty language that the Eastern Church assenteth to this wicked notion—for which purpose the Tenth Chapter was written by Cyril —we explicitly declare according to the mind which hath obtained from the beginning in the Eastern Church:—

That the dignity of the Bishop is so necessary in the Church, that without him, neither Church nor Christian could either be or be spoken of. For he, as a successor of the Apostles, having received in continued succession by the imposition of hands and the invocation of the All-holy Spirit the grace that is given him of the Lord of binding and loosing, is a living image of God upon the earth, and by a most ample participation of the operation of the Holy Spirit, who is the chief functionary, is a fountain of all the Mysteries (Sacraments) of the Catholic Church, through which we obtain salvation.

And he is, we suppose, as necessary to the Church as breath is to man, or the sun to the world. Whence it hath also been elegantly said by some in commendation of the dignity of the High Priesthood, 'What God is in the heavenly Church of the first-born, and the sun in the world, that every High Priest is in his own particular Church, as through him the flock is enlightened, and nourished, and becometh the temple of God.'

And that this great mystery and dignity of the Episcopate hath descended unto us by a continued succession is manifest. For since the Lord hath promised to be with us always, although He be with us by other means of grace and Divine operations, yet in a more eminent manner doth He, through the Bishop as chief functionary, make us His own and dwell with us, and through the divine Mysteries is united with us; of which the Bishop is the first minister, and chief functionary, through the Holy Spirit, and suffereth us not to fall into heresy. And, therefore (John) the Damascen, in his Fourth Epistle to the Africans, hath said, the Catholic Church is everywhere committed to the care of the Bishops; and that Clement, the first Bishop of the Romans, and Evodius, at Antioch, and Mark at Alexandria, were successors of Peter is acknowledged. Also that the divine Andrew seated Stachys on the Throne of Constantinople, in his own stead; and that in this great holy city of Jerusalem our Lord Himself appointed James, and that after James another succeeded, and then another, until our own times. And, therefore, Tertullian in his Epistle to Papianus called all Bishops the Apostles' successors. To their succession to the Apostles' dignity and authority Eusebius, the (friend) of Pamphilus, testifieth, and all the Fathers testify, of whom it is needless to give a list; and this the common and most ancient custom of the Catholic Church confirmeth.

And that the dignity of the Episcopate differeth from that of the simple Priest, is manifest. For the Priest is ordained by the Bishop, but a Bishop is not ordained by a Priest, but by two or three High Priests, as the Apostolic Canon directeth. And the Priest is chosen by the Bishop, but the High Priest is not chosen by the Priests or Presbyters, nor is he chosen by secular Princes, but by the Synod of the Primatial Church of that country, in which is situated the city that is to receive the ordinand, or at least by the Synod of the Province in which he is to become a Bishop. Or, if ever the city choose him, it doth not this absolutely; but the election is referred to the Synod; and if it appear that he hath obtained this agreeably to the Canons, the Elect is advanced by ordination by the Bishops, with the invocation of the All-holy Spirit; but if not, he is advanced whom the Synod chooseth. And the Priest, indeed, retaineth to himself the authority and grace of the Priesthood, which he hath received; but the Bishop imparteth it to others also. And the one having received the dignity of the Priesthood from the Bishop, can only perform Holy Baptism, and Prayer-oil, minister sacrificially the unbloody Sacrifice, and impart to the people the All-holy Body and Blood of our Lord Jesus Christ, anoint the baptised with the Holy Myron (Chrism), crown the Faithful legally marrying, pray for the sick, and that all men may be saved and come to the knowledge of the truth, and especially for the remission and forgiveness of the sins of the Faithful, living and dead. And if he be eminent for experience and virtue, receiving his authority from the Bishop, he directeth those Faithful that come unto him, and guideth them into the way of possessing the heavenly kingdom, and is appointed a preacher of the sacred Gospel. But the High Priest is also the minister of all these, since he is in fact, as hath been said before, the fountain of the Divine Mysteries and graces, through the Holy Spirit, and he alone consecrateth the Holy Myron. And the ordinations of all orders and degrees in the Church are proper to him; and in a primary and highest sense he bindeth and looseth, and his sentence is approved by God, as the Lord hath promised. And he preacheth the Sacred Gospel, and contendeth for the Orthodox faith, and those that refuse to hear he casteth out of the Church as heathens and publicans, and he putteth heretics under excommunication and anathema, and layeth down his own life for the sheep. From which it is manifest, that without contradiction the Bishop differeth from the simple Priest, and that without him all the Priests in the world could not exercise the pastorate in the Church of God, or govern it at all.

But it is well said by one of the Fathers, that it is not easy to find a heretic that hath understanding. For when these forsake the Church, they are forsaken by the Holy Spirit, and there remaineth in them neither understanding nor light, but only darkness and blindness. For if such had not happened to them, they would not have opposed things that are most plain; among which is the truly great mystery of Episcopacy, which is taught by Scripture, written of, and witnessed to, both by all Ecclesiastical history and the writings of holy men, and always held and acknowledged by the Catholic Church.

Decree XI.

We believe to be members of the Catholic Church all the Faithful, and only the Faithful; who, forsooth, having received the blameless Faith of the Saviour Christ, from Christ Himself, and the Apostles, and the Holy Œcumenical Synods, adhere to the same without wavering; although some of them may be guilty of all manner of sins. For unless the Faithful, even when living in sin, were members of the Church, they could not be judged by the Church. But now being judged by her, and called to repentance, and guided into the way of her salutary precepts, though they may be still defiled with sins, for this only, that they have not fallen into despair, and that they cleave to the Catholic and Orthodox faith, they are, and are regarded as, members of the Catholic Church.

Decree XII.

We believe the Catholic Church to be taught by the Holy Spirit. For he is the true Paraclete; whom Christ sendeth from the Father, to teach the truth, and to drive away darkness from the minds of the Faithful. The teaching of the Holy Spirit, however, doth not immediately, but through the holy Fathers and Leaders of the Catholic Church, illuminate the Church. For as all Scripture is, and is called, the word of the Holy Spirit; not that it was spoken immediately by Him, but that it was spoken by Him through the Apostles and Prophets; so also the Church is taught indeed by the Life-giving Spirit, but through the medium of the holy Fathers and Doctors (whose rule is acknowledged to be the Holy and Œcumenical Synods; for we shall not cease to say this ten thousand times); and, therefore, not only are we persuaded, but do profess as true and undoubtedly certain, that it is impossible for the Catholic Church to err, or at all be deceived, or ever to choose falsehood instead of truth. For the All-holy Spirit continually operating through the holy Fathers and Leaders faithfully ministering, delivereth the Church from error of every kind.

Decree XIII.

We believe a man to be not simply justified through faith alone, but through faith which worketh through love, that is to say, through faith and works. But [the notion] that faith fulfilling the function of a hand layeth hold on the righteousness which is in Christ, and applieth it unto us for salvation, we know to be far from all Orthodoxy. For faith so understood would be possible in all, and so none could miss salvation, which is obviously false. But on the contrary, we rather believe that it is not the correlative of faith, but the faith which is in us, justifieth through works, with Christ. But we regard works not as witnesses certifying our calling, but as being fruits in themselves, through which faith becometh efficacious, and as in themselves meriting, through the Divine promises, that each of the Faithful may receive what is done through his own body, whether it be good or bad, forsooth.

Decree XIV.

We believe man in falling by the [original] transgression to have become comparable and like unto the beasts, that is, to have been utterly undone, and to have fallen from his perfection and impassibility, yet not to have lost the nature and power which he had received from the supremely good God. For otherwise he would not be rational, and consequently not man; but to have the same nature, in which he was created, and the same power of his nature, that is free-will, living and operating. So as to be by nature able to choose and do what is good, and to avoid and hate what is evil. For it is absurd to say that the nature which was created good by Him who is supremely good lacketh the power of doing good. For this would be to make that nature evil—than which what could be more impious? For the power of working dependeth upon nature, and nature upon its author, although in a different manner. And that a man is able by nature to do what is good, even our Lord Himself intimateth, saying, even the Gentiles love those that love them.

But this is taught most plainly by Paul also, in Romans chap. i. [ver.] 19, and elsewhere expressly, saying in so many words, 'The Gentiles which have no law do by nature the things of the law.' From which it is also manifest that the good which a man may do cannot forsooth be sin. For it is impossible that what is good can be evil. Albeit, being done by nature only, and tending to form the natural character of the doer, but not the spiritual, it contributeth not unto salvation thus alone without faith, nor yet indeed unto condemnation, for it is not possible that good, as such, can be the cause of evil. But in the regenerated, what is wrought by grace, and with grace, maketh the doer perfect, and rendereth him worthy of salvation.

A man, therefore, before he is regenerated, is able by nature to incline to what is good, and to choose and work moral good. But for the regenerated to do spiritual good—for the works of the believer being contributory to salvation and wrought by supernatural grace are properly called spiritual—it is necessary that he be guided and prevented by grace, as hath been said in treating of predestination; so that he is not able of himself to do any work worthy of a Christian life, although he hath it in his own power to will, or not to will, to co-operate with grace.

Decree XV.

We believe that there are in the Church Evangelical Mysteries [i.e., Sacraments of the Gospel Dispensation], and that they are seven. For a less or a greater number of the Mysteries we have not in the Church; since any number of the Mysteries other than seven is the product of heretical madness. And the seven of them were instituted in the Sacred Gospel, and are gathered from the same, like the other dogmas of the Catholic Faith. For in the first place our Lord instituted Holy Baptism by the words, 'Go ye and make disciples of all the nations, baptising them in the name of the Father, and of the Son, and of the Holy Spirit;' and by the words, 'He that believeth and is baptised shall be saved, but he that disbelieveth shall be condemned.'

And that of Confirmation, that is to say, of the Holy Myron or Holy Chrism, by the words, 'But ye—tarry ye in the city of Jerusalem, until ye be endued with power from on high.' With which they were endued by the coming of the Holy Spirit, and this the Mystery of Confirmation signifieth; concerning which Paul also discourseth in the Second Epistle to the Corinthians, chap. i., and Dionysius the Areopagite more explicitly.

And the Priesthood by the words, 'This do ye for My Memorial;' and by the words, 'Whatsoever ye shall bind and loose upon the earth shall be bound and loosed in the heavens.'

And the unbloody Sacrifice by the words, 'Take, eat ye; This is My Body;' and, 'Drink ye all of It; This is My Blood of the New Testament;' and by the words, 'Except ye eat the Flesh of the Son of Man, ye have not life in yourselves.'

And Marriage, when, having recited the things which had been spoken thereof in the Old [Testament], He, as it were, set His seal thereto by the words, 'Those whom God hath joined together, let not man put asunder,' and this the divine Apostle also calleth a great Mystery.

And Penance, with which is joined sacramental confession, by the words, 'Whose soever sins ye remit, they are remitted unto them; and whose soever sins ye retain, they are retained;' and by the words, 'Except ye repent, ye shall [all] likewise perish.'

And, lastly, the Holy Oil or Prayer-Oil is spoken of in Mark, and is expressly witnessed to by the Lord's brother.

And the Mysteries consist of something natural, and of something supernatural; and are not bare signs of the promises of God. For then they would not differ from circumcision—than which [notion] what could be worse? And we acknowledge them to be, of necessity, efficient means of grace to the receivers. But we reject, as alien to Christian doctrine, the notion that the integrity of the Mystery requireth the use of the early thing [i.e., dependeth upon its reception]; for this is contrary to the Mystery of the Offering [i.e., the Sacrament of the Eucharist], which being instituted by the Substantial Word, and hallowed by the invocation of the Holy Spirit, is perfected by the presence of the thing signified, to wit, of the Body and Blood of Christ. And the perfecting thereof necessarily precedeth its use. For if it were not perfect before its use, he that useth it not aright could not eat and drink judgment unto himself; since he would be partaking of mere bread and wine. But now, he that partaketh unworthily eateth and drinketh judgment unto himself; so that not in its use, but even before its use, the Mystery of the

Eucharist hath its perfection. Moreover, we reject as something abominable and pernicious the notion that when faith is weak the integrity of the Mystery is impaired. For heretics who abjure their heresy and join the Catholic Church are received by the Church; although they received their valid Baptism with weakness of faith. Wherefore, when they afterwards become possessed of the perfect faith, they are not again baptised.

Decree XVI.

We believe Holy Baptism, which was instituted by the Lord, and is conferred in the name of the Holy Trinity, to be of the highest necessity. For without it none is able to be saved, as the Lord saith, 'Whosoever is not born of water and of the Spirit, shall in no wise enter into the Kingdom of the Heavens.' And, therefore, it is necessary even for infants, since they also are subject to original sin, and without Baptism are not able to obtain its remission. Which the Lord shewed when he said, not of some only, but simply and absolutely, 'Whosoever is not born [again],' which is the same as saying, 'All that after the coming of Christ the Saviour would enter into the Kingdom of the Heavens must be regenerated.' And forasmuch as infants are men, and as such need salvation; needing salvation, they need also Baptism. And those that are not regenerated, since they have not received the remission of hereditary sin, are, of necessity, subject to eternal punishment, and consequently cannot without Baptism be saved; so that even infants ought, of necessity, to be baptised. Moreover, infants are saved, as is said in Matthew; but he that is not baptised is not saved. And consequently even infants must of necessity be baptised. And in the Acts it is said that the whole houses were baptised, and consequently the infants. To this the ancient Fathers also witness explicitly, and among them Dionysius in his Treatise concerning the Ecclesiastical Hierarchy; and Justin in his fifty-sixth Question, who saith expressly, 'And they are vouchsafed the benefits of Baptism by the faith of those that bring them to Baptism.' And Augustine saith that it is an Apostolical tradition, that children are saved through Baptism; and in another place, 'The Church giveth to babes the feet of others, that they may come; and the hearts of others, that they may believe; and the tongues of others, that they may promise;' and in another place, 'Our mother, the Church, furnisheth them with a particular heart.'

Now the matter of Baptism is pure water, and no other liquid. And it is performed by the Priest only, or in a case of unavoidable necessity, by another man, provided he be Orthodox, and have the intention proper to Divine Baptism. And the effects of Baptism are, to speak concisely, firstly, the remission of the hereditary transgression, and of any sins whatsoever which the baptised may have committed. Secondly, it delivereth him from the eternal punishment, to which he was liable, as well for original sin, as for mortal sins he may have individually committed. Thirdly, it giveth to such immortality; for in justifying them from past sins, it maketh them temples of God. And it may not be said, that any sin is not washed away through Baptism, which may have been previously committed; but to remain, though not imputed. For that were indeed the height of impiety, and a denial, rather than a confession of piety. Yea, forsooth, all sin existing, or committed before Baptism, is blotted out, and is to be regarded as never existing or committed. For the forms of Baptism, and on either hand all the words that precede and that perfect Baptism, do indicate a perfect cleansing. And the same thing even the very names of Baptism do signify. For if Baptism be by the Spirit and by fire, it is manifest that it is in all a perfect cleansing; for the Spirit cleanseth perfectly. If it be light, it dispelleth the darkness. If it be regeneration, old things are passed away. And what are these except sins? If the baptised putteth off the old man, then sin also. If he putteth on Christ, then in effect he becometh free from sin through Baptism. For God is far from sinners. This Paul also teacheth more plainly, saying: 'As through one [man] we, being many, were made sinners, so through one [are we made] right-eous.' And if righteous, then free from sin. For it is not possible for life and death to be in the same [per-son]. If Christ truly died, then remission of sin through the Spirit is true also.

Hence it is evident that all who are baptised and fall asleep while babes are undoubtedly saved, being predestinated through the death of Christ. Forasmuch as they are without any sin;—without that common [to all], because delivered therefrom by the Divine laver, and without any of their own, because as babes they are incapable of committing sin;—and conse-quently are saved. Moreover, Baptism imparteth an indelible character, as doth also the Priesthood. For as it is impossible for any one to receive twice the same order of the Priesthood, so it is impossible for any once rightly baptised, to be again baptised, al-though he should fall even into myriads of sins, or even into actual apostasy from the Faith. For when he is willing to return unto the Lord, he receiveth again through the Mystery of Penance the adoption of a son, which he had lost.

Decree XVII.

We believe the All-holy Mystery of the Sacred Eu-charist, which we have enumerated above, fourth in order, to be that which our Lord delivered in the night wherein He gave Himself up for the life of the world. For taking bread, and blessing, He gave to His Holy Disciples and Apostles, saying: 'Take, eat ye; This is My Body.' And taking the chalice, and giving thanks, He said: 'Drink ye all of it: This is My Blood, which for you is being poured out, for the remission of sins.'

In the celebration whereof we believe the Lord Jesus Christ to be present, not typically, nor figura-tively, nor by superabundant grace, as in the other Mysteries, nor by a bare presence, as some of the Fa-thers have said concerning Baptism, or by impanation, so that the Divinity of the Word is united to the set forth bread of the Eucharist hypostatically, as the followers of Luther most ignorantly and wretchedly suppose, but truly and really, so that after the consecration of the bread and of the wine, the bread is transmuted, transubstantiated, converted and transformed into the true Body Itself of the Lord, Which was born in Bethlehem of the ever-Virgin, was baptised in the Jordan, suffered, was buried, rose again, was received up, sitteth at the right hand of the God and Father, and is to come again in the clouds of Heaven; and the wine is converted and transubstantiated into the true Blood Itself of the Lord, Which as He hung upon the Cross, was poured out for the life of the world.

Further [we believe] that after the consecration of the bread and of the wine, there no longer remaineth the substance of the bread and of the wine, but the Body Itself and the Blood of the Lord, under the species and form of bread and wine; that is to say, under the accidents of the bread.

Further, that the all-pure Body Itself, and Blood of the Lord is imparted, and entereth into the mouths and stomachs of the communicants, whether pious or impious. Nevertheless, they convey to the pious and worthy remission of sins and life eternal; but to the impious and unworthy involve condemnation and eternal punishment.

Further, that the Body and Blood of the Lord are severed and divided by the hands and teeth, though in accident only, that is, in the accidents of the bread and of the wine, under which they are visible and tangible, we do acknowledge; but in themselves to remain entirely unsevered and undivided. Wherefore the Catholic Church also saith: 'Broken and distributed is He That is broken, yet not severed; Which is ever eaten, yet never consumed, but sanctifying those that partake,' that is worthily.

Further, that in every part, or the smallest division of the transmuted bread and wine there is not a part of the Body and Blood of the Lord—for to say so were blasphemous and wicked—but the entire whole Lord

Christ substantially, that is, with His Soul and Divinity, or perfect God and perfect man. So that though there may be many celebrations in the world at one and the same hour, there are not many Christs, or Bodies of Christ, but it is one and the same Christ that is truly and really present; and His one Body and His Blood is in all the several Churches of the Faithful; and this not because the Body of the Lord that is in the Heavens descendeth upon the Altars; but because the bread of the Prothesis set forth in all the several Churches, being changed and transubstantiated, becometh, and is, after consecration, one and the same with That in the Heavens. For it is one Body of the Lord in many places, and not many; and therefore This Mystery is the greatest, and is spoken of as wonderful, and comprehensible by faith only, and not by the sophistries of man's wisdom; whose vain and foolish curiosity in divine things our pious and God-delivered religion rejecteth.

Further, that the Body Itself of the Lord and the Blood That are in the Mystery of the Eucharist ought to be honoured in the highest manner, and adored with latria. For one is the adoration of the Holy Trinity, and of the Body and Blood of the Lord.

Further, that it is a true and propitiatory Sacrifice offered for all Orthodox, living and dead; and for the benefit of all, as is set forth expressly in the prayers of the Mystery delivered to the Church by the Apostles, in accordance with the command they received of the Lord.

Further, that before Its use, immediately after the consecration, and after Its use, What is reserved in the Sacred Pixes for the communion of those that are about to depart [i.e., the dying] is the true Body of the Lord, and not in the least different therefrom; so that before Its use after the consecration, in Its use, and after Its use, It is in all respects the true Body of the Lord.

Further, we believe that by the word 'transubstantiation' the manner is not explained, by which the bread and wine are changed into the Body and Blood of the Lord,—for that is altogether incomprehensible and impossible, except by God Himself, and those who imagine to do so are involved in ignorance and impiety,—but that the bread and the wine are after the consecration, not typically, nor figuratively, nor by superabundant grace, nor by the communication or the presence of the Divinity alone of the Only-begotten, transmuted into the Body and Blood of the Lord; neither is any accident of the bread, or of the wine, by any conversion or alteration, changed into any accident of the Body and Blood of Christ, but truly, and really, and substantially, doth the bread become the true Body Itself of the Lord, and the wine the Blood Itself of the Lord, as is said above.

Further, that this Mystery of the Sacred Eucharist can be performed by none other, except only by an Orthodox Priest, who hath received his priesthood from an Orthodox and Canonical Bishop, in accordance with the teaching of the Eastern Church. This is compendiously the doctrine, and true confession, and most ancient tradition of the Catholic Church concerning this Mystery; which must not be departed from in any way by such as would be Orthodox, and who reject the novelties and profane vanities of heretics; but necessarily the tradition of the institution must be kept whole and unimpaired. For those that transgress the Catholic Church of Christ rejecteth and anathematiseth.

Decree XVIII.

We believe that the souls of those that have fallen asleep are either at rest or in torment, according to what each hath wrought;—for when they are separated from their bodies, they depart immediately either to joy, or to sorrow and lamentation; though confessedly neither their enjoyment, nor condemnation are complete. For, after the common resurrection, when the soul shall be united with the body, with which it had behaved itself well or ill, each shall receive the completion of either enjoyment or of condemnation for-sooth.

And such as though envolved in mortal sins have not departed in despair, but have, while still living in the body, repented, though without bringing forth any fruits of repentance—by pouring forth tears, forsooth, by kneeling while watching in prayers, by afflicting themselves, by relieving the poor, and in fine by shew-ing forth by their works their love towards God and their neighbour, and which the Catholic Church hath from the beginning rightly called satisfaction—of these and such like the souls depart into Hades, and there endure the punishment due to the sins they have com-mitted. But they are aware of their future release from thence, and are delivered by the Supreme Goodness, through the prayers of the Priests, and the good works which the relatives of each do for their Departed; es-pecially the unbloody Sacrifice availing in the highest degree; which each offereth particularly for his rela-tives that have fallen asleep, and which the Catholic and Apostolic Church offereth daily for all alike; it being, of course, understood that we know not the time of their release. For that there is deliverance for such from their direful condition, and that before the common resurrection and judgment we know and be-lieve; but when we know not.

Question I.

Ought the Divine Scriptures to be read in the vul-gar tongue by all Christians?

No. For that all Scripture is divinely-inspired and profitable we know, and is of such necessity, that with-out the same it is impossible to be Orthodox at all. Nevertheless they should not be read by all, but only by those who with fitting research have inquired into the deep things of the Spirit, and who know in what manner the Divine Scriptures ought to be searched, and taught, and in fine read. But to such as are not so exercised, or who cannot distinguish, or who under-stand only literally, or in any other way contrary to Orthodoxy what is contained in the Scriptures, the

Catholic Church, as knowing by experience the mischief arising therefrom, forbiddeth the reading of the same. So that it is permitted to every Orthodox to hear indeed the Scriptures, that he may believe with the heart unto righteousness, and confess with the mouth unto salvation; but to read some parts of the Scriptures, and especially of the Old [Testament], is forbidden for the aforesaid reasons and others of the like sort. For it is the same thing thus to prohibit persons not exercised thereto reading all the Sacred Scriptures, as to require infants to abstain from strong meats.

Question II.

Are the Scriptures plain to all Christians that read them?

If the Divine Scriptures were plain to all Christians that read them, the Lord would not have commanded such as desired to obtain salvation to search the same; and Paul would have said without reason that God had placed the gift of teaching in the Church; and Peter would not have said of the Epistles of Paul that they contained some things hard to be understood. It is evident, therefore, that the Scriptures are very profound, and their sense lofty; and that they need learned and divine men to search out their true meaning, and a sense that is right, and agreeable to all Scripture, and to its author the Holy Spirit.

So that as to those that are regenerated [in Baptism], although they must know the faith concerning the Trinity, the incarnation of the Son of God, His Passion, resurrection, and ascension into the heavens, what concerneth regeneration and judgment—for which many have not hesitated to die—it is not necessary, but rather impossible, that all should know what the Holy Spirit manifesteth to those alone who are exercised in wisdom and holiness.

Question III.

What Books do you call Sacred Scripture?

Following the rule of the Catholic Church, we call Sacred Scripture all those which Cyril collected from the Synod of Laodicea, and enumerated, adding thereto those which he foolishly, and ignorantly, or rather maliciously called Apocrypha; to wit, 'The Wisdom of Solomon,' 'Judith,' 'Tobit,' 'The History of the Dragon,' 'The History of Susanna,' 'The Maccabees,' and 'The Wisdom of Sirach.' For we judge these also to be with the other genuine Books of Divine Scripture genuine parts of Scripture. For ancient custom, or rather the Catholic Church, which hath delivered to us as genuine the Sacred Gospels and the other Books of Scripture, hath undoubtedly delivered these also as parts of Scripture, and the denial of these is the rejection of those. And if, perhaps, it seemeth that not always have all been by all reckoned with the others, yet nevertheless these also have been counted and reckoned with the rest of Scripture, as well by Synods, as by how many of the most ancient and eminent Theologians of the Catholic Church; all of which we also judge to be Canonical Books, and confess them to be Sacred Scripture.

Question IV.

How ought we to think of the Holy Eikons, and of the adoration of the Saints?

The Saints being, and acknowledged by the Catholic Church to be, intercessors, as hath been said in Eighth Chapter, it is time to say that we honour them as friends of God, and as praying for us to the God of all. And the honour we pay them is twofold;—according to one manner which we call hyperdulia, we honour the Mother of God the Word. For though indeed the Theotokos be servant of the only God, yet is she also His Mother, as having borne in the flesh one of the Trinity; wherefore also is she hymned, as being beyond compare, above as well all Angels as Saints; wherefore, also, we pay her the adoration of hyperdulia. But according to the other manner, which we call dulia, we adore, or rather honour, the holy Angels, Apostles, Prophets, Martyrs, and in fine, all the Saints.

Moreover, we adore and honour the wood of the

precious and life-giving Cross, whereon our Saviour
underwent this world-saving passion, and the sign of
the life-giving Cross, the Manger at Bethlehem,
through which we have been delivered from irration-
ality, the place of the Skull [Calvary], the life-giving
Sepulchre, and the other holy objects of adoration; as
well the holy Gospels, as the sacred vessels, wherewith
the unbloody Sacrifice is performed. And by annual
commemorations, and popular festivals, and sacred
edifices and offerings; we do respect and honour the
Saints.

And then we adore, and honour, and kiss the Eikons
of our Lord Jesus Christ, and of the most holy Theotokos, and of all the Saints, also of the holy Angels,
as they appeared to some of the Forefathers and
Prophets. We also represent the All-holy Spirit, as He
appeared, in the form of a dove.

And if some say we commit idolatry in adoring the
Saints, and the Eikons of the Saints, and the other
things, we regard it as foolish and frivolous. For we
worship with latria the only God in Trinity, and none
other; but the Saints we honour upon two accounts:
firstly, for their relation to God, since we honour
them for His sake; and for themselves, because they
are living images of God. But that which is for themselves hath been defined as of dulia. But the holy
Eikons [we adore] relatively, since the honour paid
to them is referred to their prototypes. For he that
adoreth the Eikon doth, through the Eikon, adore the
prototype; and the honour paid to the Eikon is not at
all divided, or at all separated from that of him that
is pourtrayed, and is done unto the same, like that
done unto a royal embassy.

And what they adduce from Scripture in support
of their novelties, doth not help them as they would,
but rather appeareth agreeable to us. For we, when
reading the Divine Scriptures, examine the occasion
and person, the example and cause. Wherefore, when
we contemplate God Himself saying at one time,
'Thou shalt not make to thyself any idol, or likeness;
neither shalt thou adore them, nor serve them;' and at

another, commanding that Cherubim should be made; and further, that oxen and lions were placed in the Temple, we do not rashly consider the import of these things. For faith is not in assurance; but, as hath been said, considering the occasion and other circumstances, we arrive at the right interpretation of the same; and we conclude that, 'Thou shalt not make to thyself any idol, or likeness,' is the same as saying, 'Thou shalt not adore strange Gods,' or rather, 'Thou shalt not commit idolatry.' For so both the custom obtaining in the Church from Apostolic times of adoring the holy Eikons relatively is maintained, and the worship of latria reserved for God alone; and God doth not appear to speak contrarily to Himself. For if the Scripture saith [absolutely], 'Thou shalt not make,' 'Thou shalt not adore,' we fail to see how God afterwards permitted likenesses to be made, even though not for adoration. Wherefore, since the commandment concerneth idolatry only, we find serpents, and lions, and oxen, and Cherubim made, and figures and likenesses; among which Angels appear, as having been adored.

And as to the Saints whom they bring forward as saying, that it is not lawful to adore Eikons; we conclude that they rather help us; since they in their sharp disputations inveighed, as well against those that adore the holy Eikons with latria, as against those that bring the eikons of their deceased relatives into the Church, and subjected to anathema those that so do; but not against the right adoration, either of the Saints, or of the holy Eikons, or of the precious Cross, or of the other things of which mention hath been made; especially since the holy Eikons have been in the Church, and have been adored by the Faithful, even from the times of the Apostles, as is recorded and proclaimed by very many; with whom and after whom the Seventh Holy Œcumenical Synod putteth to shame all heretical impudence.

Since it giveth us most plainly to understand that it behoveth to adore the holy Eikons, and what have been mentioned above. And it anathematiseth, and subjecteth to excommunication, as well those that adore the Eikons with latria as those that say that the Orthodox commit idolatry in adoring the Eikons. We also, therefore, do anathematise with them such as adore either Saint, or Angel, or Eikon, or Cross, or Relic of Saints, or sacred Vessel, or Gospel, or aught else that is in heaven above, or aught on the earth, or in the sea, with latria; and we ascribe adoration with latria to the only God in Trinity. And we anathematise those that say that the adoration of Eikons is the latria of Eikons, and who adore them not, and honour not the Cross, and the Saints, as the Church hath delivered.

Now we adore the Saints and the holy Eikons, in the manner declared; and pourtray them in adornment of our temples, and that they may be the books of the unlearned, and for them to imitate the virtues of the Saints; and for them to remember, and have an increase of love, and be vigilant in ever calling upon the Lord, as Sovereign and Father, but upon the Saints, as his servants, and our helpers and mediators.

And so much as to the Chapters and Questions of Cyril. But the heretics do find fault with even the prayers of the pious unto God, for we know not why they should calumniate those of the Monks only. Moreover, that prayer is a conversation with God, and a petitioning for such good things as be meet for us, from Him of whom we hope to receive, an ascent too of the mind unto God, and a pious expression of our purpose towards God, a seeking what is above, the support of a holy soul, and worship most acceptable to God, a token of repentance, and of steadfast hope, we do know; and prayer is made either with the mind alone, or with the mind and voice; thereby engaging in the contemplation of the goodness and mercy of God, of the unworthiness of the petitioner, and in thanksgiving, and in realising the promises attached to obedience to God.

And it is accompanied by faith, and hope, and perseverance, and observance of the commandments; and, as already said, is a petitioning for heavenly things;

and it hath many fruits, which it is needless to enumerate; and it is made continually, and is accomplished either in an upright posture, or by kneeling.
And so great is its efficacy, that it is acknowledged to
be both the nourishment and the life of the soul. And
all this is gathered from Divine Scripture; so that if
any ask for demonstration thereof, he is like a fool,
or a blind man, who disputeth about the sun's light at
the hour of noon, and when the sky is clear.

But the heretics, wishing to leave nothing unassailed
that Christ hath enjoined, carp at this also. But being
ashamed thus openly to impiously maintain as much
concerning prayer, they do not forbid it to be made
at all, but are distributed at the prayers of the Monks;
and they act thus, that they may raise in the simple-
minded a hatred towards the Monks; so that they may
not endure even the sight of them, as though they were
profane and innovators, much less allow the dogmas
of the pious and Orthodox faith to be taught by them.
For the adversary is wise as to evil, and ingenious in
inventing calumnies. Wherefore his followers also—
such as these heretics especially—are not so much anxious about piety, as desirous of ever involving men in
an abyss of evils, and of estranging them into places,
which the Lord taketh not under his care.

They should be asked therefore, what are the
prayers of the Monks; and if they can shew that the
Monks do anything entirely different from themselves,
and not in accordance with the Orthodox worship of
Christians, we also will join with them, and say, not
only that the Monks are no Monks, but also no Christians. But if the Monks set forth particularly the glory
and wonders of God, and continually, and unremittingly, and at all times, as far as is possible for man,
proclaim the Diety, with hymns and doxologies; now
singing, forsooth, parts of Scripture, and now gathering hymns out of Scripture, or at least giving utterance
to what is agreeable to the same; we must acknowledge
that they perform a work apostolical and prophetical,
or rather that of the Lord.

Wherefore, we also, in singing the Paracletikê, the Triodion, and the Menaeon, perform a work in no wise unbecoming Christians. For all such Books discourse of the Diety as one, and yet of more than one personality, and that even in the Hymns; now gathered out of the Divine Scriptures, and now according to the direction of the Spirit; and in order that in the melodies, the words may be paralleled by other words, we sing parts of Scripture; moreover, that it may be quite plain that we always sing parts of Scripture, to every one of our Hymns, called a Troparion, we add a verse of Scripture. And if we sing, or read the Thecara [Threasury], or other prayers composed by the Fathers of old; let them say what there is in these which is blasphemous, or not pious, and we with them will prosecute these [Monks].

But if they say this only, that to pray continually and unremittingly is wrong, what have they to do with us? Let them contend with Christ—as indeed they do contend—who spake the parable of the unjust judge, how that prayer should be made continually; and taught us to watch and pray, in order to escape trials, and to stand before the Son of man. Let them contend with Paul, [who] in the [5th] Chapter of the First [Epistle] to the Thessalonians, and elsewhere in many places [exhorteth to pray unremittingly]. I forbear to mention the divine leaders of the Catholic Church, from Christ until us; for to put these [heretics] to shame sufficeth the accord of the Forefathers, Apostles, and Prophets concerning prayer.

If, therefore, what the Monks do is what the Apostles and Prophets did; and, we may say, what the holy Fathers and Forefathers of Christ Himself did; it is manifest that the prayers of the Monks are fruits of the Holy Spirit, the giver of graces. But the novelties which the Calvinists have blasphemously introduced concerning God and divine things, perverting, mutilating, and abusing the Divine Scriptures, are sophistries and invention of the devil.

Unavailing too is the assertion, that the Church cannot, without violence and tyranny, appoint fasts and abstinence from certain meats. For the Church for the mortification of the flesh and all the passions, and acting most rightly, carefully appointeth prayer and fasting, of which all the Saints have been lovers and examples; through which our adversary the devil being overthrown by the grace from on high, together with his armies and his hosts—the race that is set before the pious is the more easily accomplished. In making these provisions the undefiled Church everywhere useth neither violence nor tyranny; but exhorteth, admonisheth, and teacheth, in accordance with Scripture, and persuadeth by the power of the Spirit.

And to what hath been mentioned a certain fellow at Charenton—we mean the before-mentioned Claud —addeth certain other ridiculous objections against us, and unworthy of any consideration; but what hath been said by him we regard as idle tales; and the man himself we consider as a trifler and altogether illiterate. For from [the time of] Photius what vast numbers have there been, and there are now, in the Eastern Church, eminent for wisdom, and theology, and holiness, by the power of the Spirit.

And it is most absurd [to argue] that because certain of the Eastern Priests keep the Holy Bread in wooden vessels, within the Church, but without the Bema, hung on one of the columns; that, therefore, they do not acknowledge the real and true transmutation of the bread into the Body of the Lord. For that certain of the poor Priests do keep the Lord's Body in wooden vessels, we do not deny; for truly Christ is not honoured by stones and marbles; but asketh for a sound purpose and a clean heart.

And this is what happened to Paul. 'For we have,' saith he, 'the treasure in earthen vessels.' But where particular Churches are able, as with us here in Jerusalem, the Lord's Body is honourably kept within the Holy Bema of such Churches, and a seven-light lamp always kept burning before it.

And I am tempted to wonder, if it may be that the

heretics have seen the Lord's Body hanging in some Churches without the Bema, because perhaps the walls of the Bema were unsafe on account of age, and so have arrived at these absurd conclusions; but they did not notice Christ pourtrayed on the apse of the Holy Bema as a babe [lying] in the Paten; so that they might have known, how that the Easterns do not represent that there is in the Paten a type, or grace, or aught else, but the Christ Himself; and so believe that the Bread of the Eucharist is naught else, but becometh substantially the Body Itself of the Lord, and so maintain the truth.

But concerning all these things it hath been treated at large and most lucidly in what is called *The Confession of the Eastern Church,* by George, of Chios, from Coresius in his [Treatises] concerning the Mysteries, and of predestination, and of grace, and of freewill, and of the intercession and adoration of Saints, and of the adoration of Eikons, and in the Refutation composed by him of the illicit Synod of the heretics holden on a certain occasion in Flanders, and in many other [Treatises]; by Gabriel, of Peloponnesus, Metropolitan of Philadelphia; and by Gregory Protosyncellus of Chios in his [Treatises] concerning the Mysteries; by Jeremias, the Most Holy Patriarch of Constantinople, in three dogmatic and Synodical Letters to the Lutherans of Tübingen in Germany; by John, Priest, and Œconomus of Constantinople, surnamed Nathaniel; by Meletius Syrigus, of Crete, in the Orthodox Refutation composed by him of the Chapters and Questions of the said Cyril; by Theophanes, Patriarch of Jerusalem in his dogmatic Epistle to the Lithuanians, and in innumerable other [Epistles]. And before these hath it been spoken most excellently of these matters by Symeon, of Thessalonica, and before him by all the Fathers, and by the Œcumenical Synods, by ecclesiastical historians too; and even by writers of secular history under the Christian Autocrats of Rome, have these matters been mentioned incidently; by all of whom, without any controversy, the aforesaid were received from the Apostles; whose traditions, whether by writing, or by word, have through the Fathers descended until us.

Further, the argument derived from the heretics also confirmeth the aforesaid. For the Nestorians after the year of Salvation, 428, the Armenians too, and the Copts, and the Syrians, and further even the Æthiopians, who dwell at the Equator, and beyond this towards the tropics of Capricorn, whom those that are there commonly call Campesii, after the year . . . of the Incarnation broke away from the Catholic Church; and each of these hath as peculiar only its heresy, as all know from the Acts of the Œcumenical Synods. Albeit, as concerning the purpose and number of the Sacred Mysteries, and all what hath been said above—except their own particular heresy, as hath been said—they entirely believe with the Catholic Church; as we see with our own eyes every hour, and learn by experience and conversation, here in the Holy City of Jerusalem, in which there either dwell, or are continually sojourning, vast numbers of them all, as well learned, such as they have, as illiterate.

Let, therefore, prating and innovating heretics keep silence, and not endeavour by stealing some sentences [as] against us, from the Scriptures and the Fathers, to cunningly bolster up falsehood, as all apostates and heretics have ever done; and let them say this one thing only, that in contriving excuses for sins they have chosen to speak wickedness against God, and blasphemies against the Saints.

Epilogue.

Let this briefly suffice for the refutation of the falsehoods of the adversaries, which they have devised against the Eastern Church, alleging in support of their falsehoods the incoherent and impious Chapters of the said Cyril. And let it not be for a sign to be contradicted of those heretics that unjustly calumniate us, as though they spake truly; but for a sign to be believed, that is for reformation of their innovations, and for their return to the Catholic and Apostolic Church; in which their forefathers also were of old, and assisted at those Synods and contests against heretics, which these now reject and revile. For it was unreasonable on their part, especially as they considered themselves to be wise, to have listened to men that were lovers of self; and profane, and that spake not from the Holy Spirit, but from the prince of lies, and to have forsaken the Holy, Catholic, and Apostolic Church, which God hath purchased with the Blood of His own Son; and to have abandoned her. For otherwise there will overtake those that have separated from the Church the pains that are reserved for heathens and publicans; but the Lord who hath ever protected her against all enemies, will not neglect the Catholic Church; to Him be glory and dominion unto the ages of the ages. Amen.

THE BARMEN DECLARATION (1934)

Representatives of the Reformed and Lutheran traditions in Germany met at Barmen, May 29–30, 1934, and proclaimed a common confession of faith. The occasion for the proclamation was the rise of the Third Reich and *German* Christianity. The Barmen Declaration, as is the case with most great creedal statements, was born in very tense times and in the midst of great struggle. The Declaration is a witness, a battle cry. In the background of the Declaration is the theology of Karl Barth, with its emphasis upon the sovereign Word of God and the discontinuity of Christian faith with all other faiths. The Barmen Declaration is not a comprehensive statement of faith, but it said with clarity the one thing that needed to be said. "The Christian must listen to Jesus Christ and to Him alone."

The Declaration has continued to exert a significant influence in German theology since the Second World War.

Source: Translation printed here taken by permission of publisher from *The German Phoenix* by Franklin Hamlin Littell (Garden City, New York: Doubleday & Co., 1960), pp. 184–88. German text may be found in Beckmann, Joachim, ed., *Kirchliches Jahrbuch:* 1933–44 (Gütersloh: C. Bertelsmann Verlag, 1948), pp. 63–65. Also *Bekenntnisschriften und Kirchenordnungen* by Wilhelm Niesel (Zürich: Evangelischer Verlag, A. G. Zollikon), pp. 334–37.

Cochrane, Arthur C., *The Church's Confession under Hitler* (Philadelphia: Westminster Press, 1962).

Frey, Arthur, *Cross and Swastika* (London: SCM Press, 1938).

Kramm, H. and Cobham, J. O., *The Significance of the Barmen Declaration for the Oecumenical Church* (London: S. P. C. K., 1943).

Littell, Franklin Hamlin, *The German Phoenix* (Garden City, New York: Doubleday & Co., 1960).

THE BARMEN DECLARATION
(MAY 1934)

According to the introductory words of its constitution of 11 July 1933, the German Evangelical Church is a federal union of confessional churches which grew out of the Reformation, of equal rights and parallel existence. The theological premise of the association of these churches is given in Article 1 and Article 2, paragraph 1 of the constitution of the German Evangelical Church, recognized by the national government on 14 July 1933:

Article 1. The impregnable foundation of the German Evangelical Church is the Gospel of Jesus Christ, as it is revealed in Holy Scripture and came again to the light in the creeds of the Reformation. In this way the authorities, which the church needs for her mission, are defined and limited.

Article 2, Paragraph 1. The German Evangelical Church consists of churches (territorial churches).

We, assembled representatives of Lutheran, Reformed and United churches, independent synods, *Kirchentage* and local church groups, hereby declare that we stand together on the foundation of the German Evangelical Church as a federal union of German confessional churches. We are held together by confession of the one Lord of the one, holy, universal and apostolic church.

We declare, before the public view of all the Evangelical Churches of Germany, that the unity of this confession and thereby also the unity of the German Evangelical Church is severely threatened. In this year of the existence of the German Evangelical Church it is endangered by the more and more clearly evident style of teaching and action of the ruling ecclesiastical party of the German Christians and the church government which they run. This threat comes from the fact that the theological premise in which the German Evangelical Church is united is constantly and basically contradicted and rendered invalid, both by the leaders and spokesmen of the German Christians and also by the church government, by means of strange propositions. If they obtain, the church—according to all the creeds which are authoritative among us—ceases to be the church. If they obtain, moreover, the German Evangelical Church will become impossible as a federal union of confessional churches.

Together we may and must, as members of Lutheran, Reformed and United churches, speak today to this situation. Precisely because we want to be and remain true to our various confessions of faith, we may not keep silent, for we believe that in a time of common need and trial (*Anfechtung*) a common word has been placed in our mouth. We commit to God what this may mean for the relationship of the confessional churches with each other.

In view of the destructive errors of the German

Christians and the present national church government, we pledge ourselves to the following evangelical truths:

1. "I am the way and the truth and the life: no man cometh unto the Father, but by me." (John 14:6)

"Verily, verily, I say unto you, He that entereth not by the door into the sheepfold, but climbeth up some other way, the same is a thief and a robber. . . . I am the door: by me if any man enter in, he shall be saved." (John 10:1, 9)

Jesus Christ, as he is testified to us in the Holy Scripture, is the one Word of God, whom we are to hear, whom we are to trust and obey in life and in death.

We repudiate the false teaching that the church can and must recognize yet other happenings and powers, images and truths as divine revelation alongside this one Word of God, as a source of her preaching.

2. "But of him are ye in Christ Jesus, who of God is made unto us wisdom, and righteousness, and sanctification, and redemption." (I Cor. 1:30)

Just as Jesus Christ is the pledge of the forgiveness of all our sins, just so—and with the same earnestness —is he also God's mighty claim on our whole life; in him we encounter a joyous liberation from the godless claims of this world to free and thankful service to his creatures.

We repudiate the false teaching that there are areas of our life in which we belong not to Jesus Christ but another lord, areas in which we do not need justification and sanctification through him.

3. "But speaking the truth in love, may grow up into him in all things, which is the head, even Christ: from whom the whole body (is) fitly joined together and compacted . . ." (Eph. 4:15–16)

The Christian church is the community of brethren, in which Jesus Christ presently works in the word and sacraments through the Holy Spirit. With her faith as well as her obedience, with her message as well as her ordinances, she has to witness in the midst of the world of sin as the church of forgiven sinners that she is his alone, that she lives and wishes to live only by his comfort and his counsel in expectation of his appearance.

We repudiate the false teaching that the church can turn over the form of her message and ordinances at will or according to some dominant ideological and political convictions.

4. "Ye know that the princes of the Gentiles exercise dominion over them, and they that are great exercise authority upon them. But it shall not be so among you: but whosoever will be great among you, let him be your minister." (Matt. 20:25–26)

The various offices in the church establish no rule of one over the other but the exercise of the service entrusted and commanded to the whole congregation.

We repudiate the false teaching that the church can and may, apart from this ministry, set up special leaders (*Führer*) equipped with powers to rule.

5. "Fear God, honor the king!" (I Peter 2:17)

The Bible tells us that according to divine arrangement the state has the responsibility to provide for justice and peace in the yet unredeemed world, in which the church also stands, according to the measure of human insight and human possibility, by the threat and use of force.

The church recognizes with thanks and reverence toward God the benevolence of this, his provision. She reminds men of God's Kingdom, God's commandment and righteousness, and thereby the responsibility of rulers and ruled. She trusts and obeys the power of the word, through which God maintains all things.

We repudiate the false teaching that the state can and should expand beyond its special responsibility to become the single and total order of human life, and also thereby fulfill the commission of the church.

We repudiate the false teaching that the church can and should expand beyond its special responsibility to take on the characteristics, functions and dignities of the state, and thereby become itself an organ of the state.

6. "Lo, I am with you alway, even unto the end of the world." (Matt. 28:20) "The word of God is not bound." (II Tim. 2:9)

The commission of the church, in which her freedom is founded, consists in this: in place of Christ and thus in the service of his own word and work, to extend through word and sacrament the message of the free grace of God to all people.

We repudiate the false teaching that the church, in human self-esteem, can put the word and work of the Lord in the service of some wishes, purposes and plans or other, chosen according to desire.

The confessing synod of the German Evangelical Church declares that she sees in the acknowledgment of these truths and in the repudiation of these errors the not-to-be-circumvented theological foundation of the German Evangelical Church as a federal union of confessional churches. [The synod] calls upon all who can join in its declaration to be aware of these theological lessons in their ecclesiastical decisions. It begs all concerned to turn again in the unity of faith, of love, and of hope.

Verbum Dei manet in aeternum.

THE RELATION OF THE CHURCH TO THE WAR IN THE LIGHT OF THE CHRISTIAN FAITH (1943)

On March 16, 1943, in the midst of the Second World War, the Federal Council of the Churches of Christ in America appointed a committee of twenty-six scholars, under the Chairmanship of Professor Robert Lowry Calhoun of Yale University, to study and report upon "The Relation of the Church to the War in the Light of the Christian Faith." The assignment indicated that the commission should engage in an examination of Christian faith and its meaning for the Church in a world at war.

The resulting report is significant as an example of a catholic sharing of many theological traditions in a common theological enterprise. It is also important as a statement of the traditional Christian faith in the language of the twentieth century and for its application of Christian faith to a specific situation in such a way as to illuminate and interpret it.

The report is divided into three sections: diagnostic, doctrinal, and practical. Three chapters of the doctrinal section are printed here: The Grounds of the Christian Understanding of the War, God's Relation to the War, and Man's Part in the War.

THE CHRISTIAN FAITH AND THE WAR*

We turn now to those Christian convictions that we have found most directly relevant to our problems. The statement that follows is organized around the four main subjects just indicated: the grounds and conditions of a Christian understanding of the war; God's relation to the war; man's part in the war; the Church in a world at war.

Grounds of a Christian Understanding of the War

A. The primary ground for a distinctive Christian understanding of any situation is the revelation of God in Jesus Christ. This is not to be separated from continuing revelations of God through the work of the Holy Spirit in the history of the Hebrew people and of the Christian Church, recorded in the Old and New Testaments, and in the whole literature of Christian life. Moreover, to the eye of Christian faith and understanding, there is revelation of the same God in the histories of all peoples, in the existence, order, and growth of the whole world of nature and man, in the rise of conscience, and in every struggle for truth and

* Published in full in *Social Action*, December, 1944.

freedom. But revelation of God in Jesus Christ is the crucial disclosure, from whose light these other areas derive new meaning.

Revelation in Jesus Christ: Revelation of God in Jesus Christ takes place whenever and wherever human persons find themselves effectively confronted, through the Gospel record or some spoken word, through personal contact or social heritage, inside or outside the institutional Church, by the person Jesus of Nazareth as an embodiment of unqualified moral judgment and of regenerating power, "God's power and God's wisdom." Effectively confronted: that is to say, compelled to acknowledge him as a stubborn reality, as summons to repentance, and as source of drastic spiritual renewal. The person Jesus of Nazareth: the actual subject of that unique actual human life and death and triumph over death from which the Christian Church and the so-called Christian era of history, a new age and a new mode of life for mankind, have their beginnings. An embodiment of God's power and God's wisdom: one in whom, for Christian faith, the initiative of God for man's redemption uniquely assumed individual human form, so that uniquely and definitively "God was in Christ reconciling the world to himself."

In speaking of the revelation of God in Jesus Christ to us, we speak of a situation in which two stages of disclosure are involved. There is first the need that the man Jesus of Nazareth be disclosed to us, men of the twentieth century. This disclosure comes mainly in two ways. On the one hand, there is the written record in the New Testament of his words and deeds. There are recorded also the reactions of others, in his earthly lifetime and later, to the impact of his personal existence in history. As the record of events that are normative for Christian faith, the New Testament, though it must be interpreted by the Christian community, is itself normative for the life of that community. On the other hand, there is the Christian Church, a living community in which his spirit is still present and active. The written record and the living community cannot be separated. Each involves the other and neither can be reduced to simple dependence on, nor to simple parallelism with the other. Through both at once, the person Jesus of Nazareth makes his impress and finds his interpreters in our day, not perfectly but in the manner of all vital communication in history.

There is hidden within this historical disclosure another that gives it an added dimension of meaning and efficacy. In Jesus of Nazareth, known to us through written word and living church, was present, we believe, the redemptive Word and Will of God. Factual evidence for this conviction has been briefly indicated. Human history then and there entered a new era, became subject to divine judgment and mercy in a new way. But the conviction itself involves not only recognition of a publicly observable state of affairs. It involves a personal reorientation of the one who believes. What is meant by saying that God was in Christ is, in essential part, that Jesus Christ has been able through the centuries and is able now to awaken in men the profound personal response we call faith. Herein is made concrete and contemporary the revealing of God in Jesus Christ to us.

Like love, such faith is a personal response too inclusive and profound to be simply an overt act of either thought or will. It is a basic response of the whole self to the presence of a reality that appears overwhelmingly great and good. It is unreserved commitment in response to a Presence from which one cannot hold oneself back, any more than the eye to which light is present can withhold itself from seeing. Through this commitment, and within the personal life pervaded and conditioned by it, both knowledge and will proceed upon lines not open before, yet so related to the past life and the persisting nature of the believer that he finds in his new orientation a powerful expansion and correction of all that he has been. Through faith, as through love, he becomes a new person, in whom new insights and energies come to life, though never in simple escape from the old self nor from essential human limitations.

In a word, Christ crucified can appear as the embodiment of God's power and God's wisdom, the crucial and unique revelation of God, only to those who actually are moved by him to religious faith and who find that faith actually an enduring condition of new insight, devotion, and regenerate life. For those who are thus responsive, a basis is provided for a distinctive Christian approach to every situation that calls for understanding. As the natural scientist approaches each phenomenon, no matter how distasteful or threatening it may appear to him personally, with the confidence that in it the great regularities of the natural process will be exhibited, so the Christian comes to each event in his or mankind's history with the confidence that he is dealing with something that contains divine meaning, that is intelligible, if not in every detail yet in essence, in terms of the faithful working of God. As the former expects to have his previous understanding of natural process not only verified but also corrected and enlarged, so the latter anticipates that in each new event, loyally accepted and responded to, his understanding of God's way and will, received first in the revelation of Christ, will be corrected, widened, and particularized while it is being confirmed.

Basis of Christian Confidence: To describe in these terms the nature of revelation and of Christian faith is to make clear at once the basis for confidence and the need for caution in Christian affirmations about God and man in any complex situation, such as this war. The basis for confidence is the discovery that for oneself, for other Christians, and for the Church as enduring and expanding Christian community, the dynamic life of Jesus Christ as revelation of God has become a vital premise for all thought and action that have in view the ultimate significance of human living. Inasmuch as the actual life of Jesus must have had the specific character required to account for the actual historical results that followed and for the present personal regeneration its impact still produces, the more precisely we learn to know these historical and personal realities, their relations to the rest of nature and history, and the demands they lay upon us, the more accurately and profoundly we may hope to discern the truth and the will of God for us men. We are not dealing simply with human ideals, wishes, wistful hopes that shift like cloud-shapes, from culture to culture and from century to century. We are face to face with an actual expanding range of events in history that arise from and bear witness to an actual center, at which we believe a crucial act of God made manifest His presence and essential aspects of His nature. We affirm, then, an actual specific revelation of the abiding truth and goodness that are in God.

The revelation itself, moreover, both as an historical reality uniquely realized in space and time and as a continuing source of regenerative energy and insight for men at grips with evil today, is an ultimate objective factor in human living. As given fact, the impact of Jesus Christ on human history is not derivative from nor dependent upon some more primary presupposition such as a certain culture or a particular philosophy, within which alone it is valid. The personal commitment to which this revelation gives rise, also, is ultimate for each person who finds himself under its sway. Faith in and love for the God and Father of Jesus Christ is an ultimate inner standard, real though not external, to which the believer's life at every moment and in every decision is amenable. He cannot choose at will to be judged now by this standard and now by some other—by the standard, for example, of unqualified obedience to some national sovereign, or ultimate devotion to some racial group. Christian faith affirms that God is absolutely good, just, merciful, and that the revelation of God in Jesus Christ and the commitment which it awakens are ultimate realities and norms for every Christian. It affirms too that all these are realities and norms even for non-Christians, in the sense that human life carried on without acknowledgment of them and participation in their meaning lacks a dimension for which there is no equivalent. Thus far Christians can speak confidently.

Need for Humility: But in two obvious facts there lies a need for clear-headed humility in Christian judgments about God and human affairs. First, our apprehension of the central revelation in Jesus Christ is in many respects conditioned by our own failings. Our very faith itself, though an ultimate inner reality and norm for each of us, is variable and corruptible. Human devotion to God, though life-giving in principle and in truth, is hard to practice. Devotion to oneself is easier, and faith and insight suffer from that fact. Our understanding of the Scriptures and other records and of the living Church is conditioned in all sorts of ways by the time and place in which we live, the traditions we inherit, the lacks in our individual heredity and training, the blind spots made in us by special interests, desires, and fears. Furthermore, the written records through which the Word of God is transmitted to us, and the Church as historical community in which the spirit of Jesus Christ is alive, themselves leave room for honest differences of understanding. In the Scriptures, the Word of God is mediated through very diverse witnesses, who wrote in the midst of historical situations, known to us only in part, that helped to shape their insights and their words. The institutional Church has come to be not one community but many, and its witness in both word and deed is often confused and contradictory.

Secondly, the specific implications of the revealed truth for human understanding and conduct in a particular present situation can be discerned only by processes of thought that are liable at every step to the risk of error. Sincere Christians who agree on the primary demand of love for neighbors and enemies can disagree on its meaning for statesmen, citizens, and victims of belligerent powers. Too confident assertions about the details of Christian duty, as though human judgment could ever claim the infallibility of God, are presumptuous and self-refuting. There is need then for humility on the part of every Christian.

But to recognize clearly these limitations, and to welcome rather than to evade or suppress the criticisms they invite, can hold the way open for correction of human errors and for emergence of fresh visions of the truth. If our minds are twisted this way and that by undisciplined wishes and fears, so that we can see in the witness of Scriptures and Church only what serves our special interests, then in candid fellowship we need the more earnestly to practice self-denial and openheartedness for the sake of the very truth we profess. Though our faith can never be made perfect in this life, it can by just such persistent correction become less bound by our cravings for safety or self-justification, and more responsive to the truth that is in God. If the Scriptures and the other Jewish and Christian records of God's dealings with our fathers, through which He speaks also to us, cannot be detached from the complexities of human history, the more need for devoted, clear-eyed Christian scholarship to help us see more plainly the truth that shines through them. If the churches speak with a confusion of tongues, more patient exploration of their past and present existence is bringing to light a persisting deeper unity, and increased recognition of mutual need can make that unity still more vital and more reassuring.

In all this acknowledgment of human limitation, and hope for more light, we trust confidently in the gracious wisdom of God, who has not permitted men to rest in error, nor suffered the light of His gospel to be quenched or confined. Through the centuries of turmoil, in spite of human weakness and the opposition of demonic powers, Christian faith has grown around the globe. Herein we see the gracious Spirit of truth, in whose presence our darkness is lightened and our faith confirmed. We have no ground for claims to full knowledge of the truth that is vital to all human living, but we are assured that the Holy Spirit will continue to overrule our errors and guide us into more light.

God's Relation to the War

B. In this mood, we venture to affirm next our belief that God's relation to the war is defined in broad terms by His essential unitary activity as Creator, Redeemer, Life-Giver. These are not three activities, but one, as the Father, Son, and Holy Spirit of Christian teaching are not three Gods but one. In seeking, then, to discern God more clearly by such distinctions as these, we must never suppose that creation and redemption, or judgment and mercy, can be so separated that in a given act of God, one is present without the other. It is true that for minds like ours, some areas of history are far easier to interpret as stark fact than as regenerative action, as displaying ruthless judgment rather than forgiving mercy. But Christian faith in one God forbids taking the appearance of separate, mutually exclusive segments of divine activity as the truth. God is one, and His essential activity with respect to us men and our world is one. The infinitely diverse power and range of that activity as revealed to us we try to apprehend more concretely by attending now to one aspect, now to another, and by seeing all these manifold aspects of divine action as displaying God in three primary roles: creation, redemption, renovation. In the war, God is active in all these personal ways.

God as Creator: The doctrine of God as Maker of heaven and earth forbids any assertion that He is aloof from the war. In the first place, that doctrine holds that the existence of every situation depends on the creative energy of God's will, put forth not merely in some past moment of time but throughout all time. In the next place, it holds that as God's energy transcends and pervades all time, all history, so likewise it transcends and pervades all that we call space, in such wise that from no portion of the existing world is God absent. He is the living and present Creator of all men and all nations. Thirdly, it holds that the presence of God is never static but always active presence, not merely form or law but energy. God then is present, active, creative, in every part of nature and history, and so in this war.

But the manner of God's omnipresence as Creator is further defined by the fact that what He creates is existent as other than Himself. God is not identical with the world, nor with any part of it. If there is no event from which God is absent, equally there is no event in which God alone is present. In as far as creation is effective, it brings into existence and maintains in existence subordinate centers and fields of energy that are at once yielding and resistant to the continuing energy of their Creator, as well as embodying attraction and repulsion, partial harmony and partial discord among themselves.

This comment applies with especial pertinence to human history, and to the war, in which natural and impersonal forces are complicated in their working by the continuous cross fire of personal human decisions, and by the consequences of past decisions. The latter may go on long after the initial act, in large part as impersonally as widening and mingling ripples in a pool, so that there is always some temptation to regard them simply as natural entities devoid of moral significance. Slums can look much like swamps, caste systems like terraced hillsides, wars like hurricanes; and both popular and learned opinion has often regarded them as facts of nature or "acts of God." In protest against such easy reduction of important segments of history to natural mechanisms, other interpreters have insisted that slums, caste systems, and wars are all moral realities through and through, the direct and continuous manifestations of human choices and especially of human sins. The truth as it seems to us is that the war is neither simply a natural fact nor an act of God nor a sinful choice of man. It is a complex event in which all of these factors are present, and need to be duly recognized. God, then, acts in the war as the creative ground that continuously keeps the warring world and its members in existence, and enables them to act in accordance with their respective natures or decisions. God does not act as an all-inclusive "One-and-All," nor in any way that excludes or nullifies decision and action by His creatures. Moreover, God does not act as a world Ruler who has willed the outbreak of the war, nor all those specific antecedent conditions that made the war inescapable. Some of these conditions God directly wills, we believe—the freedom and the interdependence of men, the inseparability of moral decisions from natural consequences, and the like. Others are the resultants of natural forces that operate in relatively uniform causal networks, perhaps without complete mechanical fixity but presumably without the foresight or decision characteristic of persons: natural forces that operate, then, often in ways that enhance or destroy values, even perhaps in ways that further or hamper the will of God, but that are not themselves amenable to moral judgment. Some are the personal decisions of men, together with their antecedents and consequences, some personal, others more or less impersonal, but all identified more directly with responsible human action than with the irresponsible forces of extra-human nature, and all involving a crucial factor of human difference from, and often of opposition to, the will of God.

We notice next another aspect of God's creative action in the war. As Creator He is not only the source of existence in all creatures. He is the ground also of their respective actual natures and primary relationships. His world is a world of order, not caprice. Those causal and moral interrelations noticed in the foregoing paragraphs are established and maintained by His creative power. The particular combinations that arise within these fabrics of ordered existence and action are, in every instance, the resultants of both divine and creaturely activity, as we have seen. But the overall persistence of order, both natural and moral, in spite of local spasms of natural and personal conflict, and in the closest union with human freedom and with whatever natural fluidness this freedom may imply, is referable directly to the sovereign presence of God. There is indeed a divinely established "order of creation," a universal "law of nature" that has both natural and moral aspects, though as we have seen it will not do to assign to this order without more ado such human institutions as slums, caste systems, slavery, claims of racial inequality, or any particular social, political, or ecclesiastical pattern in history. War is not divinely ordained, any more than these other historical emergents. But in war, as in all of these, divine law and order are present and in the long run controlling, even when human law and order are damaged or demolished by human action.

Lastly, God as Creator "is good, and the Author only of good to men," as Greek wisdom affirmed long ago. His creative will and His providential rule are set to favor not all sorts of action equally, but those that make for the realization of truth, beauty, justice, mercy, good faith, devoted love, and all else that accords with His perfection whether it be known to us or not. The God revealed in Jesus Christ is not a neutral Force but the infinitely perfect Father. His goodness is indeed of a different order from that of most good men. He cares for the unthankful and the evil. He gives sun and rain alike to the just and the unjust, and lets the tares grow along with the wheat. His valuations often are puzzling to sincerely righteous men, who not unnaturally suppose that unequal work in the vineyard deserves unequal pay and that gold pieces in the alms box weigh more than a widow's coppers. He lets His best beloved Son be crucified between two men of violence because He loves them. But in spite of all appearances, He is a God of order and righteousness, who makes even the wrath of men to praise Him. For He is God above all other gods.

In this war, then, He is not neutral, and not helpless. He is maintaining invincibly an order that men cannot overthrow. Moreover, He is taking sides throughout the struggle, not with the Axis powers nor with the United Nations, nor with any government nor any institutional church or churchman, but with the impulses toward good and against the impulses toward evil in every man and every group in both camps. God is not a combatant, nor a neutral onlooker, nor a helpless victim. First of all, He is, in war as in peace, the Creator and Sovereign whose power sustains and governs, but does not annul, the activities of nature and of men.

God as Redeemer: At the same time and for the same reason, His own perfect goodness, God is in the war as Redeemer. Divine redemption of the world appears to us men under two aspects that can be distinguished but never separated. Redemption embraces both judgment and forgiveness. So we speak of divine justice and mercy, and we seek both in this war, remembering that nowhere ought we expect to find the one without the other. As Calvin wisely noted, even a human judge cannot pronounce an equitable sentence without mercy; nor can mercy work in opposition to justice, nor wait until merciless judgment is first wreaked upon the offender, and be redemptive. No doubt in human action, because it is imperfect, what is called justice is often separated from what is called mercy; but in the perfect redemptive love of God, the two are inseparable at every moment of time. We believe that this is always true as regards the divine intent and action, however difficult it may be at times for men to discern both aspects.

Divine judgment in the war can be plainly seen at two levels. First, as we have noted, there is a natural and moral order of creation that God maintains against all man's wayward efforts in peace and in war. For human persons, that order has especial significance in these respects: that every man is in his essential nature a responsible person, as well as a natural being; that all men are interdependent, as well as dependent upon their natural environment with its network of causal processes; and that the primary demand upon every man in this situation is love, for God, for men as children of God, and for nature as man's temporal home. Man may act, in both peace and war, as though these primary conditions of his life did not exist, but they hold fast and his denials in thought and act bring calamity upon himself, his fellows, and his natural home. Divine judgment is not vengeful. It is inexorable. And in war, more vividly than in quieter times, men can see its fearful majesty. In times when human conflict operates below the threshold of armed warfare, men sow with busy hands the winds of private and public aggression or negligence, of headstrong ignorance or cunning treachery. In times of open warfare, they reap the hurricane of outraged human life and divine power. In a terrible way, the fury of war vindicates the existence and inescapability of divine law.

Secondly, God's judgment in war time negates not merely the selfish conduct of men, but also their inadequate ideals for living. There are many of our accustomed ways of action that we are ready to acknowledge to be wrong, even though usually we hope that the fitting penalty for them may somehow be escaped. But other ways of ours seem to us surely right, and the ideals we hold often seem to us beyond criticism. It is hard not to think we know what is right even when we do otherwise. Service to one's country, or to one's church, for example, seems surely right, and the ideal of patriotism or of church loyalty that moves us in our most devoted moments seems wholly good. Precisely at these points of human self-confidence the judgment of God cuts deep. The very group loyalty in which we take pride and find a basis for self-righteousness is shown up in the fierce light of warfare to be tinctured with deadly poison. For uncritical group loyalty is a potent source of war, it helps to intensify hatred while war goes on, it is most characteristic of the more aggressive and tyrannous nations in the present war, and it can retard for generations our attempts to establish a peaceful world when this war has run its course. The judgment of God writ large in wartime says: "Patriotism is not enough." Human righteousness at any level thus far achieved is not enough. That is true in times of comparative quiet. It becomes glaringly evident in times of war.

Is then war itself to be called "a divine judgment," or an instrument thereof? Does God decree war to punish the waywardness of men? We have said no. War is not divinely ordained, any more than slums or slavery. God's will is always that men shall live at peace with one another and with Him. This is true at all times and without any exception. This refers not simply to armed warfare. It is not God's will that men shall carry on covert strife with one another, and with Him, under the name of peace. When that is done, His will is already being violated, and the outbreak of open war makes that fact plain. It is not God's will that war shall come upon mankind, at any time, nor that it be regarded as a suitable instrument for good. It is God's will that the primary order of natural and human life be maintained, and in presence of that order some sorts of human conduct bring war. The order itself is confirmed and vindicated. The specific decisions that make war break out are man's decisions, not God's. Moreover, the specific decisions we make thereafter, in seeking to do "the right as God gives us to see the right" are still our decisions, not God's. War is not, then, "a judgment of God" in the sense that God wills it as a punishment for men. It serves to reveal and vindicate the judgment of God that upholds inexorably the order of His world even though in the presence of that order some combinations of human decision and natural causation, in resistance to God's will for peace, bring war.

God's judgment, in a word, is never merely punitive. Man brings down punishment when he acts in violation of God's law made dynamic by God's will. Yet that very law is even in its rigor a gift without which neither natural nor personal life could go on, and the will that maintains it is even in its unyieldingness a will to more abundant life. Divine judgment is redemptive in purpose, and it becomes so in effect, as far as men are brought by its unceasing pressures to respond in repentance and faith.

To make this clear to ourselves, we seek in the war for evidences also of divine mercy. First, we find such evidence in the fact that in the midst of the terrifying bitterness and hatred, deceit and disruption of war, there are signs of recreative forces at work it would seem continuously. In part these have a character so drastic that mercy may seem a strange word for them. If that be true, there is need to remind ourselves that divine mercy means not softness but healing, not passivity but regeneration. If divine judgment is not without mercy, divine mercy is not without rigor. Its distinctive character lies in its positive purging, renovating, and reconciling power. This power is discernible in war, on the social side, in the successive breaking down of refuges for human self-sufficiency, and the positive affirmation of interdependence. Every country at war is compelled to seek internal unity, even at the cost of many vested privileges. This is not by the will of men. Self-interest is not displaced in war time. Wilful resistance to rationing laws and pressure group tactics for winning private advantages, sharpening of racial, regional, and class jealousies, and departmental factionalism bear witness to the contrary. Likewise, competition and distrust between allied nations even in the face of a dangerous foe make it clear that war does not wholly purge men and nations of divisive self-interest. Yet in spite of these symptoms of continuing illness, the very necessities of war time compel the redoubling of efforts to extend the scope of effective cooperation. Old barriers give way here and there. The self-confidence of a ruling class or the provincialism of a self-satisfied folk group is shaken by new contacts. A new sense of the meaning of wastage of natural resources for human life takes shape. So halting, reluctant, but inescapable awareness of the fact of human and natural interdependence and the need for better cooperation is forced upon men by their very struggles. This is not the purpose of warfare, but it happens in time of war and by reason of some of the special conditions of such a time. Similarly, the pressures of belligerent needs help to stimulate intellectual and technical enterprise, and to force pooling of information and resources, in such fashion that results are quickly achieved (in medicine, in the mechanical arts, in communication, and in social organization) that may be of great value when more peaceable life is resumed. These achievements may be morally neutral in themselves, but the devoted effort spent in reaching them and the new patterns of human cooperation they make possible are not neutral. And in so far as knowledge is better than ignorance, such discoveries have worth that cannot be denied a place among the gifts of God.

Secondly, to some individual men in war time there come searching insights into the meaning of human life and the will of God. Undisciplined wastrels may find new responsibility, snobbish aristocrats or proletarians new respect for their fellows, complacent worldlings a new humility in the presence of engulfing tragedy. Such change may come to men either in or out of uniform, and find expression in words and acts that long outlast the fighting. Particular episodes can be highlighted in the prevailing darkness of war so that they become more effective witnesses to the perpetual beauty of righteousness than the routine of more peaceable living is likely to provide. There must be no exaggeration of these gleams of light, and no minimizing of the horrors against which they are visible. There must be no hint that war is justifiable as a source of human betterment. The point here is rather that, for all its ghastliness, war bears the marks of a Power that works in it for good.

Underlying the two sets of detailed evidence just reviewed, and more impressive than all of them together, we are able to discern what may be called a residual health of mankind that resists and survives the fevers of war. Herein is the active mercy of God to be seen, quietly and invincibly at work. We affirm in this specific sense Augustine's judgment, "Nothing can be evil except something which is good." Disease can exist only in a living body, and the very forces of life work to resist disease and to restore health. It is so in national societies, when a despot more powerful than any Caesar cannot prevent Germans from reading the Old Testament or befriending Jews. It is so in international warfare, when the exigencies of war itself cannot altogether prevent men from acting humanely and applauding decency. This we affirm is good evidence that God is in the midst of the struggle as healing power.

Shall we say also as the victim of a new crucifixion? Is war itself a Golgotha, and suffering humanity a new embodiment of the crucified Redeemer? In particular, can we say that the men killed in battle, or the refugees driven out to wander and starve, or the children who die in bomb shelters or blockaded famine areas are vicarious redeemers of our time? We share deeply in the desire of bereaved parents and comrades, and of chaplains and pastors to say these things, but they must not be said carelessly. War is in a general sense a crucifixion of both man and God, but it is not the the crucifixion of Jesus Christ, and it is not a chief source of man's salvation. What made the tragedy on Calvary uniquely redemptive was the Man on the middle cross, and the unmixed revelation of love and power that was in him. There were crosses on either side of him, and there have been many before and after. In a sense men have been crucifying one another, and in a different sense crucifying God, from the beginning of human history. But only one crucifixion has become a central spring of light and grace for mankind. Let the Church, then, say that in the light of that Crucifixion we see more deeply and clearly the meaning of this present struggle. We see that in our world, the burden of suffering is not distributed according to guilt and innocence, but that all suffer, even the best. We see that the spirit in which suffering and death are confronted can make them vehicles of life for many rather than merely of loss. We see that as the cross of Jesus Christ demonstrated the power of God to overcome evil in its very moment of victory, there is good ground to hope for a like conquest continuing today and tomorrow. We and our brothers are not the saviors of mankind. The Savior is God, who suffers for us, with us, at our own hands, yet in such a way that the outcome is life perpetually made new. Our part is to bear witness to this saving work of God.

God as Holy Spirit: One more dominant role must be ascribed to God in the war, as in all human history: His special work as Holy Spirit, Sanctifier, Sustainer, Life-Giver. This aspect of His presence and action, once more, is not to be thought of as separate from His presence as Creator and as sovereign Redeemer. God is one, and His work is indivisible. Hence, in what has already been said of universal creation and providence, divine judgment and mercy, the work of God as Holy Spirit has been often in view. Yet it is right to recognize along with these more general activities a special range of peculiarly personal relationship between God and those men who actually respond to His presence in conscious trust. Through such men, God is able to perform works of power that are not possible in lives ruled by unbelief. This is in a special way the distinctive work of the Holy Spirit.

The chief of such miracles has already been referred to in the discussion of divine mercy: the actual remaking of persons hard hit by the war, yet quickened into faith and devotion so that they become new and better men and women. This is the Spirit's work of sanctification, springing from God's redemptive love, and issuing in human life transformed, redirected, with new dimensions in which to grow. Nurturing such growth, likewise, toward the full stature of the manhood whose norm is Jesus Christ is the work of the same Spirit, whose impulse is one and whose gifts are many. The impulse is devoted love for God and man, for all that is good, true, and right. Among the gifts are reinforced strength and courage, sharpened insight and self-forgetfulness, steadfast patience and serenity and joy, invincible security, and others too many to name. Including them all is an abiding experience of heightened, deepened, broadened fellowship with men and nature, and with God.

The undivided Source of such new life, and the abiding Sustainer of communion among men and communion of men with God, the Holy Spirit is the living Ground of community as personal fellowship and as corporate life. Where the Spirit works, there diversity becomes enrichment of a common good rather than mere conflict or mutual destruction. We see this Spirit working wherever men are faithful to one another and to the best they know, wherever recognition of human kinship is maintained in spite of separation and strife, and especially wherever men are united in devotion to the one eternal God of heaven and earth. Upon this ground rest our understanding of the existence of the Christian Church itself, and our hope that its members and constituent bodies everywhere will find themselves increasingly pervaded by one shared and growing life.

A striking way in which this divine work comes to be affirmed in war time, with varying degrees of Christian insight, is the report from many quarters of a new sense, that comes to sorely tried men, of the fellowship of the Holy Spirit in hardship and peril, a sense often of supernatural help and protection. In this war, as in earlier wars, there is first-hand testimony, much of it startling, some of it very moving, with respect to the survival of hard-pressed pilots or mariners through unforeseen and powerful aid beyond known human powers. To the minds of many, these are palpable miracles in our time, like the "mighty works" that first century Christians took as signs and gifts of the Holy Spirit. Our problem now, like St. Paul's then, is to keep clear the right lines of Christian conviction across an area in which human cravings and emotions are uncommonly strong. It seems to us right to affirm that to every devoted person in war time, Christian or non-Christian, combatant or non-combatant, the presence of God offers an accessible source of power and spiritual security. Especially through genuine prayer, however inarticulate, a human spirit is opened toward God who is never absent, and strengthened to bear rightly whatever burden must be borne. That fresh energies, beyond the shallows drawn upon in ordinary living, can be tapped under conditions of great stress has long been known, and fresh testimony to the fact is welcome. Such energies, and such guidance as the hidden perceptions within men's bodies and minds may provide in times of extreme peril or exhaustion, can indeed manifest the watchful care of the God who neither slumbers nor sleeps.

But as in St. Paul's day, so in ours it is vital to insist that no marvel of force nor of physical guidance, not even a rescue from impending bodily death, is in itself a sufficient evidence of a special working of the Holy Spirit. The crucial test is still the old one: Is the spirit of man, in the presence of these marvels, brought closer to the pattern of the spirit of Jesus Christ? Of two men confronted by the same event, one may be moved to self-searching, humility, and new devotion, the other to self-satisfaction and arrogance. It seems not too rash to say that one has heard in rescue from peril the voice of God, the other only a magnified echo of his own.

The difference becomes very clear in the differing attitudes of those who pray in war time. It is good that men are moved to pray in times of especial stress, far better if they pray continually in good times and bad, both in words and in unspoken cravings and grateful impulses. We believe that the half-involuntary, unaccustomed cry for help and the calm reaffirmation of a lifelong trust are alike understood and accepted by an infinite Father. But they can scarcely be answered alike. Prayer is a mutual relationship between personal spirits and its significance and results are necessarily dependent on the characters, attitudes, and actions of both participants. We are assured that God will unfailingly provide, in answer to every one who turns to Him sincerely in prayer, the utmost of good that the attitude of the petitioner and the whole situation permit. But that good will often be very different from what the petitioner seeks. In particular, there is no warrant for expecting that God will protect from physical harm all those who call upon Him however sincerely, nor that prayers are enough to assure military victory or avert another war. Prayers for all these things can be offered, with or without Christian insight and faith. The one kind of petition, we believe, that God cannot accept as genuine prayer at all is a presumptuous and self-righteous effort to use Him and His power for human ends, chosen without regard to His will. Humble prayer for safety or for bread can be real prayer. Yet we believe that those soldiers pray best who pray in the spirit of the young officer who wrote to his family from Bataan: "My prayer each night is that God will send you His strength and peace. During the first few days of the war, I prayed also for personal protection from physical harm, but now, that I may be given strength to bear whatever I must bear, and do whatever I must do, so that those men under me will have every reasonable chance." The models for prayer in time of trial are still the prayers in Gethsemane and on the cross: "Abba, Father, all things are possible unto thee; take away this cup from me; nevertheless not what I will, but what thou wilt." "Father, forgive them; for they know not what they do." "Father, into Thy hands I commend my spirit."

Man's Part in the War

C. In speaking of God's action in the war, we have spoken continually of man's action also. This is neither accidental nor avoidable. No sharp line can be drawn through the world nor through any part of it with God's acts on one side, man's on the other. In every historical event, both God and man are actively present though neither can at any point be simply identified with the other. Now we seek to view the same war situation from another angle, and ask what man is doing to himself and in relation to God in the struggle. In Christian terms, our concern here is man as creature, as sinner, and as subject of redemption.

Man as Creature Enjoying the Status of Responsible Freedom: First, then, we recognize the existence of man as created personal being. We think of man as emergent in the midst of nature, called into being by the creative power of God, to become a personal self. His natural status is not thus denied, but a further range of life is opened out for him: a status we know as responsible freedom. Man's freedom is visible most simply in his ability to judge his environment and himself, intellectually and morally. In perceptual judgment, in memory and anticipation, and in reasoning to new conclusions such as he has never hitherto experienced, man asserts his partial independence of the physical situation in which at any moment he stands. In self-consciousness he brings even his own thinking under review, and in moral self-criticism he compares himself with standards that he neither has attained nor can attain. In making and carrying out practical decisions, he alters what would have been the natural course of events, and makes both the world and himself different from what they would have been. In this sense, man affirms his freedom in every act of critical awareness, and especially in self-consciousness, moral judgment, and personal decision.

This freedom is not negated but complemented by the fact that as person, a man is a responsible being. For responsibility is first of all ability to respond to factors for which many living things have no capacity for response. Truth, justice, humbleness are duties for man because the meanings, the patterns of life, for which these words stand are discernible by him and awaken acknowledgment in him. The presence of other persons as persons, moreover, not as means to his pleasure but as ends for his devotion, and the presence of God beyond all natural and human goods—to these also he is capable of appropriate response, and to them he is thence responsible. Herein is his more-than-animal freedom the more concretely defined. In being thus obligated, as irresponsible creatures are not, he is the more genuinely free—free, as they are not, to be a person intent upon freely chosen good, whose constraint upon him is not compulsion but obligation, that can be denied though not escaped.

This paradox of freedom and constraint runs throughout man's existence as social being. Not only is he under obligation to the law of God—the ingrained patterns of the world and his own being that require of him willing affirmation of what is true and right—but he is bound up so intimately with the lives of his fellow-men that apart from them he cannot be himself. Only in community can persons be persons. Yet in human community, growing individuals achieve maturity as persons only through both yielding and resistance to the demands of fellowship. Tension between individual and group, between person and person, between group and group is a constant pattern of growing human life. Group loyalty and individual self-assertion are both indispensable to such personal life as we know, even at its best. This dependence of each person upon the social groups in which he is a member obviously limits his freedom by committing him in advance to specific folkways, in which he is nurtured and which enter into him as presuppositions for action. He becomes a child of his people, his nation, his culture, with his decisions partly predetermined by this social parentage; yet without some such determinations he could not achieve the freedom of personal living at all.

In rigidly authoritarian societies or groups, this sort of moulding through conscious training and the pressure of custom can make it extremely hard for individual persons to act, or even to think freely in relation to the nurturing group. So it is in our day for the young people of both Germany and Japan. Among them, group loyalty has been stressed and personal dissent discouraged until the very meaning of critical independence, one may suppose, has still to be learned. Yet even under extreme conditions, there are two ways in which a person can find a new lease of freedom with respect to his nation or people. One way is through human contacts that make him realize that his nation is one member of a world society in which diverse national and cultural patterns exist in a wider human context. He is himself, therefore, a member of that world society as well as of his smaller group, and the scope of his loyalty is widened, the details of it modified, by this realization. He can still be a devoted patriot if the well-being of his nation is clearly seen to be inseparable from the well-being of the wider society and its other members. But this is different from the patriotism of the unawakened nationalist. A second way to such liberation is through direct conscious dependence on God and His universal laws. This is "the liberty of a Christian man," that sets one free from any cultural, political, or secular absolutism, though not from the demands of God.

In still another way man's freedom is restricted: by his dependence upon nature and history through his particular place in space and time. That he can transcend this location in some fundamental respects we have seen. He has power to think his way out beyond any specifiable limits of spatial or temporal extent. But he cannot escape the actual impacts and restraints, the defects and frustrations that are part and parcel of the world-scene into which he is born. In war time, he cannot escape the special impacts and frustrations of such a time; nor in any given age of history can he live as though the conditions that help to bound his life were not real. Attempts to escape from reality, in this sense, can lead indeed to an irresponsibility of weakness and false comfort but not to an increase of personal freedom. On the other hand, loyal acceptance of the actual place in nature and history into which one is born and grows, and at the same time persistent effort to discern the truth and right that are God's law for human living, can extend one's freedom even though one's finiteness is never left behind. The fact of bodily death is the perpetual reminder that one is finite. Yet even in the presence of death, men can be free moral selves.

Man who is thus at once finite and free becomes a genuine person, then, growing in wisdom and stature, in awareness and integrity, by accepting his responsible status and willingly affirming as his own good the truth and right that are involved in God's world-order. The law is at once around him and within him. He is summoned to obey God and thus to become more fully himself. Through love toward God and his fellow-men, and appreciation of his natural home, his own life is widened, deepened, and carried on toward fulfilment.

Man as Sinner: Conversely, man is a sinner when he denies his responsibility to God and men, and so violates his own nature and his own good as personal self. Such violation is always wrought by personal decision. It is never the automatic result of natural impacts, as bodily injury or disease may be. In these latter instances a person does not actively identify himself with the corrupting change and make it his own. But in asserting his interests without due regard to his neighbor's, in seeking pleasure or profit or power in defiance of equity, in treating persons as things or the will of God as though it were the will of man, a person affirms as his own the falsehoods that such conduct involves. This is sin, and through such commitment to falsehood a person becomes bound in a different way from the ways that mark his finiteness. As sinner he has corrupted his own powers and become less fully a person than before, less able to see truth and right clearly, and less resistant to the pressures of nature and human society that continually threaten his integrity and personal freedom.

What men thus do as individuals, they do also in groups. Human society as we know it is organized on the understanding that both loyalty and disloyalty are to be expected. We build vast credit systems that presuppose general good faith, and parallel them with police courts and prisons to deal with expected violations. We form voluntary associations for business, education, research, communal worship, held together mainly by voluntary ties, and we organize elaborate coercive machinery in the name of the State to keep the peace when quarrels arise. Within the modern nation, most disputes can be settled either by agreement or by legal coercion. But since no effective government yet runs beyond the frontiers of a state, when international disputes arise, with major collisions of national interests, the stresses and conflicts of ordinary times are likely to deteriorate sooner or later into war.

If we ask how man's sinfulness is manifest in this war, our answer can only select from the appalling tangle a few typical threads. Without minimizing the fateful consequences of the policies and decisions of the Axis governments, we can say that war came not because the peoples on both sides deliberately willed it, but because enough people on each side willed, half-gropingly, half-wittingly, their own apparent advantage without due regard to the obligations of human community and divine order. This involved both deep-seated lack of trust in God and neighbor, and faithlessness to promises given or implied, each act of faithlessness itself prompted in part by suspicion of the others' good faith. To this mesh of distrust all peoples have contributed through all history to the present outbreak, and the weaving of the web still goes on. Bad faith between men presupposes, in large part, men's distrust of God. Instead of seeking security and fullness of life through acceptance of His ways, they have tried to seize and hold these good things by defrauding or subjugating other men. And other men have sought to secure themselves against loss by more subtle deceptions or more powerful retaliations.

Add to faithlessness the kindred sins of pride and idolatry. In pride men seek to achieve fulfilment through the exercise of power above their fellows. During ordinary times, the means are economic, intellectual, social, political, ecclesiastical. The unending struggle for preferment, and assertion of superiority, develops in each people a tradition—almost an ethic—of ambition and domination, a half-articulate *Herrenmoral* in which children are reared believing that life can have savor only through the exercise of lordship. In this context, lesser dominations lead to striving for greater ones. Success already won must be protected against the resentful victim and the envious rival. Success for oneself becomes identified with dominance for one's business house, or class, or church, or nation. Small nations fear larger neighbors and make alliances against them. Large nations fear encirclement, build up armaments, and seek to use small neighbors as outposts against larger ones. Trade rivalries grow into diplomatic contests, and irredentist minorities become symbols of inferiority to be put right. And so at last to war, in which there is no self-confessed aggressor but only aggrieved defenders of imperiled security.

Another way of saying much the same thing is to say that in seeking unrivaled dominance and impregnable security, men are seeking for themselves, their church, their country the status of God. Idolatry thus underlies and aggravates human conflict, in peacetime and in war. In the degree to which one's own finite objects of devotion are treated as absolutes, the crusading temper against which Christian insight within the Church has turned, in recent years, tends to reappear on secular grounds. Defense of home and country, of capitalism, imperialism, or democracy, can become defense of "the faith."

The counterpart to pride and self-seeking, present also in all peoples in varying degree, is moral lethargy and that effort to escape irksome responsibility to which we have already referred. The very persons who are jealous of their own security and privilege are too often unconcerned about the security and freedom of others, and unwilling to share with them the task of seeking opportunity for all. Aggression and irresponsibility, tyranny and anarchy, two major forms of social sin, feed one upon the other. Deliberate wrongdoing and ignorant unconcern are a human soil in which the dragon's teeth take root and grow.

Wars, then, are not the outcome of wicked acts of particular men, in isolation from a great body of shared social evil. They grow out of that massive moral and religious wrongness which is the seed-bed of all our specific transgressions, and to which all of us and all our forebears have contributed. For in affirming as our own these war-breeding attitudes toward God and men, we have identified ourselves with the drift toward war, whether we have deliberately sought war or simply a more privileged place in the sun.

Once open war begins, under modern conditions, the malignant propagation of sin becomes a kind of perverted virtue. Systematic lying to both foes and friendly peoples becomes an implement of statecraft. Atrocious cruelties are practiced in hot blood and with cold deliberation. Reports of such cruelties are kept on file, and coined at the proper time into righteous fury and support for counter-measures. Young men are schooled in fighting methods derived from the jungle and improved by cool intelligence and careful experiment. Hatred and ruthlessness are approved, mass exterminations of enemy troops are sought and of civilians are practiced, military necessity tends to become the supreme guiding principle of conduct.

What thus comes to horrid fruitage in the war had its roots, once again, in the behavior of men and nations before the war broke out. Hideous brutalities, cold-blooded treacheries, cowardly evasions, callous stupidities—all these and more we must charge against our present enemies, our allies, and ourselves in varying proportions during the years of miscalled peace. There is no warrant for blurring the differences of situation, behavior, and objectives of the various powers during that armed truce. Some were concerned chiefly to keep advantages already won; some were more bent on revenge and the seizure of increased power at the expense of their neighbors. Some were prepared to maintain, chiefly for their own peoples, such measures of freedom and equity as they had inherited and developed; some were intent on destroying both freedom and equity for the sake of greater power at home and abroad. Though all were involved in sin, their ways of sinning were not identical in the sight of God, we believe, nor in their portent for the common life of men. In the actual course of events, dominance by the Axis powers would have fastened upon their own peoples and upon conquered lands a reign of tyranny and terror full of danger to humane living everywhere. Resistance to such rule, whether by armed force or by more peaceful means, became imperative. We speak here with keen awareness of the confusions of human motives, the mingling of good with bad intents, the differences among striving human groups that mark each new situation in history. We have in view at the same time the certainty that our own judgment of all these matters is biased and incomplete. Yet one judgment concerning the years of uneasy truce seems clear. Every nation then was concerned more for the immediate advantage of self than for the larger welfare of mankind and for the glory of God as Lord of all. Every nation, moreover, thus jeopardized even its own well-being, along with that of its neighbors, since none can long prosper alone.

To the sins of the prewar years, also, the conduct of the war itself has added greatly. It is not to be thought that with the outbreak of war, the distinction between sin and suffering temporarily disappears, so that all who are involved become helpless victims of unmoral necessity because all chance for significant decision is ended until hostilities cease. War is not hell, save in metaphor. It displays horrors, indeed, that are worthy of hell, but they are in essential part the results of continuing decisions of men who are at once bound and free in exactly the same sense in which men are bound and free in the intervals before and after a war. The specific decisions open to them are not the same nor, of course, are the specific conditions —the intellectual barriers and social pressures—under which they must decide. These become far more restrictive, and the range of choice more narrow. But as long as persons are living persons, there is no situation in which their decisions cease to be significant before God.

The view that the war is, for the persons involved in it, a morally neutral though spiritually horrible interlude in human history may seem to find a certain plausibility in another consideration: the distortions of human goodness in war as we know it. On the one hand, spiritual excellences of many sorts are intrinsic, not accidental, to the conduct of war. This war is the outcome and the scene not only of sin and of natural necessity, but also of impulses to good among many plain people. Besides the faithlessness that leads to the breakdown of peaceable ways, there is the loyalty that keeps men together under fire. There are promises honored at heavy cost as well as promises broken. There is concern for one's own country and children, and also for weaker peoples abroad, with whose security one's own is involved. This kind of faithfulness of men to one another is characteristic of all armies not demoralized into mobs. Without it war could not go on. There is courage of many grades, up to the lambent heroism of soldiers who smother grenades with their bodies in order that the men beside them may live, or the quiet faith of chaplains who give their lifebelts to others and go down with a sinking troop ship. There is love and self-sacrifice and generosity—even at times toward the enemy. The spirit of man is not simply bad in war.

But the good that men do in war has to be done mainly at the expense of genuine elements of good in what other men are seeking. Moreover, the good that one seeks for one's own part is likely then, even more obviously than at other times, to be so entangled in evil that it produces Dead Sea fruit. It is almost never possible to will good in war time without seeing the good that one wills bring evil in its train. Neither fighting in defense of the weak, nor refusing to fight while abuse of them goes on, can provide a way that is unambiguously good. The active participant, the pacifist, and the victim in war all may seek recognizable goods and all help to propagate different sorts of evil. Herein is man's misery. But though in time of war this moral plight is most acutely felt, it is in essence the same at all other times as well. War intensifies the tragedy of imperfect personal living. It does not annul its personal character, nor obliterate the permanent difference between evil and good while the fighting lasts.

Man as a Subject of Redemption: A practically urgent question arises from all that has been said about man in war: whether war itself is inevitable, by reason of human nature or of the corruption to which it has already been subjected. We believe that it is not. Particular wars become inevitable only by reason of a particular series of decisions and causal processes within the framework of the divine order. Given the freedom and interdependence of men, either aggression or neglect of obligation by national governments can result in dangerous tensions. In the absence of international community and effective means for maintaining international order, wars eventually result. But in two ways this situation can be changed, by human decisions and divine grace. On the one hand, the human sources from which war-making tensions develop can be altered by the slow processes of personal regeneration and re-education. It is an essential article of Christian faith that the hearts of men, though corrupted, can be renewed through the power of God; and only because this is so dare we hope for the ultimate elimination of war. But this hope, especially if it be held for the calculable future, requires that personal regeneration go forward in vital union with institutional change. As in widening areas through mediaeval and modern history, effective government and living community have been developed, the danger of armed conflict within such areas has decreased. For the world society now crowded into an uneasy physical entanglement, a similar need is evident. World society must become world community, and a way must be found to maintain lawful order and equity as a common trust. What men under God have achieved on the smaller but enlarging scale of provincial and national life we believe is not impossible on the international scale required by the conditions of our time.

Meanwhile, one other question demands an answer. Supposing that a more peaceful time for a future generation is not impossible, what shall we say of the men who are killing and being killed now? Is death for them an ultimate frustration, or does the Christian faith see for them some fulfilment?

There is for us no easy answer. We have felt the shock of untimely death, the pain of broken ties, the loss of unique and irreplaceable companions in our human lot. We have known the cruel disappointment and the lingering regret over powers undeveloped, promises unrealized, when young lives are cut short. We grieve with the parents, wives, and children of all countries who are suffering such pangs today. Their sorrow is not to be quieted by words of ours. It will be quieted, we believe, wherever trust in God becomes the basic premise for understanding life and death alike. For some, the death of a beloved may be the first real doorway to such faith. For some, it will long be like a blank wall that only time can dissolve. For some, there is vivid assurance that resurrection or eternal life means restoration and fulfilment of all that has been lost. For all, it is good to be assured that the souls of the righteous are in the hands of God. Christian faith provides no secret knowledge and no promise of immunity from sorrow and loss. It does provide a wisdom and power in whose presence even death can lose its sting. For we are assured that in the everlasting mercy of God, no faithful servant will have died in vain.

A CREED OF THE YOUNGER CHURCHES

Almost all the Christian creeds have been written in the cultural context of Western civilization with its legacies from Hebraic, Greek, and Roman civilization. The twentieth century has witnessed the maturing of indigenous churches in other cultural contexts. As yet, these churches have produced few creeds. Many of those that they have produced are in Western idiom.

One of the most authentic creeds of the Younger Churches was produced by the Great Synod of the Huria Kristen Batak Protestant (Batak Church) in 1951. This creed was drawn up without the help of Western theologians, and it speaks to the actual situation in which the Church exists.

Source: Translation is based on text in *Das Bekenntnis der Huria Kristen Batak Protestant (Batak-Kirche) auf Sumatra/Indonesien,* übersetzt und herausgegeben von Missions-Inspektor H. F. de Kleine, Verlag der Rheinischen Missions-Gesellschaft, 1952. Translation in *Theological Discussions and Confessional Developments in the Churches of Asia and Africa* by G. C. Oosthuizen, pp. 315–21, and the translation of the Missionary Research Library, New York, have been consulted. Scripture references are omitted.

Oosthuizen, Gerhardus Cornelis, *Theological Discussions and Confessional Developments in the Churches of Asia and Africa* (Franeker: T. Wever, 1958). A very valuable discussion of creedal developments in the Younger Churches that contains a discussion of the Batak Creed.

CONFESSION OF FAITH OF THE HURIA KRISTEN BATAK PROTESTANT

Preamble

1. This Confession of Faith of the H. K. B. P. is the continuation of existing confessions of faith, namely the three confessions of faith which were acknowledged by the Fathers of the Church: (1) the Apostles' Creed, (2) the Nicene Creed, (3) the Athanasian Creed.

2. This Confession of Faith is the summary of what we believe and hope in this life and the life to come.

3. This Confession of Faith is the basis of the H. K. B. P. which must be preached, taught, and lived.

4. This Confession of Faith is the basis of the H. K. B. P. by which all false doctrine and heresy, contrary to God's Word, is rejected and opposed.

I. The Doctrine of God.

We believe and we confess:

God is one, without beginning and without end, almighty, unchangeable, trustworthy, omniscient, inscrutable, a righteous Judge, gracious, all bountiful. He fills heaven and earth. He is true, perfect in Holiness, full of love.

We reject and refute with this doctrine: the custom of calling God "grandfather," and the idea that God is only a good God contained in the conviction that "blessing may also be expected from the spirits of the grandfathers," as the heathen maintains. We also reject lucky days, fortune-telling, and reading fate in the lines of one's hands.

We also reject with this doctrine the teaching that God's power is greater than his holiness and his love.

II. The Trinity of God.

We believe and we confess:

God is one and at the same time a Triune God, namely God the Father, God the Son, and God the Holy Spirit.

The Father has begotten his Son of his own being from all eternity, that is, just as the Father is without beginning and without end, so also is the Son. Likewise the Holy Spirit, proceeding from God the Father and the Son, is without beginning and end.

We refute and reject with this doctrine the interpretation of the Trinity which speaks about the one God (Maha Esa), the only God, with the understanding that it means that the Son and the Spirit are subordinated to the Father.

We refute at the same time the doctrine which teaches that the essence of the Trinity is as follows: God the Father, his Son, the Lord Jesus Christ and the Mother, the Holy Spirit.

III. The Special Acts of the Triune God.

We believe and confess:

A. God, the Father, created, preserves, and governs all things visible and invisible. With this doctrine we reject and refute the doctrine of Fatalism (Takdir = determinism, sibaran = fate, bagian = predestined lot).

B. God, the Son, who became man, born of the Virgin Mary, conceived by the Holy Spirit, called the Lord Jesus. Two natures are found in him, God and man inseparable in one Person; Christ is true God but at the same time true man. He has suffered under Pilate, who judged him. He was crucified on the cross in order to deliver us from our sins, from death, and from the rule of the Devil. He became the perfect sacrifice for reconciliation with God because of all the sin of mankind. He descended into hell after being buried and rose again the third day, ascended into heaven to sit on the right hand of God Jehovah, his Father, who is glorious forever. He is our intercessor in heaven. He rules all things until he will come again to this earth to judge the quick and the dead.

With the doctrine we reject and refute:

1. The doctrine of the Roman Catholics which teaches that Mary, the mother of the Lord Jesus or, as they called her, the Blessed may intercede for us with God.

2. The doctrine of the Roman Catholics which teaches that the priest can sacrifice Christ in the Mass.

3. The false doctrine of the Roman Catholics which teaches that the Pope in Rome is the Vicar of Christ on this earth.

4. With this doctrine is refuted and rejected the human conception that the Lord Jesus is comparable with the prophets of the world.

C. God, the Holy Spirit, calls and teaches the congregation (Church) and preserves it in faith and in holiness through the Gospel to the honour of God.

With this doctrine we refute and reject the doctrine which teaches that the Holy Spirit can descend upon man through his own power without the Gospel. In the same way we refute and reject the doctrine which teaches that the Holy Spirit only descends in times of ecstasy and speaking in tongues. Likewise we reject and refute the doctrine which teaches that the use of medicine is unnecessary and that it is sufficient to pray to the Holy Spirit. We reject and refute also the false prophecies made in the name of the Holy Spirit; also the dissolute life of people who teach that they are filled by the Holy Spirit. What we refute and reject here are the doctrines that falsely call upon the name of the Holy Spirit.

IV. The Word of God.

We believe and confess:

The words written in the Bible, the Old and New Testaments, are truly the Word of God. "No prophecy ever came by the impulse of man, but men moved by the Holy Spirit spoke from God." (II Peter 1:21.)

"All scripture is inspired by God and profitable for teaching, for reproof, for correction, and for training in righteousness, that the man of God may be complete, equipped for every good work." (II Timothy 3:16–17.)

With this we emphasize: The Holy Scripture is completely sufficient to reveal God's being and his will, and the Holy Scripture is also completely sufficient to teach what man must believe in order to receive eternal life. The Holy Scripture is the beginning and the end of all thoughts, wisdom, and activity in the congregation (Church) and with the believers.

With this doctrine we refute and reject any wisdom and cleverness of men which differs from the Word of God.

V. Origin of Sin.

The Devil is the source of sin. He desires that all men become sinners and turn away from God.

Thus, although the first human beings, Adam and Eve, were good and able to act in conformity with God's will, they nevertheless transgressed the commandment which God had given them because of the seduction by the Devil and turned away from God. Sin is transgression.

VI. Original Sin.

We believe and confess:

Since Adam and Eve fell into sin, sin has been passed on to all their descendants. Therefore all men are conceived in sin, and this sin enslaves all men in such a way that they trespass against God's commandments. Sin causes judgment and eternal death.

With this doctrine we refute and reject the idea that newborn children are without sin, and also the idea, which is not according to God's word, which teaches that sin is caused only by poverty, penury, or distress and that consequently sin cannot be taken as sin. Also the doctrine which teaches that the heart of men is at the time of birth pure as blank paper.

VII. Redemption from Sin.

We believe and confess:

Man cannot gain redemption from sin by means of good works or through his own power, but only from the grace of God and through the redemption of Jesus Christ. Man obtains this redemption through faith, which is the work of the Holy Spirit. In this way the believer receives remission of sin which Jesus Christ procured through his death. God regards such faith as righteousness before him.

VIII. The Church.

A. We believe and confess:

The Church is the assembly of believers in Jesus Christ, who are called, gathered, sanctified, and preserved by God through the Holy Spirit.

With this doctrine we refute and reject:

1. The congregation (Church) which was established by men through their own caprice, namely the one which has separated from our church for that reason and not because there is any false doctrine which does not harmonize with God's Word.

2. The interpretation which teaches that the ministerial office of the leader or the different assemblies or the right of the members rules the Church: only Christ is the Lord of the Church and the Church must follow only such orders as harmonize with his Word. The Church is not a democracy but a Christocracy.

3. The interpretation which teaches that our Church is a State Church. There is a difference between the obligations of a State and the office of the Church.

4. The interpretation which teaches that the Church is an assembly which is based upon and associated with the ancestral customs (*adat*) and the false thought that expects organization alone to impart life to the Church.

B. We believe and confess:

The Church is holy. The Church is not holy because its members as such are holy, but because Jesus Christ, its Head, is holy. The Church thus became holy because Christ has sanctified her. God considers the members as holy who, because of the holiness of the Church, are also called a "holy people," "temple of the Holy Spirit," and "habitation of God."

With this doctrine we refute and reject the doctrine which teaches that man can gain holiness through his own works. In the same way we reject pessimism and schisms based on the fact that there is still sin among the church members.

C. We believe and confess:

The Church is a universal Church. The universal

Church is the assembly of all saints who have already a share in the Lord Jesus Christ and in his gifts, namely the Gospel, the Holy Spirit, faith, love, and hope. They [the saints] come out of every country, people, tribe, generation, and language with their various ceremonies and orders.

With this doctrine we refute and reject the interpretation which considers the Church as a national religious community and the idea that there exists no fellowship among the churches.

D. We believe and confess:

There is one Church. It is based on what is taught in Eph. 4:4, I Cor. 12:20, "There is one body. . . ." that is the Church. "But now they are many members, yet but one body." This unity of the Church mentioned here is different from the secular unity, as men usually understand it, because it is a spiritual unity.

With this doctrine we refute and reject divisions that are not based on differences of faith but only on external regulations (laws).

E. Marks of the true Church:

We believe and confess:

The signs of the true Church are:

    a. the pure preaching of the Gospel;

    b. the right administration of the two sacraments, which the Lord Jesus commanded;

    c. the exercise of church discipline to combat sin.

IX. The Servants of the Church

We believe and confess:

Every Christian is called to be a witness for Christ. In order to administer the ministry in the Church effectively, God called servants through the Church according to the offices of Christ: Prophet, Priest, and King. These shall be exercised in the Church.

The offices comprehend:

    1. The preaching of the Gospel to the members of the Church and to those who are not yet members,

    2. The administering of the two Sacraments,

namely Holy Baptism and Holy Communion,
3. The pastoral care of the members of the Church,
4. The preserving of the pure doctrine through the exercise of spiritual discipline and the opposing of false doctrines,
5. The doing of works of mercy (*diakonia*).

For this work Apostles, Prophets, Evangelists, Pastors, and Teachers were appointed. With this doctrine we refute and reject the idea of those who capriciously and obstinately reject the office of those officers who have done nothing which contradicts their office.

With this doctrine we refute and reject anyone in the congregation rising to preach, teach, and administer the Sacraments without being called to these services by the Church.

X. The Sacraments.

We believe and confess:

There are only two Sacraments ordered by the Lord Jesus which we have to administer: the Holy Baptism and the Holy Communion. These the Lord Jesus has ordered for his congregation in order to grant his invisible grace through visible signs, namely the remission of sin, redemption, life and glory which are to be received by faith.

With this doctrine we refute and reject the Roman Catholic doctrine which speaks about seven Sacraments.

A. The Holy Baptism.

We believe and confess:

The holy baptism is a means of God's grace toward man. For by means of baptism the believer is granted remission of sin, regeneration, redemption from death and the Devil and he also receives life everlasting.

According to this doctrine we confess that children also should be baptized since through baptism they are taken up into the communion of those for whom Christ has suffered. Children are likewise accepted through the Lord Jesus.

It is not necessary to baptize by immersion.

B. The Holy Supper.

We believe and confess:

The Holy Supper is the eating of the bread by means of which we are given the Body of our Lord Jesus Christ and the drinking of the wine by means of which we are given the blood of our Lord Jesus Christ.

With this doctrine we refute and reject the doctrine which teaches that the members of the Church should only be given the bread and not also the wine. For the Lord Jesus himself at the institution of the Holy Supper said: "Drink ye all of it." The first congregation has acted in accordance with this.

The mass is not based on the Word of God when one says that our Lord is sacrificed again in the Mass. Therefore we absolutely reject this doctrine.

XI. With Regard to the Church Order.

We confess:

In the Church there must be a church order which is based upon God's Word. It is instrumental in giving order and peace to the Church. The church festivals which are to be celebrated are the Birth, the Death, the Resurrection and Ascension of the Lord Jesus and the feast of the pouring out of the Holy Spirit. Nevertheless, everyone should remember that no one can win remission of sins even by observation of all these festivals.

XII. About the Secular Government.

We confess:

All authority comes from God. This means an authority who opposes the evil and does right, who helps the believer to live in peace and security; in accordance with what is written in Romans 13 and I Tim. 2:2. Nevertheless, at the same time, it should be remembered what is written in Acts 5:29: "We ought to obey God rather than man." With this doctrine we confess the Church ought to pray for the government that it may walk in righteousness. The

Church should also let its voice be heard by the government.

With this doctrine we refute and reject the idea which teaches that the State is a religious State. For the State remains a state, and the Church remains a church.

Whenever it is necessary, a Christian is permitted to take an oath before the judge because the right judgment is sought. The same may be done at the time of induction into an office or a responsibility.

XIII. About Sunday.

We keep Sunday holy, the Day of the Lord (on which God began creation), the day of the Resurrection of the Lord Jesus, and the day of the outpouring of the Holy Spirit, which has been celebrated by the Christians from the very beginning of the Church. We refuse to return to the Jewish Sabbath, for we are Christians.

With this doctrine we refute and reject the doctrine of the Seventh Day Adventists, who teach that Saturday is the Holy Sabbath day.

XIV. About Food.

We believe and confess:

Everything God created is good. No food which man receives with thanksgiving is prohibited since it is sanctified by God's Word and by prayer.

No man becomes holy by abstaining from certain foods. Faith receives holiness from God. Man does not become holy by abstaining from food. For this reason the apostle Paul opposed the Jewish food laws. The Gospel should not be perverted by rules that demand abstention from food, by heritage or tradition.

With this doctrine we refute and reject the doctrine of those who teach this.

XV. With Regard to Faith and Good Works.

We believe and confess:

Good works must be fruits of faith. Whosoever hopes to receive righteousness, life, comfort, or salvation by doing good works is in error. The Lord Jesus

Christ alone can grant remission of sins and can reconcile man with God.

We have to follow the Ten Commandments. However, man lives by faith and not by good works alone. The Holy Spirit moves men to do good works. (If not urged by the Spirit, which moves thereto, good works become sin.)

XVI. With Regard to the Remembering of the Dead.

We believe and confess:

Men are destined to die, but after that there will be the Judgment. Then they rest from their work. Jesus Christ is the Lord of the living and the dead. When we thus remember the dead, then we remind ourselves of our own death and put our hope on the communion of believers with God and thus strengthen our hearts in our struggle in this life.

With this doctrine we refute and reject the heathenish concept which teaches that the souls of the dead have influence on the living, as well as the doctrine which teaches that the soul of a dead person remains in the grave. We refute and reject also the doctrine of the Roman Catholics which teaches that there is a purgatory which must be experienced in order to purify the souls of the dead and to win eternal life, and that man may conduct a mass to intercede for the dead so that they come out of the purifying life earlier. We refute and reject the practice of praying to the souls of the saints and the hope that power or holiness may come from the dead (from their graves, from their clothes, their bones, mementos, relics).

XVII. With Regard to the Angels.

We believe and confess:

God created the angels to serve him. They are ministering spirits sent by God to help those who are heirs of salvation.

XVIII. The Future Day of Judgment.

We believe and confess:

The Lord Jesus Christ will come in the latter day to

awake the dead and to judge all men. Then he will call the believers to everlasting life.

Those who do not believe, however, will go to everlasting torment. The sure destination of those who believe will be the side of God in eternity.

With this doctrine we refute and reject the doctrine which teaches:

a. Man can compute the time of Christ's coming again.

b. After death there is still a period of grace.

We confirm with emphasis: His coming will be unexpected.

Therefore, let us always be ready, as he has warned us.

THE ECUMENICAL MOVEMENT

One of the most significant theological developments of the twentieth century is the Ecumenical Movement. The concern for the unity of the Church called for theological study to uncover the grounds for unity and disunity. It has especially focused attention upon the doctrine of the Church. One of the more important developments has been the recovery of some measure of catholicity in theological conversation and labor.

The documents of the Ecumenical Movement fill volumes. The selections that are produced here are limited to the messages of the most important assemblies. Summary statements on the nature of the unity of the Church from three Faith and Order Conferences have also been included. The Edinburgh statement on the Grace of our Lord Jesus Christ is a clear and important example of the consensus that can result from a theological study that is representative of various traditions.

In part, the Ecumenical Movement is an internal development within the Church. In part, it is the result of external pressures, such as the demonic movements of our time. In part, it arises out of the mission of the Church, especially the missionary movement. These sources of ecumenism are apparent in the documents produced here.

Sources: The documents printed in this section are taken from the following sources and are used by permission:

"The Call to Unity," *Faith and Order, Proceedings of the World Conference, Lausanne, August 3–21, 1927* (Garden City, N.Y.: Doubleday, Doran & Co., 1928).

"The Grace of Our Lord Jesus Christ" and "Affirmation of Union," *The Second World Conference on Faith and Order, Held at Edinburgh, August 3–18, 1937*, ed. by Leonard Hodgson (New York: The Macmillan Co., 1938), pp. 224–27, 275–76.

"Message of the First Assembly of the World Council of Churches," *Man's Disorder and God's Design, the Amsterdam Assembly Series* (New York: Harper & Bros., no date). Message printed as Appendix.

"The Unity We Have and the Unity We Seek," *The Third World Conference on Faith and Order, Held at Lund, August 15th to 28th, 1952*, ed. by Oliver S. Tomkins, D. D. (London: SCM Press, 1953), pp. 33–34.

"A Message from the Second Assembly of the World Council of Churches, *The Evanston Report*, ed. by W. A. Visser 't Hooft (London: SCM Press, 1955).

The statement on unity by the Faith and Order Commission at St. Andrews, 1960, is taken from *Faith and Order Trends*, published by National Council of Churches: New York, December 1960), p. 5.

"The Church's Unity, World Council of Churches, New Delhi (1961)," *New Delhi Speaks about Christian Witness, Service, and Unity*, ed. by Visser 't Hooft (New York: Association Press, 1962).

Rouse, Ruth, and Neill, Stephen C., editors, *A History*

of the Ecumenical Movement, 1517–1948 (London: S. P. C. K., 1954).

THE CALL TO UNITY
FAITH AND ORDER CONFERENCE
[LAUSANNE],
AUGUST 20TH, 1927

God wills unity. Our presence in this Conference bears testimony to our desire to bend our wills to His. However we may justify the beginnings of disunion, we lament its continuance and henceforth must labour, in penitence and faith, to build up our broken walls.

God's Spirit has been in our midst. It was He who called us hither. His presence has been manifest in our worship, our deliberations and our whole fellowship. He has discovered us to one another. He has enlarged our horizons, quickened our understanding, and enlivened our hope. We have dared and God has justified our daring. We can never be the same again. Our deep thankfulness must find expression in sustained endeavour to share the visions vouchsafed us here with those smaller home groups where our lot is cast.

More than half the world is waiting for the Gospel. At home and abroad sad multitudes are turning away in bewilderment from the Church because of its corporate feebleness. Our missions count that as a necessity which we are inclined to look on as a luxury. Already the mission field is impatiently revolting from the divisions of the Western Church to make bold adventure for unity in its own right. We of the Churches represented in this Conference cannot allow our spiritual children to outpace us. We must gird ourselves to the task, the early beginnings of which God has so richly blessed, and labour side by side with the Christians who are working for indigenous Churches until our common goal is reached.

Some of us, pioneers in this undertaking, have grown old in our search for unity. It is to youth that we look to take the torch of unity from our failing hands. We men have carried it too much alone through many years. The women henceforth should be accorded their share of responsibility. And so the whole Church will be enabled to do that which no section can hope to perform.

It was God's clear call that gathered us. With faith stimulated by His guidance to us here, we move forward.

THE GRACE OF OUR LORD JESUS CHRIST

EDINBURGH (1937)

With deep thankfulness to God for the spirit of unity, which by His gracious blessing upon us has guided and controlled all our discussions on this subject, we agree on the following statement and recognise that there is in connection with this subject no ground for maintaining division between Churches.

(i) *The Meaning of Grace*

When we speak of God's grace, we think of God Himself as revealed in His Son Jesus Christ. The meaning of divine grace is truly known only to those who know that God is Love, and that all that He does is done in love in fulfilment of His righteous purposes. His grace is manifested in our creation, preservation and all the blessings of this life, but above all in our redemption through the life, death and resurrection of Jesus Christ, in the sending of the holy and life-giving Spirit, in the fellowship of the Church and in the gift of the Word and Sacraments.

Man's salvation and welfare have their source in God alone, who is moved to His gracious activity towards man not by any merit on man's part, but solely by His free, outgoing love.

(ii) *Justification and Sanctification*

God in His free outgoing love justifies and sanctifies us through Christ, and His grace thus manifested is appropriated by faith, which itself is the gift of God.

Justification and Sanctification are two inseparable

aspects of God's gracious action in dealing with sinful man.

Justification is the act of God, whereby He forgives our sins and brings us into fellowship with Himself, who in Jesus Christ, and by His death upon the Cross, has condemned sin and manifested His love to sinners, reconciling the world to Himself.

Sanctification is the work of God, whereby through the Holy Spirit He continually renews us and the whole Church, delivering us from the power of sin, giving us increase in holiness, and transforming us into the likeness of His Son through participation in His death and in His risen life. This renewal, inspiring us to continual spiritual activity and conflict with evil, remains throughout the gift of God. Whatever our growth in holiness may be, our fellowship with God is always based upon God's forgiving grace.

Faith is more than intellectual acceptance of the revelation in Jesus Christ; it is wholehearted trust in God and His promises, and committal of ourselves to Jesus Christ as Saviour and Lord.

(iii) The Sovereignty of God and Man's Response

In regard to the relation of God's grace and man's freedom, we all agree simply upon the basis of Holy Scripture and Christian experience that the sovereignty of God is supreme. By the sovereignty of God we mean His all-controlling, all-embracing will and purpose revealed in Jesus Christ for each man and for all mankind. And we wish further to insist that this eternal purpose is the expression of God's own loving and holy nature. Thus we men owe our whole salvation to His gracious will. But, on the other hand, it is the will of God that His grace should be actively appropriated by man's own will and that for such decision man should remain responsible.

Many theologians have made attempts on philosophical lines to reconcile the apparent antithesis of God's sovereignty and man's responsibility, but such theories are not part of the Christian Faith.

We are glad to report that in this difficult matter

we have been able to speak with a united voice, so that we have found that here there ought to be no ground for maintaining any division between Churches.

(iv) The Church and Grace

We agree that the Church is the Body of Christ and the blessed company of all faithful people, whether in heaven or on earth, the communion of saints. It is at once the realisation of God's gracious purposes in creation and redemption, and the continuous organ of God's grace in Christ by the Holy Spirit, who is its pervading life, and who is constantly hallowing all its parts.

It is the function of the Church to glorify God in its life and worship, to proclaim the gospel to every creature, and to build up in the fellowship and life of the Spirit all believing people, of every race and nation. To this end God bestows His Grace in the Church on its members through His Word and Sacraments, and in the abiding presence of the Holy Spirit.

(v) Grace, the Word and the Sacraments

We agree that the Word and the Sacraments are gifts of God to the Church through Jesus Christ for the salvation of mankind. In both the grace of God in Christ is shown forth, given and through faith received; and this grace is one and indivisible.

The Word is the appointed means by which God's grace is made known to men, calling them to repentance, assuring them of forgiveness, drawing them to obedience and building them up in the fellowship of faith and love.

The Sacraments are not to be considered merely in themselves, but always as sacraments of the Church, which is the Body of Christ. They have their significance in the continual working of the Holy Spirit, who is the life of the Church. Through the sacraments God develops in all its members a life of perpetual communion lived within its fellowship, and thus enables them to embody His will in the life of the world; but the loving-kindness of God is not to be conceived as limited by His sacraments.

Among or within the Churches represented by us there is a certain difference of emphasis placed upon the Word and the sacraments, but we agree that such a difference need not be a barrier to union.

(vi) Sola Gratia

Some Churches set great value on the expression *sola gratia*, while others avoid it. The phrase has been the subject of much controversy, but we can all join in the following statement: Our salvation is the gift of God and the fruit of His grace. It is not based on the merit of man, but has its root and foundation in the forgiveness which God in His grace grants to the sinner whom He receives to sanctify Him. We do not, however, hold that the action of the divine grace overrides human freedom and responsibility; rather, it is only as response is made by faith to divine grace that true freedom is achieved. Resistance to the appeal of God's outgoing love spells, not freedom, but bondage, and perfect freedom is found only in complete conformity with the good and acceptable and perfect will of God.

AFFIRMATION OF UNION

IN ALLEGIANCE TO OUR LORD JESUS CHRIST, ADOPTED BY THE CONFERENCE [AT EDINBURGH] BY A STANDING VOTE ON 18TH AUGUST 1937, NEMINE CONTRADICENTE

The Second World Conference on Faith and Order, held in Edinburgh in August 1937, brought together four hundred and fourteen delegates from one hundred and twenty-two Christian communions in forty-three different countries. The delegates assembled to discuss together the causes that keep Christian communions apart, and the things that unite them in Christian fellowship. The Conference approved the following statement *nemine contradicente:*

We are one in faith in our Lord Jesus Christ, the incarnate Word of God. We are one in allegiance to

Him as Head of the Church, and as King of kings and Lord of lords. We are one in acknowledging that this allegiance takes precedence of any other allegiance that may make claims upon us.

This unity does not consist in the agreement of our minds or the consent of our wills. It is founded in Jesus Christ Himself, Who lived, died and rose again to bring us to the Father, and Who through the Holy Spirit dwells in His Church. We are one because we are all the objects of the love and grace of God, and called by Him to witness in all the world to His glorious gospel.

Our unity is of heart and spirit. We are divided in the outward forms of our life in Christ, because we understand differently His will for His Church. We believe, however, that a deeper understanding will lead us towards a united apprehension of the truth as it is in Jesus.

We humbly acknowledge that our divisions are contrary to the will of Christ, and we pray God in His mercy to shorten the days of our separation and to guide us by His Spirit into fulness of unity.

We are thankful that during recent years we have been drawn together; prejudices have been overcome, misunderstandings removed, and real, if limited, progress has been made towards our goal of a common mind.

In this Conference we may gratefully claim that the Spirit of God has made us willing to learn from one another, and has given us a fuller vision of the truth and enriched our spiritual experience.

We have lifted up our hearts together in prayer; we have sung the same hymns; together we have read the same Holy Scriptures. We recognise in one another, across the barriers of our separation, a common Christian outlook and a common standard of values. We are therefore assured of a unity deeper than our divisions.

We are convinced that our unity of spirit and aim must be embodied in a way that will make it manifest to the world, though we do not yet clearly see what outward form it should take.

We believe that every sincere attempt to co-operate in the concerns of the kingdom of God draws the severed communions together in increased mutual understanding and goodwill. We call upon our fellow-Christians of all communions to practise such co-operation; to consider patiently occasions of disunion that they may be overcome; to be ready to learn from those who differ from them; to seek to remove those obstacles to the furtherance of the gospel in the non-Christian world which arise from our divisions; and constantly to pray for that unity which we believe to be our Lord's will for His Church.

We desire also to declare to all men everywhere our assurance that Christ is the one hope of unity for the world in face of the distractions and dissensions of this present time. We know that our witness is weakened by our divisions. Yet we are one in Christ and in the fellowship of His Spirit. We pray that everywhere, in a world divided and perplexed, men may turn to Jesus Christ our Lord, Who makes us one in spite of our divisions; that He may bind in one those who by many worldly claims are set at variance; and that the world may at last find peace and unity in Him; to Whom be glory for ever.

MESSAGE OF THE FIRST ASSEMBLY OF THE WORLD COUNCIL OF CHURCHES (1948)

The World Council of Churches, meeting at Amsterdam, sends this message of greeting to all who are in Christ, and to all who are willing to hear.

We bless God our Father, and our Lord Jesus Christ Who gathers together in one the children of God that are scattered abroad. He has brought us here together at Amsterdam. We are one in acknowledging Him as our God and Saviour. We are divided from one another not only in matters of faith, order and tradition, but also by pride of nation, class and race. But Christ has made us His own, and He is not divided. In seeking Him we find one another. Here at Amsterdam we have committed ourselves afresh to Him, and have covenanted with one another in constituting this World Council of Churches. We intend to stay together. We call upon Christian congregations everywhere to endorse and fulfill this covenant in their relations one with another. In thankfulness to God we commit the future to Him.

When we look to Christ, we see the world as it is— His world, to which He came and for which He died. It is filled both with great hopes and also with disillusionment and despair. Some nations are rejoicing in new freedom and power, some are bitter because freedom is denied them, some are paralysed by division, and everywhere there is an undertone of fear. There are millions who are hungry, millions who have no home, no country and no hope. Over all mankind hangs the peril of total war. We have to accept God's judgment upon us for our share in the world's guilt. Often we have tried to serve God and mammon, put other loyalties before loyalty to Christ, confused the Gospel with our own economic or national or racial interests, and feared war more than we have hated it. As we have talked with one another here, we have begun to understand how our separation has prevented us from receiving correction from one another in Christ. And because we lacked this correction, the world has often heard from us not the Word of God but the words of men.

But there is a word of God for our world. It is that the world is in the hands of the living God, Whose will for it is wholly good; that in Christ Jesus, His incarnate Word, Who lived and died and rose from the dead, God has broken the power of evil once for all, and opened for everyone the gate into freedom and joy in the Holy Spirit; that the final judgment on all human history and on every human deed is the judgment of the merciful Christ; and that the end of history will be the triumph of His Kingdom, where alone we shall understand how much God has loved the world. This is God's unchanging word to the world. Millions of our fellow men have never heard it. As we are met here from many lands, we pray God to stir up His whole Church to make this Gospel known to the whole world, and to call on all men to believe in Christ, to live in His love and to hope for His coming.

Our coming together to form a World Council will be vain unless Christians and Christian congregations everywhere commit themselves to the Lord of the Church in a new effort to seek together, where they live, to be His witnesses and servants among their neighbours. We have to remind ourselves and all men that God has put down the mighty from their seats and exalted the humble and meek. We have to learn afresh together to speak boldly in Christ's name both to those in power and to the people, to oppose terror, cruelty and race discrimination, to stand by the outcast, the prisoner and the refugee. We have to make of the Church in every place a voice for those who have no voice, and a home where every man will be at home. We have to learn afresh together what is the duty of the Christian man or woman in industry, in agriculture, in politics, in the professions and in the home. We have to ask God to teach us together to say No and to say Yes in truth. No to all that flouts the love of Christ, to every system, every programme and every person that treats any man as though he were an irresponsible thing or a means of profit, to the defenders of injustice in the name of order, to those who sow the seeds of war or urge war as inevitable; Yes, to all that conforms to the love of Christ, to all who seek for justice, to the peacemakers, to all who hope, fight and suffer for the cause of man, to all who—even without knowing it—look for new heavens and a new earth wherein dwelleth righteousness.

It is not in man's power to banish sin and death from the earth, to create the unity of the Holy Catholic Church, to conquer the hosts of Satan. But it is within the power of God. He has given us at Easter the certainty that His purpose will be accomplished. But, by our acts of obedience and faith, we can on earth set up signs which point to the coming victory. Till the day of that victory our lives are hid with Christ in God, and no earthly disillusion or distress or power of hell can separate us from Him. As those who wait in confidence and joy for their deliverance, let us give ourselves to those tasks which lie to our hands, and so set up signs that men may see.

Now unto Him that is able to do exceeding abundantly above all that we ask or think, according to the power that worketh in us, unto Him be glory in the Church by Christ Jesus, throughout all ages, world without end.

THE UNITY WE HAVE AND THE UNITY WE SEEK

LUND (1952)

We affirm that throughout Christendom there is, despite divisions, a unity already given by God in Christ, through whom 'the powers of the age to come' are already in our midst. Concerning the fact of this unity and of the participation in it of every Christian we have no doubt. The co-operation in the Ecumenical Movement is one practical proof that this unity is here. We affirm also our faith that the crucified and risen Christ is already working through His Holy Spirit to deliver us from the divisions which obscure this unity, and our sure hope that at His return in glory He will enable the manifestation of this unity to be complete. This very hope lays upon us all the inescapable duty of working and praying for the shortening of the days of our separation, in obedience to Him in whom we affirm ourselves to be one.

We differ, however, in our understanding of the relation of our unity in Christ to the visible holy, Catholic and Apostolic Church. We are agreed that there are not two Churches, one visible and the other invisible, but one Church which must find visible expression on earth, but we differ in our belief as to whether certain doctrinal, sacramental and ministerial forms are of the essence of the Church itself. In consequence, we differ in our understanding of the character of the unity of the Church on earth for which we hope . . . , though none of us looks forward to an institution with a rigid uniformity of governmental structure and all of us look forward to a time when all Christians can have unrestricted communion in Sacrament and fellowship with each other.

Yet our differences in the doctrinal and sacramental content of our faith and of our hope do not prevent us from being one in the act of believing and of hoping. For our faith and our hope are in the crucified and risen Jesus Christ, who is already working in us the purpose of His perfect will, and is already gathering up every fragment of obedient endeavour into the consummation of that purpose.

A MESSAGE FROM THE SECOND ASSEMBLY OF THE WORLD COUNCIL OF CHURCHES (1954)

To all our fellow Christians, and to our fellowmen everywhere, we send greetings in the name of Jesus Christ. We affirm our faith in Jesus Christ as the hope of the world, and desire to share that faith with all men. May God forgive us that by our sin we have often hidden this hope from the world.

In the ferment of our time there are both hopes and fears. It is indeed good to hope for freedom, justice and peace, and it is God's will that we should have these things. But He has made us for a higher end. He has made us for Himself, that we might know and love Him, worship and serve Him. Nothing other than God can ever satisfy the heart of man. Forgetting this, man becomes his own enemy. He seeks justice but creates oppression. He wants peace, but drifts towards war. His very mastery of nature threatens him with ruin. Whether he acknowledges it or not, he stands under the judgment of God and in the shadow of death.

Here where we stand, Jesus Christ stood with us. He came to us, true God and true Man, to seek and to save. Though we were the enemies of God, Christ died for us. We crucified Him, but God raised Him from the dead. He is risen. He has overcome the powers of sin and death. A new life has begun. And in His risen and ascended power, He has sent forth into the world a new community, bound together by His Spirit, sharing His divine life, and commissioned to make Him known throughout the world. He will come again as Judge and King to bring all things to their consummation. Then we shall see Him as He is and know as we are known. Together with the whole creation we wait for this with eager hope, knowing that God is faithful and that even now He holds all things in His hand.

This is the hope of God's people in every age, and we commend it afresh today to all who will listen. To accept it is to turn from our ways to God's way. It is to live as forgiven sinners, as children growing in His love. It is to have our citizenship in that Kingdom which all man's sin is impotent to destroy, that realm of love and joy and peace which lies about all men, though unseen. It is to enter with Christ into the suffering and despair of men, sharing with them the great secret of that Kingdom which they do not expect. It is to know that whatever men may do, Jesus reigns and shall reign.

With this assurance we can face the powers of evil and the threat of death with a good courage. Delivered from fear we are made free to love. For beyond the judgment of men and the judgment of history lies the judgment of the King who died for all men, and who will judge us according to what we have done to the least of His brethren. Thus our Christian hope directs us towards our neighbour. It constrains us to pray daily, "Thy will be done on earth as it is in heaven," and to act as we pray in every area

of life. It begets a life of believing prayer and expect-
ant action, looking to Jesus and pressing forward to
the day of His return in glory.

Now we would speak through our member churches
directly to each congregation. Six years ago our
churches entered into a covenant to form this Council,
and affirmed their intention to stay together. We thank
God for His blessing on our work and fellowship during these six years. We enter now upon a second stage.
To stay together is not enough. We must go forward.
As we learn more of our unity in Christ, it becomes
the more intolerable that we should be divided. We
therefore ask you: Is your church seriously considering its relation to other churches in the light of
our Lord's prayer that we may be sanctified in the
truth and that we may all be one? Is your congregation, in fellowship with sister congregations around
you, doing all it can do to ensure that your neighbours
shall hear the voice of the one Shepherd calling all
men into the one flock?

The forces that separate men from one another are
strong. At our meeting here we have missed the presence of Chinese churches which were with us at Amsterdam. There are other lands and churches unrep-
resented in our Council, and we long ardently for
their fellowship. But we are thankful that, separated
as we are by the deepest political divisions of our time,
here at Evanston we are united in Christ. And we
rejoice also that, in the bond of prayer and a common
hope, we maintain communion with our Christian
brethren everywhere.

It is from within this communion that we have to
speak about the fear and distrust which at present divide our world. Only at the Cross of Christ, where
men know themselves as forgiven sinners, can they be
made one. It is there that Christians must pray daily
for their enemies. It is there that we must seek deliverance from self-righteousness, impatience and fear.
And those who know that Christ is risen should have

the courage to expect new power to break through every human barrier.

It is not enough that Christians should seek peace for themselves. They must seek justice for others. Great masses of people in many parts of the world are hungry for bread, and are compelled to live in conditions which mock their human worth. Does your church speak and act against such injustice? Millions of men and women are suffering segregation and discrimination on the ground of race. Is your church willing to declare, as this Assembly has declared, that this is contrary to the will of God and to act on that declaration? Do you pray regularly for those who suffer unjust discrimination on grounds of race, religion or political conviction?

The Church of Christ is today a world-wide fellowship, yet there are countless people to whom He is unknown. How much do you care about this? Does your congregation live for itself, or for the world around it and beyond it? Does its common life, and does the daily work of its members in the world, affirm the Lordship of Christ or deny it?

God does not leave any of us to stand alone. In every place He has gathered us together to be His family, in which His gifts and His forgiveness are received. Do you forgive one another as Christ forgave you? Is your congregation a true family of God, where every man can find a home and know that God loves him without limit?

We are not sufficient for these things. But Christ is sufficient. We do not know what is coming to us. But we know Who is coming. It is He who meets us every day and who will meet us at the end—Jesus Christ our Lord.

Therefore we say to you: Rejoice in hope.

THE UNITY OF THE CHURCH
FAITH AND ORDER
ST. ANDREWS (1960)

The Faith and Order movement was born in the hope that it would be, under God, a help to the churches in realizing His will for the unity of the Church. . . . We have become convinced that the time has come for a fuller statement of this purpose. . . .

The Commission on Faith and Order understands that the unity which is both God's will and His gift to His Church is one which brings all in each place who confess Christ Jesus as Lord into a fully committed fellowship with one another through one baptism into Him, holding the one apostolic faith, preaching the one Gospel and breaking the one bread, and having a corporate life reaching out in witness and service to all; and which at the same time unites them with the whole Christian fellowship in all places and all ages in such wise that ministry and members are acknowledged by all, and that all can act and speak together as occasion requires for the tasks to which God calls the Church.

It is for such unity that we believe we must pray and work. Such a vision has indeed been the inspiration of the Faith and Order movement in the past, and we reaffirm that this is still our goal. We recognize that the brief definition of our objective which we have given above leaves many questions unanswered. In particular we would state emphatically that the unity we seek is not one of uniformity, nor a monolithic power structure, and that on the interpretation and the means of achieving certain of the matters specified in the preceding paragraph we are not yet of a common mind. The achievement of unity will involve nothing less than a death and rebirth for many forms of church life as we have known them. We believe that nothing less costly can finally suffice.

THE CHURCH'S UNITY,
WORLD COUNCIL OF CHURCHES
New Delhi (1961)

The love of the Father and the Son in the unity of the Holy Spirit is the source and goal of the unity which the triune God wills for all men and creation. We believe that we share in this unity in the Church of Jesus Christ, who is before all things and in whom all things hold together. In him alone, given by the Father to be Head of the Body, the Church has its true unity. The reality of this unity was manifest at Pentecost in the gift of the Holy Spirit, through whom we know in this present age the first fruits of that perfect union of the Son with his Father, which will be known in its fulness only when all things are consummated by Christ in his glory. The Lord who is bringing all things into full unity at the last is he who constrains us to seek the unity which he wills for his Church on earth here and now.

We believe that the unity which is both God's will and his gift to his Church is being made visible as all in each place who are baptized into Jesus Christ and confess him as Lord and Saviour are brought by the Holy Spirit into ONE fully committed fellowship, holding the one apostolic faith, preaching the one Gospel, breaking the one bread, joining in common prayer, and having a corporate life reaching out in witness and service to all and who at the same time are united with the whole Christian fellowship in all places and all ages in such wise that ministry and members are accepted by all, and that all can act and speak together as occasion requires for the tasks to which God calls his people. It is for such unity that we believe we must pray and work.

This brief description of our objective leaves many questions unanswered. We are not yet of a common mind on the interpretation and the means of achieving the goal we have described. We are clear that unity does not imply simple uniformity of organization, rite or expression. We all confess that sinful self-will operates to keep us separated and that in our human ignorance we cannot discern clearly the lines of God's design for the future. But it is our firm hope that through the Holy Spirit God's will as it is witnessed to in Holy Scripture will be more and more disclosed to us and in us. The achievement of unity will involve nothing less than a death and rebirth of many forms of church life as we have known them. We believe that nothing less costly can finally suffice.

A Commentary Upon This Picture of Unity

The foregoing paragraph must be understood as a brief description of the sort of unity which would correspond to God's gift and our task. It is not intended as a definition of the Church, and it does not presuppose any one particular doctrine of the Church. It is based upon a statement worked out by the Commission on Faith and Order, accepted by the Central Committee at St. Andrews in 1960 and sent to the member churches for consideration and comment. The 'Toronto Statement'[1] was a landmark in the World Council's thinking about itself and its relation to work for unity. Here we seek to carry that thought a stage further, not by dictating to the churches their conception of unity, but by suggesting for further study an attempt to express more clearly the nature of our common goal. Christian unity has been the primary concern of the Faith and Order movement from the beginning, and the vision of the one Church has become the inspiration of our ecumenical endeavor. We reaffirm that we must go forward to seek the full implications of this vision. We present this statement in the hope that the churches both inside and outside the World Council of Churches will study it with care and, should it be found inadequate, will formulate alternative statements which more fully comprehend 'both God's will and his gift.'

In him alone . . . the Church has its true unity.

[1] *The Church, the Churches and the World Council of Churches,* statement received by the Central Committee at Toronto, 1950.

It is in Jesus Christ, God's Son and our only Mediator, that we have union with God. It is he who has given this gift to us through his coming into our world. Unity is not of our making, but as we receive the grace of Jesus Christ we are one in him. We are called to bear witness to the gift of unity through offering our lives as sacrifices to his glory. The fact that we are living in division shows that we have not realized God's gift of unity, and we acknowledge our disobedience before him. Our union with God is a mystery which passes our understanding and defeats our efforts to express it adequately. But as Christ has come visibly into this world and has redeemed men of flesh and blood, this union must find visible expression.

It is the living Christ who impels us to work and pray for a fuller manifestation among us of 'the one hope which belongs to our calling.' Thus the Faith and Order movement has found the focal point of its study in the person and work of Jesus Christ. Through its Commission on Christ and the Church it has sought to explore the biblical and historical witnesses to Christ, to determine what unity in the one Lord actually means. The unity which is given is the unity of the one triune God from whom and through whom and to whom are all things. It is the unity which he gives to his people through his decision to dwell among them and to be their God. It is the unity which he gives to his people through the gift of his Son, who by his death and resurrection binds us together in him in his Sonship to the one Father. It is the unity given to his people through his Spirit, and through all the gifts of the Spirit which enliven, edify and empower the new humanity in Christ.

All in each place. This statement uses the word 'place' both in its primary sense of local neighborhood and also, under modern conditions, of other areas in which Christians need to express unity in Christ. Thus being one in Christ means that unity among Christians must be found in each school where they study, in each factory or office where they work and in each con-

gregation where they worship, as well as between congregations. 'Place' may further imply not only local
communities but also wider geographical areas such
as states, provinces or nations, and certainly refers to
all Christian people in each place regardless of race
and class.

Who are baptized into Christ. The mutual recognition of baptism, in one sense or another, has been a
foundation stone in the ecumenical discussions of the
present century. However, closer examination of the
assumptions and implications of this fact invariably
brings to light deep and wide divergences in theory
and practice amongst the churches of the World Council of Churches. Much progress has already been made
through the studies of Faith and Order in the understanding of the one baptism.[2] We would urge that
these studies be widely circulated among the churches
and that the churches in each place study the meaning
of baptism together, and in the light of such studies
seek to come to a deeper understanding of the one
baptism by which all have been sealed into the one
Lord through their one faith and the gift of the Holy
Spirit.

By the Holy Spirit. The Church exists in time and
place by the power of the Holy Spirit, who effects in
her life all the elements that belong to her unity, witness and service. He is the gift of the Father in the
name of Jesus Christ to build up the Church, to lead
her into the freedom and fellowship which belong to
her peace and joy. For any achievement of a fuller
unity than that now manifest, we are wholly dependent
upon the Spirit's presence and governance.

Fully committed fellowship. The word 'fellowship'
(*koinonia*) has been chosen because it describes what
the Church truly is. 'Fellowship' clearly implies that
the Church is not merely an institution or organization. It is a fellowship of those who are called together

[2] *The Nature of the Unity We Seek,* Oberlin Conference Report,
1957; and *One Lord, One Baptism* (London: SCM Press;
Minneapolis: Augsburg Publishing House, 1960).

by the Holy Spirit and in baptism confess Christ as Lord and Saviour. They are thus 'fully committed' to him and to one another. Such a fellowship means for those who participate in it nothing less than a renewed mind and spirit, a full participation in common praise and prayer, the shared realities of penitence and forgiveness, mutuality in suffering and joy, listening together to the same Gospel, responding in faith, obedience and service, joining in the one mission of Christ in the world, a self-forgetting love for all for whom Christ died, and the reconciling grace which breaks down every wall of race, color, caste, tribe, sex, class and nation. Neither does this 'fellowship' imply a rigid uniformity of structure, organization or government. A lively variety marks corporate life in the one Body of one Spirit.

The one apostolic faith. The Holy Scriptures of the Old and New Testaments witness to the apostolic faith. This is nothing else than those events which constitute God's call of a people to be his people. The heart of the *kerygma* is Jesus Christ himself; his life and teaching, his death, resurrection, *parousia* and the justification and sanctification which he brings and offers to all men. The creeds of the Church witness to this apostolic faith. There are important studies now being undertaken of the relationship between Scripture and Tradition (which is Christian confession down the ages), and attention is drawn to the work of Faith and Order's Theological Commission on Tradition and Traditions.[8]

Preaching the one Gospel. Preaching proclaims anew to men in each generation the Gospel of our Lord Jesus Christ. In the faithful preaching of the Word the living Christ is present as our contemporary in every age; he grants us his grace, comforts us and calls us to a renewed decision for him. In the human words of the preacher every new generation is con-

[8] *The Old and the New in the Church* (London: SCM Press; Minneapolis; Augsburg Publishing House, 1961).

fronted by the Christ as one who speaks to them where they actually are.

Breaking the one bread. Nowhere are the divisions of our churches more clearly evident and painful than at the Lord's Table. But the Lord's Table is one, not many. In humility the churches must seek that one Table. We would urge the Commission on Faith and Order to continue study and consultation to help us identify and remove those barriers which now keep us from partaking together of the one bread and sharing the one cup.

Joining in common prayer. God is to be praised in every tongue and in the setting of every culture and age in an inexhaustible diversity of expression. Yet there are certain common factors in Christian worship, such as adoration, penitence, intercession, petition and thanksgiving, which are grounded inevitably in the unique acts of God in Christ, discernible still in our divided traditions. As we learn more of each other, we shall more clearly discern this common heritage and express it more fully.

A corporate life reaching out. Mission and service belong to the whole Church. God calls the Church to go out into the world to witness and serve in word and deed to the one Lord Jesus Christ, who loved the world and gave himself for the world. In the fulfillment of our missionary obedience the call to unity is seen to be imperative, the vision of one Church proclaiming one Gospel to the whole world becomes more vivid and the experience and expression of our given unity more real. There is an inescapable relation between the fulfillment of the Church's missionary obligation and the recovery of her visible unity.

Ministry and members accepted by all. All agree that the whole Body is a royal priesthood. *Yet* one of the most serious barriers to unity is our diverse understanding of the nature of the ministry within the corporate priesthood. All who have been engaged in church union negotiations testify to this fact. There are those, for example, who affirm the necessity of an episcopally ordained ministry in the apostolic succession, while others deny that it is essential for the true Church. How can two such divergent positions on so important a matter be settled? In this, as in all matters relating to Christ's Church, it is upon the Holy Spirit we must rely. He will, if we faithfully search, reveal to us the ways in which we can have a ministry accepted by all. Here biblical, theological and historical studies must be continued to seek to lay before the churches that which is necessary to have a true ministry according to God's Word. The mutual acceptance of members, though not so formidable an obstacle as mutual recognition of ministries, still raises problems for some communions. The achievement of a ministry accepted by all would largely resolve the issues involved in the mutual recognition of members.

In all places and all ages. Every church and every Christian belongs to Christ. Because we belong to him we are bound through him to the Church and the Christians in all places and all ages. Those who are united in each place are at the same time one with believers in all places. As members of the one Body they share both in each other's joys and sufferings. The Church as a universal fellowship means also that we are part of the people of God of all ages, and as such are one with Abraham, Isaac and Jacob, and all their descendants in the faith until the end of the age. Work for unity in Christ is continually attacked by all the evil forces which fear the light of truth and holiness and obscure our own vision also. We now see our unity only darkly, but we know that then we shall see it clearly when we see him face to face. But it is also our hope which gives us courage to expose our differences and our divisions and call upon God to reveal to us even now that which has hitherto been hidden from our eyes. We pray, with the praying Christ, that *all* may be one. To this end we must work while it is day.

• • • •

THE HOLY SPIRIT AND THE
CATHOLICITY OF THE CHURCH
Uppsala (1968)

Source: Complete text in *The Uppsala Report 1968* edited by Norman Goodall (Geneva: World Council of Churches, 1968), pp. 11-18.

(Paragraphs 1-6 omitted)

. . . .

7. Since Christ lived, died and rose again for all mankind, catholicity is the opposite of all kinds of egoism and particularism. It is the quality by which the Church expresses the fullness, the integrity and the totality of life in Christ. The Church is catholic, and should be catholic, in all her elements and in all aspects of her life, and especially in her worship. Members of the Church should reflect the integrity and wholeness which is the essential character of the Church. One measure of her internal unity is that it is said of believers that they have but one heart and one soul (Acts 4:32; Phil. 2:1-12). There are then two factors in it: the unifying grace of the Spirit and the humble efforts of believers, who do not seek their own, but are united in faith, in adoration, and in love and service of Christ for the sake of the world. Catholicity is a gift of the Spirit, but it is also a task, a call and an engagement.

. . . .

9. God's gift of catholicity is received in faith and obedience. The Church must express this catholicity in its worship by providing a home for all sorts and conditions of men and women; and in its witness and service by working for the realization of genuine humanity. The Church hinders the manifestation of its given catholicity when it breaks down at any of these points.

10. God offers this gift to men in their freedom. The activity of the Spirit never forces men, but opens

before them the doors of God's love and gives them the power to cooperate in God's creative and redeeming action. Such power is needed to overcome individual and collective egoism, to reconcile enemies, and to free slaves of habit from their chains. But men misuse this freedom, refusing the gift of catholicity both individually and corporately. This happens whenever Christians confuse the unity and catholicity of the Church with other solidarities and communities. Examples of this confusion occur wherever Christian communities

allow the Gospel to be obscured by prejudices which prevent them from seeking unity;

allow their membership to be determined by discrimination based on race, wealth, social class or education;

do not exhibit in all the variety of their life together the essential oneness in Christ of men and women;

allow cultural, ethnic or political allegiances to prevent the organic union of churches which confess the same faith within the same region;

prescribe their own customary practices as binding on other Christians as the condition for cooperation and unity;

permit loyalty to their own nation to hinder or to destroy their desire for mutual fellowship with Christians of another nation;

allow themselves to be forced into a unity by the State for nationalistic ends, or break their unity for political reasons.

By recognizing these confusions and by seeking to eliminate them, our churches may find themselves on the way to overcoming the forces which still keep us apart from each other.

. . . .

The Quest for Diversity

12. The quest for catholicity faces us with the question whether we betray God's gift by ignoring the diversities of the Spirit's working. Diversity may be a perversion of catholicity but often it is a genuine expression of the apostolic vocation of the Church. This is illustrated by the New Testament, where through a wide range of doctrinal and liturgical forms, relevant to differing situations, the one unchanging apostolic heritage finds expression. Behind the variety of apostolic activities we discern a double movement: the Church is always «being called out of the world and being sent into the world» (Lund 1952). This double movement is basic to a dynamic catholicity. Each of the two movements requires different words and actions in different situations, but always the two movements belong together. The constitutive centre of this double movement is corporate worship in which Christ himself is the one who both calls and sends.

. . . .

The Quest for Continuity

14. We give thanks that down the ages the continuing life of the people of God can be discerned. For the Holy Spirit, who created this people in time, has continued with it through the centuries, preserving its worship and enabling it to bring God's good news to the world. The Church is revealed as the one body of Christ, the one people of God in every age, and so its continuity is made actual

in the «faith once given to the saints», embodied in the Scriptures, confessed in the Church and proclaimed to the world;

in the liturgical life of the Church, its worship and sacraments;

in the continuous succession of the apostolic ministry of Word and Sacrament;

in constantly preparing the people of God to go into the world and meet human needs;

in the unbroken witness of the lives of prophets, martyrs and saints.

15. The Holy Spirit has not only preserved the Church in continuity with her past; He is also continuously present in the Church, effecting her inward renewal and re-creation. The Church in heaven is indeed one with the Church on earth, yet the Church on earth does not stand outside the historical process. As the pilgrim people of God she finds herself at every point of time implicated in the varying hopes, problems and fears of men and women, and in the changing patterns of human history. The Church is faced by the twin demands, of continuity in the one Holy Spirit, and of renewal in response to the call of the Spirit amid the changes of human history.

16. The Church is apostolic in the sense that all that makes the Church the Church is derived from Christ through the apostles. Apostolicity also means the continuous transmission of the Gospel to all men and nations through acts of worship, witness and human service in the world. The Church is therefore apostolic because she remains true to the faith and mission of the apostles. We are now called afresh to repentance and humility in the search for one ministry recognized by the whole Church, and for an understanding of ministry more adequate to the New Testament, to the Church and to the needs of our own times. We seek to present the apostolic faith unimpaired: we must beware among ourselves of a perversion of catholicity into a justification for a blind defence of political and religious establishments, as well as being watchful against distortions of the apostolic faith by those who confuse the novel with the new.

The Quest for the Unity of the Whole Church

17. The New Delhi Assembly emphasized with good effect the need to manifest the unity of «all Christians in each place». Even so, much still needs to be done in drawing separated congregations to recognize each other and to share in such activities as common worship, Bible study, ecumenical offerings and joint response to human needs. We must continue to seek the unity of all Christians in a common profession of the faith in the observance of Baptism and the Eucharist, and in recognition of a ministry for the whole Church.

18. So to the emphasis on «all in each place» we would now add a fresh understanding of the unity of all Christians in all places. This calls the churches in all places to realize that they belong together and are called to act together. In a time when human interdependence is so evident, it is the more imperative to make visible the bonds which unite Christians in universal fellowship.

19. But there are hindrances. No church can properly avoid responsibility for the life of its own nation and culture. Yet if that should militate against fellowship with churches and Christians of other lands, then distortion has entered the Church's life at a vital point. But the clearest obstacle to manifestation of the churches' universality is their inability to understand the measure in which they already belong together in one body. Some real experience of universality is provided by establishing regional and international confessional fellowships. But such experiences of universality are inevitably partial. The ecumenical movement helps to enlarge this experience of universality, and its regional councils and its World Council may be regarded as a transitional opportunity for eventually actualizing a truly universal, ecumenical, conciliar form of common life and witness. The members of the World Council of

Churches, committed to each other, should work for the time when a genuinely universal council may once more speak for all Christians, and lead the way into the future.

The Quest for the Unity of Mankind

20. The Church is bold in speaking of itself as the sign of the coming unity of mankind. However well founded the claim, the world hears it sceptically, and points to «secular catholicities» of its own. For secular society has produced instruments of conciliation and unification which often seem more effective than the Church itself. To the outsider, the churches often seem remote and irrelevant, and busy to the point of tediousness with their own concerns. The churches need a new openness to the world in its aspirations, its achievements, its restlessness and its despair.

. . . .

WHAT UNITY REQUIRES
Nairobi (1975)

Source: Official text may be found in *Breaking Barriers, Nairobi 1975* edited by David M. Paton (Grand Rapids: Eerdmans, 1976), pp. 59-69.

I. FOREWORD

1. We thank God for his presence with us in our Assembly. Our gathering, more than any of our previous Assemblies, has been representative of the nations and the total membership of the Church— younger and older, men and women, lay and ordained. The privilege of meeting in Africa has enhanced our awareness of the rich diversity of God's family. Meeting in small groups for Bible study, we have been guided and comforted by the word and presence of our living Lord. Through music, praise, and prayer we have been knit together in adoration of our God. We have learned to know him better as

the one who frees us for unity in himself and as the one who unites us in his freedom. He himself precedes both the freedom for which he sets us free and the unity which binds us together; it is as we are in him that we find the liberty which does not tear us apart from one another and a unity which does not impose uniformity upon desirable diversity. We are grateful also for much that has happened in the wider life of the Church, for fresh signs of the presence of the Holy Spirit, for the advance in mutual understanding, theological agreement, closer bonds, and in some cases even unions among the churches. For all this, God be praised!

II. UNITY REQUIRES A COMMONLY ACCEPTED GOAL

2. We believe that we are called to the goal of visible unity and have therefore struggled, as previous Assemblies have done, to describe more fully that goal. We recall and reaffirm the statement made at the Third Assembly at New Delhi which described God's will for unity in terms of one fully committed fellowship of all God's people in each place, in all places, and in all ages. The Fourth Assembly spoke of a deeper internal dimension of unity which is expressed by the term "catholicity". "Catholicity", the Assembly said, "is the opposite of all kinds of egotism and particularism. It is the quality by which the Church expresses the fullness, the integrity, and the totality of life in Christ. . . . The Church must express this catholicity in its worship by providing a home for all sorts and conditions of men and women; and in its witness and service by working for the realization of genuine humanity" (*Uppsala Speaks*, pp. 13, 14, paragraphs 7 and 9). True catholicity involves a quest for diversity in unity and continuity. In its catholicity the Church "is bold in speaking of itself as the sign of the coming unity of mankind" (*ibid.*, p. 20).

3. The Faith and Order Commission at its meeting in Louvain made a considered attempt to describe the unity which we seek in terms of "conciliar fellowship". The Conference at Salamanca on "Concepts of Unity and Models of Union" has recommended the concept in the following terms: "The one Church is to be envisioned as a conciliar fellowship of local churches which are themselves truly united. In this conciliar fellowship, each local church possesses, in communion with the others, the fullness of catholicity, witnesses to the same apostolic faith, and therefore recognizes the others as belonging to the same Church of Christ and guided by the same Spirit. As the New Delhi Assembly pointed out, they are bound together because they have received the same baptism and share in the same Eucharist; they recognize each other's members and ministries. They are one in their common commitment to confess the gospel of Christ by proclamation and service to the world. To this end, each church aims at maintaining sustained and sustaining relationships with her sister churches, expressed in conciliar gatherings whenever required for the fulfilment of their common calling" (cited in *Uppsala to Nairobi*, p. 79).

4. The term "conciliar fellowship" has been frequently misunderstood. It does *not* look towards a conception of unity different from that full organic unity sketched in the New Delhi statement, but is rather a further elaboration of it. The term is intended to describe an aspect of the life of the one undivided Church *at all levels*. In the first place, it expresses the unity of church separated by distance, culture, and time, a unity which is publicly manifested when the representatives of these local churches gather together for a common meeting. It also refers to a quality of life within each local church; it underlines the fact that true unity is not monolithic, does not override the special gifts given

to each member and to each local church, but rather cherishes and protects them.

5. True conciliar fellowship presupposes the unity of the Church. We describe this unity in different ways. One description given in our meeting in which we all share, even though it is not yet expressed in the language of all, is the following: "True conciliarity is the reflection in the life of the Church of the triune being of God. It is that unity for which Christ prayed when he asked the Father that his disciples might be one *as* the Father and the Son are one. The source of the Church's unity, as of her faith and her joy, is the meeting of the Apostles with the risen Christ who bears the marks of his cross, and the continued encounter with the disciples today with his living presence in the midst of the eucharistic fellowship. He brings its members into the communion of the Holy Spirit, and makes them children of the Father. Thereby, they share a common participation in the divine nature and become living members in the one living Body of the risen Christ. Though different members in each local community, and different local communities, do and should manifest a rich diversity, and develop their own proper personality, nevertheless no cultural, sociological, psychological, political, or historical difference can alter the integrity of the one apostolic faith. By the working of the Holy Spirit, the One Living Word and Son of God is incarnate in the One Church, the One Body of which Christ is the Head and the true worshippers of the Father the members. They commune with him who said: 'I am the truth.' This Living Truth is the goal towards which all churches who seek for unity tend together. Conciliarity expresses this interior unity of the churches separated by space, culture, or time, but living intensely this unity in Christ and seeking, from time to time, by councils of representatives of all the local churches at various

geographical levels to express their unity visibly in a common meeting."

6. Our present interconfessional assemblies are not councils in this full sense, because they are not yet united by a common understanding of the apostolic faith, by a common ministry, and a common Eucharist. They nevertheless express the sincere desire of the participating churches to herald and move towards full conciliar fellowship, and are themselves a true foretaste of such fellowship.

7. It is because the unity of the Church is grounded in the divine triunity that we can speak of diversity in the Church as something to be not only admitted but actively desired. Since Christ died and rose for all and his Church is to be the sign of the coming unity of humankind, it must be open to women and men of every nation and culture, of every time and place, of every sort of ability and disability. In its mission it must actively seek them wherever and whoever they are, and in its company they must find their true home. It follows that, in order to be faithful to our calling to unity, we must consider this calling within the wider context of the unity and diversity of humankind. It is because we have often failed to do this that many have dismissed the quest for church unity as irrelevant to their real concerns.

III. UNITY REQUIRES A FULLER UNDERSTANDING OF THE CONTEXT

8. *The Handicapped and the Wholeness of the Family of God.* The Church's unity includes both the "disabled" and the "able". A Church which seeks to be truly united within itself and to move towards unity with others must be open to all; yet able-bodied church members, both by their attitudes and by their emphasis on activism, marginalize and often exclude those with mental or physical disabilities. The disabled are treated as the weak to be served, rather than as fully committed, integral members of the

Body of Christ and the human family; the specific contribution which they have to give is ignored. This is the more serious because disability—a world-wide problem—is increasing. Accidents and illnesses leave adults and children disabled; many more are emotionally handicapped by the pressures of social change and urban living; genetic disorders and famine leave millions of children physically or mentally impaired. The Church cannot exemplify "the full humanity revealed in Christ", bear witness to the interdependence of humankind, or achieve unity in diversity if it continues to acquiesce in the social isolation of disabled persons and to deny them full participation in its life. The unity of the family of God is handicapped where these brothers and sisters are treated as objects of condescending charity. It is broken where they are left out. How can the love of Christ create in us the will to discern and to work forcefully against the causes which distort and cripple the lives of so many of our fellow human beings? How can the Church be open to the witness which Christ extends through them?

9. *The Community of Women and Men and the Wholeness of the Body of Christ.* The Church's unity includes women and men in a true mutuality. As a result of rapid cultural, economic, and social change, women (and many men) reject the passive or restrictive roles formerly assigned to women, and search for fuller participation in the life of the Church and in society at large. The relations of women and men must be shaped by reciprocity and not by subordination. The unity of the Church requires that women be free to live out the gifts which God has given to them and to respond to their calling to share fully in the life and witness of the Church. This raises fundamental dogmatic issues on which we are not agreed, but which are further pursued in the study, "The Community of Women and Men in the Church", which will include the significance of the Virgin

Mary in the Church and the question of the ordination of women. It will be important for the churches to discuss the implications of this study for their teaching on family life and on religious vocation.

10. *Organization and Personal Community in the Unity of the Church.* The Church's unity enhances and does not hinder personal freedom and community. Church unity is often misunderstood as implying larger bureaucratic structures incompatible with spiritual freedom and personal community. In essence, the Church is not bureaucratic, but gathers God's people in each place and in all places around the personal presence of Christ in the ministry of word and sacrament acknowledged and accepted by all. The heart of any proposal for church union is the integrity of this fundamental personal community. The fresh search, especially among young people, for an authentic spirituality and a sense of community can contribute to that "fully committed fellowship" which is intended by the term "organic union". It is true that there is no community without structure, but structure must serve and facilitate good church order, which is itself essentially and properly the expression of committed personal fellowship in Christ. Organic union of separate denominations to form one body does mean a kind of death which threatens the denominational identity of its members, but it is dying in order to receive a fuller life. That is literally the "crux of the matter".

11. *Political Struggle and the Unity of the Church.* The Church's unity is lived in the tension of political struggle. The Church is called to discern and attest God's purpose of justice in history and in the created world, but it is frequently tempted to remain silent in order to preserve "unity", or to divide in a crusading spirit for or against some particular cause. On these difficulties, we have three things to say:

(*a*) Christians are sinners judged and forgiven, accepting one another as such in Christ. At the

Eucharist we are all equal, a company who have
no righteousness of our own but who receive by
faith and in love the righteousness of God. The
Church is thus the place where people with sharply
opposed commitments can meet at the foot of the
cross within the divine mercy which sustains them
all.

(*b*) But the Church is also a company under
Christ's discipline. We are not permitted to ignore
or to compromise with sin. We are called to open
and vigorous mutual criticism, bearing the pain of
controversy, openly testing ethical decisions (including political ones) under the truth of Christ,
and seeking always the way of obedience in each
concrete situation. Individual Christians may and
often should take more radical positions than the
Church as a whole can or should do. But there are
political issues on which the Church itself must
speak and act on behalf of the dignity of God's
creatures. To do this is not to "politicize" the
Church. Rather the Church is politicized when it
is so tied to a party or a government, a class or
an ideology, that it is not free so to speak and act.

(*c*) Open and honest controversy on political issues may lead to agreement or it may lead to polar-
ization. When all things are brought into the light,
some will find their refuge in a retreat into darkness. The Church has to learn to distinguish in the
light of God's Word between sin which can be
exposed and forgiven, and apostasy which rejects
God's forgiveness and must therefore be rejected
by the Church. How can we learn to exercise this
discipline and this discernment in situations where
our churches are involved in racism, in social,
political, or religious oppression, and in economic
exploitation?

12. *The Search for Cultural Identity and the Oneness of the Church Universal.* The Church's oneness
has to include and to transcend every culture, but the

gospel cannot be wholly separated from those cultures through which it has in fact come to us. For the sake of witnessing to the gospel of Christ the Church is free to ground itself firmly in the culture and life style of every people to whom it is sent. Otherwise it would die like a potted plant with no roots in the local soil, rather than find life as a seed which dies to bear fruit. There is no single culture peculiarly congenial to the Christian message; each culture is to be both shaped and transcended by that message. But cultures change, and the Church's alertness to cultural development is essential to healthy oneness.

No church should become so identified with its own or another particular culture, present or past, as to frustrate its critical dialogue with that culture. When a church's loyalty to a given culture becomes uncritical, the oneness of the Church Universal suffers. Indeed, there may be situations of dependence between churches where, for the sake of the integrity of a church's witness in its own culture, there should be a temporary moratorium on existing dependencies in order to prepare for a more mature independence. Yet, the people of God will always find their first and primary identity through their baptism into the one Body of Christ. How does this understanding of culture and unity shape our life in liturgy and mission, increase our understanding of diverse theological understandings of the One Faith, free us in situations, such as Ireland, where cultural identification has become an imprisonment making it profoundly costly for the churches to exercise their ministry of reconciliation?

IV. UNITY REQUIRES COMPANIONSHIP IN
STRUGGLE AND HOPE

13. There are some who question the wisdom of
placing the discussion of issues of church unity within
the wider context of the secular struggles of humankind for peace and justice, just as there are those
who question the relevance of the decades of patient
theological work which have brought us to the place
where we are. To the first we must say that the purpose for which we are called to unity is "that the
world may believe". A quest for unity which is not
set in the context of Christ's promise to draw all
people to himself would be false. To the second we
say that it is only within the reality of a forgiven
community that humankind can find true liberty. It
is as a community which is itself being healed that
the Church can be God's instrument for the healing
of the nations.

(Paragraphs 14-22 omitted)

. . . .

BAPTISM, EUCHARIST AND MINISTRY
Commission on Faith and Order
World Council of Churches (1982)

Source: The official text was published by the World
Council of Churches, Geneva, Switzerland, 1982. Reprinted by permission.

PREFACE

. . . .

The three statements are the fruit of a 50-year
process of study stretching back to the first Faith
and Order Conference at Lausanne in 1927. The
material has been discussed and revised by the Faith
and Order Commission at Accra (1974), Bangalore
(1978) and Lima (1982). Between the Plenary

Commission meetings, the Standing Commission and its steering group on Baptism, Eucharist and Ministry under the presidency of Frère Max Thurian of the Taizé Community, have worked further on the drafting.

. . . .

This Lima Text represents the significant theological convergence which Faith and Order has discerned and formulated. Those who know how widely the churches have differed in doctrine and practice on baptism, eucharist and ministry, will appreciate the importance of the large measure of agreement registered here. Virtually all the confessional traditions are included in the Commission's membership. That theologians of such widely different traditions should be able to speak so harmoniously about baptism, eucharist and ministry is unprecedented in the modern ecumenical movement. Particularly noteworthy is the fact that the Commission also includes among its full members theologians of the Roman Catholic and other churches which do not belong to the World Council of Churches itself.

In the course of critical evaluation the primary purpose of this ecumenical text must be kept in mind. Readers should not expect to find a complete theological treatment of baptism, eucharist and ministry. That would be neither appropriate nor desirable here. The agreed text purposely concentrates on those aspects of the theme that have been directly or indirectly related to the problems of mutual recognition leading to unity. The main text demonstrates the major areas of theological convergence; the added commentaries either indicate historical differences that have been overcome or identify disputed issues still in need of further research and recognition.

* * * * *

. . . .

BAPTISM

I. *The Institution of Baptism*

1. Christian baptism is rooted in the ministry of Jesus of Nazareth, in his death and his resurrection. It is incorporation into Christ, who is the crucified and risen Lord; it is entry into the New Covenant between God and his people. Baptism is a gift of God, and is administered in the name of the Father, the Son, and the Holy Spirit. St. Matthew records that the risen Lord, when sending his disciples into the world, commanded them to baptize (Matt. 28:18-20). The universal practice of baptism by the apostolic Church from its earliest days is attested in letters of the New Testament, the Acts of the Apostles, and the writings of the Fathers. The churches today continue this practice as a rite of commitment to the Lord who bestows his grace upon his people.

II. *The Meaning of Baptism*

2. Baptism is the sign of new life through Jesus Christ. It unites the one baptized with Christ and with his people. The New Testament scriptures and the liturgy of the Church unfold the meaning of baptism in various images which express the riches of Christ and the gifts of his salvation. These images are sometimes linked with the symbolic uses of water in the Old Testament. Baptism is participation in Christ's death and resurrection (Rom. 6:3-5; Col. 2:12); a washing away of sin (I Cor. 6:11); a new birth (John 3:5); an enlightenment by Christ (Eph. 5:14); a reclothing in Christ (Gal. 3:27); a renewal by the Spirit (Titus 3:5); the experience of salvation from the Flood (I Peter 3:30-21); an exodus from bondage (I Cor. 10:1-2) and a liberation into a new humanity in which barriers of division whether of sex or race or social status are transcended (Gal.

3:27-28; I Cor. 12:13). The images are many but the reality is one.

A. Participation in Christ's Death and Resurrection

3. Baptism means participating in the life, death and resurrection of Jesus Christ. Jesus went down into the river Jordan and was baptized in solidarity with sinners in order to fulfill all righteousness (Matt. 3:15). This baptism led Jesus along the way of the Suffering Servant, made manifest in his sufferings, death and resurrection (Mark 10:38-40, 45). By baptism, Christians are immersed in the liberating death of Christ where their sins are buried, where the "old Adam" is crucified with Christ, and where the power of sin is broken. Thus those baptized are no longer slaves to sin, but free. Fully identified with the death of Christ, they are buried with him and are raised here and now to a new life in the power of the resurrection of Jesus Christ, confident that they will also ultimately be one with him in a resurrection like his (Rom. 6:3-11; Col. 2:13, 3:1; Eph. 2:5-6).

B. Conversion, Pardoning and Cleansing

4. The baptism which makes Christians partakers of the mystery of Christ's death and resurrection implies confession of sin and conversion of heart. The baptism administered by John was itself a baptism of repentance for the forgiveness of sins (Mark 1:4). The New Testament underlines the ethical implications of baptism by representing it as an ablution which washes the body with pure water, a cleansing of the heart of all sin, and an act of justification (Heb. 10:22; I Peter 3:21; Acts 22:16; I Cor. 6:11). Thus those baptized are pardoned, cleansed and sanctified by Christ and are given as part of their baptismal experience a new ethical orientation under the guidance of the Holy Spirit.

C. The Gift of the Spirit

5. The Holy Spirit is at work in the lives of people before, in and after their baptism. It is the same Spirit who revealed Jesus as the Son (Mark 1:10-11) and who empowered and united the disciples at Pentecost (Acts 2). God bestows upon each person the anointing and the promise of the Holy Spirit, marks them with his seal and implants in their hearts the first instalment of their inheritance as sons and daughters of God. The Holy Spirit nurtures the life of faith in their hearts until the final deliverance when they will enter into its full possession, to the praise of the glory of God (II Cor. 1:21-22; Eph. 1:13-14).

D. Incorporation into the Body of Christ

6. Administered in obedience to our Lord, baptism is a sign and seal of our common discipleship. Through their own baptism, Christians are brought into union with Christ, with each other and with the Church of every time and place. Our common baptism, which unites us to Christ in faith, is thus a basic bond of unity. We are one people and are called to confess and serve one Lord in each place and in all the world. The union with Christ which we share through baptism has important implications for Christian unity. "There is . . . one baptism, one God and Father of us all . . ." (Eph. 4:4-6). When baptismal unity is realized in one holy, catholic, apostolic Church, a genuine Christian witness can be made to the healing and reconciling love of God. Therefore, our one baptism into Christ constitutes a call to the churches to overcome their divisions and visibly manifest their fellowship.

Commentary

The inability of the churches mutually to recognize their various practices of baptism as sharing in the one baptism, and their actual dividedness in spite of mutual baptismal recognition, have given dramatic visibility to the broken witness of the Church. The readiness of the churches in some places and times to allow differences of sex, race, or social status to divide the body of Christ has further called into question genuine baptismal unity of the Christian community (Gal. 3:27-28) and has seriously compromised its witness. The need to recover baptismal unity is at the heart of the ecumenical task as it is central for the realization of genuine partnership within the Christian communities.

E. The Sign of the Kingdom

7. Baptism initiates the reality of the new life given in the midst of the present world. It gives participation in the community of the Holy Spirit. It is a sign of the Kingdom of God and of the life of the world to come. Through the gifts of faith, hope and love, baptism has a dynamic which embraces the whole of life, extends to all nations, and anticipates the day when every tongue will confess that Jesus Christ is Lord to the glory of God the Father.

III. *Baptism and Faith*

8. Baptism is both God's gift and our human response to that gift. It looks towards a growth into the measure of the stature of the fullness of Christ (Eph. 4:13). The necessity of faith for the reception of the salvation embodied and set forth in baptism is acknowledged by all churches. Personal commitment is necessary for responsible membership of the body of Christ.

9. Baptism is related not only to momentary experience, but to life-long growth into Christ. Those baptized are called upon to reflect the glory of the Lord as they are transformed by the power of the

Holy Spirit, into his likeness, with ever increasing splendour (II Cor. 3:18). The life of the Christian is necessarily one of continuing struggle yet also of continuing experience of grace. In this new relationship, the baptized live for the sake of Christ, of his Church and of the world which he loves, while they wait in hope for the manifestation of God's new creation and for the time when God will be all in all (Rom. 8:18-24; I Cor. 15:22-28, 49-57).

10. As they grow in the Christian life of faith, baptized believers demonstrate that humanity can be regenerated and liberated. They have a common responsibility, here and now, to bear witness together to the Gospel of Christ, the liberator of all human beings. The context of this common witness is the Church and the world. Within a fellowship of witness and service, Christians discover the full significance of the one baptism as the gift of God to all his people. Likewise, they acknowledge that baptism, as a baptism into Christ's death, has ethical implications which not only call for personal sanctification, but also motivate Christians to strive for the realization of the will of God in all realms of life (Rom. 6:9ff; Gal. 3:26-28; I Peter 2:21—4:6).

IV. *Baptismal Practice*

A. Baptism of Believers and Infants

11. While the possibility that infant baptism was also practiced in the apostolic age cannot be excluded, baptism upon personal profession of faith is the most clearly attested pattern in the New Testament documents. In the course of history, the practice of baptism has developed in a variety of forms. Some churches baptize infants brought by parents or guardians who are ready, in and with the Church, to bring up the children in the Christian faith. Other churches practice exclusively the baptism of believers who are able to make a personal confession of

faith. Some of these churches encourage infants or children to be presented and blessed in a service which usually involves thanksgiving for the gift of the child and also the commitment of the mother and father to Christian parenthood. The churches baptize believers coming from other religions or from unbelief who accept the Christian faith and participate in catechetical instruction.

12. Both the baptism of believers and the baptism of infants take place in the Church as the community of faith. When one who can answer for himself or herself is baptized, a personal confession of faith will be an integral part of the baptismal service. When an infant is baptized, the personal response will be offered at a later moment in life. In both cases, the baptized person will have to grow in the understanding of faith. For those baptized upon their own confession of faith, there is always the constant requirement of a continuing growth of personal response in faith. In the case of infants, personal confession is expected later, and Christian nurture is directed to the eliciting of this confession. All baptism is rooted in and declares Christ's faithfulness unto death. It has its setting within the life and faith of the Church and, through the witness of the whole Church, points to the faithfulness of God, the ground of all life in faith. At every baptism the whole congregation reaffirms its faith in God and pledges itself to provide an environment of witness and service. Baptism should, therefore, always be celebrated and developed in the setting of the Christian community.

Commentary

When the expressions "infant baptism" and "believers' baptism" are used, it is necessary to keep in mind that the real distinction is between those who baptize people at any age and those who baptize only those able to make a confession of faith for themselves. The differences between infant and believers' baptism become less sharp when it is recognized that both forms of baptism embody God's own initiative in Christ and express a response of faith made within the believing community.

The practice of infant baptism emphasizes the corporate faith and the faith which the child shares with its parents. The infant is born into a broken world and shares in its brokenness. Through baptism, the promise and claim of the Gospel are laid upon the child. The personal faith of the recipient of baptism and faithful participation in the life of the Church are essential for the full fruit of baptism.

The practice of believers' baptism emphasizes the explicit confession of the person who responds to the grace of God in and through the community of faith and who seeks baptism. Both forms of baptism require a similar and responsible attitude towards Christian nurture. A rediscovery of the continuing character of Christian nurture may facilitate the mutual acceptance of different initiation practices.

In some churches which unite both infant-baptist and believer-baptist traditions, it has been possible to regard as equivalent alternatives for entry into the Church both a pattern whereby baptism in infancy is followed by later profession of faith and a pattern whereby believer baptism follows upon a presentation and blessing in infancy. This example invites other churches to decide whether they, too, could not recognize equivalent alternatives in their reciprocal relationships and in church union negotiations.

13. Baptism is an unrepeatable act. Any practice which might be interpreted as "re-baptism" must be avoided.

Commentary

Churches which have insisted on a particular form of baptism or which have held serious questions about the authenticity of other churches' sacraments and ministries have at times required persons coming from other church traditions to be baptized before being received into full communicant membership. As the churches come to fuller mutual understanding and acceptance of one another and enter into closer relationships in witness and service, they will want to refrain from any practice which might call into question the sacramental integrity of the other churches or which might diminish the unrepeatability of the sacrament of baptism.

B. Baptism — Chrismation — Confirmation

14. In God's work of salvation, the paschal mystery of Christ's death and resurrection is inseparably linked with the pentecostal gift of the Holy Spirit. Similarly, participation in Christ's death and resurrection is inseparably linked with the receiving of the Spirit. Baptism in its full meaning signifies and effects both.

Christians differ in their understanding as to where the sign of the gift of the Spirit is to be found. Different actions have become associated with the giving of the Spirit. For some it is the water rite itself. For others, it is the anointing with chrism and/or the imposition of hands, which many churches call confirmation. For still others it is all three, as they see the Spirit operative throughout the rite. All agree that Christian baptism is in water and the Holy Spirit.

Commentary

(a) Within some traditions it is explained that as baptism conforms us to Christ crucified, buried and risen, so through chrismation Christians receive the gift of the pentecostal Spirit from the anointed Son.

(b) If baptism, as incorporation into the body of Christ, points by its very nature to the eucharistic sharing of Christ's body and blood, the question arises as to how a further and separate rite can be interposed between baptism and admission to communion. Those churches which baptize children but refuse them a share in the eucharist before such a rite may wish to ponder whether they have fully appreciated and accepted the consequences of baptism.

(c) Baptism needs to be constantly reaffirmed. The most obvious form of such reaffirmation is the celebration of the eucharist. The renewal of baptismal vows may also take place during such occasions as the annual celebration of the paschal mystery or during the baptism of others.

C. Towards Mutual Recognition of Baptism

15. Churches are increasingly recognizing each other's baptism as the one baptism into Christ when Jesus Christ has been confessed as Lord by the candidate or, in the case of infant baptism, when confession has been made by the church (parents, guardians, godparents and congregation) and affirmed later by personal faith and commitment. Mutual recognition of baptism is acknowledged as an important sign and means of expressing the baptismal unity given in Christ. Wherever possible, mutual recognition should be expressed explicitly by the churches.

16. In order to overcome their differences, believer baptists and those who practice infant baptism should reconsider certain aspects of their practices. The first may seek to express more visibly the fact that children are placed under the protection of God's grace. The latter must guard themselves against the practice of apparently indiscriminate

baptism and take more seriously their responsibility for the nurture of baptized children to mature commitment to Christ.

V. *The Celebration of Baptism*

17. Baptism is administered with water in the name of the Father, the Son and the Holy Spirit.

18. In the celebration of baptism the symbolic dimension of water should be taken seriously and not minimalized. The act of immersion can vividly express the reality that in baptism the Christian participates in the death, burial and resurrection of Christ.

Commentary

As seen in some theological traditions, the use of water, with all its positive associations with life and blessing, signifies the continuity between the old and the new creation, thus revealing the significance of baptism not only for human beings but also for the whole cosmos. At the same time, the use of water represents a purification of creation, a dying to that which is negative and destructive in the world: those who are baptized into the body of Christ are made partakers of a renewed existence.

19. As was the case in the early centuries, the gift of the Spirit in baptism may be signified in additional ways; for example, by the sign of the laying on of hands, and by anointing or chrismation. The very sign of the cross recalls the promised gift of the Holy Spirit who is the instalment and pledge of what is yet to come when God has fully redeemed those whom he has made his own (Eph. 1:13-14). The recovery of such vivid signs may be expected to enrich the liturgy.

20. Within any comprehensive order of baptism at least the following elements should find a place: the proclamation of the scriptures referring to baptism;

an invocation of the Holy Spirit; a renunciation of evil; a profession of faith in Christ and the Holy Trinity; the use of water; a declaration that the persons baptized have acquired a new identity as sons and daughters of God, and as members of the Church, called to be witnesses of the Gospel. Some churches consider that Christian initiation is not complete without the sealing of the baptized with the gift of the Holy Spirit and participation in holy communion.

21. It is appropriate to explain in the context of the baptismal service the meaning of baptism as it appears from scriptures (i.e., the participation in Christ's death and resurrection, conversion, pardoning and cleansing, gift of the Spirit, incorporation into the body of Christ and sign of the Kingdom).

Commentary

Recent discussion indicates that more attention should be given to misunderstandings encouraged by the socio-cultural context in which baptism takes place.

(a) In some parts of the world, the giving of a name in the baptismal liturgy has led to confusion between baptism and customs surrounding name-giving. This confusion is especially harmful if, in predominantly non-Christian cultures, the baptized are required to assume Christian names not rooted in their cultural tradition. In making regulations for baptism, churches should be careful to keep the emphasis on the true Christian significance of baptism and to avoid unnecessarily alienating the baptized from their local culture through the imposition of foreign names. A first name which is inherited from one's original culture roots the baptized in that culture, and at the same time manifests the universality of baptism, incorporation into the one Church, holy, catholic and apostolic, which stretches over all the nations of the earth.

(b) In many large European and North American majority churches infant baptism is often practiced in an apparently indiscriminate way. This contributes to the reluctance of churches which practice believers' baptism to acknowledge the validity of infant baptism; this fact should lead to more critical reflection on the meaning of baptism within those majority churches themselves.

(c) Some African churches practice baptism of the Holy Spirit without water, through the laying on of hands, while recognizing other churches' baptism. A study is required concerning this practice and its relation to baptism with water.

22. Baptism is normally administered by an ordained minister, though in certain circumstances others are allowed to baptize.

23. Since baptism is intimately connected with the corporate life and worship of the Church, it should normally be administered during public worship, so that the members of the congregation may be reminded of their own baptism and may welcome into their own fellowship those who are baptized and whom they are committed to nurture in the Christian faith. The sacrament is appropriate to great festival occasions such as Easter, Pentecost and Epiphany, as was the practice in the early Church.

EUCHARIST

I. *The Institution of the Eucharist*

1. The Church receives the eucharist as a gift from the Lord. St. Paul wrote: "I have received from the Lord what I also delivered to you, that the Lord Jesus on the night when he was betrayed took bread, and when he had given thanks, he broke it, and said: 'This is my body, which is for you. Do this in

remembrance (*anamnesis*) of me.' In the same way also the cup, after supper, saying: 'This cup is the new covenant in my blood. Do this, as often as you drink it, in remembrance of me.' " (I Cor. 11:23-25; cf. Matt. 26:26-29; Mark 14:22-25; Luke 22:14-20).

The meals which Jesus is recorded as sharing during his earthly ministry proclaim and enact the nearness of the Kingdom, of which the feeding of the multitudes is a sign. In his last meal, the fellowship of the Kingdom was connected with the prospect of Jesus' suffering. After his resurrection, the Lord made his presence known to his disciples in the breaking of the bread. Thus the eucharist continues these meals of Jesus during his earthly life and after his resurrection, always as signs of the Kingdom. Christians see the eucharist prefigured in the Passover memorial of Israel's deliverance from the land of bondage and in the meal of the Covenant on Mount Sinai (Ex. 24). It is the new paschal meal of the Church, the meal of the New Covenant, which Christ gave to his disciples as the *anamnesis* of his death and resurrection, as the anticipation of the Supper of the Lamb (Rev. 19:9). Christ commanded his disciples thus to remember and encounter him in this sacramental meal, as the continuing people of God, until his return. The last meal celebrated by Jesus was a liturgical meal employing symbolic words and actions. Consequently the eucharist is a sacramental meal which by visible signs communicates to us God's love in Jesus Christ, the love by which Jesus loved his own "to the end" (John 13:1). It has acquired many names: for example, the Lord's Supper, the breaking of bread, the holy communion, the divine liturgy, the mass. Its celebration continues as the central act of the Church's worship.

II. *The Meaning of the Eucharist*

2. The eucharist is essentially the sacrament of the gift which God makes to us in Christ through the

power of the Holy Spirit. Every Christian receives this gift of salvation through communion in the body and blood of Christ. In the eucharistic meal, in the eating and drinking of the bread and wine, Christ grants communion with himself. God himself acts, giving life to the body of Christ and renewing each member. In accordance with Christ's promise, each baptized member of the body of Christ receives in the eucharist the assurance of the forgiveness of sins (Matt. 26:28) and the pledge of eternal life (John 6:51-58). Although the eucharist is essentially one complete act, it will be considered here under the following aspects: thanksgiving to the Father, memorial of Christ, invocation of the Spirit, communion of the faithful, meal of the Kingdom.

A. The Eucharist as Thanksgiving to the Father

3. The eucharist, which always includes both word and sacrament, is a proclamation and a celebration of the work of God. It is the great thanksgiving to the Father for everything which he accomplished in creation, redemption and sanctification, for everything which he accomplishes now in the Church and in the world in spite of the sins of human beings, for everything that he will accomplish in bringing his Kingdom to fulfillment. Thus the eucharist is the benediction (*berakah*) by which the Church expresses its thankfulness to God for all his benefits.

4. The eucharist is the great sacrifice of praise by which the Church speaks on behalf of the whole creation. For the world which God has reconciled to himself is present at every eucharist: in the bread and wine, in the persons of the faithful, and in the prayers they offer for themselves and for all people. Christ unites the faithful with himself and includes their prayers within his own intercession so that the faithful are transfigured and their prayers accepted. This sacrifice of praise is possible only through Christ, with him and in him. The bread and wine, fruits of

the earth and of human labour, are presented to the Father in faith and thanksgiving. The eucharist thus signifies what the world is to become: an offering and hymn of praise to the Creator, a universal communion in the body of Christ, a kingdom of justice, love and peace in the Holy Spirit.

B. The Eucharist as *Anamnesis* or Memorial of Christ

5. The eucharist is the memorial of the crucified and risen Christ, i.e., the living and effective sign of his sacrifice, accomplished once and for all on the cross and still operative on behalf of all humankind. The biblical idea of memorial as applied to the eucharist refers to this present efficacy of God's work when it is celebrated by his people in a liturgy.

6. Christ himself with all that he has accomplished for us and for all creation (in his incarnation, servanthood, ministry, teaching, suffering, sacrifice, resurrection, ascension and sending of the Spirit) is present in this *anamnesis*, granting us communion with himself. The eucharist is also the foretaste of his parousia and of the final kingdom.

7. The *anamnesis* in which Christ acts through the joyful celebration of his Church is thus both representation and anticipation. It is not only a calling to mind of what is past and of its significance. It is the Church's effective proclamation of God's mighty acts and promises.

8. Representation and anticipation are expressed in thanksgiving and intercession. The Church, gratefully recalling God's mighty acts of redemption, beseeches him to give the benefits of these acts to every human being. In thanksgiving and intercession, the Church is united with the Son, its great High Priest and Intercessor (Rom. 8:34; Heb. 7:25). The eucharist is the sacrament of the unique sacrifice of Christ, who ever lives to make intercession for us. It is the

memorial of all that God has done for the salvation
of the world. What it was God's will to accomplish
in the incarnation, life, death, resurrection and ascension of Christ, he does not repeat. These events are
unique and can neither be repeated nor prolonged.
In the memorial of the eucharist, however, the
Church offers its intercession in communion with
Christ, our great High Priest.

Commentary

It is in the light of the significance of the eucharist
as intercession that references to the eucharist in
Catholic theology as "propitiatory sacrifice" may
be understood. The understanding is that there is
only one expiation, that of the unique sacrifice of
the cross, made actual in the eucharist and presented before the Father in the intercession of
Christ and of the Church for all humanity. In the
light of the biblical conception of memorial, all
churches might want to review the old controversies about "sacrifice" and deepen their understanding of the reasons why other traditions than
their own have either used or rejected this term.

9. The *anamnesis* of Christ is the basis and source of
all Christian prayer. So our prayer relies upon and is
united with the continual intercession of the risen
Lord. In the eucharist, Christ empowers us to live
with him, to suffer with him and to pray through
him as justified sinners, joyfully and freely fulfilling
his will.

10. In Christ we offer ourselves as a living and holy
sacrifice in our daily lives (Rom. 12:1; I Peter 2:5);
this spiritual worship, acceptable to God, is nourished in the eucharist, in which we are sanctified and
reconciled in love, in order to be servants of reconciliation in the world.

11. United to our Lord and in communion with all
the saints and martyrs, we are renewed in the covenant sealed by the blood of Christ.

12. Since the *anamnesis* of Christ is the very content of the preached Word as it is of the eucharistic meal, each reinforces the other. The celebration of the eucharist properly includes the proclamation of the Word.

13. The words and acts of Christ at the institution of the eucharist stand at the heart of the celebration; the eucharistic meal is the sacrament of the body and blood of Christ, the sacrament of his real presence. Christ fulfills in a variety of ways his promise to be always with his own even to the end of the world. But Christ's mode of presence in the eucharist is unique. Jesus said over the bread and wine of the eucharist: "This is my body . . . this is my blood . . ." What Christ declared is true, and this truth is fulfilled every time the eucharist is celebrated. The Church confesses Christ's real living and active presence in the eucharist. While Christ's real presence in the eucharist does not depend on the faith of the individual, all agree that to discern the body and blood of Christ, faith is required.

Commentary

Many churches believe that by the very words of Jesus and by the power of the Holy Spirit, the bread and wine of the eucharist become, in a real though mysterious manner, the body and blood of the risen Christ, i.e., of the living Christ present in all his fullness. Under the signs of bread and wine, the deepest reality is the total being of Christ who comes to us in order to feed us and transform our entire being. Some other churches, whilst affirming a real presence of Christ at the Eucharist, do not link that presence so definitely with the signs of bread and wine. The decision remains for the churches whether this difference can be accommodated within the convergence formulated in the text itself.

C. The Eucharist as Invocation of the Spirit

14. The Spirit makes the crucified and risen Christ really present to us in the eucharistic meal, fulfilling the promise contained in the words of institution. The presence of Christ is clearly the centre of the eucharist, and the promise contained in the words of institution is therefore fundamental to the celebration. Yet it is the Father who is the primary origin and final fulfillment of the eucharistic event. The incarnate Son of God by and in whom it is accomplished is its living centre. The Holy Spirit is the immeasurable strength of love which makes it possible and continues to make it effective. The bond between the eucharistic celebration and the mystery of the Triune God reveals the role of the Holy Spirit as that of the One who makes the historical word of Jesus present and alive. Being assured by Jesus' promise in the words of institution that it will be answered, the Church prays to the Father for the gift of the Holy Spirit in order that the eucharistic event may be a reality: the real presence of the the crucified and risen Christ giving his life for all humanity.

Commentary

This is not to spiritualize the eucharistic presence of Christ but to affirm the indissoluble union between the Son and the Spirit. This union makes it clear that the eucharist is not a magical mechanical action but a prayer addressed to the Father, one which emphasizes the utter dependence of the Church on him. There is an intrinsic relationship between the words of institution, Christ's promise, and the *epiklesis*, the invocation of the Spirit, in the liturgy. The *epiklesis* in relation to the words of institution is located differently in various liturgical traditions. In the early liturgies the whole "prayer action" was thought of as bringing about the reality promised by Christ. The invocation of the Spirit was made both on the community and on the elements of bread and wine. Recovery of such an understanding may help us overcome our difficulties concerning a special moment of consecration.

15. It is in virtue of the living word of Christ and by the power of the Holy Spirit that the bread and wine become the sacramental signs of Christ's body and blood. They remain so for the purpose of communion.

Commentary

In the history of the Church there have been various attempts to understand the mystery of the real and unique presence of Christ in the eucharist. Some are content merely to affirm this presence without seeking to explain it. Others consider it necessary to assert a change wrought by the Holy Spirit and Christ's words, in consequence of which there is no longer just ordinary bread and wine but the body and blood of Christ. Others again have developed an explanation of the real presence which, though not claiming to exhaust the significance of the mystery, seeks to protect it from damaging interpretations.

16. The whole action of the eucharist has an "epikletic" character because it depends upon the work of the Holy Spirit. In the words of the liturgy, this aspect of the eucharist finds varied expression.

17. The Church, as the community of the new covenant, confidently invokes the Spirit, in order that it may be sanctified and renewed, led into all justice, truth and unity, and empowered to fulfill its mission in the world.

18. The Holy Spirit through the eucharist gives a foretaste of the Kingdom of God: the Church receives the life of the new creation and the assurance of the Lord's return.

D. The Eucharist as Communion of the Faithful

19. The eucharistic communion with Christ present, who nourishes the life of the Church, is at the same time communion within the body of Christ which is the Church. The sharing in one bread and the common cup in a given place demonstrates and effects the oneness of the sharers with Christ and with their fellow sharers in all times and places. It is in the eucharist that the community of God's people is fully manifested. Eucharistic celebrations always have to do with the whole Church, and the whole Church is involved in each local eucharistic celebration. In so far as a church claims to be a manifestation of the whole Church, it will take care to order its own life in ways which take seriously the interests and concerns of sister churches.

Commentary

Since the earliest days, baptism has been understood as the sacrament by which believers are incorporated into the body of Christ and are endowed with the Holy Spirit. As long as the right of the baptized believers and their ministers to participate in and preside over eucharistic celebration in one church is called into question by those who preside over and are members of other eucharistic congregations, the catholicity of the eucharist is less manifest. There is discussion in many churches today about the inclusion of baptized children as communicants at the Lord's Supper.

20. The eucharist embraces all aspects of life. It is a representative act of thanksgiving and offering on behalf of the whole world. The eucharistic celebration demands reconciliation and sharing among all those regarded as brothers and sisters in the one family of God and is a constant challenge in the search for appropriate relationships in social, economic and political life (Matt. 5:23f; I Cor. 10:16f; I Cor.

11:20-22; Gal. 3:28). All kinds of injustice, racism, separation and lack of freedom are radically challenged when we share in the body and blood of Christ. Through the eucharist the all-renewing grace of God penetrates and restores human personality and dignity. The eucharist involves the believer in the central event of the world's history. As participants in the eucharist, therefore, we prove inconsistent if we are not actively participating in this ongoing restoration of the world's situation and the human condition. The eucharist shows us that our behaviour is inconsistent in face of the reconciling presence of God in human history: we are placed under continual judgment by the persistence of unjust relationships of all kinds in our society, the manifold divisions on account of human pride, material interest and power politics and, above all, the obstinacy of unjustifiable confessional oppositions within the body of Christ.

21. Solidarity in the eucharistic communion of the body of Christ and responsible care of Christians for one another and the world find specific expression in the liturgies: in the mutual forgiveness of sins; the sign of peace; intercession for all, the eating and drinking together; the taking of the elements to the sick and those in prison or the celebration of the eucharist with them. All these manifestations of love in the eucharist are directly related to Christ's own testimony as a servant, in whose servanthood Christians themselves participate. As God in Christ has entered into the human situation, so eucharistic liturgy is near to the concrete and particular situations of men and women. In the early Church the ministry of deacons and deaconesses had a special responsibility in giving expression to this aspect of the eucharist. The place of such ministry between the table and the needy properly testifies to the redeeming presence of Christ in the world.

E. The Eucharist as Meal of the Kingdom

22. The eucharist opens up the vision of the divine rule which has been promised as the final renewal of creation, and is a foretaste of it. Signs of this renewal are present in the world wherever the grace of God is manifest and human beings work for justice, love and peace. The eucharist is the feast at which the Church gives thanks to God for these signs and joyfully celebrates and anticipates the coming of the Kingdom in Christ (I Cor. 11:26; Matt. 26:29).

23. The world, to which renewal is promised, is present in the whole eucharistic celebration. The world is present in the thanksgiving to the Father, where the Church speaks on behalf of the whole creation; in the memorial of Christ, where the Church, united with its great High Priest and Intercessor, prays for the world; in the prayer of the gift of the Holy Spirit, where the Church asks for sanctification and new creation.

24. Reconciled in the eucharist, the members of the body of Christ are called to be servants of reconciliation amongst men and women and witnesses of the joy of resurrection. As Jesus went out to publicans and sinners and had table-fellowship with them during his earthly ministry, so Christians are called in the eucharist to be in solidarity with the outcast and to become signs of the love of Christ who lived and sacrificed himself for all and now gives himself in the eucharist.

25. The very celebration of the eucharist is an instance of the Church's participation in God's mission to the world. This participation takes everyday form in the proclamation of the Gospel, service of the neighbour, and faithful presence in the world.

26. As it is entirely the gift of God, the eucharist brings into the present age a new reality which transforms Christians into the image of Christ and

therefore makes them his effective witnesses. The eucharist is precious food for missionaries, bread and wine for pilgrims on their apostolic journey. The eucharistic community is nourished and strengthened for confessing by word and action the Lord Jesus Christ who gave his life for the salvation of the world. As it becomes one people, sharing the meal of the one Lord, the eucharistic assembly must be concerned for gathering also those who are at present beyond its visible limits, because Christ invited to his feast all for whom he died. Insofar as Christians cannot unite in full fellowship around the same table to eat the same loaf and drink from the same cup, their missionary witness is weakened at both the individual and the corporate levels.

III. *The Celebration of the Eucharist*

27. The eucharistic liturgy is essentially a single whole, consisting historically of the following element in varying sequence and of diverse importance:

—hymns of praise;

—act of repentance;

—declaration of pardon;

—proclamation of the Word of God, in various forms;

—confession of faith (creed);

—intercession for the whole Church and for the world;

—preparation of the bread and wine;

—thanksgiving to the Father for the marvels of creation, redemption and sanctification (deriving from the Jewish tradition of the *berakah*);

—the words of Christ's institution of the sacrament according to the New Testament tradition;

—the *anamnesis* or memorial of the great acts of redemption, passion, death, resurrection, ascension and Pentecost, which brought the Church into being;

—the invocation of the Holy Spirit on the community, and the elements of bread and wine (*epiklesis*, either before the words of institution or after the memorial, or both, or some other reference to the Holy Spirit which adequately expresses the "epikletic" character of the eucharist);

—consecration of the faithful to God;

—reference to the communion of saints;

—prayer for the return of the Lord and the definitive manifestation of his Kingdom;

—the Amen of the whole community;

—the Lord's prayer;

—sign of reconciliation and peace;

—the breaking of the bread;

—eating and drinking in communion with Christ and with each member of the Church;

—final act of praise;

—blessing and sending.

28. The best way towards unity in eucharistic celebration and communion is the renewal of the eucharist itself in the different churches in regard to teaching and liturgy. The churches should test their liturgies in the light of the eucharistic agreement now in the process of attainment. The liturgical reform movement has brought the churches closer together in the manner of celebrating the Lord's Supper. However, a certain liturgical diversity compatible with our common eucharistic faith is recognized as a healthy and enriching fact. The affirmation of a common eucharistic faith does not imply uniformity in either liturgy or practice.

Commentary

Since New Testament days, the Church has attached the greatest importance to the continued use of the elements of bread and wine which Jesus used at the Last Supper. In certain parts of the world, where bread and wine are not customary or obtainable, it is now sometimes held that local food and drink serve better to anchor the eucharist in everyday life. Further study is required concerning the question of which features of the Lord's Supper were unchangeably instituted by Jesus, and which features remain within the Church's competence to decide.

29. In the celebration of the eucharist, Christ gathers, teaches and nourishes the Church. It is Christ who invites to the meal and who presides at it. He is the shepherd who leads the people of God, the prophet who announces the Word of God, the priest who celebrates the mystery of God. In most churches, this presidency is signified by an ordained minister. The one who presides at the eucharistic celebration in the name of Christ makes clear that the rite is not the assemblies' own creation or possession; the eucharist is received as a gift from Christ living in his Church. The minister of the eucharist is the ambassador who represents the divine initiative and expresses the connection of the local community with other local communities in the universal Church.

30. Christian faith is deepened by the celebration of the Lord's Supper. Hence the eucharist should be celebrated frequently. Many differences of theology, liturgy and practice are connected with the varying frequency with which the Holy Communion is celebrated.

31. As the eucharist celebrates the resurrection of Christ, it is appropriate that it should take place at least every Sunday. As it is the new sacramental meal of the people of God, every Christian should be encouraged to receive communion frequently.

32. Some churches stress that Christ's presence in the consecrated elements continues after the celebration. Others place the main emphasis of the act of celebration itself and on the consumption of the elements in the act of communion. The way in which the elements are treated requires special attention.

Regarding the practice of reserving the elements, each church should respect the practices and piety of the others. Given the diversity in practice among the churches and at the same time taking note of the present situation in the convergence process, it is worthwhile to suggest:

—that, on the one hand, it be remembered, especially in sermons and instruction, that the primary intention of reserving the elements is their distribution among the sick and those who are absent, and

—on the other hand, it be recognized that the best way of showing respect for the elements served in the eucharistic celebration is by their consumption, without excluding their use for communion of the sick.

33. The increased mutual understanding expressed in the present statement may allow some churches to attain a greater measure of eucharistic communion among themselves and so bring closer the day when Christ's divided people will be visibly reunited around the Lord's Table.

MINISTRY

I. *The Calling of the Whole People of God*

1. In a broken world God calls the whole of humanity to become God's people. For this purpose God chose Israel and then spoke in a unique and decisive way in Jesus Christ, God's Son. Jesus made his own the nature, condition and cause of the whole human race giving himself as a sacrifice for all. Jesus' life of service, his death and resurrection, are the foundation of a new community which is built up continually by the good news of the Gospel and the gifts of the sacraments. The Holy Spirit unites in a single body those who follow Jesus Christ and sends them as witnesses into the world. Belonging to the Church means living in communion with God through Jesus Christ in the Holy Spirit.

2. The life of the Church is based on Christ's victory over the powers of evil and death, accomplished once for all. Christ offers forgiveness, invites to repentance and delivers from destruction. Through Christ, people are enabled to turn in praise to God and in service to their neighbours. In Christ they find the source of new life in freedom, mutual forgiveness and love. Through Christ their hearts and minds are directed to the consummation of the Kingdom where Christ's victory will become manifest and all things made new. God's purpose is that, in Jesus Christ, all people should share in this fellowship.

3. The Church lives through the liberating and renewing power of the Holy Spirit. That the Holy Spirit was upon Jesus is evidenced in his baptism, and after the resurrection that same Spirit was given to those who believed in the Risen Lord in order to recreate them as the body of Christ. The Spirit calls people to faith, sanctifies them through many gifts, gives them strength to witness to the Gospel, and empowers them to serve in hope and love. The Spirit keeps the Church in the truth and guides it despite the frailty of its members.

4. The Church is called to proclaim and prefigure the Kingdom of God. It accomplishes this by announcing the Gospel to the world and by its very existence as the body of Christ. In Jesus the Kingdom of God came among us. He offered salvation to sinners. He preached good news to the poor, release to the captives, recovery of sight to the blind, liberation to the oppressed (Luke 4:18). Christ established a new access to the Father. Living in this communion with God, all members of the Church are called to confess their faith and to give account of their hope. They are to identify with the joys and sufferings of all people as they seek to witness in caring love. The members of Christ's body are to

struggle with the oppressed towards that freedom and dignity promised with the coming of the Kingdom. This mission needs to be carried out in varying political, social and cultural contexts. In order to fulfill this mission faithfully, they will seek relevant forms of witness and service in each situation. In so doing they bring to the world a foretaste of the joy and glory of God's Kingdom.

5. The Holy Spirit bestows on the community diverse and complementary gifts. These are for the common good of the whole people and are manifested in acts of service within the community and to the world. They may be gifts of communicating the Gospel in word and deed, gifts of healing, gifts of praying, gifts of teaching and learning, gifts of serving, gifts of guiding and following, gifts of inspiration and vision. All members are called to discover, with the help of the community, the gifts they have received and to use them for the building up of the Church and for the service of the world to which the Church is sent.

6. Though the churches are agreed in their general understanding of the calling of the people of God, they differ in their understanding of how the life of the Church is to be ordered. In particular, there are differences concerning the place and forms of the ordained ministry. As they engage in the effort to overcome these differences, the churches need to work from the perspective of the calling of the whole people of God. A common answer needs to be found to the following question: How, according to the will of God and under the guidance of the Holy Spirit, is the life of the Church to be understood and ordered, so that the Gospel may be spread and the community built up in love?

II. *The Church and the Ordained Ministry*

7. Differences in terminology are part of the matter

under debate. In order to avoid confusion in the discussions on the ordained ministry in the Church, it is necessary to delineate clearly how various terms are used in the following paragraphs.

(a) The word *charism* denotes the gifts bestowed by the Holy Spirit on any member of the body of Christ for the building up of the community and the fulfillment of its calling.

(b) The word *ministry* in its broadest sense denotes the service to which the whole people of God is called, whether as individuals, as a local community, or as the universal Church. Ministry or ministries can also denote the particular institutional forms which this service may take.

(c) The term *ordained ministry* refers to persons who have received a charism and whom the church appoints for service by ordination through the invocation of the Spirit and the laying on of hands.

(d) Many churches use the word *priest* to denote certain ordained ministers. Because this usage is not universal, this document will discuss the substantive questions in paragraph 17.

A. The Ordained Ministry

8. In order to fulfill its mission, the Church needs persons who are publicly and continually responsible for pointing to its fundamental dependence on Jesus Christ, and thereby provide, within a multiplicity of gifts, a focus of its unity. The ministry of such persons, who since very early times have been ordained, is constitutive for the life and witness of the Church.

9. The Church has never been without persons holding specific authority and responsibility. Jesus chose and sent the disciples to be witnesses of the Kingdom (Matt. 10:1-8). The Twelve were promised that they would "sit on thrones judging the tribes of Israel" (Luke 22:30). A particular role is attributed to the

Twelve within the communities of the first generation. They are witnesses of the Lord's life and resurrection (Acts 1:21-26), they lead the community in
prayer, teaching, the breaking of bread, proclamation
and service (Acts 2:42-47; 6:2-6, etc.). The very
existence of the Twelve and other apostles shows
that, from the beginning, there were differentiated
roles in the community.

Commentary

In the New Testament the term "apostle" is variously employed. It is used for the Twelve but also
for a wider circle of disciples. It is applied to Paul
and to others as they are sent out by the risen
Christ to proclaim the Gospel. The roles of the
apostles cover both foundation and mission.

10. Jesus called the Twelve to be representatives of
the renewed Israel. At that moment they represent
the whole people of God and at the same time exercise a special role in the midst of that community.
After the resurrection they are among the leaders of
the community. It can be said that the apostles prefigure both the Church as a whole and the persons
within it who are entrusted with the specific authority
and responsibility. The role of the apostles as witnesses to the resurrection of Christ is unique and
unrepeatable. There is therefore a difference between
the apostles and the ordained ministers whose ministries are founded on theirs.

11. As Christ chose and sent the apostles, Christ
continues through the Holy Spirit to choose and call
persons into the ordained ministry. As heralds and
ambassadors, ordained ministers are representatives
of Jesus Christ to the community, and proclaim his
message of reconciliation. As leaders and teachers
they call the community to submit to the authority
of Jesus Christ, the teacher and prophet, in whom
law and prophets were fulfilled. As pastors, under
Jesus Christ the chief shepherd, they assemble and

guide the dispersed people of God, in anticipation of the coming Kingdom.

Commentary

The basic reality of an ordained ministry was present from the beginning (cf. para. 8). The actual forms of ordination and of the ordained ministry, however, have evolved in complex historical developments (cf. para. 19). The churches, therefore, need to avoid attributing their particular forms of the ordained ministry directly to the will and institution of Jesus Christ.

12. All members of the believing community, ordained and lay, are interrelated. On the one hand, the community needs ordained ministers. Their presence reminds the community of the divine initiative, and of the dependence of the Church on Jesus Christ, who is the source of its mission and the foundation of its unity. They serve to build up the community in Christ and to strengthen its witness. In them the Church seeks an example of holiness and loving concern. On the other hand, the ordained ministry has no existence apart from the community. Ordained ministers can fulfill their calling only in and for the community. They cannot dispense with the recognition, the support and the encouragement of the community.

13. The chief responsibility of the ordained ministry is to assemble and build up the body of Christ by proclaiming and teaching the Word of God, by celebrating the sacraments, and by guiding the life of the community in its worship, it mission and its caring ministry.

Commentary

These tasks are not always exercised by the ordained ministry in an exclusive way. Since the ordained ministry and the community are inextricably related, all members participate in fulfilling these functions. In fact, every charism serves to assemble and build up the body of Christ. Any member of the body may share in proclaiming and teaching the Word of God, may contribute to the sacramental life of that body. The ordained ministry fulfills these functions in a representative way, providing the focus for the unity of the life and witness of the community.

14. It is especially in the eucharistic celebration that the ordained ministry is the visible focus of the deep and all-embracing communion between Christ and the members of his body. In the celebration of the eucharist, Christ gathers, teaches and nourishes the Church. It is Christ who invites to the meal and who presides at it. In most churches this presidency is signified and represented by an ordained minister.

Commentary

The New Testament says very little about the ordering of the eucharist. There is no explicit evidence about the presidency of the eucharist. Very soon it is clear that an ordained ministry presides over the celebration. If the ordained ministry is to provide a focus for the unity of the life and witness of the Church, it is appropriate that an ordained minister should be given this task. It is intimately related to the task of guiding the community, i.e., supervising its life (*episkopè*) and strengthening its vigilance in relation to the truth of the apostolic message and the coming of the Kingdom.

B. Ordained Ministry and Authority

15. The authority of the ordained minister is rooted in Jesus Christ, who has received it from the Father (Matt. 28:18), and who confers it by the Holy Spirit through the act of ordination. This act takes place within a community which accords public recognition to a particular person. Because Jesus came as one who serves (Mark 10:45; Luke 22:27), to be set

apart means to be consecrated to service. Since ordination is essentialy a setting apart with prayer for the gift of the Holy Spirit, the authority of the ordained ministry is not to be understood as the possession of the ordained person but as a gift for the continuing edification of the body in and for which the minister has been ordained. Authority has the character of responsibility before God and is exercised with the cooperation of the whole community.

16. Therefore, ordained ministers must not be autocrats or impersonal functionaries. Although called to exercise wise and loving leadership on the basis of the Word of God, they are bound to the faithful in interdependence and reciprocity. Only when they seek the response and acknowledgement of the community can their authority be protected from the distortions of isolation and domination. They manifest and exercise the authority of Christ in the way Christ himself revealed God's authority to the world; by committing their life to the community. Christ's authority is unique. "He spoke as one who has authority (*exousia*), not as the scribes (Matt. 7:29). This authority is an authority governed by love for the "sheep who have no shepherd" (Matt. 9:36). It is confirmed by his life of service and, supremely, by his death and resurrection. Authority in the Church can only be authentic as it seeks to conform to this model.

Commentary

Here two dangers must be avoided. Authority cannot be exercised without regard for the community. The apostles paid heed to the experience and the judgment of the faithful. On the other hand, the authority of ordained ministers must not be so reduced as to make them dependent on the common opinion of the community. Their authority lies in their responsibility to express the will of God in the community.

C. Ordained Ministry and Priesthood

17. Jesus Christ is the unique priest of the new covenant. Christ's life was given as a sacrifice for all. Derivatively, the Church as a whole can be described as a priesthood. All members are called to offer their being "as a living sacrifice" and to intercede for the Church and the salvation of the world. Ordained ministers are related, as are all Christians, both to the priesthood of Christ and to the priesthood of the Church. But they may appropriately be called priests because they fulfill a particular priestly service by strengthening and building up the royal and prophetic priesthood of the faithful through word and sacraments, through their prayers of intercession, and through their pastoral guidance of the community.

Commentary

The New Testament never uses the term "priesthood" or "priest" (*hiereus*) to designate the ordained ministry or the ordained minister. In the New Testament, the term is reserved, on the one hand, for the unique priesthood of Jesus Christ and, on the other hand, for the royal and prophetic priesthood of all baptized. The priesthood of Christ and the priesthood of the baptized have in their respective ways the function of sacrifice and intercession. As Christ has offered himself, Christians offer their whole being "as a living sacrifice". As Christ intercedes before the Father, Christians intercede for the Church and the salvation of the world. Nevertheless, the difference between these two kinds of priesthood cannot be overlooked. While Christ offered himself as a unique sacrifice once and for all for the salvation of the world, believers need to receive continually as a gift of God that which Christ has done for them.

In the early Church the terms "priesthood" and "priest" came to be used to designate the ordained ministry and minister as presiding at the eucharist. They underline the fact that the ordained ministry is related to the priestly reality of Jesus Christ and the whole community. When the terms are used in connection with the ordained ministry, their meaning differs in appropriate ways from the sacrificial priesthood of the Old Testament, from the unique redemptive priesthood of Christ and from the corporate priesthood of the people of God. St. Paul could call his ministry "a priestly service of the gospel of God, so that the offering of the Gentiles may be acceptable by the Holy Spirit" (Rom. 15:16).

D. The Ministry of Men and Women in the Church

18. Where Christ is present, human barriers are being broken. The Church is called to convey to the world the image of a new humanity. There is in Christ no male or female (Gal. 3:28). Both women and men must discover together their contributions to the service of Christ in the Church. The Church must discover the ministry which can be provided by women as well as that which can be provided by men. A deeper understanding of the comprehensiveness of ministry which reflects the interdependence of men and women needs to be more widely manifested in the life of the Church.

Though they agree on this need, the churches draw different conclusions as to the admission of women to the ordained ministry. An increasing number of churches have decided that there is no biblical or theological reason against ordaining women, and many of them have subsequently proceeded to do so. Yet many churches hold that the tradition of the Church in this regard must not be changed.

Commentary

Those churches which practice the ordination of women do so because of their understanding of the Go: el and of the ministry. It rests for them on the deeply held theological conviction that the ordained ministry of the Church lacks fullness when it is limited to one sex. This theological conviction has been reinforced by their experience during the years in which they have included women in their ordained ministries. They have found that women's gifts are as wide and varied as men's and that their ministry is as fully blessed by the Holy Spirit as the ministry of men. None has found reason to reconsider its decision.

Those churches which do not practice the ordination of women consider that the force of nineteen centuries of tradition against the ordination of women must not be set aside. They believe that such a tradition cannot be dismissed as a lack of respect for the participation of women in the Church. They believe that there are theological issues concerning the nature of humanity and concerning Christology which lie at the heart of their convictions and understanding of the role of women in the Church.

The discussion of these practical and theological questions within the various churches and Christian traditions should be complemented by joint study and reflection within the ecumenical fellowship of all churches.

III. *The Forms of the Ordained Ministry*

A. Bishops, Presbyters and Deacons

19. The New Testament does not describe a single pattern of ministry which might serve as a blueprint or continuing norm for all future ministry in the Church. In the New Testament there appears rather a variety of forms which existed at different places and times. As the Holy Spirit continued to lead the Church in life, worship and mission, certain elements from this early variety were further developed

and became settled into a more universal pattern of ministry. During the second and third centuries, a threefold pattern of bishop, presbyter and deacon became established as the pattern of ordained ministry throughout the Church. In succeeding centuries, the ministry by bishop, presbyter and deacon underwent considerable changes in its practical exercise. At some points of crisis in the history of the Church, the continuing functions of ministry were in some places and communities distributed according to structures other than the predominant threefold pattern. Sometimes appeal was made to the New Testament in justification of these other patterns. In other cases, the restructuring of the ministry was held to lie within the competence of the Church as it adapted to changed circumstances.

20. It is important to be aware of the changes the threefold ministry has undergone in the history of the Church. In the earliest instances, where threefold ministry is mentioned, the reference is to the local eucharistic community. The bishop was the leader of the community. He was ordained and installed to proclaim the Word and preside over the celebration of the eucharist. He was surrounded by a college of presbyters and by deacons who assisted in his tasks. In this context the bishop's ministry was a focus of unity within the whole community.

21. Soon, however, the functions were modified. Bishops began increasingly to exercise *episkopè* over several local communities at the same time. In the first generation, apostles had exercised *episkopè* in in the wider Church. Later Timothy and Titus are recorded to have fulfilled a function of *episkopè* in a given area. Later again this apostolic task is carried out in a new way by the bishops. They provide a focus for unity in life and witness within areas comprising several eucharistic communities. As a consequence, presbyters and deacons are assigned new roles. The presbyters become the leaders of the

local eucharistic community, and as assistants of the bishops deacons receive responsibilities in the larger area.

Commentary

The earliest Church knew both the travelling ministry of such missionaries as Paul and the local ministry of leadership in places where the Gospel was received. At local level, organizational patterns appear to have varied according to circumstances. The Acts of the Apostles mention for Jerusalem the Twelve and the Seven, and later James and the elders; and for Antioch, prophets and teachers (Acts 6:1-6; 15:13-22; 13:1). The letters to Corinth speak of apostles, prophets and teachers (I Cor. 12:28); so too does the letter to the Romans, which also speaks of deacons or assistants (Rom. 16:1). In Philippi, the secular terms *episkopoi* and *diakonoi* were together used for Christian ministers (Phil. 1:1). Several of these ministries are ascribed to both women and men. While some were appointed by the laying on of hands, there is no indication of this procedure in other cases. Whatever their names, the purpose of these ministries was to proclaim the Word of God, to transmit and safeguard the original content of the Gospel, to feed and strengthen the faith, discipline and service of the Christian communities, and to protect and foster unity within and among them. These have been the constant duties of ministry throughout the developments and crisis of Christian history.

22. Although there is no single New Testament pattern, although the Spirit has many times led the Church to adapt its ministries to contextual needs and although other forms of the ordained ministry have been blessed with the gifts of the Holy Spirit, nevertheless the threefold ministry of bishop, presbyter and deacon may serve today as an expression

of the unity we seek and also as a means for achieving it. Historically, it is true to say, the threefold ministry became the generally accepted pattern in the Church of the early centuries and is still retained today by many churches. In the fulfillment of their mission and service the churches need people who in different ways express and perform the tasks of the ordained ministry in its diaconal, presbyteral and episcopal aspects and functions.

23. The Church as the body of Christ and the eschatological people of God is constituted by the Holy Spirit through a diversiy of gifts or ministries. Among these gifts a ministry of *episkopè* is necessary to express and safeguard the unity of the body. Every church needs this ministry of unity in some form in order to be the Church of God, the one body of Christ, a sign of the unity of all in the Kingdom.

24. The threefold pattern stands evidently in need of reform. In some churches the collegial dimension of leadership in the eucharistic community has suffered diminution. In others, the function of deacons has been reduced to an assistant role in the celebration of the liturgy: they have ceased to fulfill any function with regard to the diaconal witness of the Church. In general, the relation of the presbyterate to the episcopal ministry has been discussed throughout the centuries, and the degree of the presbyter's participation in the episcopal ministry is still for many an unresolved question of far-reaching ecumenical importance. In some cases, churches which have not formally kept the threefold form have, in fact, maintained certain of its original patterns.

25. The traditional threefold pattern thus raises questions for all the churches. Churches maintaining the threefold pattern will need to ask how its potential can be fully developed for the most effective witness of the Church in this world. In this task

churches not having the threefold pattern should also participate. They will further need to ask themselves whether the threefold pattern as developed does not have a powerful claim to be accepted by them.

B. Guiding Principles for the Exercise of the Ordained Ministry in the Church

26. Three considerations are important in this respect. The ordained ministry should be exercised in a personal, collegial and communal way. *Personal* in that the presence of Christ among his people can most effectively be pointed to by the person ordained to proclaim the Gospel and to call the community to serve the Lord in unity of life and witness. *Collegial,* for there is need for a college of ordained ministers sharing in the common task of representing the concerns of the community. Finally, the intimate relationship between the ordained ministry and the community must find expression in a *communal* dimension where the exercise of the ordained ministry must be rooted in the life of the community and requires the community's effective participation in the discovery of God's will and the guidance of the Spirit.

Commentary

These three aspects need to be kept together. In various churches, one or the other has been over-emphasized at the expense of the others. In some churches, the personal dimension of the ordained ministry tends to diminish the collegial and communal dimensions. In other churches, the collegial or communal dimension takes so much importance that the ordained ministry loses its personal dimension. Each church needs to ask itself in what way its exercise of the ordained ministry has suffered in the course of history.

An appreciation of these three dimensions lies

behind a recommendation made by the first World Conference on Faith and Order at Lausanne in 1927: "In view of (i) the place which the episcopate, the council of presbyters and the congregation of the faithful, respectively, had in the constitution of the early Church, and (ii) the fact that episcopal, presbyteral and congregational systems of government are each today, and have been for centuries, accepted by great communions in Christendom, and (iii) the fact that episcopal, presbyteral and congregatonal systems are each believed by many to be essential to the good order of the Church, we therefore recognize that these several elments must all, under conditions which require further study, have an appropriate place in the order of life of a reunited Church . . ."

27. The ordained ministry needs to be constitutionally or canonically ordered and exercised in the Church in such a way that each of these three dimensions can find adequate expression. At the level of the local eucharistic community there is need for an ordained minister acting within a collegial body. Strong emphasis should be placed on the active participation of all members in the life and the decision-making of the community. At the regional level there is again need for an ordained minister exercising a service of unity. The collegial and communal dimensions will find expression in regular representative synodal gatherings.

C. Functions of Bishops, Presbyters and Deacons

28. What can then be said about the functions and even the titles of bishops, presbyters and deacons? A uniform answer to this question is not required for the mutual recognition of the ordained ministry. The following considerations on functions are, however, offered in a tentative way.

29. *Bishops* preach the Word, preside at the sacraments, and administer discipline in such a way as to

be representative pastoral ministers of oversight, continuity and unity in the Church. They have pastoral oversight of the area to which they are called. They serve the apostolicity and unity of the Church's teaching, worship and sacramental life. They have responsibility for leadership in the Church's mission. They relate the Christian community in their area to the wider Church, and the universal Church to their community. They, in communion with the presbyters and deacons and the whole community, are responsible for the orderly transfer of ministerial authority in the Church.

30. *Presbyters* serve as pastoral ministers of Word and sacraments in a local eucharistic community. They are preachers and teachers of the faith, exercise pastoral care, and bear responsibility for the discipline of the congregation to the end that the world may believe and that the entire membership of the Church may be renewed, strengthened and equipped in ministry. Presbyters have particular responsibility for the preparation of members for Christian life and ministry.

37. *Deacons* represent to the Church its calling as servant in the world. By struggling in Christ's name with the myriad needs of societies and persons, deacons exemplify the interdependence of worship and service in the Church's life. They exercise responsibility in the worship of the congregation: for example by reading the scriptures, preaching and leading the people in prayer. They help in the teaching of the congregation. They exercise a ministry of love within the community. They fulfill certain administrative tasks and may be elected to responsibilities for governance.

Commentary

In many churches there is today considerable uncertainty about the need, the rationale, the status and the functions of deacons. In what sense can the diaconate be considered part of the ordained ministry? What is it that distinguishes it from other ministries in the Church (catechists, musicians, etc.)? Why should deacons be ordained while these other ministries do not receive ordination? If they are ordained, do they receive ordination in the full sense of the word or is their ordination only the first step towards ordination as presbyters? Today, there is a strong tendency in many churches to restore the diaconate as an ordained ministry with its own dignity and meant to be exercised for life. As the churches move closer together there may be united in this office ministries now existing in a variety of forms and under a variety of names. Differences in ordering the diaconal ministry should not be regarded as a hindrance for the mutual recognition of the ordained ministries.

D. Variety of Charisms

32. The community which lives in the power of the Spirit will be characterized by a variety of charisms. The Spirit is the giver of diverse gifts which enrich the life of the community. In order to enhance their effectiveness, the community will recognize publicly certain of these charisms. While some serve permanent needs in the life of the community, others will be temporary. Men and women in the communities of religious orders fulfill a service which is of particular importance for the life of the Church. The ordained ministry, which is itself a charism, must not become a hindrance for the variety of these charisms. On the contrary, it will help the community to discover the gifts bestowed on it by the Holy Spirit and will equip members of the body to serve in a variety of ways.

33. In the history of the Church there have been times when the truth of the Gospel could only be

preserved through prophetic and charismatic leaders. Often new impulses could find their way into the life of the Church only in unusual ways. At times reforms required a special ministry. The ordained ministers and the whole community will need to be attentive to the challenge of such special ministries.

IV. *Succession in the Apostolic Tradition*

A. Apostolic Tradition in the Church

34. In the Creed, the Church confesses itself to be apostolic. The Church lives in continuity with the apostles and their proclamation. The same Lord who sent the apostles continues to be present in the Church. The Spirit keeps the Church in the apostolic tradition until the fulfillment of history in the Kingdom of God. Apostolic tradition in the Church means continuity in the permanent characteristics of the Church of the apostles: witness to the apostolic faith, proclamation and fresh interpretation of the Gospel, celebration of baptism and the eucharist, the transmission of ministerial responsibilities, communion in prayer, love, joy and suffering, service to the sick and the needy, unity among the local churches and sharing the gifts which the Lord has given to each.

Commentary

The apostles, as witnesses of the life and resurrection of Christ and sent by him, are the original transmitters of the Gospel, of the tradition of the saving words and acts of Jesus Christ which constitute the life of the Church. This apostolic tradition continues through history and links the Church to its origins in Christ and in the college of the apostles. Within this apostolic tradition is an apostolic succession of the ministry which serves the continuity of the Church in its life in Christ and its faithfulness to the words and acts of Jesus transmitted by the apostles. The ministers appointed by the apostles, and then the *episkopoi* of the churches, were the first guardians of this transmission of the apostolic tradition; they testified to the apostolic succession of the ministry which was continued through the bishops of the early Church in collegial communion with the presbyters and deacons within the Christian community. A distinction should be made, therefore, between the apostolic tradition of the whole Church and the succession of the apostolic ministry.

B. Succession of the Apostolic Ministry

35. The primary manifestation of apostolic succession is to be found in the apostolic tradition of the Church as a whole. The succession is an expression of the permanence and, therefore, of the continuity of Christ's own mission in which the Church participates. Within the Church the ordained ministry has a particular task of preserving and actualizing the apostolic faith. The orderly transmission of the ordained ministry is therefore a powerful expression of the continuity of the Church throughout history; it also underlines the calling of the ordained minister as guardian of the faith. Where churches see little importance in orderly transmission, they should ask themselves whether they have not to change their conception of continuity in the apostolic tradition. On the other hand, where the ordained ministry does not adequately serve the proclamation of the apostolic faith, churches must ask themselves whether their ministerial structures are not in need of reform.

36. Under the particular historical circumstances of the growing Church in the early centuries, the succession of bishops became one of the ways, together with the transmission of the Gospel and the life of the community, in which the apostolic tradition of the Church was expressed. This succession was un-

derstood as serving, symbolizing and guarding the continuity of the apostolic faith and communion.

Commentary

In the early Church the bond between the episcopate and the apostolic community was understood in two ways. Clement of Rome linked the mission of the bishop with the sending of Christ by the Father and the sending of the apostles by Christ (Cor. 42:44). This made the bishop a successor of the apostles, ensuring the permanence of the apostolic mission in the Church. Clement is primarily interested in the means whereby the *historical* continuity of Christ's presence is ensured in the Church thanks to the apostolic succession. For Ignatius of Antioch (Magn. 6:1, 3:1-2; Trall. 3:1), it is Christ surrounded by the Twelve who is permanently in the Church in the person of the bishop surrounded by the presbyters. Ignatius regards the Christian community assembled around the bishop in midst of the presbyters and the deacons as the *actual* manifestation in the Spirit of the apostolic community. The sign of apostolic succession thus not only points to historical continuity; it also manifests an actual spiritual reality.

37. In churches which practice the succession through the episcopate, it is increasingly recognized that a continuity in apostolic faith, worship and mission has been preserved in churches which have not retained the form of historic episcopate. This recognition finds additional support in the fact that the reality and function of the episcopal ministry have been preserved in many of these churches, with or without the title "bishop". Ordination, for example, is always done in them by persons in whom the Church recognizes the authority to transmit the ministerial commission.

38. These considerations do not diminish the importance of the episcopal ministry. On the contrary, they

enable churches which have not retained the episcopate to appreciate the episcopal succession as a sign,
though not a guarantee, of the continuity and unity
of the Church. Today churches, including those engaged in union negotiations, are expressing willingness to accept episcopal succession as a sign of the
apostolicity of the life of the whole Church. Yet, at
the same time, they cannot accept any suggestion
that the ministry exercised in their own tradition
should be invalid until the moment that it enters
into an existing line of episcopal succession. Their
acceptance of the episcopal succession will best
further the unity of the whole church if it is part
of a wider process by which the episcopal churches
themselves also regain their lost unity.

V. *Ordination*

A. The Meaning of Ordination

39. The Church ordains certain of its members for
the ministry in the name of Christ by the invocation
of the Spirit and the laying on of hands (I Tim.
4:14; II Tim. 1:6); in so doing it seeks to continue
the mission of the apostles and to remain faithful to
their teaching. The act of ordination by those who
are appointed for this minisry attests the bond of the
Church with Jesus Christ and the apostolic witness,
recalling that it is the risen Lord who is the true
ordainer and bestows the gift. In ordaining, the
Church, under the inspiration of the Holy Spirit,
provides for the faithful proclamation of the Gospel
and humble service in the name of Christ. The laying on of hands is the sign of the gift of the Spirit,
rendering visible the fact that the ministry was
instituted in the revelation accomplished in Christ,
and reminding the Church to look to him as the
source of its commission. This ordination, however,
can have different intentions according to the specific tasks of bishops, presbyters and deacons as indicated in the liturgies of ordination.

Commentary

It is clear that churches have different practices of ordination, and that it would be wrong to single out one of those as exclusively valid. On the other hand, if churches are willing to recognize each other in the sign of apostolic succession, as described above, it would follow that the old tradition, according to which it is the bishop who ordains, with the participation of the community, will be recognized and respected as well.

40. Properly speaking, then, ordination denotes an action by God and the community by which the ordained are strengthened by the Spirit for their task and are upheld by the acknowledgement and prayers of the congregation.

Commentary

The original New Testament terms for ordination tend to be simple and descriptive. The fact of appointment is recorded. The laying on of hands is described. Prayer is made for the Spirit. Different traditions have built different interpretations on the basis of these data.

It is evident that there is a certain difference between the unspoken cultural setting of the Greek *cheirotonein* and that of the Latin *ordo* or *ordinare*. The New Testament use of the former term borrows its basic secular meaning of "appointment" (Act 14:23; II Cor. 8:19), which is, in turn, derived from the original meaning of extending the hand, either to designate a person or to cast a vote. Some scholars see in *cheirotonein* a reference to the act of laying on of hands, in view of the literal description of such action in such seemingly parallel instances as Acts 6:6, 8:17, 13:3, 19:6; I Tim. 4:14; II Tim. 1:6. *Ordo* and *ordinare*, on the other hand, are terms derived from Roman law where they convey the notion of the special status of a group distinct from the plebs, as in the term *ordo clarissimus* for the Roman senate. The starting point of any conceptual construction using these terms will strongly influence what is taken for granted in both the thought and action which result.

B. The Act of Ordination

41. A long and early Christian tradition places ordination in the context of worship and especially of the eucharist. Such a place for the service of ordination preserves the understanding of ordination as an *act* of the *whole* community, and not of a certain order within it or of the individual ordained. The act of ordination by the laying on of hands of those appointed to do so is at one and the same time: invocation of the Holy Spirit (*epiklesis*); sacramental sign; acknowledgement of gifts and commitment.

42. (a) Ordination is an invocation to God that the new minister be given power of the Holy Spirit in the new relation which is established between this minister and the local Christian community and, by intention, the Church universal. The otherness of God's initiative, of which the ordained ministry is a sign, is here acknowledged in the act of ordination itself. "The Spirit blows where it wills" (John 3:3): the invocation of the Spirit implies the absolute dependence on God for the outcome of the Church's prayer. This means that the Spirit may set new forces in motion and open new possibilities "far more abundantly than all that we ask or think" (Eph. 3:20).

43. (b) Ordination is a sign of the granting of this prayer by the Lord who gives the gift of the ordained ministry. Although the outcome of the Church's *epiklesis* depends on the freedom of God, the Church ordains in confidence that God, being faithful to his promise in Christ, enters sacramentally into contingent, historical forms of human relationship and uses them for his purpose. Ordination

is a sign performed in faith that the spiritual relationship signified is present in, with and through the words spoken, the gestures made and the forms employed.

44. (c) Ordination is an acknowledgement by the Church of the gifts of the Spirit in the one ordained, and a commitment by both the Church and the ordinand to the new relationship. By receiving the new minister in the act of ordination, the congregation acknowledges this minister's gifts and commits itself to responsibility to be open towards these gifts. Likewise those ordained offer their gifts to the Church and commit themselves to the burden and opportunity of new authority and responsibility. At the same time, they enter into a collegial relationship with other ordained ministers.

C. The Conditions for Ordination

45. People are called in differing ways to the ordained ministry. There is a personal awareness of a call from the Lord to dedicate oneself to the ordained ministry. This call may be discerned through personal prayer and reflection, as well as through suggestion, example, encouragement, guidance coming from family, friends, the congregation, teachers, and other Church authorities. This call must be authenticated by the Church's recognition of the gifts and graces of the particular person, both natural and spiritually given, needed for the ministry to be performed. God can use people both celibate and married for the ordained ministry.

46. Ordained persons may be professional ministers in the sense that they receive their salaries from the Church. The Church may also ordain people who remain in other occupations or employment.

47. Candidates for the ordained ministry need appropriate preparation through study of Scripture and theology, prayer and spirituality, and through ac-

quaintance with the social and human realities of the contemporary world. In some situations, this preparation may take a form other than that of prolonged academic study. The period of training will be one in which the candidate's call is tested, fostered and confirmed or its understanding modified.

48. Initial commitment to ordained ministry ought normally to be made without reserve or time limit. Yet leave of absence from service is not incompatible with ordination. Resumption of ordained ministry requires the assent of the Church, but no re-ordination. In recognition of the God-given charism of ministry, ordination to any one of the particular ordained ministries is never repeated.

49. The discipline with regard to the conditions for ordination in one church need not be seen as universally applicable and used as grounds for not recognizing ministry in others.

50. Churches which refuse to consider candidates for the ordained ministry on the grounds of handicap or because they belong, for example, to one particular race or sociological group should re-evaluate their practices. This re-evaluation is particularly important today in view of the multitude of experiments in new forms of ministry with which the churches are approaching the modern world.

VI. *Towards the Mutual Recognition of the Ordained Ministries*

51. In order to advance towards the mutual recognition of ministries, deliberate efforts are required. All churches need to examine the forms of ordained ministry and the degree to which they are faithful to its original intentions. Churches must be prepared to renew their understanding and their practice of the ordained ministry.

52. Among the issues that need to be worked on as churches move towards mutual recognition of ministries, that of apostolic succession is of particular

importance. Churches in ecumenical conversations can recognize their respective ordained ministries if they are mutually assured of their intention to transmit the ministry of Word and Sacrament in continuity with apostolic times. The act of transmission should be performed in accordance with the apostolic tradition, which includes the invocation of the Spirit and the laying on of hands.

53. In order to achieve mutual recognition, different steps are required of different churches. For example:

(a) Churches which have preserved the episcopal succession are asked to recognize both the apostolic content of the ordained ministry which exists in churches which have not maintained such succession and also the existence in these churches of a ministry of *episkopè* in various forms.

(b) Churches without the episcopal succession, and living in faithful continuity with the apostolic faith and mission, have a ministry of Word and Sacrament, as is evident from the belief, practice, and life of those churches. These churches are asked to realize that the continuity with the Church of the apostles finds profound expression in the successive laying on of hands by bishops and that, though they may not lack the continuity of the apostolic tradition, this sign will strengthen and deepen that continuity. They may need to recover the sign of the episcopal succession.

54. Some churches ordain both men and women, others ordain only men. Differences on this issue raise obstacles to the mutual recognition of ministries. But those obstacles must not be regarded as substantive hindrance for further efforts towards mutual recognition. Openness to each other holds the possibility that the Spirit may well speak to one church through the insights of another. Ecumenical consideration, therefore, should encourage, not restrain, the facing of this question.

55. The mutual recognition of churches and their ministries implies decision by the appropriate authorities and a liturgical act from which point unity would be publicly manifest. Several forms of such public act have been proposed; mutual laying on of hands, eucharistic con-celebration, solemn worship without a particular rite of recognition, the reading of a text of union during the course of a celebraton. No one liturgical form would be absolutely required, but in any case it would be necessary to proclaim the accomplishment of mutual recognition publicly. The common celebration of the eucharist would certainly be the place for such an act.

THE MISSION OF THE CHURCH

Reflection on the mission of the church has been elicited by the breakup of established cultural patterns, by the new awareness of living religions, as well as by theological developments within the church. The following developments are illustrative of this reflection and debate.

DECREE ON THE MISSIONARY ACTIVITY OF THE CHURCH
Vatican Council II (1965)

Source: Text may be found in *The Documents of Vatican II* edited by Walter M. Abbott, S. J. (New York: Corpus Books, 1966), pp. 584–630.

PREFACE

1. The Church has been divinely sent to all nations that she might be "the universal sacrament of salva-

tion." Acting out of the innermost requirements of her own catholicity and in obedience to her Founder's mandate (cf. Mk. 16:16), she strives to proclaim the gospel to all men. For the Church was founded upon the apostles, who, following in the footsteps of Christ, "preached the message of truth and begot Churches." Upon their successors devolves the duty of perpetuating this work through the years. Thus "the word of God may run and be glorified" (2 Th. 3:1) and God's kingdom can be everywhere proclaimed and established.

The present historical situation is leading humanity into a new stage. As the salt of the earth and light of the world (cf. Mt. 5:13-14), the Church is summoned with special urgency to save and renew every creature. In this way all things can be restored in Christ, and in Him mankind can compose one family and one people.

Hence this holy Synod gives thanks to God for the splendid accomplishments already achieved through the noble energy of the whole Church. At the same time she wishes to sketch the principles of missionary activity and to marshal the forces of all the faithful. Her intention is that God's people, undertaking the narrow way of the cross, may spread everywhere the kingdom of Christ, the Lord and Overseer of the ages (cf. Sir. 36:19), and may prepare the way for His coming.

CHAPTER I

DOCTRINAL PRINCIPLES

2. The pilgrim Church is missionary by her very nature. For it is from the mission of the Son and the mission of the Holy Spirit that she takes her origin, in accordance with the decree of God the Father.

This decree flows from "that fountain of love" or charity within God the Father. From Him, who is "the origin without origin," the Son is begotten and the Holy Spirit proceeds through the Son. Freely

creating us out of His surpassing and merciful kindness, and graciously calling us moreover to communicate in life and glory with Himself, He has gener-
ously poured out His divine goodness and does not
cease to do so. Thus He who made all things may
at last be "all in all" (1 Cor. 15:28), procuring at
one and the same time His own glory and our
happiness.

But it has not pleased God to call men to share
His life merely as individuals without any mutual
bonds. Rather, He wills to mold them into a people
in which His sons, once scattered abroad, can be
gathered together (cf. John 11:52).

3. This universal design of God for the salvation of
the human race is not carried out exclusively in the
soul of a man, with a kind of secrecy. Nor is it
achieved merely through those multiple endeavors,
including religious ones, by which men search for
God, groping for Him that they may by chance find
Him (though He is not far from any one of us)
(cf. Acts 17:27). For these attempts need to be enlightened and purified, even though, through the
kindly workings of Divine Providence, they may
sometimes serve as a guidance course toward the
true God, or as a preparation for the gospel.

In order to establish peace or communion between
sinful human beings and Himself, as well as to
fashion them into a fraternal community, God determined to intervene in human history in a way both
new and definitive. For He sent His Son, clothed in
our flesh, in order that through this Son He might
snatch men from the power of darkness and of Satan
(cf. Col. 1:13; Acts 10:38) and that in this Son He
might reconcile the world to Himself (cf. 2 Cor.
5:19). Through Him, God made all orders of existence. God further appointed Him heir of all things,
so that in the Son He might restore them all (cf.
Eph. 1:10).

For Jesus Christ was sent into the world as a real Mediator between God and men. Since he is God, all divine fullness dwells bodily in Him (Col. 2:9). According to His human nature, He is the new Adam, made head of a renewed humanity, and full of grace and of truth (Jn. 1:14). Therefore the Son of God walked the ways of a true Incarnation that He might make men sharers in the divine nature. He became poor for our sakes, though He had been rich, in order that His poverty might enrich us (2 Cor. 8:9). The Son of Man came not that He might be served, but that He might be a servant, and give His life as a ransom for the many—that is, for all (cf. Mk. 10:45).

The sainted Fathers of the Church firmly proclaim that what was not taken up by Christ was not healed. Now, what He took up was our entire human nature such as it is found among us in our misery and poverty, though without our sin (cf. Heb. 4:15; 9:28). For Christ said concerning Himself, whom the Father made holy and sent into the world (cf. Jn. 10:36): "The Spirit of the Lord is upon me because he anointed me; to bring good news to the poor he sent me, to heal the broken-hearted, to proclaim to the captives release, and sight to the blind" (Lk. 4:18). And again: "The Son of Man came to seek and to save what was lost" (Lk. 19:10).

But what was once preached by the Lord, or what was once wrought in Him for the saving of the human race, must be proclaimed and spread abroad to the ends of the earth (Acts 1:8), beginning from Jerusalem (cf. Lk. 24:47). Thus, what He once accomplished for the salvation of all may in the course of time come to achieve its effect in all.

4. To accomplish this goal, Christ sent the Holy Spirit from the Father. The Spirit was to carry out His saving work inwardly and to impel the Church toward her proper expansion. Doubtless, the Holy

Spirit was already at work in the world before Christ was glorified. Yet on the day of Pentecost, He came down upon the disciples to remain with them forever (cf. Jn. 14:16). On that day the Church was publicly revealed to the multitude, the gospel began to spread among the nations by means of preaching, and finally there occurred a foreshadowing of that union of all peoples in a universal faith.

That union was to be achieved by the Church of the New Covenant, a Church which speaks all tongues, which lovingly understands and accepts all tongues, and thus overcomes the divisiveness of Babel. For it was from Pentecost that the "Acts of the Apostles" took their origin. In a similar way Christ was conceived when the Holy Spirit came upon the Virgin Mary. Thus too Christ was impelled to the work of His ministry when the same Holy Spirit descended upon Him at prayer.

Now, before freely giving His life for the world, the Lord Jesus so arranged the ministry of the apostles and so promised to send the Holy Spirit, that both they and the Spirit were to be associated in effecting the work of salvation always and everywhere. Throughout all ages, the Holy Spirit gives the entire Church "unity in fellowship and in service; He furnishes her with various gifts, both hierarchical and charismatic." He vivifies ecclesiastical institutions as a kind of soul and instills into the hearts of the faithful the same mission spirit which motivated Christ Himself. Sometimes He visibly anticipates the apostles' action, just as He unceasingly accompanies and directs it in different ways.

5. From the very beginning, the Lord Jesus "called to him men of his own choosing. . . . And he appointed twelve that they might be with him, and that he might send them forth to preach" (Mk. 3:13; cf. Mt. 10:1-42). Thus the apostles were the first members of the New Israel, and at the same time

the beginning of the sacred hierarchy.

By His death and His resurrection the Lord completed once for all in Himself the mysteries of our salvation and of the renewal of all things. He had received all power in heaven and on earth (cf. Mt. 28:18). Now, before He was taken up into heaven (cf. Acts 1:11), He founded His Church as the sacrament of salvation, and sent His apostles into all the world just as He Himself had been sent by His Father (cf. Jn. 20:21). He gave them this command: "Go, therefore, and make disciples of all nations, baptizing them in the name of the Father, and of the Son, and of the Holy Spirit, teaching them to observe all that I have commanded you" (Mt. 28:19 f.). "Go into the whole world; preach the gospel to every creature. He who believes and is baptized shall be saved, but he who does not believe shall be condemned" (Mk. 16:15 f.).

Since then the duty has weighed upon the Church to spread the faith and the saving work of Christ. This duty exists not only in virtue of the express command which was inherited from the apostles by the order of bishops, assisted by priests and united with the successor of Peter and supreme shepherd of the Church. It exists also in virtue of that life which flows from Christ into His members: "From him the whole body (being closely joined and knit together through every joint of the system according to the functioning in due measure of each single part) derives its increase to the building up of itself in love" (Eph. 4:16).

The mission of the Church, therefore, is fulfilled by that activity which makes her fully present to all men and nations. She undertakes this activity in obedience to Christ's command and in response to the grace and love of the Holy Spirit. Thus, by the example of her life and by her preaching, by the sacraments and other means of grace, she can lead them to the faith, the freedom, and the peace of

Christ. Thus there lies open before them a free and trustworthy road to full participation in the mystery of Christ.

This mission is a continuing one. In the course of history it unfolds the mission of Christ Himself, who was sent to preach the gospel to the poor. Hence, prompted by the Holy Spirit, the Church must walk the same road which Christ walked: a road of poverty and obedience, of service and self-sacrifice to the death, from which death He came forth a victor by His resurrection. For thus did all the apostles walk in hope. On behalf of Christ's body, which is the Church, they supplied what was wanting of the sufferings of Christ by their own many trials and sufferings (cf. Col. 1:24). Often, too, the blood of Christians was like a seed.

6. This duty must be fulfilled by the order of bishops, whose head is Peter's successor, and with the prayer and cooperation of the whole Church. This duty is one and the same everywhere and in every situation, even though the variety of situations keeps it from being exercised in the same way. Hence, the differences to be found in this activity of the Church do not result from the inner nature of her mission itself, but are due rather to the circumstances in which this mission is exercised.

These circumstances depend sometimes on the Church, sometimes on the peoples or groups or individuals to whom the mission is directed. For although the Church includes within herself the totality or fullness of the means of salvation, she does not and cannot always and instantly bring all of them into action.

Rather, she knows what it means to make beginnings and to advance step by step in the work by which she strives to make God's plan a reality. In fact there are times when, after a happy beginning, she must lament another setback, or is at least detained in a certain state of partial and insufficient fulfillment. As for the men, groups, and peoples concerned, only by degrees does she touch and pervade them, and thus take them up into full catholicity. The appropriate actions and tools must be brought to bear on any given circumstance or situation.

"Missions" is the term usually given to those particular undertakings by which the heralds of the gospel are sent out by the Church and go forth into the whole world to carry out the task of preaching the gospel and planting the Church among peoples or groups who do not yet believe in Christ. These undertakings are brought to completion by missionary activity and are commonly exercised in certain territories recognized by the Holy See.

The specific purpose of this missionary activity is evangelization and the planting of the Church among those peoples and groups where she has not yet taken root. Thus from the seed which is the Word of God, particular native Churches can be adequately established and flourish the world over, endowed with their own vitality and maturity. Thus too, sufficiently provided with a hierarchy of their own which is joined to a faithful people, and adequately fitted out with requisites for living a full Christian life, they can make their contribution to the good of the Church universal.

The chief means of this implantation is the preaching of the gospel of Jesus Christ. The Lord sent forth His disciples into the whole world to preach this gospel. Thus reborn by the Word of God (cf. 1 Pet. 1:23), men may through baptism be joined to that Church which, as the body of the Word Incarnate, is nourished and lives by the word of God and by the Eucharistic bread (cf. Acts 2:43).

In this missionary activity of the Church various stages are sometimes found side by side: first, that of the beginning or planting, then that of newness or youth. When these stages have passed, the Church's missionary activity does not cease. Rather, there lies upon the particular Churches which are already set up the duty of continuing this activity and of preaching the gospel to those still outside.

Moreover, the groups among which the Church dwells often undergo radical changes for one reason or other, and an entirely new set of circumstances can arise. Then the Church must deliberate whether these conditions call for a renewal of her missionary activity. Besides, circumstances are sometimes such that, for the time being, there is no possibility of expounding the gospel directly and immediately. Then, missionaries can and must at least bear witness to Christ by charity and by works of mercy, with all patience, prudence, and great confidence. Thus they will prepare the way for the Lord and make Him present in some manner.

It is plain, then, that missionary activity wells up from the Church's innermost nature and spreads abroad her saving faith. It perfects her Catholic unity by expanding it. It is sustained by her apostolicity. It gives expression to the collegial awareness of her hierarchy. It bears witness to her sanctity while spreading and promoting it.

Thus, missionary activity among the nations differs from pastoral activity exercised among the faithful, as well as from undertakings aimed at restoring unity among Christians. And yet these two other activities are most closely connected with the missionary zeal of the Church, because the division among Christians damages the most holy cause of preaching the gospel to every creature and blocks the way to the faith for many. Hence, by the same mandate which makes missions necessary, all the baptized are called to be gathered into one flock, and thus to be able to bear unanimous witness before the nations to Christ their Lord. And if they are not yet capable of bearing full witness to the same faith, they should at least be animated by mutual esteem and love.

7. This missionary activity finds its reason in the will of God, "who wishes all men to be saved and to come to the knowledge of the truth. For there is one God, and one Mediator between God and men, himself man, Christ Jesus, who gave himself a ransom for all" (1 Tim. 2:4-5), "neither is there salvation in any other" (Acts 4:12).

Therefore, all must be converted to Him as He is made known by the Church's preaching. All must be incorporated into Him by baptism, and into the Church which is His body. For Christ Himself "in explicit terms . . . affirmed the necessity of faith and baptism (cf. Mk. 16:16; Jn. 3:5) and thereby affirmed also the necessity of the Church, for through baptism as through a door men enter the Church. Whosoever, therefore, knowing that the Catholic Church was made necessary by God through Jesus Christ, would refuse to enter her or to remain in her could not be saved."

Therefore, though God in ways known to Himself can lead those inculpably ignorant of the gospel to that faith without which it is impossible to please Him (Heb. 11:6), yet a necessity lies upon the Church (cf. 1 Cor. 9:16), and at the same time a sacred duty, to preach the gospel. Hence missionary activity today as always retains its power and necessity.

By means of this activity, the Mystical Body of Christ unceasingly gathers and directs its forces toward its own growth (cf. Eph. 4:11-16). The members of the Church are impelled to carry on such missionary activity by reason of the love with which they love God and by which they desire to share wtih all men in the spiritual goods of both this life and the life to come.

Finally, by means of this missionary activity God

is fully glorified, provided that men consciously and fully accept His work of salvation, which He has accomplished in Christ. Through this activity that plan of God is thus fulfilled to which Christ was obediently and lovingly devoted for the glory of the Father who sent Him. According to this plan, the whole human race is to form one people of God, coalesce into the one body of Christ, and be built up into one temple of the Holy Spirit. Since it concerns brotherly concord, this design surely corresponds with the inmost wishes of all men.

And so the plan of the Creator, who formed man to His own image and likeness, will be realized at last when all who share one human nature, regenerated in Christ through the Holy Spirit and beholding together the glory of God, will be able to say "Our Father."

8. Missionary activity is closely bound up too with human nature itself and its aspirations. By manifesting Christ, the Church reveals to men the real truth about their condition and their total vocation. For Christ is the source and model of that renewed humanity, penetrated with brotherly love, sincerity, and a peaceful spirit, to which all aspire. Christ and the Church, which bears witness to Him by preaching the gospel, transcend every particularity of race or nation and therefore cannot be considered foreign anywhere or to anybody. Christ Himself is the Truth and the Way. The preaching of the gospel opens them up to all when it proclaims to all these words of the same Christ: "Repent, and believe in the gospel" (Mk. 1:15).

Now, since he who does not believe is already judged (cf. Jn. 3:18), the words of Christ are at one and the same time words of judgment and of grace, of death and of life. For it is only by putting to death what is old that we are able to come to a newness of life. This fact applies first of all to persons, but it holds for the various goods of this world, which bear the mark both of man's sin and of God's blessing; for "all have sinned and have need of the glory of God" (Rom. 3:23). By himself and by his own power, no one is freed from sin or raised above himself, or completely rid of his sickness or his solitude or his servitude. On the contrary, all stand in need of Christ, their Model, their Mentor, their Liberator, their Savior, their Source of life.

The gospel has truly been a leaven of liberty and progress in human history, even in its temporal sphere, and always proves itself a leaven of brotherhood, of unity, and of peace. Therefore, not without cause is Christ hailed by the faithful as "the expected of the nations, and their Savior."

9. And so the time for missionary activity extends between the first coming of the Lord and the second. Then from the four winds the Church will be gathered like a harvest into the kingdom of God. For the gospel must be preached to all nations before the Lord returns (cf. Mk. 13:10).

Missionary activity is nothing else and nothing less than a manifestation or epiphany of God's will, and the fulfillment of that will in the world and in world history. In the course of this history God plainly works out the history of salvation by means of mission. By the preaching of the word and by the celebration of the sacraments, whose center and summit is the most holy Eucharist, missionary activity brings about the presence of Christ, the Author of salvation.

But whatever truth and grace are to be found among the nations, as a sort of secret presence of God, this activity frees from all taint of evil and restores to Christ its maker, who overthrows the devil's domain and wards off the manifold malice of vice. And so, whatever good is found to be sown in the hearts and minds of men, or in the rites and cultures peculiar to various peoples, is not lost. More than that, it is healed, ennobled, and perfected for the glory of God, the shame of the demon, and the bliss of men.

Thus, missionary activity tends toward the fulfillment which will come at the end of time. For by it the People of God advances toward that degree of growth and that time of completion which the Father has fixed in His power (cf. Acts 1:7). To this people it was said in prophecy: "Enlarge the space for your tent, spread out your tent cloths unsparingly" (Is. 54:2). By missionary activity, the mystical body grows to the mature measure of the fullness of Christ (cf. Eph. 4:13). The spiritual temple, where God is adored in spirit and in truth (cf. Jn. 4:23), grows and is built up upon the foundation of the apostles and prophets with Christ Jesus Himself remaining the chief cornerstone (Eph. 2:20).

CHAPTER II
MISSION WORK ITSELF

. . . .

CHAPTER III
PARTICULAR CHURCHES

. . . .

CHAPTER IV
MISSIONARIES

. . . .

CHAPTER V
PLANNING

. . . .

CHAPTER VI
MISSIONARY COOPERATION

. . . .

RENEWAL IN MISSION
Uppsala (1968)

The International Missionary Council was integrated into the World Council of Churches in 1961. Hence, the Council assumed responsibility for interpreting and sponsoring missionary activity amid the changing political, economic and social situation of the second half of the twentieth century. The Assembly at Uppsala, in 1968, debated the report, "Renewal in Missions," adopted it with some modifications as the judgment of the Council. The Uppsala statement continued to be debated in the churches as well as at the conference of the Commission on World Mission and Evangelism of the World Council of Churches at Bangkok in 1973, and at the meeting of the Council in Nairobi (1975). It represents the official direction of the churches represented in the World Council of Churches.

Source: Complete text may be found in *The Uppsala Report 1968* edited by Norman Goodall (Geneva: World Council of Churches, 1968), pp. 27–36.

The Report as adopted by the Assembly

1. A MANDATE FOR MISSION

1. We belong to a humanity that cries passionately and articulately for a fully human life. Yet the very humanity of man and of his societies is threatened by a greater variety of destructive forces than ever. And the acutest moral problems all hinge upon the question: What is man? We Christians know that we are in this worldwide struggle for meaning, dignity, freedom and love, and we cannot stand aloof. We have been charged with a message and a ministry that have to do with more than material needs, but we can never be content to treat our concern for physical and social needs as merely secondary to our responsibility for the needs of the spirit. There is a

burning relevance today in describing the mission of God, in which we participate, as the gift of a new creation which is a radical renewal of the old and the invitation to men to grow up into their full humanity in the new man, Jesus Christ.

2. Men can know their true nature only if they see themselves as sons of God, answerable to their Father for one another and for the world. But because man refuses both the obedience and the responsibility of sonship his God-given dominion is turned into exploitation, and harmony into alienation in all his relationships. In this condition man, with all his amazing power, suffers an inescapable dread of his own helplessness and his deepest cry, albeit often unrecognized, is for the Triune God.

3. Jesus Christ, incarnate, crucified and risen, is the new man. In him was revealed the image of God as he glorified his Father in a perfect obedience. In his total availability for others, his absolute involvement and absolute freedom, his penetrating truth and his triumphant acceptance of suffering and death, we see what man is meant to be. Through that death on the Cross, man's alienation is overcome by the forgiveness of God and the way is opened for the restoration of all men to their sonship. In the resurrection of Jesus a new creation was born, and the final goal of history was assured, when Christ as head of that new humanity will sum up all things.

4. But the new manhood is not only a goal. It is also a gift and like all God's gifts it has to be appropriated by a response of faith. The Holy Spirit offers this gift to men in a variety of moments of decision. It is the Holy Spirit who takes the Word of God and makes it a living, converting word to men. Our part in evangelism might be described as bringing about the occasions for men's response to Jesus Christ. Often the turning point does not appear as a religious choice at all. Yet it is a new birth. It sets a

pattern of dying and rising which will continually be repeated. For we have to be torn out of the restricted and perverted life of «the old man». We have to «put on the new man» and this change is always embodied in some actual change of attitude and relationship. For there is no turning to God which does not at the same time bring a man face to face with his fellow men in a new way. The new life frees men for community unabling them to break through racial, national, religious and other barriers that divide the unity of mankind.

5. Mission bears fruit as people find their true life in the Body of Christ, in the Church's life of Word and Sacrament, fellowship in the Spirit and existence for others. There the signs of the new humanity are experienced and the People of God reach out in solidarity with the whole of mankind in service and witness. The growth of the Church, therefore, both inward and outward, is of urgent importance. Yet our ultimate hope is not set upon this progress, but on the mystery of the final event which remains in the hand of God.

6. The meeting with men of other faiths or of no faith must lead to dialogue. A Christian's dialogue with another implies neither a denial of the uniqueness of Christ, nor any loss of his own commitment to Christ, but rather that a genuinely Christian approach to others must be human, personal, relevant and humble. In dialogue we share our common humanity, its dignity and fallenness, and express our common concern for that humanity. It opens the possibility of sharing in new forms of community and common service. Each meets and challenges the other; witnessing from the depths of his existence to the ultimate concerns that come to expression in word and action. As Christians we believe that Christ speaks in this dialogue, revealing himself to those who do not know him and connecting the

limited and distorted knowledge of those who do. Dialogue and proclamation are not the same. The one complements the other in a total witness. But sometimes Christians are not able to engage either in open dialogue or proclamation. Witness is then a silent one of living the Christian life and suffering for Christ.

7. Man is one indivisible whole. Science today furnishes us with constantly increasing knowledge about man's inner being and his interdependence with society. We must see achievements of greater justice, freedom and dignity as a part of the restoration of true manhood in Christ. This calls for a more open and humble partnership with all who work for these goals even when they do not share the same assumptions as ourselves. But it also calls for a clearer acceptance of the diversity of gifts of the spirit within the Church. «He gave some to be apostles» — the bearers and strategists of the Gospel in a modern age, «some to be prophets» — to equip the saints for their ministry in the world and to be the protesting conscience of society, «some to be pastors» — to heal spiritual and psychological ills, «some to be evangelists» — the interpreters of the Gospel for the secular man or the man of another faith, «some to be teachers» — equipped with biblical light on contemporary perplexities. Each, knowing his need of the gifts of the others, contributes his own in a single, saving outreach to bring men to the measure of the fullness of the stature of Christ.

II. OPPORTUNITIES FOR MISSION

1. The Church in mission is the Church for others

The Church in mission is for all people everywhere; for those who have not heard the Gospel and for those who have; for those who, unknowing, serve the «man for others», and for those who name his Name and yet turn away from his mission; and even for those who reject the church, and yet continue to wait for the new humanity.

Since the Church is for others, its mission must both challenge and include men and women where they are:

— a Reformed banker in Zürich and his Roman Catholic colleague in Buenos Aires
— a Baptist policeman in the Congo, an Orthodox teacher in India
— a Methodist professor at Columbia, a Lutheran art student at the Sorbonne
— a pastor evangelist in New Guinea, a minister in industrial Tokyo
— a Spanish migrant worker in Holland, a West Indian bus conductor in London
— a nurse in Johannesburg, a housewife in Moscow
— a hungry child in Rio, an unemployed farm worker in Mississippi.

Localities for mission are such in variety and setting — where there is human need, an expanding population, tension, forces in movement, institutional rigidities, decision-making about the priorities and uses of power, and even open human conflict.

2. Here we describe a few priority situations for mission today

a) Centres of power

Centres of power control human life for good or evil. Increasingly men struggle over this control. For example, the mass media can be employed for either powerful communication or deceitful manipulation. All existing centres of power such as government, business, industry, military establishments, labour, and the churches, must be called to account for their uses of power, especially by those affected. Frustration grows in proportion to human powerlessness and lack of dignity. For the sake of the new humanity the powerless must exercise power.

b) Revolutionary movements

The longing for a just society is causing revolutions

all over the world. Since many Christians are deeply rooted in the *status quo* they tend to be primarily concerned for the maintenance of law and order. Where the maintenance of order is an obstacle to a *just* order, some will decide for revolutionary action against that injustice, struggling for a just society without which the new humanity cannot fully come. The Christian community must decide whether it can recognize the validity of their decision and support them.

c) The University everywhere is in change

The quest for a just society and a meaningful life ahead is erupting in all places of higher learning and research. Student rebellions reflect the insistence that maturing students share in decisions about the form and content of university life. In the intellectual centres of an emerging world culture, such movements require Christian presence and witness.

d) Rapid urbanization and industrialization

All over the world men are on the move from tribal village to township, from rural area to urban sprawl. The migrant worker, the sufferer from racial prejudice in housing, the child in a crowded school, the lonely student in his crowded dormitory, the watchers of the TV screens, the inmates, nurses and medical specialists of the hospital wards — all these make the emerging urban centres a locality for mission.

The material handler shifting ingots of steel; the woman assembling a transistor; the manager racing against time and spending his Sunday planning production targets — all these are in need of seeing the inter-relatedness of their role with that of others in building a just industrial society.

e) Suburbia, rural areas

The pupil in rural areas, starving for education; the village pastor, looking for his young people who have moved to the town; the farmer struggling to develop intermediate agricultural technology; the prematurely aged labourer in an area of famine — *and* the prematurely retired and bored pensioner; suburban wives trapped in the small world of their children and chores — these too constitute localities for mission where there are pressures for conformity, social prejudice and the threat of a clouded future.

f) *Relations between developed and developing countries*

Centres of decision and forces of public opinion influencing the relations between the developing countries and the developed countries are a locality for mission, which demands new motivations and a new international missionary strategy.

g) *The churches as an arena for mission*

The words of proclamation are doubted when the church's own life fails to embody the marks of the new humanity. The church is rightly concerned for the world's hundreds of millions who do not know the Gospel of Christ. It is constantly sent out to them in witness and service. But that concern becomes suspect when the church is preoccupied with its own numerical and institutional strength. It is called to be the servant body of Christ given to and for the world.

Too many of our discussions are about the internal concerns of our fellowship; too many statistical forms ask only about the budget and the fluctuations in attendance and not about outreach and service. Too often we send only doctors and teachers where today's need calls also for town planners. Traditional mission board structures tend to commit the churches to institutional continuity. Too many traditional churches neglect relationships with independent, rapidly growing indigenous Christian movements. The Christian community desperately needs renewal, lest it become a spiritual ghetto, unaware of its true responsibilities.

3. How to find criteria for missionary priorities

Because the world is always changing, it is always necessary to evaluate missionary priorities. That evaluation will often require willingness to face loss in prestige and finance and detachment from monuments of faithfulness in mission localities of the past. We suggest the following criteria for such evaluation:

— do they place the church alongside the poor, the defenceless, the abused, the forgotten, the bored?

— do they allow Christians to enter the concerns of others to accept their issues and their structures as vehicles of involvement?

— are they the best situations for discerning with other men the signs of the times, and for moving with history towards the coming of the new humanity?

III. FREEDOM FOR MISSION

A new Stance needed in Church Life

Mobilizing the people of God for mission today means releasing them from structures that inhibit them in the Church and enabling them to open out in much more flexible ways to the world in which they live. In this world we need to meet others, across all the frontiers, in new relationships that mean both listening and responding, both giving and receiving. This necessitates:

1. A continuing re-examination of the structures of church life at all levels, i.e. the local parish, the denominational synods and conferences and their agencies, the councils of churches at national, regional and world levels. All these must ask, not «Have we the right structures for mission?» but «Are we totally structured for mission?»

2. A re-examination of the variety of tasks to which the people are called in their ministry in the world. Laymen and women express their full commitment to mission, not primarily through the ser-

vice they give within the church structures, but pre-eminently through the ways in which they use their professional skills and competence in their daily work and public service. We need to employ all the gifts God has given to his people — whether it be gifts of proclamation, or healing, or political activity, or administration, or running a home, etc. We need to explore how, in the diverse roles in which we find ourselves, we can creatively and with integrity express our full humanity — whether it be as young people, or women, or members of minority groups, or people in positions of authority, and so on. In all these, we need to recognize what is our Christian obedience in the total ministry of the Church.

3. A re-examination of the whole scope and purpose of theological education. This is to be seen as preparation of the whole people of God for their ministry in the world. The training of the clergy cannot be considered apart from the training of the laity and both should be understood as one enterprise. This means:

a) Clergy need to be trained in an understanding of the world in which the people will minister and of their own responsibility for pointing the people to that ministry and equipping them for it.

b) Lay training needs to be understood in terms of preparing the people for the increasing complexity of their ministry in the world.

c) Provision must be made for training both clergy and laity for specialized tasks.

The Church in the Local Situation

Though some believe that the basic structures of church life are given and therefore unchangeable, others are convinced that all institutional forms of church life are provisional and open to change. In a given locality the ministry of the church may be exercised in many forms, including congregations, chaplaincies, health and welfare services, youth projects, political and economic pressure groups, functional and professional groups and others. These have often inherited a pattern of life which was the response of a past generation to a situation which is now fast changing. In all the contemporary localities of mission, we must find new and effective ways in which the Gospel can be proclaimed today and understood in all these areas of life. This will mean:

1. that the congregation must recognize its own missionary role in proclaiming the Gospel in word and deed and as a caring community for all whom they meet across the different frontiers. Related to this community there need to be groups which will help individuals to feel accepted and to accept others. There people will find through dialogue a common basis for their task and be encouraged to develop new forms of service within the social structures for the sake of their fellow men;

2. that there will be a programme of education which at all levels directs people towards their ministry in the world. This needs to be rooted in a biblical understanding of mission, so that people share the encouragement and insights which Bible study can give;

3. that we get to know the social structures in order to cooperate with all the forces working for good and to discover new tasks needing to be done;

4. that we discover the creative possibilities in the points of tension, conflict and decision in society, and try to make real our profession of love through the active pursuit of justice;

5. that teams come together to undertake specific tasks in society;

6. that we encourage a global understanding of the ministry of the Church.

No local situation or ministry is sufficient unto itself. No local group can isolate itself from the larger structures of planning and decision-making in society. It is in response to these that the Church needs to express its ministry in new ways, for example:

a) The need for specialization is recognized in areas of special concern such as education, rural development, industry, leisure, automation, the mass media.

b) Specialization without coordination is useless. There need to be joint planning and action between the diverse agencies involved in the localities as part of a total coordinated strategy of mission.

The Worldwide Situation

The missionary societies originated in a response of a past generation to the call to take the Gospel to the ends of the earth. Changing political, economic and ecclesiastical circumstances demand new responses and new relationships. Our understanding of the mission in six continents means that the resources of the whole Church in terms of men, money and expertise are available for the use of the whole Church. Their deployment must be determined by need and not by historic relationships or traditional procedures. This means in terms of structures and relationships:

1. Experiments in new forms of witness and service must be encouraged. Initiatives for such experiments may come from any quarter, but should, where possible, be carried through by joint consultation and strategy.

2. The old division between sending and receiving churches is now breaking down. More creative relationships between churches, and between churches and mission boards have developed. Now we must move to multilateral relations and decision making. These relations will be of many kinds, some national, some regional and some worldwide.

3. Where people and resources come from outside a community they must be related to the needs

of that community and incorporated into its life. Mutual understanding and relationships have to be built up between the Church in the local situation and those who bring the resources of skill and technical knowledge from outside. In this sharing the unity of all Christians in each place can be deepened, tested and realized.

Never go it alone

There is but one mission on all six continents. This makes it now imperative that Christians engage effectively in joint planning and action in both local and international situations. Only ecumenical cooperation can be adequate for the immensity of our task.

Some joint action for mission has already taken place, but the churches are still too reluctant to implement the call to joint action sounded so strongly in 1963 at the Mexico City Meeting of the Commission of World Mission and Evangelism. Present structures obviously do not provide adequate vehicles for developing joint strategy. We must determine to find ways in which joint action can become operative. We urge consultation with regional and national councils, mission boards and societies and churches, resolved to find ways and means for such joint planning and action. We recommend that more specific areas be marked out as soon as possible for experiments in ecumenical action.

In fact, we find it impossible to envisage any situation where it would not be more effective to act together across all frontiers rather than going it alone.

In a world where the whole of mankind is struggling to realize its common humanity, facing common despairs and sharing common hopes, the Christian Church must identify itself with the whole community in expressing its ministry of witness and service, and in a responsible stewardship of our total resources.

The Certain Hope

Called as we are to take up our responsibility for mission in the future which God opens up before us, we do so in the firm and certain hope that the new humanity revealed in our risen Lord and Saviour will surely come to its glorious fulfilment in him. So we humbly serve, in patience and in joy, confidently expecting his final victory.

THE FRANKFURT DECLARATION
(1970)

This declaration is the product of a Theological Convention which met at Frankfurt in 1970. The declaration, written largely by Peter Beyerhaus, Professor of Missions, Tubingen University, was in reaction to the statement of Uppsala. It is not an official document of the churches, but it has received the endorsement of many persons prominent in missions and of missionary societies. Its intention was to affirm the biblical basis, content and goal of missions.

Source: The text is taken from *Mission: Which Way?* by Peter Beyerhaus (Grand Rapids: Zondervan Publishing House, 1971).

Donald Anderson McGavran, ed., *Eye of the Storm: The Great Debate in Mission* (Waco: Word Books, 1972).

The Church of Jesus Christ has the sacred privilege and irrevocable obligation to participate in the mission of the triune God, a mission which must extend into all the world. Through the Church's outreach, his name shall be glorified among all people, mankind shall be saved from his future wrath and led to a new life, and the lordship of his Son Jesus Christ shall be established in the expectation of his second coming.

This is the way that Christianity has always understood the Great Commission of Christ, though, we must confess, not always with the same degree of fidelity and clarity. The recognition of the task and the total missionary obligation of the Church led to the endeavor to integrate missions into the German Protestant churches and the World Council of Churches, whose Commission and Division of World Mission and Evangelism was established in 1961. It is the goal of this division, by the terms of its constitution, to insure "the proclamation to the whole world of the Gospel of Jesus Christ, to the end that all men may believe in him and be saved." It is our conviction that this definition reflects the basic apostolic concern of the New Testament and restores the understanding of mission held by the fathers of the Protestant missionary movement.

Today, however, organized Christian world missions is shaken by a fundamental crisis. Outer opposition and the weakening spiritual power of our churches and missionary societies are not solely to blame. More dangerous is the displacement of their primary tasks by means of an insidious falsification of their motives and goals.

Deeply concerned because of their inner decay, we feel called upon to make the following declaration.

We address ourselves to all Christians who know themselves through the belief in salvation through Jesus Christ to be responsible for the continuation of his saving work among nonchristian people. We address ourselves further to the leaders of churches and congregations, to whom the worldwide perspective of their spiritual commission has been revealed. We address ourselves finally to all missionary societies and their coordinating agencies, which are especially called, according to their spiritual tradition, to oversee the true goals of missionary activity.

We urgently and sincerely request you to test the following theses on the basis of their biblical foundations, and to determine the accuracy of this description of the current situation with respect to the errors and modes of operation which are increasingly evident in churches, missions, and the ecumenical movement. In the event of your concurrence, we request that you declare this by your signature and join with us in your own sphere of influence, both repentant and resolved to insist upon these guiding principles.

SEVEN INDISPENSABLE BASIC ELEMENTS OF MISSION

1 *Full authority in heaven and on earth has been committed to me. Go forth therefore and make all nations my disciples; baptize men everywhere in the name of the Father and the Son and the Holy Spirit, and teach them to observe all that I have commanded you. And be assured, I am with you always, to the end of time (Matt. 28: 18-20; this Scripture quotation and those that follow are from the New English Bible).*

We recognize and declare:

Christian mission discovers its foundation, goals, tasks, and the content of its proclamation solely in the commission of the resurrected Lord Jesus Christ and his saving acts as they are reported by the witness of the apostles and early Christianity in the New Testament. Mission is grounded in the nature of the Gospel.

We therefore oppose the current tendency to determine the nature and task of mission by sociopolitical analyses of our time and from the demands of the nonchristian world. We deny that what the Gospel has to say to people today at the deepest level is not evident before its encounter with them. Rather, according to the apostolic witness, the Gospel is normative and given once for all. The situation of encounter contributes only new aspects in the application of the Gospel. The surrender of the Bible as our primary frame of reference leads to the shapelessness of mission and a confusion of the task of mission with a general idea of responsibility for the world.

2   *Thus will I prove myself great and holy and*
     make myself known to many nations; they shall
     know that I am the Lord (Ezek. 38:23).
     Therefore, Lord, I will praise thee among the
     the nations and sing psalms to thy name (Ps.
     18:49 and Rom. 15:9).

We recognize and declare:

The first and supreme goal of mission is the *glori-fication* of the name of the one *God* throughout the entire world and the proclamation of the lordship of Jesus Christ, his Son.

We therefore oppose the assertion that mission today is no longer so concerned with the disclosure of God as with the manifestation of a new man and the extension of a new humanity into all social realms. *Humanization* is not the primary goal of mission. It is rather a product of our new birth through God's saving activity in Christ within us, or an indirect result of the Christian proclamation in its power to perform a leavening activity in the course of world history.

A one-sided outreach of missionary interest toward man and his society leads to atheism.

3   *There is no salvation in anyone else at all, for*
     there is no other name under heaven granted to
     men, by which we may receive salvation (Acts
     4:12).

We recognize and declare:

Jesus Christ our Saviour, true God and true man, as the Bible proclaims him in his personal mystery and his saving work, is the basis, content, and author-ity of our mission. It is the goal of this mission to make known to all people in all walks of life the gift of his salvation.

We therefore challenge all nonchristians, who be-long to God on the basis of creation, to believe in him and to be baptized in his name, for in him alone is eternal salvation promised to them.

We therefore oppose the false teaching (which is spreading in the ecumenical movement since the Third General Assembly of the World Council of Churches in New Delhi) that Christ himself is anonymously so evident in world religions, historical changes, and revolutions that man can encounter him and find salvation in him without the direct news of the Gospel.

We likewise reject the unbiblical limitation of the person and work of Jesus to his humanity and ethical example. In such an idea the uniqueness of Christ and the Gospel is abandoned in favor of a humanitarian principle which others might also find in other religions and ideologies.

4 *God loved the world so much that he gave his only Son, that everyone who has faith in him may not die but have eternal life (John 3:16). In Christ's name, we implore you, be reconciled to God (II Cor. 5:20).*

We recognize and declare:

Mission is the witness and presentation of eternal salvation performed in the name of Jesus Christ by his church and fully authorized messengers by means of preaching, the sacraments, and service. This salvation is due to the sacrificial crucifixion of Jesus Christ, which occurred once for all and for all mankind.

The appropriation of this salvation to individuals takes place first, however, through proclamation, which calls for decision, and through baptism, which places the believer in the service of love. Just as belief leads through repentance and baptism to eternal life, so unbelief leads through its rejection of the offer of salvation to damnation.

We therefore oppose the universalistic idea that in the crucifixion and resurrection of Jesus Christ all

men of all times are already born again and already
have peace with him, irrespective of their knowledge
of the historical saving activity of God or belief in it.
Through such a misconception the evangelizing commission loses both its full, authoritative power and
its urgency. Unconverted men are thereby lulled into
a fatal sense of security about their eternal destiny.

5   *But you are a chosen race, a royal priesthood,*
     a dedicated nation, and a people claimed by God
     for his own, to proclaim the triumphs of him
     who has called you out of darkness into his
     marvelous light (I Pet. 2:9).
     Adapt yourselves no longer to the pattern of
     this present world (Rom. 12:2).

We recognize and declare:

The primary visible task of mission is *to call out*
the messianic, saved community from among all
people.

Missionary proclamation should lead everywhere
to the establishment of the Church of Jesus Christ,
which exhibits a new, defined reality as salt and light
in its social environment.

Through the Gospel and the sacraments, the Holy
Spirit gives the members of the congregation a new
life and an eternal, spiritual fellowship with each
other and with God, who is real and present with
them. It is the task of the congregation through its
witness to move the lost—especially those who live
outside its community—to a saving membership in
the body of Christ. Only by being this new kind of
fellowship does the Church present the Gospel
convincingly.

We therefore oppose the view that the Church, as
the fellowship of Jesus, is simply a part of the world.
The contrast between the Church and the world is
not merely a distinction in function and in knowledge of salvation; rather, it is an essential difference

in nature. We deny that the Church has no advantage over the world except the knowledge of the alleged future salvation of all men.

We further oppose the one-sided emphasis on salvation which stresses only this world, according to which the Church and the world together share in a future, purely social, reconciliation of all mankind. That would lead to the self-dissolution of the Church.

6   *Remember then your former condition: . . . you were at that time separate from Christ, strangers to the community of Israel, outside God's covenants and the promise that goes with them. Your world was a world without hope and without God (Eph. 2:11, 12).*

We recognize and declare:

The offer of salvation in Christ is directed without exception to all men who are not yet bound to him in conscious faith. The adherents to the nonchristian religions and world views can receive this salvation only through participation in faith. They must let themselves be freed from their former ties and false hopes in order to be admitted by belief and baptism into the body of Christ. Israel, too, will find salvation in turning to Jesus Christ.

We therefore reject the false teaching that the nonchristian religions and world views are also ways of salvation similar to belief in Christ.

We refute the idea that "Christian presence" among the adherents to the world religions and a give-and-take dialogue with them are substitutes for a proclamation of the Gospel which aims at conversion. Such dialogues simply establish good points of contact for missionary communication.

We also refute the claim that the borrowing of Christian ideas, hopes, and social procedures—even if they are separated from their exclusive relationship to the person of Jesus—can make the world religion and ideologies substitutes for the Church of Jesus Christ. In reality they give them a syncretistic and therefore antichristian direction.

7 *And this gospel of the kingdom will be proclaimed throughout the earth as a testimony to all nations; and then the end will come (Matt. 24:14).*

We recognize and declare:

The Christian world mission is the decisive, continuous saving activity of God among men between the time of the resurrection and second coming of Jesus Christ. Through the proclamation of the Gospel, new nations and people will progressively be called to decision for or against Christ.

When all people have heard the witness about him and have given their answer to it, the conflict between the Church of Jesus and the world, led by the Antichrist, will reach its climax. Then Christ himself will return and break into time, disarming the demonic power of Satan and establishing his own visible, boundless messianic kingdom.

We refute the unfounded idea that the eschatological expectation of the New Testament has been falsified by Christ's delay in returning and is therefore to be given up.

We refute at the same time the enthusiastic and utopian ideology that either under the influence of the Gospel or by the anonymous working of Christ in history, all of mankind is already moving toward a position of general peace and justice and will finally—before the return of Christ—be united under him in a great world community.

We refute the identification of messianic salvation with progress, development, and social change. The fatal consequence of this is that efforts to aid development and revolutionary involvement in the places of tension in society are seen as the contemporary forms of Christian mission. But such an identification would be a self-deliverance to the utopian movements of our time in the direction of their ultimate destination.

We do, however, affirm the determined advocacy of justice and peace by all churches, and we affirm that developmental aid is a timely realization of the divine demand for mercy and justice as well as of the command of Jesus "Love thy neighbor."

We see therein an important accompaniment and authentication of mission. We also affirm the humanizing results of conversion as signs of the coming messianic peace.

We stress, however, that unlike the eternally valid reconciliation with God through faith in the Gospel, all of our social achievements and partial successes in politics are restricted by the eschatological "not yet" of the coming kingdom and the not yet annihilated power of sin, death, and the devil, who still is the "prince of this world."

This establishes the priorities of our missionary service and causes us to extend ourselves in the expectation of Him who promises, "Behold! I make all things new" (Rev. 21:5, RSV).

A CALL TO CONFESS AND PROCLAIM
(Nairobi, 1975)

Source: Text is copy from *Breaking Barriers, Nairobi, 1975, The Official Report of the Fifth Assembly of the World Council of Churches* (Grand Rapids: Wm. B. Eerdmans, 1976).

(Paragraphs 1-52 omitted)

. . . .

A CALL TO CONFESS AND PROCLAIM

53. We do not have the option of keeping the good news to ourselves. The uncommunicated gospel is a patent contradiction.

54. We are called to preach Christ crucified, the power of God and the wisdom of God (1 Cor. 1:23-24).

55. Evangelism, therefore, is rooted in gratitude for God's self-sacrificing love, in obedience to the risen Lord.

56. Evangelism is like a beggar telling another beggar where they both can find bread.

The Whole Gospel

57. The gospel is good news from God, our Creator and Redeemer. On its way from Jerusalem to Galilee and to the ends of the earth, the Spirit discloses ever new aspects and dimensions of God's decisive revelation in Jesus Christ. The gospel always includes: the announcement of God's Kingdom and love through Jesus Christ, the offer of grace and forgiveness of sins, the invitation to repentance and faith in him, the summons to fellowship in God's Church, the command to witness to God's saving words and deeds, the responsibility to participate in the struggle for justice and human dignity, the obligation to denounce all that hinders human wholeness, and a commitment to risk life itself. In our time, to the oppressed the gospel may be new as a message of courage to persevere in the struggle for liberation in this world as a sign of hope for God's inbreaking Kingdom. To women the gospel may bring news of a Christ who empowered women to be bold in the midst of cultural expectations of submissiveness. To children the gospel may be a call of love for the "little ones" and to the rich and powerful it may reveal the responsibility to share the poverty of the poor.

58. While we rejoice hearing the gospel speak to our particular situations and while we must try to communicate the gospel to particular contexts, we must remain faithful to the historical apostolic witness as we find it in the holy Scriptures and traditions

as it is centered in Jesus Christ—lest we accommodate them to our own desires and interests.

The Whole Person

59. The gospel, through the power of the Holy Spirit, speaks to all human needs, transforms our lives. In bringing forgiveness, it reconciles us to our Creator, sparks within us the true joy of knowing God, and promises eternal life. In uniting us as God's people, it answers our need for community and fellowship. In revealing God's love for all persons, it makes us responsible, critical, and creative members of the societies in which we live. The good news of Jesus' resurrection assures us that God's righteous purpose in history will be fulfilled and free us to work for that fulfilment with hope and courage.

The Whole World

60. The world is not only God's creation; it is also the arena of God's mission. Because God loved the whole world, the Church cannot neglect any part of it—neither those who have heard the saving Name nor the vast majority who have not yet heard it. Our obedience to God and our solidarity with the human family demand that we obey Christ's command to proclaim and demonstrate God's love to every person, of every class and race, on every continent, in every culture, in every setting and historical context.

The Whole Church

61. Evangelism cannot be delegated to either gifted individuals or specialized agencies. It is entrusted to the "whole Church", the body of Christ, in which the particular gifts and functions of all members are but expressions of the life of the whole body.

62. This wholeness must take expression in every particular cultural, social, and political context. Therefore, the evangelization of the world starts at

the level of the congregation, in the local and ecumenical dimensions of its life: worship, sacrament, preaching, teaching and healing, fellowship and service, witnessing in life and in death.

63. Too often we as churches and congregations stand in the way of the gospel—because of our lack of missionary zeal and missionary structures, because of our divisions, our self-complacency, our lack of catholicity and ecumenical spirit.

64. The call to evangelism, therefore, implies a call to repentance, renewal, and commitment for visible unity. We also deplore proselytism of any sort which further divides the Church.

65. Yet, even imperfect and broken, we are called to put ourselves humbly and gladly at the service of the unfinished mission. We are commissioned to carry the gospel to the whole world and to allow it to permeate all realms of human life. We recognize the signs that the Holy Spirit is in these days calling the Church to a new commitment to evangelism, as evidenced by his voice to the Bangkok Conference on "Salvation Today" (1973), the Accra conference on "Giving account of the hope that is within us" (1974), the Lausanne Congress on "The Evangelization of the World" (1974), and the Synod of Bishops of the Roman Catholic Church on "Evangelization in the Modern World" (1974). Clearly this is a common mandate which deserves common support.

On Methodology

66. In our times many churches, Christian individuals, and groups find themselves under pressures and challenges which demand a clear choice between confessing or denying Christ. Others, however, face ambiguous situations in which the question arises: When is the appropriate time to confess and how should we do it? This leads to the question of education for mission. Programmes of lay training ought to be encouraged in order to equip lay workers for com-

municating the gospel at their particular place in everyday life, including those who, for professional reasons, cross cultural frontiers.

67. Never before has the Church universal had at its disposal such a comprehensive set of means of communication as we have today—literature, audio-visuals, electronic media. While we need to improve our use of such media, nothing can replace the living witness in words and deeds of Christian persons, groups, and congregations who participate in the sufferings and joys, in the struggles and celebrations, in the frustrations and hopes of the people with whom they want to share the gospel. Whatever "methodologies" of communication may seem to be appropriate in different situations, they should be directed by a humble spirit of sensitivity and participation.

68. Careful listening is an essential part of our witness. Only as we are sensitive to the needs and aspirations of others will we know what Christ is saying through our dialogue. What we should like to call "holistic methodology" or "methodology in wholeness" transcends mere techniques or tactics. It is rooted in God's own "strategy of love" which liberates us to tactics. It is rooted in God's own "strategy of love" which liberates us to respond freely to his call to union with him and our fellow human beings.

A Sense of Urgency

69. We need to recover the sense of urgency. Questions about theological definitions there may be. Problems of precise implementation will arise. But neither theoretical nor practical differences must be allowed to dampen the fires of evangelism.

70. Confessing Christ must be done *today*. "Behold, now is the acceptable time; behold, now is the day of salvation" (2 Cor. 6:2). It cannot wait for a time that is comfortable for us. We must be prepared to proclaim the gospel when human beings need to

hear it. But in our zeal to spread the good news, we must guard against fanaticism which disrupts the hearing of the gospel and breaks the community of God. The world requires, and God demands, that we recognize the urgency to proclaim the saving word of God—today. God's acceptable time demands that we respond in all haste. "And how terrible it would be for me if I did not preach the gospel!" (1. Cor. 9:16).

RECENT STATEMENTS OF THE FAITH

STATEMENT OF FAITH UNITED CHURCH OF CHRIST (1959)

The Statement of Faith was written in connection with the merger of the Congregational Christian Churches and the Evangelical and Reformed Church to form the United Church of Christ. It was approved by the Second General Synod of the United Church of Christ, July 5–9, 1959. It combines felicity of expression with theological sensitivity.

STATEMENT OF FAITH

We believe in God, the Eternal Spirit, Father of our Lord Jesus Christ and our Father, and to his deeds we testify:

He calls the worlds into being,
creates man in his own image
and sets before him the ways of life and death.

He seeks in holy love to save all people from
    aimlessness and sin.
He judges men and nations by his righteous will
    declared through prophets and apostles.
In Jesus Christ, the man of Nazareth, our crucified
    and risen Lord,
  he has come to us
  and shared our common lot,
  conquering sin and death
  and reconciling the world to himself.
He bestows upon us his Holy Spirit,
    creating and renewing the Church of Jesus
      Christ,
    binding in covenant faithful people of all ages,
      tongues, and races.
He calls us into his Church
    to accept the cost and joy of discipleship,
    to be his servants in the service of men,
    to proclaim the gospel to all the world
    and resist the powers of evil,
    to share in Christ's baptism and eat at his table,
    to join him in his passion and victory.
He promises to all who trust him
    forgiveness of sins and fullness of grace,
    courage in the struggle for justice and peace,
    his presence in trial and rejoicing,
    and eternal life in his kingdom which has no
      end.
Blessing and honor, glory and power be unto him.
Amen.

THE CONFESSION OF 1967

This confession was written by a committee of the
United Presbyterian Church in the United States of
America under the chairmanship of Professor Edward
A. Dowey, Jr., during a time of social unrest. In the
section reprinted here, the confession focuses its
theological resources on four critical social issues.

Sources:*The Constitution of the United Presbyterian Church in the United States of America* (Philadelphia: The Office of the General Assembly of the United Presbyterian Church in the United States of America, 1970).

Edward A. Dowey, Jr., *A Commentary on the Confession of 1967 and An Introduction to the Book of Confessions* (Philadelphia: The Westminster Press, 1968).

Preface

• • • •

The Confession

• • • •

Part I

GOD'S WORK OF RECONCILIATION

• • • •

Part II

THE MINISTRY OF RECONCILIATION

Section A. The Mission of the Church

1. DIRECTION

To be reconciled to God is to be sent into the world as his reconciling community. This community, the church universal, is entrusted with God's message of reconciliation and shares his labor of healing the enmities which separate men from God and from each other. Christ has called the church to this mission and given it the gift of the Holy Spirit. The Church maintains continuity with the apostles and with Israel by faithful obedience to his call.

The life, death, resurrection, and promised coming of Jesus Christ has set the pattern for the church's mission. His life as man involves the church in the common life of men. His service to men commits the church to work for every form of human well-being. His suffering makes the church sensitive to all the sufferings of mankind so that it sees the face of

Christ in the faces of men in every kind of need. His crucifixion discloses to the church God's judgment on man's inhumanity to man and the awful consequences of its own complicity in injustice. In the power of the risen Christ and the hope of his coming the church sees the promise of God's renewal of man's life in society and of God's victory over all wrong.

The church follows this pattern in the form of its life and in the method of its action. So to live and serve is to confess Christ as Lord.

2. FORMS AND ORDER

The institutions of the people of God change and vary as their mission requires in different times and places. The unity of the church is compatible with a wide variety of forms, but it is hidden and distorted when variant forms are allowed to harden into sectarian divisions, exclusive denominations, and rival factions.

Wherever the church exists, its members are both gathered in corporate life and dispersed in society for the sake of mission in the world.

The church gathers to praise God, to hear his word for mankind, to baptize and to join in the Lord's Supper, to pray for and present the world to him in worship, to enjoy fellowship, to receive instruction, strength, and comfort, to order and organize its own corporate life, to be tested, renewed, and reformed, and to speak and act in the world's affairs as may be appropriate to the needs of the time.

The church disperses to serve God wherever its members are, at work or play, in private or in the life of society. Their prayer and Bible study are part of the church's worship and theological reflection. Their witness is the church's evangelism. Their daily action in the world is the church in mission to the world. The quality of their relation with other persons is the measure of the church's fidelity.

Each member is the church in the world, endowed by the Spirit with some gift of ministry and is responsible for the integrity of his witness in his own particular situation. He is entitled to the guidance and support of the Christian community and is subject to its advice and correction. He in turn, in his own competence, helps to guide the church.

In recognition of special gifts of the Spirit and for the ordering of its life as a community, the church calls, trains, and authorizes certain members for leadership and oversight. The persons qualified for these duties in accordance with the polity of the church are set apart by ordination or other appropriate act and thus made responsible for their special ministries.

The church thus orders its life as an institution with a constitution, government, officers, finances, and administrative rules. These are instruments of mission, not ends in themselves. Different orders have served the gospel, and none can claim exclusive validity. A presbyterian polity recognizes the responsibility of all members for ministry and maintains the organic relation of all congregations in the church. It seeks to protect the church from exploitation by ecclesiastical or secular power and ambition. Every church order must be open to such reformation as may be required to make it a more effective instrument of the mission of reconciliation.

3. REVELATION AND RELIGION

The church in its mission encounters the religions of men and in that encounter becomes conscious of its own human character as a religion. God's revelation to Israel, expressed within Semitic culture, gave rise to the religion of the Hebrew people. God's revelation in Jesus Christ called forth the response of Jews and Greeks and came to expression within Judaism and Hellenism as the Christian religion. The Christian religion, as distinct from God's revelation of himself, has been shaped throughout its history by the cultural forms of its environment.

The Christian finds parallels between other religions and his own and must approach all religions with openness and respect. Repeatedly God has used the insight of non-Christians to challenge the church to renewal. But the reconciling word of the gospel is God's judgment upon all forms of religion, including the Christian. The gift of God in Christ is for all men. The church, therefore, is commissioned to carry the gospel to all men whatever their religion may be and even when they profess none.

4. RECONCILIATION IN SOCIETY

In each time and place there are particular problems and crises through which God calls the church to act. The church, guided by the Spirit, humbled by its own complicity and instructed by all attainable knowledge, seeks to discern the will of God and learn how to obey in these concrete situations. The following are particularly urgent at the present time.

a. God has created the peoples of the earth to be one universal family. In his reconciling love he overcomes the barriers between brothers and breaks down every form of discrimination based on racial or ethnic difference, real or imaginary. The church is called to bring all men to receive and uphold one another as persons in all relationships of life: in employment, housing, education, leisure, marriage, family, church, and the exercise of political rights. Therefore the church labors for the abolition of all racial discrimination and ministers to those injured by it. Congregations, individuals, or groups of Christians who exclude, dominate, or patronize their fellowmen, however subtly, resist the Spirit of God and bring contempt on the faith which they profess.

b. God's reconciliation in Jesus Christ is the ground of the peace, justice, and freedom among nations which all powers of government are called to serve and defend. The church, in its own life, is called to practice the forgiveness of enemies and to commend to the nations as practical politics the search for cooperation and peace. This requires the pursuit of fresh and responsible relations across every line of conflict, even at risk to national security, to reduce areas of strife and to broaden international understanding. Reconciliation among nations becomes peculiarly urgent as countries develop nuclear, chemical, and biological weapons, diverting their manpower and resources from constructive uses and risking the annihilation of mankind. Although nations may serve God's purposes in history, the church which identifies the sovereignty of any one nation or any one way of life with the cause of God denies the Lordship of Christ and betrays its calling.

c. The reconciliation of man through Jesus Christ makes it plain that enslaving poverty in a world of abundance is' an intolerable violation of God's good creation. Because Jesus identified himself with the needy and exploited, the cause of the world's poor is the cause of his disciples. The church cannot condone poverty, whether it is the product of unjust social structures, exploitation of the defenseless, lack of national resources, absence of technological understanding, or rapid expansion of populations. The church calls every man to use his abilities, his possessions, and the fruits of technology as gifts entrusted to him by God for the maintenance of his family and the advancement of the common welfare. It encourages those forces in human society that raise men's hopes for better conditions and provide them with opportunity for a decent living. A church that is indifferent to poverty, or evades responsibility in economic affairs, or is open to one social class only, or expects gratitude for its beneficence makes a mockery of reconciliation and offers no acceptable worship to God.

d. The relationship between man and woman exemplifies in a basic way God's ordering of the inter-personal life for which he created mankind. Anarchy in sexual relationships is a symptom of man's aliena-tion from God, his neighbor, and himself. Man's perennial confusion about the meaning of sex has been aggravated in our day by the availability of new means for birth control and the treatment of infec-tion, by the pressures of urbanization, by the exploi-tation of sexual symbols in mass communication, and by world overpopulation. The church, as the house-hold of God, is called to lead men out of this alienation into the responsible freedom of the new life in Christ. Reconciled to God, each person has joy in and respect for his own humanity and that of other persons; a man and woman are enabled to marry, to commit themselves to a mutually shared life, and to respond to each other in sensitive and lifelong concern; parents receive the grace to care for children in love and to nurture their individuality. The church comes under the judgment of God and invites rejection by man when it fails to lead men and women into the full meaning of life together, or withholds the compassion of Christ from those caught in the moral confusion of our time.

Section B. The Equipment of the Church

• • • •

Part III
THE FULFILLMENT OF RECONCILIATION

• • • •

ADDENDUM

ATHANASIAN CREED
(Quicunque vult)

The creed has been widely criticized for its intellectualism, identifying Christian faith with right belief, and for its anathemas upon those who believe the wrong. Its defects are the obverse side of its virtues. It does underscore the seriousness of decisions of faith. Its theological excellence has been well-stated by J.N.D. Kelly, "No other official document or creed sets forth, so incisively and with such majestic clarity, the profound theology implicit in the New Testament affirmation that 'God was in Christ reconciling the world to Himself.' . . . Its sole concern is to assert a conception of the triune Godhead which is free from anthropomorphic polytheism and a conception of the Incarnation which holds in tension the absolutely vital data about our Lord's divinity and humanity." (Kelly, *The Athanasian Creed*, p. 125).

The authorship and date of the creed are uncertain. The recent study of Professor Kelly confirms its relationship to the monastery at Lerins and to Augustine's theology, its indebtedness to Vincent, its acquaintance with the problems of Nestorianism. Kelly concludes it was written by a single person between 440 and the "high noon" of the activity of Caesarius of Arles (d. 542) by someone in his milieu and possibly at his instigation.

Source: The text printed here is from *The Athanasian Creed*, a translation by J. N. D. Kelly (London: Adam & Charles Black, 1964), pp. 17–20. Used by permission.

THE ATHANASIAN CREED

Whoever desires to be saved must above all things hold the Catholic faith. Unless a man keeps it in its entirety inviolate, he will assuredly perish eternally.

Now this is the Catholic faith, that we worship one God in Trinity and Trinity in unity, without either confusing the persons or dividing the substance. For the Father's person is one, the Son's another, the Holy Spirit's another; but the Godhead of the Father, the Son and the Holy Spirit is one, their glory is equal, their majesty coeternal.

Such as the Father is, such is the Son, such also the Holy Spirit. The Father is increate, the Son increate, the Holy Spirit increate. The Father is infinite, the Son infinite, the Holy Spirit infinite. The Father is eternal, the Son eternal, the Holy Spirit eternal. Yet there are not three eternals, but one eternal; just as there are not three increates or three infinites, but one increate and one infinite. In the same way the Father is almighty, the Son almighty, the Holy Spirit almighty; yet there are not three almighties, but one almighty.

Thus the Father is God, the Son God, the Holy Spirit God; and yet there are not three Gods, but there is one God. Thus the Father is Lord, the Son Lord, the Holy Spirit Lord; and yet there are not three Lords, but there is one Lord. Because just as we are obliged by Christian truth to acknowledge each person separately both God and Lord, so we are forbidden by the Catholic religion to speak of three Gods or Lords.

The Father is from none, not made nor created nor begotten. The Son is from the Father alone, not made nor created but begotten. The Holy Spirit is from the Father and the Son, not made nor created nor begotten but proceeding. So there is one Father, not three Fathers; one Son, not three Sons; one Holy

Spirit, not three Holy Spirits. And in this trinity there is nothing before or after, nothing greater or less, but all three persons are coeternal with each other and coequal. Thus in all things, as has been stated above, both Trinity in unity and unity in Trinity must be worshipped. So he who desires to be saved should think thus of the Trinity.

It is necessary, however, to eternal salvation that he should also faithfully believe in the Incarnation of our Lord Jesus Christ. Now the right faith is that we should believe and confess that our Lord Jesus Christ, the Son of God, is equally both God and man.

He is God from the Father's substance, begotten before time; and he is man from his mother's substance, born in time. Perfect God, perfect man composed of a rational soul and human flesh, equal to the Father in respect of his divinity, less than the Father in respect of his humanity.

Who, although he is God and man, is nevertheless not two but one Christ. He is one, however, not by the transformation of his divinity into flesh, but by the taking up of his humanity into God; one certainly not by confusion of substance, but by oneness of person. For just as rational soul and flesh are a single man, so God and man are a single Christ.

Who suffered for our salvation, descended to hell, rose from the dead, ascended to heaven, sat down at the Father's right hand, whence he will come to judge living and dead: at whose coming all men will rise again with their bodies, and will render an account of their deeds; and those who have behaved well will go to eternal life, those who have behaved badly to eternal fire.

This is the Catholic faith. Unless a man believes it faithfully and steadfastly, he will not be able to be saved.

THE LONDON CONFESSION
(1644)

This confession, produced by members of seven Particular Baptist Churches in London, has been called one of the chief landmarks of Baptist history (Vedder). Its moderate Calvinism was attractive to English Protestants in the 1640s. Yet, it was an excellent statement of distinctively Baptist convictions. With some modifications, it was submitted to Parliament and was the basis for the legal toleration granted in 1647.

Source: The complete text with Scripture references and notes can be found in *Baptist Confessions of Faith* by William L. Lumpkin (Chicago: The Judson Press, 1959).

THE CONFESSION OF FAITH
OF THOSE CHURCHES WHICH ARE COMMONLY
(THOUGH FALSLY) CALLED ANABAPTISTS.

I.

That God as he is in himselfe, cannot be comprehended of any but himselfe, dwelling in that inaccessible light, that no eye can attaine unto, whom never man saw, nor can see; that there is but one God, one Christ, one Spirit, one Faith, one Baptisme; one Rule of holinesse and obedience for all Saints, at all times, in all places to be observed.

II.

That God is of himselfe, that is, neither from another, nor of another, nor by another, nor for another: But is a Spirit, who as his being is of himselfe, so he gives being, moving, and preservation to all other things, being in himselfe eternall, most holy, every way infinite in greatnesse, wisdome, power, justice, goodnesse, truth, &c. In this God-head, there is the Father, the Sonne, and the Spirit; being every one of them one and the same God; and therefore not divided, but distinguished one from another by their severall properties; the Father being from himselfe, the Sonne of the Father from everlasting, the holy Spirit proceeding from the Father and the Sonne.

III.

That God hath decreed in himselfe from everlasting touching all things, effectually to work and dispose them according to the counsell of his owne will, to the glory of his Name; in which decree appeareth his wisdome, constancy, truth, and faithfulnesse; Wisdome is that whereby he contrives all things; Constancy is that whereby the decree of God remaines alwayes immutable; Truth is that whereby he declares that alone which he hath decreed, and though his sayings may seeme to sound sometimes another thing, yet the sense of them doth always agree with the decree; Faithfulnesse is that whereby he effects that he hath decreed, as he hath decreed. And touching his creature man, God had in Christ before the foundation of the world, according to the good pleasure of his will, foreordained some men to eternall life through Jesus Christ, to the praise and glory of his grace, leaving the rest in their sinne to their just condemnation, to the praise of his Justice.

IV.

In the beginning God made all things very good, created man after his own Image and likenesse, filling him with all perfection of all naturall excellency and uprightnesse, free from all sinne. But long he abode not in this honour, but by the subtiltie of the Serpent, which Satan used as his instrument, himselfe with his Angels having sinned before, and not kept their first estate, but left their owne habitation; first *Eve,* then *Adam* being seduced did wittingly and willingly fall into disobedience and transgression of the Commandement of their great Creator, for the which death came upon all, and reigned over all, so that all since the Fall are conceived in sinne, and brought forth in iniquitie, and so by nature children of wrath, and servants of sinne, subjects of death, and all other calamities due to sinne in this world and for ever, being considered in the state of nature, without relation to Christ.

V.

All mankind being thus fallen, and become altogether dead in sinnes and trespasses, and subject to the eternall wrath of the great God by transgression; yet the elect, which God hath loved with an everlasting love, are redeemed, quickened, and saved, not by themselves, neither by their own workes, lest any man should boast himselfe, but wholly and onely by God of his free grace and mercie through Jesus Christ, who of God is made unto us wisdome, righteousnesse, sanctification and redemption, that as it is written, Hee that rejoyceth, let him rejoyce in the Lord.

VI.

This therefore is life eternall, to know the onely true God, and whom he hath sent Jesus Christ. And on the contrary, the Lord will render vengeance in flaming fire to them that know not God, and obey not the Gospel of our Lord Jesus Christ.

VII.

The Rule of this Knowledge, Faith, and Obedience, concerning the worship and service of God, and all other Christian duties, is not mans inventions, opinions, devices, lawes, constitutions, or traditions unwritten whatsoever, but onely the word of God contained in the Canonicall Scriptures.

VIII.

In this written Word God hath plainly revealed whatsoever he hath thought needfull for us to know, beleeve, and acknowledge, touching the Nature and Office of Christ, in whom all the promises are Yea and Amen to the Praise of God.

IX.

Touching the Lord Jesus, of whom *Moses* and the

Prophets wrote, and whom the Apostles preached, is the Sonne of God the Father, the brightnesse of his glory, the ingraven forme of his being, God with him and with his holy Spirit, by whom he made the world, by whom he upholds and governes all the workes hee hath made, who also when the fulnesse of time was come, was made man of a woman, of the Tribe of *Judah*, of the seed of *Abraham* and David, to wit, of *Mary* that blessed Virgin, by the holy Spirit comming upon her, and the power of the most High overshadowing her, and was also in all things like unto us, sinne only excepted.

X.

Touching his Office, Jesus Christ onely is made the Mediator of the new Covenant, even the everlasting Covenant of grace between God and Man, to be perfectly and fully the Prophet, Priest and King of the Church of God for evermore.

XI.

Unto this Office hee was fore-ordained from everlasting, by the authority of the Father, and in respect of his Manhood, from the womb called and separated, and anointed also most fully and abundantly with all gifts necessary, God having without measure poured the Spirit upon him.

XII.

In this Call the Scripture holds forth two speciall things considerable; first, the call to the Office; secondly, the Office it self. First, that none takes this honour but he that is called of God, as was *Aaron*, so also Christ, it being an action especially of God the Father, whereby a speciall covenant being made, hee ordaines his Sonne to this office: which Covenant is, that Christ should be made a Sacrifice for sinne, that hee shall see his seed, and prolong his dayes, and the pleasure of the Lord shall prosper

in his hand; which calling therefore contains in it
selfe chusing, fore-ordaining, sending. Chusing respects the end, fore-ordaining the means, sending the
execution it self, all of meere grace, without any
condition fore-seen either in men, or in Christ
himselfe.

XIII.

So that this Office to be Mediator, that is, to be
Prophet, Priest, and King of the Church of God, is
so proper to Christ, as neither in the whole, nor in
any part thereof, it can be transferred from him to
any other.

XIV.

This Office it self to which Christ was called, is
threefold, of a Prophet, of Priest, & of a King: this
number and order of Offices is shewed; first, by
mens necessities grievously labouring under ignorance, by reason whereof they stand in infinit necessity of the Prophetical office of Christ to relieve
them. Secondly, alienation from God, wherein they
stand in need of the Priestly Office to reconcile them:
Thirdly, our utter disability to return to him, by
which they stand in need of the power of Christ in
his Kingly Office to assist and govern them.

XV.

Touching the Prophesie of Christ, it is that whereby he hath perfectly revealed the whole will of God
out of the bosome of the Father, that is needful for
his servants to know, beleeve, and obey; and therefore is called not onely a Prophet and a Doctor, and
the Apostle of our profession, and the Angel of the
Covenant; but also the very wisdome of God, and
the treasures of wisdome and understanding.

XVI.

That he might be such a Prophet as thereby to be

every way compleat, it was necessary that he should bee God, and withall also that he should be man; for unlesse hee had been God, he could never have perfectly understood the will of God, neither had he been able to reveale it throughout all ages; and unlesse hee had been man, hee could not fitly have unfolded it in his own person to man.

XVII.

Touching his Priesthood, Christ being consecrated, hath appeared once to put away sinne by the offering and sacrifice of himself, and to this end hath fully performed and suffered all those things by which God, through the blood of that his Crosse in an acceptable sacrifice, might reconcile his elect onely; and having broken downe the partition wall, and therewith finished & removed all those Rites, Shadowes, and Ceremonies, is now entred within the Vaile, into the Holy of Holiest, that is, to the very Heavens, and presence of God, where he for ever liveth and sitteth at the right hand of Majesty, appearing before the face of his Father to make intercession for such as come to the Throne of Grace by that new and living way; and not that onely, but makes his people a spirituall House, an holy Priesthood, to offer up spirituall sacrifice acceptable to God through him; neither doth the Father accept, or Christ offer to the Father any other worship or worshippers.

XVIII.

This Priesthood was not legall, or temporary, but according to the order of *Melchisedec*; not by a carnall commandement, but by the power of an endlesse life; not by an order that is weak and lame, but stable and perfect, not for a time but for ever, admitting no successor, but perpetuall and proper to Christ, and of him that ever liveth. Christ himselfe was the Priest, Sacrifice and Altar: he was Priest, according to both natures, hee was a sacrifice most properly according to his humane nature: whence in the Scripture it is wont to be attributed to his body, to his blood; yet the chiefe force whereby this sacrifice was made effectuall, did depend upon his divine nature, namely, that the Sonne of God did offer himselfe for us: he was the Altar properly according to his divine nature, it belonging to the Altar to sanctifie that which is offered upon it, and so it ought to be of greater dignity then the Sacrifice it selfe.

XIX.

Touching his Kingdome, Christ being risen from the dead, ascended into heaven, sat on the right hand of God the Father, having all power in heaven and earth, given unto him, he doth spiritually govern his Church, exercising his power over all Angels and Men, good and bad, to the preservation and salvation of the elect, to the overruling and destruction of his enemies, which are Reprobates, communicating and applying the benefits, vertue, and fruit of his Prophesie and Priesthood to his elect, namely, to the subduing and taking away of their sinnes, to their justification and adoption of Sonnes, regeneration, sanctification, preservation and strengthening in all their conflicts against Satan, the World, the Flesh, and the temptations of them, continually dwelling in, governing and keeping their hearts in faith and filiall feare by his Spirit, which having given it, he never takes away from them, but by it still begets and nourisheth in them faith, repentance, love, joy, hope, and all heavenly light in the soule unto immortality, notwithstanding through our own unbeliefe, and the temptations of Satan, the sensible sight of this light and love be clouded and overwhelmed for the time. And on the contrary, ruling in the world over his enemies, Satan, and all the vessels of wrath, limiting, using, restraining them by his mighty power, as seems good in his divine wisdome & justice to the execution of his determinate counsell, delivering them up to a reprobate mind, to be kept through their own deserts, in darknesse and sensuality unto judgement.

XX.

This Kingdome shall be then fully perfected when hee shall the second time come in glory to reigne amongst his Saints, and to be admired of all them which doe beleeve, when he shall put downe all rule and authority under his feet, that the glory of the Father may be full and perfectly manifested in his Sonne, and the glory of the Father and the Sonne in all his members.

XXI.

That Christ Jesus by his death did bring forth salvation and reconciliation onely for the elect, which were those which God the Father gave him; & that the Gospel which is to be preached to all men as the ground of faith, is that Jesus is the Christ, the Sonne of the ever-blessed God, filled with the perfection of all heavenly and spirituall excellencies, and that salvation is onely and alone to be had through the beleeving in his Name.

XXII.

That Faith is the gift of God wrought in the hearts of the elect by the Spirit of God, whereby they come to see, know, and beleeve the truth of the Scriptures, & not onely so, but the excellencie of them above all other writings and things in the world, as they hold forth the glory of God in his attributes, the excellency of Christ in his nature and offices, and the power of the fulnesse of the Spirit in its workings and operations; and thereupon are inabled to cast the weight of their soules upon this truth thus beleeved.

XXIII.

Those that have this pretious faith wrought in them by the Spirit, can never finally nor totally fall away; and though many stormes and floods do arise and beat against them, yet they shall never be able to take them off that foundation and rock which by faith they are fastened upon, but shall be kept by the power of God to salvation, where they shall enjoy their purchased possession, they being formerly engraven upon the palms of Gods hands.

XXIV.

That faith is ordinarily begot by preaching of the Gospel, or word of Christ, without respect to any power or capacitie in the creature, but it is wholly passive, being dead in sinnes and trespasses, doth beleeve, and is converted by no lesse power, [than] that which raised Christ from the dead.

XXV.

That the tenders of the Gospel to the conversion of sinners, is absolutely free, no way requiring, as absolutely necessary, any qualifications, preparations, terrors of the Law, or preceding Ministry of the Law, but onely and alone the naked soule, as a sinner and ungodly to receive Christ, as crucified, dead, and buried, and risen againe, being made a Prince and a Saviour for such sinners.

XXVI.

That the same power that converts to faith in Christ, the same power carries on the soule still through all duties, temptations, conflicts, sufferings, and continually what ever a Christian is, he is by grace, and by a constant renewed operation from God, without which he cannot performe any dutie to God, or undergoe any temptations from Satan, the world, or men.

XXVII.

That God the Father, and Sonne, and Spirit, is one with all beleevers, in their fulnesse, in relations, as head and members, as house and inhabitants, as husband and wife, one with him, as light and love, and one with him in his inheritance, and in all his glory; and that all beleevers by vertue of this union and onenesse with God, are the adopted sonnes of God, and heires with Christ, co-heires and joynt heires with him of the inheritance of all the promises of this life, and that which is to come.

XXVIII.

That those which have union with Christ, are justified from all their sinnes, past, present, and to come, by the bloud of Christ; which justification wee conceive to be a gracious and free acquittance of a guiltie, sinfull creature, from all sin by God, through the satisfaction that Christ hath made by his death; and this applyed in the manifestation of it through faith.

XXIX.

That all beleevers are a holy and sanctified people, and that sanctification is a spirituall grace of the new Covenant, and effect of the love of God, manifested to the soule, whereby the beleever is in truth and realitie separated, both in soule and body, from all sinne and dead workes, through the bloud of the everlasting Covenant, whereby he also presseth after a heavenly and Evangelicall perfection, in obedience to all the Commands, which Christ as head and King in this new Covenant has prescribed to him.

XXX.

All beleevers through the knowledge of that Justification of life given by the Father, and brought forth by the bloud of Christ, have this as their great priviledge of that new Covenant, peace with God, and reconciliation, whereby they that were afarre off, were brought nigh by that bloud, and have (as the Scripture speaks) peace passing all understanding, yea, joy in God, through our Lord Jesus Christ, by whom wee have received the Atonement.

XXXI.

That all beleevers in the time of this life, are in a continuall warfare, combate, and opposition against sinne, selfe, the world, and the Devill, and liable to all manner of afflictions, tribulations, and persecutions, and so shall continue untill Christ comes in his Kingdome, being predestinated and appointed thereunto; and whatsoever the Saints, any of them doe possesse or enjoy of God in this life, is onely by faith.

XXXII.

That the onely strength by which the Saints are inabled to incounter with all opposition, and to overcome all afflictions, temptations, persecutions, and tryalls, is onely by Jesus Christ, who is the Captain of their salvation, being made perfect through sufferings, who hath ingaged his strength to assist them in all their afflictions, and to uphold them under all their temptations, and to preserve them by his power to his everlasting Kingdome.

XXXIII.

That Christ hath here on earth a spirituall Kingdome, which is the Church, which he hath purchased and redeemed to himselfe, as a peculiar inheritance: which Church, as it is visible to us, is a company of visible Saints, called & separated from the world, by the word and Spirit of God, to the visible profession of the faith of the Gospel, being baptized into that faith, and joyned to the Lord, and each other, by mutuall agreement, in the practicall injoyment of the

Ordinances, commanded by Christ their head and King.

XXXIV.

To this Church he hath made his promises, and given the signes of his Covenant, presence, love, blessing, and protection: here are the fountains and springs of his heavenly grace continually flowing forth; thither ought all men to come, of all estates, that acknowledge him to be their Prophet, Priest, and King, to be inrolled amongst his houshold servants, to be under his heavenly conduct and government, to lead their lives in his walled sheepfold, and watered garden, to have communion here with the Saints, that they may be made to be partakers of their inheritance in the Kingdome of God.

XXXV.

And all his servants are called thither, to present their bodies and soules, and to bring their gifts God hath given them; so being come, they are here by himselfe bestowed in their severall order, peculiar place, due use, being fitly compact and knit together, according to the effectuall working of every part, to the edification of itselfe in love.

XXXVI.

That being thus joyned, every Church has power given them from Christ for their better well-being, to choose to themselves meet persons into the office of Pastors, Teachers, Elders, Deacons, being qualified according to the Word, as those which Christ has appointed in his Testament, for the feeding, governing, serving, and building up of his Church, and that none other have power to impose them, either these or any other.

XXXVII.

That the Ministers aforesaid, lawfully called by

the Church, where they are to administer, ought to continue in their calling, according to Gods Ordinance, and carefully to feed the flock of Christ committed to them, not for filthy lucre, but of a ready mind.

XXXVIII.

That the due maintenance of the officers aforesaid, should be the free and voluntary communication of the Church, that according to Christs Ordinance, they that preach the Gospel, should live on the Gospel and not by constraint to be compelled from the people by a forced Law.

XXXIX.

That Baptisme is an Ordinance of the new Testament, given by Christ, to be dispensed only upon persons professing faith, or that are Disciples, or taught, who upon a profession of faith, ought to be baptized.

XL.

The way and manner of the dispensing of this Ordinance the Scripture holds out to be dipping or plunging the whole body under water: it being a signe, must answer the thing signified, which are these: first, the washing the whole soule in the bloud of Christ: Secondly, that interest the Saints have in the death, buriall, and resurrection; thirdly, together with a confirmation of our faith, that as certainly as the body is buried under water, and riseth againe, so certainly shall the bodies of the Saints be raised by the power of Christ, in the day of the resurrection, to reigne with Christ.

XLI.

The persons designed by Christ, to dispense this Ordinance, the Scriptures hold forth to be a preaching Disciple, it being no where tyed to a particular

Church, Officer, or person extraordinarily sent, the Commission injoyning the administration, being given to them under no other consideration, but as considered Disciples.

XLII.

Christ has likewise given power to his whole Church to receive in and cast out, by way of Excommunication, any member; and this power is given to every particular Congregation, and not one particular person, either member or Officer, but the whole.

XLIII.

And every particular member of each Church, how excellent, great, or learned soever, ought to be subject to this censure and judgement of Christ; and the Church ought with great care and tendernesse, with due advice to proceed against her members.

XLIV.

And as Christ for the keeping of this Church in holy and orderly Communion, placeth some speciall men over the Church, who by their office are to governe, oversee, visit, watch; so likewise for the better keeping thereof in all places, by the members, he hath given authoritie, and laid dutie upon all, to watch over one another.

XLV.

That also such to whom God hath given gifts, being tryed in the Church, may and ought by the appointment of the Congregation, to prophesie, according to the proportion of faith, and so teach publickly the Word of God, for the edification, exhortation, and comfort of the Church.

XLVI.

Thus being rightly gathered, established, and still proceeding in Christian communion, and obedience

of the Gospel of Christ, none ought to separate for
faults and corruptions, which may, and as long as
the Church consists of men subject to failings, will
fall out and arise amongst them, even in true constituted Churches, untill they have in due order sought
redresse thereof.

XLVII.

And although the particular Congregations be distinct and severall Bodies, every one a compact and
knit Citie in it selfe; yet are they all to walk by one
and the same Rule, and by all meanes convenient to
have the counsell and help one of another in all
needfull affaires of the Church, as members of one
body in the common faith under Christ their onely
head.

XLVIII.

That a civill Magistracie is an ordinance of God
set up by God for the punishment of evill doers, and
for the praise of them that doe well; and that in all
lawfull things commanded by them, subjection ought
to be given by us in the Lord: and that we are to
make supplication and prayer for Kings, and all that
are in authority, that under them we may live a
peaceable and quiet life in all godliness and honesty.

XLIX.

The supreme Magistracie of this Kingdome we
beleeve to be the King and Parliament freely chosen
by the Kingdome, and that in all those civill Lawes
which have been acted by them, or for the present is
or shall be ordained, we are bound to yeeld subjection and obedience unto in the Lord, as conceiving
our selves bound to defend both the persons of
those thus chosen, and all civill Lawes made by
them, with our persons, liberties, and estates, with all
that is called ours, although we should suffer never
so much from them in not actively submitting to

some Ecclesiasticall Lawes, which might be conceived by them to be their duties to establish which we for the present could not see, nor our consciences could submit unto; yet are we bound to yeeld our persons to their pleasures.

L.

And if God should provide such a mercie for us, as to incline the Magistrates hearts so far to tender our consciences, as that we might bee protected by them from wrong, injury, oppression and molestation, which long we formerly have groaned under by the tyranny and oppression of the Prelaticall Hierarchy, which God through mercy hath made this present King and Parliament wonderfull honourable, as an instrument in his hand, to throw downe; and we thereby have had some breathing time, we shall, we hope, look at it as a mercy beyond our expectation, and conceive our selves further engaged for ever to bless God for it.

LI.

But if God with-hold the Magistrates allowance and furtherance herein; yet we must notwithstanding proceed together in Christian communion, not daring to give place to suspend our practice, but to walk in obedience to Christ in the profession and holding forth this faith before mentioned, even in the midst of all trialls and afflictions, not accounting for goods, lands, wives, children, fathers, mothers, brethren, sisters, yea, and our own lives dear unto us, so we [may] finish our course with joy: remembering alwayes we ought to obey God rather then men, and grounding upon the commandement, commission and promise of our Lord and master Jesus Christ, who as he hath all power in heaven and earth, so also hath promised, if we keep his commandements which he hath given us, to be with us to the end of the world: and when we have finished our course, and kept the faith, to give us the crowne of righteousnesse, which is laid up for all that love his appearing, and to whom we must give an account of all our actions, no man being able to discharge us of the same.

LII.

And likewise unto all men is to be given whatsoever is their due; tributes, customes, and all such lawful duties, ought willingly to bee by us paid and performed, our lands, goods, and bodies, to submit to the Magistrate in the Lord, and the Magistrate every way to bee acknowledged, reverenced, and obeyed, according to godlinesse; not because of wrath onely but for conscience sake. And finally, all men so to be esteemed and regarded, as is due and meet for their place, age estate and condition.

LII [sic].

And thus wee desire to give unto God that which is Gods, and unto *Cesar* that which is *Cesars*, and unto all men that which belongeth unto them, endevouring our selves to have alwayes a cleare conscience void of offence towards God, and towards man. And if any take this that we have said, to be heresie, then doe wee with the Apostle freely confesse, that after the way which they call heresie, worship we the God of our Fathers, beleeving all things which are written in the Law and in the Prophets and Apostles, desiring from our soules to disclaime all heresies and opinions which are not after Christ, and to be stedfast, unmoveable, alwayes abounding in the worke of the Lord, as knowing our labour shall not be in vain in the Lord.

I Cor. 1.24.

Not that we have dominion over your faith, but are helpers of your joy: for by faith we stand.

DOGMATIC CONSTITUTION ON
DIVINE REVELATION
Vatican Council II (1965)

This important document is not only theology but also proclamation. It seeks to relate the church's conviction about revelation and about Scripture to the church's knowledge especially about Scripture and tradition.

Source: Text from *The Documents of Vatican II* edited by Walter M. Abbott, S. J. (New York: Corpus Books, 1966), pp. 111–128.

DOGMATIC CONSTITUTION ON DIVINE REVELATION

PREFACE

. . . .

CHAPTER 1
REVELATION ITSELF

. . . .

2. In His goodness and wisdom, God chose to reveal Himself and to make known to us the hidden purpose of His will (cf. Eph. 1:9) by which through Christ, the Word made flesh, man has access to the Father in the Holy Spirit and comes to share in the divine nature (cf. Eph. 2:18; 2 Pet. 1:4). Through this revelation, therefore, the invisible God (cf. Col. 1:15; 1 Tim. 1:17) out of the abundance of His love speaks to men as friends (cf. Ex. 33:11; Jn. 15:14–15) and lives among them (cf. Bar. 3:38), so that He may invite and take them into fellowship with Himself. This plan of revelation is realized by deeds and words having an inner unity: the deeds wrought by God in the history of salvation manifest and confirm the teaching and realities signified by the words, while the words proclaim the deeds and clarify the mystery contained in them. By this revelation then, the deepest truth about God and the salvation of man is made clear to us in Christ, who

is the Mediator and at the same time the fullness of all revelation.

3. God, who through the Word creates all things (cf. Jn. 1:3) and keeps them in existence, gives men an enduring witness to Himself in created realities (cf. Rom. 1:19–20). Planning to make known the way of heavenly salvation, He went further and from the start manifested Himself to our first parents. Then after their fall His promise of redemption aroused in them the hope of being saved (cf. Gen. 3:15), and from that time on He ceaselessly kept the human race in His care, in order to give eternal life to those who perseveringly do good in search of salvation (cf. Rom. 2:6–7). Then, at the time He had appointed, He called Abraham in order to make of him a great nation (cf. Gen. 12:2). Through the patriarchs, and after them through Moses and the prophets, He taught this nation to acknowledge Himself as the one living and true God, provident Father and just Judge, and to wait for the Savior promised by Him. In this manner He prepared the way for the gospel down through the centuries.

4. Then, after speaking in many places and varied ways through the prophets, God "last of all in these days has spoken to us by his son" (Heb. 1:1–2). For he sent His Son, the eternal Word, who enlightens all men, so that He might dwell among men and tell them the innermost realities about God (cf. Jn. 1:1–18). Jesus Christ, therefore, the Word made flesh, sent as "a man to men," "speaks the words of God" (Jn. 3:34), and completes the work of salvation which His Father gave Him to do (cf. Jn. 5:36, 17:4). To see Jesus is to see His Father (Jn. 14:9). For this reason Jesus perfected revelation by fulfilling it through His whole work of making Himself present and manifesting Himself: through His words and deeds, His signs and wonders, but especially through His death and glorious resurrec-

tion from the dead and final sending of the Spirit of truth. Moreover, He confirmed with divine testimony what revelation proclaimed: that God is with us to free us from the darkness of sin and death, and to raise us up to life eternal.

The Christian dispensation, therefore, as the new and definitive covenant, will never pass away, and we now await no further new public revelation before the glorious manifestation of our Lord Jesus Christ (cf. 1 Tim. 6:14 and Tit. 2:13).

5. "The obedience of faith" (Rom. 16:26; cf. 1:5; 2 Cor. 10:5–6) must be given to God who reveals, an obedience by which man entrusts his whole self freely to God, offering "the full submission of intellect and will to God who reveals," and freely assenting to the truth revealed by Him. If this faith is to be shown, the grace of God and the interior help of the Holy Spirit must precede and assist, moving the heart and turning it to God, opening the eyes of the mind, and giving "joy and ease to everyone in assenting to the truth and believing it." To bring about an ever deeper understanding of revelation, the same Holy Spirit constantly brings faith to completion by His gifts.

6. Through divine revelation, God chose to show forth and communicate Himself and the eternal decisions of His will regarding the salvation of men. That is to say, He chose "to share those divine treasures which totally transcend the understanding of the human mind."

This sacred Synod affirms, "God, the beginning and the end of all things, can be known with certainty from created reality by the light of human reason" (cf. Rom. 1:20); but the Synod teaches that it is through His revelation "that those religious truths which are by their nature accessible to human reason can be known by all men with ease, with solid certitude, and with no trace of error, even in the present state of the human race."

CHAPTER 2

THE TRANSMISSION OF DIVINE REVELATION

7. In His gracious goodness, God has seen to it that what He had revealed for the salvation of all nations would abide perpetually in its full integrity and be handed on to all generations. Therefore Christ the Lord, in whom the full revelation of the supreme God is brought to completion (cf. 2 Cor. 1:20; 3:16; 4:6), commissioned the apostles to preach to all men that gospel which is the source of all saving truth and moral teaching, and thus to impart to them divine gifts. This gospel had been promised in former times through the prophets, and Christ Himself fulfilled it and promulgated it with His own lips. This commission was faithfully fulfilled by the apostles who, by their oral preaching, by example, and by ordinances, handed on what they had received from the lips of Christ, from living with Him, and from what He did, or what they had learned through the prompting of the Holy Spirit. The commission was fulfilled, too, by those apostles and apostolic men who under the inspiration of the same Holy Spirit committed the message of salvation to writing.

But in order to keep the gospel forever whole and alive within the Church, the apostles left bishops as their successors, "handing over their own teaching role" to them. This sacred tradition, therefore, and sacred Scripture of both the Old and the New Testament are like a mirror in which the pilgrim Church on earth looks at God, from whom she has received everything, until she is brought finally to see Him as He is, face to face (cf. 1 Jn. 3:2).

8. And so the apostolic preaching, which is expressed in a special way in the inspired books, was to be preserved by a continuous succession of preachers until the end of time. Therefore the apostles, handing on what they themselves had received, warn

the faithful to hold fast to the traditions which they have learned either by word of mouth or by letter (cf. 2 Th. 2:15), and to fight in defense of the faith handed on once and for all (cf. Jude 3). Now what was handed on by the apostles includes everything which contributes to the holiness of life, and the increase in faith of the People of God; and so the Church, in her teaching, life, and worship, perpetuates and hands on to all generations all that she herself is, all that she believes.

This tradition which comes from the apostles develops in the Church with the help of the Holy Spirit. For there is a growth in the understanding of the realities and the words which have been handed down. This happens through the contemplation and study made by believers, who treasure these things in their hearts (cf. Lk. 2:19, 51), through the intimate understanding of spiritual things they experience, and through the preaching of those who have received through episcopal succession the sure gift of truth. For, as the centuries succeed one another, the Church constantly moves, forward toward the fullnes of divine truth until the words of God reach their complete fulfillment in her.

The words of the holy Fathers witness to the living presence of this tradition, whose wealth is poured into the practice and life of the believing and praying Church. Through the same tradition the full canon of the sacred books becomes known to the Church, and the sacred writings themselves are more profoundly understood and unceasingly made active in her; and thus God, who spoke of old, uninterruptedly converses with the Bride of His beloved Son; and the Holy Spirit, through whom the living voice of the gospel resounds in the Church, and through her, in the world, leads unto all truth those who believe and makes the word of Christ dwell abundantly in them (cf. Col. 3:16).

9. Hence there exist a close connection and communication between sacred tradition and sacred Scripture. For both of them, flowing from the same divine wellspring, in a certain way merge into a unity and tend toward the same end. For sacred Scripture is the word of God inasmuch as it is consigned to writing under the inspiration of the divine Spirit. To the successors of the apostles, sacred tradition hands on in its full purity God's word, which was entrusted to the apostles by Christ the Lord and the Holy Spirit. Thus, led by the light of the Spirit of truth, these successors can in their preaching preserve this word of God faithfully, explain it, and make it more widely known. Consequently, it is not from sacred Scripture alone that the Church draws her certainty about everything which has been revealed. Therefore both sacred tradition and sacred Scripture are to be accepted and venerated with the same sense of devotion and reverence.

10. Sacred tradition and sacred Scripture form one sacred deposit of the word of God, which is committed to the Church. Holding fast to this deposit, the entire holy people united with their shepherds remain always steadfast in the teaching of the apostles, in the common life, in the breaking of the bread, and in prayers (cf. Acts 2, 42, Greek text), so that in holding to, practicing, and professing the heritage of the faith, there results on the part of the bishops and faithful a remarkable common effort.

The task of authentically interpreting the word of God, whether written or handed on, has been entrusted exclusively to the living teaching office of the Church, whose authority is exercised in the name of Jesus Christ. This teaching office is not above the word of God, but serves it, teaching only what has been handed on, listening to it devoutly, guarding it scrupulously, and explaining it faithfully by divine commission and with the help of the Holy

Spirit; it draws from this one deposit of faith every-thing which it presents for belief as divinely revealed.

It is clear, therefore, that sacred tradition, sacred Scripture, and the teaching authority of the Church, in accord with God's most wise design, are so linked and joined together that one cannot stand without the others, and that all together and each in its own way under the action of the one Holy Spirit contribute effectively to the salvation of souls.

CHAPTER 3
THE DIVINE INSPIRATION AND THE
INTERPRETATION OF SACRED SCRIPTURE

11. Those divinely revealed realities which are con-tained and presented in sacred Scripture have been committed to writing under the inspiration of the Holy Spirit. Holy Mother Church, relying on the belief of the apostles, holds that the books of both the Old and New Testament in their entirety, with all their parts, are sacred and canonical because, having been written under the inspiration of the Holy Spirit (cf. Jn. 20:31, 2 Tim. 3:16; 2 Pet. 1:19–21; 3:15–16) they have God as their author and have been handed on as such to the Church herself. In composing the sacred books, God chose men and while employed by Him they made use of their powers and abilities, so that with Him acting in them and through them, they, as true authors, consigned to writing everything and only those things which He wanted.

Therefore, since everything asserted by the inspired authors or sacred writers must be held to be asserted by the Holy Spirit, it follows that the books of Scrip-ture must be acknowledged as teaching firmly, faith-fully, and without error that truth which God wanted put into the sacred writings for the sake of our salvation. Therefore "all Scripture is inspired by God and useful for teaching, for reproving, for correcting, for instruction in justice; that the man of God may be perfect, equipped for every good work" (2 Tim. 3:16–17, Greek text).

12. However, since God speaks in sacred Scripture through men in human fashion, the interpreter of sacred Scripture, in order to see clearly what God wanted to communicate to us, should carefully investigate what meaning the sacred writers really intended, and what God wanted to manifest by means of their words.

Those who search out the intention of the sacred writers must, among other things, have regard for "literary forms". For truth is proposed and expressed in a variety of ways, depending on whether a text is history of one kind or another, or whether its form is that of prophecy, poetry, or some other type of speech. The interpreter must investigate what meaning the sacred writer intended to express and actually expressed in particular circumstances as he used contemporary literary forms in accordance with the situation of his own time and culture. For the correct understanding of what the sacred author wanted to assert, due attention must be paid to the customary and characteristic styles of perceiving, speaking, and narrating which prevailed at the time of the sacred writer, and to the customs men normally followed at that period in their everyday dealings with one another.

But, since holy Scripture must be read and interpreted according to the same Spirit by whom it was written, no less serious attention must be given to the content and unity of the whole of Scripture, if the meaning of the sacred texts is to be correctly brought to light. The living tradition of the whole Church must be taken into account along with the harmony which exists between elements of the faith. It is the task of exegetes to work according to these rules toward a better understanding and explanation of the meaning of sacred Scripture, so that through preparatory study the judgment of the Church may mature. For all of what has been said about the way of interpreting Scripture is subject finally to the judgment of the Church, which carries out the divine commission and ministry of guarding and interpreting the word of God.

13. In sacred Scripture, therefore, while the truth and holiness of God always remain intact, the marvelous "condescension" of eternal wisdom is clearly shown, "that we may learn the gentle kindness of God, which words cannot express, and how far He has gone in adapting His language with thoughtful concern for our weak human nature". For the words of God, expressed in human language, have been made like human discourse, just as of old the Word of the eternal Father, when he took, to Himself the weak flesh of humanity, became like other men.

CHAPTER 4
THE OLD TESTAMENT

. . . .

CHAPTER 5
THE NEW TESTAMENT

. . . .

CHAPTER 6
SACRED SCRIPTURE IN THE LIFE OF THE CHURCH

21. The Church has always venerated the divine Scriptures just as she venerates the body of the Lord, since from the table of both the word of God and of the body of Christ she unceasingly receives and offers to the faithful the bread of life, especially in the sacred liturgy. She has always regarded the Scriptures together with sacred tradition as the su-

preme rule of faith, and will ever do so. For, inspired by God and committed once and for all to writing, they impart the word of God Himself without change, and make the voice of the Holy Spirit resound in the words of the prophets and apostles. Therefore, like the Christian religion itself, all the preaching of the Church must be nourished and ruled by sacred Scripture. For in the sacred books, the Father who is in heaven meets His children with great love and speaks with them; and the force and power in the word of God is so great that it remains the support and energy of the Church, the strength of faith for her sons, the food of the soul, the pure and perennial source of spiritual life. Consequently, these words are perfectly applicable to sacred Scripture: "For the word of God is living and efficient" (Heb. 4:12) and is "able to build up and give the inheritance among all the sanctified" (Acts 20:32; cf. 1 Th. 2:13).

22. Easy access to sacred Scripture should be provided for all the Christian faithful. That is why the Church from the very beginning accepted as her own that very ancient Greek translation of the Old Testament which is named after seventy men; and she has always given a place of honor to other Eastern translations, and to Latin ones, especially that known as the Vulgate. But since the word of God should be available at all times, the Church with maternal concern sees to it that suitable and correct translations are made into different languages, especially from the original texts of the sacred books. And if, given the opportunity and the approval of Church authority, these translations are produced in cooperation with the separated brethren as well, all Christians will be able to use them.

23. The Bride of the incarnate Word, and the Pupil of the Holy Spirit, the Church is concerned to move ahead daily toward a deeper understanding of the

sacred Scriptures so that she may unceasingly feed her sons with the divine words. Therefore, she also rightly encourages the study of the holy Fathers of both East and West and of sacred liturgies. Catholic exegetes then and other students of sacred theology, working diligently together and using appropriate means, should devote their energies, under the watchful care of the sacred teaching office of the Church, to an exploration and exposition of the divine writings. This task should be done in such a way that as many ministers of the divine word as possible will be able effectively to provide the nourishment of the Scriptures for the People of God, thereby enlightening their minds, strengthening their wills, and setting men's hearts on fire with the love of God. This sacred Synod encourages the sons of the Church who are biblical scholars to continue energetically with the work they have so well begun, with a constant renewal of vigor and with loyalty to the mind of the Church.

24. Sacred theology rests on the written word of God, together with sacred tradition, as its primary and perpetual foundation. By scrutinizing in the light of faith all truth stored up in the mystery of Christ, theology is most powerfully strengthened and constantly rejuvenated by that word. For the sacred Scriptures contain the word of God and, since they are inspired, really are the word of God; and so the study of the sacred page is, as it were, the soul of sacred theology. By the same word of Scripture the ministry of the word also takes wholesome nourishment and yields fruits of holiness. This ministry includes pastoral preaching, catechetics, and all other Christian instruction, among which the liturgical homily should have an exceptional place.

25. Therefore, all the clergy must hold fast to the sacred Scriptures through diligent sacred reading and careful study, especially the priests of Christ

and others, such as deacons and catechists, who are legitimately active in the ministry of the word. This cultivation of Scripture is required lest any of them become "an empty preacher of the word of God outwardy, who is not a listener to it inwardly" since they must share the abundant wealth of the divine word with the faithful committed to them, especially in the sacred liturgy. This sacred Synod earnestly and specifically urges all the Christian faithful, too, especially religious, to learn by frequent reading of divine Scriptures the "excelling knowledge of Jesus Christ" (Phil. 3:8). "For ignorance of the Scriptures is ignorance of Christ". Therefore, they should gladly put themselves in touch with the sacred text itself, whether it be through the liturgy, rich in the divine word, or through devotional reading, or through instructions suitable for the purpose and other aids which, in our time, are commendably available everywhere, thanks to the approval and active support of the shepherds of the Church. And let them remember that prayer should acompany the reading of the sacred Scripture, so that God and man may talk together; for "we speak to Him when we pray; we hear Him when we read the divine sayings".

It devolves on sacred bishops, "who have the apostolic teaching", to give the faithful entrusted to them suitable instruction in the right use of the divine books, especially the New Testament and above all the Gospels, through translations of the sacred texts. Such versions are to be provided with necessary and fully adequate explanations so that the sons of the Church can safely and profitably grow familiar with the sacred Scriptures and be penetrated with their spirit.

Furthermore, editions of the sacred Scriptures, provided with suitable comments, should be prepared also for the use of non-Christians and adapted to their situation. Both pastors of souls and Christians generally should see to the wise distribution of these in one way or another.

26. In this way, therefore, through the reading and study of the sacred books, let "the word of the Lord run and be glorified" (2 Th. 3:1) and let the treasure of revelation entrusted to the Church increasingly fill the hearts of men. Just as the life of the Church grows through persistent participation in the Eucharistic mystery, so we may hope for a new surge of spiritual vitality from intensified veneration for God's word, which "lasts forever" (Is. 40:8; cf. 1 Pet. 1:23–25).

Each and every one of the things set forth in this Constitution has won the consent of the Fathers of this most sacred Council. We too, by the apostolic authority conferred on us by Christ, join with the Venerable Fathers in approving, decreeing and establishing these things in the Holy Spirit, and we direct that what has thus been enacted in synod be published to God's glory.

Rome, at St. Peter's, November 18, 1965
I, Paul Bishop of the Catholic Church